REFERENCE
FOR
USE IN LIBRARY ONLY

D1290159

American Family History

This bibliography was conceived and compiled from the periodicals database of the American Bibliographical Center by editors at ABC-Clio Information Services

Jessica S. Brown and Susan K. Kinnell, project coordinators

Pamela R. Byrne
Gail A. Schlachter

American Family History

a historical bibliography

ABC-Clio Information Services

Santa Barbara, California
Denver, Colorado
Oxford, England

WILLIAM MADISON RANDALL LIBRARY UNC AT WILMINGTON

Library of Congress Cataloging in Publication Data
Main entry under title:

American family history.

    (ABC-Clio research guides; 12)
    Drawn from ABC-Clio Information Services' 1973-1982
history database.
    Includes index.
    1. Family--United States--History--Abstracts.
2. Family--Canada--History--Abstracts.   3. Family--Services
for--United States--Abstracts.   4. Family--Services for--
Canada--Abstracts.   I. ABC-Clio Information Services.
II. Series.
HQ535.A587   1984   016.3068'5'0973   84-2955
ISBN   0-87436-380

Copyright ©1984 by ABC-Clio, Inc.

All rights reserved. No part of this publication may be
reproduced, stored in a retrieval system, or transmitted,
in any form, or by any means, electronic, mechanical,
photo-copying, recording or otherwise, without the prior
written permission of ABC-Clio, Inc.

ABC-Clio Information Services
2040 Alameda Padre Serra, Box 4397
Santa Barbara, California 93103

Clio Press Ltd.
55 St. Thomas Street
Oxford OX1 1JG, England

Printed and bound in the United States of America.

HQ535
.A587
1984

ABC-CLIO RESEARCH GUIDES

The ABC-Clio Research Guides are a new generation of annotated bibliographies that provide comprehensive control of the recent journal literature on high-interest topics in history and the related social sciences. These publications are compiled by editor/historians and other subject specialists who examine article entries in ABC-Clio Information Services' vast history data base and select abstracts of all citations that relate to the particular topic of study.

Each entry selected from this data base—the largest history data base in the world—has been reviewed to ensure consistency in treatment and completeness of coverage. The subject profile index (ABC-SPIndex) accompanying each volume has been evaluated and revised in terms of the specific subject presented to allow precise and rapid access to the entries.

The titles in this series are prepared to save researchers, students, and librarians the considerable time and expense usually associated with accessing materials manually or through online searching. ABC-Clio's Research Guides offer unmatched access to significant scholarly articles on the topics of most current interest to historians and social scientists.

266382

ABC-CLIO RESEARCH GUIDES

Gail Schlachter, Editor
Pamela R. Byrne, Executive Editor

11.
The Third Reich at War
1984   ISBN 0-87436-393-4

12.
American Family History
1984   ISBN 0-87436-380-2

13.
The Sino-Soviet Conflict
1984   ISBN 087436-382-9

CONTENTS

LIST OF ABBREVIATIONS

A.	Author-prepared Abstract	*Illus.*	Illustrated, Illustration
Acad.	Academy, Academie, Academia	*Inst.*	Institute, Institut-.
Agric.	Agriculture, Agricultural	*Int.*	International, Internacional,
AIA	Abstracts in Anthropology		Internationaal, Internationaux,
Akad.	Akademie		Internazionale
Am.	America, American	*J.*	Journal, Journal-prepared Abstract
Ann.	Annals, Annales, Annual, Annali	*Lib.*	Library, Libraries
Anthrop.	Anthropology, Anthropological	*Mag.*	Magazine
Arch.	Archives	*Mus.*	Museum, Musee, Museo
Archaeol.	Archaeology, Archaeological	*Nac.*	Nacional
Art.	Article	*Natl.*	National, Nationale
Assoc.	Association, Associate	*Naz.*	Nazionale
Biblio.	Bibliography, Bibliographical	*Phil.*	Philosophy, Philosophical
Biog.	Biography, Biographical	*Photo.*	Photograph
Bol.	Boletim, Boletin	*Pol.*	Politics, Political, Politique, Politico
Bull.	Bulletin	*Pr.*	Press
c.	century (in index)	*Pres.*	President
ca.	circa	*Pro.*	Proceedings
Can.	Canada, Canadian, Canadien	*Publ.*	Publishing, Publication
Cent.	Century	*Q.*	Quarterly
Coll.	College	*Rev.*	Review, Revue, Revista, Revised
Com.	Committee	*Riv.*	Rivista
Comm.	Commission	*Res.*	Research
Comp.	Compiler	*RSA*	Romanian Scientific Abstracts
DAI	Dissertation Abstracts	*S.*	Staff-prepared Abstract
	International	*Sci.*	Science, Scientific
Dept.	Department	*Secy.*	Secretary
Dir.	Director, Direktor	*Soc.*	Society, Societe, Sociedad,
Econ.	Economy, Econom-.		Societa
Ed.	Editor, Edition	*Sociol.*	Sociology, Sociological
Educ.	Education, Educational	*Tr.*	Transactions
Geneal.	Genealogy, Genealogical,	*Transl.*	Translator, Translation
	Genealogique	*U.*	University, Universi-.
Grad.	Graduate	*US*	United States
Hist.	History, Hist-.	*Vol.*	Volume
IHE	Indice Historico Espanol	*Y.*	Yearbook

INTRODUCTION

The evolution of American values since the late sixties has given rise to a new emphasis on the family as a legitimate subject for scholarly inquiry. Among social historians, focal points of study have been redefined to include social institutions related specifically to the family, the development of the concept of childhood, households and lifestyles, sex roles, the structures of extended and nuclear families, and the emergence of the single-parent family.

At the same time there has been a surge of interest in genealogy—popularized first in Alex Haley's *Roots: The Saga of An American Family* (Doubleday, 1976). Genealogical research, practiced both by professionals and buffs, has in turn promoted more generalized methodological approaches to family history. Relatively untapped sources of documentation—such as diaries, oral narratives, and other autobiographical data—have, literally, become the tools of the historian's trade. "More than ever," notes historian James C. Klotter in his review article, "Old Families and the New History" (*Reviews in American History* 1983 11(3): 345–350), "family history is fulfilling its long-ignored promise and regaining a place of honor at Clio's table."

Within the context of dynamic change in American society, the newly-acquired status of family history among scholars has inspired a prolific body of periodical literature on the subject during the last decade. *American Family History: A Historical Bibliography*, Number 12 of the ABC-Clio Research Guides, makes efficient access to this tremendous body of scholarship possible. The volume contains 1,167 abstracts and citations of journal articles drawn from ABC-Clio Information Services' history data base, a vast bibliographic resource with coverage of over 2,000 periodicals published in some 90 countries. In creating this volume, editors reviewed thousands of abstracts of articles published 1973–1982 and selected those relevant to the study of the American family. The result is the most thorough representation of recent historical scholarship from the periodical literature on the American family.

Article abstracts and citations in *American Family History* are arranged alphabetically by author, in four chapters. The first, "The Family in Historical Perspective," dates from the colonial period through the last decade. Chapter 2, "The Family and Other Social Institutions," focuses on the interaction between socioeconomic forces and the family. Chapter 3, "Familial Roles and Relationships," is where information on internal family dynamics can be found; and the final chapter, "Individual Family Histories," lists individual genealogical studies. Differences in the size of the chapters represents no editorial predisposition, but rather the relative volume of journal scholarship produced during the decade 1973–1982.

Additional access to the abstracts and citations in *American Family History* is through ABC-SPIndex (Subject Profile Index), a highly specific subject index. Key subject terms are linked with the historical dates to form a complete profile of the article. Each set of index terms is rotated alphabetically so that the complete profile appears under each of the subject terms. Thus, the accuracy and specificity of subject access is enhanced as compared to conventional, hierarchical indexes. Care has been taken to eliminate inconsistencies that might have appeared in the subject index as a result of merging a decade of data base material. Cross-references have been included to ensure fast and thorough searching. The explanatory note at the beginning of the subject index provides further information for using ABC-SPIndex.

This volume represents the collaboration of a skilled and diverse group. Pamela R. Byrne, Executive Editor of the ABC-Clio Research Guides, had overall responsibility for the creation of this volume and provided guidance essential to its production. Assistant Editors, Susan K. Kinnell and Lance J. Klass were responsible for conceptualizing the chapter headings, selecting and organizing the entries, reviewing the subject index, and designing the cover. Eric Schlachter, Student Assistant, carried out essential paste-up corrections. Jessica S. Brown, newly-appointed Managing Editor of the ABC-Clio Research Guides, oversaw the final stages of production of the volume. The Data Processing Services Department, under the supervision of Ken Baser, Director, and Deborah Looker, Production Supervisor, ably manipulated the data base to fit the editorial specifications of this bibliography. David R. Blanke, Applications Programmer, provided critical support in assuring high-quality photocomposition.

Sincere appreciation is extended to the worldwide community of scholars who wrote the abstracts that comprise this volume. Without their ceaseless efforts, this contribution to the scholarship on the American family would not have been possible.

1

THE FAMILY IN HISTORICAL
PERSPECTIVE

1. Abu-Laban, Sharon McIrvin.   ARAB-CANADIAN FAMILY LIFE.
Arab Studies Q. 1979 1(2): 135-156. Examines the interrelation between an Arab past and a Canadian present as the base for the distinctive family pattern and trends of contemporary Arab Canadian family life.

2. Adams, John. POINT ELLICE HOUSE, VICTORIA, B.C.   *Material Hist. Bull. [Canada] 1981 (12): 88-97.* Describes a late Victorian house, restored and reopened in 1968, which portrays the material wealth of the home life of a well-to-do civil servant and his family, ca. 1861-89.

3. Adamski, Władysław. RODZINA AMERYKAŃSKA: PRZEMIANY W STRUKTURZE I FUNKCJACH SOCJALIZACYJNO-WYCHOWAWC-ZYCH [The American family: changes in the socializing-educational structure and functions]. *Kultura i Społeczeństwo [Poland] 1976 20(3): 173-192.* The American family has undergone drastic changes in the last 30 years. Now smaller, more isolated, and financially more secure, it is undergoing an internal crisis. The parents absorbed in their professional careers have less contact with their children; consequently the education of youth is left increasingly to the outside world. Because there is greater freedom, favoring liberation from traditional norms and cultural values, one can expect fast changes in the dominant culture and principles of American society.   M. Swiecicka-Ziemianek

4. Åkerman, Sune; Kronborg, Bo; and Nilsson, Thomas.   EMIGRATION, FAMILY AND KINSHIP. *Am. Studies in Scandinavia [Norway] 1977 9(1-2): 105-122.* Instead of relying on an aggregate analysis, traces individual emigrating groups from Finland and Sweden to North America, to shed some light on the importance of kinship ties for migrational patterns.

5. Alger, Hugh Wesley.   CROPS AND CHORES: PENNSYLVANIA FARM LIFE IN THE 1890'S. *Pennsylvania Mag. of Hist. and Biog. 1961 85(4): 367-410.* A transcript, with brief introductory notes, of a selection from the reminiscences of Hugh Wesley Alger, which portray the difficulties of farm life in Bradford County, Pennsylvania, during the 1890's.

6.   Alter, Jonathan.   STAND BY FOR THE NON-EVENT OF THE YEAR. *Washington Monthly 1980 12(4): 22-24.* Issues discussed at the White House Conference on Families held in June, 1980, considered a farce both because of the controversial choice of the first conference director, Patsy Fleming, a black divorcee who finally quit, and because of the debate over defining the family, and other nonissues, leaving unexamined realistic alternatives to the breakup of the traditional family begun in the 1960's.

7.   Anderson, Michael.   FAMILY AND CLASS IN NINETEENTH-CEN-TURY CITIES. *J. of Family Hist. 1977 2(2): 139-149.* Reviews the first book-length product of the Canadian Social History Project at the University of Toronto, Michael B. Katz's *The People of Hamilton, Canada West: Family and Class in a Mid-Nineteenth-Century City.* Analyzes each of Katz's main themes: the distribution of wealth and power, social and geographic mobility, and the structure and role of the family. 10 notes, biblio.   T. W. Smith

8.   Anderson, Solena.   BACK IN 'DEM DAYS: A BLACK FAMILY REMI-NISCES.   *J. of Mississippi Hist. 1974 36(2): 179-185.* Describes "the folkways of blacks living in the Homochitto River Valley of southwestern Mississippi," including home cures, superstitions, and miscellaneous social customs. Based on the author's interviews with relatives.   J. W. Hillje

9.   Andrews, Dale K., ed.   FAMILY TRAITS: VERMONT FARM LIFE AT THE TURN OF THE CENTURY: THE SKETCHES OF STANLEY HO-RACE LYNDES.   *Vermont Hist. 1980 48(1): 5-27.* While at Pratt Institute, 1918-22, Stanley Horace Lyndes (1898-1975) made sketches for an art assign-ment, reproduced here with his captions, of his family doing chores, haying, racing, trapping, sugaring off, playing practical jokes; of the ragman, the swim-ming hole, the snow-roller, and the neighbors. Raised on farms in Cabot, Calais, and Marshfield, Vermont, he taught manual arts in secondary schools and sum-mer camps and retired to Plainfield, Vermont. Introduction by his granddaugh-ter, the editor, based on family tradition, her memories of the artist's stories, and town records.   T. D. S. Bassett

10.   Andrews, Peter.   GENEALOGY: THE SEARCH FOR A PERSONAL PAST.   *Am. Heritage 1982 33(5): 10-17.* A history of genealogical research in America that concludes that the current surge of interest in tracing one's roots is linked directly to a feeling of uncertainty and a desire to "go home." Genealo-gists, given impetus by the nation's centennial and bicentennial celebrations, seek their pasts for various reasons. Earlier, the hope was to find gentility, but now adverse findings are often considered preferable. The current surge of interest has resulted in tougher standards and greater acceptance of the historical value of genealogy.   Photo, 7 illus.   J. F. Paul

11.   Angel, Ronald and Tienda, Marta.   DETERMINANTS OF EXTENDED HOUSEHOLD STRUCTURE: CULTURAL PATTERN OR ECONOMIC NEED?   *Am. J. of Sociol. 1982 87(6): 1360-1383.* Discusses the income distribu-tion in Hispanic, black, and non-Hispanic white extended-family households, concluding that nonnuclear members of both poor and nonpoor black and His-panic households contribute significantly to the household income, contrary to the practice of the non-Hispanic whites; evidence suggests that the income contri-bution is due to economic need.

12.　Appleby, Joyce O.; commentary by Lindstrom, Diane E.　THE CHANG-
ING PROSPECT OF THE FAMILY FARM IN THE EARLY NATIONAL
PERIOD.　*Working Papers for the Regional Econ. Hist. Res. Center 1981 4(3):
1-25.* Discusses the growth of American agriculture from 1776 to the early 19th
century, traces Thomas Jefferson's espousal of natural rights and limited government back to the ideal prospects open to farm families during this period, and
compares the situation in Great Britain; commentary, pp. 61-69.

13.　Aquino, Salvatore A.　THE THIRD OF TWELVE.　*Italian Americana
1978 4(1): 65-71.* Reminiscences of an Italian immigrant family's daily life in New
York City in 1914, including the house, chores, and family relations.

14.　Armstrong, Frederick H.　THE OLIGARCHY OF THE WESTERN
DISTRICT OF UPPER CANADA, 1788-1841.　*Can. Hist. Assoc. Hist. Papers
[Canada] 1977: 86-103.* An early elite controlled government in the Western
District of Upper Canada, maintaining what was essentially an oligarchy. The
control was maintained at all levels of government by "Family Compact," a
self-perpetuating arrangement. Several factors affected original family involvement: ethnic to some extent, merchant class (because of literacy and wealth),
military and government connections, and, above all, family connections. Magis-
tracy became practically hereditary. All of this is illustrated by the histories of
three families. 14 notes.　　　　　　　　　　　　　　　　R. V. Ritter

15.　Armstrong, Thomas F. and Fennell, Janice C.　HISTORICAL AND
GENEALOGICAL GOLD MINE: AN INDEX PROJECT FOR A SMALL-
TOWN NEWSPAPER.　*RQ 1982 22(2): 140-145.* Access to the information of
small-town newspapers is limited by both availability of the papers and the lack
of suitable indexes. In an effort to solve these problems, the authors have started
an index-abstract, obtained funding, and are computerizing the index for the
Milledgeville *Southern Recorder,* in Georgia. The project and its successor newspapers (1820-present) will be of value to librarians, historians, genealogists, and
public officials.　　　　　　　　　　　　　　　　　　　　J/S

16.　Auwarter, Ruth.　A GENEALOGICAL FILE.　*Nova Scotia Hist. Q.
[Canada] 1976 6(2): 167-172.* Author discusses her experience in compiling a
genealogy for the family of Waitsill Lewis of Yarmouth, Nova Scotia, giving tips
on finding sources and methodology, 1976.

17.　Baca Zinn, Maxine.　POLITICAL FAMILIALISM: TOWARD SEX
ROLE EQUALITY IN CHICANO FAMILIES.　*Aztlan 1975 6(1): 13-37.*
Interprets changes in the Chicano family in light of the family's self-conscious
efforts to resist colonial oppression and discrimination. Political familialism is the
fusion of cultural and political resistance within the family unit. The family, for
Mexican Americans, has come to have a broader meaning than in the past, since
it incorporates loyalty to political or cultural organizations. Chicanos have been
changing their own values regarding *machismo* and women's roles. 37 notes.
　　　　　　　　　　　　　　　　　　　　　　R. Griswold del Castillo

18.　Bacchi, Carol.　LIBERATION DEFERRED: THE IDEAS OF THE EN-
GLISH-CANADIAN SUFFRAGISTS, 1877-1918.　*Social Hist. [Canada] 1977
10(20): 433-434.* The Canadian suffrage movement, initially committed to sexual
equality, was infiltrated by social reformers in the 1880's. Mainly middle class

traditionalists, the reformers wanted to preserve and strengthen the old order and their own positions. They regarded the family as the fundamental social unit and believed woman suffrage would give mothers a political voice and strengthen the family by doubling its representation. Feminists reactivated the movement in 1906 after an 11-year lull, but feminist concerns declined.   D. F. Chard

19.   Bahr, Howard M.   RELIGIOUS CONTRASTS IN FAMILY ROLE DEFINITIONS AND PERFORMANCE: UTAH MORMONS, CATHOLICS, PROTESTANTS AND OTHERS.   *J. for the Sci. Study of Religion 1982 21(3): 200-217.* Examines differences in family attitudes, using questionnaires from 1974, and finds the Mormons to be more family centered in attitude though not in behavior.

20.   Barclay, Richard L.   ACCESS TO INFORMATION WITH A GENEALOGY AND HISTORY INFORMATION FILE.   *RQ 1978 18(2): 153-155.* The Bristol Public Library's (Bristol, Virginia-Tennessee) Genealogy and History Referral File, covering parts of Virginia, Tennessee, and Georgia, so far lists 850 different names, more than 235 biographical references, 120 historical items, and more than 175 voluntary participants willing to assist researchers.
                                                                                                          D. J. Engler

21.   Barney, William L.   PATTERNS OF CRISIS: ALABAMA WHITE FAMILIES AND SOCIAL CHANGE, 1850-1870.   *Sociol. and Social Res. 1979 63(3): 524-543.* This essay focuses on a generation of Alabama whites, drawn from four distinctive ecological and cultural zones, who lived through the period of intensifying sectionalism, the Civil War, and its legacy of defeat and poverty. Such an examination of various contexts of white Southern community life permits the investigation of the impact on the Southern social order of two ongoing crises—the first related to the role of slavery as an agent of socio-economic change which precipitated a Southern version of a modernization crisis hitherto identified primarily with the North; and the second related to the traumatic experience of defeat in the Civil War. The essay seeks to demonstrate that the pattern of white responses to these crises was a function of the contrasting strengths and stabilities of regional cultures markedly different in family and household structures and in stages of economic development.   J

22.   Beall, Pamela; Leon, Warren; O'Connell, Peter; and Rothman, Ellen. STUDENTS AND FAMILY HISTORY: THE VIEW FROM OLD STURBRIDGE VILLAGE.   *J. of Family Hist. 1981 6(1): 5-14.* Discusses methods of teaching family history and sources for its study. Covers traditional literary sources and documents but emphasizes physical artifacts. Biblio.
                                                                                                          T. W. Smith

23.   Bean, Frank D. and Swicegood, Gray.   GENERATION, FEMALE EDUCATION AND MEXICAN-AMERICAN FERTILITY.   *Social Sci. Q. 1982 63(1): 131-144.* The decrease in Mexican-American fertility is due to the length of exposure to the receiving society (measured by generation) and to rising socioeconomic status (measured by female education); moreover, most Mexican-American women of later generations and greater education manifest even lower cumulative fertility than would be expected considering indicators of these variables separately, which suggests a modified theory of minority group status effects on fertility.

24. Bellard, Lewis and Ford, Judy, comp. INDEX TO "DECLARATIONS OF MARRIAGE OF NEGROES AND MULATTOES, 1866-1884, TODD COUNTY, COUNTY COURT CLERK". *J. of the Afro-American Hist. and Geneal. Soc. 1980 (1): 26-29.* Records from Kentucky.

25. Bellard, Lewis and Ford, Judy, comp. INDEX TO "MARRIAGE BONDS FOR NEGROES AND MULATTOES, 1866-1872, TODD COUNTY, COUNTY COURT CLERK". *J. of the Afro-American Hist. and Geneal. Soc. 1980 (1): 21-26.* Kentucky records.

26. Bernard, Jessie. FACING THE FUTURE. *Society 1981 18(2): 53-59.* Discusses the collapse of the traditional family during the 1960's and 1970's, examining public and government responses; focuses on the efforts of the New Right to oppose liberal programs which it feels are detrimental to the family; and argues that attempts to turn back the clock are futile.

27. Bigham, Darrel E. THE BLACK FAMILY IN EVANSVILLE AND VANDERBURGH COUNTY, INDIANA, IN 1880. *Indiana Mag. of Hist. 1979 75(2): 117-146.* Traditionally, sociologists have argued that slavery was the cause of the instability of Afro-American families. Analysis of the 1880 federal census for Vanderburgh County, Indiana, demonstrates that Afro-American family instability resulted from the urban experience rather than from the legacy of slavery. The census data offers considerable support for the integrity and strength of the Afro-American family in post-Civil War Indiana. 49 notes.   J. Moore

28. Bigham, Darrel E. THE BLACK FAMILY IN EVANSVILLE AND VANDERBURGH COUNTY, INDIANA: A 1900 POSTSCRIPT. *Indiana Mag. of Hist. 1982 78(2): 154-169.* A comparison of census returns for 1880 and 1900 shows that although most black families were male-headed at both times, the percentage had declined by 1900. The division of blacks among various occupational groups did not shift notably during the interval. There was a definite shift from rural to urban residence for blacks. Although life for black families continued to be harsh in economic terms, the two-parent family dominated among both urban and rural blacks. Based on US Census, 1880 and 1900; 12 notes, 9 tables, 2 pictures.   A. Erlebacher

29. Bigham, Darrel E. FAMILY STRUCTURE OF GERMANS AND BLACKS IN EVANSVILLE AND VANDERBURGH COUNTY, INDIANA, IN 1880: A COMPARATIVE STUDY. *Old Northwest 1981 7(3): 255-275.* Compares the effect that urbanization had on the family structure of German Americans and blacks in Evansville. Census records indicate that black and white families were not significantly different in proportion of male-headed families as is traditionally assumed. Social and economic circumstances, rather than family conditions, were the basis for differences between black and white families. Because of poverty and discrimination, blacks had smaller families, took in more lodgers, and had a higher percentage of working wives and children than did whites. Based on the manuscript census for Vanderburgh County, 1880, and other primary sources; 48 notes.   P. L. McLaughlin

30. Billman, Carol. WOMEN AND THE FAMILY IN AMERICAN DRAMA. *Arizona Q. 1980 36(1): 35-48.* Gives various views of women's positions and attitudes in American drama from 1920 through the 1960's. Clare

Boothe and Lillian Hellman are female playrights who have depicted women as wicked and dependent beings. Rachel Crothers contributed to the stage more liberated women or women struggling to become liberated, than has any other playwright. Some authors present pictures of women's powerless domesticity. Some plays look at women's changing relationship with their mothers, and at the "feminine birthright of domesticity." 24 notes.   E. P. Stickney

31.   Bitton, Davis.   ZION'S ROWDIES: GROWING UP ON THE MOR-MON FRONTIER.   *Utah Hist. Q. 1982 50(2): 182-195.* Numerous visitors in Salt Lake City noted many children on its streets. Accounts related most were noisy, boisterous, and disrestful. Acts of vandalism and property destruction were reported. To discourage idleness and disrespect, the Primary (for children under 12), Young Women's and Young Men's Mutual Improvement Association, and Sunday School were instituted. Rowdyism resulted largely as a reaction to the high degree of religious emphasis in family and community life, obedience expected from children, work ethic emphasis, and the singular role of mother in family control. Mormon children, especially from large families, were more programmed than in other western frontier societies.   Photo, 48 notes.
K. E. Gilmont

32.   Blumin, Stuart M.   RIP VAN WINKLE'S GRANDCHILDREN: FAM-ILY AND HOUSEHOLD IN THE HUDSON VALLEY 1800-1860.   *J. of Urban Hist. 1975 1(3): 293-315.* Troy, Kingston, and Marlborough represent industrial, commercial and agricultural towns respectively. Concludes that similarities in family characteristics among the three—household size, boarding houses as a transient experience, and four-fifths of the population living in nuclear families—outweigh the differences. 11 tables, 20 notes.   S. S. Sprague

33.   Bogardus, Carl R., Sr.   BLACK MARRIAGES, GALLATIN COUNTY, KENTUCKY, 1866 TO 1913.   *J. of the Afro-American Hist. and Geneal. Soc. 1981 2(3): 117-122, (4): 161-175.* Alphabetical list by bridegroom's last name of marriages from the "Record Book for Colored Marriages" in Gallatin County; includes a bride index and an index of people officiating.

34.   Boocock, Sarane Spence.   HISTORICAL AND SOCIOLOGICAL RE-SEARCH ON THE FAMILY AND THE LIFE CYCLE: METHODOLOGI-CAL ALTERNATIVES.   Demos, John and Boocock, Sarane Spence, ed. *Turning Points: Historical and Sociological Essays on the Family* (Chicago: U. of Chicago Pr., 1978): 366-394. Discusses data sources, selection of cases for research, and data analysis in the historical methodology of some of the historical papers in this volume, and suggests some sociological approaches to enhance the historians' data analysis; 1950's-70's.

35.   Bosher, J. F.   FRENCH PROTESTANT FAMILIES IN CANADIAN TRADE 1740-1760.   *Social Hist. [Canada] 1974 7(14): 179-201.* Protestant merchants in Quebec increased in number after the end of the War of Austrian Succession in 1748. By the time Quebec fell in 1759 they may have been preponderant in Franco-Canadian trade. Information on the origins, family ties, and business connections of the 16 identifiable Protestant firms indicates they came from and maintained ties with southwestern France (La Rochelle, Bordeaux, and Montauban) and were willing to trade with anyone, but formed companies and

married only with other Protestants. Based on secondary sources and on documents in the Archives nationales, Public Record Office, Bibliothèque de l'Arsenal (Paris), Public Archives of Canada, and departmental and town archives in France; 82 notes. W. K. Hobson

36. Bosworth, Timothy W. THE GENEALOGY AS A SOURCE FOR RESEARCH ON MIGRANTS BEFORE 1850: A RESEARCH NOTE. *Hist. Methods 1978 11(4): 177-179.* Given the data limitation of the census before 1850, and its nonexistence before 1790, Bosworth has used the *New England Historical and Genealogical Register,* the *Pennsylvania Genealogical Magazine,* and the *Virginia Genealogist* in his statistical research; unfortunately, the data is usually on the upper class, white, male, Protestant, and descendants of those residing in America before 1825. Other groups are ignored. Table, 8 notes.
D. K. Pickens

37. Bouchard, Gérard. FAMILY STRUCTURE AND GEOGRAPHIC MOBILITY AT LATERRIÈRE, 1851-1935. *J. of Family Hist. 1977 2(4): 350-369.* Using both family reconstitution and census records, examines demographic trends in Laterrière, Quebec. There was a high degree of population turnover and net migration was the key determinant of the rate of population change. Examines the influence of the community's hybrid system of farming and lumbering on its general economic development. Map, 8 tables, 4 graphs, 26 notes, biblio. T. W. Smith

38. Boyers, Robert. THE LAINGIAN FAMILY. *Partisan R. 1974 41(1): 109-118.* Critique of R. D. Laing's ideas on authority and the nuclear family. Notes the tendency of counterculture spokesmen to confuse authoritarian political institutions with simple restraints and limitations within the family unit. The two institutions are different. Many patients "have been brought to their confusion precisely by the failure of parents and others to set limits and make clear distinctions." D. K. Pickens

39. Boyers, Robert. THE WOMAN QUESTION AND THE DEATH OF THE FAMILY. *Dissent 1973 20(1): 57-66.*

40. Boylan, Anne M. FAMILY HISTORY QUESTIONNAIRES: TWO EXAMPLES. *Hist. Teacher 1977 10(2): 211-219.* Discusses survey questionnaires on family history. Tells about two classroom situations in which the questionnaires have been implemented and concludes that questionnaires enable students to acquire a consciousness of themselves and their families. They also spark discussion on topics such as class structure and mobility. Primary and secondary sources; 2 illus., 4 notes. P. W. Kennedy

41. Boylan, Anne M. THE FAMILY OF WOMAN. *Rev. in Am. Hist. 1980 8(4): 431-436.* Review essay of Carl N. Degler's *At Odds: Women and the Family in America from the Revolution to the Present* (New York: Oxford U. Pr., 1980).

42. Brackbill, Yvonne and Howell, Embry M. RELIGIOUS DIFFERENCES IN FAMILY SIZE PREFERENCE AMONG AMERICAN TEENAGERS. *Sociol. Analysis 1974 35(1): 35-44.* "This paper analyzes differences between Catholic and non-Catholic young people in attitudes toward family formation. A sample of 941 students in junior high schools, high schools, and

colleges in the Washington, D.C. area responded to a self-administered questionnaire in 1971. Data were obtained on students' background, attitudes toward family formation, girls' career aspirations, and population awareness. In general, results emphasize and reemphasize the continuing importance of a religious differential in family size preference. Religious affiliation was more predictive of preferred family size than was race, sex, age, socio-economic status, number of siblings, type of school, maternal work history, or girls' career aspirations. These results differ from those obtained in recent studies based on short term trends in religious conformity but are consistent with longer term trends."   J

43.   Brandes, Stanley H.   FAMILY MISFORTUNE STORIES IN AMERICAN FOLKLORE.   *J. of the Folklore Inst. 1975 12(1): 5-17.* Discusses the theme of family misfortune in folktales in the 20th century, including the role of the Protestant Ethic, values, and attitudes toward success and social status.

44.   Breines, Wini; Cerullo, Margaret; and Stacey, Judith.   SOCIAL BIOLOGY, FAMILY STUDIES, AND ANTIFEMINIST BACKLASH. *Feminist Studies 1978 4(1): 43-67.* The *Daedalus* issue on "The Family" (Spring 1977) expresses bioevolutionary and modernization theory which reverses the feminist perspective on the family as shaped historically, not biologically. Concludes with remarks on Christopher Lasch's articles in the *New York Review of Books* (Nov.-Dec. 1975) and *Salmagundi* (Fall 1976-Winter 1977), and excerpts from his *Haven in a Heartless World: The Family Besieged* (1977). The breakdown of the patriarchal family is interpreted as a more positive development than Lasch believes. 76 notes.   L. M. Maloney

45.   Brewster-Walker, Sandi J. and McDuffie-Hare, Mary.   BRIDGEPORT, CONNECTICUT, BIRTHS OF BLACKS: ABSTRACTS OF RECORDS 1855-1864 AND 1871-1885.   *J. of the Afro-American Hist. and Geneal. Soc. 1983 4(1): 23-31.* Gives the following information: name of child, date of birth; mother's name, age, birthplace, color or race; father's name, age, birthplace, occupation, race or color; other children in the family; and physician's name.

46.   Brewster-Walker, Sandi J.   INDEXES OF SOME RECORDS OF CONNECTICUT BLACKS.   *J. of the Afro-American Hist. and Geneal. Soc. 1983 4(1): 35-38.* Includes blacks found in Patten's *1840 New Haven Directory* and headstone inscriptions from Charles R. Hale's *Connecticut Headstone Inscriptions* (1934).

47.   Brobeck, Stephen.   IMAGES OF THE FAMILY: PORTRAIT PAINTINGS AS INDICES OF AMERICAN FAMILY CULTURE, STRUCTURE AND BEHAVIOR, 1730-1860.   *J. of Psychohistory 1977 5(1): 81-106.* Utilizes portrait paintings of the 18th and 19th centuries to study issues in American family history, including childrearing practices, family structure and relationships, and changing aspects of material culture. Based on 251 portraits commissioned between 1730 and 1860, and secondary sources; 2 tables, 47 notes, appendix.   R. E. Butchart

48.   Brody, Elaine M.   THE AGING OF THE FAMILY.   *Ann. of the Am. Acad. of Pol. and Social Sci. 1978 438: 13-27.* A central policy issue is the development of services for older people in the United States, specifically the extent to which families can be expected to continue to provide the bulk of needed

services vis-à-vis community responsibility. Though there has been thorough documentation of continuing responsible family behavior toward their aged, the development of services provided by the community has been hampered by the myth of widespread family abandonment. Historically, adult children, primarily daughters and daughters-in-law, have provided the vast majority of care services for the old. The oldest segment of the elderly population has been increasing proportionately at a much more rapid rate than the older population as a whole and this trend will continue. Those on whom they depend, therefore, also are older—often in the aging phase of life themselves. The fact that there now exist many of these aging families in which the adult children as well as parent(s) are old serves to reduce family resources for service provision. Another relevant social trend is the increasing entry of women into the work force, a trend which is bound to make them less available as care givers. Though family concerns, caring, and affectional ties have not diminished, the community must develop supportive services to supplement and buttress the family's efforts to care for its aged members.   J

49.   Brown, Janet and Loy, Pamela.   CINDERELLA AND SLIPPERY JACK: SEX ROLES AND SOCIAL MOBILITY THEMES IN EARLY MUSI-CAL COMEDY.   *Int. J. of Women's Studies [Canada] 1981 4(5): 507-516.* Early musical comedy, depicting marriage as the ideal feminine state, functioned as a medium of wish fulfillment, combining the changing social reality with older, patriarchal values, characterizing women with the passive qualities of charm and beauty, toiling in humble service professions.

50.   Brunger, Alan G.   GEOGRAPHICAL PROPINQUITY AMONG PRE-FAMINE CATHOLIC IRISH SETTLERS IN UPPER CANADA.   *J. of Hist. Geog. 1982 8(3): 265-282.* Large pauper families made up the bulk of a second Irish emigration to Ontario in 1825. Although Irish society valued kinship ties, these immigrants dispersed to several sites over a wide area in the uninhabited new land. Nonetheless, nuclear family members settled in close proximity. Other factors contributing to settlement locations included membership in social institu-tions in Ireland and the existence of a previous Irish immigration, although the latter was less evident. Absent is any consideration as to land quality. Based on documents and published primary and secondary sources; 4 maps, 6 tables, graph, 44 notes.   A. J. Larson

51.   Campbell, D'Ann and Jensen, Richard.   COMMUNITY AND FAMILY HISTORY AT THE NEWBERRY LIBRARY: SOME SOLUTIONS TO A NATIONAL NEED.   *Hist. Teacher 1977 11(1): 47-54.* Discusses efforts of the Newberry Library in Chicago to revitalize the study of community and family history. Includes discussion of the Newberry Workshops in community history, the more recent program in state and community history, and the projected Chicago History Fair.   P. W. Kennedy

52.   Carter, Barbara L.   REFORM SCHOOL FAMILIES.   *Society 1973 11(1): 36-43.* Describes the establishment of make-believe families in a girls' reform school.   S

53.   Cassity, Michael J.   SLAVES, FAMILIES, AND "LIVING SPACE": A NOTE ON EVIDENCE AND HISTORICAL CONTEXT.   *Southern Studies 1978 17(2): 209-215.* The family was an extremely important institution within slavery which both black slaves and white owners recognized. "Living space" is that latitude possessed by slaves for the exercise of autonomy and initiative within the restraints of slavery. Whether the family was an agency of social control which served to stabilize and perpetuate slavery or whether it was potentially assertive as a culture within the slave community has not yet been clearly demonstrated by historians. A true understanding of the slave family depends on further research into the family structure and life of slaves within particular environments such as a plantation, a group of farms, or single communities. Based on the Eugene Genovese book *Roll, Jordan, Roll* (1974) and the Herbert Gutman book *The Black Family in Slavery and Freedom, 1750-1925* (1976); 15 notes.
J. Buschen

54.   Castonguay, Charles.   EXOGAMIE ET ANGLICISATION CHEZ LES MINORITÉS CANADIENNES-FRANÇAISES   [Exogamy and anglicization among the French Canadian minorities]. *Can. Rev. of Sociol. and Anthrop. [Canada] 1979 16(1): 21-46.* Relying on data derived from the 1971 census, the causal relations between linguistic exogamy and assimilation among the nine provincial minorities of French mother tongue are investigated. Rates of anglicization, matrimonial cohabitation, exogamy, and precocious anglicization are first defined, then calculated for different age groups. Anglicization rates for francophone spouses in linguistically homogeneous and heterogeneous marriages are also established for each province. It is observed that among those minorities which best resist anglicization, mixed marriages indeed appear to be the principal factor initiating transfer to English as the home language. Among the less resistant minorities, however, this causal relation is less evident, if not outright reversed, with exogamy appearing instead to accompany, or even to follow from a number of other anglicizing factors which lead the minorities towards a type of language transfer which is rather more evolutionary in nature than catastrophic. 6 tables, ref.
J

55.   Castonguay, Charles.   LA MONTÉE DE L'EXOGAMIE CHEZ LES JEUNES FRANCOPHONES HORS QUÉBEC   [The increase in exogamy among young Francophones outside Quebec]. *Action Natl. [Canada] 1978 68(3): 219-224.* The 1971 census shows that in all Canadian provinces outside Quebec except New Brunswick, more than 90% of French Canadians with non-French spouses had adopted English as their primary language. In addition, the tendency for Francophones to enter such mixed marriages has increased each decade. The 1976 census shows, for the first time in Canada's history, an absolute decline in the French population outside Quebec. It appears that neither federal nor provincial policies will be able to preserve a French minority in any province except New Brunswick. Based on the 1971 and 1976 Canadian censuses; table.
A. W. Novitsky

56.   Castonguay, Charles and Veltman, Calvin.   L'ORIENTATION LINGUISTIQUE DES MARIAGES MIXTES DANS LA REGION DE MONTREAL   [Linguistic orientation of mixed marriages in the Montreal region]. *Recherches Sociographiques [Canada] 1980 21(3): 225-251.* English dominates as the language of usage in Montreal area families made up of partners from two

different language groups even when the mother tongue of both partners is not English. Marriages between English and French partners diminish when the English male comes from a higher socioeconomic category. Based on 1971 Canada Census figures; 9 tables, 34 notes.   A. E. LeBlanc

57.   Cauthers, Janet, ed.   A TIME OF FAMILY LIFE: MAKING THEIR OWN AMUSEMENTS. *Sound Heritage [Canada] 1978 7(3): 46-59.* The recreation of Victoria's families between 1880 and 1914 included picnics, dances, concerts, and sports events.

58.   Cherlin, Andrew J.   EXPLAINING THE POSTWAR BABY BOOM. *Social Sci. Res. Council Items 1981 35(4): 57-63.* Notes causes and effects of the postwar baby boom, and how historical circumstances have shaped trends in family life since the Depression; the Depression influenced the attitudes of men and women growing up in the 1930's regarding home and family life, thus resulting in an emphasis on childbearing in the 1950's.

59.   Chudacoff, Howard P.   NEW BRANCHES ON THE TREE: HOUSEHOLD STRUCTURE IN EARLY STAGES OF THE FAMILY CYCLE IN WORCESTER, MASSACHUSETTS, 1860-1880. *Pro. of the Am. Antiquarian Soc. 1976 86(2): 303-320.* Links family history and urban history by examining family adjustment to change in a growing city. The nuclear family prevailed here, but living arrangements varied among families in different stages of development. Contextual factors, such as housing supplies, physical growth of the city, and economic change, caused household structures to fluctuate. Primary and secondary sources; 35 notes.   J. Andrew

60.   Cole, Thomas R.   FAMILY, SETTLEMENT, AND MIGRATION IN SOUTHEASTERN MASSACHUSETTS, 1650-1805: THE CASE FOR REGIONAL ANALYSIS. *New England Hist. and Geneal. Register 1978 132(July): 171-185.* Instead of comparing periodic community listings, this study uses biographical analyses of five generations of descendants from eight early settlers in Sandwich, Massachusetts. Factors such as birth order and inheritance, family size, age at first marriage, and age at death demonstrate the closeness and strength of family ties. Migration patterns indicate descendants tended to remain in Sandwich or close by. Computer analysis of primary and secondary sources; 7 tables, chart, 40 notes.   A. E. Huff

61.   Coleman, Michael C.   CHRISTIANIZING AND AMERICANIZING THE NEZ PERCE: SUE L. MC BETH AND HER ATTITUDES TO THE INDIANS. *J. of Presbyterian Hist. 1975 53(4): 339-361.* Discusses the personal attitudes of Sue L. McBeth, a Scotland-born American Presbyterian missionary to the Nez Percé Indians, as well as those of the Mission Board of the Presbyterian Church in the last quarter of the 19th century. Her attitude to the Indian culture was one of sustained and relentless hostility. Christianity was equated with Americanism. The only "good" Indian was the converted one. Conversion embraced the totality of life—religion, eating habits, dress, family living, agriculture. The Indian was urged to forsake his old customs and enter the mainstream of American life. Miss McBeth gave a score of years to the training of Nez Percé Christians so that they would become leaders in their church. Based on documents in the Presbyterian Historical Society (American Indian Correspondence Collection) and secondary works; illus., 85 notes.   H. M. Parker, Jr.

62.   Conk, Margo.   ESSAY REVIEW: INDUSTRIAL PHILADELPHIA. *Pennsylvania Mag. of Hist. and Biog. 1982 106(3): 423-432. Philadelphia: Work, Space, Family, and Group Experience in the Nineteenth Century* (1981), edited by Theodore Hershberg, an interdisciplinary cooperative venture, represents the first collected results of the Philadelphia Social History Project. Though it provides details of life in an expanding city, it lacks historical narrative and periodization, most apparent in its discussion of blacks. Secondary works; 10 notes.
                                                                T. H. Wendel

63.   Copeley, William.   FAMILY NAMES IN NEW HAMPSHIRE TOWN HISTORIES, 1947-1980.   *Hist. New Hampshire 1980 35(4): 417-439.* A supplement to "Family Names in New Hampshire Town Histories," *Historical New Hampshire,* (1946). This index includes family names from 65 town histories published between 1947 and 1980. Families were included where a book gave at least three generations, and where the family was traced back earlier than 1900.
                                                                D. F. Chard

64.   Coty, Ellen M.   RESEARCH AIDS: GENEALOGY IN WESTERN MASSACHUSETTS.   *Hist. J. of Western Massachusetts 1978 6(2): 42-48.* Reviews the sources for genealogical research in the following western Massachusetts libraries: Springfield City Library, Forbes Library, Connecticut State Library, the Berkshire Atheneum, local historical societies, municipal agencies, and court houses.   W. H. Mulligan, Jr.

65.   Cremin, Lawrence A.   THE FAMILY AS EDUCATION: SOME COMMENTS ON RECENT HISTORIOGRAPHY.   *Teachers Coll. Record 1974 76(2): 250-265.* Examines the recent literature in the history of the family with a special focus on America. Values the focus on the role of the family as educator in Bernard Bailyn's *Education in the Forming of American Society* (New York: Norton, 1972), a theme which has rarely been dealt with.
                                                                W. H. Mulligan, Jr.

66.   Culbert, David H.   THE INFINITE VARIETY OF MASS EXPERIENCE: THE GREAT DEPRESSION, W.P.A. INTERVIEWS, AND STUDENT FAMILY HISTORY PROJECTS.   *Louisiana Hist. 1978 19(1): 43-63.* Both the Works Progress Administration life histories and the 240 family histories written by the author's Louisiana State University students are excellent sources for the history of the common people during the Depression. Analyzes these sources, comparing them on the basis of area of coverage, persons interviewed, interviewers, documentation, attitudes of interviewers, focus, language, and historical value. Concludes that the "life histories offer an extraordinary record of those who survived the 1930s outside, for the most part, conventional society," while "the family histories provide a rich account of entire families during the 1930s." 10 photos, 48 notes.   R. L. Woodward

67.   Culpepper, Betty M.   GENEALOGICAL RESOURCES AT THE MOORLAND-SPINGARN RESEARCH CENTER.   *J. of the Afro-American Hist. and Geneal. Soc. 1981 2(3): 93-98.* Brief history of Howard University, founded in 1867, and its Moorland-Spingarn Research Center, focusing on the center's purpose and rich resources for Afro-American genealogy.

68.   Curtis, Bruce.   VICTORIANS ABED: WILLIAM GRAHAM SUMNER ON THE FAMILY, WOMEN AND SEX.   *Am. Studies [Lawrence, KS] 1977 18(1): 101-122.* Did a Victorian consensus concerning sexuality exist? Sumner's life reveals many tensions and inconsistencies, although he generally supported the sexual status quo. His ideal of the middle class family, nonetheless, led him to oppose the double sexual standard and to question the idea of a stable Victorian consensus on sexuality. He supported humane divorce policies and kinder treatment for prostitutes, and recognized women as sexual beings. Primary and secondary sources; 4 notes.   J. Andrew

69.   Daniels, Bruce C.   FAMILY DYNASTIES IN CONNECTICUT'S LARGEST TOWNS, 1700-1760.   *Can. J. of Hist. 1973 8(2): 99-110.* Historiographical examination of theses on the nature of colonial American politics based on an analysis of office-holding patterns in three of the four leading towns of Connecticut, (Norwich, Hartford, and Fairfield, with New Haven excluded). Concludes that the same families dominated politics in these towns throughout the 18th century up to the American Revolution. Based on printed and MS. sources; 2 tables, 23 notes.   J. A. Casada

70.   D'Antonio, William V.   CONFESSIONS OF A THIRD-GENERATION ITALIAN AMERICAN.   *Society 1975 13(1): 57-63.* Describes the impact of the author's Italian American family life in Connecticut on his attitudes toward assimilation and ethnicity from approximately 1926-73.

71.   Davis, James A. and Smith, Tom W.   LOOKING BACKWARD: A NATIONAL SAMPLE SURVEY OF ANCESTORS AND PREDECESSORS, 1980-1850.   *Hist. Methods 1980 13(3): 145-162.* This article provides background to the survey and explains the confluence of history and sociology in the study of the family. This genealogical approach to American social history should allow for a validity check of several theories found in the historical scholarship. 4 tables, 60 notes, 4 appendixes.   D. K. Pickens

72.   Davisson, Lori.   THE APACHES AT HOME: A PHOTOGRAPHIC ESSAY.   *J. of Arizona Hist. 1973 14(2): 113-132.* Their environment and religious beliefs shaped the daily lives of the Apache before the arrival of Europeans. Contact with the Spanish and the Anglo-Americans brought irreversible destruction or modification of the old patterns of life and introduced new ones. The transition can be documented from the 1880's when photographers began making pictorial records. 25 illustrations with accompanying textual comment show some of the changes in the Arizona Apache, especially the women.

D. L. Smith

73.   Dearborn, David C.   NEW HAMPSHIRE GENEALOGY: A PERSPECTIVE.   *New England Hist. and Genealogical Register 1976 130(October): 244-258.* Evaluates published sources for New Hampshire family and local history, including genealogical dictionaries, bibliographic surveys, state papers, periodicals, military records, atlases, directories, local histories, and genealogies. The towns of southern New Hampshire, especially in the southwestern area, have the most complete town histories, but (except for scattered counties) the rest of the state remains to be done. Based on published sources; 2 maps, 5 notes, biblio.

S. L. Patterson

74.   Degler, Carl N.   WOMEN AND THE FAMILY.   Kammen, Michael, ed. *The Past Before Us: Contemporary Historical Writing in the United States* (Ithaca, N.Y.: Cornell U. Pr., 1980): 308-326. Women's history and family history are relatively recent additions to the field of US history, because the greatest volume of work in these areas appeared in the 1960's. Although they would seem to be related, they arose out of different needs and developed separately. Women's history developed to meet a need for a past in response to changes in American society. Family history grew out of demographic history and developed more slowly because it lacked active promotion by a social group. Both grew in response to a new perspective of the past which recognizes the importance of family studies and women's contributions. A new definition of the past remains to be formed before these subdisciplines become fully integrated into general history. 50 notes.   S

75.   Delude-Clift, Camille and Champoux, Edouard.   LE CONFLIT DES GÉNÉRATIONS   [The generations conflict]. *Recherches Sociographiques [Canada] 1973 14(2): 157-201.* An analysis of the perceptions of adults and adolescents with respect to family, religion, and education shows that the socio-economic milieu of the individual determines attitudes concerning social integration, whereas age is an important factor in the quest for identity. Intergenerational tension is largely due to this emergence of a private self among members of the younger generation. Based on 196 interviews conducted in Québec City.   A. E. LeBlanc

76.   Demos, John.   THE AMERICAN FAMILY IN PAST TIME.   *Am. Scholar 1974 43(3): 422-446.* Traces the history of the family in the United States from colonial times to the 20th century, discussing the tremendous changes in life and culture which have put great pressures on the family. Examines authority relations in the family, the role of children, women, sex, and the impact made upon the family by immigration and Negroes. Denies there is a continuous decline and decay in the family as both conservatives and counterculturists claim.
                                                                                                C. W. Olson

77.   Doucette, Laurel.   FAMILY STUDIES AS AN APPROACH TO ORAL HISTORY.   *Can. Oral Hist. Assoc. J. [Canada] 1976/77 2: 24-31.* Excerpts a tape-recorded collection from research on the James Kealey family in Hull, Quebec, whose history lends itself to both folklore and oral history, 1974-75.

78.   Douglas, Elinor Thompson.   GROWING UP AT BROOKWOOD. *Delaware Hist. 1979 18(4): 267-274.* The author, the daughter of Mary Wilson Thompson, describes her childhood at Brookwood Farm in Delaware, near Wilmington. Notes the family diet, the family regimen of work and leisure, farm life, and the train of visitors to the family estate. Adds comments on her travels in Egypt and in the Philippines. Covers 1900's-20's.   R. M. Miller

79.   Drago, Edmund L.   THE BLACK HOUSEHOLD IN DOUGHERTY COUNTY, GEORGIA, 1870-1900.   *Prologue 1982 14(2): 81-88.* Freedmen had two primary goals: to earn sufficient money to buy a piece of land and to improve the structure and quality of black family life. Manuscript federal census returns for Dougherty County in 1870, 1880, and 1900 are used in determining how successful the blacks were, after emancipation, in achieving these goals. Based

on congressional records, censuses, and newspapers; illus., 5 photos, 27 notes.

M. A. Kascus

80. Dunlevy, J. A. and Gemery, H. A. BRITISH-IRISH SETTLEMENT PATTERNS IN THE U.S.: THE ROLE OF FAMILY AND FRIENDS. *Scottish J. of Pol. Econ. [Great Britain] 1977 24(3): 257-263.* Statistically examines Richard Vedder and Lowell Gallaway's study of British and Irish settlement patterns, using steerage passenger immigrants for 1898. The exclusion of cabin passengers and those who entered via Canada may limit the study. British and Irish immigrants were attracted to densely populated areas of high income and high employment. Although the Scots and Welsh avoided the South, Irish and English immigrants did not. After 1880 friends and families who had settled outside the South encouraged English and Irish immigrants to do likewise. 8 notes, biblio.

J. D. Neville

81. Duvall, Scott H. MORMON BIBLIOGRAPHY 1981. *Brigham Young U. Studies 1982 22(2): 227-249.* A comprehensive collection of books and articles on Mormons and Mormonism published in 1980 and 1981, divided into nine sections: arts and literature, contemporary, biographical and family history, inspirational, historical, doctrinal, bibliography, indexes, and new periodicals.

E. R. Campbell

82. Early, Frances H. THE FRENCH-CANADIAN FAMILY ECONOMY AND STANDARD OF LIVING IN LOWELL, MASSACHUSETTS, 1870. *J. of Family Hist. 1982 7(2): 180-199.* One of the lesser known rural-to-urban migrations of the 19th century was the influx of French-Canadian farmers to the mills of New England. While traditionally seen as a negative experience (driven from the land to the slums, diverted from simple rural virtues to chaotic urban vices), the French Canadians successfully managed to adapt and some prospered. Yet success was only possible through the continued use of child labor. 3 tables, 23 notes, appendix.

T. W. Smith

83. Easterlin, Richard A. THE CHANGING CIRCUMSTANCES OF CHILD-REARING. *J. of Communication 1982 32(3): 86-98.* Discusses the circumstances behind alterations in the familial structure over two decades, most noticeably a growing divorce rate, a sharp rise in work outside the home for mothers of two-parent families, and a rapid decline in the rate of child-bearing.

84. Ebel, Henry. BEING JEWISH. *J. of Psychohistory 1980 8(1): 67-76.* Contemplates "being Jewish" from the perspectives of history and of autobiographical family history. "Being Jewish is as dangerous a sport as ever."

F. F. Harling

85. Ecklein, Joan Levin and Giele, Janet Zollinger. WOMEN'S LIVES AND SOCIAL POLICY IN EAST GERMANY AND THE UNITED STATES. *Studies in Comparative Communism 1981 14(2-3): 191-207.* East Germany is one of the top 10 industrial countries in the world with a per capita income of 9,500 marks in 1980 (including subsidized or free benefits). The birth rate is growing as the state offers aid to mothers. Almost half of all students in higher education are women, but they are concentrated in education, commerce, textiles, and light industry. Married couples receive interest-free loans. The divorce rate has grown. In the United States women receive half of all the bachelors' and masters' degrees

granted. Over 20% are professionals or managers. The birth rate has declined, and the availability of child care systems has increased. Biblio.   D. Balmuth

86.   Edlefsen, L. E.   AN INVESTIGATION OF THE TIMING PATTERN OF CHILDBEARING.   *Population Studies [Great Britain] 1981 35(3): 375-386.* Examines four samples of women from the United States and the Philippines to determine the relation between the number of live births during a woman's reproductive period and her age at the time of those births; childbearing usually occurs around the middle of the fertile period regardless of the number of children, family size, and economic, social, and cultural differences.

87.   Edwards, Ozzie L.   FAMILY   FORMATION   AMONG   BLACK YOUTH.   *J. of Negro Educ. 1982 51(2): 111-122.* Although the percentage of black men and women who marry young is decreasing, the absolute number of these marriages is increasing with larger numbers of black teenagers. This issue deserves more research. Blacks who marry young have larger families, more divorces, less education, and lower socioeconomic status. Based on US Census Reports; 5 tables, biblio.   R. G. Sherer

88.   Ehrlich, Clara Hilderman.   MY CHILDHOOD ON THE PRAIRIE. *Colorado Mag. 1974 51(2): 115-140.* A descriptive autobiographical social history of the late 19th- and early 20th-century life of German-Russian immigrant farmers who settled in the South Platte Valley of northeastern Colorado. Described are sodhouses, sugar beet farming, kraut-making, butchering, hay-making, laundering, baking and shopping visits to the nearby village. Based upon reminiscences; 9 illus., 5 notes.   O. H. Zabel

89.   Elder, Glen H., Jr.   APPROACHES TO SOCIAL CHANGE AND THE FAMILY.   Demos, John and Boocock, Sarane Spence, ed. *Turning Points: Historical and Sociological Essays on the Family* (Chicago: U. of Chicago Pr., 1978): 1-38. Discusses new methodological approaches in family studies that emerged during the 1960's, and focuses on three of them: critical theory, social theory and history in an urban-industrial context, and the social historical implications of age.

90.   Eller, Ronald D.   LAND AND FAMILY: AN HISTORICAL VIEW OF PREINDUSTRIAL APPALACHIA.   *Appalachian J. 1979 6(2): 83-110.* Views social organization in Appalachia during the 1880's-90's.

91.   Ericksen, Julia and Klein, Gary.   WOMEN'S ROLES AND FAMILY PRODUCTION AMONG THE OLD ORDER AMISH.   *Rural Sociol. 1981 46(2): 282-296.* Discusses how the social roles of women help maintain Old Order Amish society in Lancaster County, Pennsylvania, examines how these roles vary according to the life cycle, and suggests that a study of this community could be useful in providing clues about women's roles in general.

92.   Etheridge, Carolyn F.   EQUALITY IN THE FAMILY: COMPARATIVE ANALYSIS AND THEORETICAL MODEL.   *Int. J. of Women's Studies [Canada] 1978 1(1): 50-63.* Couples who wish to cohabit, bear children, and maintain parent-child relations have different attitudes toward egalitarian philosophy, economic independence of men and women, equal task allocation in public and private, and collective child-rearing; covers 1849-1977.

93. Faragher, Johnny and Stansell, Christine. WOMEN AND THEIR FAMILIES ON THE OVERLAND TRAIL TO CALIFORNIA AND OREGON, 1842-1867. *Feminist Studies 1975 2(2/3): 150-166.* Examines the efforts of women to maintain a separate sphere of their own on the Overland Trail. Life on the trail expanded the work roles of women from purely domestic duties to numerous male jobs, but only drastic circumstances forced men to take on traditionally female chores. Rather than use the expanded work roles to free themselves from narrow definitions of "woman's place," women tried to preserve their circumscribed role. Their journals testify to the importance of the female sphere and the tribulations of integration. Based on diaries, journals, memoirs, and secondary works; 75 notes. J. D. Falk

94. Featherstone, Joseph. FAMILY MATTERS. *Harvard Educ. Rev. 1979 49(1): 20-52.* Discusses the current focus on the family as a symbol of stability by educators, policy makers, and researchers, based on American tradition and events of the 1960's.

95. Finkelstein, Barbara and Clignet, Remi. THE FAMILY AS INFERNO: THE DOUR VISIONS OF FOUR FAMILY HISTORIANS. *J. of Psychohistory 1981 9(1): 135-141.* Reviews Elizabeth Badinter's *L'Amour en Plus: Histoire de l'Amour Maternel* (1980), Jacques Donzelot's *The Policing of Families* (1979), Christopher Lasch's *The Culture of Narcissism: American Life in an Age of Diminishing Expectations* (1979), Lasch's *Haven in a Heartless World: The Family Besieged* (1979), and Richard Sennett's *Authority* (1980). These books focus on the negative aspects of the family and do not discuss positive values such as nurture, love, friendship, and humor between family members. L. F. Velicer

96. Fiske, Jane Fletcher. GENEALOGICAL RESEARCH IN RHODE ISLAND. *New England Hist. and Geneal. Register 1982 136(July): 173-219.* Presents a comprehensive survey of available materials, frequently designating specific locations. Some historical background is included, pointing to the essential need for familiarity with general and local history of the state. Lists archival repositories in towns and cities in Rhode Island and provides a bibliography for 100 colonial Rhode Island families. 35 notes, 2 appendixes. J/S

97. Fitzpatrick, John J. TEACHING METHODS. *Psychohistory Rev. 1976 5(1): 23-27.* Provides a list of readings for a course taught at Adelphi University in Spring 1976 called "Social History of the American Family."

98. Fogel, Robert W. and Engerman, Stanley L. RECENT FINDINGS IN THE STUDY OF SLAVE DEMOGRAPHY AND FAMILY STRUCTURE. *Sociol. and Social Res. 1979 63(3): 566-589.* Examines recent works on the demographic patterns of slave and white populations in the United States and the slave population of the British West Indies in order to summarize the principal new findings and to highlight several still unresolved issues. Studies presenting new data on fertility, mortality, and family structure are analyzed to determine the relative contributions of different factors to the differing demographic performance of US and British West Indian slaves, and to point to certain similarities in patterns between US slaves and southern whites. Table, 3 fig., 18 notes, biblio. J/S

99. Foner, Anne. AGE STRATIFICATION AND THE CHANGING FAMILY. Demos, John and Boocock, Sarane Spence, ed. *Turning Points: Historical and Sociological Essays on the Family* (Chicago: U. of Chicago Pr., 1978): 340-365. Discusses "the importance of the age structure of a family at a given period; changing family patterns over the family cycle; and the impact of the succession of cohorts of families"; 19th and 20th centuries.

100. Friedman, Reena Sigman. "SEND ME MY HUSBAND WHO IS IN NEW YORK CITY": HUSBAND DESERTION IN THE AMERICAN JEW-ISH IMMIGRANT COMMUNITY, 1900-1926. *Jewish Social Studies 1982 44(1): 1-18.* Although many American Jewish historians maintain that the Jewish family emerged unscathed from the twin traumas of migration and Americaniza-tion, the evidence suggests otherwise. The records of the National Desertion Bureau, established in 1911, shed light on the extent of desertion in the East European Jewish community in the United States, as well as on the phenomenon's causes and impact. Based on National Desertion Bureau annual reports and other primary and secondary sources; 97 notes. J. D. Sarna

101. Frisbie, Charlotte J. TRADITIONAL NAVAJO WOMEN: ETHNO-GRAPHIC AND LIFE HISTORY PORTRAYALS. *Am. Indian Q. 1982 6(1-2): 11-33.* Assesses the quality and quantity of information about traditional Navajo women in view of feminist concerns about the treatment of women in ethnography. Reviews 10 basic ethnographies and 14 published life histories. Finds treatment not "inadequate or dismal," but unbalanced. Too much emphasis is placed on traditional, domestic life and not enough on extradomestic roles, such as politics and military. Based on published ethnographies and life histories; 19 notes. G. L. Olson

102. Frost, John Eldridge. MAINE GENEALOGY: SOME DISTINCTIVE ASPECTS. *New England Hist. and Geneal. Register 1977 131(Oct): 243-266.* Evaluates research facilities and sources for Maine genealogical histories, includ-ing genealogical dictionaries, vital records, church records, bibliographic surveys, serials, family papers, military records, cemetery indexes, census data, court, probate and land records, and genealogies. As the state in New England which retained its frontier the longest, and the last to be created, Maine has compara-tively poor vital records despite its long history. Includes check lists of genealo-gies. S. Wheeler

103. Fryer, Judith E. *TAUFSCHEINE:* A NEW INDEX FOR PEOPLE HUNTERS. *Pennsylvania Folklife 1978-79 28(2): 36-47.* Part 2. Continued from a previous article. A listing of birth and baptismal certificates found in the Pennsylvania Folklife Society at Ursinus College.

104. Fuerst, J. S. CLASS, FAMILY, AND HOUSING. *Society 1974 12(1): 48-53.* Discusses public housing programs for the poor in the United States, drawing examples from Europe. S

105. Gaffield, Chad M. CANADIAN FAMILIES IN CULTURAL CON-TEXT: HYPOTHESES FROM THE MID-NINETEENTH CENTURY. *Hist. Papers [Canada] 1979: 48-70.* The townships of Alfred and Caledonia in Prescott County, Ontario, are studied to examine stereotypes of francophone and anglophone Canadians. The French Canadian family is commonly thought to

exhibit high fertility, extended structure, cohesive organization, and an otherworldly focus. English Canadians are assumed to exhibit average fertility, nuclear family composition, detached interpersonal relationships, and a strong marital focus. Empirical comparisons do not support these stereotypes. There were many similarities between the groups between 1800 and 1881, but among the differences are the tendency of the French Canadians to immigrate to the area as families rather than as individuals as the English did, the relatively earlier age of marriage (and consequent larger families) among the French Canadians, and the tendency of younger offspring among the English Canadians to emigrate from the area rather than remain and attempt to farm what they regarded as inferior land. Based on manuscript census returns; map, 5 tables, 5 graphs, 38 notes. French summary. S

106. Gallerano, Nicola. SCHIAVITÙ E FAMIGLIA NERA IN AMERICA: UN DIBATTITO SULLA "RADICAL HISTORY REVIEW" [Slavery and the black family in America: a debate in the *Radical History Review*]. *Movimento Operaio e Socialista [Italy] 1978 1(4): 426-437.* The *Radical History Review,* founded in the United States in 1973, is attempting to present a more leftist, partly Marxist, interpretation of American history and society than that found in conventional historical periodicals. In 1974, a debate began in the pages of this journal on slavery and the black family, a debate inspired by three books: Stanley L. Engerman's and Robert W. Fogel's *Time on the Cross: The Economics of American Negro Slavery* (Boston, 1974); Eugene Genovese's *Roll Jordan Roll* (New York, 1974); and Herbert Gutmans *The Black Family in Slavery and Freedom, 1750-1925* (New York, 1976). The first was torn apart by the RHR's reviewers; the second two were criticized for certain features and praised for others; 19 notes. J. C. Billigmeier

107. Garcia-Bahne, Betty. LA CHICANA AND THE CHICANO FAMILY. Sánchez, Rosaura and Martinez Cruz, Rosa, eds. *Essays on la Mujer* (Los Angeles, Ca.: Chicano Studies Center Publ., 1977): 30-47. Emphasizes socioeconomic factors as determinants of family organization rather than describing certain qualities of Mexican Americans' families as being cultural and inherent. Lower incomes mean fewer options, consequently the majority of Chicanas marry young. Women are usually subject to male domination and are expected to cooperate and help to unify the family. Any attempt to assert independence is seen as a threat to the protective role that the family plays for the Chicanos in an otherwise hostile society. "The Chicano family can thus be seen as a vehicle which incorporates those strengthening qualities that are necessary for social units to survive under exploitative conditions and paradoxically embodies those values which mitigate against the development and exercise of self-determination." Table, 14 notes. M. T. Wilson

108. Garrison, Vivian and Weiss, Carol I. DOMINICAN FAMILY NETWORKS AND UNITED STATES IMMIGRATION POLICY: A CASE STUDY. *Int. Migration Rev. 1979 13(2): 264-283.* Studies the migration methods of a Dominican family which came to the United States during 1962 and 1976 and concludes that the family felt forced to use questionable or illegal means to remain united because its definition of "family" differs from the US Immigration and Naturalization Service's definition of "immediate family."

109. Gavelis, Vytautus.   A DESCRIPTIVE STUDY OF THE EDUCA-TIONAL ATTAINMENT, OCCUPATION, AND GEOGRAPHICAL LO-CATION OF THE CHILDREN OF LITHUANIAN DISPLACED PERSONS AND OF AMERICAN BORN PARENTS WHO ATTENDED IMMACU-LATE CONCEPTION PRIMARY SCHOOL IN EAST ST. LOUIS FROM 1948 TO 1968. *Lituanus 1976 22(1): 72-75.* Discusses the summary results of a Ph.D. dissertation comparing the educational and occupational attainment of two groups of children of Lithuanian family background. The parents of one group were American born and English speaking, the other Lithuanian born and non-English speaking. Recommendations for further research based on the results of the study are made.   K. N. T. Crowther

110. Gee, Ellen M. Thomas.   MARRIAGE IN NINETEENTH-CENTURY CANADA. *Can. Rev. of Sociol. and Anthrop. [Canada] 1982 19(3): 311-325.* Examines census data concerning marriage in Canada during 1851-91. The Canadian nuptiality experience is viewed in the light of the unique, historical Western European marriage pattern, with the finding that Canadian nuptiality levels are low, in keeping with the Western European pattern. Factors accounting for nuptiality level and trend are discussed, with a particular focus on demographic variables. Provincial variation in 19th-century marriage behavior is described and analyzed.   J/S

111. Gildrie, Richard.   FAMILY STRUCTURE AND LOCAL HISTORY IN AMERICA. *Hist. of Educ. Q. 1973 13(4): 433-439.* Reviews Bernard Farber's *Guardians of Virtue: Salem Families in 1800* (New York: Basic Books, 1972) and Paul Boyer and Stephen Nissenbaum's *Salem-Village Witchcraft: A Documentary Record of Local Conflict in Colonial New England* (Belmont, California: Wadsworth Publishing Company, 1972).

112. Gillis, John R.   YOUTH IN HISTORY: PROGRESS AND PROS-PECTS. *J. of Social Hist. [Great Britain] 1974 7(2): 201-207.* Reviews Oscar and Mary Handlin's *Facing Life: Youth and the Family in American History* (Boston: Little, Brown, 1971), Joseph M. Hawes's *Children in Urban Society: Juvenile Delinquency in Nineteenth Century America* (New York: Oxford U. Pr. 1971), Jack M. Hall's *Juvenile Reform in the Progressive Era: William R. George and the Junior Republic Movement* (Ithaca: Cornell U. Pr., 1971), Robert Mennel's *Thorns and Thistles: Juvenile Delinquents in the United States, 1825-1940* (Hanover: U. Pr. of New England, 1973), and Anthony M. Platt's *The Child Savers: The Invention of Delinquency* (Chicago: U. of Chicago Pr., 1969). "Platt's work is the only one that explores its subject in full social and cultural context, asking questions about the nature of youthful conformity and deviancy that reveal the true complexity of age relationships."   R. V. Ritter

113. Gilman, Sander L.   MADNESS AND RACIAL THEORY IN I. J. SINGER'S *THE FAMILY CARNOVSKY. Modern Judaism 1981 1(1): 90-100.* Israel Joshua Singer's *The Family Carnovsky,* written in the United States in 1943, incorporated both the literary paradigm of the family novel and the quasi-scientific medical paradigm of Jewish racial identity, attempting to analyze the myth of race, its application to the stereotype of the Jew, and the value-laden problems of assimilation.

114. Gingerich, Melvin. **MENNONITE FAMILY NAMES IN IOWA.** *Ann. of Iowa 1974 42(5): 397-403.* Describes the settlement of Mennonites in Iowa from 1839 by tracing family names. Mennonite genealogy in the United States has its origins in Dutch and ethnic Swiss names, both of which are present in Iowa. 4 notes. C. W. Olson

115. Gordon, Linda. **DOMESTIC REVOLUTION: HISTORY OF A GOOD IDEA.** *Radical Am. 1981 15(6): 63-68.* Reviews Dolores Hayden's *The Grand Domestic Revolution: A History of Feminist Designs for American Homes, Neighborhoods, and Cities* (1981). The single family house or apartment is neither eternal nor inevitable; it is merely a means by which our class system has been stabilized. This book describes a host of changing socialist and feminist designs for the sharing of domestic space and work. Note, 3 illus. C. M. Hough

116. Gordon, Suzanne. **THE FEMINIST MYSTIQUE.** *Working Papers Mag. 1981 8(4): 61-64.* Criticizes the new feminism expounded by Betty Freidan, author of *The Feminine Mystique,* in which women, after winning success in careers, independence from men, and depending on other women for support, are now turning to family and child-rearing concerns, which addresses the concerns of an upwardly mobile minority elite but excludes most American women, 1960's-81.

117. Grabb, Edward G. **SUBORDINATE GROUP STATUS AND PERCEIVED CHANCES FOR SUCCESS: THE FRENCH CANADIAN CASE.** *Ethnicity 1979 6(3): 268-280.* Generally low socioeconomic status promotes pessimism, but French-speaking Canadians, who tend to occupy lower social positions, are more positive about their chances for success than are English-speaking Canadians. Factors contributing to this sense of optimism include parental interest in the achievements of children and the supportive role of the family in French Canadian culture. Based on 1965-66 survey of Canadian high school students; 3 notes, biblio.

118. Greathouse, Betty and Young, Barbara Goldman. **"ROOTS": A STIMULUS FOR COMMUNITY INVOLVEMENT.** *Social Studies 1979 70(2): 76-80.* Suggests ways that multiethnic studies can be made effective in schools. The use of genealogists, the construction of family trees, and the use of other resource persons to talk on family descent can be effective in tracing the origins of families or persons. The libraries and services of special organizations can help in such research. 7 notes. L. R. Raife

119. Greene, Jack P. **AUTONOMY AND STABILITY: NEW ENGLAND AND THE BRITISH COLONIAL EXPERIENCE IN EARLY MODERN AMERICA.** *J. of Social Hist. [Great Britain] 1974 7(2): 171-194.* Reviews John Demos's *A Little Commonwealth; Family Life in Plymouth Colony* (New York: Oxford U. Press, 1974), Philip J. Greven, Jr.'s *Four Generations: Population, Land, and Family in Colonial Andover, Massachusetts* (Ithaca: Cornell U. Press, 1970), Kenneth A. Lockridge's *A New England Town: The First Hundred Years; Dedham, Massachusetts, 1636-1736* (New York: W. W. Norton, 1970), and Michael Zuckerman's *Peaceable Kingdoms: New England Towns in the Eighteenth Century* (New York: Alfred A. Knopf, 1970). These books suggest new

interest in early New England society. They share a shift of the focus of inquiry from the intellectual and the political to the social and thereby "bring the search for the nature of colonial New England to a new and deeper level of analysis." They record a behavioral revolution in the direction of increasing autonomy of action. 26 notes.   R. V. Ritter

120. Griffith, Elisabeth. ELIZABETH CADY STANTON ON MARRIAGE AND DIVORCE: FEMINIST THEORY AND DOMESTIC EXPERIENCE. Kelley, Mary, ed. *Woman's Being, Woman's Place: Female Identity and Vocation in American History* (Boston: G. K. Hall, 1979): 233-251. A woman who became the principal philosopher of the 19th-century women's movement, Elizabeth Cady Stanton's ambitions did not loom large at the outset of her marriage. Yet, even before marriage she was beginning to develop a strong sense of her own independence and looking toward total autonomy. Stanton did not enjoy an egalitarian marriage, and her feminism developed into an indictment of traditional marriage. Stanton came to believe that partriarchal marriage was the primary obstacle to female emancipation, and she pushed vigorously for reform of divorce laws. In her efforts to improve women's overall economic, legal, and social status she sought foremost to gain for women full recognition as human beings, first, and wives and mothers second. Mainly secondary sources; 64 notes.
                                                                J. Powell

121. Grinde, Donald. A GUIDE TO FAMILY HISTORY. *Afro-Am. in New York Life and Hist. 1977 1(2): 213-216.* Short examination of methodology and materials available for tracing personal ancestries, 1977.

122. Griswold, Robert L. APART BUT NOT ADRIFT: WIVES, DIVORCE, AND INDEPENDENCE IN CALIFORNIA, 1850-1890. *Pacific Hist. Rev. 1980 49(2): 265-283.* Nineteenth-century California divorce records reveal that alternatives to a life of submission and obedience to husbands were available to women. The divorce courts enabled women to start new lives, and desertion was the method many women used to escape an intolerable marriage. Estranged wives were either self-supporting or received help from neighbors, friends, or relatives. Although employment opportunities were poor, three-fourths of estranged wives earned at least part of their livelihood. Based on divorce records of courts in San Mateo and Santa Clara counties; 36 notes.
                                                                R. N. Lokken

123. Gustavus, Susan O. and Mommsen, Kent G. BLACK-WHITE DIFFERENTIALS IN FAMILY SIZE PREFERENCES AMONG YOUTH. *Pacific Sociol. Rev. 1973 16(1): 107-119.*

124. Gutman, Herbert G. PERSISTENT MYTHS ABOUT THE AFRO-AMERICAN FAMILY. *J. of Interdisciplinary Hist. 1975 6(2): 181-210.* Evidence from both northern cities and southern rural regions, towns, and cities refutes the argument that makes of black family life "little more than a crude speculation about the relationship between slavery and twentieth-century experience." Slavery and quasifreedom did put many burdens on American blacks, but the high proportion of two-parent households between 1855 and 1880 reveals how little is known about the slave family, its relation to white family structure, and the ways in which freedmen and freedwomen adapted, retained, transformed, or rejected older forms of family life. 5 tables, 39 notes.   R. Howell

125. Haines, Michael A. FERTILITY, MARRIAGE, AND OCCUPATION IN THE PENNSYLVANIA ANTHRACITE REGION, 1850-1880. *J. of Family Hist. 1977 2(1): 28-55.* Historians have been able to distinguish only the crudest outline of fertility in 19th-century America. Most of their early works were aggregate level analysis in which differences between states or counties were used to explain the fertility transition and to uncover correlates of fertility. Using the child-women ratio on the household level is promising but risky. The potential for bias (e.g. mortality differentials) is great, yet the possibility of significant scholarly progress into this veiled subject is sufficient to justify the attempt. The author finds that strong occupational differentials in fertility did exist. Professionals' families had the lowest fertility, farmers' and miners' the highest. 49 notes.
T. W. Smith

126. Hale, Judson. THE BEST BACKGROUND. *Am. Heritage 1982 33(5): 16-20.* A satirical look at family snobbery in New England. Photo, 2 illus.
J. F. Paul

127. Hamori, Paul A. THE AMERICAN FAMILY IN COMPARISON WITH A EUROPEAN VARIANT. *Indiana Social Studies Q. 1980 33(2): 25-46.* Compares the typical American family with a typical middle-class Hungarian family based on the author's impressions when he emigrated to the United States in 1956 from Hungary as a political scientist, focusing on family roles and functions.

128. Handler, Ellen. FAMILY SURROGATES AS CORRECTIONAL STRATEGY. *Social Service Rev. 1974 48(4): 539-549.* "Presents evidence to support the development of long-term halfway programs to function as extensions of or substitutes for deficient nuclear families of ex-offenders." S

129. Hanson, Edward W. and Rutherford, Homer V. GENEALOGICAL RESEARCH IN MASSACHUSETTS: A SURVEY AND BIBLIOGRAPHICAL GUIDE. *New England Hist. & Geneal. Register 1981 135 (July): 163-198.* 32 notes, 2 tables, appendix listing town histories, single family and multiancestor genealogies.
A. E. Huff

130. Hanson, Edward W. VERMONT GENEALOGY: A STUDY IN MIGRATION. *New England Hist. and Geneal. Register 1979 133(Jan): 3-19.* Covers migration patterns into and out of Vermont, beginning in 1760 when permanent settlement began. Discusses why settlers moved to Vermont and why they moved on, many to the west. Vital records are incomplete but some good work has been done by individuals, the D.A.R., and the Vermont Historical Society. Lists genealogies in town histories. 2 tables, 17 notes.
A. E. Huff

131. Hareven, Tamara K. and Vinovskis, Maris A. ETHNICITY, AND OCCUPATION IN URBAN FAMILIES: AN ANALYSIS OF SOUTH BOSTON MARITAL FERTILITY, AND THE SOUTH END IN 1880. *J. of Social Hist. 1975 8(3): 69-93.* Quantitative study of fertility in South Boston and the South End in 1880 "suggest that ethnicity was a major determinant of fertility differentials at the household levels." Occupation and location in the city also had an impact on fertility ratios. More work is needed on the relationship of fertility and women's work and also on evaluating the importance of the "level of education, religion, and income." 7 tables, 6 graphs, 29 notes, appendix.
L. Ziewacz

132.   Hareven, Tamara K.   THE FAMILY PROCESS: THE HISTORICAL STUDY OF THE FAMILY CYCLE.   *J. of Social Hist. [Great Britain] 1974 7(3): 322-329.* Proposes a new mode of analysis of family patterns in 19th-century society. The family is viewed as a process over time rather than as a static unit within certain time periods. This model "assumes fluidity, change and transition in family structure . . . that individuals live through a variety of patterns of family structure and household organization during different stages of their life cycle, and that families and households evolve different types of organization, structure and relationships which are generally obscured in cross-sectional analysis." Supports the validity of this approach by data from a study of family structure in 19th-century Boston. 15 notes.   R. V. Ritter

133.   Hareven, Tamara K.   INTRODUCTION: THE HISTORICAL STUDY OF THE FAMILY IN URBAN SOCIETY.   *J. of Urban Hist. 1975 1(3): 259-267.* Considers "the family . . . a critical variable" shedding "light on . . . migration . . . patterns which determine population change." This overview covers ca. 1750-1975 and introduces five papers in the same issue. 17 notes.
S. S. Sprague

134.   Hareven, Tamara K.   MODERNIZATION AND FAMILY HISTORY: PERSPECTIVES ON SOCIAL CHANGE.   *Signs: J. of Women in Culture and Soc. 1976 2(1): 190-206.* The concept of modernization can be a valuable framework in which to study society and particularly the history of the family. It is often assumed in modernization theory that traditional values and patterns of behavior are replaced by modern ones in a continuous and consistent way. However, historical reality is always more complex and illustrates the uneven changes in individual and societal patterns of behavior. Family history must acknowledge diverse patterns of change from pre- to post-modern behavior within families as well as taking into account differences in class and ethnicity. An attempt must be made to evaluate the means by which families balance traditional and modern attitudes and it must be remembered that families did not modernize as units, but that men and women modernized at different rates within the family structure. 38 notes.   S. R. Herstein

135.   Hareven, Tamara K. and Tilly, Louise A.   SOLITARY WOMEN AND FAMILY MEDIATION IN AMERICA AND FRENCH TEXTILE CITIES.   *Ann. de Démographie Hist. [France] 1981: 253-271.* Compares patterns of women's position in households around 1900 in two industrial textile cities, Manchester, New Hampshire, and Roubaix, France. For the great majority of women in both cities, the customary residential pattern was that of a familial or surrogate familial setting. Nevertheless, there were proportionately more women living alone or as heads of their own households in Roubaix than in Manchester. Transition into the labor force by native born women was not generally accompanied by departure from parents' households, but there were different patterns of work and residence for young migrant women. In both cities, the most common form of woman-headed household was that of older women who lived with their unmarried children. The familial strategies which enabled older women to continue headship of their households also prevented young women from living alone. It was older women who were most likely to live alone when these strategies failed.   J/S

136. Harris, Barbara J. RECENT WORK ON THE HISTORY OF THE FAMILY: A REVIEW ARTICLE. *Feminist Studies 1976 3(3/4): 159-172.* Gerda Lerner has recently warned against equating family history and women's history. However, family history is certainly an important element in the history of women. Only when changes in the modern family are understood will we have an accurate picture of women's role in the transition to modern society. Christopher Lasch attacked the "modernization theory" and supported much current work on family history in a series of articles in the *New York Times Review of Books* in 1975. The theory assumes that the change from an extended to a nuclear family marks the transition from traditional to industrial society. Lasch is mistaken in questionning the importance of current research on family structure, in that structure in itself is vital because of its connection with demography. The question of the relation of family history to women's history remains. The changing role of women in modern family structures is a study vitally needed to complete our understanding of the total history of modern women. 51 notes.

S. R. Herstein

137. Harris, Irving D. THE PSYCHOLOGIES OF PRESIDENTS. *Hist. of Childhood Q. 1976 3(3): 337-350.* Eminent men such as Presidents act in accordance with personal psychologies largely shaped by position in the family as children. First sons, such as Lyndon B. Johnson, have a high sense of self-worth, while later sons, such as Richard M. Nixon, have a lower self-regard bordering on inferiority. The self-image often is reflected in the ways the President pictures the nation in his public statements. Other leaders included in this analysis are Kennedy, Madison, Hamilton, Jay, Polk, Lincoln, Wilson, Franklin D. Roosevelt, Truman, and McKinley, as well as some foreign leaders. First sons are more likely to lead nations to war. Secondary sources; 10 notes.   R. E. Butchart

138. Harris, William G. RESEARCH ON THE BLACK FAMILY: MAINSTREAM AND DISSENTING PERSPECTIVES. *J. of Ethnic Studies 1979 6(4): 45-64.* Black family research has endorsed historically either a mainstream or a dissenting ideology. The mainstream looks primarily at the black family itself to explain its overall difficulty in society, while the dissenting emphasizes the effects of societal factors such as racial and class oppression. The concentration on black family deficiencies, and the negative depiction of black family life, tended to restrict black mobility and to undermine integration. Dissenting integrationists challenged this monolithic and sordid image by empirically showing different family life-styles in the black community. Surveys the evolution of this dualistically natured research, from W. E. B. Du Bois and George Edmund to Gunnar Myrdal, E. F. Frazier, Daniel Moynihan, and Herbert Gutman. Table, 71 notes.

G. J. Bobango

139. Henretta, James A. FAMILIES AND FARMS: *MENTALITÉ* IN PRE-INDUSTRIAL AMERICA. *William and Mary Q. 1978 35(1): 3-32.* Recent works on early American frontier communities claim that settlers had extensive entrepreneurial and individualistic values. Interpretations of early northern agricultural societies should emphasize economic existence rather than specific mentalities. Subsistence farming was predominant until about 1750; after that, trade relationships were limited. Discusses the gradual formation of agricultural capital and its effects on family and society. The agricultural family remained an extended lineal one, which was the basis for the cultural outlook. 71 notes.

H. M. Ward

140.   Hensley, J. Clark.   TRENDS IN BAPTIST FAMILY LIFE.   *Baptist Hist. and Heritage 1982 17(1): 3-12, 62.* Traces trends in Baptist family life in America from the 19th century to the present, focusing on the influences of modernization, doctrinal and ecclesiological attitudes, education, Bible study, the minister's work, marriage trends, and parenting.

141.   Hijiya, James A.   ROOTS: FAMILY AND ETHNICITY IN THE 1970S.   *Am. Q. 1978 30(4): 548-556.* A bibliographic essay reviewing a variety of titles that reflect a common preoccupation with human heritage whether family or ethnic as an obvious and significant phenomenon of this decade. Explores what this significance might be and its effect on our society. The interest in family is accompanied by a complementary interest in ethnic groups. Some see relatively little influence of the family or ethnic group on the character of an individual. Others strongly disagree. The idea of the self-made man will no doubt surface again shortly, rising from its temporary overshadowing before the power of family and ethnicity.   R. V. Ritter

142.   Hill, May Davis.   HIDDEN STORIES IN YOUR PHOTOGRAPHS. *Family Heritage 1978 1(1): 8-12, (2):39-44, (3): 86-94.* Part I. Describes how to read old family photographs for information about the subjects of the photographs, and provides some examples of photos with significant clues. Part II. "Portraits" of buildings (interior and exterior) including homes, shops, factories, and farms often provide valuable information about social status, work habits, and lifestyles. Part III. Discusses how arrangement of photographs in family albums can reveal significant insight into the character of a family.

143.   Hollander, Paul.   FAMILY AND SEX IN THE SOVIET UNION AND THE USA.   *Survey [Great Britain] 1973 19(3): 186-215.* Soviet women have progressed much farther outside the home in the labor force than have American women, who are more advanced in regard to status and authority within the family. One of the goals of the Soviet regime is to free women from onerous housework. Discusses the reasons for the high divorce rate in the USSR. "Drunkenness plays a far more important part in the breakup of marriage in the USSR than it does in the United States. Birth rates have declined significantly in the Soviet Union since 1940." 73 notes.   E. P. Stickney

144.   Horton, James Oliver.   GENERATIONS OF PROTEST: BLACK FAMILIES AND SOCIAL REFORM IN ANTE-BELLUM BOSTON. *New England Q. 1976 49(2): 242-256.* Traces the roles of the Hall, Paul, Dalton, Neit, Snowden, Bayley, and Lewis families in Boston reform movements. Early leaders established and developed entirely black educational, religious, and masonic organizations. With William Lloyd Garrison's (1805-79) establishment of the New England Anti-Slavery Society during the 1830's they changed to integrated organizations advocating abolitionism and racial integration. Following the passage of the Fugitive Slave Act of 1850 black leaders became willing to take illegal action to assist runaways. Based on the records of black organizations and on secondary sources; 29 notes.   J. C. Bradford

145.   Howard, James H.   SOME FURTHER THOUGHTS ON EASTERN DAKOTA "CLANS."   *Ethnohistory 1979 26(2): 133-140.* While it is now clear that the Eastern Dakota did not possess patrilineal clans in the historic period,

the village groups of this division of the Sioux possessed many of the attributes of patri-clans.

J/S

146.   Ignatieff, Michael.   THE FAMILY ALBUM.   *Queen's Q. [Canada] 1982 89(1): 54-70.* A second-generation Canadian member of the Russian family of the last liberal minister in the czarist government describes the family history of the various relatives who fled Russia.   L. V. Eid

147.   Ignatius, David.   THE TWILIGHT OF THE RICH.   *Washington Monthly 1977 9(4): 14-21.* Discusses the fall from power of American family dynasties such as the Rockefellers and Kennedys, and the rise of meritocrats as the new ruling class.

148.   Ingalls, Joan.   FAMILY LIFE ON THE SOUTHWEST FRONTIER. *Military Hist. of Texas and the Southwest 1978 14(4): 203-213.* Describes several families' lives on Army outposts.

149.   Jackson, Jacquelyn J.   CHANGES IN THE AMERICAN FAMILY. *Public Welfare 1978 36(2): 18-22.* Examines changes during 1970-74 in family structure, assesses how public policy affects it, and speculates on how to make it more responsive to black families and female-headed families.

150.   Jeffrey, Julie Roy.   WOMEN ON THE TRANS-MISSISSIPPI FRONTIER: A REVIEW ESSAY.   *New Mexico Hist. Rev. 1982 57(4): 395-400.* The history of women in American westward movement has reflected stereotyped images, which Sandra L. Myres's *Westering Women and the Frontier Experience, 1800-1915* (1982), part of the Histories of the American Frontier series, attempts to correct as women met other minorities and fashioned lives for themselves, their families, and growing communities.   13 notes.   K. E. Gilmont

151.   Jeffrey, Kirk.   FAMILY BIOGRAPHY: GUIDE TO THE RESOURCES.   *New England Social Studies Bull. 1976-77 34(3): 30-48.* Discusses genealogy in the teaching of history courses; expands this to community-wide projects and offers guidelines and sources available for such studies; includes assignment given to college students at Washington University.

152.   Jensen, Joan; Baca, Beverly; and Bolin, Barbara.   FAMILY HISTORY AND ORAL HISTORY.   *Frontiers 1977 2(2): 93-97.* Students of women's history at New Mexico State University interview their grandmothers in a class project; part of a special issue on women's oral history.

153.   Johnson, Graham E.   CHINESE FAMILY AND COMMUNITY IN CANADA: TRADITION AND CHANGE.   Elliott, Jean Leonard, ed. *Two Nations, Many Cultures: Ethnic Groups in Canada* (Scarborough, Ont.: Prentice-Hall, 1979): 358-371. Traces the history of Chinese immigration to Canada since the late 1850's when the first Chinese community was founded at Barkerville, British Columbia, and discusses the social changes affecting their traditional peasant life.

154.   Johnston, A. Montgomery.   GENEALOGY: AN APPROACH TO HISTORY.   *Hist. Teacher 1978 11(2): 193-200.* Using personal genealogies in history teaching makes history relevant to students, and introduces them to historical method. Includes basic types of genealogical charts. Primary and secondary sources; 4 fig.   P. W. Kennedy

155. Jones, Walter L.   GROWING UP IN THE FLATWOODS: JACK SMITH'S MEMORIES OF THE 1860S.   *J. of Mississippi Hist. 1980 42(2): 145-151.* Andrew Jackson Smith was born in 1858 in Pontotoc County, Mississippi. Smith's account preserves memories of his father's return from the Civil War in 1864 as well as military skirmishes near his home. He describes the family's home and rural life, educational pursuits, and activities of the Shady Grove Baptist Church. Smith's observations of medical practices, death, and activities around the southern country store preserve an interesting picture of life in the Mississippi flatwoods. Based on a typewritten account of his life that Andrew Jackson Smith sent his daughter, Lida, on his 77th birthday in 1935.
M. S. Legan

156. Jones, Yvonne V.   KINSHIP AFFILIATION THROUGH TIME: BLACK HOMECOMINGS AND FAMILY REUNIONS IN A NORTH CAROLINA COUNTY.   *Ethnohistory 1980 27(1): 49-66.* Annual homecomings and family reunions have reinforced ties of kinship and affinity over time among the black residents of a rural hamlet in Montgomery County, North Carolina. These annual ceremonies show the status one holds as a resident of the hamlet, in opposition to other such hamlets in the country, one's status as a member of a specific kin unit within the hamlet vis-a-vis other such units, and one's status as an affine. Utilizes historical sources (census records, oral histories, and local church and family records), in addition to participant observation, to analyze the formation of kin units and their subsequent segmentation over time.
J/S

157. Jordan, Winthrop D.   FAMILIAL POLITICS: THOMAS PAINE AND THE KILLING OF THE KING, 1776.   *J. of Am. Hist. 1973 60(2): 294-308.* Thomas Paine's pamphlet, *Common Sense,* has a subliminal level which explains its great popularity and the sudden willingness of many Americans to shed monarchy for republicanism. Passages suggest the primordial ritual of killing and eating the king. Further evidence for this view stems from the need of many Americans to have their paternal symbol of sovereignty destroyed before real independence could be obtained, from a subconscious rejection of paternal authority and a passion for destroying authoritarian figures, and from the obsession with the destruction of symbols of rooted and paternal authority by the rebels. All of this suggests an aspect of historical reality which should not be ignored. 59 notes.
K. B. West

158. Kanter, Rosabeth Moss.   ROOTS VERSUS RESTLESSNESS: COOPERATIVE HOUSEHOLDS, THE CITY, AND RECURRENT ISSUES IN AMERICAN FAMILY LIFE.   *Massachusetts Rev. 1976 17(2): 331-351.* Roots and restlessness have been for years the dominant warring factions in American family life: the small-town extended family of nostalgia versus the big-city cooperative "families." Cooperative households in cities are as valid a part of the American tradition as town picket fences. The early cooperatives were boarding and rooming houses, and residential hotels. In the 20th century the urban communes have come to the fore. A cooperative house is more task-sharing and more public. Their fragility makes it unlikely that they will achieve an ever-increasing popularity, but they reflect a trend away from biological imperatives in households. Secondary sources; 18 notes, biblio.
E. R. Campbell

159. Katz, Michael B. and Stern, Mark J. HISTORY AND THE LIMITS OF POPULATION POLICY. *Pol. & Soc. 1980 10(2): 225-245.* Summarizes the theoretical and data bases of a case study of declining American fertility between 1855 and 1915. Fertility behavior can best be understood as a function of class position and rational family adaptation to the realities of class position, rather than a function of modernization and education regarding birth control techniques. Table, 30 notes.

D. G. Nielson

160. Kaurouma, Patricia. RESOURCES FOR RESEARCHING AFRO-AMERICAN GENEALOGY. *Afro-Am. in New York Life and Hist. 1977 1(2): 217-224.* Compilation of information and institutions available for Afro-Americans interested in tracing their genealogy.

161. Kedro, M. James. CZECHS AND SLOVAKS IN COLORADO, 1860-1920. *Colorado Mag. 1977 54(2): 92-125.* Czech Americans and Slovak Americans in Colorado were never numerous and most came from other midwestern states rather than directly from Europe to work in mines, smelters, or agriculture. Uses specific immigrants to illustrate "a complicated network of religious, lodge and family interaction . . ." which created close-knit ethnic communities. However, upward mobility and Americanization also occurred. Secondary sources; 20 illus., 61 notes.

O. H. Zabel

162. Kellerman, Barbara. CAMPAIGNING SINCE KENNEDY: THE FAMILY AS "SURROGATE." *Presidential Studies Q. 1980 10(2): 244-253.* The nature of presidential campaigning changed in 1960. To a large extent, this was done by turning the candidate's family into a permanent political resource. With factors such as the decline of the party, the increase of primaries, the personalization of the presidency, the influence of the media, and cultural changes toward women and families, the candidate's families became much more active. This phenomenon is to the advantage of everyone, and is here to stay. 37 notes.

D. H. Cline

163. Kellerman, Barbara. THE POLITICAL FUNCTIONS OF THE PRESIDENTIAL FAMILY. *Presidential Studies Q. 1978 8(3): 303-318.* With the advent of television, the growing visibility of the presidency, the increasing number of primaries, and the rise of the women's movement, the President's family has assumed a political function during the last 18 years. Six roles are defined: Decorations, Extensions, Humanizers, Helpmates, Moral Supporters, and Alter Egos. Examines the political functions of six family members from the administrations of John F. Kennedy to Jimmy Carter and predicts the continuing political impact of presidential relatives. Fig., 63 notes.

S. C. Strom

164. Kelley, Denise and Bobbitt, Randy. FUNERAL HOME RECORDS AND THEIR VALUE IN GENEALOGICAL RESEARCH. PART 1. *Tampa Bay Hist. 1981 3(2): 84-87.* Provides a partial listing of funeral homes in Florida and explains their importance in documenting family relationships.

165. Kelley, Denise and Bobbitt, Randy. FUNERAL HOME RECORDS AND THEIR VALUE IN GENEALOGICAL RESEARCH, PART II. *Tampa Bay Hist. 1982 4(1): 78-83.* Continued from a previous article. Part 2. Continues a listing of funeral homes in Florida; records are listed in alphabetical order by county dating to the late 1800's.

166. Kern, Stephen. THE HISTORY OF CHILDHOOD: A REVIEW AR-
TICLE. *J. of the Hist. of the Behavioral Sciences 1973 9(4): 406-412.* Discusses
writings about childhood in psychology and history 1960-71, emphasizing the
theories of Erik Erikson and David Hunt.

167. Kett, Joseph F. THE BLACK FAMILY UNDER SLAVERY. *Hist.
of Educ. Q. 1977 17(4): 455-460.* Review article prompted by Herbert G. Gutman's *The Black Family in Slavery and Freedom, 1750-1925* and Eugene D.
Genovese's *Roll, Jordan, Roll* on the black family and the effects of slavery upon
it. Gutman believes that the black family structure is basically traditional and that
the "matriarchy" described by Frazier and Moynihan is not a pervasive phenomenon. Genovese sees black family structure coming from a dialectical relationship
between masters and slaves. Each presents evidence which sometimes fits the
theories of the other better, while neither explains all aspects of the structure of
the black family. Note.   J. C. Billigmeier

168. Kidwell, Clara Sue. THE POWER OF WOMEN IN THREE AMERI-
CAN INDIAN SOCIETIES. *J. of Ethnic Studies 1978 6(3): 113-121.* Uses
three anthropological studies of the Ojibwe, or Chippewa, of Canada, and the
Winnebago and Menominee in Wisconsin to discuss traditional Indian women's
roles and the impact of acculturation on these roles. Shows that the woman's role
as mother and keeper of the home has persisted and provided a strain of continuity in Indian cultures throughout times of pressures toward acculturation to the
dominant society. Contrary to what many presume, role descriptions for men in
these tribes were far more rigid; women were subject to narrow expectations only
in their biological functions as wife and mother while enjoying a good deal of
freedom in other activities of the society. The persistence of this anatomical
emphasis, however, means the Indian woman remains a bearer of her culture and
her people's identity, which gives her power. Secondary writings; 11 notes.
                                                              G. J. Bobango

169. Kitchen, Mary M. and Boyer, Dorothy M. THE HISTORY AND PUR-
POSE OF THE FLORIDA SOCIETY FOR GENEALOGICAL RESEARCH,
INC. *Tampa Bay Hist. 1979 1(1): 76-77.* Formed in 1972 in Pinellas Park,
Florida, the Florida Society for Genealogical Research, Inc., seeks to promote the
recording of family history, share genealogical experiences, provide instructional
materials, and publish, through its journal, the *Quarterly,* primary records—
birth, death, and baptismal material.

170. Klotter, James C. FEUDS IN APPALACHIA: AN OVERVIEW.
Filson Club Hist. Q. 1982 56(3): 290-317. Presents a detailed overview and
analysis of the 19th-century family wars in Kentucky and West Virginia. Prominent among these vendettas were the Hatfield-McCoy feud, the Hargis-Marcum-
Cockrell-Callahan feud, and the Rowan County war. Examines a variety of
explanations for this violence including those of Henry D. Shapiro, John A.
Williams, and Gordon B. McKinney. Finds all previous explanations not comprehensive enough and suggests that the breakdown of the legal system was the
primary cause of the family murders. Based on contemporary newspaper accounts.   G. B. McKinney

171. Kriebel, Martha B. WOMEN, SERVANTS AND FAMILY LIFE IN EARLY AMERICA. *Pennsylvania Folklife 1978 28(1): 2-9.* A view of German female immigrants who settled in colonial Pennsylvania and their status in the family, using statistical data on the households of members of the Schwenkfelder sect, wills, and indentured servant agreements; religion was to be at the center of family life and a woman's duties in this regard.

172. Kulikoff, Allan. THE ORIGINS OF AFRO-AMERICAN SOCIETY IN TIDEWATER MARYLAND AND VIRGINIA: 1700 TO 1790. *William and Mary Q. 1978 35(2): 226-259.* Argues that early slaves developed their own social institutions and culture within the context of white rule. Examines factors that shaped the lives of the slaves, particularly patterns of immigration, population distribution of whites, and the economy. Community life emerged slowly during three periods: 1650-90, assimilation amid white repression; 1690-1740, heavy immigration, social conflict among blacks and disruption of slave communities; and 1740-90, decline of immigration, the rise of black population, and the appearance of settled black communities. Various facets of family life and demography are discussed. Primary and secondary sources; 5 tables, 72 notes.
H. M. Ward

173. Labinjoh, Justin. THE SEXUAL LIFE OF THE OPPRESSED: AN EXAMINATION OF THE FAMILY LIFE OF ANTE-BELLUM SLAVES. *Phylon 1974 35(4): 375-397.* Antebellum black slaves had fairly stable families. Although slavery in its abstraction and in its practice was unconducive to the stability of black social institutions, the paternalism of the slaveholders, the indestructible human desires of the slaves, and the mature economic considerations of the society conspired to sustain family cohesion. Amidst the chaos of slavery there existed stability, though only on the large plantations which contained 25 per cent of the slaves did everything conspire to give them cohesion. Slave narratives especially revealed the respect of black family members for each other and for the institution of marriage. Yet, the main function of slave family life was to provide emotional gratification. Based on primary and secondary sources, including plantation records and slave narratives; 61 notes.
B. A. Glasrud

174. Lacey, Barbara E. WOMEN IN THE ERA OF THE AMERICAN REVOLUTION: THE CASE OF NORWICH, CONNECTICUT. *New England Q. 1980 53(4): 527-543.* Discusses trends in the condition of women in Norwich, ca. 1750-1800. Whereas at the beginning of this era most women were housewives, spending their time with their families, by the end of the era fewer women were married. Families were smaller, and many women did not have a home of their own. Divorce rates rose. Women also increased their property holdings and became interested in outside activities, such as religious and educational pursuits. They also became increasingly engaged in developing relationships with other women. Primary sources; 42 notes.
J. Powell

175. Lackey, Richard S. GENEALOGICAL RESEARCH: AN ASSESSMENT OF POTENTIAL VALUE. *Prologue 1975 7(4): 221-225.* Genealogists should accept a mutually beneficial partnership with researchers in all related fields. Too often, genealogists fail to make their discoveries available. Although historians and genealogists possess separate areas of expertise, each can serve the

other by suggesting the potential value of records which one or the other may discover. Uses several primary sources uncovered by genealogists to illustrate the potential benefits to historians, and suggests published aids that could be usefully consulted. Based on documents in the National Archives and on secondary sources; illus., 28 notes.   W. R. Hively

176. Lackey, Richard S.   THE GENEALOGIST'S FIRST LOOK AT FEDERAL LAND RECORDS. *Prologue 1977 9(1): 43-45.* The use of the federal land records in genealogical work can be most valuable if the organization and arrangement of the records are understood by the user. Users should have a good working knowledge of the operation of the rectangular survey system as well as the knowledge that the records are separated into uniform disposal-related records and administrative records. Jurisdictions of local land offices must be established and the meaning and scope of entry records understood.

N. Lederer

177. Lantz, Herman R.; Keyes, Jane; and Schultz, Martin.   THE AMERICAN FAMILY IN THE PREINDUSTRIAL PERIOD: FROM BASE LINES IN HISTORY TO CHANGE. *Am. Sociol. Rev. 1975 40(1): 21-36.* This research parallels two earlier investigations of preindustrial American family patterns during the periods of 1741-1794 and 1794-1825. The present investigation involves a content analysis of magazines for the third period, 1825-1850. Special attention is given to power patterns between husband and wife, romantic love, motivations for marriage, and advocated and actual sanctions implemented toward individuals involved in premarital and extramarital sexual relationships. The results suggest a marked increase in the power of the woman. Romantic love and personal happiness emerge as important criteria in mate selection. It is suggested that in the period 1825-1850 magazine content indicates a significant move from a traditional to a more emancipated family with new alternatives. The limitations of these findings are discussed and include the problem of identifying the precise period in which industrialization in America emerged, the implications which this difficulty poses for the interpretation of our data. The special problems of causal analysis in understanding family change are also noted. A

178. Lantz, Herman R.; Schultz, Martin; and O'Hara, Mary.   THE CHANGING AMERICAN FAMILY FROM THE PREINDUSTRIAL TO THE INDUSTRIAL PERIOD: A FINAL REPORT. *Am. Sociol. Rev. 1977 42(3): 406-421.* This report represents the completion of a content analysis of magazines designed to examine the American family from 1741 to 1865. The final report compares the last period, 1850-1865, with previous periods and includes a new discussion of family conflict in magazine content. It is suggested that the period 1850-1865 may have been a period of significant family change. The theoretical synthesis of findings for the 1741-1865 period is presented. Significant variables include the family as a change agent and the role of ideology and developmental factors (i.e., urbanization and industrialization). Some observations on causal relationships are made and basic limitations in the use of literary sources of data are noted.

179. Lantz, Herman R.   FAMILY AND KIN AS REVEALED IN THE NARRATIVES OF EX-SLAVES. *Social Sci. Q. 1980 60(4): 667-675.* To assess the extent to which slavery in the United States created black family dismember-

ment, the author counts the number of ex-slaves and children of ex-slaves—interviewed as part of a Works Progress Administration (WPA) project during the 1930's—who could identify their parents, siblings, and kin. The results support the view that black families before the Civil War were more stable than had earlier been thought. Based on 1,735 WPA narratives of ex-slaves and 537 narratives of children of ex-slaves; 2 tables, 16 notes, biblio.   L. F. Velicer

180.   Laslett, Barbara.   FAMILY MEMBERSHIP, PAST AND PRESENT. *Social Problems 1978 25(5): 476-490.* Summarizes contemporary attitudes toward the US family. Factors affecting the family include lower mortality rates, younger marriage age, declining fertility rates, urbanization, and migration. The contemporary family represents the contradiction between its traditional and nontraditional forms. Questions whether it can sustain and satisfy the search for meaning and the weight of expectation. Primary and secondary sources; 12 notes; refs.
                                                                        A. M. Osur

181.   Laslett, Barbara.   HOUSEHOLD STRUCTURE ON AN AMERICAN FRONTIER: LOS ANGELES, CALIFORNIA, IN 1850. *Am. J. of Sociol. 1975 81(1): 109-128.* Based on individual United States federal census schedules, this paper reports on the way in which economic and demographic variables relate to different types of household organization in Los Angeles in 1850. While the findings confirm the results of other recent research that the nuclear family predominated in preindustrial societies, they also emphasize the need to focus on variation rather than on modality in order to understand household organization. Methodological problems of working with this kind of data are discussed, as are the implications of the results for the study of social change.   J

182.   Laslett, Barbara.   SOCIAL CHANGE AND THE FAMILY: LOS ANGELES, CALIFORNIA, 1850-1870. *Am. Sociol. Rev. 1977 42(2): 268-291.* Using Marx's description of "the so-called primitive accumulation" which he associates with the development of capitalism in the West, a theoretical formulation is presented which explores the impact on the family of changes in the individual's access to actual and potential wealth. A multivariate analysis, based on the individual census schedules for the city of Los Angeles in 1850 and 1870, is used to explore the changing relationships between economic, demographic and other structural variables on household structure. The findings suggest that a dynamic, Marxian model can help explain the effects of social change on the family.   J

183.   Lazerwitz, Bernard.   JEWISH-CHRISTIAN MARRIAGES AND CONVERSIONS. *Jewish Social Studies 1981 43(1): 31-46.* New data on Jewish-Christian intermarriage in the United States emerged from the National Jewish Population Study. Intermarriage is increasing. The educated, and partners entering second marriages, are likely candidates. Marriages involving the Christian spouse's conversion to Judaism rank consistently higher on measures of Jewish religious expression, and far more of the resulting children remain Jewish. Divorce is much more likely in cases of intermarriage, particularly for Jewish women. 3 tables, 23 notes.
                                                                        J. D. Sarna

184.   Leacock,   Eleanor.   THE   CHANGING   FAMILY   AND   LÉVI-STRAUSS, OR WHATEVER HAPPENED TO FATHERS? *Social Res. 1977 44(2): 235-259.* Based on evidence from the North American Montagnais, Cherokee, and Iroquois, during the 17th-19th centuries, disputes Claude Lévi-Strauss's formulations of woman-exchange and incest prohibitions as "unwarranted teleology reminiscent of eighteenth-century social-contract theorizing."

185.   Leon, Warren.   PICTURING THE FAMILY: PHOTOGRAPHS AND PAINTINGS IN THE CLASSROOM. *J. of Family Hist. 1981 6(1): 15-27.* Discusses iconography as a research tool and as an instructional aid. Describes how students are taught to analyze paintings and photographs to gain insights about the historical period and families involved. A bibliographic essay is included. 2 fig., biblio.   T. W. Smith

186.   Levine, Gene N. and Montero, Darrel M.   SOCIOECONOMIC MOBILITY AMONG THREE GENERATIONS OF JAPANESE AMERICANS. *J. of Social Issues 1973 29(2): 33-48.* "Data from a three generational survey of Japanese Americans indicate that the occupational and educational attainments of the first generation (Issei) are reflected in the achievements of the second and third generations. Findings suggest that two different currents flow in the Japanese American community, one relatively traditional, the other more assimilationist. It is expected that only assimilationists will survive—but in a modified fashion. The majority of the Sansei queried indicate an interest in Japanese ways while still embracing the primary goals of American society and its emphasis on socioeconomic success in particular. Although the ban on outmarriage is breaking down, a majority of Sansei have married or intend to marry within the fold. While the Japanese Americans have successfully accommodated to the American situation—especially by correctly gauging the great importance of education, there is little evidence that the subculture will soon wither away."   J

187.   Li, Peter S.   IMMIGRATION LAWS AND FAMILY PATTERNS: SOME DEMOGRAPHIC CHANGES AMONG CHINESE FAMILIES IN CANADA, 1885-1971. *Can. Ethnic Studies [Canada] 1980 12(1): 58-73.* Ethnic families are frequently seen as products of a slum culture or a transplanted heritage. Neither view explains the changes of the Chinese family in Canada. The patterns of broken families among Chinese males in Canada before World War II and the subsequent disrupted social lives resulting from the absence of Chinese women largely resulted from a restrictive immigration system which imposed various constraints on the familial organization of the Chinese. Postwar changes in the Canadian immigration policy removed some of the structural barriers, gradually restoring conjugal family life among the Chinese community.   J/S

188.   Li, Wen L. and Yu, Linda.   INTERPERSONAL CONTACT AND RACIAL PREJUDICE: A COMPARATIVE STUDY OF AMERICAN AND CHINESE STUDENTS. *Sociol. Q. 1974 15(4): 559-566.* "The extent of the causal relation between interpersonal contact and racial prejudice is examined with emphasis on how this relation is intervened by the effects of family socioeconomic status. A cross-cultural, comparative study of American and [Taiwanese] Chinese students is attempted using a stereotype questionnaire adapted, with some modifications, from Katz and Braly's adjective list. The data indicate that a) family socioeconomic status is significantly related to cross-national contact

among both the Americans and Chinese, b) increased contact does not linearly reduce prejudice for both the Americans and Chinese and c) family socioeconomic status is, relatively speaking, more important than interpersonal contact in its relation to prejudice and significantly so in the American sample."   J

189. Lichter, Daniel T. THE MIGRATION OF DUAL-WORKER FAMILIES: DOES THE WIFE'S JOB MATTER? *Social Sci. Q. 1982 63(1): 48-57.* Brings women into the family migration equation; migration is inhibited in families in which the wife works, but specific job attributes of the wife do not aid in explaining family migration differentials.

190. Light, Beth. AN INVENTORY OF SOURCES ON WOMEN IN THE PERSONAL PAPERS, FAMILY PAPERS AND MANUSCRIPT COLLECTION IN THE ARCHIVES OF ONTARIO. *Can. Newsletter of Res. on Women [Canada] 1977 6(1, supplement): 171-196.* Provides a bibliography of sources on women, 18th-20th centuries, in the manuscript collection of the Archives of Ontario.

191. Lincoln, C. Eric. THE BLACK FAMILY, THE BLACK CHURCH AND THE TRANSFORMATION OF VALUES. *Religion in Life 1978 47(4): 486-496.* In studying the survival of the black family and the black church, examines the implications of the impact of war on social change and the distinctiveness of the black subculture in the context of American society.

192. Lowe, Richard and Campbell, Randolph. HEADS OF FAMILIES IN ANTEBELLUM TEXAS: A PROFILE. *Red River Valley Hist. Rev. 1980 5(2): 68-80.* Provides statistics from the 1850 and 1860 censuses on the heads of households in antebellum eastern Texas, where most of the non-Mexican Texas population was concentrated, focusing on birthplace, economic and social status, urban or rural residence, etc.

193. Lystad, Mary. VIOLENCE IN THE HOME: A MAJOR PUBLIC PROBLEM. *Urban & Social Change Rev. 1982 15(2): 21-25.* Discusses the incidence, causes, intervention measures, and prevention of family violence based on research from the last 15 years.

194. Malvern, Robert. OF MONEY NEEDS AND FAMILY NEWS: BRIGHAM FAMILY LETTERS, 1800-1820. *Vermont Hist. 1973 41(3): 113-122.* Cites and comments on 19 out of 30 family letters of migrants in late 1790's from Marlboro, Massachusetts, to Bakersfield, Vermont. Letters mention eight children, crops, stock, schooling, mail, cash shortages and a Massachusetts inheritance, the boys' learning trades, and only one visit home in more than 20 years.

T. D. S. Bassett

195. Marcum, John P. EXPLAINING FERTILITY DIFFERENCES AMONG U.S. PROTESTANTS. *Social Forces 1981 60(2): 532-543.* The hypothesis that Protestant fertility patterns result from differences in social characteristics among denominations is set against the hypothesis that doctrinal differences lead members of conservative denominations to have both higher wanted and unwanted fertility. Data for white couples from the 1965 National Fertility Survey support the doctrine hypothesis for wanted fertility among conservative Protestants low in formal church participation. Couples who follow

conservative doctrine and have larger families participate less frequently because of conflicting demands associated with larger families. Further analysis with a measure of participation less sensitive to differences in family size produces results consistent with this argument.   J

196.   Marietta, Jack.   QUAKER FAMILY EDUCATION IN HISTORICAL PERSPECTIVE.   *Quaker Hist. 1974 63(1): 3-16.* As New England became less homogeneous, the Puritan denomination failed to transmit its culture by family training and turned to schools. Pennsylvania Quaker sectarians, living "in the world" rather than isolated like the German sects, suffered similar dilution by accommodation. At the cost of nearly 2000 disownments for marrying non-Quakers during 1740-75, they succeeded in insulating the young through family discipline supplemented by practical schooling under Quaker masters. "The Society emerged from the Revolution (after disowning 420 armsbearing Quakers) smaller, more uniform, more endogamous, and more strictly disciplined." 31 notes.   T. D. S. Bassett

197.   Markle, G. E. and Pasco, Sharon.   FAMILY LIMITATION AMONG THE OLD ORDER AMISH.   *Population Studies [Great Britain] 1977 31(2): 267-280.* This paper shows that the Indiana Amish, a high-fertility Anabaptist population, regulate their marital fertility according to their family finances. We linked demographic data from the Indiana Amish Directory with personal property tax records at 5, 15 and 25 years after marriage and found fertility differences by occupation and wealth. Correlations between family size and wealth at the beginning, middle and end of childbearing years were positive. Wealthier women exhibited higher marital fertility, had longer first birth intervals, were older at the birth of their last child, and had larger families than poorer women. Over the past 30 years, marital fertility has remained constant among older women; but birth rates among younger women have been rising rapidly.   J

198.   Markusen, Ann R.   CITY SPATIAL STRUCTURE, WOMEN'S HOUSEHOLD WORK, AND NATIONAL URBAN POLICY.   *Signs 1980 5(3): supplement 23-44.* Of the two types of urban space, household reproduction of labor power is more complex and less understood than wage-labor production. The nuclear, patriarchal family type in the United States has defined most modern space utilization, but the household is not simply a "passive consumption unit." Because of that belief, however, women are caught in conflicting roles. Because the Carter administration policy is aimed at business incentives to change employment patterns, women will not be helped. Encouraging day-care facilities and discouraging discrimination must become the central aims of national urban policy. Secondary sources; table, 29 notes.   S. P. Conner

199.   Marsden, Michael T.   THE CONCEPT OF THE FAMILY IN THE FICTION OF LOUIS L'AMOUR.   *North Dakota Q. 1978 46(3): 12-21.* The western novels by Louis L'Amour since the 1950's emphasize the importance of the nuclear family.

200.   Martin-Perdue, Nancy.   THE USE OF AUTOBIOGRAPHY IN FAMILY HISTORY.   *Family Heritage 1979 2(3): 82-91, (4): 116-122.* Part I. Discusses genealogy and family history research; excerpts from the autobiography of Frances Martha Atkinson Martin, 1857-70, reveal details of daily life, kinship

structure, and social organization in Cooke County, Texas. Part II. Demonstrates the historical uses of personal accounts by analyzing the impact of the Civil War as recorded by a Texas girl.

201. Matossian, Mary K. and Schafer, William D. FAMILY, FERTILITY, AND POLITICAL VIOLENCE, 1700-1900. *J. of Social Hist. 1977 11(2): 137-178.* Political violence can be studied through "ecological perspective, family system theory, and quantitative methods." An analysis of the families of writers in France, Great Britain, and the United States, 1700-1900, indicates that population pressure, particularly an increase in the number of young males, can be a precondition to political violence. This situation may be alleviated by such factors as emigration but exacerbated by other factors such as immigration. 18 tables, 9 charts, 52 notes.   L. E. Ziewacz

202. Mattessich, Paul W. CHILDLESSNESS AND ITS CORRELATES IN HISTORICAL PERSPECTIVE: A RESEARCH NOTE. *J. of Family Hist. 1979 4(3): 299-307.* Childlessness has ranged between 10-20% during 1910-70. The childless tend to be poor, educated, late marrying, and employed. The decline of fertility from post-World War II "baby boom" peaks to current lows is more a return to normal than a great fertility depression. 5 tables, 5 notes, biblio.
T. W. Smith

203. Mays, Herbert J. "A PLACE TO STAND": FAMILIES, LAND AND PERMANENCE IN TORONTO GORE TOWNSHIP, 1820-1890. *Hist. Papers [Canada] 1980: 185-211.* Studies population stability in the township of Toronto Gore, Ontario. During this time of great migration a few families became permanent residents. Certain factors were crucial to this: early settlement, kinship, and the ability of later generations to acquire land. As economic stress grew, particular inheritance practices insured a good life for the children of these permanent families. The result was a high degree of stability in the township. Presented at the Annual Meeting of the Canadian Historical Association, 1980; 2 maps, 10 tables, graph, 47 notes.   A. Drysdale

204. Mazuzan, George T. and Twomey, Gerald. ORAL HISTORY IN THE CLASSROOM. *Social Studies 1977 68(1): 14-19.* Examines methodology for recording oral history and suggests forms, such as local and family histories, for classroom projects.

205. McGettigan, James William. BOONE COUNTY SLAVES: SALES, ESTATE DIVISIONS AND FAMILIES, 1820-1865. *Missouri Hist. Rev. 1978 72(2): 176-197; (3): 271-295.* Part I. In *Slave Trading in the Old South,* Frederic Bancroft said Missouri exported many slaves to the deep South, a position reasserted by Kenneth Stampp in *The Peculiar Institution.* Slavery apparently was not dying in Boone County, Missouri. An examination of census data, the probate court records, and the subscription lists of the Columbia *Missouri Statesman* reveal that very few slaves were traded out of the county and that there was a marked tendency for the slaves of a deceased owner to pass to family members in the county. Primary and secondary sources. Illus., 4 tables, 48 notes. Part II. Newspapers, personal correspondence, and estate sale records show that slave hiring was popular in Boone County, because it made a pool of labor available to men who did not want to own slaves themselves. The same records show that

most slaves tended to pass to other owners in Boone County by sale or by estate distribution. Most of the slaves might have remained in Boone County, but this did not mean that slave families remained together. Few slaveowners responded to humanitarian sentiments when there were economic and legal pressures that made it seem more advantageous to break family ties. Illus., table, 59 notes.

W. F. Zornow

206. McGovern, James R.   JOHN PIERCE: YANKEE SOCIAL HIS-TORIAN. *Old-Time New England 1974 64(3/4): 77-86.* Reverend John Pierce preserved a detailed record of New England men, institutions, social activities, and family economics during 1800-50. Although extensive and available, the Pierce manuscripts have been relatively ignored by scholars. The author offers samples of their value in the study of 19th-century New England social history. 59 notes.

R. N. Lokken

207. Metcalf, Ann.   NAVAJO WOMEN IN THE CITY: LESSONS FROM A QUARTER-CENTURY OF RELOCATION.   *Am. Indian Q. 1982 6(1-2): 71-89.* Reviews the program of the Bureau of Indian Affairs to relocate Indians and their families in urban areas, which began in the mid-1950's. Navajo women who had moved to the San Francisco Bay area and found families appeared to have made a successful adjustment to urban living. Acculturation studies will have to deal with the complexities of people who exist simultaneously in more than one cultural system.   Based on field research; 2 notes, biblio.

G. L. Olson

208. Miller, Roger.   HOUSEHOLD ACTIVITY PATTERNS IN NINE-TEENTH-CENTURY SUBURBS: A TIME-GEOGRAPHIC EXPLORA-TION.   *Ann. of the Assoc. of Am. Geog. 1982 72(3): 355-371.* Discusses the effect of suburban location in mid- to late 19th-century Philadelphia on housewife accessibility to five hypothetical activity programs, finding that the time available to each woman is more dependent on household structure and socioeconomic status than transportation availability or the time-geography of the urban environment.

209. Miranda, Gloria E.   GENTE DE RAZÓN MARRIAGE PATTERNS IN SPANISH AND MEXICAN CALIFORNIA: A CASE STUDY OF SANTA BARBARA AND LOS ANGELES.   *Southern California Q. 1981 63(1): 1-21.* Traces marriage patterns of Californians in the Spanish and Mexican periods, focusing on the Santa Barbara Mission and Presidio and the Los Angeles pueblo. Women were considered at age 13 to be marriageable, and men by their midteens, although men usually waited until their late 20's before marrying. Men averaged about 10 years older than women at time of marriage. "Cradle marriages," a popular sterotype of the era, were exceptions to the norm. Couples desiring to be married had to obtain parental consent; love matches were more common than arranged marriages. The Catholic Church conducted investigative tribunals about motives for marriage and to insure that no close blood ties existed. Between 1786 and 1848, Santa Barbara missionaries performed 306 marriages. 4 charts, 50 notes.

A. Hoffman

210. Mogey, John. RESIDENCE, FAMILY, KINSHIP: SOME RECENT RESEARCH. *J. of Family Hist. 1976 1(1): 95-105.* With family reconstitution techniques and household level analysis of census lists, historians have begun to devise precise and sophisticated means to examine the form, organization, and function of households and residential family units. Drawing on work from sociology and anthropology, the author argues that for a fuller understanding of the family it is necessary to examine the kinship system and related extra-household networks as well. Advances no concrete method to accomplish this, but strongly supports the need for such study. Biblio.   T. W. Smith

211. Moran, Gerald F. RELIGIOUS RENEWAL, PURITAN TRIBAL-ISM, AND THE FAMILY IN SEVENTEENTH-CENTURY MILFORD, CONNECTICUT. *William and Mary Q. 1979 36(2): 236-254.* The First Church of Milford, Connecticut, has complete records going back to the 17th century, and hence provides a model study for answering many questions, such as those raised by Edmund S. Morgan concerning the whole social and religious context of a Puritan community. Structural restrictiveness actually did not re-strain admissions to any large degree. Eventually, however, admissions did de-cline and the church became isolated from the community at large. In attempts to recapture its earlier vitality the church became increasingly exclusive. There appears to have been an inbred membership and a tribal spirit. Based on church records; 3 tables, graph, 53 notes.   H. M. Ward

212. Mormino, Gary R. and Pozzetta, George E. IMMIGRANT WOMEN IN TAMPA: THE ITALIAN EXPERIENCE, 1890-1930. *Florida Hist. Q. 1983 61(3): 296-312.* Italian women played a significant role in the cigar industry of Tampa, Florida. The Italian family structure was able to adjust to New World conditions. Italian women demonstrated frugality, hard work, and a retention of family bonds in coping with the new conditions of Florida. Based on personal interviews and other sources; 4 fig., 57 notes.   N. A. Kuntz

213. Mostwin, Danuta. THE PROFILE OF A TRANSPLANTED FAM-ILY. *Polish Rev. 1974 19(1): 77-89.* Studies the families of immigrants from Poland to the United States after World War II.

214. Mueller, B. Jeanne. RURAL FAMILY LIFE STYLE AND SONS' SCHOOL ACHIEVEMENT. *Rural Sociol. 1974 39(3): 362-372.* "A study of rural working-class families showed a general consensus on values related to parenting styles, desirable attributes for preadolescent sons, and expectations and aspirations for educational and occupational attainment. Actual characteristics of the preadolescent sons, however, differed between those whose school achieve-ment fell below grade level and those who were average or better. In particular, the latter were relatively homogeneous. Those boys operating at below average levels were rather heterogeneous in traits and circumstances."   J

215. Mulder, William. MORMON SOURCES FOR IMMIGRATION HIS-TORY. *Immigration Hist. Newsletter 1978 10(2): 1-8.* As an offspring from a basic religious tenet, the library at Brigham Young University (associated with the Mormon Church) contains extensive research and geneological materials with important source material for immigration studies.

216. Munzer, Rosa Pereira. IMMIGRATION, FAMILISM AND IN-GROUP COMPETITION: A STUDY OF THE PORTUGUESE IN THE SOUTHERN OKANAGAN. *Can. Ethnic Studies [Canada] 1981 13(2): 98-111.* Previous literature on the Portuguese in Canada has suggested that Portuguese immigrants actively seek to reunite the scattered extended family in Canada. This would suggest that familism should be as strong among the Portuguese in Canada as it was among the Portuguese in Portugal. Using the Portuguese community in the Oliver-Osoyoos area of British Columbia, the present study found that the Canadian Portuguese acted as the facilitators and not the instigators of extended family immigration to Canada. The level of familism among the Portuguese in this sample was not as strong as that found by Aldrich, Lipman, and Goldman (1973) in Portugal. Economic competition, status rivalry and jealousy were the reasons for decreased familism.   J

217. Myres, Sandra L. ROMANCE AND REALITY ON THE AMERICAN FRONTIER: VIEWS OF ARMY WIVES. *Western Hist. Q. 1982 13(4): 409-427.* The journals, diaries, and letters of army wives contain perceptive observations, comments, and insights that provide vivid, detailed, and intimate accounts of western military and related civilian life on the 19th-century frontier. They help to correct much of the romantic mythology about Western life, especially the role of women. Army women were an integral part of the unfolding frontier. 51 notes.   D. L. Smith

218. Nash, Gary B. and Smith, Billy G. THE POPULATION OF EIGHTEENTH-CENTURY PHILADELPHIA. *Pennsylvania Mag. of Hist. and Biog. 1975 99(3): 362-368.* Suggests that the ratio of people per house at the time the 1790 census was taken may not be applicable earlier in the 18th century. Family size, the decline of slavery and indentured servitude, and the rise of a free labor system in which large numbers of workers rented rooms in tenements, are variables that must to considered. Table, 15 notes.   C. W. Olson

219. Neil, J. Meredith. COMMUNES AND FAMILIES: REVIEW ESSAY. *J. of Popular Culture 1973 6(4): 865-870.* Reviews 10 books published 1969-72 on communes, counter culture, and attempts to found an alternative society.

S

220. Neville, John D., ed. AN ISLE OF WIGHT QUITRENT ROLL, 1714. *Virginia Mag. of Hist. and Biog. 1979 87(2): 174-181.* Reproduces a roll which lists proprietor and patentee's names, number of acres, and amount of tax paid in money, bills, or tobacco. Discusses family relationships and comparisons with 1704 rolls. Note.   P. J. Woehrmann

221. Olwig, Karen Fog. WOMEN, "MATRIFOCALITY" AND SYSTEMS OF EXCHANGE: AN ETHNOHISTORICAL STUDY OF THE AFRO-AMERICAN FAMILY ON ST. JOHN, DANISH WEST INDIES. *Ethnohistory 1981 28(1): 59-78.* This ethnohistorical case study of the American, formerly Danish, West Indian island of St. John examines the position of Afro-American women during a 260-year period from European colonization of the island to the present. It focuses on the system of social reproduction as it has evolved since slavery and the role of women as agents of production and reproduction, as seen against the background of the socioeconomic units and exchange networks within

which women have functioned. The conclusions drawn question the usefulness and validity of the concept of "matrifocality." J

222. O'Rand, Angela M. and Henretta, John C. WOMEN AT MIDDLE AGE: DEVELOPMENTAL TRANSITIONS. *Ann. of the Am. Acad. of Pol. and Social Sci. 1982 (464): 57-64.* The shapes of women's lives have changed over the 20th century as a result of declining fertility, extended longevity, new lifestyles in marriage and family formation, and increased attachment to the labor force. Midlife role transitions for women are dependent upon earlier life events. Trends such as the postponement of marriage and childbearing, divorce and separation, and early career entry have changed the traditional family life cycle. Low fertility among women with patterns of early childbirth has led to an extended empty nest period and to increased labor participation at midlife. J/S

223. Osborne, Gwendolyn E. MOTHERHOOD IN THE BLACK COMMU-NITY. *Crisis 1977 84(10): 479-484.* Current statistics suggest that 35% of all black families in the United States are headed by women. The majority have at least two children. These women are at the bottom of the socioeconomic ladder and are victimized by sexism, racism, and the biases associated with single-parent households. These conditions arise from black male suicides, unemployment, war deaths, public welfare policies, or criminal incarceration. The majority of black women are in the labor market. Problems of housing and health contribute to a bleak situation. Black motherhood is a complex and serious national concern.
A. G. Belles

224. Ostergren, Robert C. LAND AND FAMILY IN RURAL IMMI-GRANT COMMUNITIES. *Ann. of the Assoc. of Am. Geog. 1981 71(3): 400-411.* Studies the transfer of land among Swedish immigrants in seven Swedish communities in east-central Minnesota; the variations among communities in land transfer practices was linked to practices established in the various districts in Sweden where the immigrants originated.

225. Osterud, Nancy and Fulton, J. FAMILY LIMITATION AND AGE AT MARRIAGE: FERTILITY DECLINE IN STURBRIDGE, MASSACHU-SETTS, 1730-1850. *Population Studies [Great Britain] 1976 30(3): 481-494.* Rising female age at marriage combined with declining fertility within marriage led to a substantial decline in fertility in Sturbridge, Massachusetts, 1730-1850.

226. Otto, John Solomon. THE CASE FOR FOLK HISTORY: SLAVERY IN THE HIGHLANDS SOUTH. *Southern Studies 1981 20(2): 167-173.* Traditional histories of the Old South describe the plantation belt of the lowlands and are written from an upper-class viewpoint. The poorer area of the highlands in the upper South, such as the Blue Ridge Mountains and the Ozark Plateaus, were the domain of small farmers who grew few cash crops. Few written records about them exist, but the oral record of present occupants is valuable and valid under certain conditions—geographic continuity in population, parallel conditions existing in more than one ethnic group, and when traditions can be corroborated with written records. Such a situation exists for Yell County, Arkansas, where parallel white and black family traditions from the same antebellum farms have been gathered. Based on interviews and other primary sources; 25 notes.
J. J. Buschen

227. Passi, Michael M. MYTH AS HISTORY, HISTORY AS MYTH: FAMILY AND CHURCH AMONG ITALO-AMERICANS. *J. of Ethnic Studies 1975 3(2): 97-103.* Reviews Silvano Tomasi's *Piety and Power: The Role of the Italian Parishes in the New York Metropolitan Area, 1880-1930* (1975), Richard Gambino's *Blood of My Blood: The Dilemma of the Italian Americans* (1974), and Carla Bianco's *The Two Rosetos* (1974). All three attempt to explain the nature of Italian-American society. Tomasi finds the core to be the Catholic Church and its ethnic parishes, Gambino sees the family system as the central element, and Bianco tackles the issue by comparing Rosetos, Italy, with its namesake in Pennsylvania. Of these three finds Bianco's to be the most illuminating and promising. 14 notes.   T. W. Smith

228. Payne, Harry C. THE EIGHTEENTH-CENTURY FAMILY: AN ELUSIVE OBJECT. *Eighteenth-Century Life 1978 5(2): 48-61.* Review article prompted by four books dealing with the early American family and 18th-century attitudes towards child-rearing, education, religion, and sex.

229. Peebles, Minnie K. BLACK GENEALOGY. *North Carolina Hist. Rev. 1978 55(2): 164-173.* Black genealogists encounter more obstacles than white researchers because records on blacks are scarce or nonexistent. It is easier to trace a free black than a slave family as the records are better. Descendants of slaves must look at black and white (slaveowner) family records to determine lineage. Government documents are most helpful in searching out black genealogy. These include the manuscript federal census, state pension and voter registration records, and birth, marriage, and death certificates.
                                                                    T. L. Savitt

230. Penna, Anthony N. DISCOVERING ROOTS: THE FAMILY IN HISTORY. *Social Educ. 1977 41(6): 478-481.* Deals with the use of family history in history teaching; examines ways of introducing historical methodology to students.

231. Perdue, Theda. REMEMBERING REMOVAL, 1867. *J. of Cherokee Studies 1982 7(2): 69-73.* Cornelia C. Chandler, in 1937, recounted how she, her family, and about 72 North Carolina Cherokee Indians immigrated to Arkansas in 1867 to the Goingsnake District, where economic and social conditions were poor. Her account includes food gathering, a meeting with Stand Watie, primitive schools, marriage to John A. Chandler, and birth of her children. In later years, she lived in Prairie City, now Ogechee, and Fairland, Arkansas. 26 notes.
                                                                  K. E. Gilmont

232. Pessen, Edward. THE LIFESTYLES OF THE ANTEBELLUM URBAN ELITE. *Mid-Am. 1973 55(3): 163-183.* Studies the lifestyles of the wealthy upper class of Boston, New York, Brooklyn, and Philadelphia during the second quarter of the 19th century, indicating that they rejected egalitarianism. Wealth married wealth, mingled socially with wealth, joined like clubs, formed socially purposeful voluntary associations, and established elite residential concentrations. The rich and eminent were a group apart, owning roughly one-half the wealth of the northeastern cities. Based on the Philip Hone diary in the New York Historical Society, published sources and secondary works; 43 notes.
                                                                  T. H. Wendel

233. Peters, Thomas C. THE AFFECTIONAL FUNCTION HYPOTHE-SIS: AN UNTESTED TRADITION IN FAMILY SOCIOLOGY. *J. of the Hist. of Sociol. 1982 4(1): 52-65.* Discusses the wide, and almost unquestioned, acceptance of William F. Ogburn's theory of "the modern family's specialization in the affectional function," initiated in the 1920's; Ogburn's hypothesis has not been empirically tested.

234. Pfaelzer, Jean. REBECCA HARDING DAVIS: DOMESTICITY, SO-CIAL ORDER, AND THE INDUSTRIAL NOVEL. *Int. J. of Women's Studies [Canada] 1981 4(3): 234-244.* Discusses the novella written by Rebecca Harding Davis, an unmarried 30-year-old middle-class woman, *Life in the Iron Mills,* published in 1861 in The Atlantic Monthly, which tells the story of a Welsh family employed in Wheeling, West Virginia's iron and cotton mills, and intro-duced the workers to the industrial revolution, and American readers to literary realism, particularly the role of women workers.

235. Porter, Dorothy B. FAMILY RECORDS, A MAJOR RESOURCE FOR DOCUMENTING THE BLACK EXPERIENCE IN NEW ENGLAND. *Old-Time New England 1973 63(3): 69-72.* Discusses New England black family records and other collections useful for research in the history of New England blacks. R. N. Lokken

236. Posadas, Barbara M. CROSSED BOUNDARIES IN INTERRACIAL CHICAGO: PILIPINO AMERICAN FAMILIES SINCE 1925. *Amerasia J. 1981 8(2): 31-52.* Presents the general circumstances and characteristics of the Filipino migrants to Chicago in the 1920's. Notes how they differed from those that settled on the West Coast. Most were male and well educated and were able to marry white females in multiethnic Chicago. Describes how these interracial marriages occurred and some of the problems that the couples experience. Based on secondary sources and interviews with mixed couples; 2 tables, 43 notes. E. S. Johnson

237. Purvis, Thomas L. "HIGH-BORN, LONG-RECORDED FAMI-LIES": SOCIAL ORIGINS OF NEW JERSEY ASSEMBLYMEN, 1703 TO 1776. *William and Mary Q. 1980 37(4): 592-615.* All the legislators of the period of New Jersey's royal government (256 assemblymen) held high economic status. Livelihood, income, wealth, religion, and kinship connections of the assemblymen are examined. Most assemblymen were descended from families long resident. Most assemblymen began as county magistrates. A leader's rise resulted from legislative experience and a commitment to spend much time in political activity. The American Revolution reversed the trend toward oligarchic consolidation. Based on local and colony records and monographs; 5 tables, 65 notes. H. M. Ward

238. Quitt, Martin H. THE CONTEMPORARY "CRISIS" OF THE AMERICAN FAMILY: THE PERSPECTIVE OF A FAMILY HISTORIAN AND PSYCHOHISTORIAN. *J. of Psychohistory 1976 4(1): 101-110.* Argues that the traditional nuclear family is not in danger of collapsing, despite negative statistical indices, and discusses the connections between family history and psychohistory. Primary and secondary sources; 16 notes. R. E. Butchart

239. Ramirez, Bruno.   MONTREAL'S ITALIANS AND THE SOCIO-ECONOMY OF SETTLEMENT, 1900-1930: SOME HISTORICAL HYPOTHESES.   *Urban Hist. Rev. [Canada] 1981 10(1): 39-48.* As the pattern of Italian immigration to Montreal changed from predominantly sojourners to permanent settlers, important changes occurred both in the composition of that immigrant population (sex ratio, age structure, etc.) and in its internal organization (residential patterns, kinship and *paese*-based network). These changes made possible familial economic strategies characterized by the use of extra-market resources to complement the means of life deriving from earnings. Though the magnitude of this practice escapes precise quantification, it seems to have been so widespread among Italian immigrants as to constitute a socioeconomic subsystem existing alongside the official market system. Moreover, in this sphere of economic behavior, Italian immigrants enjoyed greater autonomy of time and space and thus could more freely resort to their cultural values as an important resource for their adaptive strategies. More detailed analysis may throw light on the ethnic cohesion characterizing Italian immigrant communities in Montreal during 1900-30.   J/S

240. Rapp, Rayna.   FAMILY AND CLASS IN CONTEMPORARY AMERICA: NOTES TOWARD AN UNDERSTANDING OF IDEOLOGY. *Sci. and Soc. 1978 42(3): 278-300.* Families provide the entry point for communal engagement in productive, reproductive, and consumption relations. In households, families cope with the material relationships involving the sharing or withholding of basic poolable resources. In the working class, households reproduce and maintain labor power which is exchanged for basic resources. The working class household is "lateral" in the sense that larger numbers of real or "fictive" blood relations are involved in this effort than merely the nuclear family. Middle class and upper class families tend to more "lineal" than "lateral" in that in these households resources are pooled and exchanged for commodities on the basis of unilateral earning power, inheritances and friendship rather than blood relationships.   N. Lederer

241. Rezneck, Samuel.   A NOTE ON THE GENEALOGY OF AN EIGHTEENTH-CENTURY FAMILY OF JEWISH ORIGIN: THE NUNEZ FAMILY OF LEWES, DELAWARE.   *Am. Jewish Arch. 1978 30(1): 20-23.* In colonial America, Jews occasionally left the security of the Jewish community to migrate into the hinterland. Often, deprived of essential contacts, they ceased to be Jewish. Professor Rezneck attempts to reconstruct three generations of one such family.   J

242. Rhoads, James B.   THE IMPORTANCE OF FAMILY HISTORY TO OUR SOCIETY.   *Public Hist. 1979 1(3): 6-16.* Discusses the importance of family history to American society, and describes the ways that people interested in family history can research it; through the National Archives and Records Service, local libraries, and the Bureau of the Census, 1960's-70's.

243. Riegelhaupt, Joyce F.   WOMEN, WORK, WAR, AND FAMILY: SOME RECENT WORKS IN WOMAN'S HISTORY. A REVIEW ARTICLE. *Comparative Studies in Soc. and Hist. [Great Britain] 1982 24(4): 660-672.* Reviews Thomas Dublin's *Women at Work: The Transformation of Work and Community in Lowell, Massachusetts, 1826-1860* (1979); Susan Kennedy's *If All*

We Did Was to Weep at Home: A History of White Working-Class Women in America (1979); Carl N. Degler's *At Odds: Women and the Family in America from the Revolution to the Present* (1980); Darlene G. Levy, Harriet B. Applewhite, and Mary D. Johnson's *Women in Revolutionary Paris, 1789-1795* (1979); and *Women, War and Revolution,* edited by Carol R. Berkin and Clara M. Lovett (1980). Examining the social organization of relations among men is crucial to understanding both relations between men and women and the roles available to women in a society. Gender construction is a key element in all social systems.

S. A. Farmerie

244. Rink, Oliver A. THE PEOPLE OF NEW NETHERLAND: NOTES ON NON-ENGLISH IMMIGRATION TO NEW YORK IN THE SEVENTEENTH CENTURY. *New York Hist. 1981 62(1): 5-42.* Analysis of immigrants in New Netherland reveals the colony's demographic problems. Early attempts to settle families in the colony went awry as the West India Company failed to develop a consistent settlement policy. The patroonship system also failed, except for Rensselaerswyck. The New England type nuclear family migration did not occur in Rensselaerswyck prior to 1644. Most immigrants were single young men. Between 1644 and the 1650's, immigrant families appeared, as did black slaves, who did not remain long before they were sold to planters in Maryland and Virginia. The immigration of the non-Dutch gave New Netherland a culturally heterogeneous society. Based on archival sources in Amsterdam and The Hague, the Netherlands and published primary sources; 2 illus., map, 4 tables, 73 notes.

R. N. Lokken

245. Roberts, Warren E. HOOSIER, YANKEE, AND YOHO: SOME COMMENTS ON FAMILY NAMES IN INDIANA. *Kansas Q. 1981 13(2): 73-83.* Discusses the kinds of information that can be culled in Indiana from surnames, particularly those from Great Britain and Ireland; focuses on the origins of the family names Hoosier, Yankee, and Yoho; 18c-1981.

246. Robertson, Matthew and Roy, Arun S. FERTILITY, LABOR FORCE PARTICIPATION AND THE RELATIVE INCOME HYPOTHESIS: AN EMPIRICAL TEST OF THE EASTERLIN-WACHTER MODEL ON THE BASIS OF CANADIAN EXPERIENCE. *Am. J. of Econ. and Sociol. 1982 41(4): 339-350.* Tests the relative income hypothesis, which states that fertility and labor force participation depend upon relative income. The results tend to provide empirical support for the relative income hypothesis. The postwar baby boom, which led to a decline in the income of young adults relative to that of older age groups, had the effect of increasing participation rates of young adults, especially of young (married) women.

J/S

247. Robinson, Raymond H. THE FAMILIES OF COMMONWEALTH AVENUE. *Massachusetts Hist. Soc. Pro. 1981 93: 80-94.* Provides a progress report on the research completed thus far on the history of elite Boston families who resided on Commonwealth Avenue from 1861 to 1981. A sampling taken of the records for the decennial census of 1900 of 50 odd-numbered houses indicated that residents came from Beacon Hill and the surrounding towns; 40% were college graduates (almost all from Harvard), and their occupations in order of frequency included merchant, banking and brokerage, lawyer, doctor, real estate, insurance, railroading, and navy. Social lives were clearly intertwined through church groups, civic clubs, and recreational activities.

G. A. Glovins

248. Rogler, Lloyd H.; Cooney, Rosemary Santana; and Ortiz, Vilma. IN-TERGENERATIONAL CHANGE IN ETHNIC IDENTITY IN THE PUERTO RICAN FAMILY. *Int. Migration Rev. 1980 14(2): 193-214.* Derived from a New York City survey of 1976-78, notes that education and age at arrival are significant factors upon ethnicity and that these same factors in children are related to changes in ethnicity in the family.

249. Rosenwaike, Ira. THE JEWS OF BALTIMORE TO 1810. *Am. Jewish Hist. Q. 1975 64(4): 291-320.* The systematic examination of the Jewish population of Baltimore from 1770 to 1810 reveals that by 1810 a rough outline of the communal trends in the next stage of development had been shaped: differentiation had taken place between the relatively well-off older "American" Jews and the recent immigrant arrivals. Another two decades passed, however, before the first congregation was set up. Over 40 individuals and their families provide material for this study. 85 notes.   F. Rosenthal and S

250. Ross, Ellen. RETHINKING "THE FAMILY." *Radical Hist. Rev. 1979 (20): 76-84.* Review essay of Mark Poster's *Critical Theory of the Family* (New York: Seabury, 1978) examines social theorists and psychoanalytical theories of family, 1930's-60's and the evolution of male and female roles within the family.

251. Rossi, Peter H. and Shlay, Anne B. RESIDENTIAL MOBILITY AND PUBLIC POLICY ISSUES: "WHY FAMILIES MOVE" REVISITED. *J. of Social Issues 1982 38(3): 21-34.* Early 20th century concerns with social problems and pathologies perceived as stemming from rural to urban migration, neighborhood transiency, and an absence of spatially stable communities fueled the early study of residential mobility. Knowing why people moved, it seemed, presented a potential for fostering neighborhood stability, place oriented community and a cure for urban ills such as crime, delinquency, and other forms of anomic behavior. The finding that residential mobility was neither pathological nor indicative of normlessness but was a normal process through which families improve their housing situations set the tone for later mobility research. The myriad of studies on mobility precipitants and housing adjustment processes have, today, firmly established the finding that residential shifts are driven by family compositional changes accompanying family life cycle stages.   J/S

252. Roy, Raymond and Charbonneau, Hubert. LE CONTENU DES REGISTRES PAROISSIAUX CANADIENS DU XVIIᵉ SIÈCLE [The contents of Canadian parish registers of the 17th century]. *Rev. d'Hist. de l'Am. Française [Canada] 1976 30(1): 85-97.* From about 1616 to 1700, more than 26,000 acts of baptism, marriage, and burial affecting Europeans were recorded in Quebec's parish registers. Attempts to analyze Canada's 17th-century population from parish registers. Based on parish registers and secondary works; 3 figs., 12 notes.   L. B. Chan

253. Ruffin, C. Bernard. RECORDS OF THE SELLERS FUNERAL HOME, CHAMBERSBURG, PENNSYLVANIA, RELATING TO THE BLACK FAMILIES OF FRANKLIN COUNTY, 1866-1933. *J. of the Afro-American Hist. and Geneal. Soc. 1982 3(4): 165-182; 1983 4(1): 32-34.* Continued from a previous article (see following entry). Includes data on home address, stature, and age of deceased; cause of death; and place of burial.

254. Ruffin, C. Bernard. RECORDS OF THE SELLERS FUNERAL HOME, CHAMBERSBURG, PENNSYLVANIA, RELATING TO THE BLACK FAMILIES OF FRANKLIN COUNTY, 1866-1933. *J. of the Afro-American Hist. and Geneal. Soc. 1982 3(2): 73-83, (3): 106-116.* Lists the Negroes buried by the Sellers Funeral Home in Chambersburg.

255. Rushdoony, Rousas J. THE FAMILY. *Freeman 1973 23(7): 429-432.* The foundation of the social order, the family, is under attack, but there is no cause for alarm; the attack on the family is merely the last hapless charge of statism. "The approaching collapse of the age of humanism and the state will see the strong revival of familism, and the United States is already giving evidence of this." Reprinted from *Applied Christianity* (December 1972).

D. A. Yanchisin

256. Russell-Wood, A. J. R. THE BLACK FAMILY IN THE AMERICAS. *Jahrbuch für Geschichte von Staat, Wirtschaft und Gesellschaft Lateinamerikas [West Germany] 1979 16: 267-309.* Recently there has been a great deal of interest in the slave family, much of it general in nature. These studies have revealed blacks who ran away to form separate black settlements and who selected surnames reflecting their past or present culture. Significantly, despite the quantity of new work, no definitive history has been written for any region or republic in Spanish or Portuguese America. Secondary sources; 50 notes.

T. D. Schoonover

257. Russell-Wood, A. J. R. THE BLACK FAMILY IN THE AMERICAS. *Societas 1978 8(1): 1-38.* Generally, though tentatively and not uncritically expands to the rest of the Americas Herbert Gutman's thesis in *The Black Family in Slavery and Freedom, 1750-1925* that in the English-speaking North American mainland the black family was much stronger, more independent of whites, and more tied to its African heritage than in Latin America, as many authorities have asserted. Based on printed primary and secondary sources in four languages; 50 notes.

J. D. Hunley

258. Ryan, Mary P. A WOMEN'S AWAKENING: EVANGELICAL RELIGION AND THE FAMILIES OF UTICA, N.Y., 1800-1840. *Am. Q. 1978 30(5): 602-623.* A demographic and statistical analysis and interpretation of women's place in the Second Evangelical Awakening as seen in Oneida County, New York, and more particularly in Utica and environs. The study reveals that the Utica women, as wives and mothers and as trustees of an extensive missionary organization, were the ones "who orchestrated the domestic revivals," yet also remained true to a narrowly maternal role and image for their sex. Concludes that "women were more than the majority of the converts, more even than the private guardians of America's souls. The combination and consequence of all these roles left the imprint of a women's awakening on American society as well as on American religion." 7 tables, 29 notes.

R. V. Ritter

259. Ryant, Carl. ORAL HISTORY AND FAMILY HISTORY. *Family Heritage 1979 2(2): 50-53.* Excerpts the transcript of a taped interview with Lillian and Louis Perry by their daughter, Barbara Perry, as part of a project in oral and family history at the University of Louisville, 1977.

260. Salerno, Anthony. THE SOCIAL BACKGROUND OF SEVEN-TEENTH-CENTURY EMIGRATION TO AMERICA. *J. of British Studies 1979 19(1): 31-52.* Summarizes age, sex, family and marital status, place of origin, and occupation of two groups of emigrants from the western English county of Wiltshire to America during the 1630's and 1650's. Both groups were predominantly young, male, and single, with a substantial minority of married couples traveling with children. Emigrants were mainly urban artisans and husbandmen from pastoral regions, with close kinship and neighborhood ties. Population pressure on land and declining apprenticeship opportunities, probably connected to religious nonconformity, motivated migration within the county and emigration. Based on parish archives in the Wiltshire Record Office and published and unpublished emigrant passenger lists; 2 maps, 5 tables, fig., 69 notes.

D. M. Cregier

261. Sarachek, Bernard. JEWISH AMERICAN ENTREPRENEURS. *J. of Econ. Hist. 1980 40(2): 359-372.* This note contrasts the familial origins of 136 Jewish American entrepreneurs with those of 187 American non-Jewish entrepreneurs described in a previous study of mine. Information on both groups was drawn from published biographies. In addition, manuscript biographies were used to gather information on Jewish entrepreneurs.   J

262. Schaefer, Richard T. INTERMARRIAGE IN BRITAIN AND THE UNITED STATES. *Patterns of Prejudice [Great Britain] 1981 15(2): 8-15.* Using an intermarriage index first presented in English by Franco Savorgnan in 1950, describes the frequency of intermarriage in Great Britain and makes some tentative comparisons between Britain and the United States.

263. Schelbert, Leo and Leubking, Sandra. SWISS MENNONITE FAMILY NAMES: AN ANNOTATED CHECKLIST. *Swiss Am. Hist. Soc. Newsletter 1978 14(2): 2-32.* Lists the major family names of the Swiss Brethren, a body of Mennonites who migrated to North America, 1680-1880; gives variant names, Swiss origins, and names of successive first migrated family members.

264. Schlenker, Jon A. AN HISTORICAL ANALYSIS OF THE FAMILY LIFE OF THE CHOCTAW INDIANS. *Southern Q. 1975 13(4): 323-334.* Divides Choctaw history into five categories: Primitive Period, European Contact Period, Treaty and Missionary Period, Removal and Reservation Period, and US Citizenship Period. Studies each period in terms of kinship systems and family cycles and examines such factors as birth rates, marriage customs, role assignments, and rituals. 48 notes.   R. W. Dubay

265. Schlesinger, Benjamin. ONE-PARENT FAMILIES: KNOWNS AND UNKNOWNS. *Social Sci. 1980 55(1): 25-28.* For the past 18 years we have been involved in examining the one-parent family in English-speaking industrialized countries. These countries include Australia, Canada, Britain, New Zealand, and the United States. We have published in 1978 (Schlesinger, 1978) a comprehensive annotated bibliography which surveyed 750 items related to one-parent families in these countries. From examining this literature, we have developed 20 factors in the "knowns and unknowns" related to one-parent families. These have been selected as some of the major items for consideration in examining the growing phenomenon of one-parent families as an alternate family style in the 1970's. Ref.   J

266. Schlesinger, Keith R. SOURCES AT THE NATIONAL ARCHIVES FOR GENEALOGICAL AND LOCAL HISTORY RESEARCH. *Prologue 1981 13(4): 251-262.* Social forces play an important role in the study of history. The importance of the federal population census as a historical document is generally accepted, but there are factors that make its efficient and effective use very difficult. Accelerated indexes have helped to overcome some of the difficulties in using the census, but they are not the entire solution to the problem. The urban finding aid is offered as a solution because it allows the user to locate individuals efficiently in the schedules, while it permits the effective reconstruction of geographical communities. Based on National Archives and Records Service's descriptions of census districts and cartographic records of the Bureau of Census; 2 photos, 2 fig., 25 notes. M. A. Kascus

267. Schueler, Donald G. OUR FAMILY TREES HAVE ROOTS IN UTAH'S MOUNTAIN VAULTS. *Smithsonian 1981 12(9): 87-95.* The Mormons are gathering extensive pre 20th-century genealogical information in their Granite Mountain Record Vault, in Utah, and are using microfilm and microfiche to aid in the storage of these records.

268. Scobie, Ingrid Winther. FAMILY AND COMMUNITY HISTORY THROUGH ORAL HISTORY. *Public Hist. 1979 1(4): 29-39.* Historians largely ignored family and community history until the 1950's; interest in oral history as a method of preservation did not become widespread until 1948, when historian Allan Nevins of Columbia University founded the Oral History Project.

269. Scott, John W. THE HISTORY OF THE FAMILY AS AN AFFECTIVE UNIT. *Social Hist. [Great Britain] 1979 4(3): 509-516.* A review article which examines and compares Jacques Donzelot's *La Police des Familles* (Paris: Eds. de Minuit, 1977), Christopher Lasch's *Haven in a Heartless World: The Family Besieged* (New York: Basic Books, 1977), and Lawrence Stone's *The Family, Sex, and Marriage in England 1500-1800* (London: Weidenfeld & Nicolson, 1977). Donzelot and Lasch discuss the weakened position of the family in America and France respectively in terms of its invasion by social theorists and philanthropic reformers, but both suffer from reliance on ideological rather than real evidence of changes in the historical family. Stone, by contrast, employs a wealth of real evidence to illustrate an increase in "affective feelings," but produces an idealized version of past families by assuming a straightforward equation between affective expression and the quality of emotional life. A. P. Oxley

270. Scozzari, Carole. GENEALOGICAL RESEARCH MATERIALS IN THE LONG ISLAND HISTORICAL SOCIETY. *J. of Long Island Hist. 1981 17(2): 43-49.* Description of the genealogical materials, focusing on but not limited to Brooklyn, Long Island, and New York City, available in the reading room collection of the society. This excludes, however, the numerous manuscript sources. Illus. G. R. Schroeder

271. Shaw, Peter. THE NEW FAMILY. *Antioch Rev. 1983 41(1): 20-27.* Writers and psychologists of the late 70's have discovered the prestige of maturity and the family, but only as a variation of youth and youthful self-discovery.

272. Shifflett, Crandall A. THE HOUSEHOLD COMPOSITION OF RU-
RAL BLACK FAMILIES: LOUISA COUNTY, VIRGINIA, 1880. *J. of Interdisciplinary Hist. 1975 6(2): 235-260.* Explores the economic and social forces
which have shaped black family structures, especially in the rural area of Louisa
County, Virginia. Investigates the extent to which such forces conditioned family
residence choice and suggests that more useful categories than "bi-parent" and
"woman-headed" are needed for analysis. The complexity of household composition is not captured by the simple division into the categories of nuclear or
extended. A dynamic model is needed which is keyed to changes in the family
between formation and maturation. 6 tables, 3 graphs, 31 notes.   R. Howell

273. Siegel, Fred. THE AGONY OF CHRISTOPHER LASCH. *Rev. in
Am. Hist. 1980 8(3): 285-295.* Christopher Lasch's two most recent books, *Haven
in a Heartless World* (1977) and *The Culture of Narcissism* (1979), focus on "the
decline of the family, paternal authority, and genuine individualism," which he
links with the growth of government; 1880's-1979.

274. Sitton, Thad. ORAL LIFE HISTORY: FROM TAPE RECORDER TO
TYPEWRITER. *Social Studies 1981 72(3): 121-126.* Oral history offers a
unique source for understanding the community, the culture, and the genealogy
of a given group of people. 12 notes.   L. R. Raife

275. Skolnick, Arlene. THE FAMILY AND ITS DISCONTENTS. *Society
1981 18(2): 42-47.* Discusses myths and recent scholarship concerning the family
in the 20th century; comments on the impact of technology and economic trends
upon the family structure; and argues that the family is experiencing not a decline,
but a transitional period, as it learns to adapt to changing times and circumstances.

276. Skolnick, Mark L.; Bean, Lee L.; Dintelman, Sue M.; and Mineau, Geraldine. A COMPUTERIZED FAMILY HISTORY DATA BASE SYSTEM.
Sociol. and Social Res. 1979 63(3): 506-523. Describes the development of a
unique, computer-based, data management system designed to increase the ability
of scholars in social history and historical demography to collate and analyze
large bodies of historical data. This system extends efforts, largely mounted in
Europe, to develop computerized systems for data manipulation and record
linkage. Describes the Mormon historical demography research project, for
which this system was developed, and the system's file structure, input systems,
and data access facilities. Includes an illustration of the possible types of analysis.
                                                                              J/S

277. Slater, Peter G. "FROM THE CRADLE TO THE COFFIN": PAREN-
TAL BEREAVEMENT AND THE SHADOW OF INFANT DAMNATION
IN PURITAN SOCIETY. *Psychohistory Rev. 1977-78 6(2-3): 4-24.* High
mortality rates among infants in Puritan society confronted parents with a complex and stressful process of bereavement. Anxiety was raised by the principles
of original sin, natural iniquity of children, and the uncertainty of salvation or
damnation of deceased children. Parents went through psychological processes
of idealization, rationalization, and gratification through masochism during the
cycle of mourning. Though the Puritan system made successful completion of
bereavement difficult, it seems that most parents reached a final stage of equilib-

rium. Based on contemporary diaries, sermons and poems, and secondary works; 71 notes.   J. B. Street

278.   Smelser, Neil J. and Halpern, Sydney.   THE HISTORICAL TRIANGU-
LATION OF FAMILY, ECONOMY, AND EDUCATION.   Demos, John and
Boocock, Sarane Spence, ed. *Turning Points: Historical and Sociological Essays
on the Family* (Chicago: U. of Chicago Pr., 1978): 288-315. Discusses the relationship among the family, education, and economy (industrialization) to develop
a methodological model of social change and its effects on family structure and
relationships; 1920's-70's.

279.   Smith, Daniel B.   THE STUDY OF THE FAMILY IN EARLY AMER-
ICA: TRENDS, PROBLEMS, AND PROSPECTS.   *William and Mary Q.
1982 39(1): 3-28.* Reviews the literature on family history of the 17th and 18th
centuries, with emphasis on the publications of the 1960's and 70's. Until mid-
1970, studies focused on historical demography and New England. Since then
there has been a shift to demographic foundations and the rest of the colonies.
Especially there has been recent interest in parent-child relations and sex-role
patterns. Cites the significant interpretive trends, and discusses the leading studies. Secondary literature; 76 notes.   H. M. Ward

280.   Smith, Daniel Blake.   MORTALITY AND FAMILY IN THE COLO-
NIAL CHESAPEAKE.   *J. of Interdisciplinary Hist. 1978 8(3): 403-427.* Analyzes the demographic history of Charles Parish, York County, Virginia, in the
colonial period in comparison with other Chesapeake areas and with New England. Mortality rates were high in contrast to improving conditions elsewhere
in the 18th-century Chesapeake. The population barely managed to reproduce
itself throughout the colonial era. Reviews the impact of this situation on family
structure and attitudes. 11 tables, graph, 41 notes.   R. Howell

281.   Smith, Daniel Blake.   PERSPECTIVES IN AMERICAN FAMILY
HISTORY.   *Working Papers from the Regional Econ. Hist. Res. Center 1979
3(1): 1-28.* Discusses the divergent paths of family historians in methodology and
recent findings on early American family patterns; 1750-1979.

282.   Smith, Daniel Scott.   A COMMUNITY-BASED SAMPLE OF THE
OLDER POPULATION FROM THE 1880 AND 1900 UNITED STATES
MANUSCRIPT CENSUS.   *Hist. Methods 1978 11(2): 67-74.* After a lenghty
discussion of methodology and sampling techniques, this study concludes that the
subject of old age needs reliable historical data which, within discussed limits, the
census provides and secondly, that only in recent decades has the family status
of the older population begun to change. In this study "old age" is not just being
65 but it is rather a process in which individual variations, marital status, sex,
and ethnicity contribute to a stage of life concept. Table, 30 notes.
                                                               D. K. Pickens

283.   Smith, Daniel Scott.   LIFE COURSE, NORMS, AND THE FAMILY
SYSTEM OF OLDER AMERICANS IN 1900.   *J. of Family Hist. 1979 4(3):
285-298.* There was more variation in the living arrangements of the aged in 1900
than today. More of the elderly lived with married children than today, but this
living situation was adopted by only one-sixth of the married elderly. As advanced age increased fewer members of the elderly were self-employed, household
heads, and married. 7 tables, 2 notes, biblio.   T. W. Smith

284.   Smith, J. E. and Kunz, P. R.   POLYGYNY AND FERTILITY IN NINETEENTH-CENTURY AMERICA.   *Population Studies [Great Britain] 1976 30(3): 465-480.* Statistics indicate a slightly lower completed marital fertility in polygynous than in monogamous unions among 19th-century Mormons.

285.   Spanier, Graham B. and Glick, Paul C.   THE LIFE CYCLE OF AMERICAN FAMILIES: AN EXPANDED ANALYSIS.   *J. of Family Hist. 1980 5(1): 97-112.* Studies the life cycle progressions of birth cohorts of American women born in the first half of the 20th century. Women are crossclassified by race, educational level, and number of times married. Differences between whites and blacks are diminished when education is controlled. Blacks show more variation in their patterns than do whites. 4 tables, biblio.   T. W. Smith

286.   Sprague, Stewart Seely.   OLD POSTCARDS: A LOOK AT YOUR AN-CESTORS' WORLD.   *Family Heritage 1979 2(4): 100-105.* Lists and discusses techniques for isolating possible locations of postcards and commercial photographs useful in re-creating family albums.

287.   Sprey, Jetse and Metthews, Sarah H.   CONTEMPORARY GRAND-PARENTHOOD: A SYSTEMIC TRANSITION.   *Ann. of the Am. Acad. of Pol. and Social Sci. 1982 (464): 91-103.* The transition to grandparenthood is presented as a stage in the family life cycle in which meaning comes from outside the boundaries of the original nuclear family through alliances initiated and produced by offspring. The transition is likely to occur in middle age and to overlap less with active parenting than was the case in the past. The ages of both grandparents and new parents are important variables affecting transition. The grandparent-grandchild bond is initially mediated by the parents. As time passes, however, the bond becomes more direct, although it continues to be negotiated within the extended family system.   J/S

288.   Stannard, David E.   CALM DWELLINGS.   *Am. Heritage 1979 30(5): 42-55.* Reflecting subtle social changes, rural cemeteries began to appear in the 1830's as an attempt to maintain the symbols, if not the reality, of the viable, traditional family. Tombstones reflect that concern. By the 1840's, there were so many small, fenced-in family cemeteries that complaints began. Economics and changing views on religion led to their eventual decline. 10 illus.

J. F. Paul

289.   Staples, James C.   USE OF THE COMPUTER BY THE FAMILY HISTORIAN: AN APPLICATION TO GENEALOGICAL DATA.   *New England Hist. and Geneal. Register 1979 133(July): 194-210.* The computer can be a useful tool in family history. Discusses techniques for organizing data and suggests programs for putting it into a computer. Biographical material can be maintained as text in a separate file and coded under the appropriate names. Compares costs between completing a genealogy with traditional methods and using a computer. 10 fig., 7 notes.   J

290.   Staples, Robert.   THE BLACK FAMILY IN EVOLUTIONARY PER-SPECTIVE.   *Black Scholar 1974 5(9): 2-9.* The black family has been an adaptive unit and its form and dynamics have varied according to conditions. While the structure and function of the black family changed under slavery, the importance of the family to African peoples in the New World did not change. Contem-

porary stresses have made the institution of marriage less than viable for Negroes. The decrease in the black fertility rate will probably continue. Conceptual models must be developed that can put these various changes in black family life into perspective. Secondary sources; 23 notes.　　　　　　　　　　　M. M. McCarthy

291. Steinmetz, Suzanne K. and Straus, Murray A. THE FAMILY AS CRA-DLE OF VIOLENCE. *Society 1973 10(6): 50-56.*

292. Stevens, Cj. BLACK BIRTHS AND BAPTISMS IN MANNIKIN-TOWN. *J. of the Afro-American Hist. and Geneal. Soc. 1983 4(1): 15-20.* Reprints pages from a birth register of 1721 in Mannikintown, Virginia.

293. Stinehelfer, Karen. FINDING YOUR ANCESTORS IN THE CEME-TERY. *Family Heritage 1978 1(3): 75-79.*

294. Strauss, Alena Janet. INFLUENCES ON JEWISH IDENTITY. *J. of Baltic Studies 1979 10(1): 51-59.* Discusses the development of Jewish identity among Jews in North American society. The main force insuring Jewish survival and transmitting Jewish identity has been the family. The influence of the family is gradually replaced by Jewish schools and youth groups. A profound role on Jewish identity is played by the existence of the state of Israel. The retention of Jewish identity in the open and liberal North American society is unique. Being a Jew in America is totally voluntary and must be based on a need to belong to the Jewish ethnic group. 23 ref.　　　　　　　　　　　R. Vilums

295. Sturino, Franc. A CASE STUDY OF A SOUTH ITALIAN FAMILY IN TORONTO, 1935-60. *Urban Hist. Rev. [Canada] 1978 78(2): 38-57.* City directories are used to trace the occupational and residential history of one immigrant family. Part of a larger research project, the history of this one family seems typical. The family was upwardly mobile in residence, moving from a working-class to a middle-class district, and in occupation, the sons moving from factory to white collar jobs. Many of the upward moves were a result of aid given because of kinship ties. Interviews, city directories, and secondary sources; illus., 2 tables, fig., 18 notes.　　　　　　　　　　　C. A. Watson

296. Surber, Astrid. FATTIGDOMS PROBLEMET I U.S.A. [The problem of poverty in the United States]. *Samtiden [Norway] 1971 80(7): 445-458.* There are more families below the poverty line in the cities than in the country, and more poor black families than white ones.

297. Swagerty, William R. MARRIAGE AND SETTLEMENT PAT-TERNS OF ROCKY MOUNTAIN TRAPPERS AND TRADERS. *Western Hist. Q. 1980 11(2): 159-180.* Statistical analysis of the mountain men is a useful tool to dispel the stereotyping and compartmentalizing that has dominated the literature since the 1830's. It is employed here to determine the relationship between nationalities of the fur trappers and traders and their status or position in the business on the one hand, with their marriage and ultimate settlement patterns on the other hand. Most accepted the family obligations of their last marriage and became as responsible in their homes as they had been in trapping and trading. 28 notes.　　　　　　　　　　　D. L. Smith

298.   Targ, Dena B.   IDEOLOGY AND UTOPIA IN FAMILY STUDIES
SINCE THE SECOND WORLD WAR.   *Women's Studies Int. Q. 1981 4(2):
191-200.* Examines the debate within family studies, centered around issues of
stability and change; discusses recent books which define the family and roles
within it for both men and women.

299.   Taylor, Robert M., Jr.   GENEALOGICAL SOURCES IN AMERICAN
SOCIAL HISTORY RESEARCH: A REAPPRAISAL.   *New England Hist.
and Geneal. Register 1981 135(Jan): 3-15.* The value of genealogical material in
historical interpretation is finally being acknowledged by historians. Statistics on
migration patterns, education, occupation, and religion, to name a few, may be
readily drawn through study and comparison of family genealogies. Difficulty of
access to material may still be a problem, but increasing use of computers will
help solve it. Mainly secondary sources; 2 tables, 26 notes.   J/A. E. Huff

300.   Temply-Trujillo, Rita E.   CONCEPTIONS OF THE CHICANO FAM-
ILY.   *Smith Coll. Studies in Social Work 1974 45(1): 1-20.* Reviews a range of
formulations about the Chicano family drawn from a sample of social science
literature (1968-74), and criticizes the stereotyped conception of ideal family
models used as criteria for study of Mexican Americans.   S

301.   Thavenat, Dennis.   A SEARCH FOR ALL THE PEOPLE: FAMILY
HISTORY COMES OF AGE.   *Family Heritage 1978 1(2): 58-62.* Collaboration of genealogists and historians in the 1970's has resulted in renewed interest
in history of the masses through family history, adding perspectives on the
general population's effect of national affairs, social structure, kinship patterns,
and value formation.

302.   Thomas, Robert David.   JOHN HUMPHREY NOYES AND THE
ONEIDA COMMUNITY: A 19TH-CENTURY AMERICAN FATHER
AND HIS FAMILY.   *Psychohistory Rev. 1977-78 6(2-3): 68-87.* Describes the
attempts of John Humphrey Noyes, a major utopian reformer, to create a utopian
community modeled on the family and Perfectionist religious ideology at the
Oneida Community in New York (1848-80). Noyes tried to create a perfect world
of inner and outer harmony by regulating the sex, love, marriage, and procreative
habits of his community. Order in the community was based on passivity, dependence, and familial submission to Noyes, and through him to God. Based on
Noyes's writings and secondary works; 89 notes.   J. B. Street

303.   Tienda, Marta.   FAMILISM AND STRUCTURAL ASSIMILATION
OF MEXICAN IMMIGRANTS IN THE UNITED STATES.   *Int. Migration
Rev. 1980 14(3): 383-408.* Assesses the connections between geographic mobility,
kinship ties, and social status among a sample of 820 people who were interviewed
upon entry in 1973-74 and were reinterviewed three years later.

304.   Tilly, Charles and Tilly, Louise A.   STALKING THE BOURGEOIS
FAMILY.   *Social Sci. Hist. 1980 4(2): 251-260.* Reviews and criticizes the work
of two major interpreters of the modern bourgeois family, Christopher Lasch and
Lawrence Stone. Both are charged with participating in an idealist reaction
against recent social science, and are criticized primarily for their failure to make
better use of the tools and methods of the new social history. Ref.

L. K. Blaser

305. Toll, William. MOBILITY, FRATERNALISM AND JEWISH CULTURAL CHANGE: PORTLAND, 1910-1930. *Am. Jewish Hist. 1979 68(4): 459-491.* Using the manuscript records and membership lists of B'nai B'rith, demonstrates social and cultural changes as well as family and occupational patterns in Portland, Oregon. Rising economic and social status is suggested by changes in the occupational profile of lodge members, persistence rates, and patterns of residential mobility. 4 photos, 51 notes. F. Rosenthal

306. Tolnay, Steward E. and Guest, Avery M. CHILDLESSNESS IN A TRADITIONAL POPULATION: THE UNITED STATES AT THE TURN OF THE CENTURY. *J. of Family Hist. 1982 7(2): 200-219.* An analysis of childlessness in 1900 finds that regional variations were the result of voluntary choice. The most economically advanced regions, New England and the Middle Atlantic, had a high rate of childlessness as a result of changes in social and economic structures and values. By contrast almost all childlessness in the rural South was involuntary. 6 tables, 2 fig., 7 notes, biblio. T. W. Smith

307. Torgoff, Stella DeRosa. IMMIGRANT WOMEN, THE FAMILY, AND WORK: 1850-1950. *Trends in Hist. 1982 2(4): 31-47.* Reviews recent articles that challenge the stereotype of immigrant women as passive victims of their sex and ethnicity.

308. Twombly, Robert C. SAVING THE FAMILY: MIDDLE CLASS ATTRACTION TO WRIGHT'S PRAIRIE HOUSE 1901-1909. *Am. Q. 1975 27(1): 57-72.* Despite the widely accepted view that Frank Lloyd Wright's prairie houses were unpopular, the upper middle class provided the architect with many commissions. The house appealed to conventional suburbanites owing to its harkening back to their rural origins, its close association with nature, and its emphasis on securing the family from the real and alleged dangers of a rapidly changing urban environment. The house stressed shelter, internal intimacy, and togetherness with motifs of strength, security, and durability. N. Lederer

309. Vinovskis, Maris A. FROM HOUSEHOLD SIZE TO THE LIFE COURSE: SOME OBSERVATIONS ON RECENT TRENDS IN FAMILY HISTORY. *Am. Behavioral Scientist 1977 21(2): 263-288.* Analysis of household size and composition, study of generations, use of family-cycle models, and development of life-course perspectives are primary components of the framework used to study family history, 1970-80.

310. Vinovskis, Maris A. MARRIAGE PATTERNS IN MID-NINETEENTH-CENTURY NEW YORK STATE: A MULTIVARIATE ANALYSIS. *J. of Family Hist. 1978 3(1): 51-61.* Uses the New York state censuses of 1845, 1855, 1865, and 1875, and the federal census of 1850, to carry out an ecological analysis of the demographic and socioeconomic determinants of the marriage pattern. Finds that the sex ratio was the single best predictor of the proportion married. Two measures of agricultural opportunity also were strong predictors. The foreign-native distribution was a moderate predictor. Urbanness, industrialization, and economic development were not good predictors. 3 tables, 16 notes, biblio., appendix. T. W. Smith

311. Waldman, Elizabeth.   PROFILE OF THE CHICANA: A STATISTI-CAL FACT SHEET.   Mora, Magdalena and DelCastillo, Adelaida R., ed. *Mexican Women in the United States: Struggles Past and Present* (Los Angeles: U. of California Chicano Studies Res. Center, 1980): 195-204. Provides information of the number, marital status, education, employment status, median earnings, and family status of Mexican American women in the United States in 1975. Based on US Bureau of the Census records; 8 tables.   J. Powell

312. Walker, James Dent.   FAMILY HISTORY AND GENEALOGY: AV-OCATION OR NECESSITY?   *J. of the Afro-American Hist. and Geneal. Soc. 1981 2(3): 99-105.* Discusses the necessity to preserve family heritage by researching family history and genealogy and suggests places to start looking for information.

313. Walters, Ronald G.   THE FAMILY AND ANTE-BELLUM REFORM: AN INTERPRETATION.   *Societas 1973 3(3): 221-232.* From the 1820's to after the Civil War, an unprecedented flood of nonfiction writing analyzed the family. Conservatives and reformers agreed on the redeeming value of the family and that something was wrong or about to go wrong with the family. All hoped that the family rightly ordered would lead to stability and moral progress. Concern for the family was largely the product of the turbulent economics of Jacksonian America. 16 notes.   E. P. Stickney

314. Wander, Philip.   COUNTERS IN THE SOCIAL DRAMA: SOME NOTES ON "ALL IN THE FAMILY."   *J. of Popular Culture 1974 8(3): 602-607.* Examines the characters and plot of "All in the Family" and inspects the character of the program as it both reflects and belies American society during the 1970's.

315. Ward, Robert E.   FINDING YOUR GERMAN ANCESTORS. *Family Heritage 1978 1(1): 13-17.* Provides basic guidelines and helpful hints for those tracing their German ancestors as far back as the 1600's.

316. Ward, Robert Elmer.   THE CITY DIRECTORY: A KEY TO FAMILY HISTORY.   *Family Heritage 1979 2(2): 54-59.* Uses the Buschow family in Cleveland, Ohio, 1883-1900, to demonstrate the value and use of city directories as sources of local and family history.

317. Waters, John J.   THE TRADITIONAL WORLD OF THE NEW EN-GLAND PEASANTS: A VIEW FROM SEVENTEENTH-CENTURY BARNSTABLE.   *New England Hist. and Genealogical Register 1976 130(1): 3-21.* Explores the values which governed the 17th-century and early 18th-century life of Barnstable County (Cape Cod), Massachusetts. The importance of land, the idea of patrilineage, the reliance on stem families, and the emphasis on religion suggest the Old World background of these immigrants. Property was the most dominant factor, affecting dowries, independence of either the eldest or youngest son, ability of sons and daughters to marry, care of the elderly, and wills. The world of the Barnstable inhabitant was the world of the English peasant. Based on primary sources, especially probate and land records, and on published works; 67 notes.   S. L. Patterson

318. Watkins, Susan Cotts. ON MEASURING TRANSITIONS AND TURNING POINTS. *Hist. Methods 1980 13(3): 181-187.* In this review essay of John Demos and Sarane Spence Boocock, ed., *Turning Points: Historical and Sociological Essays on the Family* (Chicago: U. of Chicago Pr., 1978) and Tamara K. Hareven, ed., *Transitions: The Family and Life Course in Historical Perspective* (New York: Academic Pr., 1978), the central issue is the life course approach, its conceptual promise, and its methodological limitations. Both books advocate the life course approach, but current data is inadequate to meet that challenge. 23 notes.   D. K. Pickens

319. Webb, Bernice Larson. I REMEMBER SAPPA VALLEY. *Kansas Q. 1980 12(2): 25-34.* Recalls family life in rural Decatur County, Kansas, in the 1930's.

320. Weitzman, Murray S. FINALLY THE FAMILY. *Ann. of the Am. Acad. of Pol. and Social Sci. 1978 (435): 61-82.* The family makes a belated but welcome appearance in *Social Indicators, 1976* after being all but ignored in *Social Indicators, 1973.* In recent years, statistics on the family have recorded a steady increase in the divorce rate, a decline in both the marriage and birth rates, and a rising proportion of premarital births to total births. These trends translate into family structures in which an increasing proportion of children are members of single-parent families. Although not inevitable, on balance some harmful spillover effects are probably generated such as less attractive human personal qualities, declining domestic tranquility in the community, and decreasing individual capability for educational achievement, work accomplishment, and earning power. After this second run through of social indicators, there seems to be sufficient evidence that, while the work was conducted by very competent people, the operational structure is far from optimal for achieving sustained progress in this field. Producing social indicators requires more than a process of searching and soliciting statistical tables from the statistical networks, assembling them in packages of charts, tables, and texts and marketing them in attractive publications. In the end it may come down to the fact that insufficient resources have been committed to these social indicator projects, precluding the formation of proper operational goals, rather than concluding that social indicator efforts are bereft of potential.   J

321. Wells, Robert V. FAMILY HISTORY AND THE DEMOGRAPHIC TRANSITION. *J. of Social Hist. 1975 9(1): 1-20.* The study of the family is emerging but still needs tighter integration of its separate themes: kinship, fertility rates, child-rearing, and women. Attempts a critique and possible revision of the role conventionally attributed to demographic transition. This transition, a sequence conventionally described as a decline in the death rate and then in the birth rate, has been attributed to changed material conditions. Proposes various clues that indicate a more plausible connection with changed motivation. US examples primarily are from the colonial era. 58 notes.   M. Hough

322. Wells, Robert V. WOMEN'S LIVES TRANSFORMED: DEMOGRAPHIC AND FAMILY PATTERNS IN AMERICA, 1600-1970. Berkin, Carol Ruth and Norton, Mary Beth, ed. *Women of America: A History* (Boston: Houghton Mifflin Co., 1979): 16-33. Demographically examines the changes in the lives of American women, focusing on 1770-1920. Childbearing has been

dramatically reduced since 1800. Patterns of first marriages have remained stable, but, during 1890-1970, divorce has increased 15 times. Women's life cycles and households are far different from those of their forebears. 2 photos, 12 notes.

K. Talley

323. White, John.   WHATEVER HAPPENED TO THE SLAVE FAMILY IN THE OLD SOUTH?   *J. of Am. Studies [Great Britain] 1974 8(3): 383-390.* Reviews a wide range of literature on Negro slavery, beginning with Abolitionist writings of the 1850's and concluding with the revisionist and Marxist studies published in the 1960's and 1970's. Slavery was inimical to the Negro family, but the actions of slave masters and the personal resilience of the slaves ensured the perpetuation of family life among the slaves. Economic and cultural forces following the Civil War produced more familial deterioration among American Negroes than did pre-Civil War slavery. Based on secondary sources; 38 notes.

H. T. Lovin

324. Wilke, Arthur S.   FAMILY AND CIVILIZATION: THIRTY YEARS LATER.   *Int. J. of Contemporary Sociol. 1976 13(3-4): 224-238.* Reviews post-World War II confusion between the orientations of individualism and collectivism regarding the state of family life, basing most of the information on Carle C. Zimmerman's *Family and Civilization* (New York: Harper & Brothers).

325. Williamson, Billie.   FUN AND GAMES OF MOUNTAIN CHILDREN.   *Kentucky Folklore Record 1975 21(2): 43-55.* Describes songs and children's games common in eastern Kentucky.   S

326. Woodrow, Karen; Hastings, Donald W.; and Tu, Edward J.   RURAL-URBAN PATTERNS OF MARRIAGE, DIVORCE, AND MORTALITY: TENNESSEE, 1970.   *Rural Sociol. 1978 43(1): 70-84.* Assesses differences in rural and urban patterns of marriage, divorce, remarriage, and mortality, according to age and sex.

327. Worth, Judith.   THE USE OF THE FAMILY IN HISTORY.   *New England Social Studies Bull. 1976/77 34(2): 19-22.* Examines personal genealogical studies in aiding students to understand broader concepts applied to the study of families through history (composition, internal functions, and social functions), 1977.

328. Wright, Raymond S.   AN INTERNATIONAL CENTER FOR THE STUDY OF THE FAMILY.   *J. of Family Hist. 1977 2(2): 169-171.* The archives of the Genealogical Society of Utah, supported by the Church of Jesus Christ of Latter-Day Saints, are unparalleled in the fields of genealogy, family history, and many related areas. The Mormon archives should be consulted as a source of primary data about much of American history. It also covers many other countries. Table.

T. W. Smith

329. Young, Mary E.   WOMEN, CIVILIZATION, AND THE INDIAN QUESTION.   Deutrich, Mabel E. and Purdy, Virginia C., ed. *Clio Was a Woman: Studies in the History of American Women* (Washington, D.C.: Howard U. Pr., 1980): 98-110. Nineteenth-century US citizens labored to convert Indians to an idealized model of Christian civilization. They accomplished this by changing the Indians' relationship to property, work, and law. If Indian

families could be confined to small farms and induced by private possession to work the land, they would convert millions of acres of hunting ground to land for use by white farmers. But with this sense of property, comes a sense of home, and it was felt that the female Indians, especially, should be educated according to the ideal of domestic femininity. An outstanding illustration of the US Indian Office's concern for modifying sex role definitions can be found in the work of agents and Presbyterian-Congregationalist missionaries among the Cherokee Indians: intermarriage, the rise to social prominence and political power of a mixed-blood elite of planters, merchants, millers, and ferry-keepers, and the shift to male agriculture changed the status as well as the work of the Cherokee women. A discussion summary follows. 36 notes.   J. Powell

330. Ziegler, Suzanne. THE FAMILY UNIT AND INTERNATIONAL MIGRATION: THE PERCEPTIONS OF ITALIAN IMMIGRANT CHILDREN. *Int. Migration Rev. 1977 11(3): 326-333.* Examines through a series of interviews with children of Italian immigrants the postwar migratory process to Canada, the centrality of the 20th-century family, and the importance of intergenerational ties and commitments; family ties have survived migration and even been fortified because of it.

331. Zinn, Maxine Baca. CHICANO FAMILY RESEARCH: CONCEPTUAL DISTORTIONS AND ALTERNATIVE DIRECTIONS. *J. of Ethnic Studies 1979 7(3): 59-71.* Criticizes social sciences studies of Mexican Americans, particularly studies of the Chicano family which have led to negative stereotyping, and suggests alternative methodologies for examining the role of the Chicano family in acculturation and assimilation; 1970's.

332. —. AMERICAN INDIAN GENEALOGY: SELECTED SOURCES ON THE EASTERN CHEROKEE. *Prologue 1982 14(4): 227-236.* Discusses American Indian genealogy, focusing on selected sources on the eastern Cherokee Indians. Records documenting relations between the federal government and the Indians are a rich source of genealogical information. Two series of such Cherokee records are outlined: "Records Relating to the Enrollment of Eastern Cherokee by Guion Miller, 1908-1910" and "Eastern Cherokee Applications of the U.S. Court of Claims, 1906-1909." A wealth of other such records available at the National Archives are listed in the "Select Catalog of Microfilm Publications Relating to American Indians." Based on National Archives records; illus., photos, 5 notes.   M. A. Kascus

333. —. [BENEFITS OF WOMEN'S EDUCATION WITHIN MARRIAGE]. *J. of Pol. Econ. 1974 82(2, part II): 57-75.*
Benham, Lee. BENEFITS OF WOMEN'S EDUCATION WITHIN MARRIAGE, pp. 57-71.
Welch, Finis. COMMENT, pp. 72-75.
Proceedings of a conference on marriage, family, human capital, and fertility on 4-5 June, 1973.   S

334. —. CERTIFICATES OF MARRIAGE ISSUED AT OWENSBORO, DAVIESS COUNTY. *J. of the Afro-American Hist. and Geneal. Soc. 1980 (1): 29-35.* Lists Kentucky marriages of freedmen.

335. —. A COLLOQUIUM ON HERBERT GUTMAN'S *THE BLACK FAMILY IN SLAVERY AND FREEDOM, 1750-1925. Social Sci. Hist. 1979 3(3-4): 45-85.*
Modell, John. DEMOGRAPHIC PERSPECTIVES, *pp. 45-55.* Criticizes the lack of demographic rigor and sophistication of Gutman's work.
Gudeman, Stephen. AN ANTHROPOLOGIST'S VIEW, *pp. 56-65.* Supports the anthropological tendencies of Gutman's work, especially the emphasis on family, and gives added suggestions on how an anthropological perspective could aid historical work.
Sanderson, Warren C. A CLIOMETRIC RECONSIDERATION, *pp. 66-85.* Refines, qualifies, and challenges several major theses of Gutman's work based on cliometric analysis. Especially emphasizes economic factors in shaping the black experience.   L. K. Blaser

336. —. [EFFECTS OF CHILD-CARE PROGRAMS ON WOMEN'S WORK EFFORT]. *J. of Pol. Econ. 1974 82(2, part II): 136-169.*
Heckman, James J. EFFECTS OF CHILD-CARE PROGRAMS ON WOMEN'S WORK EFFORT, pp. 136-163.
Rosen, Sherwin. COMMENT, pp. 164-169.
Proceedings of a conference on marriage, family, human capital, and fertility held on 4-5 June 1973.   S

337. —. [FAMILIES AND FARMS]. *William and Mary Q. 1980 37(4): 688-700.*
Lemon, James T. COMMENT ON JAMES A. HENRETTA'S "FAMILIES AND FARMS: *MENTALITÉ* IN PRE-INDUSTRIAL AMERICA," *pp. 688-696.* The central argument of Henretta (see abstract 16A:200) was that early frontier America to 1750 was dominated by the lineal family (precommercial). Desire for capital accumulation and the power of commercial leaders prevented building society simply on yeomanry, according to Lemon. Lemon accuses Henretta of populism in detaching self-sufficient families from society. 43 notes.
Henretta, James A. REPLY, *pp. 696-700.* Defends his thesis and intentions, and urges more rigorous history than that of Lemon and others. 3 notes.
                                                                    H. M. Ward/S

338. —. FAMILY HISTORY PROJECTS. *New England Social Studies Bull. 1977-78 35(1): 5-14.*
Haley, Alex. ALEX HALEY GIVES *INSTRUCTOR* HIS TIPS FOR LAUNCHING FAMILY HISTORY PROJECTS, *pp. 5-8.* Interview with Alex Haley in which he details difficulties in his own family history project; gives recommendations on research and resource materials available.
—. FAMILY HISTORY PROJECTS ARE IN SCHOOL COAST TO COAST, *pp. 8-14.* Examines current family history projects and their use in history teaching, on all educational levels.

339. —. [FAMILY INVESTMENTS IN HUMAN CAPITAL: EARNINGS OF WOMEN]. *J. of Pol. Econ. 1974 82(2, part II): 76-110.*
Mincer, Jacob and Polachek, Solomon. FAMILY INVESTMENTS IN HUMAN CAPITAL: EARNINGS OF WOMEN, pp. 76-108.

Duncan, Otis Dudley. COMMENT, pp. 109-110.
Proceedings of a conference on marriage, family, human capital, and fertility on 4-5 June, 1973.
S

340. —. THE FAMILY REVISITED. *J. of Interdisciplinary Hist. 1975 5(4): 703-709; 1977 7(4): 747-750.*
Skolnick, Arlene. THEMES IN RECENT SOCIAL SCIENCE RESEARCH, pp. 703-719. Reviews recent work on the history of the family. The various strands of research and theory suggest that both more and less is known about the family than was thought to be known a decade ago. Work on the family has helped to close some gaps separating the work of historians and social scientists and, at the same time, has introduced concepts the historian may find helpful in his work. 36 notes.
Handel, Gerald. AGAIN AND A REPLY, pp. 747-750. Suggests that Skolnick's account of the development of a social psychology of the family is misleading. In reply it is agreed that the emphasis on pathology is a limitation on the work to date but urged that such cases can still provide insight into normal functioning. 12 notes from printed sources.   R. Howell

341. —. [HOUSEHOLD AND ECONOMY: TOWARD A NEW THEORY OF POPULATION AND ECONOMIC GROWTH]. *J. of Pol. Econ. 1974 82(2, part II): 200-221.*
Nerlove, Marc. HOUSEHOLD AND ECONOMY: TOWARD A NEW THEORY OF POPULATION AND ECONOMIC GROWTH, pp. 200-218.
Griliches, Zvi. COMMENT, pp. 219-221.
Proceedings of a conference on marriage, family, human capital, and fertility on 4-5 June 1973.
S

342. —. [MARRIAGE IN AMERICA]. *J. of Pol. Econ. 1974 82(2, part II): 34-56.*
Freiden, Alan. THE UNITED STATES MARRIAGE MARKET, pp. 34-53.
Wallace, T. Dudley. COMMENT, pp. 54-56.
Proceedings of a conference on marriage, family, human capital, and fertility on 4-5 June, 1973.
S

343. —. MARRIAGES CONSUMMATED BETWEEN FREEDMEN, PADUCAH, KENTUCKY. *J. of the Afro-American Hist. and Geneal. Soc. 1980 (1): 36-37.*

344. —. SLAVE FAMILY AND ITS LEGACIES. *Hist. Reflections [Canada] 1979 6(1): 183-211.*
Gutman, Herbert G. SLAVE FAMILY AND ITS LEGACIES, pp. 183-199. Traces US historiography of the slave family and analyzes various kinds of data to show that slaves' and ex-slaves' real choices on the record suggest the nature of their marriage and family customs. Freedman's Bureau reformers, the retrogressionist theses of scholars like Ulrich B. Phillips, and the subsequent work of sociologist E. Franklin Frazier and his followers all concentrated on the social deprivation and subjection of slave life. Historians began in the 1960's to seek evidence of slaves' own history-making, including the development of family mores internal to slave culture. Freedmen's marriage registers in postbellum North Carolina, intensive study of particular

plantations, and examination of 18th-century slave naming practices give clues to important regularities in slave family and society.

Higman, Barry W.   COMMENTARY ONE,   *pp. 200-203.* Adds West Indian comparative data, particularly parallels to the succeeding historiographical generations. We need to look more closely at the influence of postemancipation social change—urbanization and the concentration of Negro women in domestic service—on the black family.

Engerman, Stanley L.   COMMENTARY TWO,   *pp. 204-211.* The slave family was always a central concern of pro-slavery defense as well as abolitionist critique, and Frazier's own views changed over time. Summarizes recent work on slave family and fertility, primarily in the United States. 6 notes.

S

2

THE FAMILY AND OTHER SOCIAL INSTITUTIONS

345. Abbott, Walter F.   INCOME LEVEL AND INFLATION STRAIN IN THE UNITED STATES: 1971-1975. *Am. J. of Econ. and Sociol. 1981 40(2): 97-106.* Estimates net inflationary effects, 1971-75, by income level. The central concept is inflation strain, or the difference between the percentage of change in prices and incomes. The inflation strain was substantially greater for lower budget families. The primary source of this strain was food, whereas the primary source of strain for the higher budget family was taxes, income and Social Security.

J/S

346. Allen, Walter R.   FAMILY ROLES, OCCUPATIONAL STATUSES, AND ACHIEVEMENT ORIENTATIONS AMONG BLACK WOMEN IN THE UNITED STATES. *Signs 1979 4(4): 670-686.* Because black women belong to two minority groups, they are excellent subjects for "research into the dynamics of discrimination, motivation, and occupational achievement." Black female achievement orientations differ substantially from other sex-race groups. During 1964-74, the greatest number of black women changed from service work to other professions, with increased entry into white-collar work. They remain in the least prestigious positions, however. Based on the National Longitudinal Study of the High School Class of 1972, the Bureau of Census and Bureau of Labor statistics, and secondary sources; 6 tables, 28 notes.   S. P. Conner

347. Anderson, Kristine L.   EDUCATIONAL GOALS OF MALE AND FEMALE ADOLESCENTS: THE EFFECTS OF PARENTAL CHARAC-TERISTICS AND ATTITUDES. *Youth & Soc. 1980 12(2): 173-188.* Uses separate measures for each parent's socioeconomic status, aspirations, and expec-tations to test current models of influences on youths' educational goals. Income has little effect, while the same-sex parent's education is very important. Mothers' expectations have more influence on both sexes than do fathers'. Sex role stereoty-ping is very evident. Based on 1974 interviews of graduating high school students in Orange County, California, and Chicago, and on secondary sources; fig., 2 tables, note, biblio.   J. H. Sweetland

348. Antler, Joyce.   "AFTER COLLEGE, WHAT?": NEW GRADUATES AND THE FAMILY CLAIM. *Am. Q. 1980 32(4): 409-434.* Describes the postgraduate experiences of the first generation of women college graduates,

1880-1910. Most found that their families reasserted control over their lives once they graduated. Aspirations of these women for achievement outside the home were largely unfulfilled, leaving many with a feeling of worthlessness. Those who did manage to establish a career either were fortunate to have supportive parents or broke away from their families. An analysis of the experience of some notable women graduates predicts well the pattern found among a larger group of college women, the Wellesley class of 1897. Based on classbooks of the Wellesley College class of 1897 and other primary sources; table, 34 notes.   D. K. Lambert

349.   Ariés, Philippe.   THE FAMILY AND THE CITY.   *Daedalus 1977 106(2): 227-235.* The 20th-century family is burdened with "the task of trying to satisfy all the emotional and social needs of its members." This phenomenon can be traced to "the decline of the city and the urban forms of social intercourse it had once provided" in institutions such as the cafe. The decline itself occurred during the 19th century in the process of decentralization, where the bourgeois and middle classes escaped to the privacy and rural surroundings of the suburb. Finally, with the advent of television and the automobile in the 20th century, the city's chief function as provider for social intercourse is now nonexistent and the balance between community life and family is destroyed, thus resulting in an all-inclusive family structure which can no longer fulfill all of its functions.
G. Fox

350.   Bair, Barbara.   THE PARENTS' COUNCIL FOR RETARDED CHILDREN AND SOCIAL CHANGE IN RHODE ISLAND, 1951-1970.   *Rhode Island Hist. 1981 40(4): 144-159.* Chronicles Rhode Island's parents' council from its inception in 1951 to 1970. Parents of retarded children were frustrated in the 1950's with the quality of available services and with the medical profession, which had limited knowledge about the therapeutic treatment of retardation. Professionals worked with blue-collar workers effectively. The close friendship of Arthur Trudeau, a charismatic leader in the parents' council, and John E. Fogarty, Rhode Island congressman, resulted in Fogarty becoming an avid champion of retarded citizens' needs and rights. Activists of the 1950's and 1960's gave way in the 1970's to a formal bureaucracy with paid staffs. Based on a major public education project entitled "Days of Darkness, Days of Hope," sponsored by the Rhode Island Department of Mental Health, Retardation and Hospitals and the John E. Fogarty Papers, Philips Memorial Library, Providence College; 3 photos, 32 notes.   C. R. Gunter, Jr.

351.   Baker, Katharine Gratwick.   MOBILITY AND FOREIGN SERVICE WIVES.   *Foreign Service J. 1976 53(2): 12-14, 27-29.* Discusses the views held by the wives of Foreign Service officers primarily in 1974 on the impact of their husband's occupational mobility on themselves and their families.

352.   Baker, Mary Holland.   MOTHER'S OCCUPATION AND CHILDREN'S ATTAINMENTS.   *Pacific Sociol. Rev. 1981 24(2): 237-254.* Using data collected from families in a midwestern city, analyzes the effect of mother's occupation on children's attainments, finding that in dual-employment families the mothers' occupation had a significant effect on both daughters' and sons' academic achievements.

353. Baker, Therese L. CLASS, FAMILY, EDUCATION, AND THE PRO-CESS OF STATUS ATTAINMENT: A COMPARISON OF AMERICAN AND BRITISH WOMEN COLLEGE GRADUATES. *Sociol. Q. 1982 23(1): 17-31.* Examines the impact of marriage, motherhood, and the relationship between higher education and social mobility on US and British women college graduates, relying on data collected from 1961 to 1968, and comments on a 1960 study of education and social status.

354. Bane, Mary Jo et al. CHILD-CARE ARRANGEMENTS OF WORKING PARENTS. *Monthly Labor Rev. 1979 102(10): 50-56.* Examines how families have achieved a balance of outside and parental child care, focusing on the costs and the role of the government, 1970's.

355. Bane, Mary Jo; Rainwater, Lee; and Rein, Martin. FILLING THE CRACKS. *Wilson Q. 1981 4(3): 136-142, 145-146.* Traces the federal government's activities regarding the family since the 1930's, including concerns about day care, food stamps, and social security.

356. Barrett, Carol J. WOMEN IN WIDOWHOOD. *Signs 1977 2(4): 856-868.* Review essay of selected periodical and book-length literature (1970's) on widowhood discusses aspects of economics, social readjustment, physical and mental health, and governmental and institutional support possibilities, 1960's-70's.

357. Bartlett, Robin L. and Poulton-Callahan, Charles. CHANGING FAMILY STRUCTURES AND THE DISTRIBUTION OF FAMILY INCOME, 1951-1976. *Social Sci. Q. 1982 63(1): 28-38.* The recent increase in the proportion of families with employed wives has tended to decrease income inequality among male-headed families; concurrently, the recent increases in female-headed families has tended to increase overall family income inequality, offsetting the former trend and creating an illusion of distributional stability.

358. Bayer, Alan E. and McDonald, Gerald W. COHABITATION AMONG YOUTH: CORRELATES OF SUPPORT FOR A NEW AMERICAN ETHIC. *Youth & Soc. 1981 12(4): 387-402.* Examines the accumulation of research results on cohabitation. Religious factors, political attitudes, and regional location emerge as principal predictors of cohabitation attitudes, operating differentially for men and women. The major finding of the study confirms the significant impact of religion on cohabitation attitudes. Covers 1974-80.   J/S

359. Bean, Frank D. COMPONENTS OF INCOME AND EXPECTED FAMILY SIZE AMONG MEXICAN AMERICANS. *Social Sci. Q. 1973 54(1): 103-116.* "Considering alternative hypotheses relevant to the income-fertility relationship, husband's income is partitioned into two components, each of which bears special salience to alternative hypotheses. The different relations of the components to expected family size among Mexican Americans underscores the notion that social processes of a reference group nature need to be better taken into account in the socioeconomic theory of family formation."

J

360. Beck, E. M.   LABOR UNIONISM AND RACIAL INCOME IN-EQUALITY: A TIME SERIES ANALYSIS OF THE POST-WORLD WAR II PERIOD. *Am. J. of Sociol. 1980 85(4): 791-814.* Labor union activity in the United States, 1947-74, has increased between-race inequality in family income and reduced within-race inequality.

361. Becker, Gary S.   ON THE RELEVANCE OF THE NEW ECONOM-ICS OF THE FAMILY. *Am. Econ. R. 1974 64(2): 317-319.* Discusses new work in economics on the family in order to show the increasing relevancy of economic theory for the understanding of human behavior.

362. Beckett, Joyce O. and Smith, Audrey D.   WORK AND FAMILY RO-LES: EGALITARIAN MARRIAGE IN BLACK AND WHITE FAMILIES. *Social Service Rev. 1981 55(2): 314-326.* Using statistical data collected in a 1976 survey, presents evidence that although whites are more egalitarian in theory, blacks tend in fact to devise egalitarian arrangements in employment and household duties; black husbands share domestic and child-care roles more often than their white counterparts.

363. Bell, Carolyn Shaw.   THE NEXT REVOLUTION. *Social Policy 1975 6(2): 5-11.* Following the equalization of employment opportunities, women's liberation must attempt to equalize family responsibilities between the sexes.

364. Bell, Carolyn Shaw.   SHOULD EVERY JOB SUPPORT A FAMILY? *Public Interest 1975 (40): 109-118.* Considers public welfare and the relationship of employment to family support.   S

365. Belzile, Bertrand and Larouche, Viateur.   MOTIVATION AU TRA-VAIL DES PARENTS DE FAMILLES À FAIBLE REVENU: MODÈLE CONCEPTUEL [Motivation to work of parents of low-income families: Con-ceptual framework]. *Industrial Relations [Canada] 1974 29(4): 643-670.* "The authors attempt to discover the factors that motivate parents of low-income families to find jobs (to work), or not to find them (to not work)." Presents a motivation model relying on a literary magazine and interviews with key infor-mants. In addition, "the authors formulate a hypothesis on the relation between motivation and the rate of participation in manpower."

366. Bennett, Carol T. F.   THE SOCIAL SECURITY BENEFIT STRUC-TURE: EQUITY CONSIDERATIONS. *Am. Econ. Rev. 1979 69(2): 227-231.* Family pattern determines the contributions to Social Security, with individuals and smaller families subsidizing the benefits for larger families. If equity is a future policy consideration, then an alternative financing of Social Security in-creased costs should be created. The alternative program might incorporate with the income tax system. 2 tables, 5 ref.   D. K. Pickens

367. Bennett, Sheila Kishler and Elder, Glen H., Jr.   WOMEN'S WORK IN THE FAMILY ECONOMY: A STUDY OF DEPRESSION HARDSHIP IN WOMEN'S LIVES. *J. of Family Hist. 1979 4(2): 153-176.* Drawing on the Berkeley Guidance Study that covers a group of families from 1928-29 to the present (the most recent panel wave was 1969-71). Examines the impact of the Great Depression on the lives on mothers and daughters. They find that the Great Depression had perhaps as much impact on increased female employment as

World War II did. They show that Depression-caused changes in the employment status of mothers influenced the employment pattern of their daughters. 5 tables, 3 fig., 9 notes, biblio.

T. W. Smith

368. Ben-Or, Joseph. THE LAW OF ADOPTION IN THE UNITED STATES: ITS MASSACHUSETTS ORIGINS AND THE STATUTE OF 1851. *New England Hist. and Genealogical Register 1976 130(October): 259-272.* Although the common law of colonial America, following its English antecedents, did not recognize the process of adoption, the citizens of Massachusetts Bay used three legal devices to accomplish the same result. The systems of indentured servitude and apprenticeship extended the natural family, and ties of affection could develop which could transform the master-servant relationship to one of parent-child. The last will and testament provided a means to transfer inheritance to the "new" child, and the General Court passed private laws permitting a change of name. The result in Massachusetts was to circumvent the English common law and to make adoption a part of the legal process in fact long before the General Court enacted the Adoption of Children Act in 1851. Primary and secondary sources; 27 notes, appendix.

S. L. Patterson

369. Berger, Alan S. BLACK FAMILIES AND THE MOYNIHAN REPORT: A RESEARCH EVALUATION. *Social Problems 1974 22(2): 145-161.* Contrary to the Moynihan Report (1965), black families are not dramatically different from white families in the treatment of children. Data was used from a sample of Illinois youths, 14-18 years old, analyzing a tangle of pathology centered around illegitimacy, female-headed families, and unemployment rates. Other, non-family factors are responsible for these problems. Notes, bibliography.

A. M. Osur

370. Berger, Brigitte. FAMILY, BUREAUCRACY, AND THE "SPECIAL CHILD." *Public Interest 1975 (40): 96-108.* Proposes methods of helping the child with learning disabilities, primarily through professional support to families.

S

371. Bernstein, Blanche. SHOULDN'T LOW INCOME FATHERS SUPPORT THEIR CHILDREN? *Public Interest 1982 (66): 55-71.* Discusses the role of public welfare programs in providing support for single-parent families and the debate over whether or not such support discourages low-income fathers from supporting their children. Title 4-D of the Social Security Act, which became law in 1975, demanded that applicants for the Aid for Dependent Children program comply with state efforts to establish paternity and to secure child support. Some members of the New York City professional social welfare community felt that adherence to Title 4-D could violate the civil rights of mothers or children. Social welfare professionals used these issues as a smokescreen to allow indiscriminate use of public funds to redistribute income. New York City judicial politics prevented establishment of an effective mechanism for obtaining child support from fathers. Other states and jurisdictions have better child support programs.

J. M. Herrick

372. Berryman, Jack W. and Brislin, Joann. THE LADIES' DEPARTMENT OF THE *AMERICAN FARMER,* 1825-1830: A LOCUS FOR THE ADVOCACY OF FAMILY HEALTH AND EXERCISE. *J. of NAL Assoc. 1977*

2(2): 8-15. Discusses the themes of family health and exercise, particularly for women, in the "Ladies' Department," inaugurated in John Stuart Skinner's *American Farmer* newspaper in 1825, during the early feminist movement.

373.   Bieker, Richard F.   WORK AND WELFARE: AFDC PARTICIPA- TION RATES IN DELAWARE.   *Social Sci. Q. 1981 62(1): 169-176.* Aid to Families with Dependent Children (AFDC) participation is partly a function of labor market conditions and financial eligibility criteria as well as the appeal of the program itself. Data from the Delaware Division of Social Services and the Statistical Abstract of the United States for 1949-75 indicate that recipients found AFDC eligibility to be more attractive than welfare. Primary sources; table, 16 notes.   M. Mtewa

374.   Bissell, Linda Auwers.   FROM ONE GENERATION TO ANOTHER: MOBILITY IN SEVENTEENTH-CENTURY WINDSOR, CONNECTICUT. *William and Mary Q. 1974 31(1): 79-110.* The social and community structure of Windsor determined geographic mobility. People left, regardless of status, usually because of little involvement in community affairs, lack of family ties, or deaths in the family. Those with institutional ties stayed longer. Migration from Windsor was heaviest before 1650. Settlers who stayed provided stability for the town. Compares family responses to stability on a generational basis and analyzes the economy and landholding. Chart, 10 tables, 25 notes.   H. M. Ward

375.   Bodnar, John.   IMMIGRATION, KINSHIP, AND THE RISE OF WORKING CLASS REALISM IN INDUSTRIAL AMERICA.   *J. of Social Hist. 1980 14(1): 45-66.* Class formulation rather than class conflict needs atten- tion in understanding the attitudes and actions of immigrant workers and their children. After reviewing the literature stressing the shift from idealistic militancy in the late 19th century and the greater realism of the 1920's and 30's, the author examines the family ties of immigrant workers in various industries. Job security for several family members was a key goal. This often outweighed concern about power relationships, work routines, occupational advancement, or social transfor- mation. Based on oral interviews conducted in Pittsburgh and other sources in 1976; 31 notes.   C. M. Hough

376.   Bodnar, John E.   SOCIALIZATION AND ADAPTATION: IMMI- GRANT FAMILIES IN SCRANTON, 1880-1890.   *Pennsylvania Hist. 1976 43(2): 147-162.* Studies the social mobility of the Irish and Welsh in Scranton during 1880-90 in order to test hypotheses advanced by Talcott Parsons, Philippe Aries, and Richard Sennett regarding the role of family structure in preparing children for adulthood in industrial society. Children from Irish and Welsh nuclear families enjoyed greater economic success than those reared in extended families. The sons of Welsh parents were more successful than those of Irish background because they were exposed to industrial life at an earlier age. The Welsh were somewhat more inclined to live in nuclear families than were the Irish. Based on census data and other sources; illus., 7 tables, 30 notes.
D. C. Swift

377.   Bolin, Winifred D. Wandersee.   THE ECONOMICS OF MIDDLE- INCOME FAMILY LIFE: WORKING WOMEN DURING THE GREAT DEPRESSION.   *J. of Am. Hist. 1978 65(1): 60-74.* Despite the traditionally

conservative attitude among whites regarding working wives, the depression decade witnessed an increase in both the number and the proportion of married women in the labor force. With many families this was necessary just for survival. But with middle-income families, those earning at least $1,000 a year, this increase is attributable not to absolute economic need, but to a change in values. Wives from middle-income families entered the labor force not to procure necessities like food and clothing for their families, but to purchase items such as refrigeration, modern plumbing, and lighting. They worked to enable their families to pursue a higher standard of living, a value acquired during the late 1920's. 5 tables, 21 notes.   T. P. Linkfield

378. Borman, Kathryn M.; Lippincott, Nancy T.; and Matey, Christopher M. FAMILY AND CLASSROOM CONTROL IN AN URBAN APPALACHIAN NEIGHBORHOOD. *Educ. and Urban Soc. 1978 11(1): 61-86.* Examines the socializing or social control function of schooling by studying the kindergarten experience of a group of children from working-class families who lived in an unspecified Appalachian area.

379. Bouchard, Gérard and La Rose, André. LA RÉGLEMENTATION DU CONTENU DES ACTES DE BAPTÊME, MARIAGE, SÉPULTURE, AU QUÉBEC, DES ORIGINES À NOS JOURS [Regulation of the contents of the acts of baptism, marriage, and burial in Quebec from the beginning to our day]. *Rev. d'Hist. de l'Am. Française [Canada] 1976 30(1): 67-77.* From the 16th century to the present, both the Church and the state have been concerned with registering baptisms, marriages, and burials. Church regulation of these practices has always been more detailed than that of the state. Vicars have been recording performances of these acts, and the state has benefited from such assistance. Based on published Church and state documents and secondary works; 6 tables, 37 notes.   L. B. Chan

380. Bould, Sally. BLACK AND WHITE FAMILIES: FACTORS AFFECTING THE WIFE'S CONTRIBUTION TO THE FAMILY INCOME WHERE THE HUSBAND'S INCOME IS LOW TO MODERATE. *Sociol. Q. 1977 18(4): 536-547.* The economic role of the black wife in contrast to her husband's weak economic position is a key assumption in Moynihan's thesis of a black matriarchy. Using the National Longitudinal Survey of women, aged 30 to 44, in 1967, this paper examines the factors affecting the wife's contribution to the family income for both black and white families where the husband's income is below the median of all male-headed families. The results suggest that black wives and white wives respond similarly with respect to their overall contribution, the demand for female labor, and the effect of children. There is no support, moreover, for Moynihan's assumption that black wives are compensating for their husband's weak economic position. It appears, however, that the definition of the provider may differ among black families and white families.
                                                           J

381. Bradbury, Bettina. THE FAMILY ECONOMY AND WORK IN AN INDUSTRIALIZING CITY: MONTREAL IN THE 1870S. *Hist. Papers [Canada] 1979: 71-96.* Describes the kinds of industries that developed in Montreal in the late 19th century and provides statistics about the work force by age, sex, and ethnic and class background. Families were often employed as a group,

especially in the textile trade, wages were low, and women and children were the poorest paid. The surplus of this source of unskilled labor depressed wages. Based on the 1871 Manuscript Census in the Public Archives of Canada, newspapers of the period, and secondary sources; 10 tables, 83 notes. French summary.

S

382. Brandt, Gail Cuthbert. "WEAVING IT TOGETHER": LIFE CYCLE AND THE INDUSTRIAL EXPERIENCE OF FEMALE COTTON WORKERS IN QUEBEC, 1910-1950. *Labour [Canada] 1981 7(Spr): 113-126.* Between 1891 and 1951, women constituted a large proportion of the work force in the Quebec cotton industry. By the 1940's a transition was occurring from a two-stage life cycle (gainful employment before marriage, permanent withdrawal from the work force after marriage) to a three-stage life cycle (employment before marriage, temporary withdrawal after marriage for child-rearing, and a subsequent return to work).

J

383. Brandwein, Ruth A. AFTER DIVORCE: A FOCUS ON SINGLE PARENT FAMILIES. *Urban and Social Change Rev. 1977 10(1): 21-25.* Examines the economic problems of child care in the single-parent family, particularly those headed by women, in the 1970's; considers the psychological effects of divorce on both children and parents.

384. Bromet, Evelyn and Dunn, Leslie. MENTAL HEALTH OF MOTHERS NINE MONTHS AFTER THE THREE MILE ISLAND ACCIDENT. *Urban & Social Change Rev. 1981 14(2): 12-15.* Presents the results of a study on the mental health of mothers with children living near the Three Mile Island power plant in Pennsylvania during the nuclear accident of 1979; the accident "had both acute and chronic mental health effects among mothers of small children living near the plant" due to stress.

385. Bruce-Briggs, B. "CHILD CARE": THE FISCAL TIME BOMB. *Public Interest 1977 (49): 87-102.* "Child care" is a combination of day care and a broad range of remedial services for the disadvantaged, such as health care, nutrition, assistance to handicapped children, as well as education. The need for such a social policy is dubious, as four out of five American children are cared for by their mothers during the day, the death of the extended family has been greatly exaggerated, each day more than a million children are already cared for by nursery schools, and most women do not want their children in day care centers, but prefer more informal arrangements closer to home. All serious policy research on day care refutes the day care advocates, as illustrated by Meredith A. Larson's summary of the studies available in early 1974. In 1977 prices, "acceptable quality" care and "desirable" day care per child per year are very high at $3,250 and $4,000 respectively. With talk of vacation and evening care, it is understandable why Andrew Hacker has called day care a "fiscal time bomb." The best explanation of the growth of the day care movement is the support it receives from its beneficiaries, those who staff the day care centers.

S. Harrow

386. Buckley, Suzann. EFFORTS TO REDUCE INFANT MATERNITY MORTALITY IN CANADA BETWEEN THE TWO WORLD WARS. *Atlantis [Canada] 1977 2(2, pt. 2): 76-84.* Focuses on the work of Dr. Helen

MacMurchy, head of the Dominion Department of Health's Child Welfare Division, and Dr. Charlotte Whitton, director of the Child and Family Welfare Council.

387. Buerkel-Rothfuss, Nancy L.; Greenberg, Bradley S.; Atkin, Charles K.; and Neuendorf, Kimberly. LEARNING ABOUT THE FAMILY FROM TELEVISION. *J. of Communication 1982 32(3): 191-201.* Shows how children's views about family roles are reinforced by television, and how parental guidance and control can limit learning about aggressive, nonaffiliative behavior from television families.

388. Bullamore, Henry W. THREE TYPES OF POVERTY IN METROPOLITAN INDIANAPOLIS. *Geographical Rev. 1974 64(4): 536-556.* "The breakdown of poor families in the Indianapolis, Indiana, SMSA by source of income (earnings, social security, and public assistance) was expected to reveal sharp differences in the spatial distribution of residence. Instead, all three types of poverty families are similarly distributed in space, with similar ecological correlates. Consideration of poverty types in relation to housing types failed to identify any differences, but it was established that poor families with income from public assistance tend to live in areas with a high proportion of very poor families. Policy implications of the study were identified in terms of welfare-office location, community centers, and welfare reform."   J

389. Bunkle, Phillida. SENTIMENTAL WOMANHOOD AND DOMESTIC EDUCATION, 1830-1870. *Hist. of Educ. Q. 1974 14(1): 13-31.* Attacks the thesis that industrialization and its displacement of the household and family farm as productive centers alone caused the antifeminist ideal of sentimental womanhood to develop. Argues instead that the new domestic education of the 1830's-70's had strong religious influences coming from the second Great Awakening that helped to foster the ideas of morality, motherhood, and domesticity. Based on primary and secondary sources; 43 notes.   L. C. Smith

390. Bushman, Richard L. FAMILY SECURITY IN THE TRANSITION FROM FARM TO CITY, 1750-1850. *J. of Family Hist. 1981 6(3): 238-256.* Home ownership was one of the most important answers to urban and industrial life in the 19th century. Besides being the single largest form of savings, the home also provided a form of social security for the elderly. As the children grew up and departed and/or when a spouse (especially the main earner) died, the excess rooms would be used for boarders. This provided an income for widows and the elderly. 14 notes, biblio.   T. W. Smith

391. Caplovitz, David. MAKING ENDS MEET: HOW FAMILIES COPE WITH INFLATION AND RECESSION. *Ann. of the Am. Acad. of Pol. and Social Sci. 1981 (456): 88-98.* A survey of almost 2,000 families in 1976 found that 59% had fallen behind rising prices and almost as many, 52%, were hurting because of inflation. A variety of coping mechanisms were identified, ranging from income-raising strategies such as taking second jobs, having additional family members go to work, and working more overtime, to lowering consumption, greater self-reliance, bargain hunting, and sharing with others. Tensions in the family and hostility to government were products of inflation.   J/S

392. Caplow, Theodore and Chadwick, Bruce A.   INEQUALITY AND LIFE-STYLES IN MIDDLETOWN, 1920-1978. *Social Sci. Q. 1979 60(3): 367-386.* Studies the distribution of occupations and occupational prestige in Middletown (Muncie, Indiana) from 1920 to 1970, and compares certain aspects of the life-styles of working-class and business-class families in 1924 and 1978 by replicating the 1924 survey of Middletown's housewives by Robert S. Lynd and Helen Merrell Lynd. The average occupational level of Middletown's families improved, but the distribution of occupations was more unequal in 1970 than in 1920. Most of the differences in life-style between working-class and business-class families reported by the Lynds in 1924 had diminished or disappeared by 1978. Based on Decennial Censuses, 1920-1970; Robert S. Lynd and Helen Merrell Lynd's *Middletown: A Study in American Culture* (New York: Harcourt and Brace, 1929); and a 1978 survey of Middletown housewives; 12 tables, 14 notes.
                                                                L. F. Velicer

393. Carlson, Allan C.   FAMILIES, SEX, AND THE LIBERAL AGENDA. *Public Interest 1980 (58): 62-79.* Assesses the liberal notion that a comprehensive family policy, initiated by the federal government, is essential to strengthen American family life. Examines the arguments and evidence used by liberals to support their family policy recommendations and finds them based on faulty interpretations of statistics. The instability of family life since 1960 has not resulted from phenomena such as poverty or unemployment, but from: the baby boom, whose members reached adolescence in the 1960's; the "second" sex revolution, which produced shifts in sexual attitudes and behavior; and the collapse of the nuclear family norm. None of these developments can be altered by government intervention. Lists the "post-bourgeois" values of sociologists and family counselors and concludes that government intervention on behalf of families actually weakens or destroys them. Secondary sources.   J. M. Herrick

394. Censer, Jane Turner.   "SMILING THROUGH HER TEARS": ANTE-BELLUM SOUTHERN WOMEN AND DIVORCE. *Am. J. of Legal Hist. 1981 25(1): 24-47.* An analysis of early 19th-century Southern divorce law, and the state supreme courts' interpretation of those laws, with special attention to attitudes towards women expressed in court cases and the problem of victimized women of the lower classes. A research base of 109 divorce cases in the supreme courts of the 11 Confederate states, 1800-1860, reveals how divorce suits diverged from British precedent, how state legislation concentrated on remedies for "wronged wives," questions of mental cruelty, the problems of respectability and propriety, alimony custody and property settlements. Judges, believing in the Southern social organization, significantly modified legal concepts dealing with women, helping them to escape subordination. 82 notes, appendix.
                                                                L. A. Knafla

395. Cerullo, Margaret and Ewen, Phyllis.   "HAVING A GOOD TIME": THE AMERICAN FAMILY GOES CAMPING. *Radical Am. 1982 16(1-2): 13-44.* Examines camping as seen in New England by two observers searching for insights into democracy in normal communities, or neighborhoods, a topic of concern to political activists who make assumptions about the need for a new populism. This article focuses on the more congested camp grounds that are cities created of equals accidentally, or deliberately as in the case of the Worcester Family Camping Association. These families in search for equality distrusted

elites and "others" (minorities). They shared an anticapitalistic dream, yet the glue that held that dream together was the nuclear family, internally as undemocratic as ever. Based on observation and participation; 7 notes, 15 illus.

C. M. Hough

396. Clark, Vernon L. REVELATIONS, RESPONSES, REFINEMENT: AN OVERVIEW OF THE RESEARCH PERTAINING TO THE YOUNG CHILD, 1960-79. *J. of Negro Educ. 1979 48(3): 288-305.* Research pertaining to the young child in the 1960's was involved in the controversy between heredity and environment as determining factors in the development of intelligence. Project Head Start emerged as a strategy to intervene in the preschool development of poor children so that they would not suffer developmentally. The research of the 1970's emphasized advocacy for children regardless of ethnicity, racial identification, or socioeconomic background. Intervention strategies that were successful emphasized clearly stated objectives, small groups, parental participation, careful training of the teachers, and high expectations for the children. The Children's Defense Fund emerged as the advocacy organization for children during the 1970's. 38 notes.

J. Powell

397. Clarke, James W. FAMILY STRUCTURE AND POLITICAL SOCIALIZATION AMONG URBAN BLACK CHILDREN. *Am. J. of Pol. Sci. 1973 17(2): 302-315.* "The results of this study of 94 urban black children suggest that father absence is an important variable in their political socialization. Father-absent children tend to be more cynical and also express much stronger preferences for a racially segregated environment. Beyond this, the results underscore the importance of intra-family relationships in the political socialization process."

J

398. Clement, Priscilla Ferguson. FAMILIES AND FOSTER CARE: PHILADELPHIA IN THE LATE NINETEENTH CENTURY. *Social Service Rev. 1979 53(3): 406-420.* The Home Missionary Society of Philadelphia and the Children's Aid Society of Pennsylvania placed poor, urban, usually white Protestant children in country homes as servants or farm laborers, 1880-1905.

399. Clifford, Geraldine Jonçich. HOME AND SCHOOL IN 19TH-CENTURY AMERICA: SOME PERSONAL HISTORY REPORTS FROM THE UNITED STATES. *Hist. of Educ. Q. 1978 18(1): 3-35.* Attacks the view that the family lost power and control in educational matters because of economic and demographic changes in 19th-century America. Stresses the importance of other life experiences. The family "web" was strong even in an increasingly mobile America. Families continued to be important in the selection and the control of teachers. Based on primary sources, particularly family journals; 102 notes.

L. C. Smith

400. Clinton, Catherine. EQUALLY THEIR DUE: THE EDUCATION OF THE PLANTER DAUGHTER IN THE EARLY REPUBLIC. *J. of the Early Republic 1982 2(1): 39-60.* The polish and frivolity of female instruction which characterized colonial times was replaced in the postrevolutionary period by a system that demanded women play a larger role in nation building and become good republican mothers. Fostered by community spirit and monetary contributions, female academies emerged throughout the South. Fathers in the Southern

planter class were particularly insistent on their daughters' schooling since education served as a substitute for wealth in marriage arrangements. The academies usually provided a rigorous and broad curriculum that stressed writing, penmanship, arithmetic, and languages, especially French. By 1840, the female academics succeeded in producing a cultivated, well-read female elite ready for their roles as wives and mothers in southern aristocratic society. Primary and secondary sources; 46 notes.   G. A. Glovins

401.   Cohen, David K. and Farrar, Eleanor.   POWER TO THE PARENTS? THE STORY OF EDUCATION VOUCHERS.   *Public Interest 1977 (48): 72-97.* Education vouchers are direct aids to families so that they can enroll their children in schools of their own choice. The vouchers provide an alternative to the requirement of either mandatory public school attendance or additional outlays for private schools. Vouchers were to promote competition, thereby encouraging schools to improve curricula and increase responsiveness, and help shift the balance of power from professional educators to parents. The idea gained the attention of reformers in the 1960's and a federal effort was begun in 1969. An outstanding experience with vouchers took place in Alum Rock, California, in 1972. Because the voucher idea overestimated popular discontent and the demand for educational change, it was the professional educators in Alum Rock who emerged from the experience with increased power. The parents did have more alternatives and freedom of choice, but within an authoritative framework provided by professionals. 8 notes.   S. Harrow

402.   Coser, Rose Laub.   STAY HOME, LITTLE SHEBA: ON PLACEMENT, DISPLACEMENT, AND SOCIAL CHANGE.   *Social Problems 1975 22(4): 470-480.* The busing of school children and federal support for child-care centers have the potential to create radical change by altering the social placement function of the American family—parents losing control of their children. Traveling away from home threatens the class structure and creates social disruption. Strong negative reactions from the public and government testify to the radical implications of the two issues. Notes, biblio.   A. M. Osur

403.   Coser, Rose Laub.   WOMEN'S RIGHTS AND FAMILY DEMANDS. *Dissent 1981 28(2): 225-228.* Reviews Carl N. Degler's *At Odds: Women and the Family in America from the Revolution to the Present* (1980) and Ellen Carol Du Bois's *Feminism and Suffrage: The Emergence of an Independent Women's Movement in America, 1848-1869* (1980). Degler's book discusses the evolving American family, focusing on the 19th and 20th centuries, and suggests that modern feminism conflicts with the anti-individualistic bias of the family. Du Bois's book traces the various alliances the suffragist movement made in the late 19th century and sees this movement as the beginning of an attack on the patriarchal family.

404.   Cutright, Phillips and Shorter, Edward.   THE EFFECTS OF HEALTH ON THE COMPLETED FERTILITY OF NONWHITE AND WHITE U.S. WOMEN BORN FROM 1867 THROUGH 1935.   *J. of Social Hist. 1979 13(2): 191-218.* Why, contrary to previous theories about minority group birth rates and the effect of nonassimilation on them, would the child-bearing rates for nonwhites born in the United States after the Civil War and before the end of the Depression drop to that of the whites? The authors deal with this and the subsequent baby

boom for nonwhites by stressing matters of health rather than the age of the first birth as the independent variable affecting racial differences in birth rates (live births). Infection, dietary insufficiencies, miserable conditions for childbirth, all manner of social dislocations, and discriminations which made post-Civil War conditions for blacks "only slightly more subtle than slavery," must be investigated even more thoroughly. The authors project a study of the years since World War II, when nonwhites have been in conditions where they have been physically able to conceive, carry, and deliver children better. 6 fig., 4 tables, 58 notes.

M. Hough

405. Daly, Patricia A. UNPAID FAMILY WORKERS: LONG-TERM DECLINE CONTINUES. *Monthly Labor Rev. 1982 105(10): 3-5.* Discusses demographic changes in the number of unpaid family members working in family businesses, which has dropped by more than 50% from 1950 to 1981, with special attention to occupational trends, and hours worked.

406. D'Antonio, William V.; Newman, William M.; and Wright, Stuart A. RELIGION AND FAMILY LIFE: HOW SOCIAL SCIENTISTS VIEW THE RELATIONSHIP. *J. for the Sci. Study of Religion 1982 21(3): 218-225.* Religion is viewed by sociologists more as a means of social control than as a means of social support.

407. D'Antonio, William V. and Stack, Steven. RELIGION, IDEAL FAMILY SIZE, AND ABORTION: EXTENDING RENZI'S HYPOTHESIS. *J. for the Sci. Study of Religion 1980 19(4): 397-408.* Analyzes denomination-specific attitudes within Protestantism that link ideal family size and proabortion sentiment, testing for seven related variables and concluding that, with particular exceptions for denominations with strong proabortion sentiments, Renzi's hypothesis (that family size preference was an intervening variable between religion and attitudes toward abortions) holds true; 1972-75.

408. Danziger, Sheldon. DETERMINANTS OF THE LEVEL AND DISTRIBUTION OF FAMILY INCOME IN METROPOLITAN AREAS, 1969. *Land Econ. 1976 52(4): 467-478.* Constructs a model, emphasizing industrial structure, that predicts the median value and distribution of family income. Indicates those industries that bring an increase in income, and the structural elements that affect their distribution. Findings may be of value to local industrial development efforts. 5 tables, 13 notes.

E. S. Johnson

409. Davidson, Faye Tennyson. THE AMES PLANTATION, GRAND JUNCTION. *Tennessee Hist. Q. 1979 38(3): 267-276.* Traces the history of the Ames Plantation near Grand Junction, Tennessee, in three stages: as the 19th-century farm of the Micajah Clark Moorman (1775-1826) family and their descendants, as the early 20th-century hunting lodge of New England industrialist Hobart C. Ames, and finally since 1950 as a model farm of the College of Agriculture of the University of Tennessee. Primary sources; 21 notes.

W. D. Piersen

410. Davies, Don and Zerchykov, Ross. PARENTS AS AN INTEREST GROUP. *Educ. and Urban Soc. 1981 13(2): 173-192.* Discusses why so few parental interest groups exist in the United States, the only two being local Parents' Unions and the federation of People United for Rural Education

(PURE), per the authors' definition of interest groups, and why many interest groups serve parents; and presents an approach for studying political action by and for parents, and how their interests are and are not "represented in educational policy making"; 1977-81.

411.   Davis, James A.   ACHIEVEMENT VARIABLES AND CLASS CULTURES: FAMILY, SCHOOLING, JOB, AND FORTY-NINE DEPENDENT VARIABLES IN THE CUMULATIVE GSS.   *Am. Sociol. Rev. 1982 47(5): 569-586.* Asks whether the core achievement variables, father's occupation, educational attainment, and respondent's occupation affect a variety of attitudes and behaviors identified by the 1972-80 General Social Survey (GSS). There is no evidence that these attitudes are affected by "sheer" or "score" occupational mobility, status consistency, or "return on investment" psychology. Prestige stratum of father's occupation has no net association with any of the items. Respondent's occupational stratum has nontrivial associations with about one-third of the items, but the magnitudes are small. Education is clearly the most pervasive net predictor. The notion of powerful "class cultures" receives little support from these data.   J

412.   De Jong, G. F. and Sell, R. R.   CHANGES IN CHILDLESSNESS IN THE UNITED STATES: A DEMOGRAPHIC PATH ANALYSIS.   *Population Studies [Great Britain] 1977 31(1): 129-142.* Primarily, enrollment of married women in education, labor force participation, and mean age of first marriage, and secondarily, mean educational attainment, incidence of marital disruption, and proportion of women in urban environments, affect the increase in childlessness among married women under age 30 since 1960.

413.   del Castillo, R. Griswold.   LA FAMILIA CHICANA: SOCIAL CHANGE IN THE CHICANO FAMILY IN LOS ANGELES, 1850-1880.   *J. of Ethnic Studies 1975 3(1): 41-58.* Examines the reaction of Mexican American families in light of the impact of modernization (urbanization and industrialization) during the period 1850-80. The pre-modern family is found to be paternalistic and extended. Modernization led to a decline in the proportion of extended families, a rise in the proportion of female headed families, and an increase in common law marriages. Rather than being functional adjustments to industrialization, these are interpreted as dysfunctional since both literacy and social mobility were associated with the declining extended family structure. Based largely on manuscript censuses and other primary sources; 27 notes.
                                                                                T. W. Smith

414.   DeVaus, David A.   THE IMPACT OF CHILDREN ON SEX RELATED DIFFERENCES IN CHURCH ATTENDANCE.   *Sociol. Analysis 1982 43(2): 145-154.* Considers the arguments that the child-rearing role of women does not account for their greater commitment to institutional religion in America. Data from 1972-80 show that becoming a parent, the number of children in the family, and the child-rearing stages affect frequency of church attendance; these family variables have an equal impact on both men and women.
                                                                                J/S

415. Dewey, Frank L. THOMAS JEFFERSON AND A WILLIAMSBURG SCANDAL: THE CASE OF *BLAIR* V. *BLAIR*. *Virginia Mag. of Hist. and Biog. 1981 89(1): 44-63.* Presents Thomas Jefferson's argument in this 1773 Virginia case where the widow of Dr. James Blair sued her brother-in-law, as executor of Dr. Blair's estate, for her dowry. Precedents were against the estate, but Jefferson and his colleagues argued that because the marriage was not consummated, it was nominal only. They further asserted that Mrs. Blair, who had been legally denied separate maintenance while Dr. Blair was alive, was guilty of deceit in her marriage contract. Jefferson's account is fully printed here for the first time. His appeals to English and international law, literature and the Bible in defense of Blair men were, ultimately, for the losing side. 50 notes.

P. J. Woehrmann

416. Dewey, Frank L. THOMAS JEFFERSON'S NOTES ON DIVORCE. *William and Mary Q. 1982 39(1): 212-223.* Jefferson prepared notes intended to be used on behalf of Dr. James Blair of Williamsburg for a petition to the legislature for divorce. Blair died on 26 December 1772. No legislation for the divorce was introduced during the session of February-April 1772 (the next session was March 1773). Jefferson's notes outline the case that Jefferson would have made to the legislature. The author explains Jefferson's references to treatises on international law and Scripture, and the annotation points specifically to Jefferson's sources. Reproduces the document. Based on books in Jefferson's library; 57 notes.

H. M. Ward

417. Dielman, T. E. GAMBLING: A SOCIAL PROBLEM? *J. of Social Issues 1979 35(3): 36-42.* This paper reports the results from a national survey of gambling behavior, social problems, and attitudes toward the legalization of gambling. Non-bettors perceived more negative consequences and fewer positive consequences associated with the legalization of gambling than did bettors. One negative consequence perceived by a majority of both groups was an increase in political corruption. The level of gambling activity was positively associated with several social problems such as divorce, absenteeism, and frequency of alcohol consumption. Respondents who were classified as probable compulsive gamblers reported more family problems.

J

418. Downs, Anthony. THE IMPACT OF HOUSING POLICIES ON FAMILY LIFE IN THE UNITED STATES SINCE WORLD WAR II. *Daedalus 1977 106(2): 163-180.* Government housing policies of the last 30 years have had an ambivalent impact on family life. They did help overcome the acute housing shortage of 1945. While the impact was favorable to the majority, it was very harmful to the millions living in poor households. It is the latter fact which must be remedied now through income improvement, housing assistance, and housing opportunities for the poor to move into nonpoor areas. Based on government documents and secondary sources; 15 notes.

E. McCarthy

419. Drake, W. Magruder, ed. A DISCOURSE ON DIVORCE: ORLEANS TERRITORIAL LEGISLATURE, 1806. *Louisiana Hist. 1981 22(4): 434-437.* Reproduces a speech by Samuel S. Mahon, a representative from Concordia and member of the legislature's select committee on divorce and alimony, as printed in a Natchez, Mississippi, newspaper. Examples drawn from history show that easy divorce is correlated with societal degeneracy. Divorce is justified only in

exceptional circumstances such as impotence or adultery. The legislature should invest the Superior Court with jurisdiction over divorces and free itself to deal with more important issues. 4 notes.   R. E. Noble

420.   Dublin, Thomas.   WOMEN, WORK, AND THE FAMILY: FEMALE OPERATIVES IN THE LOWELL MILLS, 1830-1860.   *Feminist Studies 1975 3(1/2): 30-39.* Between 1830 and 1860 Lowell, Massachusetts, was a leading center of textile manufacture in the United States. From 1830 to 1845 women operatives formed a majority of the mill workforce. They were native-born and lived in company-owned boarding houses, which became centers of community life, and which provided the organizational base for the Lowell labor movement. After 1845 Irish immigrant men and women became an increased portion of the mill population. Immigrant women tended to live with their families (usually parents) rather than in boarding houses. Family dependence on the income of these female children meant greater caution in strike action and discouraged labor activity in Lowell during the 1850's. Primary and secondary sources; 33 notes.
                                                                          S. R. Herstein

421.   Dubnoff, Steven.   GENDER, THE FAMILY, AND THE PROBLEM OF WORK MOTIVATION IN A TRANSITION TO INDUSTRIAL CAPITALISM.   *J. of Family Hist. 1979 4(2): 121-136.* Using data from the payrolls of a Lowell, Massachusetts, factory and the 1860 federal manuscript census, studies the adaptation of the largely preindustrial labor force to the strictures of factory labor. Men were absent from work less than women and that family position influenced one's work orientation. 3 tables, 18 notes, biblio.
                                                                          T. W. Smith

422.   Dubnoff, Steven.   A METHOD FOR ESTIMATING THE ECONOMIC WELFARE OF AMERICAN FAMILIES OF ANY COMPOSITION: 1860-1909.   *Hist. Methods 1980 13(3): 171-181.* The statistical creation of a poverty line is methodologically significant in analyzing historical data. The first estimate of the poverty line is based on the estimated elasticity between a poverty line and average earnings in the 20th century in constant dollars and then transformed logarithmically backward into the 19th century. The second strategy compares the proportion of income spent on food. After adjusting for various factors, an appendix of estimated poverty lines was presented, useful for several research purposes. 2 tables, 34 notes, 2 appendixes.   D. K. Pickens

423.   Dubovik, Paul N.   HOUSING IN HOLYOKE AND ITS EFFECTS ON FAMILY LIFE 1860-1910.   *Hist. J. of Western Massachusetts 1975 4(1): 40-50.* The poverty of the "Shanty Irish" of "The Patch," the financial difficulties of the Hadley Falls Company, inadequate transportation, and expensive land led to barracks-like tenements. High rental company housing was a method of exploiting the workers. Based on the Holyoke *Transcript*, Green's *Holyoke*, and state and local documents; 3 illus., 62 notes.   S. S. Sprague

424.   Duran, James A. and Duran, Elizabeth C.   THE MARRIAGE TAX.   *Social Policy 1981 11(5): 21-24.* Discusses the inequities built into the American tax structure for two-income families from the passage of the 1969 Tax Reform Act, which penalizes women who combine marriage and a career, to the 1981 suggestions to reform taxation.

425. Edmonds, Anthony O. POPULAR MUSIC IN THE 1950S AND THE CONTEMPORARY AMERICAN FAMILY. *Indiana Social Studies Q. 1980 33(2): 93-100.* Focuses on the influence of popular music on children who grew up during the 1950's and early 1960's, and how their attitudes and behavior from childhood are affecting the nature of the contemporary American family.

426. Feree, Myra Marx. EMPLOYMENT WITHOUT LIBERATION: CUBAN WOMEN IN THE UNITED STATES. *Social Sci. Q. 1979 60(1): 35-50.* Tests the hypothesis that women's participation in the paid labor force changes sex-role attitudes and behavior. Observation of middle-class Cuban women who immigrated to the United States after 1959 indicates that there is no necessary conflict between employment and traditional values. Traditionally, women in Cuban society had to be subservient to the needs of the family. This central role has continued in the United States, while the means have changed: the woman must work outside the family for the family's honor and upward mobility. 4 tables, biblio.
S

427. Finkelstein, Barbara J. IN FEAR OF CHILDHOOD: RELATIONSHIPS BETWEEN PARENTS AND TEACHERS IN POPULAR PRIMARY SCHOOLS IN THE NINETEENTH CENTURY. *Hist. of Childhood Q. 1976 3(3): 321-335.* American primary schools were "networks of collaborative relationships between parents and teachers" which reflected a fear of childhood and a consequent need to restrain natural inclinations and maintain constant vigilance over children. This dimension of childrearing theory was important in fostering the growth of popular schooling. Based on primary and secondary sources; 61 notes.
R. E. Butchart

428. Fraundorf, Martha Norby. THE LABOR FORCE PARTICIPATION OF TURN-OF-THE-CENTURY MARRIED WOMEN. *J. of Econ. Hist. 1979 39(2): 401-418.* The standard modern model of married women's labor force participation is modified because turn-of-the-century families had the alternatives of substituting children for the mother in the labor force and of taking in paying boarders. The modified model explained 1901 participation rates quite well. Participation rates were significantly related (negatively) to the number of older children (potential workers) but not to the number of young children. In addition, the availability of jobs was more important than high wages in inducing women to seek work. Other family income, the male unemployment rate, and literacy also were significant.
J

429. Freeman, Jo. WOMEN AND URBAN POLICY. *Signs 1980 5(3): supplement 4-21.* The Carter administration has attempted to enunciate an urban policy, but the task has been made nearly impossible by the variety of problems and the administration's failure to study the sex composition of neighborhoods and cities. Sex and race are clear indicators of central city populations where public transportation and affordable housing have made life less difficult for female-headed households and elderly women. A national policy which recognizes that women face dual roles and which supports career-family lifestyles must be developed. Based on US Department of Commerce Census Bureau statistics and secondary sources; 8 tables, 41 notes.
S. P. Conner

430. Friedberger, Mark.   THE DECISION TO INSTITUTIONALIZE: FAMILIES WITH EXCEPTIONAL CHILDREN IN 1900. *J. of Family Hist. 1981 6(4): 396-409.* Studies the growth of institutionalized care for "exceptional" children by linking institutional records and census manuscripts. Institutionalization grew because it relieved individual parents of the difficult task of rearing their handicapped children and because specialists argued that society and the child also benefit from institutional care. 3 tables, 3 notes, methodological appendix, biblio.   T. W. Smith

431. Friedberger, Mark.   THE FARM FAMILY AND THE INHERITANCE PROCESS: EVIDENCE FROM THE CORN BELT, 1870-1950. *Agric. Hist. 1983 57(1): 1-13.* Studies estate records in seven Illinois and Iowa townships to determine how farm land was inherited. About half the families studied lived in their townships long enough to pass land between generations. Inheritance laws usually gave the widow one-third of the estate and divided the rest among the children, which often made it difficult to keep the land intact so that young family members could get a good start in farming. Many farm families preferred to write wills or to settle their land divisions before death, practices which enabled transfer of the land in larger units while allowing for proper care of widows and retired farmers. Family size, land costs, and credit availability were all factors in determining the type of settlement used. Based on local tax, deed, mortgage, and probate records; table, 22 notes.   D. E. Bowers

432. Gary, Lawrence E.   POLICY DECISIONS IN THE AID TO FAMILIES WITH DEPENDENT CHILDREN PROGRAM: A COMPARATIVE STATE ANALYSIS. *J. of Pol. 1973 35(4): 886-923.* Previous studies of policy decisions at the state level have concentrated on monetary components. Definition has been largely based on conclusions derived from levels of expenditure. The author "offers a new way of operationalizing welfare policies," and mentions monetary and socioeconomic variables. Eighteen eligibility requirements for Aid to Families with Dependent Children were quantified in an effort to gain an overall picture of welfare policies at the state level. Concludes "that when policy decisions outside the budgetary process are examined, political considerations prove to play a crucial role in determining welfare policy decisions." 5 tables, 65 notes.   A. R. Stoesen

433. Gecas, Viktor.   FAMILY AND SOCIAL STRUCTURAL INFLUENCES ON THE CAREER ORIENTATIONS OF RURAL MEXICAN-AMERICAN YOUTH.   *Rural Sociol. 1980 45(2): 272-289.* Discusses a study on the effects of the family environment and obstacles from the cultural and economic situations of rural Mexican American families on the career orientations of rural Mexican American youth, based on a survey of migrant and settled rural Mexican American families in Yakima Valley, Washington, in 1971; concludes that cultural and economic situations affect career orientations as much as family influences do.

434. Giele, Janet Zollinger.   CHANGING SEX ROLES AND FAMILY STRUCTURE.   *Social Policy 1979 9(4): 32-43.* Discusses the changing role of women in the working world and the extent to which this affects child-rearing practices, division of labor, and other sex roles in the family; 20th century.

435. Gilchrist, Lewayne D. and Schinke, Steven Paul. TEENAGE PREG-
NANCY AND PUBLIC POLICY. *Social Service Rev. 1983 57(2): 307-322.*
Outlines historical policies and legislation addressing the problems of teenage
pregnancy; finds a current trend away from public involvement and a return to
family and personal responsibilities for sexual behaviors.

436. Glazer-Malbin, Nina. HOUSEWORK. *Signs 1976 1(4): 905-922.* Recent scholarship on housework centers on these issues: 1) the monetary value of
housework to the family and as an estimated contribution to the gross national
product, 2) the social role of the housewife, and 3) the integration of housework
into an analysis of capitalism. Earlier studies viewed housework as a biologically
determined task of women. Ann Oakley's study of the housewife since preindustrial times finds women dissatisfied with doing housework. John K. Galbraith
concludes that women are exploited. The housewife works for the maintenance
of capitalism, not simply for her family. The working-class man's domination of
his wife deflects his dissatisfaction with the economic system and gives him the
illusion of power. Based on secondary works; 54 notes.   J. Gammage

437. Goldin, Claudia. FAMILY STRATEGIES IN LATE NINETEENTH-
CENTURY PHILADELPHIA. *Working Papers from the Regional Econ.
Hist. Res. Center 1979 2(3): 60-106.* Analyzes the family decisionmaking process
regarding economics in late 19th century Philadelphia households, based on a
study of urban families from 1870 to 1880 United States Federal Population
Censuses.

438. Goldin, Claudia. HOUSEHOLD AND MARKET PRODUCTION OF
FAMILIES IN A LATE NINETEENTH CENTURY AMERICAN CITY.
Explorations in Econ. Hist. 1979 16(2): 111-131. Apart from the male head of
household, urban families relied upon children as an important source of labor
income. An examination of Philadelphia, Pennsylvania, in 1880 shows substitu-
tion between mothers and their daughters and the role of comparative advantage
in family decisions concerning the allocation of their members' time. Ethnic
differences were important only for daughters. Based on published documents
and secondary accounts; 4 tables, 29 notes, 23 ref.   P. J. Coleman

439. Gonzalez, Rosalinda M. and Fernandez, Raul A. U.S. IMPERIALISM
AND MIGRATION: THE EFFECTS ON MEXICAN WOMEN AND FAMI-
LIES. *Rev. of Radical Pol. Econ. 1979 11(4): 112-124.* Illegal Mexican immigration into the United States is a consequence of US imperialism. Having
destroyed the economy of Mexico, US capitalists have acted to keep the Mexican
people as a reserve force of cheap labor. Especially exploited are women and
children, who will labor for less money and are less skilled at demanding their
rights. At present, the all-powerful capitalists are striving to shut off illegal
immigration on the one hand, in order to prevent having to pay higher wages,
and to keep those who have entered in a position of second-class persons without
rights for the same purpose. 34 notes.   V. L. Human

440. Goodwin, Leonard and Moen, Phyllis. THE EVOLUTION AND IM-
PLEMENTATION OF FAMILY WELFARE POLICY. *Policy Studies J.
1980 8(4, Special no. 2): 633-651.* Examines federal public welfare programs
enacted since 1962, their implementation, and the attitudes of welfare recipients.

441.   Gordon, Linda.   THE LONG STRUGGLE FOR REPRODUCTIVE RIGHTS.   *Radical Am. 1981 15(1-2): 75-88.* An adequate defense of abortion has and will be critical to free sexuality, the family, and problems of human dependancy and gender; 19th-20th centuries. 7 notes, 7 illus.   C. M. Hough

442.   Gould, Ketayun H.   FAMILY PLANNING AND ABORTION POLICY IN THE UNITED STATES.   *Social Service Rev. 1979 53(3): 452-463.* Examines legislation, court decisions, and administrative regulations and traces obstacles to the development of a cohesive federal policy, including differences between Congress and the Health, Education, and Welfare Department, inadequate funding, lack of accountability, and bureaucratic inefficiency, 1970's.

443.   Greene, William H. and Quester, Aline O.   DIVORCE RISK AND WIVES' LABOR SUPPLY BEHAVIOR.   *Social Sci.Q. 1982 63(1): 16-27.* Investigates the risk of marital dissolution in affecting human capital accumulation, labor market supply patterns, savings, and fertility and hypothesizes that wives subject to high probabilities of marital dissolution will be more likely to be working in the labor market; since individual wives subject to high probabilities of marital dissolution have hedged in the past by working in the labor market, they have accumulated more years of labor market experience than have other wives.

444.   Grossman, Allyson Sherman.   THE EMPLOYMENT SITUATION FOR MILITARY WIVES.   *Monthly Labor Rev. 1981 104(2): 60-64.* During the 1970's the labor force participation rate of military wives advanced by 20% (now at 50%, it equals that of civilian wives); attributes this rise to rapidly increasing prices, low military pay, diminished benefits, and greater societal acceptance of working wives and mothers.

445.   Grossman, Allyson Sherman.   WORKING MOTHERS AND THEIR CHILDREN.   *Monthly Labor Rev. 1981 104(5): 49-54.* Discusses statistics related to the increasing number of working mothers during 1970-80, including racial differences, family income, the costs of child-rearing, day-care centers, changing family patterns and the proportion of children with working mothers.

446.   Gundersen, Joan R. and Gampel, Gwen V.   MARRIED WOMEN'S LEGAL STATUS IN EIGHTEENTH-CENTURY NEW YORK AND VIRGINIA.   *William and Mary Q. 1982 39(1): 114-134.* Married women in both colonies had active roles in the legal system; however, as compliance with British legal procedure increased, the legal status of women diminished. Discusses the areas in which women primarily came into contact with the civil law: property, contracts and family law. By mid-century, women were receiving less control of property and participating less frequently in the judicial process. Provides profiles of some of the women, their family, occupation, and legal experience. Based on statute law and legal records; 59 notes.   H. M. Ward

447.   Haebler, Peter.   EDUCATIONAL PATTERNS OF FRENCH-CANADIANS IN HOLYOKE, 1868 to 1910.   *Hist. J. of Massachusetts 1982 10(2): 17-29.* Examines the decisions made by French-Canadian parents concerning the education of their children in the industrial city of Holyoke as they attempted to maintain both ethnic values and economic stability.   Based on contemporary government reports, the author's dissertation, and other secondary sources.   W. H. Mulligan, Jr.

448. Haines, Michael R. INDUSTRIAL WORK AND THE FAMILY LIFE CYCLE, 1889-1890. *Res. in Econ. Hist. 1979 4: 289-356.* This paper provides an analysis of the 1889-1890 Commissioner of Labor Survey of budgets for 8544 families in nine industries in the United States and five European countries. The focus is the composition of family income over the life cycle and its relationship to family expenditures. It was found that earnings of the principal male wage earner peaked early in the life cycle whereas expenditures peaked later. The gap was made up by secondary wage earners, particularly children, entering the labor market. The pattern was same for both the U.S. and Western European families and is in marked contrast to the mid-20th century, when mostly married women reenter the labor market later in the life cycle. Finally, some analysis of the determinants of labor force participation and earnings of married women and children was conducted. 10 tables, 22 notes, biblio.   J

449. Hanson, Sandra L. THE EFFECTS OF RURAL RESIDENCE ON THE SOCIO-ECONOMIC ATTAINMENT PROCESS OF MARRIED FEMALES. *Rural Sociol. 1982 47(1): 91-113.* Compares the earnings and relative socioeconomic status of married women with rural backgrounds and urban women on the basis of a series of studies and interviews conducted in Pennsylvania from 1947 to 1971; examines the generally higher financial and social standing of urban women; discusses the variables, including education, responsible for this.

450. Harding, Susan. FAMILY REFORM MOVEMENTS: RECENT FEMINISM AND ITS OPPOSITION. *Feminist Studies 1981 7(1): 57-75.* Feminists and their opponents employ two distinct perspectives and strategies in attempting to reform family organization. Feminist strategy (set of plans) reduces the family's role in defining woman's life and identity. Feminist ("egalitarian") perspective emphasizes individuality and equality. Their opponents emphasize deference to authority and inevitability of marriage and children. This "hierarchal" perspective centralizes the family's role in woman's identity. In general, women combine "egalitarian" and "hierarchal" ideas. An uneasy truce is likely between competing strategies. Another consciousness is emerging: kinship reaching beyond the family for identity, intimacy, sexuality, and reproduction. Covers ca. 1960-80. Secondary sources; 23 notes.   P. D. Hinnebusch

451. Hareven, Tamara K. FAMILY TIME AND INDUSTRIAL TIME: FAMILY AND WORK IN A PLANNED CORPORATION TOWN 1900-1924. *J. of Urban Hist. 1975 1(3): 365-389.* Cumulative individual employee files 1910-36 of the Amoskeag Manufacturing Company of Manchester, New Hampshire, coupled with marriage and insurance records and oral histories, reveal a pervasive family influence in working. Vacancies were discovered via word-of-mouth, family members substituted for each other, family finances postponed marriages and caused babies to be dropped off so women could return to work. Young children found summer jobs in the mills, and many met their future spouses there. 45 notes.   S. S. Sprague

452. Hareven, Tamara K. THE LABORERS OF MANCHESTER, NEW HAMPSHIRE, 1912-1922: THE ROLE OF FAMILY AND ETHNICITY IN ADJUSTMENT TO INDUSTRIAL LIFE. *Labor Hist. 1975 16(2): 249-265.* A case study of the Amoskeag Mills in Manchester, New Hampshire, which

demonstrates the effect of ethnocentrism and family ties upon the modernization process. When the corporation introduced an efficiency and welfare system, the workers responded with attempts to control job mobility and hiring through their own ethnic and family affiliations. This was largely successful until the nine-month strike of 1922. Based on statistical family research, government reports and the *Amoskeag Bulletin*. Table; 25 notes.   L. L. Athey

453. Harper, John Paull. BE FRUITFUL AND MULTIPLY: ORIGINS OF LEGAL RESTRICTIONS ON PLANNED PARENTHOOD IN NINE-TEENTH-CENTURY AMERICA.   Berkin, Carol Ruth and Norton, Mary Beth, ed. *Women of America: A History* (Boston: Houghton Mifflin Co., 1979): 245-269. Describes US 19th-century legal policy to suppress demands for birth control and trade in birth control devices. Some historians have claimed that this was an act to oppress women, but there is an indication that political leaders were afraid America would be underpopulated. Robert Dale Owen was a radical espouser of planned parenthood who believed birth control would improve the lot of the individual in society. Examines the place of abortion and the effect of Comstock laws. Primary sources; 10 notes.   K. Talley

454. Harris, William.   WORK AND THE FAMILY IN BLACK AT-LANTA, 1880.   *J. of Social Hist. 1976 9(3): 319-330.* Investigates whether slavery or conditions in the post civil war environment affected the opportunities of blacks and the nature of the black family. Lack of advancement was not as much a result of a poverty of skills, which could be blamed on slavery, as the lack of political opportunities in the post civil war situation. Limitations in the census information make analysis of the slight differences in fatherless families difficult. Attempts are made to enlighten the subject with comparisons with other data and conclusions about different ethnic groups in urban situations in the late 19th century. Based on a sample of 400-500 blacks and the same number of whites in Atlanta from the censuses of 1870 and 1880.   M. Hough

455. Hayghe, Howard.   HUSBANDS AND WIVES AS EARNERS: AN ANALYSIS OF FAMILY DATA.   *Monthly Labor Rev. 1981 104(2): 46-59.* Provides a broad base of information on the increasingly prevalent dual-earner family type (especially their demographic and economic characteristics), com-pares dual-earner families with traditional families, and lists recent studies deal-ing with dual-earner families and their unique problems.

456. Hayghe, Howard.   MARITAL AND FAMILY PATTERNS OF WORKERS: AN UPDATE.   *Monthly Labor Rev. 1982 105(5): 53-56.* Statis-tics for the 12 months ending March 1981 on labor force changes due to the large number of married women with children re-entering the labor force; focuses on marital status, ethnic background, median income, and poverty level and percent-ages.

457. Hedley, Max. RELATIONS OF PRODUCTION OF THE "FAMILY FARM": CANADIAN PRAIRIES.   *J. of Peasant Studies [Great Britain] 1981 9(1): 71-85.* Studies the 20th-century development of the family farm in Alberta, to evaluate the impact of capital on domestic producers and their communities. The domination of capital in agriculture involves more than the broad processes of capitalization, proletarianization and concentration since it penetrates and

conditions the very structure of country life. Domestic producers in Western Canada created the material basis of their existence, their communities and their culture. However, their achievements are progressively undermined and their transitional status steadily revealed as the conditions of reproduction are transformed under the hegemony of capital. 27 notes, ref.   M. K. Hogg

458. Hemphill, C. Dallett. WOMEN IN COURT: SEX-ROLE DIFFEREN-TIATION IN SALEM, MASSACHUSETTS, 1636 TO 1683. *William and Mary Q. 1982 39(1): 164-175.* Essex County (Massachusetts) Quarterly Court records provide information on sex roles through cases and depositions. In Salem, sex roles conformed to the traditional, but surprisingly the roles were indistinct and overlapped during the early years. Wives were active in occupations that their husbands were engaged in that were additional to farming. Women were involved in litigation affecting property. They also often made financial and other economic decisions. Partnership and mutual obligation detracted from patriarchal deference. Women became less aggressive toward the end of the period as communities grew. Uses Essex County records; 51 notes.   H. M. Ward

459. Herring, Reuben. SOUTHERN BAPTIST CONVENTION RESOLU-TIONS ON THE FAMILY. *Baptist Hist. and Heritage 1982 17(1): 36-45, 64.* Reprints resolutions related to the family passed by the Southern Baptist Convention from 1863 to 1980, but mainly from the 1970's, on issues such as abortion, homosexuality, marriage and divorce, women's and children's rights, and sex education; discusses the Southern Baptist stand on other issues such as alcohol use, pornography, and television morality.

460. Hofferth, Sandra L. and Moore, Kristin A. WOMEN'S EMPLOY-MENT AND MARRIAGE. Smith, Ralph E., ed. *The Subtle Revolution: Women at Work* (Washington: Urban Inst., 1979): 99-124. Discusses the changing ideas about traditional marriage and how women working outside the home have affected these, using statistics on marriage and divorce since 1890, focusing on how women's employment affects marital relations and the domestic power structure, and assesses the implications.

461. Houseknecht, Sharon K. and Spanier, Graham B. MARITAL DISRUP-TION AND HIGHER EDUCATION AMONG WOMEN IN THE UNITED STATES. *Sociol. Q. 1980 21(3): 375-389.* Because during 1971-77 there was a 71% increase in the number of women completing at least five years of college, it is important to learn why the marital disruption (divorce and separation) rate for these women exceeds that for all educated women except those who did not finish high school; four possible explanations incorporate the variables of race, employment, and income: insecure identities on the part of males and a sense of status loss on the part of females, resulting from educationally hypogamous marriages; female economic independence; female career commitment; and non-shared social support systems.

462. Howe, Claude L., Jr. FAMILY WORSHIP IN BAPTIST LIFE. *Baptist Hist. and Heritage 1982 17(1): 46-53.* Focuses on family worship among Southern Baptists and the influences of Puritanism, evangelicalism, individualism, and denominationalism.

463. Howe, Ruth-Arlene W. DIVORCE: CRITICAL ISSUES FOR LEGAL AND MENTAL HEALTH PROFESSIONALS. *Urban and Social Change Rev. 1977 10(1): 15-21.* Examines the implications of recent legal decisions regarding divorce and child custody for attorneys and mental health social workers in the 1970's; considers the changing role of the family unit in social organization.

464. Huber, Joan and Spitze, Glenna. WIVES' EMPLOYMENT, HOUSEHOLD BEHAVIORS, AND SEX-ROLE ATTITUDES. *Social Forces 1981 60(1): 150-169.* Tests the effect of wives' 10-year work attachment on their current employment status, and the effect of wives' work attachment, current employment status, and earnings on perceptions of household decision-making, the household division of labor, and on sex-role attitudes. Work attachment, current employment status, and earnings affect husbands' but not wives' perceptions of decisionmaking. Both spouses' perceptions of the household division of labor are affected more by wives' current employment status than by their work attachment or earnings. Attitudes most closely related to wives' employment are most responsive to it. Based on interviews.   J/S

465. Huckle, Patricia. THE WOMB FACTOR: PREGNANCY POLICIES AND EMPLOYMENT OF WOMEN. *Western Pol. Q. 1981 34(1): 114-126.* Examines the historical treatment of pregnant or potentially pregnant women from 1908 to 1978, describes the process of amending the Civil Rights Act (US, 1964) to include pregnancy discrimination as sex discrimination, and analyzes the central arguments postulated. The resulting Pregnancy Discrimination Act (US, 1978), while barring discrimination in employment benefits based on the capacity to reproduce, and while responsive to the problem of equity for women workers, does little to restructure employment for women who must fill dual roles of worker and mother. Government sources; table, 53 notes.   J. Powell

466. Hunt, Janet G. and Hunt, Larry L. THE DUALITIES OF CAREERS AND FAMILIES: NEW INTEGRATIONS OR NEW POLARIZATIONS? *Social Problems 1982 29(5): 499-510.* The living patterns of men and women in "dual career families" are not radically different from those in "conventional sex-roles," but their careers do threaten, contrary to the literature, family life.

467. Ichioka, Yuji. AMERIKA NADESHIKO: JAPANESE IMMIGRANT WOMEN IN THE UNITED STATES, 1900-1924. *Pacific Hist. Rev. 1980 49(2): 339-357.* The number of Japanese women in the United States increased significantly between 1910 and 1920 because of immigration. Japanese men, working in the United States, summoned their wives in Japan, returned to Japan to marry and bring their wives to America, or sent for picture-brides. Probably more than half of married Japanese women immigrants were picture-brides. Disappointed women sometimes deserted their husbands. Japanese immigrant newspapers and associations attempted to exercise social control so that marital scandals would not embarrass all Japanese. Most married women, however, remained with their husbands and became the mothers of Nisei children. The Japanese government ceased to issue passports to picture-brides in December 1919. Based on interviews with Issei women in the Japanese Retirement Home in East Los Angeles, Japanese American Research Project Collection, Japanese Foreign Ministry Archival Documents, and other primary sources; 44 notes.
R. N. Lokken

468. Iglehart, Alfreda P. WIVES, HUSBANDS, AND SOCIAL CHANGE: THE ROLE OF SOCIAL WORK. *Social Service Rev. 1982 56(1): 27-38.* Examines the social change that accompanies the increasing participation of wives in the US labor force, and discusses the importance of understanding this trend for social workers as well as sociologists, demographers, and economists in the 1980's.

469. Javits, Jacob and Steinberg, Rafael. SCENES FROM A POLITICAL MARRIAGE. *Washington Monthly 1980 12(10): 20-29.* Senator Jacob Javits recounts his marriage with Marian Borris, and problems in mixing marriage and politics; 1947-80.

470. Jeffries, John W. THE SEPARATION IN THE CANTERBURY CONGREGATIONAL CHURCH: RELIGION, FAMILY, AND POLITICS IN A CONNECTICUT TOWN. *New England Q. 1979 52(4): 522-549.* Discusses the Great Awakening and resulting church schisms. In 1743, conflict over the choice of a new minister caused an irreparable division in Canterbury. The split involved more than religious beliefs, but was not along economic, age, sex, or geographical lines. It was between a group of old, important families who dominated local politics and another group of families with as much wealth but with less power in government. Thus "the religious phenomena of revivalism and separatism had important social, political, and institutional contents." Families tied to the political and religious establishment and, thus, with a stake in its continued dominance, came to oppose separation. Based on local records; 78 notes.

J. C. Bradford

471. Johnson, Beverly L. MARITAL AND FAMILY CHARACTERISTICS OF THE LABOR FORCE, MARCH 1979. *Monthly Labor Rev. 1980 103(4): 48-52.* Presents data on the reasons for the increase in multiearner families during the 1970's, particularly the rise in the number of working wives, mothers, and one-parent families, both black and white.

472. Johnson, John M. PROGRAM ENTERPRISE AND OFFICIAL COOPTATION IN THE BATTERED WOMEN'S SHELTER MOVEMENT. *Am. Behavioral Scientist 1981 24(6): 827-842.* Reports on the development of the battered women's shelter movement from 1960 to 1981, comparing earlier interest in the issue and subsequent law reforms from 1850 to the early 20th century, and comments on the adverse effect of official cooptation and corruption in running these shelters.

473. Johnstone, John W. C. SOCIAL CHANGE AND PARENT-YOUTH CONFLICT: THE PROBLEM OF GENERATIONS IN ENGLISH AND FRENCH CANADA. *Youth and Soc. 1975 7(1): 3-26.* The high degree of tension between Quebec French Canadian youth and their parents is based primarily on the decline of the Roman Catholic Church as a dominant force and significant changes in the educational system. Conflicts are strongest over dating and religion, and are strong also over politics and occupational plans. There is much less tension in English Canadian families. Based on a 1965 sample of Canadian youth (ages 13-20), and on primary and secondary sources; 5 tables, 8 notes, biblio.

J. H. Sweetland

474.   Jones, Elise F.   THE IMPACT OF WOMEN'S EMPLOYMENT ON MARITAL FERTILITY IN THE U.S. 1970-1975.   *Population Studies [Great Britain] 1981 35(2): 161-174.* The 1975 National Fertility Study concluded that employment reduced intended and unintended female fertility.

475.   Kanter, Rosabeth Moss.   FAMILIES, FAMILY PROCESSES, AND ECONOMIC LIFE: TOWARD SYSTEMATIC ANALYSIS OF SOCIAL HISTORICAL RESEARCH.   Demos, John and Boocock, Sarane Spence, ed. *Turning Points: Historical and Sociological Essays on the Family* (Chicago: U. of Chicago Pr., 1978): 316-339. Discusses variables in the family that affect the relationship between families and economic life (particularly industrialization), in order to provide a system for comparative historical analysis based on studies from the 1950's to the 1970's.

476.   Klaczynska, Barbara.   WHY WOMEN WORK: A COMPARISON OF VARIOUS GROUPS—PHILADELPHIA, 1910-1930.   *Labor Hist. 1976 17(1): 73-87.* Analyzes the reasons for women working by comparing patterns of Italian, Polish, Irish, Jewish, black, and native-born white women. Central determinants were strong ethnic familial traditions, the lack of strong familial ties, and class consciousness. Italian and Polish women worked least often, and blacks, native-born whites, and Irish most often. Jewish women tended to move from a work tradition to a nonwork position as they moved into the middle class. Based on government publications and periodicals; 20 notes.   L. L. Athey

477.   Laslett, Peter.   THE FAMILY AND THE COLLECTIVITY.   *Sociol. and Social Res. 1979 63(3): 432-442.* The collectivity is all of society outside the family. The collectivity, which includes Church, State, economic and volunteer organizations, performs welfare functions, i.e. functions which families cannot always accomplish alone. Commonly held assumptions about the relationship between the family and the collectivity seem to ignore the complex and necessary relationship between the Western nuclear family system and the collectivity. A welfare state has always existed to bolster family tasks. To study family history adequately, all social relations must be accounted for.   J/S

478.   Leibowitz, Arleen and Friedman, Bernard.   FAMILY BEQUESTS AND THE DERIVED DEMAND FOR HEALTH INPUTS.   *Econ. Inquiry 1979 17(3): 419-434.* Examines family demand for health services for children according to family income, maternal education, and price of the health service; uses 1969 data from rural and urban America.

479.   Lerner, Samuel and Kaplan, Rose.   A BRIEF HISTORY OF THE DETROIT JEWISH FAMILY AND CHILDREN'S SERVICE: AN OVERVIEW.   *Michigan Jewish Hist. 1976 16(2): 22-26.* The Jewish Family and Children's Service is a community organization interested in the education and Americanization of Detroit's Jewish community, 1876-1976.

480.   Levitan, Sar A. and Belous, Richard S.   WORKING WIVES AND MOTHERS: WHAT HAPPENS TO FAMILY LIFE?   *Monthly Labor Rev. 1981 104(9): 26-30.* Presents statistics on the working patterns and family-related obligations of women in the labor force; traditional ideas about what constitutes a family and what work roles should be no longer are realities, 1970's.

481. Lewis, Ronald L. SLAVE FAMILIES AT EARLY CHESAPEAKE IRONWORKS. *Virginia Mag. of Hist. and Biog. 1978 86(2): 169-179.* Despite a widespread belief that the institution of slavery destroyed the black family, the evidence indicates that this was not true with industrial slavery. In ironworks, the opportunity for overwork provided male slaves with money to buy additional food or clothing for their families and helped to preserve the family unit. For the majority of slave ironworkers, the family was a viable patriarchal institution. Drawn from primary material in the Maryland Historical Society, the College of William and Mary, the Library of Congress, the University of Virginia, the State Historical Society of Wisconsin, the Virginia Historical Society, and Duke University; 33 notes.
R. F. Oaks

482. Long, James E. and Jones, Ethel B. MARRIED WOMEN IN PART-TIME EMPLOYMENT. *Industrial and Labor Relations Rev. 1981 34(3): 413-425.* Deals with three aspects of the part-time employment pattern of working wives: 1) the wives' characteristics, 2) the level and structure of their earnings in part-time jobs, and 3) the duration of their employment when part-time jobs are available to them and concludes that part-time work opportunities appear to increase the length of the working life of married women.
J/S

483. Long, Larry H. WOMEN'S LABOR FORCE PARTICIPATION AND THE RESIDENTIAL MOBILITY OF FAMILIES. *Social Forces 1974 52(3): 342-348.* Families in which the wife works are more likely to undertake short-distance moving and slightly less likely to undertake long-distance migration than families in which the wife does not work. The effect of the wife's employment is greater in raising the family's local mobility rates than in lowering migration rates. The reasons behind these findings are explored, along with the implied consequences. It is concluded that the migration of husbands interferes substantially with career development among wives and in this way contributes to explaining why women earn less than men at the same age, occupation, and educational level.
J

484. Loof, David. ASSISTING APPALACHIAN FAMILIES. *Appalachian J. 1977 4(4): 102-112.* The efforts of health professionals to promote health, education, and welfare in Appalachia hinge on their ability to breach the resistance of a tight knit society by forming trusting relationships with Appalachian children and adults, despite problems of language and aggression.

485. Lueptow, Lloyd B.; McClendon, McKee J.; and McKeon, John W. FATHER'S OCCUPATION AND SON'S PERSONALITY: FINDINGS AND QUESTIONS FOR THE EMERGING LINKAGE HYPOTHESIS. *Sociol. Q. 1979 20(4): 463-475.* A study of 1,750 high school boys shows, contrary to expectation, no statistically significant effect of their fathers' job complexity on their achievement patterns or intelligence.

486. Macauley, Jacqueline. STEREOTYPING CHILD WELFARE. *Society 1977 14(2): 47-51.* Discusses the policy and attitude toward children who are the recipients of welfare, maintaining that because of the negative reinforcement received, welfare children are destined to become welfare recipients in adulthood, 1970's.

487.   Madden, Janice Fanning.   URBAN LAND USE AND THE GROWTH IN TWO-EARNER HOUSEHOLDS. *Am. Econ. Rev. 1980 70(2): 191-197.* Because two-earner families are increasing in number with an increased demand for housing, employees are moving to the suburbs. The long-term demographic effects of female labor should greatly influence urban land markets. Covers 1976. 3 tables, 2 ref.   D. K. Pickens

488.   Marcus, George E.   LAW IN THE DEVELOPMENT OF DYNASTIC FAMILIES AMONG AMERICAN BUSINESS ELITES: THE DOMESTICATION OF CAPITAL AND THE CAPITALIZATION OF FAMILY. *Law & Soc. Rev. 1980 14(4): 858-903.* Studies American dynastic business families as descent groups and argues that law has been a critical organizational resource in their development. Law becomes an integral dimension of extended family relations in the arrangements for perpetuating collective wealth as business capital, and in distributing individual entitlements to that wealth among descendants. A general model of family/business formations is presented, supported by a comparative discussion of two dynastic families of Galveston, Texas, ca. 1890-1980.
                                                                               J/S

489.   Matthies, Susan A.   FAMILIES AT WORK: AN ANALYSIS BY SEX OF CHILD WORKERS IN THE COTTON TEXTILE INDUSTRY. *J. of Econ. Hist. 1982 42(1): 173-180.* Differences in the school and work experience of young girls and boys are explained by factors related to the demand for household production including the presence of young children, boarders and lodgers, and home ownership. Gender-based differences in job characteristics and hourly earnings associated with occupational segregation contributed to the observed pattern of higher schooling investment by girls and earlier work experience by boys.   J

490.   Mayfield, Chris.   LIVING WITH DAY CARE. *Southern Exposure 1980 8(3): 22-33.* Traces the history of day care since the Depression, when day nurseries were established as part of the Works Progress Administration program, focusing on day care since the 1960's in Jacksonville, Florida; Swainsboro, Georgia; and Durham, North Carolina.

491.   McArthur, Benjamin.   THE CHICAGO PLAYGROUND MOVEMENT: A NEGLECTED FEATURE OF SOCIAL JUSTICE. *Social Service R. 1975 49(3): 376-395.* Discusses the movement in American cities, begun in Chicago in 1894, to develop playgrounds for urban children as "part of the Progressive's quest for social justice."   S

492.   McEaddy, Beverly Johnson.   WOMEN WHO HEAD FAMILIES: A SOCIOECONOMIC ANALYSIS. *Monthly Labor Rev. 1976 99(6): 3-9.* Analyzes the results of a Special Labor Force Report (1975), detailing the increase of families headed by women since 1960, giving characteristics of age, marital status, and labor force participation.

493.   Medjuck, Sheva.   THE IMPORTANCE OF BOARDING FOR THE STRUCTURE OF THE HOUSEHOLD IN THE NINETEENTH CENTURY: MONCTON, NEW BRUNSWICK AND HAMILTON, CANADA WEST. *Social Hist. [Canada] 1980 13(25): 207-213.* Michael Katz, in his study of Hamilton, Ontario (1975), argues that there was little distinction between relatives

residing with kin and boarders, and that the latter should be regarded as "an integral part of the household." When, however, comparisons are made with Moncton in 1851, 1861, and 1871, very clear distinctions emerge. Boarders tended to be young, male, foreign-born, and highly transient. Relatives tended to be native-born females under 20 years of age or over 60, and not in the labor force. The distinction is important because of what it indicates about the relationship between household structure and economic conditions. 7 tables, 7 notes.

D. F. Chard

494. Menchik, Paul L. PRIMOGENITURE, EQUAL SHARING, AND THE U.S. DISTRIBUTION OF WEALTH. *Q. J. of Econ. 1980 94(2): 299-316.* Analyzes the distribution of 1,050 large estates probated in Connecticut, 1930-46, by sex, birth order, family size, estate size, and asset composition; equal sharing among children is the rule.

495. Merelman, Richard M. THE FAMILY AND POLITICAL SOCIAL-IZATION: TOWARD A THEORY OF EXCHANGE. *J. of Pol. 1980 42(2): 461-486.* The family provides the state with both taxes and socialized children. In the predemocratic era, the family produced far more for the state than it received in return, but its control over landed property provided a secure defense against the state as well as a family bond. Since the 18th century, urbanization and the decline of the extended family reversed the balance, leading to the contemporary family's vulnerable position of dependent exploitation by the state. Because a strong family system provides a defense for individuals against the state, novel policies to redress the balance would not only further the family's role in political socialization, but would also further the cause of individual freedom. 63 notes.

A. W. Novitsky

496. Merwick, Donna. DUTCH TOWNSMEN AND LAND USE: A SPA-TIAL PERSPECTIVE ON SEVENTEENTH-CENTURY ALBANY, NEW YORK. *William and Mary Q. 1980 37(1): 53-78.* Examines early settlement on the upper Hudson River, with special attention to the Van Rensselaer patroon-ship. The Van Rensselaer family is discussed. Dutchmen and Englishmen differed on the meaning of "town," the relationship between family and property, and the responsibilities of town and rural areas. Albany and Beverwyck and their adjoin-ing areas serve as models for the interaction of rural and urban society and also for the conflict between English and Dutch culture. The author investigates land development, the fur trade, and artisan and merchant life. When the English took over, they encouraged status based on land and also weakened the idea of a tight political structure, self-contained, in the towns. Uses the early public records of New Netherland and New York; 2 maps (Van Rensselaer's Patroonship and Settlement of Beverwyck 1698), 109 notes.

H. M. Ward

497. Mitchinson, Wendy. HISTORICAL ATTITUDES TOWARD WOMEN AND CHILDBIRTH. *Atlantis [Canada] 1979 4(2, part 2): 13-34.* Examines Canadian medical textbooks and journals written during 1870's-90's, and discusses medical, social, and religious attitudes toward women and child-birth.

498.   Modell, John.   AN ECOLOGY OF FAMILY DECISIONS: SUBUR-
BANIZATION, SCHOOLING, AND FERTILITY IN PHILADELPHIA,
1880-1920.   *J. of Urban Hist. 1980 6(4): 397-417.* Studies the relationship of
three major developments in Philadelphia from 1880 to 1920: the suburban move
to distant reaches of the city not heavily settled previously, the growth of the
public schools system to handle immigrants and the expanding local population,
and fertility and childrearing decisions of families. Focuses on individual family
responses, aggregate demographic responses, and actions by political bodies,
especially the school board. 6 tables, 33 notes.   T. W. Smith

499.   Modell, John.   SUBURBANIZATION AND CHANGE IN THE
AMERICAN FAMILY.   *J. of Interdisciplinary Hist. 1979 9(4): 621-646.* Studies the extent to which cities after 1890 became more differentiated internally and
the extent to which progressive differentiation was linked to suburbanization and
to selective location of families in particular stages of their life cycles. An analysis
of Boston, Baltimore, Chicago, and St. Louis suggests that, while the populations
of large American cities did assort themselves during the period of streetcar
suburbanization as suggested by ecological theory, they did not do so to such a
degree nor with such trends that lasting consequences for preferences in family
life can be claimed. In the post-World War II period, the same patterns of spatial
differentiation continued, but this time at such a pace that tastes may well have
been affected. Printed sources and census data; 12 tables, 23 notes.
                                                                    R. Howell

500.   Moore, Kristin A. and Hofferth, Sandra L.   WOMEN AND THEIR
CHILDREN.   Smith, Ralph E., ed. *The Subtle Revolution: Women at Work*
(Washington: Urban Inst., 1979): 125-157. Discusses the issues that have arisen
over the care of children, traditionally women's responsibility, since women
began entering the labor market in large numbers, focusing on statistics on
changes in childbearing patterns from 1890-1977 and day care from 1970-77,
considering the effects of working mothers and day care on children and families.

501.   Moran, Gerald F. and Vinovskis, Maris A.   THE PURITAN FAMILY
AND RELIGION: A CRITICAL REAPPRAISAL.   *William and Mary Q.
1982 39(1): 29-63.* Evaluates recent works on the relationship between the Puritan family and religion. The author accuses most recent social historians of
writing "tunnel" history, and sets forth the need for an integration of family and
social history. Several areas of interaction between family and religions are discussed: Puritan tribalism and the core family; family strategies and life course; and
death and dying. The family had considerable influence over the course of religion. Annotates the important historiography; 106 notes.   H. M. Ward

502.   Moroney, Robert M.   THE NEED FOR A NATIONAL FAMILY
POLICY.   *Urban and Social Change Rev. 1977 10(1): 10-14.* Examines the
extent to which the welfare state has taken over traditional moral and economic
responsibilities of the family in social organization in the 1960's and 70's; advocates the need for social policies regarding the changed role of the family in
society.

503. Morrison, W. R. "THEIR PROPER SPHERE": FEMINISM, THE FAMILY, AND CHILD CENTERED SOCIAL REFORM IN ONTARIO, 1875-1900. *Ontario Hist. [Canada] 1976 68(1): 45-64; (2): 65-74.* Part I. Argues that 19th-century feminists saw family instability resulting from social changes as something women should try to correct. Mentions variations of viewpoints among feminist groups and the attitudes of antifeminists. Both outlooks saw the home as central to women's lives but with varying degrees of emphasis. Also discusses the relationships between the women's movement and other social reform movements, especially the temperance movement. 88 notes. Part II. Discusses the National Council of Women, which originated as a means of coordinating the activities of several organizations. Looks at the activities of a selection of individual women (e.g., Mrs. Hoodless in education) and organizations (e.g., the Victorian Order of Nurses) which were seen as part of the women's movement specifically, and reformism in general. A final section attempts to set the movement in perspective. Photo, 35 notes.   W. B. Whitham

504. Moynihan, Daniel Patrick. THE STATE, THE CHURCH, AND THE FAMILY. *Urban and Social Change Rev. 1977 10(1): 7-9.* Religious institutions have forsaken their traditional societal role as a moral force in favor of the government in the 1960's and 70's; examines the implications for the family unit and ethnic groups.

505. Nathanson, Constance A. MOVING PREFERENCES AND PLANS AMONG URBAN BLACK FAMILIES. *J. of the Am. Inst. of Planners 1974 40(5): 353-359.* "Data are reported from a random sample survey of residents in an average income [Baltimore, Maryland] inner-city black neighborhood. Respondents' moving preferences and moving plans were equally associated with housing and neighborhood dissatisfaction, and weakly related to family composition or demographic characteristics. The physical condition of the neighborhood and respondents' social ties to the area were most important in their moving preferences and plans. It is suggested that both movers and stayers are limited in their ability to materially change their living conditions through mobility, and some proposals for stabilizing this neighborhood are advanced."   J

506. Neitz, Mary Jo. FAMILY, STATE, AND GOD: IDEOLOGIES OF THE RIGHT-TO-LIFE MOVEMENT. *Sociol. Analysis 1981 42(3): 265-276.* Examines the differences between ideologies of elite and mass publics in the case of the abortion issue. Within the Right-to-Life movement exist two conceptual frameworks: a "prolife" framework advocated by the elite, and a "profamily" framework advocated by the mass. Ethnographic data from a Catholic Charismatic prayer group shows that the profamily framework demonstrates both range and centrality, but in regard to concerns quite different from those of the elite.
                                                                                J/S

507. Nelson, Barbara J. REVIEWING CHILD ABUSE POLICY IN AMERICA: A SOCIAL SERVICE APPROACH. *Policy Studies J. 1980 9(3): 455-463.* Remedies a lack of attention to the problem by examining child abuse policy in terms of the conflict of values involved in the formation of social service policy and the relationship between child abuse and other recent social service issues responding to familial violence or childhood dependency.

508.   Nelson, Charmeynne D.   MYTHS ABOUT BLACK WOMEN WORK-ERS IN MODERN AMERICA.   *Black Scholar 1975 6(6): 11-15.* Explores myths about Negro women workers, 1969-75, emphasizing those regarding employment and heads of families.

509.   Newell, Linda King and Avery, Valeen Tippetts.   SWEET COUNSEL AND SEAS OF TRIBULATION: THE RELIGIOUS LIFE OF THE WOMEN IN KIRTLAND.   *Brigham Young U. Studies 1980 20(2): 151-162.* Describes the role of Mormon women in Kirtland, Ohio, 1831-38. The women manifested their spirituality in several ways: in their homes; in support of their missionary husbands with encouragement and prayers; and in prophesying and speaking in tongues in church meetings. The women also assisted in building and furnishing Kirtland Temple by making draperies and carpets and by boarding and clothing the craftsmen. The women moved from Kirtland secure in the conviction that their spiritual strength would overcome all tribulation. Based on diaries, journals, letters, autobiographies, memoirs, sermons, and a master's thesis; 45 notes.
E. R. Campbell

510.   Nobles, Wade W.   AFRICANITY: ITS ROLE IN BLACK FAMILIES. *Black Scholar 1974 5(9): 10-17.* Customary analytical frameworks offer a distorted perspective of the total reality and complexion of the black family system. The black family is best understood as a unit or system deriving its primary characteristics, form, and definition from its African nature. The intrinsic nature of the black family is its sense of "continual flexibility in circularity." Scholars have been unable to appropriately reflect the actuality of the black family system because they have failed to respect the sense of Africanity in black people and families. Secondary sources; notes.   M. M. McCarthy

511.   Nock, Steven L. and Rossi, Peter H.   ASCRIPTION VERSUS ACHIEVEMENT IN THE ATTRIBUTION OF FAMILY SOCIAL STATUS. *Am. J. of Sociol. 1978 84(3): 565-590.* Evaluates status based on individual achievement versus ascribed status.

512.   Norman, Mary Anne.   PIONEER EDUCATIONAL EXPERIENCES IN THE NINETEENTH-CENTURY SOUTHWEST.   *Red River Valley Hist. Rev. 1980 5(2): 25-42.* Discusses "how and why Southwestern frontier families provided formal education for their children" during the 19th century, providing examples of parental encouragement of educational opportunities, different types of schools, their curricula, textbooks, and teaching methods.

513.   Novak, Michael.   THE FAMILY OUT OF FAVOR.   *Urban and Social Change Rev. 1977 10(1): 3-6.* Discusses the role of capitalism in diminishing the moral and economic importance of the family in social organization, particularly among ethnic groups, in the 1970's.

514.   Oberle, Wayne H.; Stowers, Kevin R.; and Darby, James P.   FAMILY INCOME AND STATUS ORIENTATIONS OF OZARKS YOUTH.   *Youth and Soc. 1974 6(1): 91-103.* Examines the relationship between the household income of the family and selected educational and occupational status orientations of youth who are the children of household heads residing in the Ozark Mountains.   S

515. Onuf, Peter S.   NEW LIGHTS IN NEW LONDON: A GROUP POR-TRAIT OF THE SEPARATISTS.   *William and Mary Q. 1980 37(4): 627-643.* The New Lights of the Congregational Church were addicted to conflict. The revival in Connecticut occurred among widespread separation within the churches; the semicommercial towns were most susceptible. Two revivals in New London, 1741 and 1742, attracted primarily the young. Ninety-nine separatists formed the Shepherd's Tent. Many of the members of the separatist church had not previously joined an established church. Family ties were the cohesive factors among the separatists. The separatists came from all sections of New London and represented a variety of occupations. The status and wealth of the separatists are examined. Based on church and court records; 3 tables, 30 notes.

H. M. Ward

516. O'Rand, Angela M. and Henretta, John C.   DELAYED CAREER EN-TRY, INDUSTRIAL PENSION STRUCTURE, AND EARLY RETIRE-MENT IN A COHORT OF UNMARRIED WOMEN.   *Am. Sociol. Rev. 1982 47(3): 365-373.* The effects of early family and work patterns and industrial pension structures on the timing of retirement among unmarried women are examined within a life course perspective. The retirement process is viewed in a longitudinal framework with similar combinations of factors influencing succes-sive stages of final withdrawal from work. Having children and delayed career entry along with late life family, pension, and health status affect retirement schedules.

J/S

517. Osmond, Marie Withers and Grigg, Charles M.   CORRELATES OF POVERTY: THE INTERACTION OF INDIVIDUAL AND FAMILY CHARACTERISTICS.   *Social Forces 1978 56(4): 1099-1120.* Characteristics of the family head are compared with those of the family as a unit in extent to which they are associated with three criteria of family poverty. Analysis of data from a sample of 561 welfare applicants in four states reveal substantial interac-tion effects among the two sets of variables. Sex of family head is a major conditional variable. For female-headed families, characteristics of the family largely account for variation in family income, work history of the head, and welfare history of the family. For male-headed families, individual characteristics of the family head take precedence over family characteristics. There is little difference in family economics by race among male-headed families. But if black families have any additional disadvantage, they show a much more pronounced decline in economic status than do white families.

J

518. Pessen, Edward.   EARLY INDUSTRIALIZATION, URBANIZA-TION, AND THE AMERICAN FAMILY.   *Rev. in Am. Hist. 1982 10(1): 49-53.* Review essay of Mary P. Ryan's *Cradle of the Middle Class: The Family in Oneida County, New York, 1790-1865* (1981).

519. Pike, Robert.   LEGAL ACCESS AND THE INCIDENCE OF DI-VORCE IN CANADA: A SOCIOHISTORICAL ANALYSIS. *Can. Rev. of Sociol. and Anthrop. 1975 12(2): 115-133.* Long-term trends in divorce rates in Canada are examined within the framework of Canadian divorce law and of changes in social attitudes and family structure. It is suggested, in particular, that an essential concept in an analysis of the changing incidence of divorce is that of 'legal access,' by which is meant the impact on divorce rates of the nature of

the legal grounds for divorce, as well as the impact of the provision, or lack of provision, of divorce court facilities. More specifically, Canadian divorce rates prior to the divorce law reforms of 1968 are shown to have provided a very poor indication of the actual rate of marriage breakdown owing to the stringent nature of the legal grounds of divorce and the lack of divorce court facilities in some provinces. Furthermore, the existence of major legal barriers to divorce fostered patterns of institutionalized evasion amongst those seeking divorces including migratory divorces and fraudulent divorce actions. However, the continued existence of large, and long-term, variations in divorce rates between the Canadian provinces highlights the need for further analysis of a wide variety of social, cultural, and demographic variables which appear to be associated with the differential regional incidence of divorce in this country.   J

520.   Pred,   Allen.   PRODUCTION,   FAMILY   AND   FREE-TIME PROJECT: A TIME-GEOGRAPHIC ON THE INDIVIDUAL AND SOCIETAL CHANGE IN NINETEENTH-CENTURY U.S. CITIES.   *J. of Hist. Geography 1981 7(1): 3-36.* Examines individual and family experience in artisan and factory modes of production. Factory workers lost the self-determination in their working conditions, which accounted for 10 or more hours daily. Life became more regimented and disciplined at work, but those traits were lost in the home where women were required to make more decisions and perform more duties. Other family members with jobs became more independent and self-centered with their income. These conditions led to a minimum of extra money and a consequent reduction in average family size. Free-time activities centered on those taking place on Sunday with little cost. Attendance at major league baseball games by industrial wage earners illustrates these constraints. Based on US Census and other sources; 3 tables, 2 graphs, 122 notes.   A. J. Larson

521.   Presser, Harriet B. and Baldwin, Wendy.   CHILD CARE AS A CONSTRAINT ON EMPLOYMENT: PREVALENCE, CORRELATES, AND BEARING ON THE WORK AND FERTILITY NEXUS.   *Am. J. of Sociol. 1980 85(5): 1202-1213.* Women with small children, especially the young, black, single, poor, or poorly educated, are constrained from seeking or taking employment because of the lack of child care facilities.

522.   Rainwater,   Lee.   MOTHERS'   CONTRIBUTION   TO   FAMILY MONEY ECONOMY IN EUROPE AND THE UNITED STATES.   *J. of Family Hist. 1979 4(2): 198-211.* Despite increased female participation in the labor force over recent decades, the contribution of mothers to family income on average remains slight. In addition most women workers do not see their occupation as a career and do not give their work experience the same significance and centrality as men do. 7 notes, biblio.   T. W. Smith

523.   Rainwater, Lee.   NOTES ON U.S. FAMILY POLICY.   *Social Policy 1978 8(5): 28-30.* The family is the basic unit of American social organization; assesses how federal policies (tax reform, employment, equal opportunity, child welfare, and housing) affect family life.

524.   Raynes, Marybeth.   GETTING UNMARRIED IN A MARRIED CHURCH.   *Dialogue 1981 14(4): 75-90.* A personal reminiscence by a divorced Mormon. In a religion which stresses marriage and successful family living,

divorce can imply total failure, as the description of daily life while terminating a marital relationship shows. The author, a full-time therapist, outlines several stages of "unmarrying," and considers the problem of being unwed in a "married church." Confusion and uncertainty become the companions of a recently divorced individual.

M. G. Bishop

525. Renzi, Mario. IDEAL FAMILY SIZE AS AN INTERVENING VARIABLE BETWEEN RELIGION AND ATTITUDES TOWARDS ABORTION. *J. for the Sci. Study of Religion 1975 14(1): 23-27.* Analyzes data defining the relationships between family size preferences, religion, and attitudes on abortion.

S

526. Rice, Robert M. A PREAMBLE TO FAMILY POLICY: ISSUES OF THE PAST AND PRESENT. *Policy Studies J. 1979 7(4): 811-820.* Overview of the social and political importance of families in American social organization offers thoughts on current needs in the area of public policy.

527. Richmond, Julius B. THE NEEDS OF CHILDREN. *Daedalus 1977 106(1): 247-259.* Although there has been a reduction in infant mortality and a decline in morbidity and mortality rates, there is still a need to improve child health care. Children of nonwhite and urban poor families have the greatest health needs. The major problem in child health care is coping with the negative effects of the environment, such as accidents, child abuse, the ubiquity of toxic substances and pollutants, and the developmental attrition among the poor. Continued research, improved community services, and a Presidential Council of Advisors on Children are suggested to meet these needs. Based on government documents and secondary sources; 20 notes, biblio.

E. McCarthy

528. Ritter, Kathleen V. and Hargens, Lowell L. OCCUPATIONAL POSITIONS AND CLASS IDENTIFICATIONS OF MARRIED WORKING WOMEN: A TEST OF THE ASYMMETRY HYPOTHESIS. *Am. J. of Sociol. 1975 80(4): 934-948.* Data for 566 married working women from the 1960, 1964, 1968, and 1970 Survey Research Center election studies . . . suggests that traditional assumptions that wives derive their class positions and identifications exclusively or predominantly from the occupational positions of their husbands do not hold for working wives.

S

529. Roistacher, Elizabeth A. and Young, Janet Spratlin. TWO-EARNER FAMILIES IN THE HOUSING MARKET. *Policy Studies J. 1979 8(2): 227-240.* The continued entrance of wives into the labor market and escalating housing prices in the 1970's will continue into the 1980's.

530. Rook, Patricia T. and Schnell, R. L. CHARLOTTE WHITTON AND THE "BABIES FOR EXPORT" CONTROVERSY, 1947-48. *Alberta Hist. [Canada] 1982 30(1): 11-16.* For over 20 years as the spokesperson for the Canadian Welfare Council (CWC), Charlotte Whitton was "Canada's leading proponent of child welfare." Her research, investigations, and exposés resulted in "a furor over conditions of child care in Alberta." The publication "Welfare in Alberta" added fuel to the fire as did Whitton's articles in the press. The results were a Judicial Commission of Inquiry into Child Welfare in 1947, the *New Liberty* trial, and, ultimately, "Report on the Child Welfare Branch." The end products were positive in that there were "changes in the policies and practices

of child care services at both the public and private levels . . . . " 3 photos, 15 notes.   E. A. Chard

531.   Rooke, Patricia T. and Schnell, R. L.   CHILD WELFARE IN EN-GLISH CANADA, 1920-1948.   *Social Service Rev. 1981 55(3): 484-506.* Traces the history of the Canadian Council on Child Welfare (CCCW) from its forma-tion in 1920 until 1948, noting the leadership of Charlotte Whitton; though devoted to voluntarism, Whitton, with her use of scientific survey method and the "emphasis on uniformity and centralization," fostered increasing state control in child and family life.

532.   Rothchild, Sylvia.   TRAVELING THROUGH MIDDLE AMERICA. *Present Tense 1975 2(2): 37-40.* Discusses patterns of assimilation in three gener-ations of Jewish families in the United States, 1925-75, and how each generation has responded to the social and religious attitudes of its parents.

533.   Rothman, Sheila M.   OTHER PEOPLE'S CHILDREN: THE DAY CARE EXPERIENCE IN AMERICA.   *Public Interest 1973 (30): 11-27.* The history of day care centers during 1854-1973 indicates that the centers may be poor institutions for promoting social reform, particularly with respect to the women's liberation movement.   S

534.   Rothman, Sheila M.   STERILIZING THE POOR.   *Society 1977 14(2): 36-40.* Examines the family planning services available to the poor as representa-tive not only of the right to have fewer children, but the right to have more children; discusses the sterilization projects among the poor, 1970's.

535.   Rowatt, G. Wade, Jr. and Bertolino-Green, Dianne.   FAMILY MINIS-TRIES AMONG SOUTHERN BAPTISTS.   *Baptist Hist. and Heritage 1982 17(1): 13-25, 62.* Defines family ministry as "any specific Christian program or activity intended to rescue, instruct, and/or undergird a family group" and traces the history and development of family ministries among Southern Baptists from 1845 to 1960; discusses local church programs on family life, their achievements, and future areas of concern.

536.   Ryan, Vernon D. and Warland, Rex H.   RACE AND THE EFFECT OF FAMILY   STATUS   AMONG   MALE   AGRICULTURAL   LABORERS. *Rural Sociol. 1978 43(3): 335-347.* Questions Daniel P. Moynihan's 1965 thesis that low-income blacks experience high divorce rates due to the man's weakening position in the family as a result of his inability to provide economic security; Moynihan's study fails to consider other causes of high divorce rates.

537.   Rytina, Nancy F.   THE ECONOMIC STATUS OF MIGRANT WI-VES: AN APPLICATION OF DISCRIMINANT ANALYSIS.   *Sociol. and Social Res. 1981 65(2): 142-152.* Views the labor force behavior of wives who experience migration in terms of economic status. The lower work rate of migrant wives after moving is a function not only of moving for husbands' job opportuni-ties, but being in the childrearing stage of the life cycle. However, the socioeco-nomic characteristics are lower for nonworking than for migrant wives, and migrant wives who work have higher levels of education and higher status jobs prior to and after moving than nonmigrants. Based on data for 1970.   J/S

538. Safilios-Rothschild, Constantina. DUAL LINKAGES BETWEEN THE OCCUPATIONAL AND FAMILY SYSTEMS: A MACROSOCIAL ANALYSIS. *Signs: J. of Women in Culture and Soc. 1976 1(3, Part 2): 51-60.* Increasing husband-and-wife linkages of family and occupational systems raise questions of structural adjustments in one or both of these systems. Such adjustments would mean important sociopsychological changes which would call up strong resistance by both men and women. But if equal status dual linkages are to become institutionalized, a combination of occupational and familial structural changes is probably necessary. Structural changes which permit both spouses equal employment and occupational options need not drastically cut down options in marital and familial alternatives. Based on secondary sources; 14 notes.

S. E. Kennedy

539. Salamon, Sonya. ETHNIC DIFFERENCES IN FARM FAMILY LAND TRANSFERS. *Rural Sociol. 1980 45(2): 290-308.* Data from studies of a German farming community 1975-77 and an Irish farming community 1977-78 in the same county in Illinois show ethnic differences in family size, interpersonal relations, land holdings size, marriage patterns, and outmigration, which affect land transfers within the family.

540. Salamon, Sonya and O'Reilly, Shirley M. FAMILY LAND AND DEVELOPMENTAL CYCLES AMONG ILLINOIS FARMERS. *Rural Sociol. 1979 44(3): 525-542.* A 1975-77 study involving an ethnic community of farmers revealed that four types of family land developmental cycles (expander, conservator, pragmatist, and convertor) are related to land transfer and overall farm management.

541. Salkever, David S. EFFECTS OF CHILDREN'S HEALTH ON MATERNAL HOURS OF WORK: A PRELIMINARY ANALYSIS. *Southern Econ. J. 1980 47(1): 156-166.* Data analyzed with a basic labor supply model indicate that children's disabilities and health problems negatively affect maternal working hours; 1972.

542. Sawhill, Isabel. DISCRIMINATION AND POVERTY AMONG WOMEN WHO HEAD FAMILIES. *Signs: J. of Women in Culture and Soc. 1976 1(3, Part 2): 201-211.* Labor market discrimination by sex and race as well as occupational segregation contribute to the lack of income which characterizes families headed by women (which have grown at twice the rate of two-parent families in the past decade). Changes in attitudes regarding sex roles in families and end of racial discrimination would be helpful in alleviating this situation, but the elimination of sex discrimination alone would improve the economic status of these women and their families. Based on government census documents, published official statistics, and secondary sources; 3 tables, 22 notes.

S. E. Kennedy

543. Schlossman, Steven. THE PARENT EDUCATION GAME: THE POLITICS OF CHILD PSYCHOLOGY IN THE 1970'S. *Teachers Coll. Record 1978 79(4): 788-808.* Parent education has recently replaced compensatory education as the accepted panacea for the educational deficiencies of poor children. The change resulted from 1) a 1969 report of the Westinghouse Learning Corporation critical of compensatory programs, 2) the growing belief that

properly trained mothers are the best educators of young children, and 3) the need of the recently created Office of Child Development for a program to fund. There is a danger that failure of parent education programs such as Home Start and Parent Child Development Centers will result in the blaming of poverty mothers. Based on original research and secondary sources; 52 notes.

E. Bailey

544. Scranton, Philip. AN IMMIGRANT FAMILY AND INDUSTRIAL ENTERPRISE: SEVILL SCHOFIELD & THE PHILADELPHIA TEXTILE MANUFACTURE, 1845-1900. *Pennsylvania Mag. of Hist. and Biog. 1982 106(3): 365-392.* Schofield's rise exemplifies the significance of family and communal environment, the difficulties encountered in a changing industrial sector, and the problems of generational transition. Based on official records, newspapers, other published sources, and secondary works; 69 notes. T. H. Wendel

545. Segal, David R. et al. TRENDS IN THE STRUCTURE OF ARMY FAMILIES. *J. of Pol. and Military Sociol. 1976 4(1): 135-139.* There have been marked changes in the structure of families of US Army personnel during the past 20 years. While little sociological research has been undertaken in this area during this period, several studies have been reported in the past two years. Continuing change in sex roles and in the utilization of women in the Army are opening new areas of exploration. J

546. Seninger, Stephen F. and Stevenson, Wayne. THE ECONOMIC IMPACT OF FAMILY-BASED RURAL EDUCATION AND TRAINING. *Social Sci. J. 1979 16(3): 91-98.* Discusses the National Institute of Education's program of experimentally relocating poor rural families to training centers to receive basic education and vocational guidance and training, 1970's.

547. Smith, Billy G. THE MATERIAL LIVES OF LABORING PHILADELPHIANS, 1750 TO 1800. *William and Mary Q. 1981 38(2): 163-202.* Philadelphia's working class was impoverished before and during the revolution, not benefiting from wealth trickling down, and suffered even worse during the Confederation period. What was gained in wages was offset by declining living standards. The author treats two categories: the less-skilled artisans—cordwainers and tailors—and two unskilled groups—laborers and mariners (the two largest occupational groups in the city). Examination of costs of food, rent, fuel, and clothing provides a reconstruction of the typical household budget. Comparison of wages and costs indicate families could barely meet the expenses of necessities. Comments on health and dietary conditions. Uses tax lists, censuses, newspapers, and business records; 6 tables, 4 fig., 126 notes. H. M. Ward

548. Smith, Judith E. OUR OWN KIND: FAMILY AND COMMUNITY NETWORKS. *Radical Hist. Rev. 1978 (17): 99-120.* Provides a study of immigrant family ties and traditions, particularly among southern Italian and eastern European Jewish immigrants as they experienced the urban industrial environment of Rhode Island during 1880-1940.

549. Smith-Rosenberg, Carroll. SEX AS SYMBOL IN VICTORIAN PURITY: AN ETHNOHISTORICAL ANALYSIS OF JACKSONIAN AMERICA. Demos, John and Boocock, Sarane Spence, ed. *Turning Points: Historical and Sociological Essays on the Family* (Chicago: U. of Chicago Pr.,

1978): 212-247. Discusses the advocacy of purity by sexual reformers during the 1830's and 1840's in the context of social and family change and of medical and familial attitudes toward adolescence, morality, marriage, and social organization.

550. Smylie, James H. "OF SECRET AND FAMILY WORSHIP": HISTORICAL MEDITATIONS. *J. of Presbyterian Hist. 1980 58(2): 95-115.* In 1788, Presbyterians adopted the *Directory of Worship*; it was used until the 1960's. The last chapter of the *Directory* declares that it is the "indispensable duty of each person, alone, in secret, and of every family, by itself, in private, to pray to and worship God." Considers three crises as they are related to the directions given by the *Directory* to Presbyterians: the crisis of the Sabbath and the secularization of time and space, the crisis of the family and the professionalization of religious services, and the crisis of faith and the trivialization of life. Traces these crises historically into the contemporary scene.

H. M. Parker, Jr.

551. Southwick, Lawrence, Jr. THE EFFECTS OF WELFARE PROGRAMS ON FAMILY STABILITY. *Rev. of Social Econ. 1978 36(1): 19-40.* Public welfare has effective incentives which encourage the breakdown of family structure; such breakups are more likely to occur in urban rather than rural environments.

552. Spatz, Marshall. CHILD ABUSE IN THE NINETEENTH CENTURY. *New York Affairs 1977 4(2): 80-90.* Discusses child abuse in New York City 1820's-80's and the establishment of the Society for the Prevention of Cruelty to Children.

553. Stetson, Dorothy M. FAMILY POLICY AND FERTILITY IN THE UNITED STATES. *Policy Studies J. 1977 6(2): 223-230.* Examines the federal government's attitudes toward population policy and how these attitudes relate to the study of childbearing behavior and fertility; the social perceptions of childbearing affect family policy.

554. Strong-Boag, Veronica. CANADA'S EARLY EXPERIENCE WITH INCOME SUPPLEMENTS: THE INTRODUCTION OF MOTHERS' ALLOWANCES. *Atlantis [Canada] 1979 4(2, part 2): 35-43.* Describes the flurry of legislation in Canada, 1916-20, which continued during the 1920's-30's, to grant mothers pensions and allowances, an important step in the history of child welfare in Canada; points out the inadequate aid for mothers in Canada during the 1960's-70's.

555. Strong-Boag, Veronica. "WAGES FOR HOUSEWORK": MOTHERS' ALLOWANCES AND THE BEGINNINGS OF SOCIAL SECURITY IN CANADA. *J. of Can. Studies [Canada] 1979 14(1): 24-34.* The first steps in Canada's formal income support programs were directed to the needs of mother-led families with inadequate means of support in the first decades of this century. Mothers' allowance legislation was introduced in every province. There was some variation in the way the need was met, and there was a slow development in the rationale as well—often "connected to a narrow vision of human potential." Weaknesses in the present Social Security system may be one of the legacies from these early years. Primary sources; 46 notes.

R. V. Ritter

556. Swann, Lee Ann Caldwell. LANDGRANTS TO GEORGIA WOMEN, 1755-1775. *Georgia Hist. Q. 1977 61(1): 23-34.* Women landowners in colonial Georgia, a majority of whom were widows receiving grants to support their families, increased in number during 1755-75. Gives statistics showing the amount of land acquired, during which years it was acquired, and the case histories of some of the recipients. Primary and secondary sources; 33 notes.

G. R. Schroeder

557. Sweig, Donald M. REASSESSING THE HUMAN DIMENSION OF THE INTERSTATE SLAVE TRADE. *Prologue 1980 12(1): 5-19.* Discusses the interstate commerce in slaves from Alexandria, Virginia, to New Orleans during 1828-36, focusing on the effects on the black family and on the practice of selling young children singly. Describes the largest firm to systematically transport slaves for sale, Franklin & Armfield. The records of 28 Alexandria manifests are analyzed according to the age, sex, and family status of the 3,570 slaves listed. The analysis of these manifests indicates that when it was good business to divide families and sell young children, Armfield did so, and when it was good business to maintain the integrity of the slave family, he did that. This changed with the passage of time as the standards for the slave trade became more restrictive. Based on records of the Alexandria manifests, records of US Customs Service and newspapers; 7 photos, 6 tables, 28 notes, 2 appendixes.

M. A. Kascus

558. Takanishi, Ruby. CHILDHOOD AS A SOCIAL ISSUE: HISTORI-CAL ROOTS OF CONTEMPORARY CHILD ADVOCACY MOVEMENTS. *J. of Soc. Issues 1978 34(2): 8-28.* The emergence of childhood as a social issue is barely a century old. The historical roots of current child advocacy movements can be found in an earlier period (1873-1914) characterized as the child-saving era. The emergence of this social issue during this period appears to be related to changing conceptualizations of the child, the developing "scientific" view of the child, as well as the influence of industrialization and urbanization. The child-saving era resulted in a number of problematic achievements regarding children's rights. The historical discussion points to the contributions which developmental and social psychology can make to the study of children's rights.

J

559. Thomas, Sari and Callahan, Brian P. ALLOCATING HAPPINESS: TV FAMILIES AND SOCIAL CLASS. *J. of Communication 1982 32(3): 184-190.* Discusses a series of television programs aired between 1978 and 1980 that show how greater happiness is enjoyed by families of lower socioeconomic strata, while their upper-class counterparts are unharmonious and problem-ridden.

560. Tomes, Nigel. THE FAMILY, INHERITANCE, AND THE INTER-GENERATIONAL TRANSMISSION OF INEQUALITY. *J. of Pol. Econ. 1981 89(5): 928-958.* Based upon a 1964-65 study, tests the model of intergenerational transmission advanced by Gary Beckner, Alan Blinder, and Tsuneo Ishikawa that implies that unequal inheritance may either increase or reduce consumption inequality; concludes that inheritance tends to have an equalizing role.

561. Trennert, Robert A. PEACEABLY IF THEY WILL, FORCIBLY IF THEY MUST: THE PHOENIX INDIAN SCHOOL, 1890-1901. *J. of Arizona Hist. 1979 20(3): 297-322.* A history of the founding, establishment, and first decade of the Phoenix Indian School, with Wellington Rich appointed as its first superintendent (despite no previous knowledge of Indian life or culture). The philosophy undergirding such ventures at that period of handling Indian affairs demanded the complete destruction of Indian culture and an assimilation into white society. The program of the school was geared to this goal plus providing the sort of industrial training as would give the students entrance into the white labor force. The first students were from the Maricopa and Pima tribes. In the first decade over a thousand had attended. There is little evidence of a significant mark on their lives. Primary sources; 10 photos, 35 notes.   R. V. Ritter

562. Tucker, Barbara M. THE FAMILY AND INDUSTRIAL DISCI-PLINE IN ANTE-BELLUM NEW ENGLAND. *Labor Hist. 1980 21(1): 55-74.* Analyzes the role of the family in industrial discipline in factories in Slatersville, Rhode Island, and Webster, Massachusetts, 1790-1840. The family assumed part of the responsibility for industrial training and discipline in these factory towns, which were modeled in a way to preserve tradition. Old practices dissolved in the 1840's as factories shifted to an individual-based work force and new immigration disrupted traditional patterns. Labor conflict accompanied the change. Based on the Samuel Slater collection, Harvard U.; 46 notes.
L. L. Athey

563. Vandepol, Ann. DEPENDENT CHILDREN, CHILD CUSTODY, AND THE MOTHERS' PENSIONS: THE TRANSFORMATION OF STATE-FAMILY RELATIONS IN THE EARLY 20TH CENTURY. *Social Problems 1982 29(3): 221-235.* Challenges the widely-held belief that government has assumed increasing authority over family life in the United States, by tracing public welfare services for dependent children from the colonial indenture system to the introduction of mothers' pensions in the early 20th century; government has moved from an initial disregard of the family unit to positive reinforcement.

564. Vickery, Clair. WOMEN'S ECONOMIC CONTRIBUTION TO THE FAMILY. Smith, Ralph E., ed. *The Subtle Revolution: Women at Work* (Washington: Urban Inst., 1979): 159-200. Discusses how women working in the paid labor force affect their families' standard of living, focusing on what a wife's employment adds to her family's security and well-being, and how it changes housework patterns; 1950-73.

565. Vine, Phyllis. THE SOCIAL FUNCTION OF EIGHTEENTH-CEN-TURY HIGHER EDUCATION. *Hist. of Educ. Q. 1976 16(4): 409-424.* Higher education was seen as a new force to be used for the proper socialization of youth in light of changes in family life.

566. Waite, Linda J. WORKING WIVES: 1940-1960. *Am. Sociol. Rev. 1976 41(1): 65-80.* Changes since 1940 in the rates and patterns of labor force participa-tion of married women are examined using retrospective work histories of wives taken from the 1960 Growth of American Families Study. The effects of certain predictor variables, such as income of the husband, wage potential of the wife and number of children under six, on the probability of a woman working are deter-

mined for life cycle stages. Changes since 1940 in the effects of these predictors are examined using a single-equation, additive linear model and analysis of covariance techniques. The major hypothesis tested in this research is that significant changes have occurred since 1940 in the effects of the factors influencing working by wives. The reseach supports this hypothesis for the early stages of marriage and childbearing only. No changes in either probability of work activity between births or the effects of all predictors when these are considered together on this activity are found for wives with three or more children. When each causal variable is considered separately, a significant decrease is noted in the effects of those factors which tend to inhibit wives' working. Among these are the presence of children under six, the age of the wife and her educational level. The factors which tend to facilitate working, past labor force activity and wife's earning power, have tended to increase in effect or have remained strongly positive influences.   J

567. Wallace, Anthony F. C.   EXTENDED FAMILY AND THE ROLE OF WOMEN IN EARLY INDUSTRIAL SOCIETIES.   *Working Papers from the Regional Econ. Hist. Res. Center 1982 5(2-3): 1-12.* Discusses the important role women played in family businesses in England and America during the 19th century, focusing on their roles as providers of "marital links," organizers at family gatherings, writers of family history, and preservers of family papers.

568. Watts, Ronald K.   JEWISH FERTILITY TRENDS AND DIFFERENTIALS: AN EXAMINATION OF THE EVIDENCE FROM THE CENSUS OF 1970.   *Jewish Social Studies 1980 42(3-4): 293-312.* Data from California confirm Calvin Goldscheider's theory about convergence of fertility behavior among different Jewish nativity groupings. Urbanization, modernization, and industrialization have served to rationalize all human behavior, fertility patterns included. America's Jewish population has become homogenized. 47 notes.
                                                                                                       J. D. Sarna

569. Wein, Roberta.   WOMEN'S COLLEGES AND DOMESTICITY, 1875-1918.   *Hist. of Educ. Q. 1974 14(1): 31-47.* Compares Bryn Mawr College and Wellesley College. Also analyzes the educational ideas of two important presidents of these institutions, Alice Freeman Palmer and Carey Thomas. Finds that Bryn Mawr graduates were more feminist and career-oriented than the Wellesley graduates, who tended to look at education as supplementary to the traditional sex roles of wife and mother. Based on primary and secondary sources; 36 notes.
                                                                                                       L. C. Smith

570. Weiss, Robert S.   HOUSING FOR SINGLE PARENTS.   *Policy Studies J. 1979 8(2): 241-248.* Discusses housing problems of divorced, widowed, and never-married parents, based on interviews with more than 200 respondents in Massachusetts.

571. Welch, Charles E., III.   THE FAMILY AND THE STATES: AN AMERICAN PERSPECTIVE.   *Int. J. of Women's Studies [Canada] 1982 5(3): 227-235.* Discusses the "discriminatory economic treatment of women in American society" evident when marriages are dissolved through no-fault divorce settlements, stating that women with children must provide total economic support for their family and that the problem will continue until fathers provide the necessary economic support.

572. Wilks, Danny. "SAVE THE CHILDREN": IMPLICATIONS OF DAY CARE. *Black Scholar 1973 4(8-9): 14-20.* Discusses the need to reform the day care system in the United States to provide adequate care and proper social and racial stimuli for the children of working parents. Compares US programs with those found in developing countries, 1967-73.

573. Williams, Herma B. and Williams, Eric. SOME ASPECTS OF CHILD-REARING PRACTICES IN THREE MINORITY SUBCULTURES IN THE UNITED STATES. *J. of Negro Educ. 1979 48(3): 408-418.* Minority groups seek to socialize their children into the values of the larger culture, but they also instill other values belonging to their particular ethnic subculture. This paper focuses on the values and child-rearing practices of Mexican Americans, Indians, and Negroes. Each group stresses different values in child-rearing, and these in turn are often in conflict with the values promoted in the schools these children must attend. Secondary sources; 22 notes. J. Powell

574. Woodrum, Eric; Rhodes, Colbert; and Feagin, Joe R. JAPANESE AMERICAN ECONOMIC BEHAVIOR: ITS TYPES, DETERMINANTS, AND CONSEQUENCES. *Social Forces 1980 58(4): 1235-1254.* This paper argues that immigrant economic adaptations should be analyzed as vehicles through which factors in the society of origin influence experiences following migration and as predictors of noneconomic characteristics. The strategy is applied to first generation Japanese Americans (Issei) with national survey data from the Japanese American Research Project. Six economic adaptive modes are isolated by cross-classifying occupational categories with class status as self-employed versus employee. Father's occupation and class status, as well as respondent's education, religion, and family background all significantly influence Issei economic adaptations. Those adopting the various economic modes differ also in other economic respects. Knowledge of economic modes facilitates prediction of Issei English fluency, religious affiliation, primary structural integration and encounters with white prejudice and discrimination. [Covers 1924-79]. 13 tables, 21 ref. J

575. Woolsey, Suzanne H. PIED-PIPER POLITICS AND CHILD-CARE DEBATE. *Daedalus 1977 106(2): 127-145.* Despite much public discussion of federal policy toward day-care, little progress has been made in defining the issues or in analyzing the evidence. Proponents of day-care believe in expanded federal support. Because of the variety of parental preferences, the idea of a single system federally financed does not appeal. Most parents prefer forms of day-care which involve family members, with parents alternating work hours. How federally funded day-care will increase the labor-force participation of women, help in the development of children, or aid AFDC mothers is not yet clear. Secondary sources; 2 tables, 41 notes. E. McCarthy

576. Zelizer, Viviana A. THE PRICE AND VALUE OF CHILDREN: THE CASE OF CHILDREN'S INSURANCE. *Am. J. of Sociol. 1981 86(5): 1036-1056.* Children's life insurance, which began in the United States in 1875, was viewed suspiciously because in Europe it had, since the 16th century, seemed an outright bet against a child's survival and, in the 19th century, it perpetuated the view of the lower class child as a mere financial asset; insurance companies overcame the opposition of child savers, however, by claiming that children's

insurance was a symbolic recognition of the sacred value of working class children's lives and a means of providing them with proper mourning rituals, a campaign so successful that in the 20th century children's insurance has become less a token of respect for dead working class children than a token of love for living middle class children.

577.   Zinn, Maxine Baca.   EMPLOYMENT AND EDUCATION OF MEXICAN-AMERICAN WOMEN: THE INTERPLAY OF MODERNITY AND ETHNICITY IN EIGHT FAMILIES.   *Harvard Educ. Rev. 1980 50(1): 47-62.* Examines and compares the role of outside employment and education on conjugal power and ethnicity in Mexican American women from eight families, 1970's.

578.   —.   [DIVORCE].   *Center Mag. 1980 13(6): 4-18.*
Kauffman, Linda and Bycel, Benjamin.   DIVORCE: AMERICAN STYLE, *pp. 4-9.* Explores discrepancies between legal theory and practice in divorce law, focusing on California's no-fault divorce Family Law Act (1970).
—.   DISCUSSION,   *pp. 9-18.* A panel discussion between the authors and others.

579.   —.   PERSPECTIVES ON *INEQUALITY: A REASSESSMENT OF THE EFFECT OF FAMILY AND SCHOOLING IN AMERICA.*   *Harvard Educ. Rev. 1973 43(1): 37-164.*
—.   INTRODUCTION, pp. 37-50.
Jackson, Philip W.   AFTER APPLE-PICKING, pp. 51-60.
Rivlin, Alice M.   FORENSIC SOCIAL SCIENCE, pp. 61-75.
—.   A BLACK RESPONSE TO CHRISTOPHER JENCKS'S *INEQUALITY* AND CERTAIN OTHER ISSUES, pp. 76-91.
Michelson, Stephen.   THE FURTHER RESPONSIBILITY OF INTELLECTUALS, pp. 92-105.
Thurow, Lester C.   PROVING THE ABSENCE OF POSITIVE ASSOCIATIONS, pp. 106-112.
Clark, Kenneth B.   SOCIAL POLICY, POWER, AND SOCIAL SCIENCE RESEARCH, pp. 113-121.
Duncan, Beverly.   COMMENTS ON *INEQUALITY,* pp. 122-128.
Coleman, James S.   EQUALITY OF OPPORTUNITY AND EQUALITY OF RESULTS, pp. 129-137.
Jencks, Christopher.   INEQUALITY IN RETROSPECT, pp. 138-164.
Commentary on Christopher Jencks' *Inequality: A Reassessment of the Effect of Family and Schooling in America* (New York: Colophon Books, 1973) and a reply by Jencks in which he reaffirms his handling of data and statistics and his conclusions about income inequality and educational opportunity.
                                                                  J. Herbst and S

3

FAMILIAL ROLES AND RELATIONSHIPS

580. Adler, Thomas A. MAKING PANCAKES ON SUNDAY: THE MALE COOK IN FAMILY TRADITION. *Western Folklore 1981 40(1): 45-54.* Observes that the increasing prominence of men in American kitchens has evolved slowly in the 20th century. Perhaps precisely because of the still-pervasive stereotype that it is the woman who is solely or principally responsible for food preparation in the home, the character of male cookery is generally seen as festal, experimental, and limited to a few specialties thought to be masculine. Initially preparing food which is regarded as appropriate to the role as a diversion or form of self-expression, Dad tends to repeat the activity if it is personally satisfying and if he receives reinforcement or if the activity is treated as festive. Lapses take place if the activity loses its novelty. Secondary sources; 25 notes.   J. Powell

581. Aguirre, B. E. THE MARITAL STABILITY OF CUBANS IN THE UNITED STATES. *Ethnicity 1981 8(4): 387-405.* Cuban marriages in the United States are quite modern. The institutional marriage model does not accurately predict marital behavior. The model of democratic, companionship marriage is more applicable than stereotypes of male-dominated, Latin marriages. One of the consequences of the modernity of Cuban marriages in the United States is a relatively high divorce rate. Table, 2 fig., 7 notes, biblio.
                                                                      T. W. Smith

582. Aldridge, Delores P. INTERRACIAL MARRIAGES: EMPIRICAL AND THEORETICAL CONSIDERATIONS. *J. of Black Studies 1978 8(3): 355-368.* Research on interracial marriages since the 1940's is often contradictory, especially on stability. These marriages declined before 1954, then increased. The 1960's black pride movement may have caused a decline, which could have been balanced by desegregation's increased contact between races. Most black men's white wives have a higher social status (reversed for black women, except entertainers), but the trend is toward equal-status partners. Interracial couples tend to be less devout, from disorganized families, urban, black male-white female, previously married, above-average status black males (reversed for others), and foreign-born white males (reversed for white females). Future research should deal with the entire United States and with the exact rates of marriages, and should compare the characteristics of interracial with same-race marriages. Secondary sources; biblio.   R. G. Sherer

583. Alston, Jon P.; McIntosh, William A.; and Wright, Louise M. EXTENT OF INTERFAITH MARRIAGES AMONG WHITE AMERICANS. *Sociol. Analysis 1976 37(3): 261-264.* The General Social Survey Program makes available data dealing with the religious preferences of respondents and their spouses from national samples of the American population. Seventeen percent of the white population have spouses with different religious preferences. Interfaith marriage is associated with lower church participation and with lower levels of perceived family satisfaction. J

584. Antler, Joyce and Fox, Daniel M. THE MOVEMENT TOWARD A SAFE MATERNITY: PHYSICIAN ACCOUNTABILITY IN NEW YORK CITY, 1915-1940. *Bull. of the Hist. of Medicine 1976 50(4): 569-595.* Maternal mortality was the subject of much study during 1915-40. Infant mortality rates had declined dramatically by then, and epidemic disease was no longer the threat it had been in the recent past. Yet, maternal mortality rates had not declined at all. In the mid-1930's, a report on maternal mortality by the New York Academy of Medicine led to an effective strategy for its reduction. The report did not blame midwives, but instead placed the blame with the medical profession itself. The Academy chose to publicize the report. This galvanized medical opinion and led to widespread reform of obstetric care in New York City and throughout the country. 86 notes. M. Kaufman

585. Armitage, Susan. HOUSEWORK AND CHILDREARING ON THE FRONTIER: THE ORAL HISTORY RECORD. *Sociol. and Social Res. 1979 63(3): 467-474.* Oral history interviews with 20 rural Colorado women concerning housework and childrearing, 1895-1920, reveal the economic importance of the female role in domestic sustenance: food production and the manufacture of clothing. Further subjects for oral history investigation are suggested. J

586. Aseltine, Gwendolyn Pamenter. FAMILY SOCIALIZATION PERCEPTIONS AMONG BLACK AND WHITE HIGH SCHOOL STUDENTS. *J. of Negro Educ. 1978 47(3): 256-265.* As part of the 1970 White House Conference on Children and Youth, this paper finds that attitudes toward family, school, community, and religion among black and white high school youth in Rutherford County, Tennessee, compare favorably, indicating a community which offers stability and opportunity for blacks.

587. Austin, Ellen. SODDY HOMEMAKER. *Am. Hist. Illus. 1982 17(3): 38-45.* Describes how pioneer Great Plains women managed their households in sodhouses, which were almost impossible to keep clean.

588. Bacon, Lloyd. EARLY MOTHERHOOD ACCELERATED ROLE TRANSITION, AND SOCIAL PATHOLOGIES. *Social Forces 1974 52(3): 333-341.* Every society prescribes the timing of critical events in the life cycle, such as those attending motherhood. Patterns of role transition at variance with social prescriptions should produce role stress. Thus, when the adult roles associated with motherhood are activated too early in a woman's life cycle, stress and resultant social pathologies should be generated in the family. This study employs national survey data, finding that early motherhood, a form of accelerated role transition, is closely associated with high incidence of marital dissolution, poverty, and truncated education. J

589. Bahr, Howard M. CHANGES IN FAMILY LIFE IN MIDDLE-TOWN, 1924-77. *Public Opinion Q. 1980 44(1): 35-52.* Characteristics of family life described by Middletown [Muncie, Indiana] high school students in 1924 and reported in Robert and Helen Lynd's *Middletown* are contrasted with data from students interviewed in 1977. Comparisons of students' responses suggest that there has been an attenuation of certain family functions and an enhancement of others. The 1977 students were more likely to earn their own spending money and less likely to receive their sex education from their parents; and females were more likely to spend evenings away from home. There were changes in definitions of women's roles, and the range of desirable parental characteristics had narrowed to focus on direct parent-child relationships of an emotional or expressive nature. Analysis of reported topics of disagreement suggest that the generation gap in 1977 is no wider than it was in 1924. 3 tables, biblio.　　　　J

590. Bahr, Howard M. RELIGIOUS INTERMARRIAGE AND DIVORCE IN UTAH AND THE MOUNTAIN STATES. *J. for the Sci. Study of Religion 1981 20(3): 251-261.* Based on data (1972-76) from sample surveys of Utah and the Mountain States as well as on Utah's annual statistical report on characteristics of divorcing couples, assesses differences in the probabilities of divorce by type of interfaith marriage, showing that same-faith marriages are more stable than interfaith marriages.

591. Barrett, Michèle and McIntosh, Mary. NARCISSISM AND THE FAMILY: A CRITIQUE OF LASCH. *New Left Rev. [Great Britain] 1982 (135): 35-48.* Challenges the concepts of human sexuality proposed by Christopher Lasch; examines societal concepts of family, mother, and father—especially the role of women.

592. Bennett, Mary. WOMEN AT HOME. *Palimpsest 1982 63(2): 42-51.* Discusses and provides photographs of Iowa women working at home, ca. 1890-1910.

593. Berardo, Donna Hodgkins. DIVORCE AND REMARRIAGE AT MIDDLE AGE AND BEYOND. *Ann. of the Am. Acad. of Pol. and Social Sci. 1982 (464): 132-139.* The occurrence of divorce at midlife brings losses and adjustments. Divorce at older ages causes similar losses and adjustments, as well as others associated with old age. In addition, the elderly experience divorce indirectly through the divorces of their children. There are problems associated with remarriage that arise from age, previous marital status, sex ratios, geographic residence, and kinship relationships. The success or failure of a second marriage depends on many factors and is affected by a lack of institutionalized norms fitting the situation.　　　　J/S

594. Bettelheim, Bruno. UNTYING THE FAMILY. *Center Mag. 1976 9(5): 5-9.* Discusses social change in middle-class family structure in the 1970's, emphasizing parent-child relations and the changing role of women.

595. Bierhorst, John. THE CONCEPT OF CHILDHOOD IN AMERICAN INDIAN LORE. *Bull. of Res. in the Humanities 1978 81(4): 395-405.* Excerpts from several stories of Native American oral tradition reveal attitudes toward childhood which emphasize attaining maturity while adults continually seek rejuvenation or a return to childhood, a preferable spiritual state.

596. Blackburn, George and Ricards, Sherman L.   THE MOTHER-HEADED FAMILY AMONG FREE NEGROES IN CHARLESTON, SOUTH CAROLINA, 1850-1860.   *Phylon 1981 42(1): 11-25.* Although much current scholarship demonstrates that the nuclear and father-headed family was widespread among blacks, the norm among free Negroes in Charleston was a mother-headed family. This was due in part because of an imbalance between the numbers of nonslave males and females and because free females had greater economic opportunities to support families. The mother-headed family was also stable over time.   A. G. Belles

597. Blake, Judith.   THE ONLY CHILD IN AMERICA: PREJUDICE VERSUS PERFORMANCE.   *Population and Development Rev. 1981 7(1): 43-54.* Single children suffered no educational, occupational, or societal disadvantages due to lack of siblings. Based on the General Social Science Surveys conducted between 1972 and 1978 by the National Opinion Research Center of the University of Chicago.

598. Blau, Peter M.; Blum, Terry C.;   and   Schwartz, Joseph E. HETEROGENEITY AND INTERMARRIAGE.   *Am. Sociol. Rev. 1982 47(1): 45-62.* Test data on intermarriage in the largest American metropolitan areas to determine if a group's relative size is inversely related to the proportion of its members who marry outside the group and if heterogeneity of a group is directly related to the rate of intermarriage in it. Heterogeneity in national origins, mother tongue, birth region, industry, and occupation raise intermarriage rates. Although racial heterogeneity does not have this predicted effect, the reason is that the great socioeconomic differences between races consolidate racial boundaries and thereby counteract the influence of heterogeneity on intermarriage. When racial income differences are controlled, the predicted positive relationship between racial heterogeneity and intermarriage becomes apparent. Based on the 1970 census.   J/S

599. Block, James E.   NEW SHAPES OF FAMILY LIFE.   *Dissent 1981 28(3): 350-357.* Discusses the demise of the American family due to the extension of authority to others beside the father within the family.

600. Bomberger, Herbert L.   THE PARSONAGE: A WAY OF CHRISTIAN FAMILY LIVING.   *Lutheran Q. 1974 26(1): 58-63.* Examines the myths, opportunities for growth, and avenues for strengthening marriage and family life within the parsonage.   S

601. Boyd, Monica.   FAMILY SIZE IDEALS OF CANADIANS: A METHODOLOGICAL NOTE.   *Can. R. of Sociol. and Anthrop. 1974 11(4): 360-370.* "Using data from Canadian Gallup Poll questions on the number of children considered ideal, this paper suggests that the frequently cited 1960 figure of 4.2 children is erroneously inflated. The discussion compares responses in 1960 to responses of an earlier 1957 poll. Comparisons are also made between American and Canadian responses to recent questions on ideal family size."   J

602. Braito, Rita and Powers, Edward A.   WHAT THE OTHER HALF THINKS: THE IMPLICATIONS OF FEMALE PERCEPTIONS FOR WORK DEMANDS.   *Sociol. Inquiry 1977 47(1): 59-64.* Surveys 353 female registered nurses in a northwestern urban center in 1968 and finds that the women

believed that their husbands would not be threatened if theirs were the greater income, and that they saw a greater need for money than did their husbands.

603. Brouwer, Merle G. MARRIAGE AND FAMILY LIFE AMONG BLACKS IN COLONIAL PENNSYLVANIA. *Pennsylvania Mag. of Hist. and Biog. 1975 99(3): 368-372.* The moral standards of white society in colonial America were not considered applicable to the black community. Marriage between Negroes had no legal status throughout the period, and when it did occur family life was often disrupted since slaves were usually sold individually. 21 notes.
C. W. Olson

604. Brown, Steven E. SEXUALITY AND THE SLAVE COMMUNITY. *Phylon 1981 42(1): 1-10.* Recent scholarship on the institution of slavery has demonstrated that slaves not only retained personality initiative and were not passive "Sambos," but also that they constructed a viable black community within the confines of slavery. Using sexual relationships, one can test the formation and existence of shared community values and codes of behavior. Slaves did follow routine procedures regarding courtship, marriage, and family despite restrictions and difficulties. Slaves considered fidelity and caring for loved ones a virtue. An analysis of sexuality demonstrates the ability of slaves to formulate community norms and patterns of shared codes of behavior.
A. G. Belles

605. Bryant, Keith L., Jr. THE ROLE AND STATUS OF THE FEMALE YEOMANRY IN THE ANTEBELLUM SOUTH: THE LITERARY VIEW. *Southern Q. 1980 18(2): 73-88.* In the past historians have given little attention to middle-class white women in the antebellum South. Using literary sources, the author finds that these women occupied significant positions in the antebellum South. For example, they worked, made money for the family, raised the children, established the moral tone in the home, and became important in religious institutions. Their early role in southern history should not be underestimated. Primary sources; 60 notes.
B. D. Ledbetter

606. Bumpass, Larry and Rindfuss, Ronald R. CHILDREN'S EXPERIENCE OF MARITAL DISRUPTION. *Am. J. of Sociol. 1979 85(1): 49-65.* Analyzes the effects of marital disruption (divorce or separation) on children, including the percentage of possibility that a child will experience marital disruption, for how long, etc., based on data from the 1973 Family Growth Survey.

607. Burnham, Dorothy. THE LIFE OF THE AFRO-AMERICAN WOMAN IN SLAVERY. *Int. J. of Women's Studies [Canada] 1978 1(4): 363-377.* Surveys the life of slave women (from narratives, interviews, and written observations), including sexual treatment by slavemasters, family and living conditions, work (both field and household), treatment of the elderly, and psychological effects, 17th century-1865.

608. Burstyn, Joan N. AMERICAN SOCIETY DURING THE EIGHTEEN-NINETIES: "THE WOMAN QUESTION." *Studies in Hist. and Soc. 1973 4(2): 34-40.* Deals with the great debate over the role of women during the last decade of the 19th century with emphasis on the impact of industrialization. Railroad expansion and the development of machinery helped liberate women from the drudgery of domestic life.
J. O. Baylen

609.   Calvert, Karin.   CHILDREN IN AMERICAN FAMILY PORTRAITURE, 1670 TO 1810. *William and Mary Q. 1982 39(1): 87-113.* Examines 334 family portraits, which include 476 children (31% from New England, 43% from the middle colonies, and 18% from the South). Compares children under age seven with those of seven to 14. Most of the paintings are late 18th century. The portraiture reveals patrons' perceptions of their children, the image of the family, the connotations of objects, dress, toys, and the like, and the metamorphosis of child into adult. As families became more private and insular, nuclear family portrait painting became more abundant. Perceptions of childhood grew more positive. Based on portraiture collections, art works, and biography; 9 illus., 2 tables, 43 notes.   H. M. Ward

610.   Campbell, Arthur A.   BOOM TO BIRTH DEARTH AND BEYOND. *Ann. of the Am. Acad. of Pol. and Social Sci. 1978 (435): 40-60.* The processes of fertility change in the United States are structured in a way that exaggerates the upward and downward trends in annual measures of fertility, relative to underlying trends in the average number of children that women have during their reproductive years of life. In the 1950's, we witnessed a period of relatively inflated fertility; in the 1970's we are apparently going through a period of relatively depressed fertility. The childbearing expectations of young women suggest that annual fertility rates will rise in the near future, but do not provide any reason to believe that there will be a substantial increase in fertility comparable to that occurring between the 1930's and the 1950's. The causes of swings in fertility rates are not yet fully known, but some promising hypotheses have been proposed and are being tested.   J

611.   Carr, Lois G. and Walsh, Lorena S.   THE PLANTER'S WIFE: THE EXPERIENCE OF WHITE WOMEN IN SEVENTEENTH-CENTURY MARYLAND. *William and Mary Q. 1977 34(4): 542-571.* Analyzes disrupting factors in 17th century Maryland society, such as, the majority of inhabitants' immigrant status; early death; late marriages; and surplus of men. Discusses the various kinds of women who immigrated, why they came, where they settled, and their status in the colony. Gives a profile of the typical planter's wife. Comments on morality, family size, property rights, and women's responsibility in household polity. Based on Maryland archives and secondary sources; 4 tables, 90 notes.
                                                                        H. M. Ward

612.   Carter, Donald E. and Walsh, James A.   FATHER ABSENCE AND THE BLACK CHILD: A MULTIVARIATE ANALYSIS. *J. of Negro Educ. 1980 49(2): 134-143.* Considers how the absence of a father influences the scholastic achievement, locus of control, and interpersonal distancing of black children, and finds that interpersonal distancing is most affected. Authors suggest strategies for teachers. Based on original research and secondary sources; 25 notes.
                                                                        R. E. Butchart

613.   Chadney, James G.   SIKH FAMILY PATTERNS AND ETHNIC ADAPTATION IN VANCOUVER. *Amerasia J. 1980 7(1): 31-50.* Fieldwork and interviews in the Vancouver Sikh community are used to identify the cultural adaptations made by the Sikhs. Finds that marriage patterns, sexual behavior, and generational precedence are strongly Sikh, while family size, residence patterns and age of marriage are becoming more Canadian. Concludes that the adaptations are largely a response to economic advantages. 2 tables, 18 notes.
                                                                        E. S. Johnson

614. Chegwidden, Paula; Felt, Lawrence F.; and Miller, Anne. BATTERED WOMEN: MYTHS, REALITIES AND NEW DIRECTIONS FOR FUTURE RESEARCH. *Atlantis [Canada] 1981 6(2): 186-193.* Intrafamilial violence is thought to occur in 16% to 50% of American families, scarcely relating to such factors as social class, alcoholism, or alleged female masochism. Most victims are female. Revision of a paper presented to the Atlantic Association of Anthropologists and Sociologists, Halifax, March 1979. Photo, 25 notes.

C. G. P. Gillespie

615. Chudacoff, Howard P. and Hareven, Tamara K. FROM THE EMPTY NEST TO FAMILY DISSOLUTION: LIFE COURSE TRANSITIONS INTO OLD AGE. *J. of Family Hist. 1979 4(1): 69-83.* There appears to be no sharp discontinuities in labor force participation or family roles in the later years of life. Also most of the elderly lived in households that they headed. There appears to be less isolation in the late 19th century of the elderly than presently. 6 tables, 8 notes, biblio.

T. W. Smith

616. Cody, Cheryll A. NAMING, KINSHIP, AND ESTATE DISPERSAL: NOTES ON SLAVE FAMILY LIFE ON A SOUTH CAROLINA PLANTATION, 1786 TO 1833. *William and Mary Q. 1982 39(1): 192-211.* The values held by slaves and the behavior of owners is seen by examining the business records of Peter Gaillard, a South Carolina planter, for his plantation, the Rocks, about 50 miles from Charleston. Slave views of their own families indicate a broad sense of extended kin, in contrast to the owner's conception of slave families in the nuclear sense. The family history of a slave couple, Nero and Binah, shows the contrast in the cultural views of slaves and masters. Naming practices of this slave family indicates kinship bonds. Of Gaillard's inherited and purchased slaves, two-parent nuclear families were dominant in both groups. The slaves showed genealogical knowledge. Names of both paternal and fraternal kin were most frequent because older male children were the first to be separated from their families by the owner. Based on plantation records; 6 tables, fig., 30 notes.

H. M. Ward

617. Cohen, Sheldon S. "TO PARTS OF THE WORLD UNKNOWN": THE CIRCUMSTANCES OF DIVORCE IN CONNECTICUT, 1750-1797. *Can. Rev. of Am. Studies [Canada] 1980 11(3): 275-293.* Although Connecticut was billed the "Land of Steady Habits," it boasted more liberal divorce laws than its neighbors by accepting reasons other than adultery as grounds for divorce. In Connecticut courts, plaintiffs most often alleged desertion, adultery allegations placed second in number, and bigamy and other fraudulent contracts formed the third most common set of complaints. Reflecting Revolutionary War social dislocations, the number of divorce petitions increased during the war and rose again in the postwar period. Based on Connecticut court records; graph, 55 notes.

H. T. Lovin

618. Cohen, Yehudi A. SHRINKING HOUSEHOLDS. *Society 1981 18(2): 48-52.* Discusses the role of technological innovations in agriculture in decreasing the average size of the American family (1689-1975); offers comparisons with Fiji, Japan, and the Israeli kibbutzim; and suggests that this decrease in family size may contribute to a feeling of loneliness prevalent in American society.

619. Cole, Johnnetta. MILITANT BLACK WOMEN IN EARLY U.S. HIS-
TORY. *Black Scholar 1978 9(7): 38-44.* Discusses stereotypes about black
women in slavery, and actual roles of black women within the family and the slave
community; outlines individual and community-supported resistance in which
women participated, in the 17th and 18th centuries.

620. Cooney, Rosemary Santana; Rogler, Lloyd H.; and Schroder, Edna.
PUERTO RICAN FERTILITY: AN EXAMINATION OF SOCIAL CHAR-
ACTERISTICS, ASSIMILATION, AND MINORITY STATUS VARI-
ABLES. *Social Forces 1981 59(4): 1094-1113.* Examines the 1969
Goldscheider-Uhlenberg theory of minority group fertility by making a direct
assessment of the importance of assimilation and minority status. The influence
of assimilation on the fertility behavior of both generations is mediated through
social conditions. Minority status insecurity, however, significantly adds to explained variance in the fertility behavior of the younger generation.   J/S

621. Cosby, Arthur G. and Marshall, Kimball P. ANTECEDENTS OF
EARLY MARITAL AND FERTILITY BEHAVIOR: THE EFFECTS OF
SOCIAL ORIGINS AND ADOLESCENT ATTITUDE FORMATION.
Youth and Soc. 1977 9(2): 191-212. Examines fertility aspirations and related
attitudes as they develop through adolescence, and their bearing on occupational
and educational goals in women.

622. Cott, Nancy F. DIVORCE AND THE CHANGING STATUS OF
WOMEN IN EIGHTEENTH-CENTURY MASSACHUSETTS. *William and
Mary Q. 1976 33(4): 586-614.* Examines 229 divorce petitions for the period
1692-1786 and discusses the legal grounds for divorce. Divorces were granted by
the legislature or the governor and the council. Increasingly, aggrieved spouses
sought divorce through official channels rather than through the traditional
means of "self divorce." More women sought divorce than men, but more men
than women succeeded. Data offer perspectives on sexual, family, marriage, and
property aspects. The Revolutionary era marked a decline in the double standard,
and there was an improvement in the condition of wives. Stricter standards for
men's marital fidelity were also evident. Based on legislative and court divorce
records; 5 tables, 84 notes.   H. M. Ward

623. Cott, Nancy F. EIGHTEENTH-CENTURY FAMILY AND SOCIAL
LIFE REVEALED IN MASSACHUSETTS DIVORCE RECORDS. *J. of
Social Hist. 1976 10(1): 20-43.* Studies family life and habits, including sex mores,
by examining depositions made in Massachusetts divorce proceedings. Considerable alteration needs to be made in commonly accepted assumptions. The second
half of the 18th century saw important transitions in family life. 73 notes.
                                                              R. V. Ritter

624. Cott, Nancy F. NOTES TOWARD AN INTERPRETATION OF AN-
TEBELLUM CHILDREARING. *Psychohistory Rev. 1978 6(4): 4-20.* In the
1830's, the child-rearing manual, already known in Great Britain, made its appearance in the United States. These handbooks emphasized moral and physical
training for children six and under, urging parents not to force their offspring to
read and write before this age (bright children were often force-fed literacy at two
or three). The manuals stressed the mother's role, which often had been ignored

in advice to parents in the 18th and 17th centuries. This increased feminine orientation in the child's education went along with an emphasis on gentler methods, leading rather than forcing the child to do what is right. Self-mastery was the goal. This is connected with a move from external to internal motivation, from elements of a shame-culture to a purer guilt-culture. 99 notes.

J. C. Billigmeier

625.   Cumming, Elaine and Lazer, Charles.   KINSHIP STRUCTURE AND SUICIDE: A THEORETICAL LINK.   *Can. Rev. of Sociol. and Anthrop. [Canada] 1981 18(3): 271-282.* The role of women in maintaining both normative and interactive integration of kinship systems on behalf of men is why marriage lowers the risk of suicide for men more than it does for women. Such an explanation is compatible with existing theories of both kinship and suicide. Rates of reported suicide for all Canada for 1951, 1956, 1961, 1966, and 1971 show that the extra protection of men is consistent through time, and the theoretical explanation offered received support from a preliminary comparison of suicide rates in English and French Canada as well as from suicide rates in matrilineal and patrilineal societies.

J/S

626.   Cunnigen, Donald.   THE POWER OF A BLACK MOTHER'S TOUCH.   *Crisis 1977 84(10): 477-478.* Black mothers who suffer from the strain of raising children and supporting a household often experience nervous breakdowns. This often results in a strength of character that touches the lives of each member of the family. It may also result in stronger determination among the children as they face the realities of a racist society.

A. G. Belles

627.   Cuthbertson, Brian C.   FATHERLY ADVICE IN POST-LOYALIST NOVA SCOTIA: RICHARD JOHN UNIACKE TO HIS SON NORMAN. *Acadiensis [Canada] 1980 9(2): 78-91.* Attorney-General Richard John Uniacke's letter to his son Norman Fitzgerald Uniacke, reproduced here, was written in 1798, just before Norman left Halifax for London to study law. The letter is a homily, full of advice for a young man leaving home for the first time, going from provincial Halifax to the then center of the world. The letter's severity comes from Richard's anguished remembrance of his own break with his father. The letter also reflects an 18th-century Halifax father's desire to protect his child from the temptations and vice that abounded there. 3 notes.

D. F. Chard

628.   Dalton, Russell J.   THE PATHWAYS OF PARENTAL SOCIALIZATION.   *Am. Pol. Q. 1982 10(2): 139-157.* Examines two pathways of family influence in the socialization process. The attitudinal pathway is based on direct interpersonal value transfer and is the major source of parental influence for partisanship, racial attitudes, and other core beliefs. The social milieu pathway represents the effects of social characteristics shared between generations and is the major source of parental influence for political efficacy, political knowledge, and civic tolerance. Socialization research is too concerned with simple comparisons of the amount of parent-child agreement. Greater attention to the nature of specific beliefs and the means of influence is necessary to understand and explain the socialization process.

J

629. Davis, Susan G. OLD-FASHIONED POLISH WEDDINGS IN UTICA, NEW YORK. *New York Folklore 1978 4(1-4): 89-102.* The traditional folk rites surrounding an old-fashioned Polish wedding in Utica, New York, would last for days; describes antecedents of the wedding, the actual ceremony, and the subsequent festivities, 1900-40's.

630. Dillon, Richard. TRAGEDY AT OATMAN FLAT: MASSACRE, CAPTIVITY, MYSTERY. *Am. West 1981 18(2): 46-54, 59.* The Roys Oatman family of nine, a Mormon splinter sect of converts, headed for a promised land in the Southwest. Gold fever changed their goal to California. In February 1851, in southwestern Arizona, Yavapai Indians massacred the family. A son survived and escaped. Two daughters, taken captive, were later sold to the Mohave. One died of starvation. The other, Olive, was bought from captivity five years later and may have left at least two half-blood children behind. Reunited with her brother who died a few years later, Olive lectured. Eventually she married. Many aspects of the Roys Oatman family, once shrouded in contradiction and mystery, are being corrected. 6 illus., map, biblio.   D. L. Smith

631. Dowdall, Jean A. WOMEN'S ATTITUDES TOWARD EMPLOYMENT AND FAMILY ROLES. *Sociol. Analysis 1974 35(4): 251-262.* "Greeley has argued that not enough is known about American ethnic group differences but that such differences exist primarily in the 'common core of assumptions' about familial role expectations. A measure of women's attitudes toward questions of female employment and family responsibilities is taken as an index of such expectations. Using a sample of 673 white, native born, married Rhode Island women, nationality, religious affiliation and social class are explored in relation to attitudes. Significant nationality-linked differences in attitudes were found. Religion was not significantly associated with attitudes, but among Catholic respondents there were significant differences associated with nationality. Taking social class into consideration, nationality group differences in attitudes were significant only among non-high school graduates and among those from non-white collar families. As Greeley predicted, there is considerable nationality-linked attitudinal variation among working class women; the reasons for it require further research."   J

632. Dwork, Deborah. THE CHILD MODEL (OR THE MODEL CHILD?) OF THE LATE NINETEENTH CENTURY IN URBAN AMERICA. *Clio Medica [Netherlands] 1977 12(2-3): 111-130.* Physicians, novelists, educators, and moralists in the late 19th century wrote extensively about child-raising. Julius Uffelman's *Manual of the Domestic Hygiene of the Child* (1881) expressed the consensus view in banning rich foods, alcohol, and prescribing active games for children. Louisa May Alcott in her novels echoed the sentiments of the day in censuring the corset and recommending household chores for girls. Elizabeth Grimmell in *How John and I Brought up the Child* (1894) gave the standard advice by linking moral development with healthy growth. 89 notes, biblio.
                      A. J. Papalas

633. Dye, Nancy Schrom. HISTORY OF CHILDBIRTH IN AMERICA. *Signs 1980 6(1): 97-108.* Reviews the following works dealing with the social aspects of childbirth: Richard W. Wertz and Dorothy C. Wertz's *Lying-In* (New York: Free Pr., 1977), Jane Donegan's *Women and Men Midwives: Medicine,*

Morality and Misogyny in Early America (Westport, Conn.: Greenwood Pr., 1978), Catherine Scholten's " 'On the Importance of the Obstetrick Art': Changing Customs of Childbirth in America, 1760-1825," *William and Mary Quarterly* 1977 (see entry 15A:6967), Janet Bogdan's "Care or Cure? Childbirth Practices in Nineteenth-Century America," *Feminist Studies* 1978 4 (see abstract 16A:3554), and Judy Barrett Litoff's *American Midwives, 1860 to the Present* (Westport, Conn.: Greenwood Pr., 1978). Secondary sources; 46 notes.

S. P. Conner

634.   Eberstein, Isaac W. and Frisbie, W. Parker.   DIFFERENCES IN MARITAL STABILITY AMONG MEXICAN AMERICANS, BLACKS AND ANGLOS: 1960 AND 1970.   *Social Problems 1976 23(5): 609-621.* The frequency of marital disruption during 1960-70 is lowest among Mexican Americans, followed by Anglos and finally Negroes.

635.   Elder, Glen H., Jr. and Rockwell, Richard C.   MARITAL TIMING IN WOMEN'S LIFE PATTERNS.   *J. of Family Hist. 1976 1(1): 34-53.* Studies the average age of first marriage for white women born in 1925-29, using data from the 1965 and 1970 National Fertility Surveys. Age at marriage is divided into early (under 19), on time (19-22), and late (23 and after). These groups differ greatly in their socioeconomic background, religion, other background variables, and subsequent life styles and fertility patterns. 7 tables, 10 notes, biblio.

T. W. Smith

636.   Elder, Glen H., Jr.   SCARCITY AND PROSPERITY IN POSTWAR CHILDBEARING: EXPLORATIONS FROM A LIFE COURSE PERSPECTIVE.   *J. of Family Hist. 1981 6(4): 410-433.* Using data from two longitudinal life history studies, examines the baby boom that followed World War II. There is a "fundamental interdependence of social change and the life course." The pattern of childbearing seems to fit Richard A. Easterlin's model of the baby boom that emphasizes the relative size and economic opportunity of successive cohorts. 2 tables, 2 fig., 6 notes, biblio.

T. W. Smith

637.   Engerman, Stanley L.   BLACK FERTILITY AND FAMILY STRUCTURE IN THE UNITED STATES, 1880-1940.   *J. of Family Hist. 1977 2(2): 117-138.* Black fertility trends over the century since emancipation are another example of the demographic revolution, dropping from an agrarian high to an urban low. The experience of American blacks differed in significant ways from other modernizing populations. For example, a large-scale decline in mortality did not precede the fertility decline; and the decline occurred while most blacks were still agricultural workers in rural areas. Also discounts the "heritage of slavery" explanation for the instability of the black family observed in the 1960's. 6 tables, 3 figs., 48 notes., biblio.

T. W. Smith

638.   Ericksen, Eugene P.; Ericksen, Julia A.; and Hostetler, John A.   THE CULTIVATION OF THE SOIL AS A MORAL DIRECTIVE: POPULATION GROWTH, FAMILY TIES, AND THE MAINTENANCE OF COMMUNITY AMONG THE OLD ORDER AMISH.   *Rural Sociol. 1980 45(1): 49-68.* Examines the Old Order Amish ideals of family farming, the value of parenting and kinship ties, the use of the *Ordnung* (the set of rules for governing Amish life), and the success of those ideals in spite of environmental changes and external pressures on the Amish in Lancaster County, Pennsylvania; 1757-1979.

639. Faragher, John Mack. "MEN AND WOMEN'S WORK ON THE OVERLAND TRAIL" FROM *FAMILIES ON THE OVERLAND TRAIL.* *Pacific Hist. 1979 23(1): 4-23.* Graphic account of the everyday tasks of pioneers in getting ready to make the trek westward (raising the money, soapmaking, selecting and mending clothing, making out diets, getting the necessary food-stuffs, and packing) as well as necessary work while on the trail (droving, getting ready for the night, cooking, and grazing). All work and responsibilities were apportioned in strict adherence to the traditional sexual division of labor, with the work of women structured around the men's. When men became sick, women often filled their places. Covers 1840's-50's. Based on many published primary accounts of people involved in wagon trains; 110 notes. H. M. Parker, Jr.

640. Fengler, Alfred P. and Wood, Vivian. CONTINUITY BETWEEN THE GENERATIONS: DIFFERENTIAL INFLUENCE OF MOTHERS AND FATHERS. *Youth and Soc. 1973 4(3): 359-372.* Discusses sex role influences on student attitudes. S

641. Fischer, Claude S. THE DISPERSION OF KINSHIP TIES IN MOD-ERN SOCIETY: CONTEMPORARY DATA AND HISTORICAL SPECU-LATION. *J. of Family Hist. 1982 7(4): 353-378.* Describes the contacts and interactions between nonresident kin. Most contacts are between immediate kin (e.g., parents or children) while little active involvement occurs between more distant kin (e.g., uncles and nephews, cousins). These contacts often occur over long distances. Attempts to work backward from this modern pattern of kinship to establish the probable pattern in the past. Based on data from a 1977 survey of kinship networks; 3 tables, 29 notes, biblio., appendix. T. W. Smith

642. Fisher, Berenice M. THE WISE OLD MEN AND THE NEW WOMEN: CHRISTOPHER LASCH BESEIGED. *Hist. of Educ. Q. 1979 19(1): 125-141.* Review article of Christopher Lasch's *Haven in a Heartless World: The Family Besieged* (New York: Basic Books, 1977), a sweeping feminist attack on the book's concepts and on Lasch's previous essays and books. Lasch argues capitalism is attacking and destroying the authority of the family through subtle social science techniques. Suggests Lasch's analyses of women intellectuals and women's roles in the family are biased. L. C. Smith

643. Flora, Cornelia Butler. RURAL WOMEN. *J. of NAL Assoc. 1977 2(2): 16-21.* "This paper will now examine the historical and literary roots that give us insights into rural women, reveal the kind of work they do and how this has shifted over time, take a look at marriage, childbearing, and childrearing of rural women, and finally analyze rural women's life styles and what implications there are for the future of rural America."

644. Folbre, Nancy. PATRIARCHY IN COLONIAL NEW ENGLAND. *Rev. of Radical Pol. Econ. 1980 12(2): 4-13.* Data from New England, 1619-1776, show a significant relationship between control over women and control over children. Although colonial women played a part in production they had no real power within the household. Table, 7 notes, biblio. D. R. Stevenson

645. Forsyth, Louise H. THE RADICAL TRANSFORMATION OF THE MOTHER-DAUGHTER RELATIONSHIP IN SOME CANADIAN WRIT-ERS. *Frontiers 1981 6(1-2): 44-49.* Since the 1950's, women writers have pro-

duced works in which the mother-figure, an important image in Quebec society, and mother-daughter relationships do not conform to traditional stereotypes; in the 1970's, other women writers succeeded in going beyond that separation to new women's affirmation and solidarity; without continuity from mother-to-daughter, women remain detached from their origins and fragmented in their being.

646. Foster, Lawrence. POLYGAMY AND THE FRONTIER: MORMON WOMEN IN EARLY UTAH. *Utah Hist. Q. 1982 50(3): 268-289.* Studies the impact of polygamy on women, using the example of Franklin D. Richards, who took 10 wives. Typically, the women adapted themselves to individual tasks and the men treated their wives in an equal manner. Women were given divorce and voting rights and became active in social and community affairs. Polygamy is seen as unifying the Mormon community, and Mormons believed the way to heaven would be easier because families worked together for spiritual and economic success. 2 photos, 42 notes. K. E. Gilmont

647. Furstenberg, Frank F., Jr.; Hershberg, Theodore; and Modell, John. THE ORIGINS OF THE FEMALE-HEADED BLACK FAMILY: THE IMPACT OF THE URBAN EXPERIENCE. *J. of Interdisciplinary Hist. 1975 6(2): 211-233.* Much of the speculation about the origins of the matrifocal black family in the 19th century has been lacking in specific historical data. The female-headed family emerged not so much as a legacy of slavery as a result of the destructive conditions of northern urban life. The matrifocal black family is the product of economic discrimination, poverty, and disease. 12 tables, 22 notes. R. Howell

648. Gallagher, Bernard J., III. AN EMPIRICAL ANALYSIS OF ATTITUDE DIFFERENCES BETWEEN THREE KIN-RELATED GENERATIONS. *Youth & Soc. 1974 5(3): 327-349.* Examines the attitude differences between Philadelphia college students and older members of their families in order to study intergenerational attitudes and family organizational change. S

649. Gallman, James M. DETERMINANTS OF AGE AT MARRIAGE IN COLONIAL PERQUIMANS COUNTY, NORTH CAROLINA. *William and Mary Q. 1982 39(1): 176-191.* Discusses various factors determining age of marriage in this northeastern North Carolina county. Most of the settlers had come from Virginia. Scarcity of land and low mortality of parents contributed to high marriage ages. With parents surviving, sons were more willing to leave their families and set up on their own. Discusses age at first marriage, male marriage ages compared to father's deaths, marriage ages elsewhere, time span between father's death and son's marriage, and times males waited to marry after owning land. Uses local records; 5 tables, 29 notes. H. M. Ward

650. Gannett, Michael R., ed. TWELVE LETTERS FROM ALTOONA, JUNE-JULY, 1863. *Pennsylvania Hist. 1980 47(1): 39-56.* Enoch and Charlotte Lewis of Altoona, Pennsylvania, sent their children to Philadelphia during Robert E. Lee's invasion of Pennsylvania in 1863. Twelve of their letters to Enoch's mother and sister are reprinted. Enoch Lewis was General Superintendent of the Pennsylvania Railroad in Altoona. 3 photos, 25 notes. D. C. Swift

651. Gilbert, Susan. CHILDREN OF THE SEVENTIES: THE AMERI-CAN FAMILY IN RECENT FICTION. *Soundings 1980 63(2): 199-213.* Critically examines the theme of the failure of the nuclear family to protect family members in modern society and how the family is implicated in the isolation of its members from contemporary human community, in John Cheever's *Falconer,* Wallace Stegner's *The Spectator Bird,* Joan Didion's *A Book of Common Prayer,* and John Irving's *The World According to Garp,* all written in the 1970's.

652. Goldman, Judy Lael. *A MOVEABLE FEAST:* THE ART OF A KNISH MAKER. *Western Folklore 1981 40(1): 11-18.* Describes a woman who has married into a Jewish family and is initiated into the art of making knishes by her mother-in-law. Draws parallels between the making of knishes and the act of artistic creation, both relying on innovation within a tradition. Based on personal experience.   J. Powell

653. Gordon, Linda. VOLUNTARY MOTHERHOOD: THE BEGIN-NINGS OF FEMINIST BIRTH CONTROL IDEAS IN THE UNITED STATES. *Feminist Studies 1973 1(3/4): 5-22.* Discusses the motives and aims of the three feminist groups—the suffragists, the moral reformers, and the Free Love movement—advocating birth control during the 1870's-80's. The groups failed to challenge traditional sex roles while motherhood "remained almost exclusively a tool for women to strengthen their positions within conventional marriages and families. . . ."   T. Simmerman

654. Gougler, Richard C. THE AMISH WEDDING. *Pennsylvania Folklife 1981 30(4): 14-16.* Amish sociability within the group manifests itself in practical events, such as barn raisings, sales, and weddings; of these, the wedding is the most important event in the life of the Amish, for a young couple embarking on marriage represents the passing on of customs and traditions from one generation to another.

655. Graham, Andrea. "LET'S EAT!" COMMITMENT AND COMMUN-ION IN COOPERATIVE HOUSEHOLDS. *Western Folklore 1981 40(1): 55-63.* The author and 10 other individuals of diverse backgrounds and varied experiences assembled to form a single household. The conscious effort of these people was to create common patterns of behavior in order to function as a unit. Part of the success of such an enterprise, on whatever scale, must be attributed to the fact that, in order to establish behavioral similarities, the participants must recognize individuality, stress novelty, and celebrate diversity; discontinuity and dissolution of the household may occur when the delicate balance between sharing and self-interest is upset. Based mainly on personal experience; 2 notes.
                                                     J. Powell

656. Grant, Mary H. DOMESTIC EXPERIENCE AND FEMINIST THE-ORY: THE CASE OF JULIA WARD HOWE. Kelley, Mary, ed. *Woman's Being, Woman's Place: Female Identity and Vocation in American History* (Boston: G. K. Hall, 1979): 220-232. Presents a paradox between Julia Ward Howe's unhappy marriage and her glorification of woman's role within the home. Despite her marital experiences with a husband who refused to allow her the married woman's traditional domestic prerogatives, and who withheld even affection and companionship, Howe emerged a champion of domesticity. For Howe, marriage,

especially motherhood, was more significant as a vehicle than as an end in itself. Through motherhood women were responsible for the moral and mental development of their children, who would comprise the nation's future. Thus her feminism looked beyond the home as much as within. Her fame and achievement as a public figure were greatest once she was widowed. With motherhood as the key to her feminism, Howe pursued a variety of reforms for women, not the least of which was to demand that society allow women to assume their unique and critical role in spheres within and without the home. Based on the Julia Ward Howe Collection in the Library of Congress; 47 notes.   J. Powell

657. Grigg, Susan. TOWARD A THEORY OF REMARRIAGE: A CASE STUDY OF NEWBURYPORT AT THE BEGINNING OF THE NINE-TEENTH CENTURY. *J. of Interdisciplinary Hist. 1977 8(2): 183-220.* Studies remarriage in Newburyport in the early 19th century and explains why some people remarried. The data are compared with similar studies of European and North American communities. Remarriage was inversely related to age and less likely for women than for men of the same age. The effects of wealth and children on remarriage are also studied. There were variations in desire, need, and opportunity, which affected the likelihood of remarriage, and such variations can be measured in economic terms. Printed sources; 12 tables, 49 notes   R. Howell

658. Haines, David; Rutherford, Dorothy; and Thomas, Patrick. FAMILY AND COMMUNITY AMONG VIETNAMESE REFUGEES. *Int. Migration Rev. 1981 15(1-2): 310-319.* Focuses on the maintenance, extent, and structure of family and community ties among Vietnamese refugees in northern Virginia; the family, in particular, extends well beyond the boundaries of the household and furnishes emotional and practical support.

659. Haines, Michael R. FERTILITY AND MARRIAGE IN A NINE-TEENTH-CENTURY INDUSTRIAL CITY: PHILADELPHIA, 1850-1880. *J. of Econ. Hist. 1980 40(1): 151-158.* This paper examines age-specific and differential fertility, both marital and total, and nuptiality for census samples of white Philadelphia families headed by native white Americans, Germans, and Irish for 1850-80. Using Philadelphia Social History Project data, own-children techniques are employed to construct age-standardized child-woman ratios and age-specific total and marital fertility rates. Conclusions are that the low fertility among native whites was due to both low marital fertility and later marriage; that rapid declines in marital fertility occurred among second generation migrants; and that variations existed in marital fertility across occupational groupings within ethnic groups.   J

660. Hankerson, Henry E. CHILDREN IN CRISIS IN THE UNITED STATES: CHILD ABUSE AND NEGLECT—A CONTINUING PROBLEM. *J. of Negro Educ. 1979 48(3): 396-407.* Provides a brief history of child abuse from Biblical times, defines child abuse, and reports on the current status of the problem. Cases of child abuse and neglect are estimated at over one million per year in the United States. The typically abusive parent has been characterized as below 30 years of age, with a family income of less than $6,000 per year, residing in the Midwest, having a high school diploma, and belonging to a minority religion or race. However, the more affluent inflict psychological harm, which may be more damaging than physical harm. Children under 4 years of age

constitute 62% of abused children. Boys are abused more than girls. There are four broad categories of public policy comprising the child welfare system: criminal law, juvenile court acts, child abuse reporting laws, and legislatively established protective services. Primary sources; 43 notes.   J. Powell

661.   Hareven, Tamara K.   FAMILY TIME AND HISTORICAL TIME. *Daedalus 1977 106(2): 57-70.* The family did not "break down" under the impact of industrialization and urbanization, but rather it contributed to both processes. Families aided in adapting their members to industrial work and to living in large urban settings. It is inaccurate to hold that the timing of family transitions was once more orderly than it is now. In fact, families are now less subject to sudden change. Some of the major problems facing the contemporary family arise from the demands placed on it by those who require that it be a haven and retreat from the outside world, which it has never been. Secondary sources; 27 notes.
                                                                        E. McCarthy

662.   Harper, Jared V.   MARRIAGE AS AN ADAPTIVE STRATEGY AMONG IRISH TRAVELERS IN SOUTH CAROLINA.   *Southern Studies 1981 20(2): 174-184.* The "Irish Travelers" or "Tinkers," an itinerant people who move on annual circuits doing odd jobs and returning to the same campsites each year form an identifiable ethnic minority in the South. They came to America just prior to the Civil War and have maintained a unique lifestyle. That is now changing under the influence of radio, television, schools, and the Catholic Church. Sexual roles especially are changing as women assume greater importance. Traditional marriage arrangements are changing as parents marry their daughters off at ever earlier ages and frequently to first cousins in an attempt to ensure the cultural, social, and economic integrity of their special lifestyle. 11 notes.
                                                                        J. J. Buschen

663.   Hartley, William.   "IN ORDER TO BE IN FASHION I AM CALLED ON A MISSION": WILFORD WOODRUFF'S PARTING LETTER TO EMMA AS HE JOINS THE "UNDERGROUND."   *Brigham Young U. Studies 1974 15(1): 110-112.* In the 1880's as the federal government began enforcing a new antipolygamy law, many Mormons, fearing arrest and conviction for "unlawful cohabitation," fled into exile or the Mormon "underground." This article reprints and describes a letter written in 1885 by Wilford Woodruff, at the time President of the Council of Twelve and Church Historian, to one of his wives, Emma Smith Woodruff, while he was in exile. Most of the letter concerns information about the family's economic affairs, his advice on how to deal with federal officers, his pride in his children's activities, and other personal matters.
                                                                        M. S. Legan

664.   Heller, Peter L. and Quesada, Gustavo M.   RURAL FAMILISM: AN INTERREGIONAL ANALYSIS.   *Rural Sociol. 1977 42(2): 220-240.* The central problem of this study is to test the hypothesis that at least two types of rural familism exist within different geographic regions of the United States. *Extended kin-oriented* familism in which secondary kin relationships for the basis of an individual's emotional and physical support, was expected to be found in the American Southeast. *Primary kin-oriented* familism, emphasizing the nuclear family as an exclusive unit, was predicted to constitute the basic form of family organization in the Far West. Six specific hypotheses were derived from the

general hypothesis. Each research hypothesis was supported by probability and strength of association measures. It is suggested that regional controls be used extensively in future rural family research.   J

665. Hess, Beth B. STEREOTYPES OF THE AGED. *J. of Communication 1974 24(4): 76-85.* Discusses misleading popular stereotypes of aged people created by the mass media and advertisements in the 1960's and 70's, emphasizing questions in family roles and problems of an overly youth-oriented culture.

666. Hilliard, Addie Suggs. ON SWALLOWING PUNKIN SEED. *Tennessee Folklore Soc. Bull. 1974 40(4): 119-121.* Discusses superstitions and folklore surrounding pregnancy and childbirth in Chester County, Tennessee.   S

667. Hirata, Lucie Cheng. FREE, INDENTURED, ENSLAVED: CHINESE PROSTITUTES IN NINETEENTH-CENTURY AMERICA. *Signs 1979 5(1): 3-29.* When Chinese prostitution developed in 19th-century America, it provided a double economic benefit. Cheap labor in California was guaranteed, while economic benefits were transmitted to China. Families of the laborers in China were supported, and the problem of an over-abundance of nonproductive women was remedied. The Chinese patriarchal system supported prostitution because daughters had no choice except to submit. In America, conditions ranged from concubinage to ruthless slavery. A period of competition during 1849-54 was followed by the creation of a rigorous and corrupt trade network, which lasted until 1925, although prostitution had begun to decline by 1880. Based on California and US census records and secondary sources; 4 tables, 126 notes.
                                                                                                            S. P. Conner

668. Honig, Alice Sterling and Mayne, Gary. BLACK FATHERING IN THREE SOCIAL CLASS GROUPS. *Ethnic Groups 1982 4(4): 229-238.* Examines reports from black fathers from lower-lower, upper-lower, and middle-class groups on their parental interactions with preschoolers. Black fathers' stimulation and provision of enriching experiences are strongly related to socioeconomic group membership. Middle-class fathers are particularly responsive to their children's developmental needs. Based on interviews.   J/S

669. Hoover, Dwight W. HOME AND FAMILY. *Indiana Social Studies Q. 1980 33(2): 7-18.* Individualism, a "central value to Americans," has "not permitted the type of close family intimacy so dear to the hearts of commentators on the American scene but which exists more rarely in reality"; focuses on the autobiographies of Benjamin Franklin, Ralph Waldo Emerson, and Malcolm X.

670. Hunter, Edna J. COMBAT CASUALTIES WHO REMAIN AT HOME. *Military Rev. 1980 60(1): 28-36.* Discusses the experiences of families of US prisoners of war (POW's) and missing in action (MIA's) of the Vietnam War. The author, only looking at families that remained intact after reunion, finds that the wives and children who coped best were those in which the wife asserted independence and control of the family while the husband was gone. The POW families that remained intact after the return of the husband were better able to handle problems in the future, but the MIA families often live in unresolved grief that will continue as long as the MIA's are not found or returned. Based on personal study; 2 photos, 3 notes.
                                                                                                            D. H. Cline

671.   Illick, Joseph E.   CHILD-REARING IN SEVENTEENTH-CENTURY
ENGLAND AND AMERICA.   deMause, Lloyd, ed. *The History of Childhood*
(New York: Psychohistory Pr., 1974): 303-350. During the 17th century life
expectancy dropped in Great Britain, and the birth rate declined, due in part to
contraception. The 17th century witnessed new methods of child-rearing, based
on the small, nuclear family, and designed to instill a strong sense of personal
responsibility in the growing child. The patriarchal family of the early 17th
century was superseded by one based on contractual relations. In both England
and America an increasing child mortality rate and a nuclear family whose
relationships were increasingly contractual suggest that parents showed greater
interest in children yet found the means to cope with frequent death through
aloofness or religion. Mainly secondary sources; 137 notes.   J. Powell

672.   Ironmonger, Elizabeth and Oxreider, Julia, ed.   AN 1890'S KITCHEN.
Tennessee Folklore Soc. Bull. 1979 45(4): 166-169. Briefly traces the background
of Elizabeth Hogg Ironmonger, born in York County, Virginia, in 1891, and
reprints an article written by Mrs. Ironmonger about the kitchen in her childhood
home.

673.   Jenkins, William D.   HOUSEWIFERY AND MOTHERHOOD: THE
QUESTION OF ROLE CHANGE IN THE PROGRESSIVE ERA.   Kelley,
Mary, ed. *Woman's Being, Woman's Place: Female Identity and Vocation in
American History* (Boston: G. K. Hall, 1979): 142-153. The emergence of home
economics as a formal discipline not only developed from the Progressive movement generally during 1900-20 but also was promoted by already acknowledged
trends within Progressivism as varied as the child study movement, John Dewey's
"New Education," the settlement house movement, and vocationalism. The introduction of home economics into secondary and collegiate curricula along with
the appearance of professional associations and journals gave added recognition
to the supposed science of domesticity and elevated it to the status of a discipline.
It meant that traditional values concerning woman's role and place were reinforced. Progressivism supported home economics and thus indicated that woman's primary social functions were a wife and mother. Mainly secondary sources;
39 notes.   J. Powell

674.   Johnson, Anna.   ROUGH WAS THE ROAD THEY JOURNEYED.
Palimpsest 1977 58(3): 66-83. Excerpts from Anna Dockal Johnson's account of
Czech family life in Pocahontas, Iowa, during the first two decades of the 20th
century. 10 photos.   D. W. Johnson

675.   Johnson, Michael P.   PLANTERS AND PATRIARCHY: CHARLES-
TON, 1800-1860.   *J. of Southern Hist. 1980 46(1): 45-72.* The planter's strong
patriarchal system required subordination of women, despite the frequent necessity of marrying a well-to-do wife, and the integration of slaves into the patriarchal family. The paternal inheritance induced the sons to adopt a lackadaisical
attitude toward work, but also required them to augment the diminished (because
divided) estate they in fact inherited. Moreover, the sons were trained in the
school of subordination, but expected to exert dominance later as the unquestioned head of a family. Based on manuscript and printed primary and secondary
sources; 2 tables, 70 notes.   T. D. Schoonover

676. Johnson, Michael P. SMOTHERED SLAVE INFANTS: WERE SLAVE MOTHERS AT FAULT? *J. of Southern Hist. 1981 47(4): 493-520.* A consideration of the high rate of infant mortality among slave infants in the antebellum South. Census takers attributed the deaths to accidental smothering by the mother. More reasonable causes are the overreporting of Negro deaths, combined with the underreporting of white smothering deaths, infant death syndrome, failure to diagnose infections and other infant diseases, and overwork of the slave mothers prior to, and immediately after, the births of their children. The latter factor may have been the most important. 6 tables, 6 fig., 66 notes.
V. L. Human

677. Kantrow, Louise. PHILADELPHIA GENTRY: FERTILITY AND FAMILY LIMITATION AMONG AN AMERICAN ARISTOCRACY. *Population Studies [Great Britain] 1980 34(1): 21-30.* Analyzes fertility trends and family limitation practices among a group of wealthy Philadelphia families from the mid-18th century until the Civil War, and compares the results with European social elites.

678. Kelley, Mary. A WOMAN ALONE: CATHARINE MARIA SEDGWICK'S SPINSTERHOOD IN NINETEENTH-CENTURY AMERICA. *New England Q. 1978 51(2): 209-225.* Catharine Maria Sedgwick (1789-1867) glorified the family and reinforced the belief that women could achieve their greatest fulfillment within the family and make their greatest contribution to society by inculcating values in the family. However, she never married and always sprinkled her works with statements affirming the legitimacy of the unmarried woman's status. Observing the unsatisfactory marriages of friends and relatives she rejected several suitors. Her brothers served as surrogate husbands and their children as her surrogate children. Together they provided her the psychological benefits of a family without the attendant responsibilities. Based on Sedgwick's papers in the Massachusetts Historical Society; 61 notes.
J. C. Bradford

679. Kerber, Linda. THE REPUBLICAN MOTHER: WOMEN AND THE ENLIGHTENMENT—AN AMERICAN PERSPECTIVE. *Am. Q. 1976 28(2): 187-205.* Western political theory even during the Enlightenment only occasionally contemplated the role of women in the civic culture, and then primarily in domestic relationships as wives and mothers. The Republican mother was devised as a means by which domesticity and politics were to be integrated. Republican Mothers devoted their efforts to service in raising sons and disciplining husbands to be virtuous citizens of the republic. Primary based on contemporary Enlightenment works of political theory.
N. Lederer

680. Kessler, Carol Farley and Rudenstein, Gail. MOTHERS AND DAUGHTERS IN LITERATURE: A PRELIMINARY BIBLIOGRAPHY. *Women's Studies 1979 6: 223-234.* The preliminary bibliography catalogues works dealing with mother-daughter relationships written in the 19th and 20th centuries by women authors. The bibliography centers on American literature, although relevant British works and English translations are included. The books are listed generically: autobiographies/biographies, drama, fiction, poetry, and interdisciplinary background such as books by anthropologists, historians, psychologists, and sociologists. Poetry and drama include only 20th century publica-

tions. Books by black, Native American, Chicana, Hispanic, Oriental, and Third World women are underrepresented. S. P. Forgus

681. Keyes, Jane. MARRIAGE PATTERNS AMONG EARLY QUAK-ERS. *Nova Scotia Hist. [Canada] 1978 8(4): 299-307.* Economic factors persuaded Quakers from Nantucket, Massachusetts, to settle in Dartmouth, Nova Scotia, in 1786; Friends meetings continued until 1789 when most of the settlers returned to Nantucket. Examination of the Minutes of the Dartmouth Friends Meetings for Business revealed that only four marriages of the 10 recorded were between members of the Society of Friends following prescribed procedures. Two were between two members of the Meeting but were not sanctioned, and four were between a member and a non-member. Based on Minutes of the Dartmouth Friends Meetings for Business; table. H. M. Evans

682. Keyssar, Alexander. WIDOWHOOD IN EIGHTEENTH-CENTURY MASSACHUSETTS: A PROBLEM IN THE HISTORY OF THE FAMILY. *Perspectives in Am. Hist. 1974 8: 83-119.* An analysis of 60 Woburn, Massachusetts, couples during 1701-10 challenges traditional views on widowhood in colonial Massachusetts. Colonial women married relatively late in life, usually only once, and for long periods of time. Widowhood was terminated by death more often than by remarriage, therefore widows could rely on society to fulfill its obligation to care for them if left destitute. 89 notes. W. A. Wiegand

683. Kikumura, Akemi and Kitano, Harry H. L. INTERRACIAL MARRIAGE: A PICTURE OF THE JAPANESE AMERICANS. *J. of Social Issues 1973 29(2): 67-82.* "The most outstanding fact about Japanese American marriage patterns prior to the 1960's was that Japanese tended to marry predominately within their own group. However, a review of past studies and an analysis of current rates of intermarriage indicate that this pattern is rapidly changing. Outgroup rates approaching 50 percent for Japanese American marriages occur in areas as diverse as Hawaii, Los Angeles, Fresno, and San Francisco. The varying rates and patterns of Japanese outmarriages are discussed." J

684. Kitagawa, Evelyn M. NEW LIFE-STYLES: MARRIAGE PATTERNS, LIVING ARRANGEMENTS, AND FERTILITY OUTSIDE OF MARRIAGE. *Ann. of the Am. Acad. of Pol. and Social Sci. 1981 (453): 1-27.* In the 1970's, the postponement of marriage by many young adults and the escalating divorce rates resulted in a large increase in the proportion of one-person households. Sharp increases in the proportion of illegitimate births—in combination with rising rates of separation and divorce—brought substantial increases in the proportion of children living in one-parent families. The total fertility rate, which had declined by 50% from 1960 to 1975, leveled off after 1975. Illegitimate birthrates, which had almost quadrupled between 1940 and 1970, decreased during the 1970's; however, the proportion of illegitimate births continued to increase. These changes are not interpreted as evidence that Americans are moving away from their basic orientation to marriage and a family existence. J/S

685. Klemmack, David L. and Edwards, John N. WOMEN'S ACQUISITION OF STEREOTYPED OCCUPATIONAL ASPIRATIONS. *Sociol. and Social Res. 1973 57(4): 510-525.* "Assuming that type of work desired by women

is increasingly problematic, a multivariate model is developed to account for the degree to which women select stereotypically feminine work roles. The model indicates that the degree of feminity of occupational aspirations is an indirect function of family background. Marriage and family plans serve a critical mediational function in determining the type of occupation desired."
                                                                                    J

686. Knowles, Sally. THE COLONIAL KITCHEN. *Daughters of the Am. Revolution Mag. 1979 113(9): 1006-1009.* Describes the importance of kitchens in colonial times; kitchen fireplaces were the centers of a family decisionmaking and social and cultural life; describes kitchen utensils.

687. Ktorides, Irene. MARRIAGE CUSTOMS IN COLONIAL NEW EN-GLAND. *Hist. J. of Western Massachusetts 1973 2(2): 5-21.* Discusses courting and marriage customs and behavior, including matrimonial advertising, courting sticks, bundling, contracts, banns, dowries, punishment for unchaste behavior, disorderly marriages, shift marriages, and wedding ceremonies. Based on secondary sources; 3 illus., 35 notes.
                                                                        S. S. Sprague

688. Kunz, Phillip R. ONE WIFE OR SEVERAL? A COMPARATIVE STUDY OF LATE NINETEENTH-CENTURY MARRIAGE IN UTAH. Alexander, Thomas G., ed. *The Mormon People: Their Character and Traditions* (Provo, Utah: Brigham Young U. Pr., 1980): 53-73. Popular images of plural marriage both inside and outside the Mormons are grossly in error. The picture which emerges from this survey of the literature and use of statistical data is of an institution which many of the Latter-Day Saints resisted, which was practiced by perhaps 10% of the men, and was entered principally by the best-educated and most able. It did not produce a larger number of children for Mormon society. Both husbands and wives seem to have been less satisfied with polygamy than with monogamy. There was little to recommend the system, other than religious conviction. It produced little or no economic advantage, happiness, or ease. Secondary sources; 7 tables, 45 notes.
                                                                        J. Powell

689. Kyriazis, Natalie. A PARITY-SPECIFIC ANALYSIS OF COM-PLETED FERTILITY IN CANADA. *Can. Rev. of Sociol. and Anthrop. [Canada] 1982 19(1): 29-43.* Studies the role of the income of husbands, wives' ages at marriage, education, places of residence, and birth cohorts in determining fertility. Examines Catholics and Protestants separately. Based on the 1971 census; note, biblio.
                                                                                    S

690. Ladner, Joyce A. MIXED FAMILIES: WHITE PARENTS AND BLACK CHILDREN. *Society 1977 14(6): 70-78.* Discusses black children, generally from adoption or foster home agencies, who are placed in white households; discusses common problems of social readjustment within the family, life-style conflicts, and differing value systems.

691. Lampe, Philip E. TOWARDS AMALGAMATION: INTERETHNIC DATING AMONG BLACKS, MEXICAN AMERICANS AND ANGLOS. *Ethnic Groups 1981 3(2): 97-109.* Ethnically homogenous marriages are favored in the United States. Mate selection is relatively open, however, and is usually accomplished through the dating process. There are some indications that interethnic dating has been on the increase in the United States. College students from the three major ethnic groups, black, Mexican American and Anglo, were

surveyed to determine the extent of such dating. The majority of the 251 students had engaged in interethnic dating with males being significantly more active than females and Mexican Americans than whites or Negroes. Those whose friends had dated interethnically were themselves more likely to have done so. Age was not a significant consideration.   J/S

692.   Lancelle, Mark and Rodefeld, Richard D.   THE INFLUENCE OF SO-CIAL ORIGINS ON THE ABILITY TO ATTAIN OWNERSHIP OF LARGE FARMS.   *Rural Sociol. 1980 45(3): 381-395.* Examines the work force of large, incorporated farms in the 1970's in an attempt to reveal relationships between familial socioeconomic status, familial support, education, and farm ownership status as primary determinants of attaining ownership of select Wisconsin farms.

693.   Lane, Patricia G.   BIRTH, MARRIAGE, AND DEATH: PAST AND PRESENT CUSTOMS IN EAST TENNESSEE.   *Tennessee Folklore Soc. Bull. 1982 48(2): 53-60.* Discusses the changes in beliefs and rituals regarding birth, marriage, and death, concluding that some elements of the old traditions survive in current practices.

694.   Lantz, Herman and Hendrix, Lewellyn.   BLACK FERTILITY AND THE BLACK FAMILY IN THE NINETEENTH CENTURY: A RE-EXAMI-NATION OF THE PAST.   *J. of Family Hist. 1978 3(3): 251-261.* Post-Civil War black families in the United States were not as matriarchal as previously believed, and most black families shared the achievement aspirations of whites. The net result was a conscious attempt by Negroes, like whites, to restrict their fertility in order to enhance intra- and intergenerational opportunities. 3 tables, biblio.   T. W. Smith

695.   LaSorte, Michael A.   NINETEENTH CENTURY FAMILY PLAN-NING PRACTICES.   *J. of Psychohist. 1976 4(2): 163-183.* The decline in the birthrate which began in the early 1800's in the United States is attributable to an increased knowledge and use of contraceptive devices and techniques. Contraception was used more frequently by native-born Protestants than by other groups. Discusses abortion, condoms, coitus interruptus, and coitus reservatus, vaginal extraction and barriers, and the rhythm method. Based on medical publications, marriage manuals, and other primary sources; 102 notes.
                                                                    R. E. Butchart

696.   Lee, Eun Sul and Roberts, Robert E.   ETHNIC FERTILITY DIFFER-ENTIALS IN THE SOUTHWEST: THE CASE OF MEXICAN AMERI-CANS REEXAMINED.   *Sociol. and Social Res. 1981 65(2):   194-210.* Socioeconomic factors exert different effects on fertility in different ethnic groups and ethnic fertility differentials vary at different stages of child progression. Based on 1970 census data.   J/S

697.   Lerner, Gerda.   MOTHERHOOD IN HISTORICAL PERSPECTIVE. *J. of Family Hist. 1978 3(3): 297-301.* Review article prompted by Adrienne Rich's *Of Woman Born: Motherhood as Experience and Institution* and Linda Gordon's *Woman's Body, Woman's Right: A Social History of Birth Control in America.* These are valuable contributions to the field of feminist studies. Although only Gordon's book is a full scholarly research monograph, both books

are found to offer significant insight into the traditional fertility role of women and the politics of sexual control. Gordon is found to have a Marxist-feminist perspective while Rich offers a radical-feminist viewpoint.   T. W. Smith

698. Levy, Barry. "TENDER PLANTS": QUAKER FARMERS AND CHILDREN IN THE DELAWARE VALLEY, 1681-1735. *J. of Family Hist. 1978 3(2): 116-135.* Examines the place of children in Quaker theology and their position in Quaker families on Pennsylvania farms in the late 17th century. Studies family organization through demographic analysis of the social, economic, and familial structure of society, and through the socializational and interactional analysis of family relationships. 7 tables, 5 notes, biblio.
T. W. Smith

699. Lewis, Diane K. THE BLACK FAMILY: SOCIALIZATION AND SEX ROLES. *Phylon 1975 36(3): 221-337.* Explores, synthesizes, and reinterprets the existing literature on sex role socialization in black families. Covers three areas: 1) the extent to which socialization patterns express a distinctive Afro-American culture, 2) whether Afro-American and Euro-American child rearing practices offer significantly contrasting bases for differentiating behavior, and 3) the role of cultural processes and macrostructural constraints in defining adult sex roles in black life. 74 notes.   R. V. Ritter

700. Lewis, Jan. DOMESTIC TRANQUILLITY AND THE MANAGEMENT OF EMOTION AMONG THE GENTRY OF PRE-REVOLUTIONARY VIRGINIA. *William and Mary Q. 1982 39(1): 135-149.* Relationships in the families of the gentry lacked emotional intensity. Peace and moderation provided a context whereby emotion might be displayed. Parents and children alike had material obligations. Evaluates such experiences as love, marriage, childbearing, and child-rearing, death, and interfamily affection. The gentry kept an intimate distance from those whom they loved, practicing restraint through manners, geniality, and self-assurance. Emotions were managed. The goal was tranquillity. Uses contemporary correspondence; 47 notes.   H. M. Ward

701. Littlefield, Daniel C. PLANTATIONS, PATERNALISM, AND PROFITABILITY: FACTORS AFFECTING AFRICAN DEMOGRAPHY IN THE OLD BRITISH EMPIRE. *J. of Southern Hist. 1981 47(2): 167-182.* The search for an explanation of why slaves reproduced themselves amply in North America (where slavery was assumed to be harsh) while they did not do so in the West Indies and Latin America has attracted much attention recently. The different characters of plantations produced different treatment and a different sex balance between men and women. North American plantations adopted an ethos which balanced men and women better and hence brought about greater reproduction. Covers data from ca. 1721-1803 about South Carolina. Based on holdings in Scotland and England and printed primary sources; 48 notes.
T. D. Schoonover

702. Lockwood, Rose A. BIRTH, ILLNESS AND DEATH IN 18TH-CENTURY NEW ENGLAND. *J. of Social Hist. 1978 12(1): 111-128.* The diary of Ebenezer Parkman (1703-82), minister of Westborough, Mass., provides the opportunity to reconstruct the social history of medicine in a New England village. The qualitative impressions of Parkman on illness and death, his discus-

sion of the treatment of disease, and the details of the birth of the Parkman children, illustrate the impact of diseases and death on 18th-century New Englanders. What emerged was a pattern of social interdependence. Residents confronted childbirth, illness, and death as a social group. Includes an appendix of the reproductive history of the Parkman family. Based on *The Diary of Ebenezer Parkman, 1703-1782,* ed., Francis G. Walett (Worcester, Ma., 1974), 3 vols., and secondary sources; 70 notes.   R. S. Sliwoski

703.   Lueptow, Lloyd B.   PARENTAL STATUS AND INFLUENCE AND THE ACHIEVEMENT ORIENTATIONS OF HIGH SCHOOL SENIORS. *Sociol. of Educ. 1975 48(1): 91-110.* "Suggests the importance of family interaction processes in achievement orientations and questions the validity of treating motive, value, and aspiration as discrete aspects of an achievement syndrome."
S

704.   Maguire, Robert E.   LES PEUPLES: LES CRÉOLES NOIRS   [The people: the black Creoles]. *Vie Française [Canada] 1980 34(7-9): 21-24.* Describes briefly the life and culture of a contemporary black Creole family in Louisiana, and compares it to Haitian and other Antilles families that have descended from French plantation slaves.

705.   Mathieu, Jacques; Cyr, Céline; Dinel, Guy; Pozzo, Jeannine; and St-Pierre, Jacques.   LES ALLIANCES MATRIMONIALES EXOGAMES DANS LE GOUVERNEMENT DE QUÉBEC 1700-1760   [Exogamous marriages in Quebec, 1700-60]. *Rev. d'Hist. de l'Amérique Française [Canada] 1981 35(1): 3-32.* Quantitative study of marriages in five Quebec parishes. In two out of five marriages, one partner came from outside the parish, generally involving a rural man marrying a parish woman. The effects of epidemics on the pool of partners and the desire for land explain this exogamy. Quebec parish registers; 4 tables, 37 notes, appendix.   R. Aldrich

706.   May, Dean L.   PEOPLE ON THE MORMON FRONTIER: KANAB'S FAMILIES OF 1874.   *J. of Family Hist. 1976 1(2): 169-192.* Kanab, Utah, a small agricultural community along the Mormon frontier, had a more normal sex-age distribution than was typical for frontier towns but shared with other frontier towns a high rate of population turnover. Discusses how to handle polygamous families and their complex household organization and the distribution of property among members in the Kanab United Order, a communal experiment initiated by Brigham Young. 6 graphs, 2 tables, 17 notes, appendix with ideographs of all 81 families.   T. W. Smith

707.   May, Elaine Tyler.   SEX IN UTOPIA: A REVIEW ESSAY.   *New York Hist. 1981 62(4): 462-467.* Lawrence Foster's *Religion and Sexuality: Three American Communal Experiments of the Nineteenth Century* (1981) and Louis J. Kern's *An Ordered Love: Sex Roles in Victorian Utopias—the Shakers, the Mormons, and the Oneida Community* (1981) view the communal experiments in terms of the sexual crisis facing Victorian America. While they vary in their approach and in the details of interpretation, they both agree that Shakers, Mormons, and Oneida perfectionists were concerned about sexual anarchy and sought to control it and they were also determined to alter the status of women in both family and society.   R. N. Lokken

708.   Mayer, Egon.   PROCESSES AND OUTCOMES IN MARRIAGES BE-TWEEN JEWS AND NON-JEWS. *Am. Behavioral Scientist 1980 23(4): 487-518.* Mixed marriages between Jews and non-Jews can best be viewed as the result of normal interpersonal relations, not as a rejection of parents or a desire for assimilation.

709.   McDonald, Gerald W.   PARENTAL POWER PERCEPTIONS IN THE FAMILY: THE INFLUENCE OF ADOLESCENT CHARACTERIS-TICS. *Youth & Soc. 1982 14(1): 3-31.* Using data from questionnaires, mea-sures the effect of sex, age, birth order, and religiosity on adolescent perceptions of parental power.

710.   McFalls, Joseph A., Jr. and Masnick, George S.   BIRTH CONTROL AND THE FERTILITY OF THE U.S. BLACK POPULATION, 1880-1980. *J. of Family Hist. 1981 6(1): 89-106.* The 1880-1980 decline in black fertility was due to several trends: an increase in effective birth control use, a decrease in stable, enduring marriages, and a rise in subfecundity. 5 tables, 7 notes, biblio.
T. W. Smith

711.   McGroarty, Jane.   METAPHORS FOR HOUSE AND HOME. *Cen-terpoint 1980 3(3-4): 181-189.* After distinguishing the house, a physical struc-ture, from the home, both residential structure and "territory where one feels safe," identifies home metaphors reflecting assumptions about women, including: home as reflection of self; as woman's body; as castle; as moral domain; as machine for living; as museum, as theater, as boudoir.

712.   Medicine, Bea.   AMERICAN INDIAN FAMILY: CULTURAL CHANGE AND ADAPTIVE STRATEGIES. *J. of Ethnic Studies 1981 8(4): 13-23.* The unsatisfactory encompassing phrase "the Indian family" blurs a wide variety of unique and viable tribal entities by creating a "monolithic family unit." Family life of Indians in contemporary society is difficult to summarize. We need a native or indigenous definition that will include all the types of extended families and the many interlocking circular forms which they display, each being an outgrowth of some successful adaptive strategy vis-à-vis white society. Secondary writings; biblio.
G. J. Bobango

713.   Miller, Michael V.   VARIATIONS IN MEXICAN AMERICAN FAM-ILY LIFE: A REVIEW SYNTHESIS OF EMPIRICAL RESEARCH. *Aztlán 1978 9: 209-231.* Major errors about the family life of Mexican Americans occur, largely because of uncritically accepted assumptions uniformly applied to Mexi-can Americans. However, social science research has revealed important devia-tions across Mexican American families. Results can be synthesized in the following areas: familism, family roles, ritual kinship relations, and intermarriage. Mexican Americans, because of a bondage to family, are not their own worst enemies: rather, stereotypes are not supported by the facts. Family systems vary considerably, conditioned by many factors. 93 notes.
R. V. Ritter

714.   Monahan, Thomas P.   SOME DIMENSIONS OF INTERRELIGIOUS MARRIAGES IN INDIANA, 1962-67. *Social Forces 1973 52(2): 195-203.* Data were selected from Indiana computer tapes, 1962-67, for detailed analysis of intrafaith as compared to interfaith marriages for four religious groups—Protestant, Catholic, Jewish, Other. The influence of age, previous marital status,

and occupational class was examined, along with other factors such as age difference and type of ceremony. Although the proportion of mixed marriages among non-Protestants was found to be high and increasing somewhat, a comparison of actual with possible random matings disclosed considerable selectivity, with Jewish persons being by far the most endogamous and Catholics the most intermarried of the minority groups.   J

715. Mooney, Kathleen A.   ETHNICITY, ECONOMICS, THE FAMILY CYCLE, AND HOUSEHOLD COMPOSITION.   *Can. Rev. of Sociol. and Anthrop. [Canada] 1979 16(4): 387-403.* Within the theoretical framework of the effects of industrialized society on kinship, compares native Indian and non-Indian household composition for most of British Columbia. In general, Indian household organization and development are shown to reflect greater solidarity in kinship relations, while non-Indian households show greater fragmentation. Though income and family-household developmental variables are demonstrated to have strong relationships to many types of household composition for both Indians and non-Indians, they do not account for the solidarity/fragmentation differences. It is suggested that Indian ethics may play a role.   J

716. Moore, Kristin A. and Waite, Linda J.   MARITAL DISSOLUTION, EARLY MOTHERHOOD AND EARLY MARRIAGE.   *Social Forces 1981 60(1): 20-40.* Among young wives, teenage parenthood did not appear to increase the risk of divorce or separation, whereas teenage marriage significantly raised the probability of disruption. This pattern held among white wives; however, for black wives a first birth before the age of 20 was found to increase instability more than a first marriage before that age. The finding that age at first marriage but not age at first birth is significantly related to the probability of marital dissolution appears robust in the total sample: among subsamples of wives all married at about the same age, the age at which they had their first birth did not influence stability of marriages.   J

717. Morgan, Myfanwy and Golden, Hilda H.   IMMIGRANT FAMILIES IN AN INDUSTRIAL CITY: A STUDY OF HOUSEHOLDS IN HOLYOKE, 1880.   *J. of Family Hist. 1979 4(1): 59-68.* From a sample of the census manuscript for 1880 studies the relationship between ethnicity and 1) household size, 2) household composition, and 3) family type in Holyoke, Massachusetts. Important differences are found among the major ethnic groups (native born whites, Irish, and Canadians). The native born had small household size, but included more non-relatives and non-immediate kin than the immigrant groups. As a result the native households were more frequently extended families than the immigrant households were. 6 tables, 8 notes, biblio.   T. W. Smith

718. Mortimer, Jeylan T.   PATTERNS OF INTERGENERATIONAL OCCUPATIONAL MOVEMENTS: A SMALLEST-SPACE ANALYSIS.   *Am. J. of Sociol. 1974 79(5): 1278-1299.* "Using the smallest-space analysis technique to investigate the relationships between fathers' occupations and male college students' career choices, three dimensions of work were found to be relevant to the interpretation of the space: autonomy, rewards, and functional foci. Further examination of the data indicated a strong pattern of occupational inheritance. When sons did not inherit their fathers' occupations, they still tended to choose work offering their fathers' vocational experiences. These findings support the

hypothesis that distinctive attributes of fathers' occupations are related to values which are transmitted to sons and reflected in their vocational decisions." J

719. Murphy, Cullen. KIDS TODAY. *Wilson Q. 1982 6(4): 61-82.* Discusses the demography of children, economics of raising children, childhood health, employment, and education, television's effects on children's behavior, children's effects on the changing family and other topics.

720. Nazzari, Muriel. THE SIGNIFICANCE OF PRESENT-DAY CHANGES IN THE INSTITUTION OF MARRIAGE. *Rev. of Radical Pol. Econ. 1980 12(2): 63-75.* Present-day changes in marriage, exemplified by the mounting divorce rate and the trend toward egalitarian partnership within marriage, is bringing about the proletarianization of women. This parallels the proletarianization of men when their feudal ties to the lord were dissolved. Women no longer provide feudal services to their lord in return for support; instead, women are working for employers, enlarging the reserve army of unemployed without increasing the population. 79 notes. D. R. Stevenson

721. Palmieri, Patricia A. PATTERNS OF ACHIEVEMENT OF SINGLE ACADEMIC WOMEN AT WELLESLEY COLLEGE, 1880-1920. *Frontiers 1980 5(1): 63-67.* Discusses the personal and professional success and achievements of the 65 single women senior and associate professors at Wellesley College during 1880 and 1920, most of whom were born during the Civil War, came from upper-middle class families, were products of professional fathers and educated mothers, and although single, were supported by their family and women friends, and encouraged to contribute to social reform, unlike the majority of young women who were expected to follow conventional patterns and be dutiful daughters.

722. Pease, William H. and Pease, Jane H. PATERNAL DILEMMAS: EDUCATION, PROPERTY, AND PATRICIAN PERSISTENCE IN JACKSONIAN BOSTON. *New England Q. 1980 53(2): 147-167.* Discusses steps taken by wealthy fathers during an intensely competitive era to prepare their sons for the business world. Most sent their sons to boarding schools (where discipline was strict) and then to Harvard. Fathers usually placed their sons in their first positions and after a time provided them with capital and other assistance in setting up independent businesses. Families also guided children into marriages. Once sons were economically established and married, their fathers could retire. Based on Lee, Lawrence, Appleton, and Amory family correspondence in the Massachusetts Historical Society and secondary sources; 39 notes.

J. C. Bradford

723. Placek, Paul J. DIRECT MAIL AND INFORMATION DIFFUSION: FAMILY PLANNING. *Public Opinion Q. 1974/75 38(4): 548-561.* "The success of family planning programs partially depends upon informal diffusion within the target population. This study examines the effects of direct mailing on knowledge, opinion leadership, and diffusion. Information about local birth control clinics, the pill, the IUD [intrauterine device], and other methods of birth control was sent to a random half of a total sample of 300 welfare mothers. Subsequent interviews showed that the direct mailing improved knowledge and increased diffusion, but had no effect on self-concept as an opinion leader."

J

724. Polzin, Theresita. THE POLISH AMERICAN FAMILY: PART I, THE SOCIOLOGICAL ASPECTS OF THE FAMILIES OF POLISH IMMI- GRANTS TO AMERICA BEFORE WORLD WAR II, AND THEIR DE- SCENDANTS. *Polish Rev. 1976 21(3): 103-122.* Examines families in terms of structure (type, size, ascribed roles, and division of labor), value orientations (social, religious, and cultural), and social control (from other family members, church, and community) in the 20th century. To be continued.

725. Pool, D. I. and Bracher, M. D. ASPECTS OF FAMILY FORMATION IN CANADA. *Can. Rev. of Sociol. and Anthrop. 1974 11(4): 308-323.* "Fertility is declining in Canada. We attempt to account for this change and to suggest policy implications. We review recent Canadian studies fitting them into an adaptation of the Davis-Blake framework. This permits the formulation of hy- potheses at two levels implicit in the framework: 1) social structural (independent variables); 2) proximate ("intermediate" variables). Hypotheses were tested against available data, but a problem remained: does the decline result from deferring or averting of births?"   J

726. Pursell, Carroll W., Jr. TOYS, TECHNOLOGY AND SEX ROLES IN AMERICA, 1920-1940. Trescott, Martha Moore, ed. *Dynamos and Virgins Revisited: Women and Technological Change in History* (Metuchen, N.J.: Scare- crow Pr., 1979): 252-267. Examines the socialization of children into traditional sex roles through the medium of toys. Little girls were consistently educated for the roles of housewife and mother by dolls and toys which simulated various household technologies. Little boys were encouraged to be scientists and engi- neers, among other professions, with chemistry sets, Erector sets, various vehi- cles, and tools. 38 notes.   J. Powell

727. Raczka, Paul. MINIPOKA: CHILDREN OF PLENTY. *Am. Indian Art Mag. 1979 4(3): 62-67, 96.* The concept of "minipoka" among American Indians means that the favorite child of parents or grandparents will be spoiled in childhood and guaranteed high social status upon maturity.

728. Reinier, Jacqueline S. REARING THE REPUBLICAN CHILD: AT- TITUDES AND PRACTICES IN POST-REVOLUTIONARY PHILADEL- PHIA. *William and Mary Q. 1982 39(1): 150-163.* Analyzes the didactic literature pertaining to child-rearing and education of the period. British books were revised to fit the American environment. Also American lesson books extolled heroes of the American Revolution. Benjamin Rush's writings serve as an example of efforts to achieve an adaptation of republican principles to child- rearing. Protestant beliefs played a central role. Authors of children's literature combined associationist psychology with Christian doctrine. Based on educa- tional literature and manuscripts of the period; 42 notes.   H. M. Ward

729. Rice, John G. MARRIAGE BEHAVIOR AND THE PERSISTENCE OF SWEDISH COMMUNITIES IN RURAL MINNESOTA. Hasselmo, Nils, ed. *Perspectives on Swedish Immigration* (Chicago: Swedish Pioneer Hist. Soc. and Duluth: U. of Minnesota, 1978): 136-150. Studies six townships in south central Kandiyoki County from 1870 to 1905 to determine the value of marriage behavior as an index of the persistence of Swedish identity among immigrants and their offspring and concludes that further investigation is warranted regarding the

article's underlying hypothesis that communities whose members stem largely from the same region in the old country exhibit greater stability than would otherwise be the case. 7 fig., 12 notes.   S

730.   Ritchey, P. Neal and Stokes, C. Shannon.   CORRELATES OF CHILD-LESSNESS AND EXPECTATIONS TO REMAIN CHILDLESS: U.S. 1967. *Social Forces 1974 52(3): 349-356.* It is widely agreed that society has strong mores proscribing couples remaining childless. Nonetheless, childlessness varies regularly by a number of sociodemographic factors. Given the virtually universal acceptance of the norm concerning the desirability of children, why does child-lessness vary so widely among social aggregates? First, it may simply be the case that this norm is not as universal as previously thought. Alternatively, if the norm is as widespread as represented, various social structural influences may operate to counter, selectively, the prevailing norms and produce deviance. Data from the 1967 *Survey of Economic Opportunity* for wives still in the childbearing years are used to explore these alternatives. Expectation data, interpreted as indicating the normative position of couples on remaining childless, are contrasted with current rates of childlessness for a number of factors. Comparisons suggest the second alternative and direct future research to include structural considerations.
                                                                                J

731.   Ritchey, P. Neal.   EFFECTS OF MARITAL STATUS ON THE FER-TILITY OF RURAL-URBAN AND URBAN-RURAL MIGRANTS.   *Rural Sociol. 1973 38(1): 26-35.* "Existing knowledge on the relationship between mi-gration and fertility has been based on studies of married women. Furthermore, research has focused on the fertility of rural-urban migrants and has tended to ignore fertility among urban-rural migrants. These two factual gaps have limited the ability to assess the contribution made by the fertility of migrants to either population growth or the urban-rural differential in fertility. This paper reports on data from the 1967 Survey of Economic Opportunity. Determining the inter-vening effects of marital status on the relation between migration and fertility was the study's major objective. Among white, married women 20 to 44 years of age, rural-urban migrants have only slightly higher fertility than that of indigenous urban women, which slightly increases the rate of population growth in urban areas. Urban-rural migrants, on the other hand, have lower fertility than indige-nous rural women and consequently serve to lower the growth rate in rural areas. The relative effect upon the growth rates at place of destination is greater for urban-rural than for rural-urban migrants. When the analysis is not restricted to married women, the impact of migration on both urban and rural fertility is considerably changed. In general, migrants were more likely than indigenous sending and receiving populations to have been ever-married and be married and living with spouse—including being in a sustained first marriage and being remar-ried. Proportionately more migrants and less indigenous women bear children. Therefore, when we examine fertility of all women, irrespective of marital status, the childbearing of rural-urban migrants makes a moderate contribution to in-creasing the population growth rate in urban areas. In rural areas, when women's marital status is ignored, the presence of urban-rural migrants sustains the rate of population growth— partially offsetting the lowering effect of the fertility of the rural indigenous women."
                                                                                J

732. Rogers, Kim Lacy. RELICTS OF THE NEW WORLD: CONDI-
TIONS OF WIDOWHOOD IN SEVENTEENTH-CENTURY NEW EN-
GLAND. Kelley, Mary, ed. *Woman's Being, Woman's Place: Female Identity
and Vocation in American History* (Boston: G. K. Hall, 1979): 26-52. Examines
values and practices associated with widowhood. Intensive analysis of records of
Essex County, Massachusetts, and the Hartford District of Connecticut between
1638 and 1681 reveals that husbands and courts protected the wife but preferred
to lodge eventual control of the estate with male descendants. A widow's actual
control of property was tightly circumscribed, often falling to sons or grandsons
when they came of age. The woman who survived her husband, however, did
receive protection through a process in which inheritances were made conditional
upon the heirs' continued support of the widow. Based mainly on probate records;
5 tables, 10 fig., 29 notes.   J. Powell

733. Rosenzweig, Mark R. THE DEMAND FOR CHILDREN IN FARM
HOUSEHOLDS. *J. of Pol. Econ. 1977 85(1): 123-146.* A multiperiod
household model of fertility behavior applicable to rural-agricultural settings in
which the pecuniary as well as the psychic returns from children are significant
is formulated. Implications regarding the effects of variables associated with the
market for agricultural labor on the demand for farm children, including techni-
cal change, agricultural wage rates, farm value, and nonfarm employment opportunities, derived from the model are tested on U.S. aggregate data covering the
period 1939-60. The empirical results obtained appear to support the theoretical
model and suggest the importance of the reduction in the value of children as
productive assets in agriculture as a factor in the postwar decline in the U.S. farm
birth rate.   J

734. Rothman, Sheila. FAMILY LIFE AS ZERO-SUM GAME. *Dissent
1978 25(4): 392-397.* Discusses the evolution of feminist thought, particularly as
expressed through the National Organization for Women, from an emphasis on
civil rights in 1966 to the struggle for complete women's liberation in 1971, and
the effects of this struggle on family relationships.

735. Rutman, Darrett B. and Rutman, Anita H. "NOW-WIVES AND SONS-
IN-LAW": PARENTAL DEATH IN A SEVENTEENTH-CENTURY VIR-
GINIA COUNTY. Tate, Thad W. and Ammerman, David L., ed. *The
Chesapeake in the Seventeenth Century: Essays on Anglo-American Society*
(Chapel Hill: U. of North Carolina Pr. for the Inst. of Early Am. Hist. and
Culture, 1979): 153-182. Paternal death was frequent in Middlesex County, Virginia. Fathers of half of the sons died before the children reached legal maturity
or married. Kin ties helped to hold the society together: family members frequently settled close to each other so that orphans could be placed in the families
of near relatives. Stability lay with the kin group rather than with transitory
parents. 4 tables, 47 notes, 2 appendixes.   S

736. Ryder, Norman B. THE FUTURE OF AMERICAN FERTILITY.
Social Problems 1979 26(3): 359-370. Describes the postwar baby boom and
assesses the decline in the birthrate during the 1970's as the result of changing
women's roles, loosening family structure, and the rise in cohabitation in place
of conventional marriage.

737. Sabagh, Georges and Lopez, David. RELIGIOSITY AND FERTILITY: THE CASE OF CHICANAS. *Social Forces 1980 59(2): 431-439.* Data from a probability sample of 1,129 Mexican American women married to Chicanos and interviewed in Los Angeles, California, in 1973 were used to analyze the effects of religious norms on the fertility of Catholic women 35-44 years old in the sample. If religiosity is a measure of adherence to the norms of the Catholic Church, then these norms do have a net impact on the fertility of Chicanas reared in the United States but not on the fertility of those brought up in Mexico. Characteristics of the country of upbringing have to be taken into account in any analyses of the effects of religious norms on the reproductive behavior of Catholics.
J/S

738. Salamon, Sonya and Lockhart, Vicki. LAND OWNERSHIP AND THE POSITION OF ELDERLY IN FARM FAMILIES. *Human Organization 1980 39(4): 324-331.* "Presents evidence that the quality of intergenerational relations in the family depends on the handling by the farm elders of those prerogatives accrued from control of land" based on a study of elderly farmers and their families in a German ethnic community in rural Illinois during 1976-77.

739. Salamon, Sonya. SIBLING SOLIDARITY AS AN OPERATING STRATEGY IN ILLINOIS AGRICULTURE. *Rural Sociol. 1982 47(2): 349-368.* Discusses sibling solidarity among Irish-American farm families in the Illinois farming community of Finnegan and the resulting formation of close-knit groups for successful agricultural and family life during the 100 years since the Irish settled in the area; "a dominant kinship interpersonal bond" affects other aspects of life.

740. Scambray, Kenneth. HE CAUGHT IT FOR THIS: FOUR LETTERS BY HENRY BLAKE FULLER. *Am. Literary Realism, 1870-1910 1980 13(2): 266-269.* In the fall of 1875, 18-year-old Henry Blake Fuller, under the name of Harry S. Free, contributed four irreverent letters to a debate on marriage in the young people's column of *The Chicago Tribune*; because of a misleading entry in Fuller's diary and because Fuller preserved two letters in response to "Free" rather than the four *by* him, scholars previously failed to attribute the four "Free" letters to Fuller.

741. Scharf, Lois. MISS HAVISHAM'S REVENGE. *Rev. in Am. Hist. 1981 9(3): 387-391.* Reviews Elaine Tyler May's *Great Expectations: Marriage and Divorce in Post-Victorian America* (1980); 1880-1920.

742. Schlesinger, Benjamin. THE SINGLE WOMAN IN SECOND MARRIAGES. *Social Sci. 1974 49(2): 104-109.* "The topic of remarriage has been neglected in the field of family sociology in North America. With more and more persons deciding to marry again, we need to examine the adjustment problems in these unions. The few available studies have focused on the person who marries for the second time. This paper examines some of the selected findings of a Canadian study which included 28 single women, who married men who had been married previously. Their feelings, attitudes, and problems in this type of union give us direction for further research in this important and growing area of family life."
J

743.   Shammas, Carole.   THE DOMESTIC ENVIRONMENT IN EARLY MODERN ENGLAND AND AMERICA.   *J. of Social Hist. 1980 14(1): 3-24.* A study of changes in household goods and practices in 16th- and 17th-century England and 18th-century Massachusetts, based on three groups of household inventories. The 16th- and 17th-century changes made the home more livable; 18th-century changes provided space and equipment suitable for sociability. The former changes included more and better bedding, linen, brass, and pewter. The latter were characterized by book ownership, tea use, and musical instruments. 4 tables, 43 notes, appendix.   C. M. Hough

744.   Shapiro, Howard M.   PERCEIVED FAMILY STRUCTURE AS AN EXPLANATION OF JEWISH INTELLECTUALITY.   *Sociol. Q. 1977 18(4): 448-463.* This paper focuses on the perceived structure of parent-adolescent relations for its effect on intellectuality in young adulthood. In addition, position in the wider societal structure and integration into a supposed intellectually oriented subculture are considered for their effects on this personality characteristic. The data reported are based on a questionnaire survey of 181 Jewish men age 22-29 residing in metropolitan St. Paul. There is a clear association between the perception structure of parent-child relations and later intellectuality. On the other hand, integration into the Jewish subculture neither leads directly to intellectuality nor is associated with the relationship between perceived family structure, and intellectuality. Position in the wider social structure, however, is important in the development of intellectuality both directly and in terms of its effect on perceived family structure.   J

745.   Shumsky, Neil Larry.   PARENTS, CHILDREN, AND THE SELECTION OF MATES IN COLONIAL VIRGINIA.   *Eighteenth-Cent. Life 1976 2(4): 83-88.* During the 17th and 18th centuries in Virginia, parents fought for a veto over their children's selection of marriage partners, a situation caused largely by the oversupply of men; by the end of the 18th century Virginians viewed marriage as a contract between two consenting individuals. 39 notes.

746.   Singer, David.   LIVING WITH INTERMARRIAGE.   *Commentary 1979 68(1): 48-53.* Discusses the issue of marriage between Jews and Christians in the United States, which was discussed at a national symposium on intermarriage in 1963, and provides data on intermarriage from studies since 1962.

747.   Skerry, Peter.   THE CLASS CONFLICT OVER ABORTION.   *Public Interest 1978 (52): 69-84.* Discusses the abortion dispute as a result of class values rather than religious sentiments. The number of Roman Catholics opposing abortion is only slightly higher than that of Protestants, yet both, particularly in the lower and lower-middle class reject it much more strongly than the professional, upper-middle class. The lower classes defend the child centered nuclear and extended family, while the middle and upper classes defend a set of values based on their experiences and beliefs. 5 tables.   J. Tull

748.   Smallwood, James M.   EMANCIPATION AND THE BLACK FAMILY: A CASE STUDY IN TEXAS.   *Social Sci. Q. 1977 57(4): 849-857.* The slave heritage cannot explain contemporary black family instability. Uses data from rural Texas to challenge the traditional historiography of the black family. The rapid disintegration of some black families after emancipation was only

temporary. By 1870, black and white family statistics are similar. Because whites were favored economically, a higher percentage of black women and children were working. Several forces strengthened the black family during Reconstruction: former slave marriages were legalized, Freedmen's Bureau agents worked as legal and marital counselors, and schools and churches stressed the virtues of a stable family life. Based on 1870 census data from three Texas counties and on secondary sources; 6 tables, 8 notes, biblio.   W. R. Hively

749. Smith, Daniel Blake. AUTONOMY AND AFFECTION: PARENTS AND CHILDREN IN EIGHTEENTH-CENTURY CHESAPEAKE FAMILIES. *Psychohistory Rev. 1977-78 6(2-3): 32-51.* In well-to-do, mainly planter, families of Virginia and Maryland in the 18th century, parents valued their children much higher than in previous epochs and in Europe. Sources indicate that parents took a deeper interest in the physical, mental, and moral development, the personal autonomy, and the self-sufficiency of their children. This resulted in closely knit families with strong filial ties. Based on diverse collections of family papers, diaries, pamphlets and sermons, and secondary works; 86 notes.
J. B. Street

750. Smith, Daniel Scott. FAMILY LIMITATION, SEXUAL CONTROL AND DOMESTIC FEMINISM IN VICTORIAN AMERICA. *Feminist Studies 1973 1(3/4): 40-57.* "Suggests the hypothesis that over the course of the 19th century the average woman experienced a great increase in power and autonomy *within* the family . . ." which is shown by the "important contribution women made to the radical decline in . . . marital fertility."   T. Simmerman

751. Smith, Daniel Scott; Dahlin, Michel; and Friedberger, Mark. THE FAMILY STRUCTURE OF THE OLDER BLACK POPULATION IN THE AMERICAN SOUTH IN 1880 AND 1900. *Sociol. and Social Res. 1979 63(3): 544-565.* This paper explores the relations between southern black and white old people and their adult children. The data derive from samples of persons over age 65 taken from the US manuscript censuses for 1880 and 1900. The families of older blacks and whites were similar in several important ways. Only half of old blacks, however, lived with children compared to nearly seventy percent of whites. Co-residence of adult generations was related to family economic activity and to the provision of welfare to needy kin. Economic factors account for part of the black-white differential and for differentials within the black population. Both black and white families served welfare functions, but welfare in the black family flowed more from older to younger generations.   J

752. Smith, Suzanne. THE CHILDREN'S HOUR. *Am. Heritage 1975 26(4): 42-51.* Childhood photographs of the James A. Drake daughters taken in the 1880's and 1890's depicting family life. 29 illus.   B. J. Paul

753. Somerville, James K. THE SALEM (MASS.) WOMAN IN THE HOME, 1660-1770. *Eighteenth-Cent. Life 1974 1(1): 11-14.* Uses wills to explore the way the position of women in the home changed through generations.
S

754. Staples, Robert. MASCULINITY AND RACE: THE DUAL DILEMMA OF BLACK MEN. *J. of Social Issues 1978 34(1): 169-183.* This article delineates the special status of black men in contemporary society. First,

considering some of the common stereotypes of black men from a historical perspective, alternative explanations are posited to counter prevailing views of the Afro-American male as emasculated, dominated by women, and lacking in positive self-esteem. The socialization process and problems of black youth are examined. Afterwards the special roles of lover, husband, and father are analyzed as black men interpret and carry them out. Finally, black male sexism and the response of black feminism are discussed, as are the problems and prospects for black men in American society.   J

755.   Steckel, Richard H.   THE FERTILITY OF AMERICAN SLAVES. *Res. in Econ. Hist. 1982 7: 239-286.* Analyzes the time trend and regional differential in slave fertility, the role of the family in fertility decisions, and slave and white behavior. Fertility declined with plantation size, possibly because fewer eligible marriage partners were availiable. Relatively higher fertility among slaves employed in tobacco may been related to selective migration out of the crop. These factors largely explain the time trend and regional differential in fertility. Slave and white child-woman ratios are poorly correlated at the county level. Different patterns of selective migration may explain part of this phenomenon. Slaves married earlier than whites, possibly because owners subsidized slave family formation, whereas whites had to acquire sufficient wealth to establish a family.   J/S

756.   Stewart, James B.   PERSPECTIVES ON BLACK FAMILIES FROM CONTEMPORARY SOUL MUSIC: THE CASE OF MILLIE JACKSON. *Phylon 1980 41(1): 57-71.* One black man satisfying the material, sexual, familial and companionship needs of two black women constitutes a social phenomenon known as sharing. In Millie Jackson's songs about the wife, the single woman, and the man they share, subjective insights enrich sociological analyses. 21 notes.
                                                                           N. G. Sapper

757.   Stoloff, Carolyn.   WHO JOINS WOMEN'S LIBERATION?   *Psychiatry 1973 36(3): 325-340.* Responses to questionnaires sent to female graduate students at the University of Michigan in order to determine the differences between members of the women's liberation movement and others who remained out of the movement indicate that there were distinct differences in socioeconomic, religious, intellectual and political background, and the political attitudes of the students' parents. Those who join the movement are most typically from middle- or upper-middle-class urban or suburban families, with a Jewish or "nonformalistically religious" Protestant background, and from homes in which religion was not strongly emphasized. Parents of those who joined the movement are most likely college graduates or employed in professional or intellectual occupations, and they are more politically liberal than parents of the nonjoiners. Most of those in each group reported that they had a close relationship with their mothers, but the participants reported that their mothers were considerably more competitive than mothers of nonparticipants, and somewhat more competitive than their husbands. The women's liberationists tend to be more sexually experienced, and they tended to be participants in the earlier Civil Rights movement and the recent Peace Movement. Subjects in each group, however, subscribed to the women's liberation view of women's rights, roles, and responsibilities. 6 notes, biblio.   M. Kaufman

758. Stone, Michael and Kestenbaum, Clarice.   MATERNAL DEPRIVATION IN CHILDREN OF THE WEALTHY: A PARADOX IN SOCIOECONOMIC VS. PSYCHOLOGICAL CLASS. *Hist. of Childhood Q. 1974 2(1): 79-106.* Examines 17 case histories involving prolonged maternal absence or a strict, aloof mother (maternal deprivation) in wealthy families. Such deprivation led to severe emotional and psychological debilities. The cases were predominantly female, probably a result of lower expectations for female offspring from upper class parents. Recent interpretations of the history of childhood may be flawed by reliance on elite sources: the elite may perpetuate maternal deprivation more than others. Based on case histories and secondary sources; biblio.
R. E. Butchart

759. Straus, Murray. VICTIMS AND AGGRESSORS IN MARITAL VIOLENCE. *Am. Behavioral Scientist 1980 23(5): 681-704.* Analyzes marital violence during the late 1970's and concludes that the incidence rate is about equal for men and women but that female violence is typically less severe and more defensive.

760. Sudarkasa, Niara. AFRICAN AND AFRO-AMERICAN FAMILY STRUCTURE: A COMPARISON. *Black Scholar 1980 11(8): 37-60.* Analyzes African family structure and compares it with the Afro-American family structure evolved since the first slaves arrived in the United States from Africa.

761. Suitor, J. Jill. HUSBANDS' PARTICIPATION IN CHILDBIRTH: A NINETEENTH-CENTURY PHENOMENON. *J. of Family Hist. 1981 6(3): 278-293.* Husbands began to accompany childbirths around 1830 and this continued until hospital births replaced homebirths in the early 20th century. The increase in husband participation is seen as a result of 1) the increase of male doctors, 2) the emergence of companionate marriage, 3) a more child centered culture, and 4) a decrease in family size. 2 tables, 19 notes, biblio., appendix.
T. W. Smith

762. Swadesh, Frances Leon. TOYS AND GAMES. *Palacio 1975 81(1): 31-34.* Describes toys and pastimes typical of Hispanic Americans and Indians in the Southwest, 16th-20th centuries: arriada, pelote, cazuleja, and matanza.

763. Sweet, James A. and Bumpass, Larry L. DIFFERENTIALS IN MARITAL INSTABILITY OF THE BLACK POPULATION: 1970. *Phylon 1974 35(3): 323-331.* Uses statistics derived from the 1970 National Fertility Study and examines the differences in separation and divorce among Negroes compared to that of whites. The differences investigated include: age at first marriage, education at the time of first marriage, status of first pregnancy, wife's religion while growing up, residence while growing up, family status at age 14, and first husband's marital history. Looks at individuals ever-separated or divorced, and those currently in those statuses. Concludes that "the majority of the racial differential in marital instability is not explicable in an additive model involving the variables considered here." Based on primary and secondary sources; 2 tables, 8 notes.
B. A. Glasrud

764. Taveggia, Thomas C. and Thomas, Ellen M. LATCHKEY CHILDREN. *Pacific Sociol. Rev. 1974 17(1): 27-34.* Synthesizes 24 studies comparing children of working and nonworking mothers.
S

765.   Thompson, Arthur N.   THE WIFE OF THE MISSIONARY.   *J. of the Can. Church Hist. Soc. 1973 15(2): 35-44.* A study of the wives of early Anglican missionaries in the Canadian Red River settlement from 1820 to 1840. Born and reared in England, some complained bitterly about their new deprivations. Yet the wives vigorously supported their husbands' work. They bore many children, managed households, taught Sunday school classes, and taught in the missionary boarding schools and cared for the students who lived with them. Although some of the women were hostile to the Indians, most missionary wives treated Indians with warmth and visited them in their homes. In short, the missionaries' wives deserve much credit for their part in maintaining the influence of education and religion in the Red River area. Based on primary and secondary sources; 50 notes.
J. A. Kicklighter

766.   Thomson, Peggy.   WHITE HOUSE CAN BE HAPPY, AS ITS TOYS REVEAL.   *Smithsonian 1973 4(9): 72-78.* Catalogs the toys of presidents' children since the 19th century.   S

767.   Tierney, Kathleen J.   THE BATTERED WOMEN MOVEMENT AND THE CREATION OF THE WIFE BEATING PROBLEM.   *Social Problems 1982 29(3): 207-220.* Wife beating has become the object of media attention and government policy, not because of an increase in its frequency, nor because the public has become more concerned, but because a social movement developed in the 1970's to help battered women.

768.   Tillman, William M., Jr.   PATTERNS IN FAMILY ETHICS IN BAPTIST LIFE.   *Baptist Hist. and Heritage 1982 17(1): 26-35, 53.* Traces changes in family life patterns, particularly the dynamics of Puritan standards of behavior and cultural standards of behavior, and how they have affected family life among Southern Baptists.

769.   Tolnay, Stewart E.; Graham, Stephen N.; and Guest, Avery M.   OWN-CHILD ESTIMATES OF U.S. WHITE FERTILITY, 1886-1899.   *Hist. Methods 1982 15(3): 127-138.* Declining fertility is a basic social fact of American history. The question remains: was the decline a result of a conscious desire or was it the result of such other "external" factors as urbanization and industrialization? By the end of the last century, control was "modern," that is, the result of conscious family limitation.   6 tables, 33 notes.   D. K. Pickens

770.   Troll, Lillian E.   FAMILY LIFE IN MIDDLE AND OLD AGE: THE GENERATION GAP.   *Ann. of the Am. Acad. of Pol. and Social Sci. 1982 (464): 38-46.* Many of the same issues and approaches used to study young children and their young-adult parents can be applied to the parallel study of parent-child relations at the later end of the age continuum, adults and their parents, and people in early old age and their parents. Generation gaps may be of the same order of magnitude, whether this term refers to value differences or to conflicts. Helping and communication patterns can be examined at both age poles, as can attitudes and feelings. The issue of geographic closeness does not usually apply to minor children who reside in the same place as their parents, but is a salient issue in later years.   J/S

771. Trussel, James and Steckel, Richard. THE AGE OF SLAVES AT MENARCHE AND THEIR FIRST BIRTH. *J. of Interdisciplinary Hist. 1978 8(3): 477-505.* Analyzes the degree of intrusion into the sexual behavior of slaves by their owners with particular attention to whether masters manipulated reproductive behavior of female slaves in order to increase their stock for sale or their own use. Reviews the methodology of Robert William Fogel and Stanley L. Engerman *(Time on the Cross,* Boston, 1974) and suggests a more unbiased estimation procedure. The evidence indicates that slave women did not bear children at the earliest possible age; this in turn raises questions about the intentions of the slave owners. 8 tables, 2 graphs, 37 notes, appendix.   R. Howell

772. Uhlenberg, Peter. DEATH AND THE FAMILY. *J. of Family Hist. 1980 5(3): 313-320.* The decline in mortality during the 20th century has had a major impact on the composition and organization of the family. The dramatic increase in the survival probability of children led to stronger emotional bonds between children and parents, orphanhood has almost disappeared, and the empty nest interval has increased greatly. 6 tables, 3 notes, biblio.

T. W. Smith

773. Vanek, Joann. WORK, LEISURE, AND FAMILY ROLES: FARM HOUSEHOLDS IN THE UNITED STATES, 1920-1955. *J. of Family Hist. 1980 5(4): 422-431.* There appears to have been little change in the work and leisure time of farmers and farm wives between the 1920's and the 1950's. In addition, the work and leisure patterns of these two groups were quite similar. Much leisure time was shared, and separate activities were similar. Table, 3 notes, biblio.

T. W. Smith

774. Vann, Richard T. QUAKER FAMILY LIFE. *J. of Interdisciplinary Hist. 1975 5(4): 739-749.* Review article prompted by J. William Frost, *The Quaker Family in Colonial America* (New York, 1973). The work has substantial virtues, but Frost has overlooked the crucial importance of theory precisely in directing attention to what can count as evidence. 11 notes.   R. Howell

775. Veevers, J. E. VOLUNTARILY CHILDLESS WIVES: AN EXPLORATORY STUDY. *Sociol. and Social Res. 1973 57(3): 356-366.* "In-depth unstructured interviews with a non-random sample of 52 voluntarily childless wives suggest that most remain childless through a series of postponements of child-bearing, involving at least four separate stages. Informal sanctioning of childless couples is most intense during the fourth and fifth years of marriage. Factors related to satisfaction with childlessness are discussed in terms of the symbolic importance of adoption and of supportive ideologies."   J

776. Vipond, Mary. YOUTH, THE FAMILY AND SOCIETY. *Can. Rev. of Am. Studies [Canada] 1979 10(3): 363-370.* In the last decade, youths have sued their parents, claiming damages for parental malpractice. Such incidents call attention to three recent studies analyzing the historical and contemporary position of children in American homes and society: *Love and the American Delinquent: The Theory and Practice of "Progressive" Juvenile Justice, 1825-1920* (U. of Chicago Pr., 1977) by Steven L. Schlossman; *The Children's Rights Movement: Overcoming the Oppression of Young People* (Garden City, N.Y.: Anchor Pr./Doubleday, 1977) edited by Beatrice Gross and Ronald Gross; and *The*

Damned and the Beautiful: American Youth in the 1920's (Oxford U. Pr., 1977) by Paula S. Fass. 7 notes.   H. T. Lovin

777.   Walsh, Lorena S.   "TILL DEATH US DO PART": MARRIAGE AND FAMILY IN SEVENTEENTH-CENTURY MARYLAND.   Tate, Thad W. and Ammerman, David L., ed. *The Chesapeake in the Seventeenth Century: Essays on Anglo-American Society* (Chapel Hill: U. of North Carolina Pr. for the Inst. of Early Am. Hist. and Culture, 1979): 126-152. The patriarchal society which characterized New England did not exist in the Chesapeake due to the special demography of the region. A majority of immigrants were young, single men who married late. Most died young. Traditional controls over sexual behavior and marriage were weakened, as was paternal control of the family: fathers died too soon to exert control. Society had the major responsibility of raising children. Table, 75 notes.   S

778.   Walzer, John F.   A PERIOD OF AMBIVALENCE: EIGHTEENTH-CENTURY AMERICAN CHILDHOOD.   deMause, Lloyd, ed. *The History of Childhood* (N.Y.: Psychohistory Pr., 1974): 351-382. In 18th-century America, there were distinct advantages in having many children. Yet, in colonial America, the attitudes of parents toward their children were shaped by the basic ambivalent wishes to retain and to reject their offspring, to hold on to them and to be rid of them. When these contradictory wishes were restrained and balanced, they can be said to have disappeared. When they were not so well-integrated, the results were less happy, resulting in abandonment, infanticide, and abuse. 196 notes.   J. Powell

779.   Waters, John J.   FAMILY, INHERITANCE, AND MIGRATION IN COLONIAL NEW ENGLAND: THE EVIDENCE FROM GUILFORD, CONNECTICUT.   *William and Mary Q. 1982 39(1): 64-86.* In Guilford and East Guilford the families staying in the area (constituting the majority of inhabitants) were those with one or two male heirs or "stem families with a chosen male heir." The minority, with more sons and daughters who could not be accommodated with property, accounted for the migration. The author provides case studies of the Meigs, Cruttenden, Lee, and Blachley families. Consciously, family lines were shaped, with parents influencing marriage through control of land and cattle. Such control determined marriages, landholding, care of the aged, and migration. Uses contemporary records and writings; 2 tables, 3 fig., 61 notes.   H. M. Ward

780.   Watson, Alan D.   WOMEN IN COLONIAL NORTH CAROLINA: OVERLOOKED AND UNDERESTIMATED.   *North Carolina Hist. Rev. 1981 58(1): 1-22.* White women in colonial North Carolina, despite the restrictions imposed by custom and law, operated with more freedom of action than has been recognized. Though married women bore the burdens of raising children and running households, they sometimes gained the opportunity to own or dispose of property, act against abusive husbands, separate from unfortunate marriages, and find extra-marital sexual and psychological satisfaction. Unmarried and widowed women enjoyed greater liberties in areas such as self-employment, education, political protests, sexual activity, and property-holding. Female servants, orphans, and apprentices had fewer liberties. Based on local county records (published and manuscript), and descriptions of contemporary travelers and observers; 6 illus., map, 66 notes.   T. L. Savitt

781. Waxman, Chaim I. THE THREADBARE CANOPY: THE VICISSI-
TUDES OF THE JEWISH FAMILY IN MODERN AMERICAN SOCIETY.
Am. Behavioral Scientist 1980 23(4): 467-486. Explains the concern of American
Jews with the future of the Jewish family by examining the role of the family in
Jewish socialization and by examining data.

782. Weiss, Nancy Pottishman. MOTHER, THE INVENTION OF NECES-
SITY: DR. BENJAMIN SPOCK'S *BABY AND CHILD CARE.* *Am. Q. 1977
29(5): 519-546.* Compares Spock's book *Baby and Child Care* (New York: Pocket
Books, 1976; originally 1946) with Mary Mills West's pamphlet *Infant Care*
(Department of Labor, Children's Bureau, Bureau Publication No. 8, Washington, D.C., G.P.O., 1914, 1921), in light of women's responses to them, as revealed
in letters to the Children's Bureau and to Spock. Views Spock's central tenet of
permissiveness in many behavioral contexts and what it means for mothers. 54
notes.
R. V. Ritter

783. Weiss, Nancy Pottishman. THE MOTHER-CHILD DYAD REVIS-
ITED: PERCEPTIONS OF MOTHERS AND CHILDREN IN THE TWEN-
TIETH CENTURY CHILD-REARING MANUALS. *J. of Soc. Issues 1978
34(2): 29-45.* While devoting substantial efforts to studying the impact of the
mother-child dyad on children's growth, development, and social and intellectual
achievements, researchers under the umbrella of child development (psychologists, pediatricians, educators) have failed to explore the impact of rearing children on mothers' lives. This article examines child-rearing manuals in America
from 1913 to 1976 viewing the literature as mother-rearing tracts which have as
much to say about the lives of women as about the children for whom they are
caring.
J

784. Westbrook, Max. THE CONFIDENCE CHILD. *Texas Q. 1976 19(3):
7-19.* Between 1965 and 1975 parents ceased to believe what they were saying,
but, lacking alternatives, continued to mouth old ideas. Parental control might
survive error, but it could not survive its own loss of conviction. Parents used a
materialistic language for philosophical values. Freedom had been material
wealth, but after World War II Americans saw that material wealth did not equal
the values of freedom or equality. Based on secondary sources.
R. H. Tomlinson

785. Wetherell, Charles. SLAVE KINSHIP: A CASE STUDY OF THE
SOUTH CAROLINA GOOD HOPE PLANTATION, 1835-1856. *J. of Fam-
ily Hist. 1981 6(3): 294-308.* Studies the kinship ties of the slaves on Good Hope
Plantation. He finds an increase in kinship inbeddedness. Secondary as well as
primary ties may have been an important source of support for the average slave.
5 tables, 4 fig., 10 notes, biblio., appendix.
T. W. Smith

786. Wiggins, David K. THE PLAY OF SLAVE CHILDREN IN THE
PLANTATION COMMUNITIES OF THE OLD SOUTH, 1820-1860. *J. of
Sport Hist. 1980 7(2): 21-39.* An analysis of slave narratives and other sources
indicates that through play slave children learned the values and mores of their
parents' world. Some of the games were role-playing which enabled them to talk
about things which disturbed them, like the slave trade. The slaves viewed themselves as a family group, and their amusements demonstrated the strength of the

family. Although the slave children often played with the white children of the master or overseer, a caste system operated so that slave children were forced into a subservient role. Through play, slave children realized a needed sense of community, developed group solidarity and fellowship, and furnished individuals with a sense of security they might not otherwise experience. Based mostly on George Rawick's 19-volume collection from the slave narrative series; 74 notes.

M. Kaufman

787.   Williams, Juanita H.   EQUALITY AND THE FAMILY.   *Int. J. of Women's Studies [Canada] 1980 3(2): 131-142.* Examines the effects and implications of the changes wrought by the new ideals of egalitarianism on the family, focusing on traditional roles in the family, the variables affecting family equality, and "birth struggles of egalitarianism in the family."

788.   Williamson, Nancy E.   SEX PREFERENCES, SEX CONTROL, AND THE STATUS OF WOMEN.   *Signs 1976 1(4): 847-862.* Since the 1930's, sex preference studies in the United States reveal a clear preference for boys, with men preferring boys more strongly than women do. Because three methods of sex control are available in America today, the quality of women's lives and the status of women could be profoundly affected. Women would bear the risk, inconvenience, and psychic costs. Preference studies indicate that first-borns would be male; therefore, females as a group might suffer, because studies of first-borns conclude that they are high achievers. If the population contains fewer women, more societal pressure to marry, have children, and function primarily within the family, could result. Age differences between husbands and wives would increase, thus placing women in a more dependent, less experienced situation. Based on sociological studies; 46 nos.

J. Gammage

789.   Withey, Lynne E.   HOUSEHOLD STRUCTURE IN URBAN AND RURAL AREAS: THE CASE OF RHODE ISLAND, 1774-1800.   *J. of Family Hist. 1978 3(1): 37-50.* Uses state and federal census manuscripts from 1774, 1782, 1790, and 1800 to study the household structure of Rhode Island. Analyzes differences in household structure by community types and finds: 1) household size varied inversely with urbanness, 2) black- and women-headed households were associated with urbanness, 3) mean household size declined as a result of fewer slaves and servants and lower fertility, and 4) the fertility decline was general, but it started in urban areas. 6 tables, 9 notes, biblio.   T. W. Smith

790.   Woehrer, Carol E.   THE INFLUENCE OF ETHNIC FAMILIES ON INTERGENERATIONAL RELATIONSHIPS AND LATER LIFE TRANSITIONS.   *Ann. of the Am. Acad. of Pol. and Social Sci. 1982 (464): 65-78.* Since a great number of older Americans are either immigrants or the children of immigrants, and many others have spent much of their lives in ethnic communities, understanding the elderly in American society requires insight into ethnic values and family patterns. Ethnic family structure and socialization of children are closely related to intergenerational interaction in adulthood. Extended family relationships in turn influence social participation outside the family throughout the life cycle and older people's responses to the later life transitions of retirement, widowhood, and decline in health.   J/S

791. Wyatt, Philip R. JOHN HUMPHREY NOYES AND THE STIR-PICULTURAL EXPERIMENT. *J. of the Hist. of Medicine & Allied Sci. 1976 31(1): 55-66.* The Oneida Community, established by John Humphrey Noyes (1811-86) emphasized the desire for perfection. Noyes developed four unique concepts to achieve this goal. These were male continence, complex marriage, community child care, and the stirpicultural experiment. The success of male continence freed women from unwanted pregnancies, and permitted the practice of complex marriage. To assure that children were as perfect as possible, Noyes developed the policy of stirpiculture, the culture of a new race, produced by carefully controlled selective breeding. During 1869-79, 58 live births occurred in the Oneida community as a result of the experiments in scientific breeding. There was a low infant mortality rate, indicating that the combination of selective breeding and community child care had good results. Noyes demonstrated that the nature of man could be improved by controlling the environment and man's biological inheritance. The children became exceptionally successful later in life. 26 notes.
M. Kaufman

792. Zanger, Jules. ON NOT MAKING IT IN AMERICA. *Am. Studies 1976 17(1): 39-48.* The Jewish mother has become a standard literary stereotype, and a boy turning his back on his mother has symbolized the rejection of a cluster of religious and cultural values. This became a necessary reaction to the Americanization process. American Jewish literature also reveals that behind every Jewish mother is a failed Jewish father. To accept an Americanness, these immigrants frequently had to reject part of their Jewishness. Primary and secondary sources; 6 notes.
J. Andrew

793. Zeitlin, Steven J. "AN ALCHEMY OF MIND": THE FAMILY COURTSHIP STORY. *Western Folklore 1980 39(1): 17-33.* Briefly traces the history of family narratives as a folklore form. Studies of family folklore are split between "genre studies" and "ethnographies of particular families." These approaches can be effectively combined; provides examples of family courtship narratives. Family courtship narratives transmute reality through the use of love at first sight, destiny, and fictional themes. Based on interview tapes in the Archives of Folklife Program, Smithsonian Institution, and on other primary sources; 39 notes.
S. L. Myres

794. —. [BRONSON ALCOTT'S CHILD-REARING PRACTICES]. *Hist. of Childhood Q. 1973 1(1): 4-61.*
Strickland, Charles. A TRANSCENDENTALIST FATHER: THE CHILD-REARING PRACTICES OF BRONSON ALCOTT, *pp. 4-51.* A narrative account of the child-rearing practices of Bronson Alcott, educator and father of Louisa May Alcott. The account highlights Alcott's attempts to appeal to love and conscience rather than to use coercion. His practices, adapted from Romantic and Transcendental views of childhood, resulted in an intensification of family identity and isolation. Based primarily on observations that Alcott made of the first years of his daughters' lives. Primary and secondary sources; 175 notes.
Ebel, Henry. COMMENT, *pp. 52-55.* Puts Strickland's essay into a broader historical context, noting the rapidly changing world-view of Western civilization in the early 19th century, and the compatibility of child-rearing practices such as Alcott's with the changes in ideas concerning hierarchical

order and authority. Emphasizes the particularly manipulative psychic domination which came to replace physical domination in child-rearing.

Despert, J. Louise. COMMENT, *pp. 56-57.* Focuses on Alcott, seeking causes for his activity. Finds significance in his constant flirtation with poverty, family rootlessness, conflict with his wife, repressed childhood experiences, and compulsive drive to achieve.

Walzer, John. COMMENT, *pp. 57-61.* Compares Alcott's notions of childhood and training with similar notions of the previous century. Argues that cruelty and neglect have epitomized parental responses to children in earlier ages; the 18th and 19th centuries mark an advance in humane conceptions of childhood. R. E. Butchart

795. —. CHILD ABUSE AND NEGLECT IN THE AMERICAN SOCIETY. *Center Mag. 1978 11(2): 70-77.* Discussion among 14 specialists on family violence and child abuse; discusses current workshops, shelters, and counseling services available to affected persons.

796. —. [EVOLUTION OF THE DIVORCE RATE IN THE UNITED STATES]. *Population [France] 1980 35(4-5): 975-984.*

Roussel, Louis. À PROPOS DE L'ÉVOLUTION DE LA DIVORTIALITÉ AUX ÉTATS-UNIS: UN ARTICLE DE E. CARLSON [Evolution of the divorce rate in the United States: an article by E. Carlson], *pp. 975-980.* A critical analysis of Elwood D. Carlson's article (see abstract 18A:5472); examines reasons for an important increase of divorces in the United States since 1967 and focuses on the problem of causality in demography.

Carlson, Elwood. LA DIVORTIALITÉ ET L'ÉVOLUTION FONDAMENTALE DU MARIAGE [The divorce rate and the basic evolution of marriage], *pp.981-984.* Comments favorably on the author's article, but criticizes a few points and offers clarification.

797. —. PREMARITAL PREGNANCY IN AMERICA, 1640-1971.

Smith, Daniel Scott and Hindus, Michael S. AN OVERVIEW AND INTERPRETATION. *J. of Interdisciplinary Hist. 1975 5(4): 537-570.* Analyzes sexual behavior and the social mechanisms controlling it, based on the cycles in premarital pregnancy. 28 notes, appendix.

Hair, P. E. H. SOME DOUBTS. *J. of Interdisciplinary Hist. 1977 7(4): 739-744.* Criticizes the conclusions of Hindus and Smith about the inhibiting effects of Puritanism and Victorian morality.

Smith, Daniel Scott and Hindus, Michael S. A REPLY. *J. of Interdisciplinary Hist. 1977 7(4): 744-746.* Urges that doubts are not equivalent to evidence, and that multiple variables must be considered. Printed sources; table, graph, 9 notes. R. Howell

4

INDIVIDUAL FAMILY HISTORIES

798.   Adams, Thomas Boylston.   LINCOLN AND THE CODMANS. *Old-Time New England 1981 71(258): 1-14.* Personal narrative about the Codman family, upperclass members of Lincoln, Massachusetts, society; includes information on social customs; 1890-1920.

799.   Alschuler, Al.   THE COLMANS AND OTHERS OF DEADWOOD, SOUTH DAKOTA.   *Western States Jewish Hist. Q. 1977 9(4): 291-298.* Nathan Colman, a German Jewish immigrant, came to Deadwood, South Dakota, in 1877 and opened a tobacco store. He was appointed postmaster in 1878, elected justice of the peace, and active in local Republican politics. In 1911 Colman's daughter Blanche became the first woman admitted to the South Dakota Bar. For more than 50 years she was a practicing attorney. Other Jews settled in frontier Deadwood in the 1870's and became prominent in businesses and industries. The Jewish community has diminished with the rest of Deadwood's population; Blanche Colman is the only remaining member of the pioneer Jewish community. Based on newspapers, family records and secondary sources; 4 photos, 20 notes.
B. S. Porter

800.   Alsop, James D.   SIR SAMUEL ARGALL'S FAMILY, 1560-1620. *Virginia Mag. of Hist. and Biog. 1982 90(4): 472-484.* A genealogical study of the ancestry of Sir Samuel Argall, an important figure in the 17th-century English colonizing movement and the Virginia Company.   Based on British Public Records, manuscripts in the British Library, biographical and other secondary sources; 78 notes.
D. J. Cimbala

801.   Ames, Marilyn G.   LINCOLN'S STEPBROTHER: JOHN D. JOHNSTON.   *Lincoln Herald 1980 82(1): 302-311.* Discusses Abraham Lincoln's stepbrother, John D. Johnston (1810-ca. 50's), son of Sarah Bush Johnston, Thomas Lincoln's second wife.

802.   Ammidown, Margot.   THE WAGNER FAMILY: PIONEER LIFE ON THE MIAMI RIVER.   *Tequesta 1982 42: 5-37.* The Wagner family, from South Carolina, were pioneers in the Miami area, having constructed the oldest known house standing in Miami today. William and Evaline Wagner met, married, and moved to Miami by 1858. Evaline, of mixed blood, was accepted in the area socially, although the members of the Adam Richard family, her daughter's family, were to be persecuted for their darker complexions. Evaline died in 1888; her husband lived until the advent of the 20th century. Based on census data, personal interviews, and contemporary newspaper accounts.   H. S. Marks

803. Anderson, Harry H.   THE MACARTHURS OF MILWAUKEE. *Milwaukee Hist. 1979 2(2): 38-42.* Provides an overview of the MacArthur family in Milwaukee, Wisconsin, 1849-1951, concentrating on the military achievements of General Douglas MacArthur; text of an address given at the dedication of a statue of General MacArthur, 8 June 1979.

804. Anderson, Irving W.   A CHARBONNEAU FAMILY PORTRAIT: PROFILES OF THE AMERICAN WEST.   *Am. West 1980 17(2): 4-13, 58-64.* The Charbonneau family accompanied the Lewis and Clark expedition on the 5,000-mile trek from Fort Mandan, North Dakota, to Fort Clatsop, Oregon, and return, 1805-06. "Incredibly, persistent contradictions cloud the facts" of their lives and of their roles on the expedition. In separate biographical sketches of Toussaint, French-Canadian fur trader and interpreter, Sacagawea, Shoshoni teenager, and Jean Baptiste, their son of eight weeks at the beginning of the journey, the significant, known facts of their lives dispel some of the romance and myth that have veiled them in mystery and speculation. 5 illus., note, biblio.
D. L. Smith

805. Anderson, James William.   IN SEARCH OF MARY JAMES.   *Psycho-history Rev. 1979 8(1-2): 63-70.* Analyzes the role and importance of William James's mother, Mary, in his life. The mother-child relationship during James's first years of life affected his career and feelings. Examination of evidence suggests that Mary James was unempathic toward William and was anxious as well. She also seemed to have encouraged illness in her family. Finds Mary James to be a much different person than her family thought. Instead of being the embodiment of "divine maternity," she is seen as a complex product of her culture and its behavioral prescriptions. 40 notes.
J. M. Herrick

806. Anderson, James William.   AN INTERVIEW WITH LEON EDEL ON THE JAMES FAMILY.   *Psychohistory Rev. 1979 8(1-2): 15-22.* Leon Edel, a leading scholar of the James family, discusses the role of illness among family members. Analyzes roles of male and female members, the genius of William and Henry, and their rivalry. Edel discusses the fusion of psychology with literary studies, his own career, his notions of what makes a successful psychobiographer, and the relationship of the diachronic and synchronic in good biographical writing. 4 notes.
J. M. Herrick

807. Anderson, Robert C.   A NOTE ON THE GAY-BORDEN FAMILIES IN EARLY NEW ENGLAND.   *New England Hist. and Geneal. Register 1976 130: 35-39.* Traces the relationship between the Borden and Gay families of early Massachusetts and Connecticut. The immigrant John Borden (d. 1635) arrived in New England with his family (a wife and two children) in the summer of 1635. By 1638 his widow, Joanna (d. 1691), had married John Gay (d. 1688). They had 10 children. The author establishes the various locales in which the two Borden children lived. Based on primary and secondary sources; 27 notes.
S. L. Patterson

808. Arguimbau, Ellen and Brennan, John A.   GUIDE TO THE DARLEY FAMILY PAPERS, 1875-1970.   *Western Hist. Collections, U. of Colorado Lib. 1974(Nov.): 1-32.* Consists of correspondence, articles, photographs, books, and manuscripts relating to the Darley family of Colorado.

809.   Arguimbau, Ellen, comp. and Brennan, John A., ed.   GUIDE TO THE THOMAS M. PATTERSON FAMILY PAPERS, 1850-1925.   *Western Hist. Coll. 1977 (March): 1-29.* Guide to the Thomas M. Patterson Family papers contained in the University of Colorado's Western Historical Collection; includes correspondence, diaries, photographs, and scrapbooks pertaining to the family, 1850-1925.

810.   Armour, David A.   DAVID AND ELIZABETH: THE MITCHELL FAMILY OF THE STRAITS OF MACKINAC.   *Michigan Hist. 1980 64(4): 17-29.* David Mitchell, a surgeon's mate in the King's Eighth Regiment stationed at Mackinac Island in 1780 chose to resign his commission and remain there with his Indian wife. He became a farmer, trader and physician. His wife Elizabeth greatly aided his economic endeavors. Mitchell retained his British loyalty and moved from Michilimackinac to Mackinac Island, to St. Joseph Island, back to Mackinac Island, to Drummond Island and then to Penetanguishene on Georgian Bay, always following the Union Jack. Based on the Port Mackinac Papers located in the Judge Joseph H. Steere Special Collection Room of the Bayliss Public Library, Sault Ste. Marie, Michigan and other primary and secondary sources; 21 photos, map.   L. E. Ziewacz

811.   Arnstein, Flora J. and Park, Susan B.   THE GODCHAUX SISTERS. *Western States Jewish Hist. Q. 1982 15(1): 40-47.* The four Godchaux sisters, Adele, Helene, Rebecca, and Josephine, were the daughters of Alsatian Jews who came to the United States in 1840. Adele was the only one who was married (to Sylvain Salomon). All four sisters taught French and music to the children of San Francisco's elite. One of their pupils was Yehudi Menuhin. In the 1920's, appreciative students and their parents raised a fund to send the three single Godchaux sisters and their brother Edmond (who served 33 years as the San Francisco County Recorder) on a trip to France. Based on the authors' recollections and communication from Godchaux family members; 3 photos, 12 notes.
                                                          B. S. Porter

812.   Ashkenazy, Elinor and Ashkenazy, Irvin.   WHEN THE CAMPBELL-JOHNSTONS CAME TO SAN RAFAEL.   *Westways 1975 67(12): 14-16.* Discusses the settlement in California near Pasadena in the 1880's of Alexander Campbell-Johnston and his family.   S

813.   Auman, Dorothy Cole and Zug, Charles G., III.   NINE GENERATIONS OF POTTERS: THE COLE FAMILY.   *Southern Exposure 1977 5(2-3): 166-174.* The Cole family has been involved in pottery manufacture in North Carolina for 200 years. The family's pottery making tradition has been traced back to 18th-century England, and some family members may have made pottery during the early 17th century in Jamestown. For most of the 19th and early 20th centuries, the Coles manufactured simply designed, utilitarian pottery for local and regional use and sale. During the 1920's-30's, a greater variety of designs was introduced along with pottery aimed at tourism, garden use, and artistic forms. Despite some modern innovations, pottery making still retains many ties to traditional modes of manufacture. Based on participant observation.
                                                          N. Lederer

814.   Baas, Jacob C., Jr.   JOHN JAY JACKSON, JR., AND THE JACK-
SONS OF PARKERSBURG: THEIR FIRST ONE HUNDRED YEARS.
West Virginia Hist. 1976 38(1): 23-34. John Jay Jackson, Jr. (1824-1907), was
born into a prominent Scotch-Irish family of western Virginia. His great-grandfather, George Jackson (b. 1757), was a congressman; his grandfather, John George
Jackson (1777-1828), served eight terms in Congress, married Dolly Madison's
sister, and was a strong Jeffersonian. His father, John Jay Jackson (b. 1800), was
illegitimate but served in the Army and became a prosperous Whig businessman,
lawyer and state legislator. John Jay Jackson, Jr., grew up in Parkersburg, was
educated at Princeton, and entered law practice in the 1840's. Primary sources;
38 notes.   J. H. Broussard

815.   Badaracco, Claire M.   SOPHIA PEABODY HAWTHORNE'S CUBA
JOURNAL: VOLUME 3, 31 OCTOBER 1834-15 MARCH 1835.   *Essex Inst.
Hist. Collections 1982 118(4): 280-315.* From the winter of 1833 until the spring
of 1835 Sophia Peabody and her sister Mary Tyler Peabody earned room and
board as governesses to the three children of Dr. Robert and Laurette de Tousard
Morrell at their Cuban sugar plantation, La Reserva. Letters sent from Cuba were
circulated among eminent Bostonians and occasionally discussed at "reading
parties." After the sisters returned to Salem in 1835, the Peabody women assembled the letters into a three-volume manuscript called the "Cuba Journal." This
manuscript was compiled "to demonstrate Sophia's achievments as a female and
her suitability as a wife." Excerpts from the third volume are presented here. The
manuscript is in the Berg Collection at the New York Public Library; 3 illus., 49
notes.   R. S. Sliwoski

816.   Baird, Anne Foster.   THE WOLFSKILLS OF WINTERS.   *Pacific
Hist. 1977 21(4): 351-358.* Biographical account of the Wolfskill family that
settled in the 19th century in California, including brothers: William, John,
Mathus, Sanchel, and Milton. Covers 1838-1900. 2 illus., 30 notes.
                                                                         G. L. Olson

817.   Baker, Donald E., ed.   THE CONINE FAMILY LETTERS, 1849-1851:
EMPLOYED IN HONEST BUSINESS AND DOING THE BEST WE CAN.
Indiana Mag. of Hist. 1973 69(4): 320-365. Twelve letters, most of which were
written to Mrs. Mary Ann Conine Seymour by her father, Derrick Conine, and
her sister Jane in New York and by her sisters Emily and Catharine and her
brother Horace in northern Indiana. The letters are all intimate, unpolished notes
dealing with family affairs and domestic life. They demonstrate considerable
privation, loneliness, and hard labor in converting a wilderness tract into a farm
and home. Concludes that Conines were representative of those who settled in
the Old Northwest during the Forties and Fifties and that their letters are the rare
exception to the rule that one generation's treasures are another's trash. Based
on primary sources; 10 photos, 105 notes.   N. E. Tutorow

818.   Baker, Donald G., ed.   THE CONINE FAMILY LETTERS, 1852-1863:
"JUST THINK HOW WE ARE SCATTERED."   *Indiana Mag. of Hist. 1974
70(2): 122-178.* These letters supplement those written 1849-51 and published in
this journal in December 1973. Attention is given to religion, marriage, births,
struggle to make a living, and death. Based on primary sources; 5 illus., 120 notes.
                                                                         N. E. Tutorow

819.   Baker, Donald F., ed.   THE CONINE FAMILY LETTERS, 1852-1863: "JUST THINK HOW WE ARE SCATTERED." *Indiana Mag. of Hist. 1974 70(2): 122-178.* Continued from a previous article. Publishes a series of letters from various members of the Conine family to Mary Ann Conine Seymour during the years 1852-63. The letters ignore the burning sociopolitical questions of the day, instead being concerned with matters of farm, home, school, and church, and are thus excellent accounts of pioneer life in the midwestern states. Based on letters in the possession of Ruth Seymour Burmester; 2 photos, 120 notes.
V. L. Human

820.   Baldwin, Alice Sharples.   THE SHARPLES. *Alberta Hist. Rev. 1973 21(1): 12-17.* Describes homesteading of horsemen Charles and William Sharples in southern Alberta, 1870's-1902. 2 illus.
D. L. Smith

821.   Baldwin, Hélène L.   "DOWN STREET" IN CUMBERLAND: THE DIARIES OF TWO NINETEENTH-CENTURY LADIES. *Maryland Hist. Mag. 1982 77(3): 222-229.* Analysis of the daily entries of Mrs. William W. McKaig, wife of the mayor of Cumberland, and Miss Mazie Bruce. Both were upper-class women of Cumberland, Maryland, and had assured social positions in the town. The diaries reveal valuable information about the social call—the "basis of social relations in the nineteenth century"—along with church-going, household life and management, the problems of servants, recreation, and the education of children. Both women lived in the characteristic manner of their time, being dependent, protected, and generally submissive, although at times they displayed unexpected reserves of strength. From the untranscribed diaries in the Allegany County Historical Society, and secondary sources; 13 notes.
G. J. Bobango

822.   Ballard, Elsie Miner.   JAMES DICK DAVIS (1810-1880): A GENEA-LOGICAL SKETCH.   *West Tennessee Hist. Soc. Papers 1975 29: 165-167.* Contains an extensive genealogy of James Dick Davis, who was born in Pennsylvania in 1810 and moved to Memphis in 1827. As municipal harbormaster he gained considerable knowledge about the history of his adopted city. He was one of the five men from Shelby County who voted against secession in 1861. During the Civil War he was identified with the federal government. In 1857 he formed the Old Folks of Shelby County—Memphis' first historical society and forerunner to the present West Tennessee Historical Society. In 1873 he wrote *History of the City of Memphis*.
H. M. Parker, Jr.

823.   Barlow, Claude W.   WILLIAM STEEVENS OF KILLINGWORTH, CONN.: A NEW *MAYFLOWER* LINE.   *New England Hist. and Genealogical Register 1975 129(January): 18-22.* Traces one branch of the fourth- and fifth-generation descendants of Governor William Bradford (1589/90-1657) and corrects published errors regarding the marriages of Melatiah Bradford (b. 1664), the granddaughter of Governor Bradford. The clarification involves recounting the history of William Steevens (d. before 3 Sept. 1751) of Killingworth, Connecticut, and his three sons, William (b. 1736), Christopher (1738-87), and Leverett (1742-99?). Primary and secondary sources.
S. L. Patterson

824. Bate, Kerry William. THE ENGLISH ORIGINS OF THE CAM-BRIDGE, MASSACHUSETTS, ERRINGTON FAMILY. *New England Hist. and Genealogical Register 1978 132(Jan): 44-50.* Traces the genealogy of the Errington family to Edward Errington of Denton, Northumberland. Seventh-generation William Errington (1592-1634) married Ann Liddell 16 September 1619 at Newcastle. He probably died before his wife settled in Cambridge with two of their six children, Abraham (1622-77) and Rebecca (1627-90). Abraham married Rebecca Cutler and had nine children. A. Huff

825. Baym, Nina. NATHANIEL HAWTHORNE AND HIS MOTHER: A BIOGRAPHICAL SPECULATION. *Am. Lit. 1982 54(1): 1-27.* Speculates that the novel *The Scarlet Letter* was Nathaniel Hawthorne's response to his mother's death and also his tribute to her memory. Hawthorne preserved his mother's image in the main character Hester, and enough resemblances exist between Hester's life and Elizabeth Hawthorne's life to suggest that the novel's origin lay in the son's deep attachment to his mother's role in life and to her memory after death. 20 notes. T. P. Linkfield

826. Bear, James A., Jr. THE HEMINGS FAMILY OF MONTICELLO. *Virginia Cavalcade 1979 29(2): 78-87.* A history of the Hemings family before, during, and after their enslavement to Thomas Jefferson, 1730's-1830's.

827. Beauchamp, Virginia Walcott. LETTERS AS LITERATURE: THE PRESTONS OF BALTIMORE. *Maryland Hist. Mag. 1982 77(3): 213-221.* The extensive correspondence between Baltimore attorney William P. Preston and his wife Madge Preston during 1847-70 shows the possibilities for serious literary achievement in epistolary form. Among surviving correspondence is a lengthy exchange of letters with their only child, May, who attended St. Joseph's Academy at Emmitsburg, and became "an accomplished artist herself in the epistolary form." The self-portrait revealed in the letters, the concreteness of detail, the self-conscious literary stances of the husband's writing set beside the sheer entertainment value of his wife's style, raise the letters to the class of literature and are invaluable for social history. Based on manuscripts and secondary sources; 24 notes. G. J. Bobango

828. Bedford, Denton R. FIRST THUNDER OF THE ROCKY BOYS. *Indian Historian 1977 10(1): 37-41.* Relates the life story of Mary Rego, a Chippewa-Cree, from her early days on a poverty stricken reservation in the early 20th century to her subsequent successful position as a leader of a large family. The family is reasserting its Indianness and taking a lead in bringing the Chippewa-Cree tribe to a realization of its heritage and future. E. D. Johnson

829. Bennett, Mildred. WHAT HAPPENED TO THE REST OF THE CHARLES CATHER FAMILY? *Nebraska Hist. 1973 54(4): 619-624.* Biographical sketches of Willa Cather's (1873-1947) brothers and sisters, relying heavily upon quotes from their children. All were successful in life, though only Willa Cather had a literary career. R. Lowitt

830. Benton, Robert M. THE JOHN WINTHROPS AND DEVELOPING SCIENTIFIC THOUGHT IN NEW ENGLAND. *Early Am. Literature 1973 7(3): 272-280.* The first-hand observations and second-hand reports in the papers of John Winthrop, Sr. (1588-1649), show him to have had scientific interests. He

was not fully a part of the growing scientific movement of the 17th century, for he did not seem interested in testing or experimentation. John Winthrop, Jr. (1606-96), however, made more significant scientific contributions than any 17th-century New England colonist. In him one sees the beginning of the evolution of scientific thought in New England. Without rejecting the religion of his father, he moved away from the restrictions of Puritanism into the light of free scientific inquiry. A later John Winthrop, the great-grandnephew of John Winthrop, Jr., achieved scientific distinction surpassing that of any in his illustrious family. Second Hollis professor of mathematics and natural philosophy at Harvard in 1738 when he was only 24, Professor John Winthrop (1714-79) represented a culmination of that development in scientific thinking which had begun with John Winthrop, Jr. Based on primary and secondary sources; 9 notes.

D. P. Wharton

831. Bern, Enid, ed. THEY HAD A WONDERFUL TIME: THE HOME-STEADING LETTERS OF ANN AND ETHEL ERICKSON. *North Dakota Hist. 1978 45(4): 4-31.* The Erickson sisters homesteaded in Hettinger County, North Dakota, in 1910 and 1911. Their correspondence with their parents in Iowa reveals the details of daily life on the treeless prairie, including life in a shack, problems with raising poultry, the vagaries of the weather, depredations on garden crops by wandering animals and the self-sufficiency necessitated by being located at the end of the route of supply. Their letters also indicate instances of neighborliness, holiday festivities, dances, socials, etc., and the popularity of single women of marriageable age in a region containing many young bachelors. Based on Erickson family correspondence.

N. Lederer

832. Berry, Carolyn. COMENHA. *Frontiers 1981 6(3): 17-19.* Details the experiences and family life of the Cheyenne woman, Comenha, daughter of Dull Knife, 1860-1900.

833. Berry, Hannah Shwayder. A COLORADO FAMILY HISTORY. *Western States Jewish Hist. Q. 1973 5(3): 158-165.* Chronicles the history of the Isaac and Rachel Shwayder family, from their emigration from Poland in 1865, to their successful business activities in Denver in 1916.

834. Bingham, Afred M. SYBIL'S BONES, A CHRONICLE OF THE THREE HIRAM BINGHAMS. *Hawaiian J. of Hist. 1975 9: 3-36.* Traces the lives of two generations of Binghams. The first Hiram Bingham and his wife Sybil were the models for James Michener's missionary sequence in his novel *Hawaii.* He made free use of the first Hiram Bingham's *A Residence of Twenty-one Years in the Sandwich Islands.* In later years the Binghams returned to New England, and were dismissed by the American Board of Commissioners for Foreign Missions. The second Hiram Bingham spent his missionary years in the Gilbert Islands until ill health forced his return to Hawaii. The third Hiram Bingham, the author's father, was responsible for moving the bones of Sybil, the first Hiram's first wife, into a grave next to her husband.

R. Alvis

835. Boucher, Neil. THE SURETTES OF EEL BROOK AND THEIR DE-SCENDANTS. *Nova Scotia Hist. Q. [Canada] 1979 9(1): 15-24.* Reviews briefly the history of the Surette family in Nova Scotia through the lives of Pierre (1679-1749), the first settler, and his son Pierre 2nd (1709-?). Grandsons of Pierre

2nd settled on Surrette's Island between 1801 and 1804. Descendants of the family are still on the island. Primary and secondary sources; 19 notes, biblio.
H. M. Evans

836. Brennan, Thomas A., Jr. BRENNANS AND BRANNANS IN WASHINGTON'S ARMY AND THE WAR OF 1812.   *Irish Sword [Ireland] 1976 12(49): 310-312.* Information in addition to that in the article by Thomas A. Brennan, Jr., "Brennans and Brannans in American Military and Naval Life" in *The Irish Sword,* 12 (48), pp. 239-246.   H. L. Calkin

837. Brennan, Thomas A., Jr.   BRENNANS AND BRANNANS IN AMERICAN MILITARY AND NAVAL LIFE, 1745-1918.   *Irish Sword [Ireland] 1976 12(48): 239-245.* Provides an account of persons whose surnames were Brennan, Brannan, or similar, who participated in military and naval activities of the American colonies and the United States, 1745-1918. 9 notes.
H. L. Calkin

838.   Brink, Andrew.   THE BRINK FAMILY IN ONTARIO.   *Halve Maen 1982 57(1): 6-9, 13, 17.* Traces the history of the Brink family in Ontario from 1797, when Nicholas Brink (1770-1834) was granted a tract of land in what is now Oxford County, until 1857.

839.   Brodie, Fawn M.   THOMAS JEFFERSON'S UNKNOWN GRANDCHILDREN.   *Am. Heritage 1976 27(6): 28-33, 94-99.* Thomas Jefferson, married only once, had two families. The second family, by his quadroon slave, Sally Hemings, numbered seven children, from a liaison lasting 38 years. Their disappearance and that of their progeny resulted from several factors, including Jefferson's desire that they eventually "escape" into white society. Much information has recently come to light concerning Jefferson's other family. Family lines are traced from each of the children. Based on primary and secondary sources; 2 illus., 36 notes.   J. F. Paul

840.   Bronner, Simon J.   THE DURLAUF FAMILY: THREE GENERATIONS OF STONECARVERS IN SOUTHERN INDIANA.   *Pioneer Am. 1981 13(1): 17-26.* Biographies of Michael Durlauf, Sr., his son Michael F. Durlauf, and grandsons, Harry, Leo, and Otto, master stonecarvers from Jasper, Dubois County, in southern Indiana from 1858 to 1962, with descriptions of some of their tombstones.

841.   Brophy, Frank Cullen.   THE RELUCTANT BANKER.   *J. of Arizona Hist. 1974 15(2): 159-184.* The Brophy family banking enterprise started when the author's Irish-born father, William Henry Brophy, was store manager for a copper mining company commissary in Bisbee in the boom years 1887-1914. The father drowned in 1922 and the author reluctantly took over the banking enterprise and the family sheep and lumber operations, for all of which he was "singularly ignorant" and unprepared. Adopted from a forthcoming book.
D. L. Smith

842.   Brubaker, Landis H.   THE BRUBAKERS AND THEIR LANDS IN EAST HEMPFIELD TOWNSHIP, LANCASTER COUNTY, PENNSYLVANIA.   *Pennsylvania Mennonite Heritage 1982 5(2): 10-29.* Traces the ownership of land by the Brubaker family, a Mennonite family, from 1717 to 1981; some land has remained in the same family for 264 years.

843. Brunk, Ivan W. BRUNK ANCESTORS. *Mennonite Hist. Bull. 1975 36(4): 5-6; 1976 37(3): 5-7.* Part I. Traces the genealogy of the Brunk family which probably goes back to immigrants from the Palatinate area of Europe, but can only be established for certain with Mennonite families in Pennsylvania in the 1750's. Part II. Examines the Brunk family genealogy, 1750-1850, their affiliation with the Mennonite Church, their spread throughout Maryland, Virginia, and Pennsylvania, and their military service.

844. Bryson, William Hamilton. A LETTER FROM LEWIS BURWELL TO JAMES BURROUGH, JULY 8, 1734. *Virginia Mag. of Hist. and Biog. 1973 81(4): 405-414.* A letter from Lewis Burwell (1710-56) to his cousin and former Cambridge tutor, James Burrough, gives information about the Burwells, a prominent Virginia family, and many financial, educational, and social aspects of 18th-century Virginia. Manuscript in Bury St. Edmunds and West Suffolk Record Office; 53 notes.   R. F. Oaks

845. Bueckner, Thomas R., ed. LETTERS FROM A POST SURGEON'S WIFE. *Ann. of Wyoming 1981 53(2): 44-63.* In 1879 Caroline Winne accompanied her surgeon husband, Charles, to his new assignment as post medico at Fort Washakie, Wyoming. Her letters capture both the excitement and mundane nature of life for an army wife. Separated from her childhood surroundings of New York and faced with the realization that only one other officer's wife lived at the post, Mrs. Winne suffered through hard times. Her descriptions of the fort, daily life, health problems, and her unflattering accounts of Indians dominate most of the letters. 5 sketches, 9 photos, 52 notes.   M. L. Tate

846. Burleigh, Anne Husted. THE FAMILY ADAMS. *Modern Age 1981 25(2): 179-188.* Describes the place of the Adams family in US history from the time of the American Revolution until (in 1927) the death of the last Adams to live in the family mansion in Quincy, Massachusetts. Several characteristics marked the Adams family. They pledged themselves to do their duty regardless of outcome to themselves. They were conscious of their roles in history as individuals and as members of a family. They sought recognition rather than fame, and they feared the effects of democracy on the nation they had helped bring into being. 19 notes.   R. D. Rahmes

847. Burrison, John A. CLAY CLANS: GEORGIA'S POTTERY DYNASTIES. *Family Heritage 1979 2(3): 70-77.* Georgia pottery communities developed along the Piedmont Plateau in the early 19th century, involving entire families who have carefully guarded secrets and intermarried to maintain family lines, as exemplified by the Ferguson and Hewell families.

848. Bushman, Claudia. THE WILSON FAMILY IN DELAWARE AND INDIANA. *Delaware Hist. 1982 20(1): 27-49.* Describes the experiences of the Wilson and Corbit families of Odessa, Delaware, as they developed their holdings in farming, tanning, and trade and their subsequent move west to Richmond, Indiana, in the early 19th century. Concludes that the move westward was also a move downward in economic terms and that eastern family members helped to sustain western ones through the first generation, but that over time family bonds weakened and even broke. 122 notes.   R. M. Miller

849.   Camden, Thomas E.   THE LANGDON-ELWYN FAMILY PAPERS. *Hist. New Hampshire 1981 36(4): 350-356.* The Langdon-Elwyn Family Papers, on deposit with the New Hampshire Historical Society since 1979, span the years 1762-1972. Much of the collection deals with the career of John Langdon, who played a major role in the revolutionary history of New Hampshire and the nation. Among other offices, he served as governor of New Hampshire and US senator. He was also a merchant-shipbuilder in Portsmouth.   3 notes.

D. F. Chard

850.   Campbell, Janet and Campbell, David G.   THE MACINTOSH FAMILY AMONG THE CHEROKEES.   *J. of Cherokee Studies 1980 5(1): 4-16.* Indian accounts of Carolina and Georgia record McIntosh as Cherokee agents during the colonial era. Ensign Lacklan McIntosh represented Georgia in the Provincial Congress, later served with Washington, led the Savannah campaign, and served as a delegate to the Continental Congress. William McIntosh also appears as Indian agent and chief of Creek Indians. Captain John McIntosh, his son, served as Creek and Cherokee leader during the War of 1812 with Jackson in the Seminole Campaign. Around the War of 1812 John McIntosh was a leader who helped negotiate the Treaty of Echota (1835) and later led Confederate Cherokees in the Civil War. In 1897 John G. McIntosh was elected last chief justice of the Cherokee Supreme Court and his son John Ross McIntosh was a Cherokee Council Cooweescoowee District Speaker. From a series of articles in *Chronicles of Oklahoma;* 3 photos, 23 notes.   K. E. Gilmont

851.   Campbell, Joan Bourque.   THE BOURQUE FAMILY OF STE. ANNE DU RUISSEAU, YARMOUTH COUNTY NOVA SCOTIA.   *Nova Scotia Hist. Q. [Canada] 1980 10(3-4): 255-271.* Traces the genealogy of the Bourque family through nine generations since 1636, when Antoine Bourg (b. 1609) arrived in Acadie. The family included artisans, woodsmen, carpenters, teachers, and nurses. Primary sources, including archives and census records.

H. M. Evans

852.   Campbell, Randolph B. and Pickens, Donald K.   "MY DEAR HUSBAND": A TEXAS SLAVE'S LOVE LETTER, 1862.   *J. of Negro Hist. 1980 65(4): 361-364.* Slave woman Fannie wrote a love letter to her bondsman husband, Norfleet, who was taken off the plantation to serve as a personal servant to his owner in the Confederate Army. This voice from slavery provides a momentary insight into the human, existential, and individual dimension of slavery.

A. G. Belles

853.   Capozzola, Barbara.   HIS CHILDREN'S CHILDREN.   *Italian Americana 1978 4(2): 203-214.* Describes three generations of the Derrico family, immigrants to the United States in 1904 from Naples, Italy; shows the changing traditions, attitudes, and values of each generation as a result of assimilation and acculturation.

854.   Carlisle, Lilian Baker.   HUMANITIES' NEEDS DESERVE OUR FORTUNE: MARY MARTHA FLETCHER AND FLETCHER FAMILY BENEVOLENCES.   *Vermont Hist. 1982 50(3): 133-142.* In 1871, Thaddeus Fletcher of Burlington, Vermont, left at least $370,000 to his widow, who died five years later leaving the estate to Mary, their only surviving daughter, a recluse

dying of consumption. Fletcher had prospered as a Chittenden County merchant and real estate dealer. Just before he died, Fletcher gave $10,000 each to the Home for Destitute Children and to the Essex Classical Institute. In 1873, Mary and her mother gave the city $24,000 for books and a library, the Fletcher Free Library. In 1876, Mary designated $185,000 to build and endow a Burlington hospital and nursing school. It was the largest gift to a Vermont public institution up to then. Mary Fletcher's will left $186,000 more in 1885 to the hospital, which was named after her. Based on newspapers and public records; 36 notes.

T. D. S. Bassett

855.   Carlsson, Sten and Nordstrom, Byron J., transl.   JOHN HANSON'S SWEDISH BACKGROUND. *Swedish Pioneer Hist. Q. 1978 29(1): 9-20.* A genealogical study based on work in 1876 by George A. Hanson, a Maryland lawyer. John Hanson was one of Maryland's two great forefathers and a political activist during the American Revolution. He was President of Congress in Philadelphia in 1781-82. He was born in either 1715 or 1721 and died in 1783. In 1903 a statue was erected over his grave in Statuary Hall in the Capitol in Washington, D.C. Concludes that George Hanson established a clear set of traditions which do include genealogical links with Sweden. Photo, chart, 46 notes.

C. W. Ohrvall

856.   Carson, Christopher Seberian.   THE OLIVER FAMILY IN PEACE AND WAR, 1632-1860. *New England Hist. and Genealogical Register 1976 130(July): 196-205.* Surveys the Oliver family of Massachusetts, beginning with the arrival of Thomas Oliver (1582-1657) and his wife, Anne (d. 1637), in Boston in 1632, and concluding with a summary of the restructured lives of the children and grandchildren of Andrew (1706-74) and Peter Oliver (1713-91) and Thomas Hutchinson (1711-80), their brother-in-law. The family's prominence in Massachusetts was lost when Hutchinson, the royal governor, and Andrew, the Lt. governor, chose to support King George III and Parliament during the American Revolution. Some family members chose exile, others remained but their influence was severely diminished. Their descendants left politics and turned to colonizing, law, medicine, and history. Based on secondary sources; 2 charts, 7 notes.

S. L. Patterson

857.   Carter, Joseph C.   MONUMENTS AND MYSTERIES. *Daughters of the Am. Revolution Mag. 1977 111(5): 454-457.* Discusses the burial plots, gravestones, and epitaphs thereon engraved of several members of the Allen Family of Vermont, associated with state, colonial, and Revolutionary War history, 1770-1834.

858.   Casper, Trudie.   THE BLOCHMAN SAGA IN SAN DIEGO. *J. of San Diego Hist. 1977 23(1): 64-79.* Gives a history of the family of Abraham Blochman, 1848-1959, with highlights of his promotion of bicycles for both leisure and sport.

859.   Cawthon, John Ardis.   FREDERICK MILLER, THE FIRST WHITE MAN BURIED IN CLAIBORNE PARISH AND HIS DESCENDANTS. *North Louisiana Hist. Assoc. J. 1975 7(1): 27-30.* In 1820, the more prosperous colonizers of the old Murrell Settlement, some 12 miles northeast of Minden near the Claiborne-Webster line, took into their homes a group of impoverished Ger-

man immigrants—Frederick Miller; his son, Frederick, Jr.; and his daughter, Maria, among them. John Murrell was the benefactor of the Miller family. Frederick Miller lived only two more years, dying in 1822. He was buried in Murrell's graveyard. While there is no known record of the name of the wife of Frederick Miller, Jr., it is known that she had at least eight children. Maria Miller married Judge Robert Lee Kilgore, and their descendants all have been through their daughters; none of the Kilgore boys married. "As late as the middle of the 20th century, several fourth-generation descendants of Frederick Miller were still living within a 25-mile radius of the old Murrell settlement sites." 20 notes.

A. N. Garland

860. Chaput, Donald. THE FAMILY OF DROUET DE RICHERVILLE: MERCHANTS, SOLDIERS, AND CHIEFS OF INDIANA. *Indiana Mag. of Hist. 1978 74(2): 103-116.* From the 1720's, when several members of the Drouet de Richerville family entered the fur trade, until the death of Jean-Baptiste Richardville in 1841, the Drouets were one of the most significant families of officers-traders in the western Great Lakes region.

861. Chaput, Donald. THE PICOTÉ DE BELESTRE FAMILY. *Louisiana Hist. 1980 21(1): 67-76.* Traces the history of a family, described as both middle class and of the lesser nobility, through five generations in the New World. The progenitor of this clan, Pierre Picoté de Belestre (1637-79), a French military officer and merchant, immigrated to Canada in 1659. For more than 150 years, his descendants ably served France, Great Britain, and Spain as military officers and merchants in contested frontier areas from Montreal to Detroit, St. Louis, New Orleans, Pensacola, and Havana. Based on microfilmed documents in the Public Archives of Canada and court and church records, St. Landry Parish, Louisiana; 50 notes.

D. B. Touchstone

862. Chipman, Donald. THE OÑATE-MOCTEZUMA-ZALDÍVAR FAMILIES OF NORTHERN NEW SPAIN. *New Mexico Hist. Rev. 1977 52(4): 297-316.* In the settlement of New Mexico, historians are well acquainted with the work done by the Zaldívar brothers, Juan and Vicente. More research needs to be done on the work of Hernán Cortes and his lieutenants. Genealogical chart, 27 notes.

J. H. Krenkel

863. Clinton, Katherine B. ILLINOIS COMMENTARY: AN ILLINOIS FAMILY OF THE 1870'S. *J. of the Illinois State Hist. Soc. 1973 66(2): 198-204.* Reprints the account of Lewis Thomas, store owner in Polo, describing small town life in the late 1870's to his father-in-law. The social history of a small northern Illinois town and its activities, entertainment, illnesses, and financial reverses are vividly depicted. Based on Lewis Thomas papers in the author's possession; illus., 2 notes.

A. C. Aimone

864. Cole, Adelaide M. ABIGAIL ADAMS: A VIGNETTE. *Daughters of the Am. Revolution Mag. 1979 113(5): 494-499.* Biography of Abigail Adams (1744-1818), wife of John Adams and mother of John Quincy Adams.

865. Cole, Glyndon. THE EASTMAN STORY. *York State Tradition 1974 28(3): 21-28.* Discusses the life and family home of George Eastman (1854-1932), founder of the Eastman Kodak Company, in Rochester, New York.   S

866. Conover, Cheryl, ed. "TO PLEASE PAPA": THE LETTERS OF
JOHN WALLER BARRY, WEST POINT CADET, 1826-1830. *Register of
the Kentucky Hist. Soc. 1982 80(2): 182-212.* Excerpts of letters from John
Waller Barry to his sister and brother-in-law. The letters tell of his studies at West
Point and of his concern for his family and his father's political career. 7 illus.,
46 notes. Article to be continued.   J. F. Paul

867. Conte, Stephen Gerald. A VISIT TO MY ANCESTORS' VILLAGE.
Family Heritage 1979 2(2): 36-39. Recounts experiences in genealogy and visiting
Andretta, Italy, 1971, the village from which his father's ancestors had origi-
nated.

868. Corbett, Katharine T. LOUISA CATHERINE ADAMS: THE AN-
GUISHED "ADVENTURES OF A NOBODY." Kelley, Mary, ed. *Woman's
Being, Woman's Place: Female Identity and Vocation in American History* (Boston: G. K. Hall, 1979): 67-84. Studies Louisa Catherine Adams, daughter-in-law
of Abigail Adams. While Abigail personified Republican motherhood, Louisa,
though fully committed to wifehood and motherhood, was unsuccessful in fulfilling the role. She considered herself an alien, possessing qualities of an upper-
middle-class-English woman, which were inappropriate for the United States.
Her relationship with her husband was strained, as was her relationship with her
children. The interest in Louisa Adams lies not so much in the experience of
failure as in her ability to articulate that experience. Her memoirs and letters for
1797-1812 shed light upon the role played by large numbers of women, the
inherent strains in the role, and its effect upon the conception of self. Based on
memoirs and letters of Louisa Adams; 64 notes.   J. Powell

869. Cousins, Leone B. THE FELLOWS FAMILY OF GRANVILLE,
NOVA SCOTIA. *Nova Scotia Hist. Q. [Canada] 1978 8(1): 81-91.* Traces the
genealogy of William Fellows, or Fellowes (1609-?) who came to Massachusetts
from Hertfordshire, England, in 1635. His great-grandson Israel Fellows (1740-
1815) emigrated to Nova Scotia in 1768 and reared a family of 11 children.
Among his descendants were members of the clergy, a ship-builder, chemist,
legislators, and a US naval officer. Includes nine generations. Primary and secondary sources; 25 notes.   H. M. Evans

870. Cowley, Malcolm. MOTHER AND SON. *Am. Heritage 1983 34(2):
28-35.* Writer Malcolm Cowley tells of his mother's life, trials, and tribulations.
From her birth in 1864 until her death in 1937, Josephine Hutmacher Cowley
led a life of compassion and generosity, yet a life filled with sorrow and deprivations. 6 photos.   J. F. Paul

871. Cox, William E. THE GREENS OF JEFFERSON COUNTY, MISSIS-
SIPPI. *J. of Mississippi Hist. 1974 36(1): 77-103.* Traces the activities of the
family of planter Thomas Marston Green, Sr. (1723-1805), including those of his
son Thomas (1758-1813), in Jefferson County, Mississippi, from 1782 to 1813.
Green's chief concerns were political power and clear titles for land he and his
sons claimed. Based on Spanish and local records; 65 notes.   J. W. Hillje

872. Crane, Elaine F. THE WORLD OF ELIZABETH DRINKER.
Pennsylvania Mag. of Hist. and Biog. 1983 107(1): 3-28. The diary of Philadel-
phian Elizabeth Sandwith Drinker for 1758-1807 indicates women's knowledge

of business and politics, their dutifulness and family orientation, the world of servants, and class and residential patterns. Based on the diary in the Historical Society of Pennsylvania and secondary sources; 2 tables, 101 notes.

T. H. Wendel

873. Crane, Robert. GALLIC ROOTS: OBSERVATIONS OF TWO NINE-TEENTH-CENTURY FRENCHMEN ON THE LOUISIANA OF THEIR DAY. *Rev. de Louisiane 1978 7(1): 65-78.* Excerpts from letters by François Ruelle, Sr. (1790-1855), and his son François (1821-77) offer insight into social organization, politics, daily life, and economic conditions of Louisiana, 1818-56.

874. Crathorne, Ethel. THE MORRIS FAMILY: SURVEYORS-GEN-ERAL. *Nova Scotia Hist. Q. [Canada] 1976 6(2): 207-216.* Genealogy of the Morris family of Great Britain, Nova Scotia, and Massachusetts in the 18th and 19th centuries.

875. Crimmins, Terence R. THE SANDERSON FAMILY AND INTER-NATIONAL RELATIONS. *Studies in Soviet Thought [Netherlands] 1980 21(1): 31-38.* Entries from the diary of a Mr. Sanderson, US delegate to an August 1937 London conference on life in the USSR, presided over by Nikolai Natuschen. Postscript by Sanderson's nephew Daryll.

876. Crock, Evelyn Bryan. MAJOR GENERAL ARTHUR ST. CLAIR: HIS LIFE AND FAMILY. *Daughters of the Am. Revolution Mag. 1975 109(2): 118-122.*

877. Crosson, David. MANUSCRIPT COLLECTIONS: THE A. J. VAN DUZEE PAPERS. *Ann. of Iowa 1979 45(1): 63-67.* Describes the Alonzo J. Van Duzee Papers in the Division of Rare Books and Special Collections of the University of Wyoming, Laramie. Originally from New York, elements of the family moved to Iowa and Minnesota during the mid-19th century. Taken as a unit, the Van Duzee Collection "provides an intimate glimpse of the westward progress of one family." The papers are paricularly strong in the Civil War era.

P. L. Petersen

878. Cuitlahuac de Hoyos, Juan. INQUIRIES INTO THOMAS ALVA EDI-SON'S ALLEGED MEXICAN ANCESTRY. *Aztlán 1978 9: 151-176.* Examines the evidence for claims of Mexican ancestry for Thomas Alva Edison, which have persisted, since the 1920's, as: the Texas orphan version, the Martinez version, and the Alva version. The first two make him entirely Mexican, the third Anglo-Mexican. In no case is the evidence conclusive, but it does include some strange, suggestive coincidences. Biblio., appendixes including correspondence, interviews, and data relevant for the various versions.

R. V. Ritter

879. Cumbler, John T. THREE GENERATIONS OF POVERTY: A NOTE ON THE LIFE OF AN UNSKILLED WORKER'S FAMILY. *Labor Hist. 1974 15(1): 78-85.* Reviews the need for more information and new methods of approach to the study of the life of the everyday laborer. The remnants of a case history of a family in Lynn from 1915-40 are published as an example of the types of material needed to understand poverty. Based on a case history from the files of the Associated Charities of Lynn, Massachusetts. 4 notes.

L. L. Athey

880. Dalin, David G. FLORINE AND ALICE HAAS AND THEIR FAMI-LIES. *Western States Jewish Hist. Q. 1981 13(2): 135-141.* Florine Haas Bransten (1881-1973) and Alice Haas Lilienthal (1885-1972), daughters of San Francisco merchant William Haas, were leaders of the city's social and cultural community as their husbands were prominent in business. The Haas-Lilienthal House on Franklin Street, commissioned by William Haas in 1886, and inherited by Alice, is a San Francisco historical landmark. Based on published sources; 4 photos, 5 notes.
B. S. Porter

881. Daniels, Almon E. and McLean, Maclean W; Harding, Anne B., ed. WILLIAM GIFFORD OF SANDWICH, MASS. (D. 1687). *New England Hist. and Geneal. Register 1981 135(Oct): 307-321.* Part 24. Continued from a previous article. All 13 members of the 5th generation of the William Gifford family were born in or near Dartmouth, Massachusetts. All but two appear to have died in the same area. John and Elihu, sons of Obediah, migrated to New York. Article to be continued.
A. E. Huff

882. Daniels, Almon E. and McLean, Maclean W. WILLIAM GIFFORD OF SANDWICH, MASS. (D. 1687). *New England Hist. and Genealogical Register 1974 128(October): 241-261; 1975 129(January): 30-44, (July): 221-237, 129(October): 335-346; 1976 130(January): 40-45, (April): 130-141, (October): 284-291; 1977 131(January): 51-57, (April): 133-141, (July): 214-220.* Part I. William Gifford (d. 1687) arrived in Sandwich, Barnstable County, Massachusetts, after 1643. Traces Gifford and his descendants through five generations. (Only male descendants with progeny are traced). The Giffords were originally Quakers, and abstracted court records reveal some of the early persecutions they suffered. This section covers William Gifford's history in England prior to immigration, his life in Massachusetts, and the history of his first three sons. Based on vital statistics, court records, probate documents, estate administrations, land deeds (the probate and land deeds are often cited in full) and secondary works. Notes are incorporated into the text. Part II. Covers the second and part of the third generation, when the Giffords began their migrations to other settlements in southeastern Massachusetts and Rhode Island. Part III. Covers part of the third generation. Part IV. The Giffords migrated to other communities in Barnstable County as well as into the eastern New York counties of Columbia, Dutchess, Putnam, and Westchester. Covers part of the third generation. Part V. Covers part of the third and fourth generations. Part VI. Covers part of the fourth generation. Part VII. Covers part of the fourth generation. Part VIII. Covers part of the fourth generation. Part IX. Covers part of the fourth generation. Part X. Covers part of the fourth and fifth generations. Article to be continued.
S. L. Patterson and R. J. Crandall

883. Daniels, Almon E. and McLean, MacLean W. WILLIAM[1] GIFFORD OF SANDWICH, MASS. (D. 1687). *New England Hist. and Geneal. Register 1977 131 (Oct): 294-298; 1978 132 (July): 211-217, 132 (Oct): 293-301; 1979 133 (Jan): 49-56, 133 (Apr): 134-140.* Continued from an earlier article. Part XI. Covers three male descendants of William Gifford in the fourth generation. Part XII. Covers four male descendants in the fourth generation. Part XIII. More fourth-generation male descendants. Part XIV. Covers two fourth-generation male descendants and three males from the fifth generation. Part XV. Covers two fifth-generation descendants. Article to be continued.
S. Wheeler/A. E. Huff/D. L. Schermerhorn

884.   Daniels, Almon E. and McLean, Maclean W.; Harding, Anne B., ed. WILLIAM[1] GIFFORD OF SANDWICH, MASS. (D. 1687).   *New England Hist. and Geneal. Register 1980 134(Oct): 310-315; 1981 135(Jan): 45-56, (Apr): 138-147.* Continued from a previous article. Part XXI. The six Gifford genealogy family members portrayed here died at Albany County, New York, Little Compton and Portsmouth, Rhode Island, two at Dartmouth, Massachusetts, and Guilford County, North Carolina. Part XXII. Documents eight fifth-generation Gifford descendants, most of them born in Dartmouth, Massachusetts. Several of them moved to New York State. Part XXIII. Traces nine fifth-generation descendants, at least six of whom were born in Freetown, Massachusetts. Two probably died in Tiverton, Rhode Island, one in Champaign County, Ohio, and the rest probably in Massachusetts. Article to be continued.   J/A. E. Huff

885.   Daniels, Almon E. and McLean, Maclean W.   WILLIAM[1] GIFFORD OF SANDWICH, MASS. (D. 1687).   *New England Hist. and Geneal. Register 1979 133(July): 211-215.* Continued from a previous article. Part XVI. Covers descendants of William Gifford in the fifth generation: Josiah Gifford (1748-95) of Rhode Island, David (1741-1814) and his brother, Jesse (1745-1821) of Falmouth, Mass. Their wives and children are also well documented. Article to be continued.   A. E. Huff

886.   Denlinger, Ralph E.   THE DENLINGER FAMILY.   *Pennsylvania Mennonite Heritage 1980 3(3): 10-16.* Genealogy of the author's family dating to 1594 in Switzerland, through the arrival of the earliest known of the family in 1715 in Pennsylvania, until 1803.

887.   Dolmetsch, Carl.   THREE BYRDS OF VIRGINIA.   *Mississippi Q. 1978 31(4): 615-622.* Reviews *The Correspondence of the Three William Byrds of Westover, Virginia, 1684-1776* (Charlottesville: U. Pr. of Virginia, 1977) edited by Marion Tinling.

888.   Dowty, Ruth Sprague.   SOME SPRAGUE RECORDS IN WEYMOUTH, TINCLETON, AND DORCHESTER, DORSET.   *New England Hist. and Geneal. Register 1980 134(July): 194-198.* Discusses three unknown, or little known, primary sources which pertain to Edward Sprague of Dorset, England, and his family, and conclusions drawn from them. There may be other undiscovered means of proving the parentage of Edward, three of whose sons were among the founders of Charlestown, Massachusetts. 14 notes.

889.   Dublin, Thomas.   THE HODGDON FAMILY LETTERS: A VIEW OF WOMEN IN THE EARLY TEXTILE MILLS, 1830-1840.   *Hist. New Hampshire 1978 33(4): 283-295.* In the mid-19th century many young New Englanders migrated from rural areas to urban centers. Sarah and Elizabeth Hodgdon, whose letters are reproduced here, left Rochester, New Hampshire, to work in a Lowell, Massachusetts, textile factory. Typical of female mill workers of the period, they apparently migrated not from economic necessity but because of rural overcrowding. Their letters reveal their strong family bonds, adjustment problems, and their economic independence. 20 notes.   D. F. Chard

890.   Duncanson, John V.   THE MAXNERS OF LUNENBURG AND WINDSOR.   *Nova Scotia Hist. Q. [Canada] 1980 10(2): 165-183.* Johann Heinrich Meichsner (1730-1815), founder of the Maxner family of Nova Scotia, emi-

grated to Canada from Saxony, East Germany in 1751. The original German spelling of the name went through various forms and pronounciations to become Maxner. The genealogy traces the family through the eldest son Andrew Leonard Maxner (1760-1840) of Windsor and John Henry Maxner (1762-1830) of Lunenberg and covers six generations. Based on census, church and probate records.

H. M. Evans

891.   Durrell, Harold Clarke and Dearborn, David Curtis, ed. PHILIP[1] DURRELL AND HIS DESCENDANTS. *New England Hist. and Geneal. Register 1979 133(Apr): 118-124; (July): 216-219.* Continued from a previous article. Part IV. This genealogical study traces the lives of three more descendants of Philip[1]. Lemuel[4], Ebenezer[4], and John[4] Durrell were all born at Durham, New Hampshire (probably) in the mid-18th century. Wives, children and places of residence are noted, some in detail. Notes incorporated in text. Part V. Discusses David[4] Durrell (ca. 1746-1833), his three marriages, and his 10 children. To be continued.

J

892.   Durrell, Harold Clarke; Dearborn, David Curtis, ed. PHILIP[1] DURRELL AND HIS DESCENDANTS. *New England Hist. and Geneal. Register 1980 134(Oct): 276-281; 1981 135(Jan): 16-22.* Continued from a previous article. Part X. Traces three more Durrell descendants and their offspring. The brothers, all born at Arundel, Maine, are: Samuel (1786-1853); Thomas, his twin (1786-1867); and William Henry (1790-1863). All three died at Kennebunkport, Maine. Part XI. The Durrell genealogy concludes with an investigation of the lives and families of three descendants. The cousins were born within a year of each other at Arundel, Maine. One died at Kennebunk, the other two at Kennebunkport. Provides an addendum of additions and corrections for articles in the previous three volumes.

J/A. E. Huff

893.   Durrell, Harold Clarke and Dearborn, David Curtis. PHILIP[1] DURRELL AND HIS DESCENDANTS. *New England Hist. and Geneal. Register 1978 132(Apr): 115-122, 132 (Oct): 264-277; 1979 133 (Jan): 40-48.* Part I. The 204 page unindexed notebook of Harold Clarke Durrell (1882-1943) is a detailed history of the Durrell family of New Hampshire and Maine. Philip is believed to have come from Guernsey around 1689. Indians attacked his family in 1703 and 1726. Several children were carried off to Canada and his wife was killed in the second attack. Philip's dates are unknown as is the identity of his wife, who bore him eleven children. Part II. Covers descendants of Philip Durrell in the second and third generations. Part III. Covers five descendants in the third generation. Article to be continued.

A. E. Huff/D. L. Schermerhorn/G. Fox

894.   Durrer, Margot Ammann. MEMORIES OF MY FATHER. *Swiss Am. Hist. Soc. 1979 15(2): 26-35.* Personal portraits of Othmar Hermann Ammann (1879-1965) by his daughter.

895.   Easley, Madeline O. A FAMILY HISTORY. *Afro-Americans in New York Life and Hist. 1982 6(2): 57-60.* Traces the author's family history from the birth of her great-great-grandfather, slave Henry Barnes, born around 1818 near or in Richmond, Virginia; the Barnes family has lived in Olean, New York, since 1900, when Oliver T. Barnes and Harry Barnes founded the Barnes Brothers Electrical and Plumbing Company.

896.   Eastwood, Elizabeth C. S.   DESCENDANTS OF ANDREW FORD OF WEYMOUTH, MASS.: ADDITIONS AND CORRECTIONS.   *New England Hist. and Geneal. Register 1983 137(Jan): 34-51.*

897.   Eaton, Ernest Lowden.   WHO WAS JACOB WALTON?   *Nova Scotia Hist. Q. 1975 5(4): 367-380.* Inquires into the identity of the two Jacob Waltons whose epitaphs appear on gravestones in the public cemetery in the Township of Cornwallis, the first a merchant who died in 1811, and the second his son, a physician, who died in 1840. They and two other Jacob Waltons are identified and the findings summarized in "The Waltons of Canard Genealogy."
R. V. Ritter

898.   Erlich, Gloria C.   HAWTHORNE AND THE MANNINGS.   *Studies in the Am. Renaissance 1980: 97-117.* Almost all biographies of Nathaniel Hawthorne begin with the first generation of Puritan ancestors on the Hathorne side. It is a rare biographer who mentions the maternal ancestor, Nicholas Manning, who reached the shores of Massachusetts only 30 years later than the better known William Hathorne. In 1680 the wife of Nicholas Manning accused him of incest with his two sisters, Anstiss and Margaret. Nicholas fled into the forest, but the sisters were tried, convicted, and sentenced to sit, during the next church service on a high stool in the middle aisle of Salem meetinghouse with paper on their heads (inscribed in capital letters) with their crime. These Mannings were ancestors of the author of *The Scarlet Letter,* who, in his autobiographical "Custom House," did not link the novel with his maternal ancestors. The Mannings were a business family, and the young Hawthorne had to hide from them the fact that he wished to be a writer. It was the Manning influence which caused a self-distrust in Hawthorne and contributed to the ambiguity of his fiction. Mainly archival and published primary sources; 35 notes.   J. Powell

899.   Fairs, Geoffrey L.   THOMAS[1] HOWELLS OF HAY AND HIS DESCENDANTS IN AMERICA.   *New England Hist. and Geneal. Register 1980 134(Jan): 27-47.* Difficulty in tracing the history of the family of the great-grandfather of William Dean Howells in Wales appears to have occurred because all but one of his offspring emigrated to America and brought the family papers along. Nevertheless the author accounts for many descendants. The illegitimate ones were troublesome, and frequent use of the same names made for confusion. Parenthetically this work illustrates the high infant mortality rate during the period. Genealogical chart, 50 notes.   J

900.   Farnam, Anne.   OLIVE PRESCOTT, WEAVER OF FORGE VILLAGE.   *Essex Inst. Hist. Collections 1979 115(3): 129-143.* Olive Adams Prescott (1780-1860) of Forge Village, Massachusetts, left no written records of herself or her life. Instead what remains is a sizeable collection of Prescott's skilled woven textiles in wool, linen, and cotton. Given to the Essex Institute in 1914, such artifacts are documents of American social history. Provides a brief history of the Prescott family, Forge Village, and Westford, examines Prescott's work as a professional weaver, and catalogues and describes the six types of weave (huck, twill, plain, woolen blankets, coverlets, and carpeting) in Prescott's work in the Essex Institute collection. Primary and secondary sources; 5 photos, 2 fig., 25 notes.   R. S. Sliwoski

901. Feder, Bernard. THE RIDGE FAMILY AND THE DEATH OF A NATION. *Am. West 1978 15(5): 28-31, 61-63.* A brief history of the Cherokee Indians after 1785. Discusses friction with whites who coveted their lands in the southern Appalachians, fighting on the American side in the War of 1812, adoption of agriculture and white culture and establishment of the Cherokee Nation, the Cherokee-Georgia confrontation, the "Trail of Tears" removal to Oklahoma, and dissolution of the Cherokee Nation in 1893. A few hundred escaped removal and now live on a reservation in western North Carolina. Major Ridge, a Cherokee warrior who earned his rank by leading volunteers in service with Andrew Jackson in the War of 1812, became a wealthy planter and government leader, and helped to convince his people to adopt white ways as the only alternative to extinction. His son John Ridge, educated in a missionary school, was an eloquent spokesman for the Cherokee cause before eastern white audiences. 4 illus.

D. L. Smith

902. Feinstein, Howard M. THE USE AND ABUSE OF ILLNESS IN THE JAMES FAMILY CIRCLE: A VIEW OF NEURASTHENIA AS A SOCIAL PHENOMENON. *Psychohistory Rev. 1979 8(1-2): 6-14.* Assuming that illness is a social phenomenon, the prevalence of invalidism in post-Civil War New England offers insights into American social history. Various nervous illnesses were commonplace among members of the James family, especially neurasthenia. Neurasthenia was peculiar to America; its occurrence and treatment were seen as related to work. Many members of the James family felt that work depleted vital energies. Rest was often taken as a cure, and members of the James family used illness to gain privileges and trips to Europe to recover. In Puritan New England, illness allowed members of the James family to enjoy themselves and seek pleasures abroad. Invalidism also allowed children to express love-hate feelings for parents. Late-19th-century invalidism symbolized the fusion of Puritanism and Romanticism. 50 notes.

J. M. Herrick

903. Feinstein, Howard. WORDS AND WORK: A DIALECTICAL ANALYSIS OF VALUE TRANSMISSION BETWEEN THREE GENERATIONS OF THE FAMILY OF WILLIAM JAMES. Albin, Mel, ed. *New Directions in Psychohistory: The Adelphi Papers in Honor of Erik H. Erikson* (Lexington, Mass.: Heath, 1980): 131-142. Focuses on familial continuity in a blend of Erik H. Erikson's developmental psychology, the communications theory of Klaus Riegel, and historical research on the conflicts surrounding work and occupational choice in the family of scientist and philosopher William James (d. 1832). Reconstructs the dialogue engaging three generations: young Henry James (1811-82) becoming middle-aged Henry James senior, becoming elderly Henry James senior, in relation to young William James (1842-1910), becoming middle-aged William James becoming elderly William James. Young Henry James senior developed his views as artist, scientist, and philosopher in relation to his father's definitions of these terms, as did the young William James. Value transmission in any family involves at least three generations. Secondary sources; fig., 17 notes.

J. Powell

904. Felton, Jacob. A FRONTIERSMAN'S MEMOIRS: JACOB FELTON'S SKETCH OF HIS EARLY LIFE. *Pennsylvania Mag. of Hist. and Biog. 1982 106(4): 539-554.* Reproduces 76-year-old Jacob Felton's memoirs, composed in 1890, which recall his family's role in the settlement of Ohio and Indiana.

T. H. Wendel

905.   Fenstermacher, J. Howard.   VESTIGES OF THE MARKLEY FAM-
ILY.   *Pennsylvania Folklife 1980 29(3): 114-119.* Describes the influence of two
families, the Kempfers and the Markleys, who founded a cemetery in 1738 on a
farm plot in the Skippack region, maintained it, and kept records of deaths in the
area; in 1926 the Markley Family Association obtained the original land and
restored the cemetery.

906.   Fierman, Floyd S.   THE SPECTACULAR ZECKENDORFS.   *J. of
Arizona Hist. 1981 22(4): 387-414.* Traces the careers of the Zeckendorf brothers,
Aaron, William, and Louis, who were prominent Arizona entrepreneurs. They
exemplify the maturation of Arizona's businessmen, and the networking common
among Jewish families and the Western character. Zeckendorf family records,
primary and secondary sources; 6 photos, 60 notes.   G. O. Gagnon

907.   Fisher, John.   THE WOLCOTT FAMILY AND THE WOLCOTT
HOUSE.   *Indiana Hist. Bull. 1975 52(12): 143-148.* Retraces the history of the
land baron Anson Wolcott and his family through the description of the Wolcott
house in Indiana, now a historical monument.

908.   Fitzgerald,   Sally.   ROOT   AND   BRANCH: O'CONNOR   OF
GEORGIA.   *Georgia Hist. Q. 1980 64(4): 377-387.* Brief history of the Georgia
ancestry of author Flannery O'Connor. Includes material on the development of
Catholicism in the state as it relates to family members. From a talk delivered
at the meeting of the Georgia Historical Society at Milledgeville in October 1980.
G. R. Schroeder

909.   Foster, Edward Halsey.   THE STEVENS FAMILY AND THE ARTS,
1820-1860.   *New Jersey Hist. 1976 94(4): 173-183.* The Stevens family of
Hoboken displayed a sophisticated knowledge of contemporary aesthetic theory
in landscape gardening and architecture. Members of this family commissioned
some of the country's finest Greek, Gothic, and Italian Revival buildings. The
grounds they landscaped at Hoboken were the most famous of their kind in the
country. Describes specific buildings and places influenced by the Stevens family.
Based on the Stevens family papers and secondary sources; 4 illus., 19 notes.
E. R. McKinstry

910.   Freidel, Frank.   THE DUTCHNESS OF THE ROOSEVELTS.   *Bijdra-
gen en Mededelingen betreffende de Geschiedenis der Nederlanden [Netherlands]
1982 97(3): 538-557.* Both Theodore and Franklin D. Roosevelt were proud of
their Dutch ancestry. The first Roosevelt to settle in America was Claes Mart-
ensen van Rosenvelt from whom both presidents descended. Franklin D. Roosevelt was active in the Netherlands-American Foundation and the Holland
Society. He was very fond of the Dutch royal family to whom he offered asylum
during World War II and who stayed with him at Hyde Park and the White
House. Published primary materials; illus., 3 photos, 39 notes. G. D. Homan

911.   French, David.   PURITAN CONSERVATISM AND THE FRON-
TIER: THE ELIZUR WRIGHT FAMILY ON THE CONNECTICUT WEST-
ERN RESERVE.   *Old Northwest 1975 1(1): 85-95.* Elizur Wright I and his
Yale-educated son, Elizur II, built pioneer farms: the father in wilderness Canaan,
Connecticut; the son in the Western Reserve. Both were orthodox congregational-
ists, scientists, and mathematicians. In the next generation, Elizur III's study of

science led to his questioning Puritan orthodoxy. Elizur II became a conservative religious leader and educator at Tallmadge, Ohio, but his son Elizur III returned to Connecticut to enter Yale University, representing the first generation to return east. Elizur III succeeded at Yale but abandoned the orthodoxy of his heritage. He became a follower of the agnostic Robert Ingersoll (1833-99). 37 notes.

J. N. Dickinson

912. Friedrich, Otto. CLOVER AND HENRY ADAMS. *Smithsonian 1977 8(1): 58-67.* Relates details of the marriage of Marian "Clover" Hooper Adams and Henry Brooks Adams from 1872 until her suicide in 1885, after which Adams commissioned a memorial statue to her by Augustus Saint-Gaudens.

913. Frost, Margaret Fullerton.   SMALL GIRL IN A NEW TOWN. *Great Plains J. 1980 19: 2-73.* Discusses the early impressions of a small girl who moved in 1901 with her family from Iowa to a farm in southwestern Oklahoma. During 1903-07 the family lived on a farm near Lawton. Margaret Fullerton Frost's reminiscences describe many country life experiences such as cooking a possum, attending a country school, prairie fires, playing with Indian children, the problems of "keeping clean and decent," and the finding of simple entertainments in a prairie environment. In 1907, after the grandfather's death, the family moved to Lawton. Based upon reminiscences, 10 photos. Article to be continued.

O. H. Zabel

914. Frost, Olivia Pleasants.   THE JOURNEY OF FIVE GENERATIONS OF A FREEDMAN'S FAMILY IN THEIR QUEST FOR HIGHER EDUCATION. *J. of the Afro-American Hist. and Geneal. Soc. 1982 3(2): 54-64.* Focuses on five generations of the ancestors of Dr. William Henry Pleasants, Jr., M.D. during 1829-1975.

915. Fuller, Constance Wadley.   JOSEPH[4] WADLEIGH OF BRENT-WOOD, NEW HAMPSHIRE AND SOME OF HIS DESCENDANTS. *New England Hist. and Geneal. Register 1978 132(July): 218-221.* Sets forth in considerable genealogical detail the lives of Joseph 4 1711-92 and three of his descendants: his only son Joseph, 1743-1821, and his eldest grandson Dole, 1783-1826, in New Hampshire; and his eldest great-grandson William Morrill Wadley, 1813-82, who moved to Georgia. Includes a wealth of information concerning wives and children. Wadleigh Family Papers, probate, military, Church and vital records, and other family papers; notes.   A. E. Huff

916. Gallardo, Florence. 'TIL DEATH DO US PART: THE MARRIAGE OF ABRAHAM LINCOLN AND MARY TODD.   *Lincoln Herald 1982 84(1):3-10.* Criticizes the 1885 book, *Life of Lincoln,* by William H. Herndon in collaboration with Jesse W. Weik, that includes a negative account of the marriage between Abraham Lincoln and Mary Todd Lincoln; it was regarded as absolutely true until 1947, when the Lincoln papers were made available and documented another version of their admittedly difficult marriage from 4 November 1842 until his assassination in 1865.

917. Garigliano, Leonard J. SWORD OF MAJOR N. E. LADD. *Military Collector & Historian 1975 27(1): 13-15.* Discusses the genealogy and life of Major Nathaniel Eustis Ladd (1840-1916) and particularly his career in the US Army during the Civil War.

918. Gass, W. Conrad.   A FELICITOUS LIFE: LUCY MARTIN BATTLE, 1805-1874.   *North Carolina Hist. R. 1975 52(4): 367-393.* During the long and distinguished career of her lawyer-judge husband, William Horn Battle, Lucy Martin Battle assumed much of the responsibility for managing his private affairs. Mrs. Battle served briefly as his amanuensis, and then ran the large household of children and slaves, first in Raleigh, then in Chapel Hill, during her husband's frequent and lengthy absences. Her success at these tasks permitted William Battle to participate fully in public life in antebellum North Carolina. Based primarily on the Battle Family Papers, as well as other manuscript collections, newspaper accounts, public documents, and secondary sources; 7 illus., 94 notes.

T. L. Savitt

919. Geelhoed, E. Bruce.   BUSINESS AND THE AMERICAN FAMILY: A LOCAL VIEW.   *Indiana Social Studies Q. 1980 33(2): 58-67.* Provides case histories of three family small businesses in Muncie, Indiana, as economic and social phenomena: Kirk's, a bicycle and sporting goods store which began in 1865; the American Lawn Mower company, started in 1902; and Riggin's Dairy, run for three generations by the Riggin family; and briefly compares these businesses with the Carter Warehouse in Plains, Georgia, and the dynasties of the Ford, Mellon, Rockefeller, and other families.

920. Geer, Emily Apt.   THE RUTHERFORD B. HAYES FAMILY.   *Hayes Hist. J. 1978 2(1): 46-51.* Compares the 19th-century family with the present era, by examining the family of Rutherford B. Hayes and Lucy Hayes; until Hayes' election to the Presidency (1877), their family life was typical of politically active, upper middle-class families of their age. Comparing the Hayes family with our own, using the factors of health, familial affection, living conditions, educational and recreational opportunities, religious training, and individual development, rejects the notion of the 19th century as the "golden age" of the American family. Primary and secondary sources; 3 photos, 23 notes.

J. N. Friedel

921. Gentry, Richard E.   EARLY FAMILIES OF UPPER MATECUMBE.   *Tequesta 1974 (34): 57-63.* Discusses the Russell, Pinder, and Parker families, the original residents of Upper Matecumbe Key, one of the islands of the upper Florida Keys. They are referred to as Conches, a term applied to people on the keys who are of "British descent by way of the Bahamas." Based on interviews with residents of Upper Matecumbe; 22 notes.   H. S. Marks

922. Giaquinta, Joyce and Peterson, Billie.   MANUSCRIPT COLLECTIONS: THE IRISH-PRESTON PAPERS, 1832-1972.   *Ann. of Iowa 1978 44(6): 475-479.* The State Historical Society of Iowa has recently acquired a large collection of materials dealing with the Iowa pioneer family of Frederick and Elizabaeth Irish and its descendants. The Irish-Preston papers include correspondence, diaries, scrapbooks, historical and literary writings, medical records, photographs, financial records, and drawings. The collection is particularly rich in women's correspondence over four generations. A descriptive inventory of the collection is available from the State Historical Society of Iowa, Iowa City.

P. L. Petersen

923. Gibson, John G. PIPER JOHN MACKAY AND RODERICK MCLENNAN: A TALE OF TWO IMMIGRANTS AND THEIR INCOMPLETE GENEALOGY. *Nova Scotia Hist. Rev. [Canada] 1982 2(2): 69-82.* Traces the genealogy of the McKay family of Scotland from Iain Dall (Blind John, ca. 1656-ca. 1754) through seven generations. John McKay (1790-1884), grandson of the Blind Piper, settled in Nova Scotia in 1805. Roderick McLennan (ca. 1778-1866), great-grandson of the Blind Piper, also came to Nova Scotia in 1812. The uncle and nephew never acknowledged their relationship although they lived in the same geographic area. Based on Public Archives of Nova Scotia manuscripts; 22 notes.   H. M. Evans

924. Glazer, Michele. THE DURKHEIMERS OF OREGON: A PICTURE STORY. *Western States Jewish Hist. Q. 1978 10(3): 202-209.* Kaufman Durkheimer brought his family from Philadelphia to Portland, Oregon, in 1862, where he opened a second-hand furniture store. In 1874 his son Julius moved to Baker City, Oregon where he opened a general mechandise store. Julius sold the store in 1887 and opened a new store in Prairie City. The next year he opened another store in Canyon City. With the expansion of his merchandising businesses to a third site, in Burns, Oregon, Julius sent for his brothers Moses, Sam, and Sigmund to help run the firm. Julius's wife, Delia, was not happy in the primitive, isolated small towns of eastern Oregon, so the family moved to Portland. In 1896 Julius purchased an interest in the wholesale grocery firm of Wadham and Company, the northwest distributor of Olympia beer. Under the management of Julius's son and grandson, the company—now, Bevhold, Inc.—continues to market Olympia beer. Primary and secondary sources; 5 photos, 3 notes.   B. S. Porter

925. Gloor, Richard D. 125 YEARS GLOOR FAMILY IN THE UNITED STATES. *Swiss Am. Hist. Soc. Newsletter 1980 16(1): 20-27.* Examines the Swiss Colonization Society founded in Cincinnati in 1856 and the genealogy and settlement in Tell City, Indiana (named for William Tell) of the Gloor family from Aargau canton, Switzerland.

926. Goerler, Raimund E. FAMILY, PSYCHOLOGY, AND HISTORY. *Group for the Use of Psychology in Hist. 1975 4(3): 31-38.* Discusses the psychological influences of Sydney Howard Gay's family on his decision in 1844 to join the abolition movement; 1830's-40's.

927. Goetsch, C. Carnahan. THE IMMIGRANT AND AMERICA: ASSIMILATION OF A GERMAN FAMILY. *Ann. of Iowa 1973 42(1): 17-27, (2): 114-125.* Part I. The story of the Goettsch family, who settled in Davenport, Iowa, after moving to the United States. Part II. Illustrates the importance of higher education to the five brothers and one sister; two have M.D.'s, three have Ph.D.'s, and one has a degree in engineering. Only through immigration to the United States would they have had this opportunity. Discusses also the anti-German feeling and its effect upon the family during World War I. The grandchildren did not share the strong bond of the Germanic background, while the great-grandchildren regarded themselves as completely American. 2 photos, 8 notes.   C. W. Olson

928.   Golden, Richard L. and Golden, Arlene A.   THE MARK I. JACOBS FAMILY: A DISCURSIVE OVERVIEW.   *Western States Jewish Hist. Q. 1981 13(2): 99-114.* Mark Israel Jacobs (1816-94) and Hannah Solomon Jacobs (1815-72) established a general store in San Diego, California, in 1851. Their children and grandchildren expanded the family business to San Francisco and to several towns in Arizona. Sons Lionel and Barron Jacobs established the first bank in Tucson, Arizona, and saw it evolve into the Valley National Bank with 190 branches throughout Arizona. Grandson Selim Franklin is known as the father of the University of Arizona. Other family members were prominent in the commercial, social, and intellectual life of Arizona and southern California. Based on material in the Jacobs Collection, University of Arizona Library, and the Arizona Historical Society; 6 photos, 46 notes.   B. S. Porter

929.   Goranson, Greta K.   IN SEARCH OF MY HERITAGE.   *Swedish Pioneer Hist. Q. 1976 27(1): 26-43.* The author had a genealogical account left by her great-great-grandfather, Gustaf Göransson (b. 1832), and wanted to discover why and how he had left Sweden. She went to Sweden as a student and discovered relatives at a house near the parish church of her ancestor. She visited the isolated and enclosed farm her ancestor had owned. They had been the only family to emigrage from the parish. 5 photos.   K. J. Puffer

930.   Graves, Ross.   THE WEATHERHEAD FAMILY OF UPPER RAW-DON.   *Nova Scotia Hist. Q. [Canada] 1975 5(2): 177-188.* Presents a genealogy of the James Weatherhead (ca. 1802-67) family from the late 1820's when he came to Hants County as a weaver from southern Scotland; carries the line down to 1946.   R. V. Ritter

931.   Gregg, Edith Emerson Webster.   EMERSON AND HIS CHILDREN: THEIR CHILDHOOD MEMORIES.   *Harvard Lib. Bull. 1980 28(4): 407-430.* Ellen, Edith and Edward Waldo Emerson, the children of Ralph Waldo Emerson, all had fond memories of childhood with their father. The two sisters' recollections are among the papers in the Ralph Waldo Emerson Memorial Association, and Edward's are found in his book *Emerson in Concord,* published in 1888. The three accounts present a picture of an affectionate father who, between the years of 1845-60, often took his children on walks in the woods and made certain that they attended to their studies in Latin and Greek with much care. Primary sources; 23 notes.   J. Powell

932.   Gregory, Sarah J.   PIONEER HOUSEWIFE: THE AUTOBIOGRA-PHY OF SALLY DODGE MORRIS.   *Gateway Heritage 1983 3(4): 24-33.* Presents the memoirs of Sally Dodge Morris, written in 1893, which focus on pioneering in Missouri and Nebraska during 1821-57. The Morris family journeyed overland to California in 1857, returned to the Midwest in 1859, and moved once more to California in 1877. Map, 13 photos, 49 notes.   H. T. Lovin

933.   Greulich, Kathleen M.   A PHILADELPHIA FAMILY AT THE "CENTRE OF THE UNIVERSE."   *Pennsylvania Heritage 1981 7(1): 18-22.* Celebrated war correspondent and reporter Richard Harding Davis (1864-1916) of Philadelphia covered the coronation of Czar Nicholas, the Spanish-American War, the Greco-Turkish War, the Boer and Belgian Congo War, the Russo-Japanese War, World War I, and other events.

934.   Groover, Mary-Agnes Brown, ed.   FROM CONCORD, MASSACHU-
SETTS, TO THE WILDERNESS: THE BROWN FAMILY LETTERS, 1792-
1852.   *New England Hist. and Genealogical Register 1977 131 (January): 28-39,
(April): 113-120, (July): 200-206.* In three parts. Thomas Browne (1601-88) and
his wife Bridget (d. 1680) had settled in Concord, Massachusetts, by 1640. The
progeny of his eldest and youngest sons, Boaz (1641/2-1724) and Thomas (1651-
1718), remained there until the fifth generation, when they began to immigrate
to the New Hampshire and Vermont wilderness in the early 1800's. These 23
letters recount some of the hardships of the frontier experience, but even more
importantly they attest to the deeply religious feelings of this family. Footnotes
identify relationships between the senders and receivers of the letters, as does a
brief chart. Primary documents.   S. L. Patterson

935.   Haliburton, Gordon.   GENEALOGY: THE DESCENDANTS OF DA-
VID FAIRWEATHER OF WEST RIVER AND RIVER JOHN, PICTOU
COUNTY.   *Nova Scotia Hist. Q. [Canada] 1979 9(4): 363-377.* Traces the
genealogy of David Fairweather (1789-1879) and his wife Janet Ross (1807-87)
to three generations. Descendants include carpenters, farmers, teachers, librarians, and ministers in British Columbia, California, Prince Edward Island, and
Nova Scotia. Based on personal letters, interviews, and Bible records.
                                                                   H. M. Evans

936.   Haliburton, Gordon M.   A TATTRIE LINE OF DESCENT.   *Nova
Scotia Hist. Rev. [Canada] 1981 1(2): 91-105.* Traces the genealogy of the Tattrie
family from George Tattrie (1722-1824) through his second son Louis (or Lewis)
Tattrie (1785-1855). The history includes members of the family through four
generations and lists a descendant born in 1977. 6 notes.   H. Evans

937.   Hamblen, Charles F.   A PIONEER FAMILY: THE RICHARDSONS
OF MOUNT DESERT.   *Maine Hist. Soc. Q. 1976 16(1): 20-28.* Traces the
migration of James Richardson and his family from Gloucester, Massachusetts,
to the Deer Isle-Mount Desert region in Maine in 1761. Notes their struggles for
survival on the Maine frontier, the arrival of the Someses, Thurstons, Gotts, and
Hamblens in the 1760's and 1770's, and their establishment of a Committee of
Correspondence, Safety, and Inspection in 1776.   P. C. Marshall

938.   Hamilton-Edwards, Gerald.   EDWARD, DUKE OF KENT, AND THE
LYONS FAMILY IN NOVA SCOTIA.   *J. of the Soc. for Army Hist. Res.
[Great Britain] 1978 56(225): 39-47.* Despite a reputation for brutal discipline
among his military underlings, Prince Edward was kind to the wives and families,
as evidenced by his careful watch over the widow and orphaned children of
Captain Charles Lyons, former Town Major of Halifax, Nova Scotia, 1812-63.

939.   Hanchett, Catherine M.   "WHAT SORT OF PEOPLE & FAMI-
LIES ... ": THE EDMONDSON SISTERS.   *Afro-Americans in New York
Life and Hist. 1982 6(2): 21-37.* Abolitionists won the freedom of Mary and
Emily Edmondson, two of the 14 slave children of freeman Paul Edmondson and
his slave wife Amelia, in 1848; the sisters attended New York Central College,
an "abolitionist school" in McGrawville, Cortland County, New York, during
1851-52.

940.   Hanson, Edward W.   THE HURDS OF BOSTON.   *New England Hist. and Geneal. Register 1978 132(Apr): 83-96.* The reason for errors in the earlier genealogy of John Hurd (d. 1690) of Boston appears to have been his repeated excommunications (for drunkenness) by the First Church. Using primary sources, Mr. Hanson traces the offspring of John and Mary Hurd through fifth-generation Isaac Hurd (1756-1844) and his children by first marriage to Sarah Thompson. The family produced notable silversmiths, and artist Peter Hurd of New Mexico is a present-day representative.   A. Huff

941.   Harvey, Robert Paton.   JOHN HARVIE (1730-1822) OF NEWPORT, NOVA SCOTIA: THREE GENERATIONS OF DESCENDANTS.   *Nova Scotia Hist. Q. [Canada] 1976 6(4): 431-442.* Genealogy of the John Harvie family (Hervie, Herve, Harvey) which originated in Great Britain and settled and flourished in Nova Scotia, 1730-1945.

942.   Harvey, Robert Paton.   WHERE CURRANT BUSHES GREW: AN INTRODUCTION TO THE SACKVILLE FULTZES.   *Nova Scotia Hist. Rev. [Canada] 1982 2(1): 74-85.* Johann Andreas Fultz reached Halifax from Germany on the Speedwell in 1751 and settled on a grant of 500 acres in what is now Windsor Junction in 1773. His sons stayed in the area and were respected citizens. The family home was restored by the Fultz County Restoration Society and is now a museum. Public Archives of Nova Scotia and family letters; 31 notes.   H. M. Evans

943.   Hatchard, Keith A.   THE HISTORY OF THE APPLE INDUSTRY OF NOVA SCOTIA.   *Nova Scotia Hist. Q. [Canada] 1977 7(3): 235-241; (4): 367-375; 1978 8(1): 39-49, (3): 195-204.* Continued from a previous article. Part III. Presents a brief history of the Starr family of Connecticut (Dr. Comfort Starr) and Nova Scotia (Samuel Starr) and their contributions to the early history of Nova Scotia. Biblio. Part IV. Ahira Calkin (1752-1828) farmed in Cornwallis and introduced the Calkin Pippin apple to the Nova Scotia apple industry. The Calkin family contributed a great deal to the early history of both Canada and the United States: John Burgess Calkin (b. 1829), educator and author in Canada; Dr. Marshal Calkins (1828-1922), pioneer in gynecology in Massachusetts; Charles Walbridge Calkins (1842-1918), lawyer and scholar in Michigan; and Benjamin Howes Calkin (1819-93), businessman in Canada, are the most prominent. The American descendants added an 's' to the family name, while the Canadian branch retained the singular. 12 notes. Part V. Charles Inglis (1734-1816), first Anglican Bishop of Nova Scotia, retired to the Annapolis Valley and through experiments produced the Bishop Pippin apple during 1796-1808. Discusses the lives of his daughters, Margaret and Ann, and his son, John. 9 notes. Part VI. In 1872 Robert Grant Halliburton (1831-1901) urged the fruit growers of Nova Scotia to form an association to control and supervise the apple industry and to widen the market to include England. 6 notes. Article to be continued.
                              H. M. Evans

944.   Hatchard, Keith A.   THE NOVA SCOTIA APPLE INDUSTRY.   *Nova Scotia Hist. Q. 1977 7(1): 31-39, (2): 125-133.* Part I. Traces the history of the apple industry in Nova Scotia from 1851 to the present time. Uses statistics of crop yields. 4 tables, 8 notes, biblio. Part II. Outlines the family history of Charles Ramage Prescott (1772-1859) and his efforts to improve the apple industry in Nova Scotia. Primary and secondary sources; 11 notes, biblio.
                              H. M. Evans

945. Hathaway, Carol Joyce. FOUR GENERATIONS OF DESCEN-
DANTS OF JEREMIAH HATHAWAY OF COVENTRY, RHODE IS-
LAND. *New England Hist. and Geneal. Register 1980 134(July): 199-210.* The
parentage and place of birth of Jeremiah Hathaway (ca. 1700-76) remain unknown but this article traces some of his descendants, through two of his sons,
most of whom lived in Washington and Kent Counties in Rhode Island. Descendants of Anthony Hathaway (b. ca. 1785 at East Greenwich) live in the same
counties, but there is no evidence linking the two families. Notes from Vital
Records, Cemetery and Probate Records and other primary sources and a few
secondary sources are included in the text.

946. Havighurst, Walter. HOWELLS OF HAMILTON. *Old Northwest
1982 8(1): 7-11.* Discusses the childhood years spent in Hamilton, Ohio, during
1841-50 by William Dean Howells. The publication of *A Boy's Town* by Howells
in 1890 reflected the happiness and importance he placed on his early years in
Hamilton.
P. L. McLaughlin

947. Hawks, Joanne Varner. LIKE MOTHER, LIKE DAUGHTER: NEL-
LIE NUGENT SOMERVILLE AND LUCY SOMERVILLE HOWORTH.
J. of Mississippi Hist. 1983 45(2): 116-128. An overview of the lives of two
Mississippi women who served in the state legislature. Nellie Somerville, the first
woman elected to the Mississippi legislature, entered public service in 1923 as
representative from Washington County through her earlier interests in the temperance and suffrage movements. She worked continuously to involve women in
civic improvement projects and other responsibilities of citizenship. Howorth, the
daughter, was elected as a state representative from Hinds County in 1931, but
her influence would spread beyond the state's boundaries. Appointed initially to
the Board of Veterans' Appeals by President Franklin D. Roosevelt, she became
an influential part of the network of women in the federal government who were
appointed by Roosevelt in the early years of the New Deal. Returning to Mississippi in 1957, she remains active in public life. Based on an interview with Lucy
Somerville Howorth, periodicals, M.A. theses, and secondary sources; 14 notes.
M. S. Legan

948. Heisey, John W. BRENNEMAN GENEALOGY AND HEIRLOOMS.
Pennsylvania Mennonite Heritage 1981 4(3): 20-22. Traces the author's ancestors
to 1631 in Switzerland when Melchior Brenneman was born and focuses on the
coverlet that Martin B. Breneman, the author's great-great-grandfather, wove in
1861, which was given to the author as a wedding present in 1971.

949. Herr, Pamela. THE LIFE OF JESSIE BENTON FRÉMONT. *Am.
West 1979 16(2): 4-13, 59-63.* Jessie Anne Benton (1824-1902) was educated and
influenced by the political, cultural, and westward-dreaming family life of Senator
Thomas Hart Benton in Washington and in their Missouri home. Her marriage
to John Charles Frémont made her the "passionate connecting link" between the
ambitious young army explorer and his powerful senator father-in-law. Having
served as her father's secretary and assistant, Jessie served her husband in the
same capacity through his stormy military and political career. She "shared in
her husband's life more fully than most women, learning to accept the limitations
that both her sex and fate enforced." 6 illus., bibliographic note.
D. L. Smith

950.   Hickey, James T.   A FAMILY ALBUM: THE DRESSERS OF SPRINGFIELD. *J. of the Illinois State Hist. Soc. 1982 75(4): 309-320.* The Illinois State Historical Society has received over 200 ambrotypes, daguerreotypes, and photographs depicting five generations descended from Nathan and Rebecca Dresser. Two generations of the family were closely associated with the family of Abraham Lincoln. Members included Episcopal priests Charles and David Walker Dresser, architect Henry Dresser, and physician Thomas Withers Dresser. Other members of the family included a county judge, a county clerk, and a state representative. Edmund Dresser served as assistant superintendent of the western division of the Wabash, St. Louis and Pacific Railroad. Thomas Dresser White served as US Air Force chief of staff during 1957-61. 16 illus., 14 notes.   A. W. Novitsky

951.   Hickey, James T., ed.   AN ILLINOIS FIRST FAMILY: THE REMINISCENCES OF CLARA MATTESON DOOLITTLE. *J. of the Illinois State Hist. Soc. 1976 69(1): 2-16.* Provides reminiscences of Mrs. James Doolittle, daughter of Illinois governor Joel Matteson (1852-56). She describes the family's comfortable and patrician style of life in Illinois and abroad in the 1850's and throughout the Civil War. The editor presents a history of the first governor's mansion, 1843-56, money for which was not appropriated until more than 20 years after statehood. The editor also describes the life-size marble statue of Stephen A. Douglas by Leonard Volk; it was first used as a touring campaign prop. Based on newspapers, family records, and *Illinois Laws;* illus., map, 43 notes.   J

952.   Hickey, James T.   ROBERT TODD LINCOLN AND THE "PURELY PRIVATE" LETTERS OF THE LINCOLN FAMILY. *J. of the Illinois State Hist. Soc. 1981 74(1): 59-79.* The papers of Abraham Lincoln were held by Elizabeth Todd Grimsley, Clark Moulton Smith, and William H. Herndon. After his assassination, his White House papers were brought to Bloomington by David Davis at the request of Robert T. Lincoln. Robert, determining that family papers should not be available for public inspection, safeguarded them. Many family papers, stored in his law office, were destroyed in the Chicago fire of 1871. Examination of the surviving papers was conducted by Charles Sweet until Robert Lincoln transferred them from Chicago to Hildene, his Vermont estate, between 1911 and 1918. In 1919, he presented eight trunks, forming the base of the *Collected Works of Abraham Lincoln,* to the Library of Congress. Robert Todd Lincoln Beckwith recently distributed the last of the Hildene material to close friends and various historical agencies. 16 illus., 41 notes.
                                                                                                        A. W. Novitsky

953.   Higgins, Anthony.   MARY WILSON THOMPSON MEMOIR. *Delaware Hist. 1978 18(1): 43-62.* The author recounts his lifelong impressions of Mary Wilson Thompson (1866-1947), an important Wilmington socialite, an opponent of women's suffrage in Delaware, and a perennial "do-gooder" responsible for historic preservation in New Castle, campaigns to fight mosquitoes in Sussex County, beautification of the state's highways, preservation of the state's beaches, and promotion of the state's heritage. Publishes part one of Mrs. Thompson's memoirs, which includes her recollections of her ancestors, the Andrews line, and particularly General James Harrison Wilson, her father. 6 notes. Article to be continued.   R. M. Miller

954. Higgins, Anthony B., ed. MARY WILSON THOMPSON MEMOIR. *Delaware Hist. 1978 18(2): 124-151; 1979 18(3): 194-217.* Continued from a previous article. Part II. Mary Wilson Thompson describes her childhood in New Castle County, Delaware, in the late 19th century. The memoirs include descriptions of trips to Wilmington, an earthquake, recreation, personalities in Wilmington, education, school and life in Farmington, Connecticut, a trip to Europe, romance, and the "gay nineties." Part III. Mary Wilson Thompson discusses life with her father in Cuba, 1899-1900, more of her family life, Delaware and national, social, and political life, and her family vis-à-vis World War I.

R. M. Miller

955. Highes, Charles W. THE CHENEYS: A VERMONT SINGING FAMILY. *Vermont Hist. 1977 45(3): 155-168.* The Cheney Family Singers consisted of Moses, four of his sons and a daughter. Moses was a Sanbornton, New Hampshire, farmer, Free Will Baptist preacher, versifier, and singer. Moses Ela taught at singing schools and common schools, directed church choirs, and pioneered musical conventions. Peripatetic as a young man, he settled in Barnard, Vermont. Simeon lived in Dorset, Vermont, was a spiritualist, and published *The American Singing Book* (Boston: White, Smith & Co., 1879). 55 notes.

T. D. S. Bassett

956. Hinckley, Ted C. A VICTORIAN FAMILY IN ALASKA. *Am. West 1979 16(1): 32-37, 60-63.* The Reverend John Green Brady went to Alaska in 1878 as a Presbyterian missionary. Business and politics beckoned. He established the forerunner of Sheldon Jackson College, became a successful lumberman, was appointed judge, and served the territory for three terms as its fifth governor. John and Elizabeth and their five children were models of "Christian upbringing," plain living, and "high thinking." The Brady family was firmly committed to the "Victorian virtues of perspiration, proficiency, and piety," despite the attractions and temptations of frontier Sitka. 7 illus, biblio, note.

D. L. Smith

957. Hinsley, Jacqueline A. THE READING TASTES OF EDUCATED WOMEN OF A MID-ATLANTIC MANUFACTURING FAMILY, 1810-1835. *Working Papers from the Regional Econ. Hist. Res. Center 1982 5(2-3): 131-138.* The literary interests of the women of Delaware's Du Pont family included French periodicals and books and English newspapers, books, and periodicals on subjects such as philosophy, history, travel, poetry, religion, and contemporary fiction; apparently differences in reading taste and opportunities were not due to gender but to class.

958. Hoard, Lyon J. HOAR-LAWTON-SOUTHWORTH AND CONNECTIONS. *New England Hist. and Geneal. Register 1980 134(Apr): 115-120.* Follows up on a study concerning William Hoar (d. 1810) of Chester, Vermont, and his descendants, published by the author in the *National Genealogical Society Quarterly* 1958 46:212-217. Further research has identified the first wife of William as Elizabeth Lawton (d. 1787), daughter of William Lawton (1701/17-1780/85) and Sarah (Southworth) Lawton of Rhode Island. These proofs provide some interesting genealogical connections. Notes from vital records, probate records, other sources incorporated in text.

J

959. Hoffecker, Carol E., ed. THE DIARIES OF EDMUND CANBY, A QUAKER MILLER, 1822-1848. *Delaware Hist. 1974 16(2): 79-131.* Selections from the diaries of Edmund Canby (1804-48), of the Canby flour milling family of Brandywine. The diaries relate weather conditions, marketing practices, the Canby's Whig principles, family history, the Hicksite schism among Quakers, and social life of New Castle County, Delaware, in the 1820's and 1830's. The first installment covers 1822-35. 2 illus., 24 notes. Article to be continued.
                                                                    Randall M. Miller

960. Hollis, Daniel W., III. THE HALL FAMILY AND TWENTIETH-CENTURY JOURNALISM IN ALABAMA. *Alabama Rev. 1979 32(2): 119-140.* The Hall family established itself in Alabama journalism in 1908. It continues so to the present, either as publishers, editors, business managers, or reporters. Some members are notable for their defense of civil liberties, one for winning the Pulitzer prize, and all for a commitment to their trade and the vitality of the human spirit. Primary and secondary sources; 75 notes.
                                                                          J. F. Vivian

961. Holsman, Virginia B. FOND RECOLLECTIONS. *Oregon Hist. Soc. 1979 80(4): 365-390.* Memoir of the author's childhood in Hillsboro, Oregon, with information on her mother, Josephine Schulmerich, and her parents, of Hillsboro, and her father, Thomas Bilyeu of Scio, Oregon, and his parents. The author includes information on child-rearing, recreation, and friends.   S

962. Horner, Patricia V. MARY RICHARDSON WALKER: THE SHATTERED DREAM OF A MISSIONARY WOMAN. *Montana 1982 32(3): 20-31.* Mary Richardson Walker wanted to be a missionary first and a housewife second. She kept a diary during 1833-79 reflecting her personal views of her life and duties at the Tshimakain Indian Mission in eastern Washington and Forest Grove, Oregon. The diaries reveal an intelligent, articulate, and pious woman whose dreams of missionary work were shattered by the tasks and obligations of a pioneer wife. Based on the Walker diary transcriptions at the Eastern Washington Historical Society, Spokane, and secondary sources; 6 illus., 10 notes.
                                                                        R. C. Myers

963. Howie, Robert L., Jr. CODMAN CONNECTIONS: PORTRAIT OF A FAMILY AND ITS PAPERS. *Old-Time New England 1981 71(258): 150-157.* Provides a genealogy of the Codmans and describes the Codman Family Manuscripts Collection, 100,000 items that the Society for the Preservation of New England Antiquities acquired with the Codman House in 1969, covering the period 1715-1969, and describes the organization of the collection.

964. Humphrys, Ruth. THE BECKTONS OF CANNINGTON MANOR. *Beaver [Canada] 1982 313(3): 42-50.* William and Ernest Beckton of Manchester returned to Cannington Manor, Saskatchewan, in 1888 to establish "what they hoped would be the finest horse-breeding ranch in Western Canada." Here at the Didsbury Stock Farm or "the Ranch," the Becktons "lived in splendid style . . .; their money gave stability to the district; their exuberance added zest to pioneer life." Descriptions are provided of the luxury life at the ranch, particularly with respect to the Cannington Manor Hunt and Turf Club's activities. By 1897 all the Becktons had returned to England with the result that "much of the spirit

and hope of Cannington Manor was lost." Most settlers soon departed also. 12 photos.

E. A. Chard

965.   Humphrys, Ruth.   [THE SHINY HOUSE].
THE SHINY HOUSE ... AND THE MAN WHO BUILT IT.   *Beaver [Canada] 1977 307(4): 49-55.* James Humphrys, retired British naval architect, moved to Assiniboia in 1888 for his health. There he acquired land for a farm. Within a few months he erected a large, comfortable home for his family of eight children and his wife, who remained in England until the home was completed. The Humphrys home was at Cannington Manor in southeastern Saskatchewan. Humphrys adjusted well, helped initiate medical and educational services, and looked forward to life in a progressive community. 8 illus.
EARLY DAYS IN THE SHINY HOUSE.   *Beaver [Canada] 1977 308(1): 20-28.* Concludes the story of the family of James Humphrys. Discusses education, church life, entertainment, and other social affairs. 17 illus.

D. Chaput

966.   Huron, Francis H.   HUGH MAHURIN OF TAUNTON, MASSACHUSETTS.   *New England Hist. and Geneal. Register 1982 136(Jan): 17-30, (Apr): 115-132, (July): 242-253.* Part 1. To date there has been no comprehensive genealogy of the descendants of Hugh Mahurin (1665-1718), although bits of information may be found in other family histories and in general works. Presents all known data on the first four generations. Part 2. Eleven more descendants are traced. Six members of the 3d generation were born at Bridgewater, Massachusetts, and five of the 4th generation at Morris County, New Jersey. Part 3. It is curious to observe that there are six different spellings of the last name in this section alone: Mahurin; Hurin; Mehurin; Manhuren; McHuron; Huron and one misspelling, "Mehruin". Primary and secondary sources.

A. E. Huff

967.   Jacobs, Julius L.   CALIFORNIA'S PIONEER WINE FAMILIES.   *California Hist. Q. 1975 54(2): 139-174.* A survey of viticulture and enology in California. Of the more than 240 bonded wineries in the state, only four which trace their origins back to the 19th century—Biane, Mirassou, Wente, and Concannon—are still under family operation. The history of these four and other pioneering wine families are described. California proved ideal for the production of fine red and white wines. Although the industry received a setback during Prohibition, it has expanded greatly since its repeal, with more than 325 million gallons being produced. Both tiny producers and giant companies have contributed to making wine production a major California industry. Primary sources, including oral history interviews and secondary studies; 5 illus., 19 photos, 37 notes.

A. Hoffman

968.   Jenson, Carol.   THE LARSON SISTERS: THREE CAREERS IN CONTRAST.   Stuhler, Barbara and Kreuter, Gretchen, ed. *Women of Minnesota: Selected Biographical Essays* (St. Paul: Minnesota Historical Society Press, 1977): 301-324. Agnes, Henrietta, and Nora Larson grew up in Minnesota. Daughters of a successful farmer-businessman and a gentle mother, they were raised in an environment of Norwegian American traditions and the Lutheran Church. They all attended St. Olaf College in Northfield, pursued graduate studies, and became teachers. Agnes Larson became a historian, taught at St.

Olaf, and wrote the meticulously researched and well-written monograph, *History of the White Pine Industry in Minnesota.* Henrietta Larson became a prominent pioneer in business history. She taught at colleges and universities. She became a noted editor and writer while working as a research associate at Harvard, where she became the first woman named as an associate professor by the business school despite that university's tradition of sex discrimination. Nora Larson became a bacteriologist. She did research at the Mayo Foundation, the Lakey Clinic, and the Takamine Laboratories before finally settling back in Minnesota in 1950, where she became the only woman among the principal scientists at the University of Minnesota's Hormel Institute. She studied swine diseases and was active in professional and community organizations. In 1960, Nora joined the faculty of St. Olaf where she taught until her retirement in 1972. Primary sources; 3 photos, 50 notes.   A. E. Wiederrecht

969.   Jessee, Dean C.   BRIGHAM YOUNG'S FAMILY: PART I, 1824-1845. *Brigham Young U. Studies 1978 18(3): 311-327.* Discusses Young as the head of his domestic household, one of the largest families in Mormondom. Many details of Young's private life are sketchy. Assesses Young's personality on the basis of how well he performed his domestic role. The years of instability, 1824-45, cover the period from his first marriage to the family's exodus from Nauvoo. These years were characterized by numerous and extended absences from his family as he served the Mormon Church in America and England. Article to be continued.   M. S. Legan

970.   Jessee, Dean C.   BRIGHAM YOUNG'S FAMILY: THE WILDERNESS YEARS. *Brigham Young U. Studies 1979 19(4): 474-500.* An account of the trials and tribulations of the family of Brigham Young during the Mormon migration from Nauvoo, Illinois, to Salt Lake City, Utah. Young already had numerous wives; the time, energy, and thought-consuming problems connected with directing the migration while simultaneously establishing a new home in the West left little time for his family. The wives and children did not leave as a unit, and several returned to Nauvoo or went from camp to camp. Their sufferings, faith, and efforts to communicate with their husband are carefully detailed.
V. L. Human

971.   Jessee, Dean C.   LUCY MACK SMITH'S 1829 LETTER TO MARY SMITH PIERCE. *Brigham Young U. Studies 1982 22(4): 455-465.* Discusses a recently discovered letter written 23 January 1829 by Lucy Mack Smith, mother of Mormon founder Joseph Smith, to her sister-in-law, Mary Smith Pierce. The letter contradicts the notion that Joseph Smith's early religious experiences were fabricated later in life, and shows that Lucy Mack Smith was an articulate woman of above-average literary ability who was aware of the *Book of Mormon* before it was translated. The letter also raises a question about the dating of *Doctrine and Covenants.* It also clarifies why they left their farm in 1829. Based on letters, speeches, and secondary sources; illus., 4 plates, 19 notes.   E. R. Campbell

972.   Jessup, Wilbur E.   THE WARREN FAMILY OF MARSHALL COUNTY, IOWA. *J. of the Afro-American Hist. and Geneal. Soc. 1982 3(3): 99-104.* Traces the history of the Warren family, Edward, Winnie, and their son George, who arrived in Iowa in the late 1800's.

973. Johnson, David R. THE EARLY EAST PETERSBURG AREA HER-
SHEY FAMILY. *Pennsylvania Mennonite Heritage 1978 1(1): 6-16.* Chronicles land patents and genealogy of various members of the Hershey family
residing in Lancaster County, Pennsylvania, 1730's-1870's.

974. Johnson, Mary. VICTORINE DU PONT: HEIRESS TO THE EDU-
CATIONAL DREAM OF PIERRE SAMUEL DU PONT DE NEMOURS.
Delaware Hist. 1980 19(2): 88-105. Argues that Victorine du Pont (b. 1792), the
granddaughter of Pierre Samuel du Pont de Nemours, the physiocrat, imbibed
du Pont de Nemours' thinking on the need for democratic education and translated her experience of growing up in France to the upbringing of the du Pont
family in America and to the mill towns of the Brandywine region. She became
an advocate of primary education in the rural manufacturing districts of the
middle Atlantic region, working particularly with the American Sunday School
Movement. Her chief legacy was the Brandywine Manufacturers' Sunday School,
incorporated in 1817, which embodied the du Pont concept that learning should
be pleasurable not corporal. Her other legacy was the liberal education of the du
Pont family, which guided them even as they attended formal schools. 60 notes.
R. M. Miller

975. Johnson, Mary Durham. MADAME E. I. DU PONT AND MADAME
VICTORINE DU PONT BAUDUY, THE FIRST MISTRESSES OF ELEU-
THERIAN MILLS: MODELS OF DOMESTICITY IN THE BRANDYWINE
VALLEY DURING THE ANTEBELLUM ERA. *Working Papers from the
Regional Econ. Hist. Res. Center 1982 5(2-3): 13-45.* Based on the household
account books and private papers of Sophie Du Pont and her oldest daughter,
Madame Victorine du Pont Bauduy, giving an account of domestic life and of the
family business, the Eleutherian Mills, in the Brandywine Valley, near Wilming-
ton, Delaware, during the early 19th century.

976. Johnson, Sherman E. A MINNESOTA IMMIGRANT AT AGE SEV-
ENTY. *Swedish Pioneer Hist. Q. 1978 29(4): 240-256.* Johan Persson (1804-85)
was an unusual immigrant from Sweden because he and his wife lived a full and
active life in Sweden and did not come to America until he was 70 years old.
Describes the life of Persson and his family—three sons and two daughters. Based
on a brief autobiography and letters written to relatives. The author is the great-
grandson of Johan on his mother's side. 4 photos, 9 notes.   C. W. Ohrvall

977. Jordan, William B., Jr., comp. SHAKING THE FAMILY TREE: THE
RECORDS OF PORTLAND'S EASTERN CEMETERY. *Maine Hist. Soc. Q.
1980 19(4): 227-250, 20(1): 41-65, (2): 101-121.* Part I. Briefly notes the history
of Eastern Cemetery, Portland, Maine, and the early surveys of its plots. The
major survey, by William A. Goodwin in 1890, which tabulated more than 4,000
graves, is the core of this compilation of names, dates of death, and ages, of people
buried in the cemetery. The compiler has combined data from the surveys and
made additions and corrections. This list includes names from Abbott to Cutter.
Part II. This list includes names from Daley to Knox. Part III. Provides names
from Lambert to Quincy. Based on Eastern Cemetery surveys and further research by the compiler. Article to be continued.   C. A. Watson

978. Joslyn, Roger D. THE DESCENDANTS OF JOHN[1] STOCK-BRIDGE. *New England Hist. and Geneal. Register 1979 133(Oct): 286-293; 1980 134(Jan): 70-73, (Apr): 135-147, (July): 228-236.* Part III. Continued from a previous article (see preceding abstract). This section of the Stockbridge genealogy details the lives of John[2] (1657-before 1715) of Boston, Massachusetts, and Hampton, New Hampshire, and Charles[3] (1663/4-1731) of Scituate and Hanover, Massachusetts, their children and grandchildren. Based on church records, probate and other court records, and histories; notes incorporated in text. Part IV. Discusses Thomas Stockbridge (1667-1717/18), third in line from John[1]. Thomas lived and died in Scituate, Massachusetts, and his children were born there. Notes incorporated in the text, based on church and town records and histories. Part V. Documents three sons of Charles[2] Stockbridge of Scituate: Joseph (1672-1773), Benjamin (1677-1725), and Samuel (1679-1758), and a cousin, Samuel (ca. 1683-1722/23) of Haverhill. Includes their wives and children. Notes included in text. Part VI. Discusses three more New Hampshire descendants and one Massachusetts descendant of John Stockbridge, including their families. Based on town records, vital records, registers, wills, military histories, and other sources. Notes incorporated in text. Article to be continued.
J/S

979. Joslyn, Roger D. THE DESCENDANTS OF JOHN[1] STOCK-BRIDGE. *New England Hist. and Geneal. Register 1980 134(Oct): 291-298; 1981 135(Jan): 36-44, (Apr): 121-132.* Continued from a previous article (see preceding entry). Part VII. Sets forth the lives and times of two fourth-generation members of the Stockbridge family. Michael (1714-63), was born in Scituate, Massachusetts and drowned in Dresden, Maine. He fathered 13 children. David (1713-88), was born in Pembroke, Massachusetts and died in Hanover, Massachusetts. He had seven children. Part VIII. Focuses on two fourth-generation cousins, Benjamin (1704-88) and Samuel, Jr. (1711-84). Both were born in Scituate, Massachusetts, and died there, as did the majority of their children. Part IX. Conclusion. Samuel[4] (d. ca. 1761) of Gloucester, Massachusetts, Charles[4] (d. ca. 1743-49) of Georgetown, Maine, and John[4] (d. 1782) of Stratham, New Hampshire, are the final Stockbridge descendants traced by the author. Provides an addendum containing additions and corrections to the articles in volumes 133 and 134.
J/A. E. Huff

980. Joslyn, Roger D. THE DESCENDANTS OF JOHN[1] STOCK-BRIDGE. *New England Hist. and Geneal. Register 1979 133(Apr): 93-101, (July): 187-193.* Part I. There is no complete genealogy in existence for the Stockbridge family who settled early in New England. This article will include new information about Charles[2], the oldest son of John[1]. John[2], the youngest child, was erroneously reported to have died soon after his birth in 1657. Notes incorporated in text. Part II. Discusses Charles[2], his wife, Abagail, and their children, 17th-18th centuries. Article to be continued.
J

981. Kenney, Alice P. A DUTCH PIONEER: ZACHARIAH PRICE DE WITT MOVES WEST. *Halve Maen 1983 57(2): 3-5, 23, 25.* The family of Zachariah Price De Witt lived in New Amsterdam in the 1650's, and migrated to New Jersey in the early 1700's, to Kentucky in the late 1780's, then to the frontier settlement of Oxford, Ohio, in 1805.

982.   Kent, D. L.   THE SPRAGUE FAMILY OF CHARLESTOWN, MAS-
SACHUSETTS.   *New England Hist. and Geneal. Register 1978 132 (Jan):
51-53.* Corrects some erroneous information concerning the origins of the
Sprague family of Charlestown, Massachusetts, by publishing research from the
parish registers at Puddletown and Fordington St. George, Dorchester. The
Reverend Richard Bartelot, vicar of Fordington St. George, made some inaccurate connections because of similarities in names. The misconceptions appear in
The Spragues of Malden, Mass. compiled by George W. Chamberlain and published in 1923. 5 notes.   A. Huff

983.   Kernaghan, Lois Y. and Punch, Terrence M.   THE FULTZ FAMILY
OF SACKVILLE, HALIFAX COUNTY, A CASE STUDY TO 1881.   *Nova
Scotia Hist. Rev. [Canada] 1982 2(1): 86-106.* Traces the genealogy of the Fultz
family from the arrival of Johann Andreas Fultz in Halifax in 1751 through five
generations to 1881. The family was predominantly Anglican and was a cohesive
group, settling in a specific geographic area. Various members were farmers,
shipwrights, carpenters, and salesmen.   Public Archives of Nova Scotia; appendix, biblio.   H. M. Evans

984.   Kersey, Harry A., Jr.   THE JOHN DUBOIS FAMILY OF JUPITER:
A FLORIDA PROTOTYPE, 1887-1981.   *Tequesta 1981 41: 5-22.* Since Harry
DuBois began living in Jupiter, Florida, during the 1880's, the DuBois family has
been an integral part of the area's social history. During the 1890's Harry DuBois
purchased a tract of 18 acres, known as Stone's Point, on the Loxahatchee River.
His home was constructed on a massive oyster-shell mound 20 feet high and over
600 feet long. His first child, John, born in 1899, still lives there. Based on oral
history interviews and family papers; 25 notes.   H. S. Marks

985.   Ketchum, William C., Jr.   THE BUELL REGISTER: CHRONICLE OF
A 19TH-CENTURY FARM FAMILY.   *Early Am. Life 1977 8(1): 72-77.*
Discusses the contents of the Buell Register, a family diary kept by John L. Buell
during 1844-48, which details his life in farming near Morristown, New York;
includes information on family history, agricultural business, and local events.

986.   Kimball, Stanley B.   HEBER C. KIMBALL AND FAMILY, THE
NAUVOO YEARS.   *Brigham Young U. Studies 1975 15(4): 447-479.* Discusses
the Heber C. Kimball family during their tenure in Nauvoo, Illinois, with the rest
of the Mormon community, 1839-46.

987.   Klotter, James C.   SLAVERY AND RACE: A FAMILY PERSPEC-
TIVE.   *Southern Studies 1978 17(4): 375-397.* Examines racial attitudes within
the upper class Breckenridge family of Kentucky for four generations. All were
prominent citizens, politicians, newspaper publishers, clergymen, educators; they
were progressive for their times. John Breckenridge (1760-1806) supported slavery, but his son Robert Jefferson Breckenridge (1800-71) was antislavery and an
educational reformer. Robert's son William C. P. Breckenridge (1837-1904)
became a Democrat and supported legal rights for blacks under a paternalistic
system. William's son Desha Breckenridge (1867-1935) was for states' rights and
opposed to rights for blacks, probably because he was nonreligious and feared for
his political career. Primary and secondary sources; 68 notes.
                                                                   J. J. Buschen

988. Kovačević, Ante. ON THE DESCENT OF JOHN OWEN DOMINIS, PRINCE CONSORT OF QUEEN LILIUOKALANI. *Hawaiian J. of Hist. 1976 10: 3-24.* Researches the origins of the Consort of the Queen of Hawaii. These origins appear to have been Croatian and more particularly Dalmatian. A family tree and photographs are included.   R. Alvis

989. Krick, Robert. THE ALRICHES OF SPOTSYLVANIA. *Lincoln Herald 1980 82(1): 311-318.* Discusses the Alrich family of Spotsylvania County, Virginia, and focuses on their participation in the Civil War, beginning with John Alrich's enrollment in Company E of the Ninth Virginia Cavalry; covers 1830-1979.

990. Kulikoff, Allan. "THROWING THE STOCKING," A GENTRY MARRIAGE IN PROVINCIAL MARYLAND. *Maryland Hist. Mag. 1976 71(4): 516-521.* Describes the wedding day of Stead Lowe and Laetitia Young, one of the highlights of the 1757 Annapolis social season, within the context of wedding celebrations in the Chesapeake region. The steps of the nuptial process included publication of banns, the ceremony at the bride's home or the local minister's house, and the celebration afterwards. The whole was "rich with rituals which structured the entire event," and by the mid-18th century "served to unite the separate kin networks of the bride and groom." Guests were usually members of the same social group; the newly-wedded couple was seldom left alone; and the celebrations, always public events, often went on for days. Based on the 1769 deposition of Katherine Jacques, wife of an Annapolis merchant. Primary sources; 16 notes.   G. J. Bobango

991. Larson, Bruce L. LITTLE FALLS LAWYER, 1884-1906: CHARLES A. LINDBERGH, SR. *Minnesota Hist. 1973 43(5): 158-174.* Traces the career of Charles A. Lindbergh, Sr., from his graduation from law school in 1883 to his entry into politics in 1906. Mentions family life, business affairs, and the development of a law practice in Minnesota. A chapter from a forthcoming biography. 13 illus., 46 notes.   D. L. Smith

992. Lazzell, Ruleen. LIFE ON A HOMESTEAD: MEMORIES OF MINNIE A. CRISP. *New Mexico Hist. Rev. 1979 54(1): 59-64.* Portrays the homestead life of Minnie A. (Cardwell) Crisp (b. 1888) from 1910 to 1933 in Union County, New Mexico. Recounts the hardships, doubts, and enjoyments of frontier living by the Crisp family. After 23 years and 12 children, the Crisp family lost their homestead by foreclosure during the Depression. Mrs. Crisp now resides in Clayton, New Mexico. Photo, 7 notes.   P. L. McLaughlin

993. Lee, David D., ed. JESSE WAUGH, WEST VIRGINIAN. *West Virginia Hist. 1974 35(2): 154-162.* Jesse Waugh's "A Brief History of My Life," a narrative written for his grandchildren, contains reminiscences of life in 19th century West Virginia and personal advice to his grandchildren. Waugh went to school at age 11, became a farmer, lumberman, teacher, and carpenter, and held minor local offices. He was a Baptist deacon for 30 years and his "History" stresses the importance of a religious life.   J. H. Broussard

994. Lee, Russell. 1946: DAY BY DAY. *Southern Exposure 1976 4(1-2): 104-113.* Presents a photo-essay on the poverty of the Sergent family of Harlan County, Kentucky, whose men were coal miners.

995. Lehman, Daniel R. BISHOP HANS LEHMAN, IMMIGRANT OF 1727. *Pennsylvania Mennonite Heritage 1980 3(4): 16-23.* Discusses Bishop Hans Lehman (1702-76) of Rapho Township, Lancaster County, Pennsylvania, who settled there in 1727 upon his arrival to the United States from Switzerland, and a genealogy of his family until the early 20th century.

996. Lentz, Lula Gillespie. ILLINOIS COMMENTARY: THE REMINIS-CENCES OF LULA GILLESPIE LENTZ. *J. of the Illinois State Hist. Soc. 1975 68(3): 267-288, (4): 353-367.* Part I. The author describes life on an Illinois farm in the late 19th century and mentions the farm homestead and furnishings, work routine and daily chores, food preparation, home manufacture of clothing, and sports and games, especially hunting. Discusses the family's practice of its Baptist faith and provides a first-hand account of rural education. Part II. The author describes her experiences of farm life and later town residency, rural education, marriage, and early married life with Eli G. Lentz, a school superin-tendent and later professor at Southern Illinois Normal University. Covers 1890 to 1929.
N. Lederer

997. Lepre, Jerome. A FAMILY PORTRAIT. *J. of Mississippi Hist. 1979 41(4): 373-382.* Discusses the pioneer families of the Mississippi Gulf Coast. Included in the discussion are the Boney, Delaunay, Fountain, LaFontaine, Moran, Lepre, Necaise, Ladner, Ryan, Fayard, Cuevas, and Saujon families. Lepre traces his main line of ancestors and recounts the difficulties he encoun-tered in seeking to resolve contradictions and disagreements in his family history.
M. S. Legan

998. Levin, Arthur. A SOVIET JEWISH FAMILY COMES TO CAL-GARY. *Can. Ethnic Studies [Canada] 1974 6(1-2): 53-66.* Describes the experi-ence of the first Soviet Jewish family to come to Calgary, Alberta, during the post-1971 wave of Jewish emigration from the USSR, as reported in interviews held in September and October 1974.

999. Lewis, Bessie M. THE WIGGS OF SOUTH CAROLINA. *South Carolina Hist. Mag. 1973 74(2): 80-97.* Traces the history of the Wigg family in South Carolina from the first appearance of Richard Wigg in court records, 1705/1706. The name figures prominently in public affairs in the state until the Civil War, when the Wiggs dispersed. 112 notes.
D. L. Smith

1000. Lieber, Constance L. "THE GOOSE HANGS HIGH": EXCERPTS FROM THE LETTERS OF MARTHA HUGHES CANNON. *Utah Hist. Q. 1980 48(1): 37-48.* Martha Hughes Cannon (1857-1932) was the fourth polyga-mous wife of Angus Munn Cannon, president of the Salt Lake Stake of the Mormon Church. To prevent Angus Cannon's arrest for polygamy, Martha exiled herself to England during 1885-87. Her letters reveal loneliness, constant fear of exposure, fear of Cannon's arrest, and jealousy of other wives. The 1890 Manifesto allowed her to live openly in Salt Lake City and continue her medical career. In 1896 she became the first woman state senator in the United States. Based on letters and diaries in the Angus Munn Cannon collection, LDS Ar-chives; 6 illus., 23 notes.
J. L. Hazelton

1001. Liggin, Edna. BERTHA PORTER BURNS—FROM THE NORTH CORNER OF SHILOH. *North Louisiana Hist. Assoc. J. 1975 6(2):81-84.* Bertha Porter Burns was born north of Shiloh on 24 October 1884. In 1974, she was the "living widow of the late M. V. Burns, country preacher . . . mother to six children" with "the courage to live alone in her house in Bernice." She taught school at Mt. Sterling, Salem, and Mt. Patrick, all Baptist church-schoolhouses, and married the Reverend Marion Van Burns on 5 December 1905. They lived first in Oakland (Louisiana) and then in Shiloh, before moving to Bernice in 1922. "Generously and courageously, Bertha Burns shared with countless people the life of her husband." He died on 7 August 1965. 2 photos.   A. N. Garland

1002. Liggin, Edna. CATHERINE COOK MABRY: MOTHER OF TWELVE, FROM THE WEST CORNER OF SHILOH. *North Louisiana Hist. Assoc. J. 1975 7(1): 23-25.* William Pierce Mabry and Catherine Cook were married in Alabama and lived for a time at Muscle Shoals, across the Dog River. They moved to Louisiana with two children and settled first at Patton Town, near present-day Lisbon. Later they moved to a farm about a mile northwest of the present town of Bernice and 10 more children were born to them; in all, they had 10 boys and 2 girls. In 1885, William Mabry was killed by bullets fired by four concealed gunmen. The four were captured and brought to trial, during which they claimed they had shot the wrong man. Catherine Cook Mabry continued to operate the farm and remained active until she was quite old. All except one of her children lived to be over 80 years of age. She eventually sold the farm and spent her remaining years with her children and grandchildren. Photo.
                                                              A. N. Garland

1003. Liggin, Edna. MARGARET FULLER ELAM, SOLDIER'S DAUGHTER: FROM THE SOUTH CORNER OF SHILOH. *North Louisiana Assoc. J. 1975 6(4): 175-177.* Margaret Fuller Elam, now 100 years old, blind, and living in a nursing home in Bernice, was born 3 February 1874 "across Middlefork Creek, south of Shiloh." As a young girl she worked on her father's farm and during the summer went to Fellowship Church School. She married Henry Clay Elam, of Missouri, and bore four children, two of whom died at early ages. Her father, Alf Fuller, became famous as a Civil War veteran and was the last surviving veteran of the Civil War in Lincoln Parish. Margaret Fuller Elam has been a member of the Fellowship Baptist Church for 87 years. Photo.
                                                              A. N. Garland

1004. Liggin, Edna. MARY EDMUNDS TABOR LEE—FROM THE EAST CORNER OF SHILOH. *North Louisiana Hist. Assoc. J. 1975 6(3): 133-135.* Mary Edmunds Tabor Lee was born in Georgia but moved with her family to settle in Union Parish, west of Farmerville, in the 1840's. On 4 December 1852, 15-year-old Mary married George Tabor, and they lived in a house on property given them by her father some three miles east of Shiloh. They had five children during 1852-61, when George went off to war. He died, apparently in 1863, in Holly Springs, Mississippi. Mary married Dan Lee, about whom little is known, in 1866; he disappeared in 1871, after having fathered three children. From time to time thereafter Mary was "involved in litigation that complicated her life." She never married again and eventually "gained a reputation as a 'medicine woman,' and was sent for wherever there was sickness." Mary died 22 January 1926 and was buried at Shiloh.   A. N. Garland

1005.   Linsenmeyer, Helen Walker.   ILLINOIS COMMENTARY: THREE GENERATIONS OF RIVER COMMERCE: THE JENKINS FAMILY OF GRAND TOWER.   *J. of the Illinois State Hist. Soc. 1980 73(1): 53-60.* Discusses the impact of the Jenkins family on the economic growth of Grand Tower, a river town in Jackson County, Illinois. Thomas Jenkins, son Herod Marshall Jenkins, and grandson Thomas Whitson Jenkins were river merchants during 1818-90's. Based on the inventory of the estate of Herod Marshall Jenkins and other primary and secondary sources; 3 drawings, 3 photos, 26 notes.

G. V. Wasson

1006.   Linsink, Judy Nolte; Kirkham, Christine M.; and Witzke, Karen Pauba. "MY ONLY CONFIDANT": THE LIFE AND DIARY OF EMILY HAWLEY GILLESPIE.   *Ann. of Iowa 1980 45(4): 288-312.* Contains excerpts from the diary (1858-88) of Iowa farm wife Emily Hawley Gillespie along with a narrative summary of her life. Based on the 10-volume Emily Gillespie diary deposited at the Iowa State Historical Department, Iowa City, Iowa; 3 photos, note.

P. L. Peterson

1007.   List, Howard M. and List, Edith M., ed.   JOHN M. SHIVELY'S MEMOIR.   *Oregon Hist. Q. 1980 81(1): 4-29, (2): 180-195.* Part I. John M. Shively (1804-93), Oregon pioneer, recorded his reminiscences in 1883. Describes some family background, his experiences on his way to Oregon in 1843, his stay in Astoria, and the beginning of his trip back East in 1845. Describes problems with Indians. 3 illus., 2 photos, map, 39 notes. Part II. Conclusion. Shively's adventures from 1845 to 1851 included advising the government on the Oregon situation during 1845-46, being the first postmaster west of the Rocky Mountains (in Astoria, Oregon), organizing the Pacific mail service, and participating in the California gold rush. Based mainly on Shively's memoir with some other primary sources; 5 illus., photo, 2 maps, 21 notes.   G. R. Schroeder

1008.   Littlefield, Daniel F., Jr. and Littlefield, Ann.   THE BEAMS FAMILY: FREE BLACKS IN INDIAN TERRITORY.   *J. of Negro Hist. 1976 6(1): 16-35.* The anomalous experience of free black people in the Indian Territory is traced in a history of the Beams family (1823-58). Despite successful recourse to the courts to protect their free status, the Beams family members were enslaved, killed, or forced to flee to Mexico. Theirs was a hollow victory. Based on primary sources in the Archives of the United States; 80 notes.   N. G. Sapper

1009.   Lopez, Claude-Anne.   A STORY OF GRANDFATHERS, FATHERS, AND SONS.   *Yale U. Lib. Gazette 1979 53(4): 177-195.* The Beinecke Library of Yale University acquired a group of letters from the heirs of Jane Persis Burn-Murdoch. When the letters were examined, it was found they related to the European adventures and education of the sons of leaders such as John Adams, Robert Morris, and Robert Montgomery, but particularly to the unhappy experiences of Samuel Cooper Johonnot and Benjamin Franklin Bache and the care provided for them in Europe by Benjamin Franklin. 47 notes.

D. A. Yanchisin

1010.   Losi, Jan Joseph.   THE VALLANDIGHAMS OF NEWARK: A DELAWARE COPPERHEAD FAMILY.   *Delaware Hist. 1979 18(4): 219-225.* The Reverend James Vallandigham and family favored the Confederates during the

Civil War. Relatives of the famous Copperhead Democrat Clement Valland-igham, and willing to enlist in the southern cause, the Vallandighams were ostracized in the pro-Union community of Newark. After the war the Valland-igham sons, James, Jr., and Edward, slowly worked their way back into the community's trust. They wrote about their war experiences and never shrank from support of the southern cause, but came to recognize the importance of war in unleashing America's economic energies and freeing the nation from the incubus of slavery. 29 notes.   R. M. Miller

1011. Marble, Allan. THE BURNS FAMILY OF WILMOT TOWNSHIP: SCOTCH-IRISH FOLK IN ANNAPOLIS COUNTY. *Nova Scotia Hist. [Canada] 1978 8(2): 171-180.* Traces the genealogy of Francis Burns (d. 1798) through four generations. He came to Wilmot Township from the North of Ireland with his brothers William and John in 1764, obtained a land grant of 450 acres, and raised his family of eight children on the land. Sources include census, church, and cemetery records.   H. M. Evans

1012. Marble, Allan E. THE BURNS FAMILY OF WILMOT TOWNSHIP: SCOTCH-IRISH FOLK IN ANNAPOLIS COUNTY. *Nova Scotia Hist. Q. [Canada] 1978 8(2): 171-180.* Traces the genealogy of the Burns family through four generations; Francis Burns (d. 1789) came to Wilmot Township with his brother William (1733-1818) from the North of Ireland in 1764. Primary and secondary sources.   H. M. Evans

1013. Marble, Allan E. and Punch, Terrence M. SIR J. S. D. THOMPSON: A PRIME MINISTER'S FAMILY CONNECTIONS. *Nova Scotia Hist. Q. [Canada] 1977 7(4): 377-388.* Outlines the genealogy of John S. D. Thompson (1844-94), a native of Halifax and Prime Minister of Canada 1892-94. The listings trace the family from 1796 in Waterford, Ireland, to 1903 and include both female and male lines. Primary and secondary sources.   H. M. Evans

1014. Marshall, J. Furber. A BANKS FAMILY OF NOVA SCOTIA. *Nova Scotia Hist. Q. 1977 7(2): 175-188.* Traces the genealogy of Moses Banks (1739-1833) and Joshua Banks (1749-1843), of Granville, Nova Scotia. Primary sources; biblio.   H. M. Evans

1015. Martin, Terry. THE RACE THAT GOD MADE MAD: A MEMOIR BY AN ARCHITECT'S GRANDDAUGHTER. *Kansas Q. 1974 6(2): 105-114.* Recounts the life of her grandfather Joseph Martin in the context of other Irish ancestors in 19th century Kansas.   S

1016. McCurdy, Mary Burton Derrickson. THE TOWNLEYS AND WARNERS OF VIRGINIA AND THEIR ENGLISH CONNECTIONS. *Virginia Mag. of Hist. and Biog. 1973 81(3): 319-367.* Reports the results of further genealogical researches into the English family pedigrees of the Townleys and Warners supplementing the original report in this journal entitled "A Discovery Concerning the Townley and Warner Families of Virginia," 1969 77(4): 473-476. Includes figures showing: 1) the pedigree of Elizabeth Sotherton Warner (ca. 1582-16??), 2) the Warners of Hoe-Next-East Dereham and their descen-dants, 3) Dugdales's pedigree chart of Townley of Barnside showing the origin of Townley of Stonehedge, and 4) Dugdale's pedigree chart of Townley of Stone-hedge. Carries the detailed family histories down to the close of the 19th century in both England and Virginia. Based on primary sources, mainly parish registers and records of wills and deeds; 4 figs., 167 notes.   R. V. Ritter

1017. McGinty, Garnie W. MARY JANE CONLY LESHE: PIONEER WOMAN OF BIENVILLE PARISH (1849-1932). *North Louisiana Hist. Assoc. J. 1976 7(2): 61-63.* Mary Jane Conly was the third child of Cullen Thomas Conly, of Savannah, Georgia. When she was about 20 she married Usir Leshe (1839-1934) and moved with him to Bienville Parish. She bore 14 children; one died in infancy, 13 reached adulthood. "The Leshe family were fervent patriots" and Mary Jane Leshe promoted "education and patriotism, instilling frugality, thrift, and industry in her descendants." She was a "deeply religious woman" and "a loyal and devoted member of the Baptist Church." Photo, 4 notes.
                                                        A. N. Garland

1018. Menard, Wilmon. THE WIDOW SINCLAIR AND HER SEA SEARCH FOR PARADISE. *Beaver [Canada] 1981 312(1): 48-55.* In 1863, Eliza Sinclair (1800-93) uprooted 12 members of her family from their home on New Zealand's South Island and departed on the *Bessie* on a "long-cherished plan [to establish] an estate in Canada." Arriving in Victoria in June 1863, the settlers soon saw that the grazing lands for sheep and cattle ranches could be cleared only with considerable time and effort; hence they departed for Hawaii, where they bought the entire island of Niihau for $10,000. "The House" was soon constructed, symbolizing the matriarchial rule of Eliza Sinclair, the "kindly, wise and beloved leader." The island remains with her descendants and is regarded by some as "a feudal island-state of serfs."
                                                        E. A. Chard

1019. Merrill, Ginette de B. THE MEETING OF ELINOR GERTRUDE MEAD AND WILL HOWELLS AND THEIR COURTSHIP. *Old Northwest 1982 8(1): 23-47.* Discusses the courtship of William Dean Howells and Elinor Gertrude Mead from their meeting in Columbus, Ohio, in 1860 to their marriage in Paris in December 1862. Howells's reluctance to introduce his fiancee to his father and his belated engagement announcement indicate that he feared some opposition from his family. Based on the Howells Papers at the Houghton Library, Harvard, and other primary sources; 4 illus., 4 photos, chronology, 24 notes.
                                                        P. L. McLaughlin

1020. Miller, Lillian B. THE PEALE FAMILY: A LIVELY MIXTURE OF ART AND SCIENCE. *Smithsonian 1979 10(1): 66-80.* Discusses the lives and careers of Charles Willson Peale and seven of his sons, including the scapegrace Charles Linnaeus Peale, 1770-1823.

1021. Miller, M. Sammye. LAST WILL AND TESTAMENT OF ROBERT REED CHURCH, SENIOR (1839-1912). *J. of Negro Hist. 1980 65(2): 156-163.* Robert Reed Church, Sr., was the most successful black businessman in Memphis, Tennessee, by the time of his death in 1912. He was one of the wealthiest Afro-Americans of his generation, and his children distinguished him as well. 8 notes.
                                                        N. G. Sapper

1022. Mills, Gary B. and Mills, Elizabeth Shown. THE FORGOTTEN PEOPLE. *Family Heritage 1979 2(3): 78-81.* Originating from the marriage of a black slave named Marie Thérèse Coincoin and a Frenchman named Claude Thomas Pierre Metoyer, ca. 1767, a free mixed-blood colony of Creoles developed in Natchitoches on Louisiana's Cane River, persisting as an integrated and self-sustained community until the Civil War; after that the land was gradually sold and the family's unique social status was greatly altered by changing race relations into the 20th century.

1023.   Mills, Gary B. and Mills, Elizabeth Shown.   LOUISE MARGUERITE: ST. DENIS' *OTHER* DAUGHTER.   *Southern Studies 1977 16(3): 321-328.* Louisiana historians have long been confused about the number and sequence of the children of Louis Antoine Juchereau de St. Denis (1676-1744), Louisiana's "Cavalier in the Wilderness." The first child was Louise Marguerite Juchereau de St. Denis, an illegitimate child probably born of a Natchitoches Indian woman ca. 1712. Church records indicate her first marriage in 1729 and her participation in various civic-religious functions. She was not included in the legitimate heirs of St. Denis, nor was she on good terms with St. Denis' wife. She had two children by her first marriage. She remarried in 1758. Based on Church records and court documents at Natchitoches and on secondary sources; 28 notes.   J. Buschen

1024.   Mitchell, J. Marcus.   THE PAUL FAMILY.   *Old-Time New England 1973 63(3): 73-77.* Tells of Thomas Paul, a black minister who organized the first black church in Boston, his brothers, Nathaniel and Shadrach, who were also ministers, and other members of the Paul family. Illus.   R. N. Lokken

1025.   Molz, Ferdinand L.   THE CHRISTIANA MACHINE COMPANY AND THE STATUS REVOLUTION.   *J. of the Lancaster County Hist. Soc. 1974 78(3): 141-152.* Details the background and social status, 1880-1900, of the Broomell family who owned the Christiana Machine Company in Christiana, Pennsylvania; analyzes the Broomell position within local social and business circles and draws parallels to the characteristics of the business community on a national level. 47 notes.

1026.   Mondone, Mrs. Raymond.   AN ITALIAN FAMILY IN PRINCETON.   *Family Heritage 1978 1(4): 118-121.* Gives the history of the author's family since 1884, when her father, Achille "Charlie" Carnevale, came to America from Petronello di Molise, Italy, and settled in Princeton, New Jersey.

1027.   Moore, Willard B.   DOWN ON THE FARM: TRADITION IN THE LIFE OF AN AMERICAN FAMILY.   *Family Heritage 1978 1(6): 164-169.* Traces the traditional Minnesota farm heritage of the Standke family, whose ancestors from Germany settled in Minnesota in 1873.

1028.   Morgan, David T.   THE SHEFTALLS OF SAVANNAH.   *Am. Jewish Hist. Q. 1973 62(4): 348-361.* Benjamin Sheftall arrived in Savannah, Georgia, in 1733. The Sheftall Papers indicate that the family acquired real estate throughout the state before the Revolution. Mordecei and Levi Sheftall suffered imprisonment, banishment, and loss of livelihood for espousing the American cause when the British captured Savannah in 1778. Although the government did not reimburse the Sheftalls for losses suffered, they prospered again after 1790 and remained active in the affairs of Savannah's Jewish community. The Sheftall Papers, Keith Reid Collection, University of Georgia; 39 notes.

F. Rosenthal

1029. Morris, Adelaide K. TWO SISTERS HAVE I: EMILY DICKIN-SON'S VINNIE AND SUSAN. *Massachusetts Rev. 1981 22(2): 323-332.* Describes the two most important women in Emily Dickinson's life: her natural sister, Lavinia Norcross Dickinson (b. ca. 1832), familiarly referred to as Vinnie, and her brother's wife, Susan Gilbert Dickinson, commonly called Sue, her lifelong friend and fascination. The three women were neighbors for 30 years, sharing each other's sufferings and triumphs. Sue represented the heavenly in Emily's life, Vinnie the earthly. These two complementary yet contradictory influences helped keep Emily on an even keel. Emily referred to Vinnie's world as a prose world and to Sue's as a poetry world. Relations between Vinnie and Sue exploded after Emily died, since Emily's role as arbitrator was vacant. Covers ca. 1850-86. Based on Emily Dickinson's letters and poetry, Vinnie Dickinson's diary, and Mabel Todd's journal; 11 notes. E. R. Campbell

1030. Morrison, Katherine L. A REEXAMINATION OF BROOKS AND HENRY ON JOHN QUINCY ADAMS. *New England Q. 1981 54(2): 163-179.* The career of John Quincy Adams provided a lens through which Henry and Brooks Adams could look back upon their family and nation. Exchanges in their letters over Brooks's manuscript, "Life of John Quincy Adams," indicate moral and intellectual positions between the brothers that are more divergent than previously believed. Flattering comments included in the letters cannot be taken seriously. The evidence is even stronger that Henry never supplied much intellectual material for Brooks. Primary sources; 36 notes. R. S. Sliwoski

1031. Moskos, Charles C., Jr. GROWING UP GREEK AMERICAN. *Society 1977 14(2): 64-71.* Author reminisces about his life as a Greek American and offers insight into the assimilation of ethnic groups, as well as family history, 1898-1976.

1032. Moyer, Willoughby W. ABSTRACT OF DIARY OF WARREN G. BEAN, 1899. *Pennsylvania Folklife 1979 28(4): 32-36.* Warren G. Bean, born in 1866, took over the management of the family farm in Skippack Township in 1896 and kept a diary, and the abstract of this document from the year 1899 reflects the weather conditions and everyday hard work encountered by a Pennsylvania farmer and his family.

1033. Munford, Kenneth and Moore, Harriet. THE BOSWELLS OF BOS-WELL SPRINGS. *Oregon Hist. Q. 1982 83(4): 340-370.* Narrates the lives of Captain Ben D. Boswell and his wife, Emma, who were owners of Boswell Springs, a health resort, in Douglas County, Oregon, at the turn of the century. Enlisting as a private at the start of the Civil War, Boswell rose to the rank of major by 1864. He was wounded and disabled during the seige of Vicksburg, and this injury, plus several misdiagnosed maladies, plagued him during his eccentric military career. Following his retirement from the service in 1878, the Boswells spent 10 years in California and then returned to Oregon to settle and manage the resort. Based on the Boswell papers, National Archives; letters in the files of Bureau of Pensions, National Archives, and numerous Oregon newspaper articles; 5 photos, map, 158 notes. C. R. Gunter, Jr.

1034. Murray, Lawrence L.   REVIEW ESSAY: THE MELLON FAMILY, MAKING AND SHAPING HISTORY: A SURVEY OF THE LITERATURE.   *Western Pennsylvania Hist. Mag. 1979 62(1): 61-66.* Covers 1885-1978.

1035. Musto, David F.   THE ADAMS FAMILY.   *Massachusetts Hist. Soc. Pro. 1981 93: 40-58.* Explores the mental outlook or "family mind" of the Adams family, which held sway through four generations to the death of Brooks Adams in 1927. Abigail Adams so recognized and identified with her husband's call to duty and sacrifice and so understood the need to prepare the children for careers in national service that she subordinated her personal loneliness and desires. Some members of the family, notably John Quincy and Charles Francis, met the challenge of the myth, lived long fruitful lives, and became successful public servants. For other members, the myth was clearly an unbearable burden. George Washington Adams, the son of John Quincy Adams, unable to separate his own nature from parental expectations, anguished over the prospects of not measuring up to the family myth, committed suicide at the age of 28.   40 notes.

G. A. Glovins

1036. Musto, David F.   CONTINUITY ACROSS GENERATIONS: THE ADAMS FAMILY MYTH.   Albin, Mel, ed. *New Directions in Psychohistory: The Adelphi Papers in Honor of Erik H. Erikson* (Lexington, Mass.: Heath, 1980): 117-129. Discusses the extent to which people are influenced by their environments, situating this dilemma in the family's quest for identity and continuity across generations. Examines four generations of the Adams family, beginning with John and Abigail Adams in 1764, attempting to understand the family's intergenerational internal stream of identity, the "family myth," and how it relates to the wider culture. Such a myth can be forged in a stressful historical period, continue for several generations as an inherited set of attitudes, and eventually be reconstructed under the impact of an incongruous environment. Secondary sources; 23 notes.   J. Powell

1037. Muth, Bell Rowan Stuart.   PLACE NAMES ON A FAMILY FARM. *Kentucky Folklore Record 1978 24(1): 15-17.* Discusses language as folklore; the Stewart family of Warren and Butler Counties, Kentucky, is an example of the survival of personal identity for more than 100 years.

1038. Nasatir, Abraham P.   THE NASATIR FAMILY IN SANTA ANA, CALIFORNIA 1898 TO 1915.   *Western States Jewish Hist. Q. 1983 15(3): 254-258.* The author's parents came from Russia and settled in 1900 in Santa Ana, where his father, Morris Nasatir, ran a men's clothing store. His mother's brothers, Sam, Isidore, and Frank Hurwitz, joined the Nasatirs in California; they worked for a while with Morris Nasatir, but soon set up their own businesses, including stores in Exeter and Visalia. In 1915, when their children were high school age, the Nasatirs left Santa Ana for Los Angeles so that the youngsters could associate with other Jewish children and more easily follow Jewish traditions.   Based on family interviews and records; 6 notes.   B. S. Porter

1039. Noon, Rozanne E.   THE BISHOP'S CHILDREN.   *Hist. Mag. of the Protestant Episcopal Church 1974 43(1): 5-20.* Reviews the life, works, and theological philosophies of Frederick Huntington, Episcopal Bishop of Central New York during 1869-1904, and his children. His daughters, Arria and Ruth, shared the Bishop's zeal and energy for good works, but not his view of woman's place as being in the home. His son James also leaned toward a religious life, but deplored the money-raising, good works aspects of the Church, causing conflict with his father; another son, George, was undecided. The death of the Bishop left James to turn to the quiet life he so much desired. 28 notes.   V. L. Human

1040.   Nordham, George Washington.   THE WEDDING OF MARTHA AND GEORGE WASHINGTON. *Daughters of the Am. Revolution Mag. 1977 111(2): 108-111.* Discusses the courtship and wedding ceremony and plans of Martha Dandridge Custis and George Washington, 1759.

1041.   Ocko, Stephanie.   CHIEF MASSASOIT'S ROYAL FAMILY. *Early Am. Life 1978 9(2): 22-25.* Presents a genealogy (1620-1931) of Wampanoag chief Massasoit who aided Pilgrims at Plymouth Plantation.

1042.   Olfert,   Sharon.   THE   HILDEBRANDS   OF   ROSENTHAL, MANITOBA. *Mennonite Life 1979 34(4): 19-26.* The Hildebrand family was centered in Neuenburg, South Russia, from 1818 until 1878 when Bernhard Hildebrand (1840-1910) and family emigrated to Rosenthal, Manitoba. A farming family, they gradually expanded their holdings until the 10 children all had nearby farms. Patriarch Bernhard Hildebrand supported education and foreign missions. Listing of Bernhard Hildebrand family; Rosenthal Village census 1878-80; farm inventory 1880-81. 7 photos, map of Rosenthal householders, late 1870's, 10 notes, biblio.   B. Burnett

1043.   Ostendorf, Lloyd.   LINCOLN AND THE HOBLITS. *Lincoln Herald 1975 77(1): 49-52.* Two generations of the Hoblit family of Logan County, Illinois, were friends of Abraham Lincoln. Lincoln frequently visited the Hoblits. Based on documentation provided by the Hoblit family; illus., 2 photos, 5 notes.
B. J. LaBue

1044.   Otto, John Solomon and Banks, Ben Wayne.   THE BANKS FAMILY OF YELL COUNTY, ARKANSAS: A "PLAIN FOLK" FAMILY OF THE HIGHLANDS SOUTH. *Arkansas Hist. Q. 1982 41(2): 146-167.* Describes the lifestyle of two generations of the Alex Banks family, small slaveholding farmers, during 1830-60. Based on oral interviews, census records, and secondary sources; 4 photos, map, 64 notes.   G. R. Schroeder

1045.   Overholser, J. Spencer.   THE TERRE HILL OBERHOLTZER FAMILY. *Pennsylvania Mennonite Heritage 1978 1(2): 2-8.* Offers a genealogy of several members of the Oberholtzer family who originated in Switzerland, immigrated to Pennsylvania, and established farms in the community of Terre Hill, 1720's-1850's.

1046.   Pace, Dick.   HENRY SIEBEN: PIONEER MONTANA STOCK-MAN. *Montana 1979 29(1): 2-15.* Henry Sieben (1847-1937) came to Montana's gold fields in 1864, was a farm laborer, prospector, and freighter, then turned to livestock raising along the Smith River in 1870. In partnership with his brothers Leonard and Jacob, Henry Sieben raised cattle and became one of the territory's pioneer sheep ranchers in 1875. The partnership was dissolved in 1879 and Henry moved his stock to the Lewistown area. He established a reputation as an excellent businessman and as someone who took care of his stock and employees. After ranching in the Culbertson area, Henry Sieben purchased ranches near Cascade and along Little Prickly Pear Creek, forming the Sieben Livestock Company. By 1907, these two ranches had become the heart of his cattle and sheep raising business which he directed from his home in Helena. Sieben became well known for his business approach to ranching and for his public and private philanthropies. His family continues to operate the Sieben Ranch Company today. Family records, contemporary newspapers, and interviews with employees and family members; 13 illus., map, 7 notes, biblio.

R. C. Myers

1047. Page, Jean Jepson. NOTES ON THE CONTRIBUTIONS OF FRANCIS BLACKWELL MAYER AND HIS FAMILY TO THE CULTURAL HISTORY OF MARYLAND. *Maryland Hist. Mag. 1981 76(3): 217-239.* Catalogs the numerous contributions of Francis Blackwell Mayer (1827-99), his father Charles Frederick (1795-1864), and his uncle Brantz (1809-79) to the artistic life and historic preservation of Annapolis. Frank Mayer's original house is now the home of Historic Annapolis, Inc., and his architectural sketches are being used today in restoring "old Annapolis." Mayer founded the well-known Allston Association and the Local Improvement Association in 1884, while his sizeable output of "history paintings" is an invaluable record of the sights and scenes of 19th-century Annapolis. Includes a catalog of Mayer's unlocated paintings. Mayer papers in Baltimore and Detroit, secondary works; 5 illus., 57 notes.

G. J. Bobango

1048. Page, Thomas More. LLOYD TILGHMAN AND SHERWOOD MANOR. *Maryland Hist. Mag. 1979 74(2): 152-174.* Traces the family background, education, probable adult activities, and court property settlement (when he died intestate) of Lloyd Tilghman (1749-1811), second son of revolutionary activist Matthew Tilghman (1718-90). Lloyd lived and died in relative obscurity, carefully managing his father's and then his own extensive landholdings in Talbot County, Maryland. His principal historical legacy is his dwelling, Sherwood Manor, still in existence and on the National Register of Historic Places. Concludes with a detailed architectural description and ownership record of Sherwood Manor. Based on contemporary correspondence, census records, tax lists, wills, land records, and court proceedings of Talbot County, Maryland; 2 illus., 114 notes.

C. B. Schulz

1049. Parramore, Thomas C. THE BARTONS OF BARTONSVILLE. *North Carolina Hist. R. 1974 51(1): 22-40.* Stephen Barton, Jr. (1806-65), brother of Clara Barton (1821-1912), moved from his native Massachusetts in 1856 to establish a short-lived mill village in Hertford County, North Carolina, based on a lumber trade with Norfolk, Virginia, and northern ports. The community and its thriving business activity were jeopardized by the commercial uncertainty of 1860 and by Barton's strict neutrality in the Civil War. The site was destroyed by Union soldiers in 1865. Primary and secondary sources; illus., map, 77 notes.

W. B. Bedford

1050. Parris, Percival J. and Shettleworth, Earle G., Jr., ed. PEDRO TOVOOKAN PARIS. *Old-Time New England 1973 63(3): 61-68.* This biographical sketch tells of an African who came to the United States in 1845 and became a member of the Parris family in Maine. The author, a member of the

family, was 11 years old when Pedro died in 1860, and wrote this account before his death in 1945. 4 illus., 12 notes.
R. N. Lokken

1051. Parsons, William T. and Heimburger, Mary Schuler. SHULER FAM-ILY CORRESPONDENCE. *Pennsylvania Folklife 1980 29(3): 98-113.* Re-produces letters exchanged by members of the Shuler family of Pennsylvania that provide information on the California gold rush, daily life in Pennsylvania, and the Civil War; texts in Pennsylvania German and English translation are pro-vided, 1849-64.

1052. Patterson, G. James. GREEK MEN IN A COFFEE HOUSE IN DEN-VER: FIVE LIFE HISTORIES. *J. of the Hellenic Diaspora 1976 3(2): 27-37.* Presents life histories of five Greek Americans in Denver, Colorado, emphasizing problems in cultural assimilation in the 20th century.

1053. Paulson, Ross Evans. "STRUCTURE" AND "STORY" IN THE SEARCH FOR THE COLONIAL FAMILY. *Rev. in Am. Hist. 1976 4(2): 171-177.* Review article prompted by Randolph Shipley Klein's *Portrait of an Early American Family: the Shippens of Pennsylvania Across Five Generations* (Philadelphia: U. of Pennsylvania Pr., 1975); discusses the use of social sciences methodology in compiling historical facts and formulating interpretations, specifically in terms of the Shippen family, 1668-1776.

1054. Pelley, Winifred F. et al. THOMAS[1] BRUCE OF SUDBURY AND MARLBOROUGH, MASSACHUSETTS. *New England Hist. and Geneal. Register 1982 136(Oct): 294-306.* Straightens out the identity of Thomas Bruce through a careful study of the Marlborough town records. He was long thought to be John Bruce, who actually turned out to be John Brewer of Sudbury. The Bruce family is traced from Thomas through three of his sons and their offspring.
A. E. Huff

1055. Pencak, William. THE MARTYROLOGY OF THOMAS HUTCH-INSON: FAMILY AND PUBLIC LIFE. *New England Hist. and Geneal. Register 1982 136(Oct): 279-293.* Analyzes Thomas Hutchinson's self-examina-tion of his life and his attempt to justify his principles and behavior. Based on the writings of Hutchinson: a family history, diaries, and correspondence; 23 notes.
A. E. Huff

1056. Petrick, Paula. MOTHERS AND DAUGHTERS OF ELDORADO: THE FISK FAMILY OF HELENA, MONTANA, 1867-1902. *Montana 1982 32(3): 50-63.* Elizabeth Fisk was an average, middle-class woman on the mining frontier. The frontier affected such women by eroding informal networks and returning women to the home and domesticity, creating a scarcity of domestic help to relieve household burdens, causing husbands to be absent from home for long periods so that women had to manage on their own, and undermining social institutions that normally were power bases for women. Elizabeth changed her views of a woman's role—she endured and rationalized. However, her daughter Grace, who grew up on the frontier, asserted herself. Based on Fisk letters in the Montana Historical Society archives, Helena; 8 illus., 91 notes.
R. C. Myers

1057.   Pinckney, Elise, ed.   LETTERS OF ELIZA LUCAS PINCKNEY, 1768-1782.   *South Carolina Hist. Mag. 1975 76(3): 143-170.* Miscellaneous letters held by the South Carolina Historical Society relate family concerns (marriages, births, and illnesses) as well as the hardships of the Revolutionary War on the homefront. Based on primary sources; 54 notes.

R. H. Tomlinson

1058.   Pister, M. Claire.   MARY.   *Pacific Hist. 1980 24(3): 325-343.* Mary W. K. D. Rhodes (13 October 1808-16 September 1893), the author's great-grandmother, was born and educated in New Hampshire. She was a teacher; when widowed in the 1830's in Charleston, South Carolina, she resumed teaching. In 1838 she married Colonel Elisha Rhodes and moved to Galveston Island, Texas. Her husband was the US Consul to the Republic of Texas. When he was ill or away, she took care of his business. When Colonel Rhodes became an invalid in 1848, Mary took over running the family of his, her, and their children. For financial reasons she went to California alone in 1850, set up a boarding house in San Francisco, and bought some property in Stockton. The family was brought west, where its fortunes went up and down. Mary built Windsor Farm in Stockton. Mary supported the South in the Civil War and lost her two younger sons in that conflict. She left the farm to Stark Blount Smith, Jr., her grandson who had cared for her and the farm. Based on family letters; 3 photos, 90 notes.

G. L. Lake

1059.   Plummer, Stephen and Julin, Suzanne.   LUCY SWAN, SIOUX WOMAN: AN ORAL HISTORY.   *Frontiers 1981 6(3): 29-32.* Parts of an interview with a Sioux woman, detailing her family life and an Indian legend, 1900-71.

1060.   Poteet, James M.   A HOMECOMING: THE BULKELEY FAMILY IN NEW ENGLAND.   *New England Q. 1974 47(1): 30-50.* Peter Bulkeley, a Puritan pastor, came to America in 1635 and settled in Concord. He viewed New England as a holy experiment directed by the hand of God. In 1646 his book of sermons expounding the covenant theology was printed in London, the first book by a New England clergyman. While his son Gershom was disillusioned by Puritanism, the third generation accepted it on its own terms. John Bulkeley "found contentment in the routine of a provincial, country preacher." 60 notes.

E. P. Stickney

1061.   Power, Patrick Victor.   MAYOR DALEY'S OTHER HOME: THE IRISH CONNECTION.   *Studies [Ireland] 1980 69(273): 79-92.* An examination of the Irish background of the Daley family in Ring and Old Parish, a Gaelic-speaking peninsula of the West Carberry coast, County Cork, Ireland, whence the family emigrated to Chicago a century ago. Mayor Richard Daley's (d. 1976) dedication to social and political achievement over 21 years as mayor, chairman of the Cook County Democratic Party, and powerbroker of the Illinois State Senate is treated against the background of his Irish roots. The hostility of the press against Daley's big city boss image is set against the more humane traits in his character. Based on the author's personal research in Daley's family background in Ireland.

J. J. N. McGurk

1062.   Prashek, James L.   THE NURNBERGERS IN DAKOTA: A FAMILY BIOGRAPHY.   *North Dakota Hist. 1979 46(4): 9-19.* Frederick Nurnberger, native of Germany (b. 1838), arrived in Wisconsin with his parents in 1854. As an adult he moved to North Dakota where he and his numerous progeny became owners of large tracts of land in Richland County. Frederick was director in the Farmers Mutual Protecive Association, was on the Board of Township supervisors, and was elected justice of the peace, getting the reputation of a troublemaker, though always honest and fairdealing. However, in later life, a suit was brought against him for fraudulant manipulation of homestead claims. Drawnout litigation clouded his old age and he died in 1923. 11 photos, 2 charts, 109 notes, ref.   H. F. Thomson

1063.   Price, Jacob M.   ONE FAMILY'S EMPIRE: THE RUSSELL-LEE-CLERK CONNECTION IN MARYLAND, BRITAIN, AND INDIA, 1707-1857.   *Maryland Hist. Mag. 1977 72(2): 165-225.* Details the life, family interrelationships, and progeny of the Scottish merchant James Russell (1708-88), who married Ann Lee, daughter of Philip Lee, founder of the Maryland branch of that famous family. Russell was one of the most important London commission merchants of his day, a pioneer of the cargo system of credit consignments. One of his sons-in-law, William Molleson, eventually surpassed him in profits and volume. Records Russell's innumerable American interests and connections, and analyzes his difficulties arising from the American Revolution. Years were consumed in seeking compensation for his confiscated property; his widow reached a settlement only long after his death. A final section describes the multifarious careers of Russell's descendants in the Indian civil and military service. The whole involved story is quite representative of the opportunities grasped by the Scottish middle class following the 1707 Act of Union which opened the hitherto closed empire as an arena for what became a veritable folk migration, and also shows the historical path for studying the bourgeois strata through the microcosm of the individual family. Largely from archival materials in British Museum and Public Records Office plus secondary works; 3 illus., 6 tables, 243 notes, appendix showing Clerks' genealogy in India.   G. J. Bobango

1064.   Propst, Nell Brown.   VOICE FROM THE FRONTIER.   *Methodist Hist. 1982 20(2): 51-59.* Missouri Powell Propst, born in Alabama and a daughter of a sometime Methodist minister, came with her husband to northeastern Colorado in 1874 to participate in taming the frontier. She helped to organize the first Methodist Episcopal Church, South in the area and later tried to serve in a meaningful way with the congregation of the northern Methodist Episcopal Church. When she found that women were used in a very limited way in the church, she sent, in 1891, an article in protest to the *Christian Advocate.* Her article, which was not accepted, is printed here. Based partly on family letters and other papers; 12 notes.   H. L. Calkin

1065.   Punch, Terrence M. and Marble, Allan E.   JOHN HOWE GENEALOGY.   *Nova Scotia Hist. Q. [Canada] 1976 6(3): 317-328.* Gives the genealogy of John Howe, a Loyalist in Nova Scotia and King's printer in Halifax, in the 18th and 19th centuries.

1066.   Punch, Terrence Michael.   TOBIN GENEALOGY.   *Nova Scotia Hist. Q. [Canada] 1975 5(1): 71-82.* Contains a genealogy of Thomas Tobin (d. 1783), merchant tailor, who established his home in Halifax about 1759. He came from Newfoundland and, earlier, Ireland. Mentions his descendants down to 1936.

R. V. Ritter

1067.   Purvis, Thomas L.   THE MAKING OF A MYTH: ABRAHAM LINCOLN'S FAMILY BACKGROUND IN THE PERSPECTIVE OF JACKSONIAN POLITICS.   *J. of the Illinois State Hist. Soc. 1982 75(2): 148-160.* The myth of Abraham Lincoln's humble origins was a product of mid-19th-century politics that glorified the common man rising by his own efforts as well as the frontier culture in which exaggeration for effect was an accepted rhetorical device. Lincoln's family was representative of the early Illinois political elite and included members of the middle class and lesser gentry. Over three generations, Lincoln's relatives held various offices in Virginia, Kentucky, Indiana, and Illinois. Lincoln's awareness of these roots led him to woo the daughters of the Kentucky elite and contributed to his political confidence and aggressiveness. 4 illus., 53 notes.

A. W. Novitsky

1068.   Quander, Rohulamin.   THE QUANDER FAMILY, 1684-1910: ITS HISTORY AND ITS ROOTS.   *J. of the Afro-American Hist. and Geneal. Soc. 1982 3(2): 47-53.* History of the Quando, Quandoe, Quander, Quanders, or Kwando (various spellings) family beginning with the first reference to the name Quando in 1684.

1069.   Ramage, James A.   THOMAS HUNT MORGAN: FAMILY INFLUENCES IN THE MAKING OF A GREAT SCIENTIST.   *Filson Club Hist. Q. 1979 53(1): 5-25.* Thomas Hunt Morgan was a Nobel Prize winner for biology in 1933. He developed the famous fruit fly experiments that confirmed much of the theoretical work of Charles Darwin and Gregor Johann Mendel. Much of the article deals with Morgan's namesake uncle, the famous Confederate raider, his father Charlton, and his uncle Basil Duke. The remainder of the account consists of anecdotes about Morgan as a scholar, teacher, father, and husband. Based on the Hunt-Morgan Papers at the University of Kentucky; 58 notes.

G. B. McKinney

1070.   Raymond, Andrew.   A NEW ENGLAND COLONIAL FAMILY: FOUR GENERATIONS OF THE PORTERS OF HADLEY, MASSACHUSETTS.   *New England Hist. and Genealogical Register 1975 129(July): 198-220.* Recounts the rise of the Porter family to prominence in western Massachusetts. Samuel (d. 1689) was one of the founders of Hadley, but it was the three generations after him—especially his son, Samuel, Jr. (1660-1722), his grandson, Eleazer (1698-1751), and his great-grandsons Eleazer (1728-97) and Elisha (b. 1742)—who took advantage of the benefits of trade, land speculation, military offices, political patronage, and marriage alliances to make the Porters almost, but never quite, the equal of the Connecticut Valley "River Gods." Eleazer's and Elisha's affirmation of the patriot cause in the American Revolution and their adamant opposition to Shays' Rebellion secured for this family its legacy of wealth and political power as the 18th century came to a close. Based on primary documents and secondary works; 2 maps, 2 charts, 98 notes.

S. L. Patterson

1071. Reese, Charles Lee, Jr., ed. AUTOBIOGRAPHY OF CHRISTO-
PHER L. WARD (1868-1943). *Delaware Hist. 1973 15(3): 157-186.* A portion
of an incomplete autobiography written by Christopher L. Ward, historian, paro-
dist, novelist, and businessman. Describes Ward's family, his family's life at
Towanda, Pennsylvania, the move to Wilmington in the 1870's, and the Ward
home and surroundings in Wilmington. Sketches of his grandfathers, father, and
younger members of the family. 10 notes. Article to be continued.

R. M. Miller

1072. Reichlin, Ellie. "READING" FAMILY PHOTOGRAPHS: A CON-
TEXTUAL ANALYSIS OF THE CODMAN PHOTOGRAPHIC COLLEC-
TION. *Old-Time New England 1981 71(258): 115-149.* Discusses the
interrelated aspects of family history and "photographic usage" in the approximately 3,000 photographs left by the last two generations of the Codman family
of Lincoln, Massachusetts, which show how and why people of the mid and late
19th century took photographs and the photographic themes of one family.

1073. Reninger, Marion Wallace. RECOLLECTIONS OF THE WILLIAM-
SONS OF UPPER LAWN. *J. of the Lancaster County Hist. Soc. 1974 78(3):
113-125.* Offers a family genealogy and history of the Henry Stackhouse Williamson family of Lancaster, Pennsylvania, 1879-1966. 2 photos.

1074. Reynolds, Gary. AN AMERICAN FAMILY OF PAINTERS: JOHN
JAMES AUDUBON AND HIS SONS. *Art & Antiques 1982 5(1): 48-57.*
Biographies of John James Audubon (1785-1851) and his two sons, Victor Gifford Audubon (1809-60) and John Woodhouse Audubon (1812-62), focusing on
the paintings of animals and birds John did in collaboration with his two sons;
he also painted portraits and gave painting lessons during 1820-26 in order to
support his family.

1075. Riley, Glenda. FAMILY LIFE ON THE FRONTIER: THE DIARY
OF KITTURAH PENTON BELKNAP. *Ann. of Iowa 1977 44(1): 31-51.* A
diary kept by Kitturah Penton Belknap (1820-1913) describes her family's journey by covered wagon from Ohio to Iowa in late 1839. During the next eight
years, Kitturah struggled as a frontier wife in Iowa, recorded the deaths of three
of her first four children, found great comfort in religious meetings, and helped
her husband construct their first home. By 1848 her husband had caught "Oregon
fever" and Kitturah was soon preparing for another long trek to the West. 9 illus.

P. L. Petersen

1076. Riley, Paul D., ed. CATHER FAMILY LETTERS. *Nebraska Hist.
1973 54(4): 585-618.* Reprints letters written in 1895 by members of her family
to Emily Ann Caroline Cather (Willa Cather's grandmother), who at age 67
decided to visit her old home in Frederick County, Virginia. She resided in
Webster County, Nebraska, as did her entire family, all of whom moved from
Virginia in the 1870's. Letters detail conditions, chiefly in Nebraska, in summer
1895. Annotations by the editor and a genealogical chart help identify members
of the Cather family.

R. Lowitt

1077. Ritchie, Jean. LIVING IS COLLECTING: GROWING UP IN A
SOUTHERN APPALACHIAN "FOLK" FAMILY. *Appalachian J. 1977
4(4): 188-198.* The author's personal remembrances of Jason Ritchie are combined with the texts of some of his unpublished folklore and folk songs.

1078.   Robertson, Allen B.   THE FAMILY OF ROLEN ROGERS, A NEW ENGLAND PLANTER IN KING'S COUNTY.   *Nova Scotia Hist. Q. [Canada] 1979 9(2): 177-187.* Traces the descendants of Rolen Rogers (d. 1805) to the fifth generation. Rolen emigrated from Connecticut to Nova Scotia in 1760, acquired land, and became involved in community affairs. He reared eight children, three of whom founded families in Horton. Church, census, and cemetery records; 9 notes.   H. M. Evans

1079.   Rodriguez, Janice Eichholtz.   THE LANCASTER OF LEONARD EICHHOLTZ, 1750-1817.   *J. of the Lancaster County Hist. Soc. 1975 79(4): 175-207.* Presents a biographical account of Lancaster, Pennsylvania, tavern-keeper, Leonard Eichholtz, his family, and their times.

1080.   Roosa, Alma Carlson and Hamilton, Henry W.   HOMESTEADING IN THE 1880'S: THE ANDERSON-CARLSON FAMILIES OF CHERRY COUNTY.   *Nebraska Hist. 1977 58(3): 371-394.* Alma Carlson Roosa was five years old when her parents and grandparents homesteaded in Cherry County, Nebraska, in the 1880's. Her uncle, photographer John A. Anderson (1869-1948), lived in 1879 in the home of a married sister, Amanda Anderson Carlson. Her daughter, Alma Carlson Roosa, contributed valuable reminiscences to the editor and his wife as they prepared their biography of Anderson.   R. Lowitt

1081.   Ross, Frances Mitchell, ed.   "A TIE BETWEEN US THAT TIME CANNOT SEVER": THE LATTA FAMILY LETTERS, 1855-1872.   *Arkansas Hist. Q. 1981 40(1): 31-78.* A collection of 19 letters, which contain family news, written mainly to Eli Chambers Latta in California by his various brothers and sisters in Arkansas, Texas, and Indian Territory. Editor's notes based on census records and published family history; 4 photos, 2 maps, 132 notes.
                                                         G. R. Schroeder

1082.   Rothschild, Janice.   PRE-1867 ATLANTA JEWRY.   *Am. Jewish Hist. Q. 1973 62(3): 242-249.* The first Jewish family—Jacob and Jeanetta Hirsch Haas with their four children—came to Atlanta in 1845, soon followed by Henry Levi, Herman Haas, David Mayer, and others, mostly from southern Germany. Sketches family, business, and social activities. Mayer was instrumental in organizing the Hebrew Benevolent Society and a Jewish cemetery, and led the small community during the Civil War. Based on contemporary newspaper data and family recollections; 26 notes.   F. Rosenthal

1083.   Rovit, Earl.   FAULKNER, HEMINGWAY, AND THE AMERICAN FAMILY.   *Mississippi Q. 1976 29(4): 483-497.* Examines the childhood in middle-class rural homes which both Ernest Hemingway and William Faulkner shared, and the effect which this had on their world views, 1900-50.

1084.   Rowell, Gladys M.   MEMORIES OF AN ENGLISH SETTLER. *Alberta Hist. [Canada] 1982 30(2): 30-36.* Continued from a previous article. Part 2. Details the experiences of the Stephenson family when homesteading on a plot of land 16 miles southwest of High River. The freedom and isolation of life is noted as well as the variety of foods available, the excitement when new settlers arrived, the reopening of classes, the attempts to augment the family income by selling bread, and the purchase of the first horse. The hardships, loneliness, and fatalities caused many people to give up, but those who stayed now "look back upon those days with nostalgic longing." 3 sketches.   E. A. Chard

1085. Rudinsky, Mary Louise. SLOVAK AND AMERICAN ROOTS: A
COMPARISON. *Jednota Ann. Furdek 1982 21: 189-197.* The author traces
her genealogy, half English-Welsh and half Slovak, from the 16th century.

1086. Rudy, Michael. THE FAMILY OF JOHN[1] BOND OF BEVERLY,
MASSACHUSETTS. *New England Hist. and Geneal. Register 1983 137(Jan):
18-33.* John Bond, whose date and place of birth are unknown, lived in Beverly,
Massachusetts in the 17th century. He had many descendants who progressed to
Worcester and Hamden counties before the Revolution. This study records 12
male descendants and their offspring.   A. E. Huff

1087. Russell, George Ely. STEPHEN RUSSELL (1749-1820) OF SOUTH-
WICK, MASSACHUSETTS, COLEBROOK, CONNECTICUT, AND LIB-
ERTY, NEW YORK. *New England Hist. and Geneal. Register 1977 131(Oct):
292-293.* An account of Stephen Russell (1749-1820) which was left out of the
Russell genealogy published in the *Register,* 1964 118 (Apr). Stephen, a Minute
Man who answered the Lexington Alarm, later emigrated with his family to
Sullivan County, New York. Based on vital statistics, land deeds, and other
primary and secondary sources.   S. Wheeler

1088. Rutherford, Homer V. THE BOLTER FAMILY OF WEYMOUTH,
BRAINTREE, BOSTON, AND SOME CONNECTIONS. *New England Hist.
and Geneal. Register 1979 133(Oct): 255-270.* There is no proof that the Bolter
Family of Massachusetts is descended from that of Norfolk, England. However,
tradition, a migration pattern, and spelling of the name make for a strong likelihood. Richard Bolter [d. 1679] of Weymouth was the earliest member found in
Massachusetts. Traces 19 of his descendants and their offspring. Based on church
records, wills, the family Bible and other family records, and state and town
records. Notes incorporated in text. Appendix.   J/S

1089. Ryan, P. J. THE MARTINEZ YEARS: THE FAMILY LIFE AND
LETTERS OF JOHN MUIR. *Pacific Hist. 1981 25(2): 79-85.* Discusses natu-
ralist John Muir's family life as revealed in his correspondence. These include
letters to his sister Mary, with whom he was close. He lived with his family in
Martinez, California, when he was not out in the wilderness. He was considered
to be somewhat eccentric by the townspeople. Muir lived in Martinez from 1890
until his death in 1914. Based on primary sources; 14 notes.   J. Powell

1090. Sarkesian, Barbara. FOUND: A LEDGER AND A FAMILY.
Family Heritage 1979 2(3): 68-69. Discovery of a work ledger kept by Welcome
Allen Shippee, 1834-70, led the author to meet several family members and to
reconstruct details of Shippee's life in Glocester, Rhode Island.

1091. Schaedel, Grace Logan. THE STORY OF ERNEST AND LIZZIE
LOGAN—A FRONTIER COURTSHIP. *Ann. of Wyoming 1982 54(2): 48-
61.* Ernest Logan arrived at Camp Carlin, Wyoming, in 1871 and subsequently
worked as a carpenter, cowboy, and stagecoach driver. In 1891 he opened a book
and stationery shop in Cheyenne that featured a soda fountain and homemade
ice cream and candy. Two years later he married Lizzie Walker who had come
west to work with her sister Jennie in a dressmaking business. Together they made
the Logan Store one of the lasting business enterprises of Cheyenne. 9 photos.
                                                                    M. L. Tate

1092. Scharnhorst, Gary. BIOGRAPHICAL BLINDSPOTS: THE CASE OF THE COUSINS ALGER. *Biography 1983 6(2): 136-147.* Biographical blindspots exist when original sources about the lives of significant historical figures do not exist. A minor figure who retires long before death (e.g., W. R. Alger) or who becomes the subject of intense public interest only long after death (e.g., Horatio Alger, Jr.) may be lost entirely in such a blindspot.   J

1093. Schweninger, Loren. A SLAVE FAMILY IN THE ANTE BELLUM SOUTH. *J. of Negro Hist. 1975 60(1): 29-44.* Recognizing the modern controversy concerning the effect of slavery upon the black family, this family history serves to shed some light on the family experiences of many slaves in the antebellum South. The Thomas-Rapier slave family experienced legal restrictions, separation, miscegenation, and sexual exploitation, but these forces served to promote feelings of family loyalty, unity, and love. Based on primary sources in the Moorland-Spingarn Research Center and secondary sources; 53 notes.
N. G. Sapper

1094. Sears, Edith Smyth and Roberts, Margaret Smyth. THE LIFE AND TIMES OF TWO EARLY CALIFORNIANS: OUR GRANDPARENTS. *Pacific Hist. 1974 18(1): 2-11.* Sketches the lives of Gerhard Frederick Terschuren of Germany, and Jane Elizabeth Cunningham from California, their marriage, his steamboat shipping business, and her life as wife and widow. Note.
S

1095. Seghesio, Susanne R. FOUR GENERATIONS OF THE SEGHESIO FAMILY IN THE WINE BUSINESS. *Pacific Hist. 1977 21(3): 248-261.* Eduardo Seghesio's family has been involved in the California winemaking industry's Chianti area since 1886, owning vineyards since 1895. Originally supplying wine to other vineyards, the business is still family-run, and recently has developed its own label. 5 photos.   G. L. Olson

1096. Seymour, R. Owen and Austin, John D. EBENEZER[4] SEYMOUR OF RUPERT, VERMONT AND HIS DESCENDANTS. *New England Hist. and Geneal. Register 1978 132 (Apr): 140-145, (July): 186-195, (Oct): 302-307; 1979 133 (Jan): 20-39.* Discusses genealogy of the Seymour family, 1760's-1860's, in New England, New York, and the Midwest; in three parts. Part IV. Traces 16 descendants and their offspring. Article to be continued.
A. E. Huff/D. L. Schermerhorn

1097. Shaffer, Janet. NARCISSA AND ROBERT OWEN: THE POINT OF HONOR YEARS. *Virginia Mag. of Hist. and Biog. 1981 89(2): 153-169.* Describes this Tennessee and Lynchburg, Virginia family headed by Robert Owen, who was president of the strategically important Virginia and Tennessee Railroad during the Civil War, focusing on the Lynchburg years. The family moved from the Point of Honor homestead to Norfolk in 1873 when the patriarch died. The widow managed to provide educations for the couple's two sons. William went into military medicine, and Robert into politics, ultimately as US Senator helping to write the Federal Reserve Bank Bill of 1913. The Lynchburg homestead is being restored. Based on Mrs. Owen's 1913 *Memoirs* and secondary sources. 76 notes.   P. J. Woehrmann

1098. Shaw, Edward C. THE KENNEDYS—AN UNUSUAL WESTERN FAMILY. *Trans. of the Hist. and Sci. Soc. of Manitoba [Canada] 1972/73 Series 3(29): 69-79.* Traces the origins of the Kennedy family from their Scottish ancestry and devotes considerable attention to the activities of those who settled in Canada in the late 18th and early 19th centuries. 2 charts.   J. A. Casada

1099. Shor, Elizabeth N. PROBLEMS IN THE LAND OF OPPORTU-NITY. *Am. West 1976 13(1): 24-29.* Francis and Sarah Sim and their children moved from Connecticut to southeastern Nebraska Territory in 1856. Their letters reveal the harsh and nearly unbearable circumstances of their first year in the raw frontier area. By spring of the second year their optimism began to return. Hardships continued but the Sim family prospered. 6 illus.   D. L. Smith

1100. Shortt, Mary. TOURING THEATRICAL FAMILIES IN CANADA WEST: THE HILLS AND THE HERONS. *Ontario Hist. [Canada] 1982 74(1): 3-25.* The problems of touring stage companies before the railroads were severe in rural Ontario, and the yields were relatively low unless the production proved popular. Some of the problems are sketched and illustrated by the experiences of the Hill family in the 1840's and 1850's and the Heron family in the 1840's. Mainly contemporary newspapers; 4 illus., 53 notes. W. B. Whitham

1101. Showalter, Grace I. THE VIRGINIA MENNONITE RHODES FAMILIES. *Pennsylvania Mennonite Heritage 1980 3(2): 15-22.* History of the Rhodes family and Rhodes descendants of Virginia since the late 1770's and early 1780's, when the first of the Mennonite Rhodes family migrated to Virginia from eastern Pennsylvania, until 1900.

1102. Sichel, Carolyn Meyberg. LOS ANGELES MEMORIES. *Western States Jewish Hist. Q. 1974 7(1): 49-58.* The author relates her experiences growing up in Los Angeles at the turn of the century. Relatives and close family friends included civic, business, and religious leaders in Los Angeles. As a second generation Jewish family, their goal was Americanization. Yiddish was not spoken in her home, but the family was very religious. 2 photos, 6 notes.
R. A. Garfinkle

1103. Simms, L. Moody, Jr. TALENTED VIRGINIANS: THE PETICO-LAS FAMILY. *Virginia Mag. of Hist. and Biog. 1977 85(1): 55-64.* Like most eastern cities in the first half of the 19th century, Richmond had miniature portrait painters, employed by wealthy Virginians who wanted to participate in this growing fashion. The Peticolas family, particularly Philippe and his son Edward, never attained the status of first-rank painters, but they still deserve to be included among the talented of this profession. Based on primary and secondary sources; 30 notes.   R. F. Oaks

1104. Sklar, Kathryn Kish. VICTORIAN WOMEN AND DOMESTIC LIFE: MARY TODD LINCOLN, ELIZABETH CADY STANTON, AND HARRIET BEECHER STOWE. Davis, Cullom; Strozier, Charles B.; Veach, Rebecca Monroe; and Ward, Geoffrey C., ed. *The Public and the Private Lincoln: Contemporary Perspectives* (Carbondale: So. Illinois U. Pr., 1979): 20-37. Examines efforts by prominent Victorian women to limit the size of their families and their public and private activities to arrive at a qualitative rather than quantitative definition of motherhood, during 1830-80. Harriet Beecher Stowe's strategy was

to abstain from sex, in part to punish her philandering husband, undertake a literary career, and foster women's education. Elizabeth Cady Stanton, like Stowe, practiced family planning and worked for feminist domestic reform, seeking the legal equality of women. Mary Todd Lincoln's approach was total commitment to her husband and children. In part she practiced family planning to aid her husband's political career, and she was indulgent of her children. She did not separate domestic from public life, participating in the political sector on Abraham's behalf, but she was unable to build an autonomous career. 40 notes.
S

1105. Slusser, Cathy Bayless. THE JOSEPH ATZEROTH FAMILY: MA-NATEE COUNTY PIONEERS. *Tampa Bay Hist. 1982 4(2): 20-44.* Joseph Atzeroth and his wife, Julia, German-American immigrants, homesteaded 160 acres on Terra Ceia Island in Manatee County, Florida in 1843; their descendants were involved in county life until ca. 1910.

1106. Smith, Jack E. STORY OF A FARMER: A PORTRAIT OF THE LIFE AND FAMILY OF J. GUY SMITH. *Colorado Heritage 1982 1(1): 52-63.* The author describes the career of his grandfather, John Guy Smith (1854-1937), who moved to Colorado in 1878 for health reasons. His diary during his first year in Colorado describes working on a ranch, in a shoe store, for the railroad, and prospecting. In 1881 he began acquiring land in what is now Denver. He and his brother, George, pioneered irrigation as truck gardeners for some 45 years, and J. Guy was known as the "Celery King" of Colorado. He became a leading citizen and, beginning in 1906, was a member of the Denver board of supervisors, serving for a time as its president. His career was similar to many others, but it illustrates early economic, political, and social history of a frontier state. Based on J. Guy Smith's diary, memory of the author, and secondary sources; 24 notes, 16 photos.   O. H. Zabel

1107. Smith, Suzanne. "BACKWARD, TURN BACKWARD, O TIME, IN YOUR FLIGHT . . ." *Am. Heritage 1975 26(5): 30-35.* Photos of a turn of the 20th-century wealthy family at leisure in Corning, New York. 13 photos.
J. F. Paul

1108. Sneed, Roseanna. TWO CHEROKEE WOMEN. *Frontiers 1981 6(3): 35-38.* Discusses Lucyann Davis Wolf and her daughter, Mary, respectively grandmother and mother of the author, and describes their family life in the Tennessee hills, 1900-35.

1109. Souder, Paul. HERITAGE: A LETTER TO MY CHILDREN. *Guam Recorder 1978 8: 15-24.* Reprints a portion of the author's letter to his children providing the family's genealogy on Guam dating to 1710.

1110. Spears, Woodridge. A POET FROM THE CLAY FAMILY OF KEN-TUCKY, SUSAN CLAY SAWITSKY. *Filson Club Hist. Q. 1983 57(2): 175-187.* Biographical sketch of Susan Clay Sawitzky, the great-granddaughter of Henry Clay. She was a poet who published most of her work before her marriage in 1927. Presents nine poems by Mrs. Sawitzky. 22 notes, 2 photos.
G. B. McKinney

1111. Sprunger, Milton F. COURTSHIP AND MARRIAGE. *Mennonite Life 1976 31(2): 13-16.* Contains the diary account of Indiana Mennonite farmer and widower David Sprunger (1857-1933) in his search for a second wife and mother for his seven children. He married Caroline Tschantz (d. 1939) of Sonneberg, Ohio, 4 April 1895. 2 photos. B. Burnett

1112. Stayner, Charles St. Clair. THE BLACKADAR FAMILY OF HALIFAX. *Nova Scotia Hist. Rev. [Canada] 1981 1(1): 67-72.* Traces the genealogy of the Blackadar family through Hugh Blackadar (1773-1818), a shipwright, and his four children. Hugh William Blackadar (1908-63) learned the printing trade and assumed management of the *Acadian Recorder* in 1937. Charles Coleman Blackadar (1847-1930) became publisher of the paper in 1901 and continued until his death. Archives' Manuscripts MG100, vol. 111, No. 36C. H. M. Evans

1113. Steffen, Charles G. THE SEWALL CHILDREN IN COLONIAL NEW ENGLAND. *New England Hist. and Geneal. Register 1977 131: 163-172.* Examines the family life of Samuel Sewall of Boston to explore the socialization of children in colonial New England. Numerous Sewall households scattered across eastern Massachusetts played an important role in the rearing of Samuel's offspring. The father frequently placed his young children in the care of relations living outside Boston. Older children were put out as maids and apprentices to extended kinsmen who then assumed parental control. Like most upper-class children, Samuel's were deeply influenced by their nurses and teachers. Based on Sewall papers, other primary and secondary sources; 8 charts, 19 notes.
R. J. Crandall

1114. Stengel, Drusilla Hartlieb. GRANDMA HARTLIEB. *Niagara Frontier 1979 26(1): 14-24, (3): 62-68.* Part I. A biography of the author's grandmother, Louise Marie Katherina Boehner Hartlieb (1825-1918), born in Bavaria, who arrived in the United States and settled in Buffalo in 1849; based on the grandmother's recollections in 1918 at age 93. Part II. Relates more of Louise Hartlieb's reminiscences of life in Buffalo.

1115. Stern, Malcolm H. ASHER LEVY, NEW JERSEY REVOLUTIONARY, AND HIS COLONIAL NAMESAKES. *New Jersey Hist. 1980 98(3-4): 233-236.* Confusion exists concerning the forebearers of Asher Levy (1756?-85) of New Jersey due to an error in understanding colonial handwriting and faulty genealogical reasoning. The descendants of an earlier Asher Levy (1630-81/2), a prominent New Amsterdam burgher, are listed to show how these two men who shared a name are related. Based on New York and Philadelphia city records and secondary sources; 13 notes. E. R. McKinstry

1116. Stern, Norton B. THE BERNSTEINS OF BAJA CALIFORNIA. *Western States Jewish Hist. Q. 1975 7(2): 108-115.* Max Bernstein (1854-1914) went to Baja California during the gold rush of 1881. He became the resident agent of the International Company of Mexico, working to develop Ensenada for the company. He married Governor Teodoro Riveroll's daughter, Guadalupe, and had seven children. Includes information about their descendants living mainly in California. 9 photos, 5 notes. R. A. Garfinkle

1117.   Stern, Norton B. and Kramer, William M.   THE LILIENTHAL FAM-
ILY PACT.   *Western States Jewish Hist. Q. 1975 7(3): 220-224.* The pact of
seven families surnamed Lilienthal created on 20 August 1880 established a
family corporation whereby the signers pooled their assets and their abilities to
aid each other and "the furtherance of the common interest." "In this document
the age-old Jewish ideal of family solidarity was formalized by a contractual
agreement under the laws of the State of New York." Included are short biographies of the Lilienthals, the text of the pact, and the individual roles of the signers
within the agreements of the pact. 5 notes.   R. A. Garfinkle

1118.   Stern, Norton B. and Kramer, William M.   THE SINSHEIMERS OF
SAN LUIS OBISPO.   *Western States Jewish Hist. Q. 1973 6(1): 3-32.* Traces
Aaron Sinsheimer's family from his German ancestors to his children who reside
in California. Aaron Zachary Sinsheimer came to America in 1845, settled in
Vicksburg, Mississippi, and then moved to San Luis Obispo, California, in 1878.
In 1884 the Sinsheimers built an iron front store that is considered one of the
best-preserved structures of its style. Aaron took over the store in 1898 and was
a leading citizen in his day. Includes short biographies of the 10 Sinsheimer
children. 2 illus., 4 photos, 90 notes.   R. A. Garfinkle

1119.   Stiffler, Liz and Blake, Tona.   FANNIE SPERRY-STEELE: MON-
TANA'S CHAMPION BRONC RIDER.   *Montana 1982 32(2): 44-57.* Fannie
Sperry-Steele rode in the professional rodeo and wild west show circuit from 1907
to 1925. Born on a Montana ranch, Fannie Sperry won the bucking horse contest
in 1912 at the Calgary Stampede and became known as Montana's champion
bronc rider. In 1913 she married Bill Steele; they toured together until 1925, and
from then until 1965 she managed a dude ranch in the Lincoln, Montana area.
Discusses the Sperry-Steele family and its professional activities. Based on the
Fannie Sperry-Steele Papers in a private collection, contemporary newspapers,
and secondary sources; 15 illus., 29 notes.   R. C. Myers

1120.   Stocker, Devera Steinberg.   THE LIPSITZ FAMILIES: EARLY JEW-
ISH SETTLERS IN DETROIT.   *Michigan Jewish Hist. 1982 22(2): 6-13.*
Traces the settlement and activities of Lithuanian born brothers, Isaac Lipsitz
(1842-1918) and Louis Lipsitz (1856-1933), Philip, their nephew, and their families, in Detroit, Michigan; from 1868 the men were successful businessmen and
active members of the Jewish community.

1121.   Strauss, Leon L., ed.   BELOVED SCRIBE: LETTERS OF THERESA
EHRMAN.   *Western States Jewish Hist. Q. 1979 12(1): 39-62; 1980 12(2):
142-160, 12(3): 229-245.* Part I. Theresa Ehrman (1884-1967) was related to Leo
and Gertrude Stein, Americans who lived in Paris, France, in the center of a
literary and artistic community. Theresa went to Paris to advance her training
as a pianist. She lived with Michael and Sarah Stein, Leo's brother and sister-in-
law. Among her acquaintances were Pablo Casals and other noted musicians of
the era. Reprints Ehrman's letters to her family in California; 5 photos, 40 notes.
Part II. In the summer of 1904, Theresa Ehrman toured Switzerland, Italy,
Holland, Belgium, and Germany with her relatives Mike and Sarah Stein. In
Germany, she visited her father's brother and sister. Back in Paris in October,
she continued piano studies with Harold Bauer. Reprints letters of Theresa
Ehrman; 2 photos, 14 notes. Part III. Late in 1904, Theresa broke off her

romantic relationship with Pablo Casals, but they maintained a lifelong friendship. Her piano studies continued in Paris with Therese Chaigneau and Harold Bauer. After her return home to San Francisco in 1905, Theresa began her career as an accompanist and piano teacher. She was a close friend to many outstanding musicians, composers, and conductors. In her last years she lived in the San Francisco Bay area. Reprints her letters; 2 photos, 31 notes.   B. S. Porter

1122. Strong, Ronald Thomas. YOUNG ADVENTURE BY LUCY ANN HENDERSON. *Nevada Hist. Soc. Q. 1973 16(2): 66-99.* An account of an overland wagon journey in 1846 from St. Joseph, Missouri, to Oregon. Supplies reminiscences by Lucy Ann Henderson (1835-1923), a member of this emigrant party. The group followed the Oregon Trail as far west as Goose Creek (a tributary of the Snake River) and then decided to travel southwestward through Nevada and to follow the Applegate Cutoff to Oregon. The emigrants' decision later proved ill-advised due to unforeseen hardships along the route. Based on interviews in 1923 with Lucy Henderson, on Henderson family records, and on Jessy Quinn Thornton's *Oregon and California in 1848* (New York: Harper and Brothers, 1855); 4 maps, photo.   H. T. Lovin

1123. Stuart, Donna Valley. SOME DESCENDANTS OF GEORGE FARLEY OF BILLERICA, MASSACHUSETTS. *New England Hist. and Geneal. Register 1982 136(Jan): 43-62, (Apr): 133-147.* Consolidates all known facts about George Farley (1615-93) and his descendants, presenting a history as complete as possible through four generations. Some erroneous surmises are refuted, particularly in regard to the original ancestor. Primary and secondary sources.   A. E. Huff

1124. Sumida, Janelle. PORTRAIT OF ONE JAPANESE-AMERICAN FAMILY. *Kroeber Anthrop. Soc. Papers 1977 49: 37-44.* Discusses the acculturation of members of a San Francisco Bay area family since 1905.

1125. Thompson, Tommy R., ed. SEARCHING FOR THE AMERICAN DREAM IN ARKANSAS: LETTERS OF A PIONEER FAMILY. *Arkansas Hist. Q. 1979 38(2): 167-181.* Information drawn from a letter collection and court records describes the wanderings of James and Margaret Lockridge, their five children, and Margaret's brother Joseph Morris. Pioneers of moderate means, they began in Kentucky and ended up in Texas, but the focus is on their residence in various places in Arkansas during 1856-68. Primary sources; 63 notes.   G. R. Schroeder

1126. Thorington, J. Monroe. A CYCLE OF TIME. *Princeton U. Lib. Chronicle 1975 37(1): 29-33.* Western Americana collector J. Monroe Thorington traces his family history during 1758-1887 and discusses its bearing on US frontier life, represented by his collection in the Princeton University Library.   S

1127. Thorpe, Grace F. THE JIM THORPE FAMILY: FROM WISCONSIN TO INDIAN TERRITORY, PART I. *Chronicles of Oklahoma 1981 59(1): 91-105.* Grace Thorpe recounts the ancestry of her famous father and renowned athlete, Jim Thorpe. The mixed-blood lineage began in 1786 when Canadian adventurer Jacques Vieux married a Potawatomi woman named Angeline LeRoy. Their 12 children included Louis Vieux who moved from Wisconsin to the Council Bluffs Agency, Iowa, in 1837 where the Potawatomis became even more dependent on white traders. They were moved again in 1845 to Kansas where they were joined by the Sauk and Fox Indians. There Hiram G. Thorpe, Sr., a white, married Wind Woman, a Sauk and Fox. Their son married Charlotte Vieux and the two gave birth to Jim Thorpe, who shared blood from both tribes as well as from his white grandfather. Secondary sources; 3 photos, 61 notes. Article to be continued.   M. L. Tate

1128.   Threlfall, John B.   THE VERIN FAMILY OF SALEM, MASSACHU-SETTS.   *New England Hist. and Genealogical Register 1977 131(April): 100-112.* Traces the six sons of Philip Verin (ca. 1580-ca. 1649) who settled in Salem, Massachusetts, in 1635. One son, Robert (b. 1606), probably died on the voyage from England. Joshua (ca. 1611-95) followed Roger Williams to Providence, Rhode Island, but his religious views were too unorthodox for even that unortho-dox settlement, and he returned to Salem; he ultimately removed to Barbados. Philip (b. 1619) had Quaker tendencies; he appears no more in the records of Essex County after 1665. Hilliard (1621-83) was a model Salem resident; he held a variety of town offices. Nathaniel (1623-ca. 1665) was a ship captain. John (ca. 1625-89) immigrated to Maine, where he was killed in an Indian ambush. Based on primary and secondary sources.   S. L. Patterson

1129.   Trautmann, Frederic, ed. and transl.   EIGHT WEEKS ON A ST. CLAIR COUNTY FARM IN 1851: LETTERS BY A YOUNG GERMAN. *J. of the Illinois State Hist. Soc. 1982 75(3): 162-178.* Letters by Carl Köhler, written in 1851 and published in Germany as *Briefe aus Amerika für Deutsche Auswanderer.* They describe life on an Illinois farm and are based on Köhler's experience at the farm of Friedrich Karl Hecker, a participant in the German revolutions of 1848 who had settled near Belleville. The leters discuss farming practices, travel, topography, wardrobes, and entertainment. Köhler notes that many German immigrants gradually purchased and expanded their holdings while additional acreage was usually available for rent or barter. Köhler con-cluded that independence compensated for inevitable hardships. 6 illus., 17 notes.
                                                              A. W. Novitsky

1130.   Tuggle, Troy S.   "SMITTY": THE LIVING LEGACY OF JEDE-DIAH AND PETER SMITH.   *Pacific Hist. 1981 25(3): 62-71.* Brief history of the Smith Bacon family of California; based on interviews with Julian Smith Bacon. 10 illus.   H. M. Evans

1131.   —.   THE GIBSON FAMILY OF MUNCY AND NISBET.   *Now and Then 1973 17(7): 295-299.*

1132.   —.   GIBSON FAMILY RECORDS.   *South Carolina Hist. Mag. 1974 75(4): 245-248.* Family record listing marriages and births from the 1750's to ca. 1800.   R. H. Tomlinson

1133.   —.   JAMES WOLCOTT AND HIS ANCESTORS.   *Northwest Ohio Q. 1973 45(4): 111-116.* Wolcott (1789-1873) was descended from a family that came to America from England in 1630 to settle in Massachusetts. He moved to Delaware, Ohio, in 1818 to open a woolen mill. After a brief period in Missouri, he returned to Ohio to make his permanent home in Maumee City (later called Maumee). He operated a retail store and owned steamboats and wharves. He was the first president of the city council, common pleas judge of Lucas County, and mayor of Maumee City. Traces six generations of Wolcotts in England and America. Based on family genealogies, newspapers, and local histories; illus., 41 notes.

W. F. Zornow

1134. —. MEMOIR OF WILLIAM LOGAN FISHER (1781-1862) FOR HIS GRANDCHILDREN. *Pennsylvania Mag. of Hist. and Biog. 1975 99(1): 92-103.* Publication of a memoir of William Logan Fisher, Pennsylvania industrialist, written to provide his grandchildren with a record of his life and activities. Fisher's life was unmarred by dramatic events. He achieved moderate success in the iron industry, the business remaining in the family after his death. He also published a number of writings with an ethical or religious theme. 3 notes.

V. L. Human

1135. Urban, William. WYATT EARP WAS BORN HERE: MONMOUTH AND THE EARPS, 1845-1859. *Western Illinois Regional Studies 1980 3(2): 154-167.* Brief outline of the Earp family in Monmouth, western Illinois, 1845-59, based on the 1853 obituary of Wyatt Earp's grandfather, Walter Earp; the family lived, worked, and died relatively unnoticed.

1136. Vacheenas, Jean and Volk, Betty. BORN IN BONDAGE: HISTORY OF A SLAVE FAMILY. *Negro Hist. Bull. 1973 36(5): 101-106.* Discusses the history of the Lewis G. Clarke family and their life in and out of slavery, 1831-82.

S

1137. Valley, Seabrook Wilkinson. THE PARENTAGE OF GOVERNOR MORTON. *South Carolina Hist. Mag. 1973 74(3): 164-169.* Joseph Morton (Mourton) (1630?-88) was one of the most enigmatic governors of colonial South Carolina (1682-84 and 1685-86). Believing that information about his English background would help to understand Morton's gubernatorial career, the author has uncovered genealogical data about his parentage. Also reproduces the will of Ambrose Mourton, hosier of Wells, Somerset, England. 20 notes.

D. L. Smith

1138. Vincent, Charles. ASPECTS OF THE FAMILY AND PUBLIC LIFE OF ANTOINE DUBUCLET: LOUISIANA'S BLACK STATE TREASURER, 1868-1878. *J. of Negro Hist. 1981 66(1): 26-36.* Antoine Dubuclet was born in 1810 into a prosperous free black family. By the end of the Civil War, he had accumulated large sugarcane plantations. Under congressional reconstruction policies, Dubuclet was elected state treasurer of Louisiana in 1868, 1870, and 1874. He died in 1887. Dubuclet survived the stormy days of Reconstruction untouched by scandal and blessed with bipartisan support. A. G. Belles

1139. Vogt, Kathryn A. THE MISSOURI SHORTHORN INDUSTRY: THE LEONARD FAMILY LEGACY. *Gateway Heritage 1982 2(4): 16-23.* In 1825, Nathaniel Leonard created Ravenswood, which later became a showplace farm in Cooper County, Missouri. There he and his descendants created great wealth and enjoyed opulent lifestyles. Their economic successes derived primarily after 1839 from astute herdsmanship of English shorthorn cattle. Based on printed histories and archival sources; 16 photos, biblio. H. T. Lovin

1140. Walne, Peter. EMIGRANTS FROM HERTFORDSHIRE 1630-1640: SOME CORRECTIONS AND ADDITIONS. *New England Hist. and Genealogical Register 1978 132(Jan): 18-24.* The study of emigrants to New England from Hertfordshire in the 1630's has been aided by the Allen Index (compiled by the late T. F. Allen) to Hertfordshire marriages before 1837. New information on the following Massachusetts families is now available: John Dane, ca. 1610-84, Ipswich; Margaret Chandler (Monk) Denison, wife of William; William Heath, d.1652, Roxbury; Isaac Perry; Joshua Tead, d.1678 at 71 years, Charlestown; Robert Titus; Laurence Whittamore, b. ca. 1572 and wife Elizabeth, Roxbury. 29 notes.   A. Huff

1141. Warren, Claude N. THE MANY WIVES OF PEDRO YANUNALI. *J. of California Anthrop. 1977 4(2): 242-248.* Analysis of births, deaths, baptisms, and Catholic marriages and native marriages confirmed at Mission Santa Barbara in California yields kinship information and information on the sociopolitical matrices of the local Chumash Indians; discusses marriages of chief Pedro Yanunali, 1787-1806.

1142. Washburn, Emory. THE JEWS IN LEICESTER, MASSACHUSETTS. *Rhode Island Jewish Hist. Notes 1975 7(1): 34-41.* Discusses three Newport, Rhode Island Jewish families of Portuguese descent: those of Abraham Mendez, Jacob Rodriguez Rivera, and Aaron Lopez, who sought refuge from the invasion of British troops during the American Revolution, 1777-83.

1143. Weissbach, Lee Shai. THE TOWNES OF MASSACHUSETTS: A PILOT STUDY IN GENEALOGY AND FAMILY HISTORY. *Essex Inst. Hist. Collections 1982 118(3): 200-220.* Kin networks provide an alternative to geographic location in examining the demographic history of colonial New England. They further answer questions not easily tested in local studies, such as frequency of migration, importance of kin connections in courtship, and the development of naming patterns. The family established by William Towne in Salem in the 1630's provides the material to demonstrate the feasibility and value of focusing on kin networks and the use of genealogical material as a database. Compares quantitative findings generated by a three-generation analysis of the Towne family with Philip Greven's previous study of Andover. A wealth of quantitative information "can be derived from a thorough analysis of data which is purely genealogical in nature." Primary sources; 2 tables, 3 graphs, 20 notes.
R. S. Sliwoski

1144. White, Elizabeth Pearson. FEARNOT AND JOSEPH SHAW OF MASSACHUSETTS. *New England Hist. and Geneal. Register 1980 134(Jan): 48-58.* The many unrelated Shaw families in colonial New England made it difficult to disentangle the ancestry of Eunice Shaw (1798-1890), who was born at Marlowe, New Hampshire. She was finally traced back to Joseph Shaw (ca. 1702-79) of Milton. His parentage is not confirmed, but, because the name Jacob, unusual in early Shaw families, appears frequently among his descendants, his father may have been Jacob Shaw, born 1672. If this was so, Fearnot Shaw (1653-ca. 1700) was his grandfather; hence the title of the article. Notes, mainly from primary sources, incorporated in text.   J

1145.   White, Stephen A.   THE LA VACHE FAMILY OF ARICHAT, CAPE BRETON. *Nova Scotia Hist. Q. 1977 7(1): 69-85.* Gives a genealogy of the LaVache family beginning in 1774. Traces the name changes from LaVache, Lavache, to Lavash. Primary and secondary sources; 9 notes.   H. M. Evans

1146.   Whitlow, Leonard A. and Whitlow, Catherine Copper, ed.   MY LIFE AS A HOMESTEADER. *Oregon Hist. Q. 1981 82(1): 65-84.* Memoirs by Fannie Adams Copper on the experiences and hardships of homesteading in various wild sections of Oregon in the 1890's. There were boundary problems, wild animals, lack of money and frequent moves for her growing family. 6 illus., photo. Article to be continued.   G. R. Schroeder

1147.   Whitman, Clifford Dale, ed.   PRIVATE JOURNAL OF MARY ANN OWEN SIMS. *Arkansas Hist. Q. 1976 35(2): 142-187, (3): 261-291.* Part I. Mary Anne Owen Sims (1830-61?), a Tennessean who moved to Arkansas in 1838, kept a diary between June 1855 (the death of her physician husband, Dr. John D. Sims) and her own death sometime in 1861. The diary describes frontier family life, especially frequent illnesses and remedies, religious and social activities, and personal affairs. Based on primary and secondary sources; 4 illus., 59 notes. Part II. Covers 1865-61 and deals with giving up the farm, hiring out the slaves, and the start of the Civil War.   T. L. Savitt

1148.   Williams, Peter W.   THE ADAMS FAMILY IN CATHOLIC CINCINNATI. *Cincinnati Hist. Soc. Bull. 1981 39(3): 195-200.* Discusses the tumultuous relationship between members of the John Quincy Adams family and Catholics: in 1843 Adams, dedicating Cincinnati's new observatory made disparaging comments offensive to Catholics; a quote by Henry Adams, John's grandson, that appeared in the *Catholic Telegraph* in 1927 also offended Catholics, although the newspaper's attitude toward Henry changed by 1930.

1149.   Williamson, Eileen M.   THE GUERIN FAMILY OF WHITEWOOD, N.W.T. *Beaver [Canada] 1979 309(4): 20-23.* John Francis Guerin, a French dentist, and his wife Angelica Mary, from England, settled in Whitewood in 1885. He had a widespread practice, and she educated most of the Guerin children. Family practices in speech and drama led to local performances. Soon the group expanded to provide Shakespeare, Dickens, and Moliere to wider audiences, often with musical accompaniment. Based on granddaughter's reminiscences; 4 illus.   D. Chaput

1150.   Wilson, W. Emerson, ed.   PHOEBE GEORGE BRADFORD DIARIES. *Delaware Hist. 1974 16(1): 1-21.* Part I. Selections (1832-33) from the diary of Phoebe George Bradford, daughter of Sidney George, Jr., of Cecil County and wife of Whig editor Moses Bradford, relating to her Mt. Harmon plantation in Maryland, life in Wilmington, family, Wilmington religious fare and ministers, gardening interests, the Female Colonization Society, and prominent or obscure state and national political figures including Henry Clay and the McLane family. 48 notes. Article to be continued.   R. M. Miller

1151.   Wittenburg, Mary Ste. Therese.   A CALIFORNIA GIRLHOOD: REMINISCENCES OF ASCENSION SEPULVEDA Y AVILA. *Southern California Q. 1982 64(2): 133-139.* Describes María Ascensión Sepúlveda y Ávila's childhood years and marriage to Thomas Mott in 1861. She descended from two of California's oldest families. Ascensión's family lived in Los Angeles and owned Rancho San Joaquin. She met Mott when she was 15; the courtship observed tradition, and the wedding climaxed a week of festivities. The marriage produced 11 children and marked the transition from a formal Spanish society into the less rigid American society. Based on unpublished memoirs and other primary and secondary sources; photos; 3 notes.   A. Hoffman

1152. Wolin, Howard E. GRANDIOSITY AND VIOLENCE IN THE KENNEDY FAMILY. *Psychohistory Rev. 1979 8(3): 27-37.* Behavior patterns of the Kennedy family, including Joseph, Sr., Rose, Joseph, Jr., John, Robert, and Edward, show evidence of fantasies of omnipotence, invulnerability, and grandiosity. These fantasies are not well-integrated with the ego or the ego-ideal and are therefore expressed in unrealistic and self-destructive actions. The Kennedy sons acted out their parents' unintegrated grandiose fantasies. Parental expectations led to incautious behavior by the Kennedy sons. Cites examples of risk-taking behavior by the Kennedy sons. Edward Kennedy's accident at Chappaquiddick island may have been an anniversary reaction of Robert Kennedy's death. Secondary sources; ref.   J. M. Herrick

1153. Wood, Stacy B. C., Jr. THE HOFF FAMILY: MASTER CLOCK-MAKERS OF LANCASTER BOROUGH. *J. of the Lancaster County Hist. Soc. 1977 81(4): 169-225.* John George Hoff and his sons, John, John Jacob, and John George, Jr., were master clockmakers in Lancaster County, Pennsylvania, 1769-1822, developing a style uniquely theirs.

1154. Woodcock, George. THE FAMILY BUSH: A PRE-AUTOBIO-GRAPHICAL EXERCISE. *Queen's Q. [Canada] 1982 89(2): 376-385.* George Woodcock, Canadian poet, had never probed far back into his ancestry because he knew there was nothing of great public interest to discover. But as he began to write his autobiography, he felt a need to explain how his life had been formed by his forebears. His parents emigrated to Winnipeg from Great Britain before his birth in 1912 but soon returned to England.   L. V. Eid

1155. Woodman, Harold D. CLASS, SOCIAL CHANGE, AND FAMILY HISTORY. *Rev. in Am. Hist. 1983 11(2): 233-237.* Reviews *The Hammonds of Redcliffe* (1981), edited by Carol Bleser, a collection of letters written by members of the Hammond family of South Carolina from the early 19th to mid-20th centuries that provides insights into social change and the attempts of Southern plantation owners to adapt to this change.

1156. Woods, H. Ted. THE MEREDITH FAMILY AND THE CREEK INDIAN WAR. *North Louisiana Hist. Assoc. J. 1974 6(1): 27-29.* In early 1812, Arthur Lott from Georgia and Thomas Meredith from South Carolina were killed in separate incidents by Indians in Alabama while moving their families to Mississippi. It has been suggested that the murders of these two men were the events which "actually caused the Creek Indian War of 1813-1814." Members of the Meredith family later moved to Louisiana and today their descendants "constitute one of the largest families in several north and central parishes of the state." There are also a number of Lott descendants living in Louisiana. 4 notes.   A. N. Garland

1157. Yeazell, Ruth Bernard; Maliszewski, Barbara; and Constantikes, Andrea. AN EXCHANGE OF LETTERS BETWEEN WILLIAM AND ALICE JAMES. *Psychohistory Rev. 1979 8(1-2): 53-59.* Alice James (1848-92), the only girl, grew up as the family invalid, an interesting role in a family plagued by neurasthenia. Four letters written between July and September 1886 between William and Alice James are reprinted, and each is annotated, in this article, for students of the James family and for those studying the role of illness among family members. Primary sources; 39 notes.
J. M. Herrick

1158. Zabriskie, George Olin. THE ACKERMAN FAMILY. *Halve Maen 1974 49(2): 5-6, 16-17, 49(3): 9-10, 16.* Discusses the David Ackerman family who first settled in New Netherland in 1662. Article in two parts.
S

1159. Zeager, Lloyd. THE SHOPE MENNONITE CEMETERY AND AREA FAMILIES. *Pennsylvania Mennonite Heritage 1983 6(1): 7-21.* Recounts the history of the Shope Mennonite Cemetery in Lower Swatara Township, Dauphin County, Pennsylvania, from its first burial in 1877 to 1981; includes a list of tombstone inscriptions and genealogical notes on nine families represented in it.

1160. Zollo, Richard P. FAMILY LIFE AT OAK KNOLL: THE POET WHITTIER AND HIS COUSINS. *Essex Inst. Hist. Collections 1983 119(2): 99-118.* Examines John Greenleaf Whittier's family life at Oak Knoll, particularly his relations with three Danvers cousins and his niece Phebe Woodman. Highlights the special relationship between Whittier and Phebe, and discusses her life after her uncle's death. Primary sources; 2 photos, illus., 28 notes.
R. S. Sliwoski

1161. Zuckerman, Michael. WILLIAM BYRD'S FAMILY. *Perspectives in Am. Hist. 1979 12: 255-311.* Analysis of William Byrd's diaries (ca. 1700-20) reveals that his conception of "family" differed significantly from the modern perception of a close-knit nuclear family where the father demonstrated affection for and control of offspring. Byrd's concern for immediate family was almost indifferent, and was only a part of his concern for a community family which included friends, neighbors, cousins, nephews and nieces, slaves, and government officials. He felt the need to expand his family beyond his own plantation, constantly invited and entertained guests, and spent much time himself in traveling and visiting others. Thsi concern for an expanded community demonstrates that Byrd felt that the community in which he lived was precarious when compared to England, and that it was the job of the plantation owner to do everything he could to bind the community together and clearly define its ties.
W. A. Wiegand

1162. —. THE LOS ANGELES BRODERS: A PICTURE STORY. *Western States Jewish Hist. Q. 1981 13(3): 225-229.* Brothers and sisters of the Broder family, including their in-laws of the Cadish family, operated a bakery and delicatessen from 1922 to the mid-1960's. They moved their place of business several times in keeping with changing settlement patterns of their Jewish customers. Based on interviews; 6 photos.
B. S. Porter

1163. —. THE MARKS BROTHERS OF LOS ANGELES, A PICTURE STORY. *Western States Jewish Hist. Q. 1979 11(4): 311-317.* Joshua H. Marks (1884-1965) and David X. Marks (1891-1977) were brought to Los Angeles by their parents in 1902. Joshua entered their father's brick business and became a building designer and contractor. Among his better known works are Grauman's Chinese and Egyptian theaters, and the Santa Anita Race Track. He also built several shopping centers, churches, business offices, and movie studios. David entered the insurance business and was active in civic affairs. He helped establish the Los Angeles Civic Light Opera Association, and contributed financially to developments at the University of Southern California, and other educational institutions. Family records and published sources; 7 photos, 8 notes.

B. S. Porter

1164. —. THE ONDERDONKS...A FAMILY OF TEXAS PAINTERS. *Southwestern Art 1976 5(1): 32-43.* Discusses the painting of the members of the Onderdonk family, Robert Jenkins (1852-1917), Robert Julian (1882-1922), and Eleanor Rogers (1884-1964).

1165. —. PRESERVING FOR THE FUTURE: AN INTERVIEW WITH THREE GENERATIONS OF THE STARKEY FAMILY. *Tampa Bay Hist. 1981 3(2): 58-75.* An interview with J. B. Starkey, Sr., J. B. Starkey, Jr., and his son, Frank Starkey, of the Umberton Ranch in Pasco and Pinellas counties, Florida.

1166. —. THE SHAFSKY BROTHERS OF FORT BRAGG: A MENDOCINO COUNTY VIGNETTE. *Western States Jewish Hist. Q. 1976 9(1): 49-54.* The Shafsky family, Russian emigrants, came to the United States by way of Canada. Starting as pack peddlers in the lumber camps of northern California, two of the brothers, Abraham Harry and Samuel, opened a general merchandise store in Fort Bragg. The business prospered and is still operated by a son and grandson of Abraham Harry Shafsky. Based on interviews, family records, and published works; 3 photos, 13 notes.

B. S. Porter

1167. —. THE WIVES OF GERONIMO. *Escribano 1973 10(3): 83-89.*

SUBJECT AND AUTHOR INDEXES

USER'S GUIDE TO THE INDEXES

All titles in this series use ABC-Clio Information Services' unique Subject Profile Index (ABC-SPIndex) and an author index. The following abstract is found in this volume:

Abstract

242. Rhoads, James B. THE IMPORTANCE OF FAMILY HISTORY TO OUR SOCIETY. *Public Hist. 1979 1(3): 6-16.* Discusses the importance of family history to American society, and describes the ways that people interested in family history can research it; through the National Archives and Records Service, local libraries, and the Bureau of the Census, 1960's-70's.

In this Subject Index, each index entry is a complete profile of the abstract and consists of one or more subject, geographic, and biographic descriptors, followed by the dates covered in the article. These descriptors are rotated so that the complete subject profile is cited under each of the terms in alphabetical order. Thus, indexing for the abstract shown above is located in five different places in the index:

Subject Index

Archives, National. Census Bureau. Family history. Libraries, local. Research. 1960's-70's. *242*

and

Census Bureau. Archives, National. Family history. Libraries, local. Research. 1960's-70's. *242*

and

Family history. Archives, National. Census Bureau. Libraries, local. Research. 1960's-70's. *242*

and

Libraries, local. Archives, National. Census Bureau. Family history. Research. 1960's-70's. *242*

and

Research. Archives, National. Census Bureau. Family history. Libraries, local. 1960's-70's. *242*

A dash replaces second and subsequent identical leading terms. Cross-references in the form of *See* and *See-also* references are provided. Refer also to the notes at the head of the Subject Index.

Intermarriage *See also* Marriage, interfaith; Marriage, interreligious; Miscegenation.
—. Christians. Converts. Jews. 1971. *183*

The separate Author Index lists the name of the author and abstract number.

Author Index

Renzi, Mario 525
Reynolds, Gary 1074
Rezneck, Samuel 241
Rhoads, James B. 242
Rhodes, Colbert 574
Ricards, Sherman L. 596

SUBJECT INDEX

Subject Profile Index (ABC-SPIndex) carries both generic and specific index terms. Begin a search at the general term but also look under more specific or related terms. Cross references are provided.

Each string of index descriptors is intended to present a profile of a given article; however, no particular relationship between any two terms in the profile is implied. Terms within the profile are listed alphabetically after the leading term. The variety of punctuation and capitalization reflects production methods and has no intrinsic meaning; e.g., there is no difference in meaning between "History, study of" and "History (study of)."

Cities, towns, and counties are listed following their respective states or provinces; e.g., "Ohio (Columbus)." Terms beginning with an arabic numeral are listed after the letter Z. The chronology of the bibliographic entry follows the subject index descriptors. In the chronology, "c" stands for "century"; e.g., "19c" means "19th century."

Note that "United States" is not used as a leading index term; if no country is mentioned, the index entry refers to the United States alone. When an entry refers to both Canada and the United States, both "Canada" and "USA" appear in the string of index descriptors, but "USA" is not a leading term. When an entry refers to any other country and the United States, only the other country is indexed.

The last number in the index string, in italics, refers to the bibliographic entry number.

A

Abolition Movement. Blacks. Edmondson, Emily. Edmondson, Mary. New York Central College. 1832-55. *939*
—. Gay, Sydney Howard. Values. 1830's-40's. *926*
Abortion. Attitudes. Family size preferences. Religion. 1972. *525*
—. Birth Control. Federal policy. 1970's. *442*
—. Birth Control (techniques). 19c. *695*
—. Family size, ideal. Proabortion sentiment. Protestant Churches. 1972-75. *407*
—. Ideology. Social Classes. 1970's. *506*
—. Sex roles. 19c-20c. *441*
—. Social Classes. Values. 1973-78. *747*
Academic achievement. Blacks. Children. Human Relations. Parents. Teachers. 1970's. *612*
—. Children. Mothers. North Central States. Occupations. Occupations. 1977. *352*
—. Fathers. IQ. Linkage hypothesis. Occupations. Personality. Sons. 1964. *485*
—. Social reform. Teachers. Wellesley College. Women. 1880-1920. *721*
Academies. Education. Planter class. South. Women. 1800-40. *400*
Acadian Recorder. Blackadar family. Newspapers. Nova Scotia (Halifax). 1773-1980. *1112*
Acculturation. British Columbia (Vancouver). Sikhs. 1904-72. *613*
—. Bureau of Indian Affairs. California (San Francisco Bay area). Indians. Navajo Indians. Relocation. Women. 1950-80. *207*
—. California (San Francisco Bay area). Japanese Americans. 1905-76. *1124*
—. Canada. Indians. Sex roles. Wisconsin. Women. 1901-70. *168*
—. Italian Americans (review article). Social Organization. 20c. *227*
Achievement. Ascription. Social status. 1970's. *511*
Achievement syndrome. Family interaction processes. Secondary Education. Social Status. 1962-73. *703*
Ackerman, David (family). New Netherland. Settlement. 1662-67. *1158*
Adams, Abigail. Massachusetts. 1744-1818. *864*

Adams, Brooks. Adams, Henry. Adams, John Quincy. Historiography. 1767-1848. 1880-1920. *1030*
Adams family. 1776-1830. *1035*
—. Attitudes. Communications Behavior. Generations. 1764-1919. *1036*
—. Massachusetts (Quincy). 1775-1927. *846*
Adams, Henry. Adams, Brooks. Adams, John Quincy. Historiography. 1767-1848. 1880-1920. *1030*
Adams, Henry Brooks. Adams, Marian Hooper. Marriage. Monuments. Saint-Gaudens, Augustus. Suicide. 1872-85. *912*
Adams, John Quincy. Adams, Brooks. Adams, Henry. Historiography. 1767-1848. 1880-1920. *1030*
Adams, John Quincy (family). Catholics. Ohio (Cincinnati). 1843-1930. *1148*
Adams, Louisa Catherine. Domesticity. Middle Classes. 1797-1812. *868*
Adams, Marian Hooper. Adams, Henry Brooks. Marriage. Monuments. Saint-Gaudens, Augustus. Suicide. 1872-85. *912*
Adams, Thomas Boylston. Codman family. Massachusetts (Lincoln). Personal Narratives. Social customs. Upper Classes. 1890-1920. *798*
Adelphi University. History Teaching. Social History. 1976. *97*
Adolescence. Attitudes. Education. Parents. ca 1954-74. *347*
—. Attitudes. Parents. 1975-76. *709*
—. Attitudes (formation). Fertility aspirations. Social origins. Women. 1977. *621*
—. Family, make-believe. Reform school, girls'. 1973. *52*
—. Marriage. Purity. Sexual reform. Social organization. 1830's-40's. *549*
—. Pregnancy. Public policy. 20c. *435*
Adoption. Legal devices. Massachusetts. 1650-1850's. *368*
Advice. Great Britain (London). Letters. Nova Scotia (Halifax). Uniacke, Norman Fitzgerald. Uniacke, Richard John. 1798. *627*
Affectional function hypothesis. Ogburn, William F. Sociology. 1920's-81. *233*
Africa. Blacks. 17c-1979. *760*

Antipolygamy campaign. Mormons. Utah.
Woodruff, Wilford (letter). 1885. *663*
Apache Indians. Arizona. Photography. 1880's. *72*
Appalachia. Cherokee Indians. Georgia. Indian-
White Relations. Oklahoma. Ridge family.
1785-1907. *901*
—. Health professionals. Social integration.
1950-77. *484*
—. Kindergarten. Social control. 1970's. *378*
—. Social organization. 1880's-90's. *90*
Appalachia, southern. Folklore. Ritchie, Jason.
Ritchie, Jean (reminiscences). 1917-49. *1077*
Apple industry. Calkin(s) family. Halliburton,
Robert Grant. Inglis, Charles. Nova Scotia.
Starr family. 19c. *943*
—. Crop yields. Genealogy. Nova Scotia. Prescott,
Charles Ramage. 1772-1970's. *944*
Aquino, Salvatore A. (reminiscences). City Life.
Immigration. Italian Americans. New York
City. 1914. *13*
Arab Canadians. Family life. 1970-79. *1*
Architects. Irish Americans. Kansas. Martin,
Joseph. 19c. *1015*
Architecture. California (Los Angeles). Insurance.
Marks, David X. Marks, Joshua H.
Philanthropy. 1902-77. *1163*
—. Land. Massachusetts (Talbot County).
Sherwood Manor. Tilghman, Lloyd. 1718-1823.
1048
—. Landscaping. New Jersey (Hoboken). Stevens
family. 1820-60. *909*
—. Middle Classes. Prairie house. Wright, Frank
Lloyd. 1900-09. *308*
Archival Catalogs and Inventories. Baptismal
certificates. Birth certificates. Genealogy.
Pennsylvania Folklife Society (archives). 19c.
103
—. Business. Elwyn family. Langdon, John
(descendants). New Hampshire Historical
Society (Langdon-Elwyn Family Papers).
Politics. 1762-1972. *849*
—. Genealogy. Long Island Historical Society.
New York City. 17c-20c. *270*
Archives. Codman Family. Massachusetts. Society
for the Preservation of New England
Antiquities (Codman Family Manuscripts
Collection). 1715-1979. *963*
—. Family history. Genealogical Society of Utah.
Mormons. 1500-1900. *328*
—. Genealogy. Mormons. Utah. 17c-20c. *267*
Archives, National. Census Bureau. Family history.
Libraries, local. Research. 1960's-70's. *242*
—. Cherokee Indians. Genealogy. Indians. North
Carolina (western). 1906-10. *332*
Archives of Ontario. Bibliographies. Ontario.
Women. 18c. *190*
Argall, Samuel (ancestors). Virginia. 1560-1620. *800*
Aristocracy. Colonial Government. New Mexico.
New Spain. Settlement. 16c. *862*
Arizona. Apache Indians. Photography. 1880's. *72*
—. Assimilation. Education. Indians. Industrial
Arts Education. Phoenix Indian School.
1890-1901. *561*
—. Business. California, southern. Jacobs, Mark
Israel (and family). Jews. 1851-94. *928*
—. Entrepreneurs. Jews. Zeckendorf, Aaron.
Zeckendorf, Louis. Zeckendorf, William.
1853-1906. *906*
Arizona (Bisbee). Banking. Brophy (family).
1887-1930's. *841*
Arizona, southwestern. Indians (captivities).
Oatman, Roys (and family). Westward
Movement. Yavapai Indians. 1851-1903. *630*
Arkansas. Diaries. Frontier and Pioneer Life.
Simms, Mary Ann Owen. 1855-61. *1147*
—. Letters. Lockridge family. Morris, Joseph.
Pioneers. 1856-68. *1125*

Arkansas (Yell County). Banks, Alex (descendants).
Farmers. 1830-60. *1044*
Armies. Benton, Thomas Hart. Frémont, Jessie
Benton. Politics. Trans-Mississippi West.
1841-1902. *949*
—. Civil War. Genealogy. Ladd, Nathaniel Eustis.
1861-65. *917*
—. Family (structure). Social Change. Women.
1950's-70's. *545*
—. Frontier and Pioneer Life. Western states.
Wives. 19c. *217*
—. Great Britain. Kent, Duke of (Edward). Lyons,
Charles (family). Nova Scotia (Halifax).
1812-63. *938*
—. Military Camps and Forts. Southwest. 19c. *148*
Art. Peale family. Science. 1770-1823. *1020*
Artifacts. Family history. History Teaching.
Massachusetts. Old Sturbridge Village.
1790-1840. 1980. *22*
Artists (miniaturists). Peticolas family. Portraits.
Virginia (Richmond). 1800-50. *1103*
Ascription. Achievement. Social status. 1970's. *511*
Assimilation. Arizona. Education. Indians.
Industrial Arts Education. Phoenix Indian
School. 1890-1901. *561*
—. California (Los Angeles). Jews. Sichel, Carolyn
Meyberg (reminiscence). 1902-31. *1102*
—. Colorado (Denver). Greek Americans. Life
histories. 20c. *1052*
—. Connecticut. D'Antonio, William V.
(autobiography). Ethnicity. Italian Americans.
ca 1926-73. *70*
—. Delaware (Lewes). Genealogy. Jews. Nunez
family. 18c. *241*
—. Derrico family. Italian Americans. 1904-1970's.
853
—. Ethnic groups. Greek Americans. Moskos,
Charles C., Jr. (reminiscences). 1898-1976. *1031*
—. Fertility. Puerto Ricans. Social Status. 1969-77.
620
—. Geographic mobility. Immigrants. Mexican
Americans. Social status. 1890-1977. *303*
—. German Americans. Goettsch family. Higher
education. Immigration. Iowa (Davenport). 20c.
927
—. Immigrants. Jews. Literature. ca 1900-20. *792*
—. Japanese Americans (Issei, Sansei). Social
Mobility. ca 1900-. *186*
—. Jews. Mental Illness. Novels. Race. Singer,
Israel Joshua *(Family Carnovsky)*. 1943. *113*
Assimilation, patterns of. Attitudes. Generations.
Jewish families. 1925-75. *532*
Attitudes. Abortion. Family size preferences.
Religion. 1972. *525*
—. Adams family. Communications Behavior.
Generations. 1764-1919. *1036*
—. Adolescence. Education. Parents. ca 1954-74.
347
—. Adolescence. Parents. 1975-76. *709*
—. Aid to Families with Dependent Children.
Delaware. Poor. Public Welfare. 1949-75. *373*
—. Assimilation, patterns of. Generations. Jewish
families. 1925-75. *532*
—. Behavior. Children. Music, popular. Popular
Culture. ca 1950-80. *425*
—. Behavior. Education. Occupations. Social
Classes. 1972-80. *411*
—. Birth Rate. Sex control. Women. 1930-70's.
788
—. Blacks. Breckenridge family. Elites. Kentucky.
Race. 1760-1935. *987*
—. Blacks. High Schools. Social Organization.
Students. Tennessee (Rutherford County). 1970.
586
—. Catholic Church. Mormons. Protestant
Churches. Utah. 1974. *19*
—. Childbirth. Physicians. Women. 1870's-90's. *497*

—. Child-rearing. 1880-99. *632*
—. Child-rearing. Education. Family (review article). Religion. Sex. 18c. *228*
—. Children. ca 1950-80. *719*
—. Children. Parents. 18c. *778*
—. Children. Stereotypes. Welfare, recipients of. 1970's. *486*
—. Cohabitation. Religion. Youth. 1974-80. *358*
—. Domesticity. Lincoln, Mary Todd. Stanton, Elizabeth Cady. Stowe, Harriet Beecher. 1830-80. *1104*
—. Family organization. Pennsylvania (Philadelphia). Students. 1970's. *648*
—. Federal government. Fertility. Population. Public Policy. 1970's. *553*
—. Federal Government. Public welfare. 1962-80. *440*
—. Fisk, Elizabeth (family). Frontier and Pioneer Life. Montana (Helena). Social Organization. Women. 1867-1902. *1056*
—. Sex roles (influences). Social Psychology. Students. 1969. *640*
—. Social Change. 1970's. *180*
Attitudes (formation). Adolescence. Fertility aspirations. Social origins. Women. 1977. *621*
Atzeroth, Joseph (family). Florida (Terra Ceia Island). German Americans. Homesteading and Homesteaders. Immigrants. 1840's-1910. *1105*
Audubon, John James. Audubon, John Woodhouse. Audubon, Victor Gifford. Painting. Wildlife. 1785-1862. *1074*
Audubon, John Woodhouse. Audubon, John James. Audubon, Victor Gifford. Painting. Wildlife. 1785-1862. *1074*
Audubon, Victor Gifford. Audubon, John James. Audubon, John Woodhouse. Painting. Wildlife. 1785-1862. *1074*
Australia. Canada. Family, one-parent. Great Britain. New Zealand. 1970's. *265*
Authority. Government. Pensions. Public welfare. ca 1900-20. *563*
Authority (symbols of). American Revolution. Paine, Thomas. 1776. *157*
Autobiography. Civil War. Daily life. Genealogy. Martin, Frances Martha Atkinson. Social organization. Texas. 1857-75. 1979. *200*
—. Emerson, Ralph Waldo. Franklin, Benjamin. Individualism. Interpersonal Relations. Malcolm X. 18c-1980. *669*

B

Bacon, Julian Smith. California. Smith, Jedediah Strong. Smith, Peter (family). 19c-20c. *1130*
Badinter, Elizabeth. Donzelot, Jacques. Family (review article). Lasch, Christopher. Sennett, Richard. 15c-20c. *95*
Bailyn, Bernard (review article). Education. Historiography. 1915-74. *65*
Bakeries. Broder family. Cadish family. California (Los Angeles). Delicatessens. Jews. Settlement. 1922-70. *1162*
Bancroft, Frederic. Missouri (Boone County). Slavery. Stampp, Kenneth. 1820-65. *205*
Banking. Arizona (Bisbee). Brophy (family). 1887-1930's. *841*
Banks, Alex (descendants). Arkansas (Yell County). Farmers. 1830-60. *1044*
Banks, Joshua. Banks, Moses. Genealogy. Nova Scotia (Granville). 1739-1843. *1014*
Banks, Moses. Banks, Joshua. Genealogy. Nova Scotia (Granville). 1739-1843. *1014*
Baptismal certificates. Archival Catalogs and Inventories. Birth certificates. Genealogy. Pennsylvania Folklife Society (archives). 19c. *103*

Baptisms. Birth. Blacks. Documents. Virginia (Mannikintown). Vital Statistics. 1721. *292*
Baptists. 19c-1981. *140*
—. Burns, Bertha Porter. Burns, Marion Van. Clergy. Louisiana (Shiloh). Teachers. 1884-1975. *1001*
—. Values. 17c-1970's. *768*
Baptists, Southern. 1845-1981. *535*
—. 1863-1980. *459*
—. Worship. 17c-1980. *462*
Barnes family. Blacks. Easley, Madeline O. (ancestors). New York (Olean). 1818-1981. *895*
Barry, John Waller. Letters. US Military Academy. 1826-30. *866*
Barton, Stephen, Jr. Lumber trade. North Carolina (Hertford County, Bartonsville). Rural Settlements. 1856-65. *1049*
Battered women's shelter movement. Law reform. Organizations. Wife beating. 1850-1981. *472*
Battle, Lucy Martin. Battle, William Horn. Daily Life. North Carolina. Plantations. 1805-74. *918*
Battle, William Horn. Battle, Lucy Martin. Daily Life. North Carolina. Plantations. 1805-74. *918*
Bauduy, Victorine Du Pont. Business. Delaware (Brandywine Valley). Domesticity. DuPont, Sophie. Eleutherian Mills. Women. 1803-52. *975*
Bavaria. Daily Life. Hartlieb, Louise Marie Katherina Boehner. Immigration. New York (Buffalo). Reminiscences. 1825-1918. *1114*
Beams family. Freedmen (status). Indian Territory. Law. 1823-58. *1008*
Bean, Warren G. Diaries. Farmers. Pennsylvania (Skippack Township). 1899. *1032*
Beckton, Ernest. Beckton, William. Ranching. Saskatchewan (Cannington Manor). Upper Classes. 1888-97. *964*
Beckton, William. Beckton, Ernest. Ranching. Saskatchewan (Cannington Manor). Upper Classes. 1888-97. *964*
Behavior. Attitudes. Children. Music, popular. Popular Culture. ca 1950-80. *425*
—. Attitudes. Education. Occupations. Social Classes. 1972-80. *411*
—. Capitalism. Labor. Massachusetts (Lowell). Sex roles. 1860. *421*
—. Child-rearing. Labor Department (Children's Bureau). Mothers. Spock, Benjamin *(Baby and Child Care)*. West, Mary Mills *(Infant Care)*. 1914-76. *782*
—. Communes. Self-interest. 1980. *655*
—. Economic theory. 1973. *361*
—. Fantasy. Kennedy family. Risk-taking. Violence. ca 1940-79. *1152*
—. Interpersonal Relations. James, Mary. James, William. ca 1842-1914. *805*
—. Missing in action. Prisoners of war. Vietnam War. 1965-80. *670*
—. Pregnancy. Sex, premarital. Social control. 1640-1971. *797*
Belknap, Kitturah Penton. Diaries. Family life. Frontier and Pioneer Life. Iowa. 1839-48. *1075*
Benton, Thomas Hart. Armies. Frémont, Jessie Benton. Politics. Trans-Mississippi West. 1841-1902. *949*
Berkeley Guidance Study. California. Depressions. Employment. Women. 1930-70. *367*
Berkin, Carol R. Degler, Carl N. Dublin, Thomas. Kennedy, Susan. Lovett, Clara M. Women (review article). 1770's-1980. *243*
Bernstein, Max. California. Gold Rushes. International Company of Mexico. Jews. Mexico (Baja California). 1854-1971. *1116*
Bibliographies. Archives of Ontario. Ontario. Women. 18c. *190*
—. Blacks. Genealogy. Research. 1977. *160*

—. Daughters. Literature. Mothers. Women. 1800-1979. *680*

—. Genealogy. Massachusetts. Research. 17c-20c. *129*

—. Genealogy. Methodology. 1977. *121*

—. Mellon family. Pennsylvania. 1885-1978. *1034*

—. Mormons. 19c-20c. *81*

Bicycles. Blochman, Abraham (family). California (San Diego). 1848-1959. *858*

Bingham family. Hawaii. Missions and Missionaries. Protestantism. 1820-1975. *834*

Biography. Alger, Horatio. Alger, William Rounseville. 1840's-1905. *1092*

—. Depressions. Family history. Interviews. Louisiana State University. Students. Works Progress Administration. 1930's. 1978. *66*

—. Diseases. Edel, Leon (interview). James, Henry (1811-82; and family). Literature. Psychology. 1811-1916. 1979. *806*

Biology. *Daedalus* (periodical). Feminism. Lasch, Christopher. Social change. 1975-77. *44*

Birth. Baptisms. Blacks. Documents. Virginia (Mannikintown). Vital Statistics. 1721. *292*

—. Death and Dying. Marriage. Rites and Ceremonies. Social Customs. Tennessee, eastern. 20c. *693*

Birth certificates. Archival Catalogs and Inventories. Baptismal certificates. Genealogy. Pennsylvania Folklife Society (archives). 19c. *103*

Birth Control. Abortion. Federal policy. 1970's. *442*

—. Blacks. Fertility. Marriage. 1880-1980. *710*

—. Childlessness. Regionalism. 1900. *306*

—. Elites. Europe. Fertility. Pennsylvania (Philadelphia). ca 1750-1869. *677*

—. Feminism, domestic. Social Status. ca 1870's-1900. *750*

—. Feminist groups. Sex roles (challenge to). 1870's-80's. *653*

—. Gordon, Linda. Motherhood (review article). Rich, Adrienne. Prehistory-1970's. *697*

—. Law. Medicine and State. Public Policy. 19c. *453*

Birth control information. Direct mail. Information diffusion. 1972. *723*

Birth Control (techniques). Abortion. 19c. *695*

Birth Rate. Attitudes. Sex control. Women. 1930-70's. *788*

—. Child care. Education. Employment. Germany, East. Women. 1970's. *85*

—. Child-rearing. Great Britain. 17c. *671*

—. Engerman, Stanley L. Fogel, Robert William. Methodology. Slavery. 19c. *771*

—. Ethnicity. Marriage. Massachusetts (Boston; South, South End). Occupations. 1880. *131*

—. Health. Minorities. Social Conditions. 1867-1935. *404*

—. Plantations. Slavery. South Carolina. ca 1721-1803. *701*

—. Women. 17c-20c. *322*

Birth Rate (decline). Agricultural labor. Children, demand for. Farm households. Models. 1939-60. *733*

—. Canada. Demography. 1961-71. *725*

—. Births. Blacks. Connecticut (Bridgeport). Vital Statistics. 1855-85. *45*

—. Gibson family records. Marriage. South Carolina. 1750-1800. *1132*

Black Capitalism. Church, Robert Reed, Sr. Tennessee (Memphis). Wealth. Wills. 1912. *1021*

Blackadar family. *Acadian Recorder*. Newspapers. Nova Scotia (Halifax). 1773-1980. *1112*

Blacks. 1855-1925. *124*

—. Abolition Movement. Edmondson, Emily. Edmondson, Mary. New York Central College. 1832-55. *939*

—. Academic achievement. Children. Human Relations. Parents. Teachers. 1970's. *612*

—. Africa. 17c-1979. *760*

—. Africanity. Family system. Scholars (inadequate perceptions of). 1974. *510*

—. Aged. Economic Structure. South. Whites. 1880-1900. *751*

—. Agricultural Labor. Divorce. Men. Moynihan, Daniel P. ("The Negro Family"). 1965-78. *536*

—. Americas (North and South). Historiography. Slavery. ca 1550-1850. *256*

—. Anglos. Marriage (instability). Mexican Americans. 1960-70. *634*

—. Anthropology. Economic Conditions. Gutman, Herbert G. *(The Black Family in Slavery and Freedom, 1750-1925)*. Quantitative Methods. 1750-1925. *335*

—. Attitudes. Breckenridge family. Elites. Kentucky. Race. 1760-1935. *987*

—. Attitudes. High Schools. Social Organization. Students. Tennessee (Rutherford County). 1970. *586*

—. Baptisms. Birth. Documents. Virginia (Mannikintown). Vital Statistics. 1721. *292*

—. Barnes family. Easley, Madeline O. (ancestors). New York (Olean). 1818-1981. *895*

—. Bibliographies. Genealogy. Research. 1977. *160*

—. Birth control. Fertility. Marriage. 1880-1980. *710*

—. Births. Connecticut (Bridgeport). Vital Statistics. 1855-85. *45*

—. Census. City Life. Historiography. Indiana (Vanderburgh County; Evansville). 1865-80. *27*

—. Census. Indiana (Vanderburgh County; Evansville). Migration, Internal. 1880-1900. *28*

—. Child-rearing. Indians. Mexican-Americans. Values. 1979. *573*

—. Children. Cities. Family structure. Socialization, political. 1973. *397*

—. Children, black. Family (white). 1977. *690*

—. Children, treatment of. Illinois. Moynihan Report (1965). Social Problems. 1965-74. *369*

—. Christianity. Social change. Values. War. 1960's-70's. *191*

—. Church, black (first). Clergy. Massachusetts (Boston). Paul, Thomas (and family). 1773-1973. *1024*

—. Cities. Family heads (female). Women. 19c. *647*

—. Cities. Poverty. 1963-71. *296*

—. Connecticut. 19c. *46*

—. Creoles. Louisiana. 1970's. *704*

—. Dating. Mexican Americans. Race Relations. Whites. 1978-79. *691*

—. Demography. Family structure. Fertility trends. 1880-1940. *637*

—. Divorce. Marriage. 1970. *763*

—. Documents. Genealogy, black. Public Records. Research. 19c-20c. *229*

—. Documents. Mortality. Pennsylvania (Chambersburg). Sellers Funeral Home. 1866-1933. *254*

—. Documents. Mortality. Pennsylvania (Franklin County; Chambersburg). Sellers Funeral Home. 1866-1933. *253*

—. Employment. Family. Women workers. 1969-75. *508*

—. Employment. Family (one-parent). Whites. Women. 1970's. *471*

—. Equality. Marriage. Sex roles. Whites. 1976. *362*

—. Family life. Marriage. Pennsylvania. 18c. *603*

—. Family life. Social Change. 1974. *290*

Brookwood Farm. Children. Country Life. Delaware. Douglas, Elinor Thompson (account). Thompson, Mary Wilson. Travel. 1900's-20's. *78*

Broomell family. Business community. Christiana Machine Company. Pennsylvania (Christiana). Social status. 1880-1900. *1025*

Brophy (family). Arizona (Bisbee). Banking. 1887-1930's. *841*

Brown family. Frontier and Pioneer Life. Letters. New England. 1792-1852. *934*

Brubaker family. Land tenure. Pennsylvania (East Hempfield Township). 1717-1981. *842*

Bruce, Mazie. Diaries. Maryland (Cumberland). McKaig, Mrs. William W. Upper Classes. Women. 1857-89. *821*

Bruce, Thomas (family). Massachusetts (Marlborough, Sudbury). 17c-19c. *1054*

Brunk family. Genealogy. Immigrants. Mennonites. 1750-1850. *843*

Bryn Mawr College. Feminism. Palmer, Alice Freeman. Sex roles, traditional. Thomas, Carey. Wellesley College. 1875-1918. *569*

Budgets. Decisionmaking. Pennsylvania (Philadelphia). 1870-80. *437*

—. Europe, Western. Income. Life cycles. 1889-90. *448*

Buell, John L. (family register). Country Life. Diaries. New York (Morristown). 1844-48. *985*

Buildings (iron front). California (San Luis Obispo). Jews. Sinsheimer, Aaron Zachary (2d family). 1878-1956. *1118*

Bulkeley, Peter. Covenant theology. Massachusetts (Concord). Puritans. 1635-1731. *1060*

Bureau of Indian Affairs. Acculturation. California (San Francisco Bay area). Indians. Navajo Indians. Relocation. Women. 1950-80. *207*

Bureaucracy. Children. Learning disabilities. Mental Illness. 1975. *370*

Burial plots. Allen Family. Epitaphs. Vermont. 1770-1834. *857*

Burns, Bertha Porter. Baptists. Burns, Marion Van. Clergy. Louisiana (Shiloh). Teachers. 1884-1975. *1001*

Burns family. Immigration. Ireland. Nova Scotia (Annapolis County; Wilmot Township). 1764-20c. *1012*

Burns, Francis (and family). Farms. Irish Canadians. Nova Scotia (Wilmot Township). 18c. *1011*

Burns, Marion Van. Baptists. Burns, Bertha Porter. Clergy. Louisiana (Shiloh). Teachers. 1884-1975. *1001*

Burrough, James. Burwell, Lewis (letter). Social History. Virginia. 1734. *844*

Burwell, Lewis (letter). Burrough, James. Social History. Virginia. 1734. *844*

Buschow family. City directories. Family history. Local History. Ohio (Cleveland). 1883-1900. 1979. *316*

Business. Alaska. Brady, John Green (and family). Morality. Politics. Presbyterian Church. 1878-1906. *956*

—. Archival Catalogs and Inventories. Elwyn family. Langdon, John (descendants). New Hampshire Historical Society (Langdon-Elwyn Family Papers). Politics. 1762-1972. *849*

—. Arizona. California, southern. Jacobs, Mark Israel (and family). Jews. 1851-94. *928*

—. Bauduy, Victorine Du Pont. Delaware (Brandywine Valley). Domesticity. DuPont, Sophie. Eleutherian Mills. Women. 1803-52. *975*

—. Bransten, Florine Haas. California (San Francisco). Culture. Jews. Lilienthal, Alice Haas. ca 1900-81. *880*

—. California (Fort Bragg). Jews. Russia. Shafsky family. 1889-1976. *1166*

—. Capital. Elites. Family dynasties. Law. Texas (Galveston). ca 1890-1980. *488*

—. Cattle Raising. Montana. Ranches. Sheep raising. Sieben, Henry. 1864-1937. *1046*

—. Education. Massachusetts (Boston). Property. Upper Classes. ca 1825-40. *722*

—. Industry. Women. 19c. *567*

Business community. Broomell family. Christiana Machine Company. Pennsylvania (Christiana). Social status. 1880-1900. *1025*

Business (family). Employment. 1950-81. *405*

Busing. Child care centers. Social change. 1975. *402*

Byrd, William, I. Byrd, William, II. Byrd, William, III. Letters. Tinling, Marion (review article). Virginia. 1684-1776. *887*

Byrd, William, II. Byrd, William, I. Byrd, William, III. Letters. Tinling, Marion (review article). Virginia. 1684-1776. *887*

—. Diaries. Social Organization. Virginia. 1700-20. *1161*

Byrd, William, III. Byrd, William, I. Byrd, William, II. Letters. Tinling, Marion (review article). Virginia. 1684-1776. *887*

C

Cadish family. Bakeries. Broder family. California (Los Angeles). Delicatessens. Jews. Settlement. 1922-70. *1162*

California. Agricultural Industry. Wine. ca 1830-1975. *967*

—. Bacon, Julian Smith. Smith, Jedediah Strong. Smith, Peter (family). 19c-20c. *1130*

—. Berkeley Guidance Study. Depressions. Employment. Women. 1930-70. *367*

—. Bernstein, Max. Gold Rushes. International Company of Mexico. Jews. Mexico (Baja California). 1854-1971. *1116*

—. Census. Fertility. Jews. 1970. *568*

—. Chinese. Economic Structure. Prostitution. Women. 1849-1925. *667*

—. Chumash Indians. Indians. Marriage. Mission Santa Barbara. Social Organization. Yanunali, Pedro. 1787-1806. *1141*

—. Civil War. Daily life. Gold Rushes. Letters. Pennsylvania. Shuler family. 1849-64. *1051*

—. Cunningham, Jane Elizabeth. Steamboat. Terschuren, Gerhard Frederick. 1860-1947. *1094*

—. Divorce. Family Law Act (1970). Law. ca 1970-80. *578*

—. Divorce. Women. 1850-90. *122*

—. Ehrman, Theresa. France (Paris). Letters. Music. Stein, Gertrude. 1901-67. *1121*

—. Frontier and Pioneer Life. Missouri. Morris, Sally Dodge. Nebraska. Overland Journeys to the Pacific. Personal narratives. 1821-77. *932*

—. Pioneers. Rhodes, Mary W. K. D. Texas. Women. 1830-93. *1058*

—. Seghesio family. Winemaking. 1886-1977. *1095*

—. Wolfskill family. 1838-1900. *816*

California (Alum Rock). Education. Parents. Public Schools. Vouchers. 1960's-70's. *401*

California (Fort Bragg). Business. Jews. Russia. Shafsky family. 1889-1976. *1166*

California (Los Angeles). Architecture. Insurance. Marks, David X. Marks, Joshua H. Philanthropy. 1902-77. *1163*

—. Assimilation. Jews. Scheuer, Carolyn Meyberg (reminiscence). 1902-31. *1102*

—. Bakeries. Broder family. Cadish family. Delicatessens. Jews. Settlement. 1922-70. *1162*

—. Catholic Church. Fertility. Mexican Americans. Religiosity. Women. 1973. *737*

—. Catholic Church. Marriage. Mission Santa Barbara. Social Customs. 1786-1848. *209*
—. Daily Life. Mott, Thomas. Sepúlveda y Ávila, María Ascensión. 1844-61. *1151*
—. Demography. Economic Conditions. Family (structure). Methodology. Social change. 1850-75. *181*
—. Demography. Economic Conditions. Marxism. Social change. 1850-70. *182*
—. Mexican Americans. Modernization. Social change. 1850-80. *413*
California (Martinez). Daily Life. Letters. Muir, John. 1890-1914. *1089*
California (Pasadena, San Rafael Ranch). Campbell-Johnston, Alexander. Settlement. 1880's. *812*
California (San Diego). Bicycles. Blochman, Abraham (family). 1848-1959. *858*
California (San Francisco). Bransten, Florine Haas. Business. Culture. Jews. Lilienthal Alice Haas. ca 1900-81. *880*
—. French language. Godchaux family. Music. Teachers. 1880's-1920's. *811*
California (San Francisco Bay area). Acculturation. Bureau of Indian Affairs. Indians. Navajo Indians. Relocation. Women. 1950-80. *207*
—. Acculturation. Japanese Americans. 1905-76. *1124*
California (San Luis Obispo). Buildings (iron front). Jews. Sinsheimer, Aaron Zachary (2d family). 1878-1956. *1118*
California (Santa Ana). Jews. Nasatir, Morris (family). Retail Trade. 1888-1915. *1038*
California, southern. Arizona. Business. Jacobs, Mark Israel (and family). Jews. 1851-94. *928*
Calkin(s) family. Apple industry. Halliburton, Robert Grant. Inglis, Charles. Nova Scotia. Starr family. 19c. *943*
Campbell-Johnston, Alexander. California (Pasadena, San Rafael Ranch). Settlement. 1880's. *812*
Camping. Democracy. New England. 1978. *395*
Canada. Acculturation. Indians. Sex roles. Wisconsin. Women. 1901-70. *168*
—. Australia. Family, one-parent. Great Britain. New Zealand. 1970's. *265*
—. Birth Rate (decline). Demography. 1961-71. *725*
—. Child welfare. Legislation. Mothers' allowances. 1916-70's. *554*
—. Childbirth. Infants. MacMurchy, Helen. Mortality. Whitton, Charlotte. 1919-39. *386*
—. Chinese Canadians. Federal Policy. Immigration. Legislation. 1885-1971. *187*
—. Chinese Canadians. Immigration. Social change. 1850's-1970's. *153*
—. Demography. Family size ideals. Social Surveys (methodology). 1945-74. *601*
—. Divorce rates. Law and Society. Legal access. 1867-1973. *519*
—. Employment. Family (low-income). Methodology. Models. 1974. *365*
—. English Canadians. Woman suffrage. 1877-1918. *18*
—. Ethnicity. Jews. Schools. Youth groups. 20c. *294*
—. Family unit. Generations. Immigrants. Italians. 20c. *330*
—. Fertility. 1971. *689*
—. Fertility. Income. Labor. 1951-76. *246*
—. Francophones. Marriage, mixed. Population. 1971-78. *55*
—. French Canadians. Social Status. Success, chances for. 1965-66. *117*
—. Genealogy. Ireland (Waterford). Prime Minister. Thompson, John S. D. 1796-1903. *1013*

—. Ignatieff family. Russian Canadians. 1900-50's. *146*
—. Interpersonal Relations. Kinship. Marriage. Suicide. 1951-71. *625*
—. Kennedy family. 18c-1973. *1098*
—. Legislation. Mothers. Public Welfare. ca 1900-39. *555*
—. Literature. Mothers (image). 1950-80. *645*
—. Marriage. 1851-91. *110*
Canadian Council on Child Welfare. Charities. Child Welfare. Whitton, Charlotte. 1920-48. *531*
Canby, Edmund (diary). Delaware (New Castle County). Friends, Society of. Milling. 1822-35. *959*
Cannon, Martha Hughes. Great Britain. Letters. Mormons. Polygamy. Utah (Salt Lake City). Women. 1885-96. *1000*
Capital. Agricultural Production. Alberta. Country life. 20c. *457*
—. Agriculture. Commerce. Frontier and Pioneer Life. Values. 1607-1758. *337*
—. Agriculture. Frontier and Pioneer Life. Values. 1607-1830. *139*
—. Business. Elites. Family dynasties. Law. Texas (Galveston). ca 1890-1980. *488*
Capitalism. Aliens, illegal. Children. Labor. Mexico. Women. ca 1950-79. *439*
—. Behavior. Labor. Massachusetts (Lowell). Sex roles. 1860. *421*
—. Ethnic groups. Social organization. 1970's. *513*
—. Galbraith, John Kenneth. Housework. Oakley, Ann. Sex roles. Women. 1950-70's. *436*
—. Lasch, Christopher (review article). Women. 1900-75. *642*
Carnevale, Achille. Immigration. Italian Americans. 1884-1978. *1026*
Carter, Jimmy (administration). Cities. Federal Policy. Women. 1977-80. *429*
Cather, Charles (and family). Nebraska. 19c-20c. *829*
Cather family (letters). Nebraska. Pioneers. 1895. *1076*
Catholic Church. Attitudes. Mormons. Protestant Churches. Utah. 1974. *19*
—. California (Los Angeles). Fertility. Mexican Americans. Religiosity. Women. 1973. *737*
—. California (Los Angeles). Marriage. Mission Santa Barbara. Social Customs. 1786-1848. *209*
—. Educational system. French Canadians. Parent-youth conflict. Quebec. Social change. 1960-70. *473*
—. Georgia. O'Connor, Flannery (ancestry). ca 1733-1949. *908*
—. Government. Parish registers. Quebec. 1539-1973. *379*
—. Parish registers. Population. Quebec. 1616-1700. *252*
Catholics. Adams, John Quincy (family). Ohio (Cincinnati). 1843-1930. *1148*
—. Family size preferences. Religious differences. Teenagers. 1971-74. *42*
Cattle Raising. Business. Montana. Ranches. Sheep raising. Sieben, Henry. 1864-1937. *1046*
—. Houses. Leonard, Nathaniel (descendants). Missouri (Cooper County). Ravenswood (residence). 1825-1980. *1139*
Cemeteries. Genealogy. 1978. *293*
—. Markley family. Pennsylvania (Skippack area). Restorations. 1738. 1926. *905*
—. Mennonites. Pennsylvania (Dauphin County; Lower Swatara Township). Shope Mennonite Cemetery. 18c-1981. *1159*
Cemeteries, rural. Social change. Tombstones. 1830's-40's. *288*
Cemetery records. Eastern Cemetery. Maine (Portland). ca 1717-1900. *977*

—. Attitudes. Parents. 18c. *778*
—. Attitudes. Stereotypes. Welfare, recipients of. 1970's. *486*
—. Blacks. Cities. Family structure. Socialization, political. 1973. *397*
—. Brookwood Farm. Country Life. Delaware. Douglas, Elinor Thompson (account). Thompson, Mary Wilson. Travel. 1900's-20's. *78*
—. Bureaucracy. Learning disabilities. Mental Illness. 1975. *370*
—. Chesapeake Bay area. Maryland. Parents. Values. Virginia. 18c. *749*
—. Child-rearing. Holsman, Virginia (reminiscences). Oregon (Hillsboro). Recreation. 19c-1920's. *961*
—. Cities. Income. Pennsylvania (Philadelphia). 1880. *438*
—. Connecticut. Inheritance. Probate. Wealth. 1930-46. *494*
—. Day care. Employment. Women. 1890-1977. *500*
—. Day care centers. Social reform. Women's liberation movement. 1854-1973. *533*
—. Day care system. Race Relations. 1967-73. *572*
—. Day nurseries. Florida (Jacksonville). Georgia (Swainsboro). North Carolina (Durham). 1960-80. *490*
—. Divorce. Separation. 1973. *606*
—. Drake, James A. (family). Family life. Photographs. 1880-1900. *752*
—. Education. Social Change. 1946-76. *3*
—. Educational Policy. Parents. Poor. 1960-78. *543*
—. Employment. Income. Literacy. Men. Wives. 1901. *428*
—. Environment. Medical care. 1970's. *527*
—. Fogarty, John E. Mentally Handicapped. Parents Council for Retarded Children. Rhode Island. Social change. Trudeau, Arthur. 1951-70. *350*
—. Folk Songs. Games. Kentucky, eastern. 20c. *325*
—. Franklin & Armfield (firm). Interstate commerce. Manifests. Slave Trade. Virginia (Alexandria). 1828-36. *557*
—. Friends, Society of. Pennsylvania (Delaware Valley). 1681-1735. *698*
—. Games. Plantations. Slaves. Socialization. South. 1820-60. *786*
—. Health. Women. Working hours. 1972. *541*
—. Life insurance. Social Classes. 1875-1980. *576*
—. Massachusetts. Sewall, Samuel (family). Socialization. 1670-1720. *1113*
—. Maternal deprivation. Upper Classes. 1950-74. *758*
—. Medical Care (costs). 1969. *478*
—. Portraits. 1670-1810. *609*
—. Presidents. Toys. 19c-20c. *766*
—. Research. 1960-79. *396*
—. Sex roles. Socialization. Technology. Toys. 1920-40. *726*
—. Television. 1982. *387*
Children, black. Blacks. Family (white). 1977. *690*
Children (comparative studies). Mothers (working, non-working). 1974. *764*
Children, demand for. Agricultural labor. Birth Rate (decline). Farm households. Models. 1939-60. *733*
Children, treatment of. Blacks. Illinois. Moynihan Report (1965). Social Problems. 1965-74. *369*
Children's Aid Society. Foster care. Home Missionary Society. Pennsylvania (Philadelphia). 1880-1905. *398*
Chinese. California. Economic Structure. Prostitution. Women. 1849-1925. *667*
Chinese Canadians. Canada. Federal Policy. Immigration. Legislation. 1885-1971. *187*

—. Canada. Immigration. Social change. 1850's-1970's. *153*
Chippewa Indians. Cree Indians. Indians. Rego, Mary. Women. 20c. *828*
Choctaw Indians. Family life. 1700-1975. *264*
Christian Biography. Episcopal Church, Protestant. Huntington, Frederick. New York. 1869-1904. *1039*
Christiana Machine Company. Broomell family. Business community. Pennsylvania (Christiana). Social status. 1880-1900. *1025*
Christianity. Blacks. Social change. Values. War. 1960's-70's. *191*
—. Cherokee Indians. Indian-White Relations. Missions and Missionaries. Property. Social Change. Women. 19c. *329*
Christians. Converts. Intermarriage. Jews. 1971. *183*
—. Jews. Marriage. 1962-79. *746*
Chumash Indians. California. Indians. Marriage. Mission Santa Barbara. Social Organization. Yanunali, Pedro. 1787-1806. *1141*
Church attendance. Child-rearing. Religion. Women. 1972-80. *414*
Church, black (first). Blacks. Clergy. Massachusetts (Boston). Paul, Thomas (and family). 1773-1973. *1024*
Church, Robert Reed, Sr. Black Capitalism. Tennessee (Memphis). Wealth. Wills. 1912. *1021*
Cigar industry. Florida (Tampa). Italian Americans. Women. 1890-1930. *212*
Cities. Blacks. Children. Family structure. Socialization, political. 1973. *397*
—. Blacks. Family heads (female). Women. 19c. *647*
—. Blacks. Poverty. 1963-71. *296*
—. Carter, Jimmy (administration). Federal Policy. Women. 1977-80. *429*
—. Census. Genealogy. Local history. Methodology. 1980. *266*
—. Children. Income. Pennsylvania (Philadelphia). 1880. *438*
—. Cooperative households. Family life. 1850-1976. *158*
—. Divorce. Marriage. Mortality. Rural Settlements. Tennessee. 1970. *326*
—. Federal Policy. Geographic space. Households. Labor. Women. 1977-80. *198*
—. Illinois (Chicago). Playgrounds. Progressivism. Social Reform. 1894-1917. *491*
—. Immigration. Italian Americans. Jews. Rhode Island. 1880-1940. *548*
—. Northeastern or North Atlantic States. Upper class. 1825-50. *232*
—. Population change. Social History. 1750-1975. *133*
—. Recreation. Social Change. Working conditions. 1830-90. *520*
Cities (decline). Social Organization. 1700-1977. *349*
City directories. Buschow family. Family history. Local History. Ohio (Cleveland). 1883-1900. 1979. *316*
City Life. Aquino, Salvatore A. (reminiscences). Immigration. Italian Americans. New York City. 1914. *13*
—. Blacks. Census. Historiography. Indiana (Vanderburgh County; Evansville). 1865-80. *27*
—. Census. Pennsylvania (Philadelphia). 1693-1790. *218*
City Life (review article). Hershberg, Theodore. Pennsylvania (Philadelphia). 19c. *62*
Civic culture. Enlightenment. Mothers, Republican. Political theory. 18c. *679*
Civil rights. National Organization for Women. Women's Liberation Movement. 1966-71. *734*
Civil War. Alabama. Slavery. Social Change. Whites. 1850-70. *21*

—. Alrich family. Virginia (Spotsylvania County).
1830-1979. *989*
—. Armies. Genealogy. Ladd, Nathaniel Eustis.
1861-65. *917*
—. Autobiography. Daily life. Genealogy. Martin,
Frances Martha Atkinson. Social organization.
Texas. 1857-75. 1979. *200*
—. Boswell, Ben D. Boswell, Emma. Boswell
Springs (resort). Military. Oregon. Spas.
1860-1908. *1033*
—. California. Daily life. Gold Rushes. Letters.
Pennsylvania. Shuler family. 1849-64. *1051*
—. Copperheads. Delaware (Newark).
Vallandigham family. 1861-69. *1010*
—. Country Life. Mississippi (Pontotoc County).
Smith, Andrew Jackson (account). 1864-69. *155*
—. Letters. Lewis, Charlotte. Lewis, Enoch.
Pennsylvania (Altoona). 1863. *650*
Clans. Indians. Sioux Indians. Social Organization.
Villages. 19c-20c. *145*
Clarke, Lewis G. (family history). Slavery. 1833-82.
1136
Clergy. Baptists. Burns, Bertha Porter. Burns,
Marion Van. Louisiana (Shiloh). Teachers.
1884-1975. *1001*
—. Blacks. Church, black (first). Massachusetts
(Boston). Paul, Thomas (and family).
1773-1973. *1024*
—. Lehman, Hans (and family). Mennonites.
Pennsylvania (Lancaster County; Rapho
Township). Swiss Americans. ca 1727-1909. *995*
Clockmaking. Hoff, John George (and sons).
Pennsylvania (Lancaster County). 1769-1822.
1153
Coal Mines and Mining. Daily Life (photo-essay).
Kentucky (Harlan County). Poor. Sergent
family. 1946. *994*
Codman family. Adams, Thomas Boylston.
Massachusetts (Lincoln). Personal Narratives.
Social customs. Upper Classes. 1890-1920. *798*
—. Archives. Massachusetts. Society for the
Preservation of New England Antiquities
(Codman Family Manuscripts Collection).
1715-1979. *963*
—. Massachusetts (Lincoln). Photographs.
1850-1900. *1072*
Cohabitation. Attitudes. Religion. Youth. 1974-80.
358
Cole family. North Carolina. Pottery. 1700's-1977.
813
Collectivism. Family (review article). Individualism.
Zimmerman, Carle C. 1945-70's. *324*
College graduates. Human Relations. Wellesley
College. Women. 1880-1910. *348*
—. Social mobility. Women. 1961-68. *353*
College students, male. Occupational movements,
intergenerational. -1974. *718*
Colman, Blanche. Colman, Nathan. Frontier and
Pioneer Life. Jews. South Dakota (Deadwood).
1877-1977. *799*
Colman, Nathan. Colman, Blanche. Frontier and
Pioneer Life. Jews. South Dakota (Deadwood).
1877-1977. *799*
Colonial experience. New England. Social History
(review article). 17c-18c. *119*
Colonial Government. Aristocracy. New Mexico.
New Spain. Settlement. 16c. *862*
Colorado. Agriculture. Czech Americans.
Migration, Internal. Mines. Slovak Americans.
1860-1920. *161*
—. Child-rearing. Frontier and Pioneer Life. Home
Economics. Oral history. Women. 1895-1920.
585
—. Daily Life. Smith, John Guy. 1878-1937. *1106*
Colorado (Denver). Assimilation. Greek Americans.
Life histories. 20c. *1052*

—. Immigration. Jews. Shwayder family.
1865-1916. *833*
Colorado, northeastern. Frontier and Pioneer Life.
Methodist Episcopal Church (North, South).
Propst, Missouri Powell. Women. 1874-91.
1064
Colorado (South Platte Valley). Farmers. Frontier
and Pioneer Life. German Russians.
Immigration. 1890-ca 1907. *88*
Colorado, University of (Western Historical
Collections). Darley family (papers). 1875-1970.
808
—. Libraries (holdings). Patterson, Thomas M.
(family). 1850-1925. *809*
Comenha (woman). Cheyenne Indians. Daily Life.
Indians. Women. 1860-1900. *832*
Commerce. Agriculture. Capital. Frontier and
Pioneer Life. Values. 1607-1758. *337*
Communes. Behavior. Self-interest. 1980. *655*
Communes (review article). Society, alternative.
1960's-70's. *219*
Communications Behavior. Adams family.
Attitudes. Generations. 1764-1919. *1036*
—. Generations. James, William (d. 1832; and
family). Values. 1811-1910. *903*
Community. Agriculture. Amish, Old Order.
Pennsylvania (Lancaster). 1757-1979. *638*
Community history. Family history. Nevins, Allan.
Oral history. 1940's-70's. *268*
Community organization. Americanization.
Education. Jewish Family and Children's
Service. Michigan (Detroit). 1876-1976. *479*
Community structure. Connecticut (Windsor).
Geographic mobility. 17c. *374*
Computers. Genealogy. 20c. *289*
Conches. Florida (Upper Matecumbe Key).
Pioneers. 1880-1940. *921*
Congregationalism. Connecticut. Frontier and
Pioneer Life. Ohio. Western Reserve. Wright,
Elizur (and family). Yale University. 1762-1870.
911
—. Connecticut (Canterbury). Great Awakening.
Local politics. Schisms. 1742-50. *470*
—. Connecticut (New London). Great Awakening.
New Lights. Separatism. Shepherd's Tent
(church). 1720-50. *515*
Congress. American Revolution. Hanson, George
A. Hanson, John. Maryland. Sweden. 18c.
1876. *855*
Conine family. Frontier and Pioneer Life. Letters.
North Central States. 1852-63. *819*
Conine family (letters). Indiana. Pioneers. 1849-51.
817
—. Indiana. Pioneers. 1852-63. *818*
Connecticut. Assimilation. D'Antonio, William V.
(autobiography). Ethnicity. Italian Americans.
ca 1926-73. *70*
—. Blacks. 19c. *46*
—. Borden family. Gay family. Massachusetts.
1635-91. *807*
—. Children. Inheritance. Probate. Wealth.
1930-46. *494*
—. Congregationalism. Frontier and Pioneer Life.
Ohio. Western Reserve. Wright, Elizur (and
family). Yale University. 1762-1870. *911*
—. Divorce. 1757-97. *617*
Connecticut (Bridgeport). Births. Blacks. Vital
Statistics. 1855-85. *45*
Connecticut (Canterbury). Congregationalism. Great
Awakening. Local politics. Schisms. 1742-50.
470
Connecticut (Colebrook). Massachusetts
(Southwick). New York (Liberty). Russell,
Stephen (and descendants). 1749-1820. *1087*
Connecticut (Guilford). Inheritance. Migration.
1650-1775. *779*

Connecticut (Hartford County). Inheritance. Massachusetts (Essex County). Property rights. Widows. 1638-81. *732*
Connecticut (Killingworth). Bradford, William (descendants). Steevens family. 1752-1800. *823*
Connecticut (Milford). Puritans. 1639-90's. *211*
Connecticut (New London). Congregationalism. Great Awakening. New Lights. Separatism. Shepherd's Tent (church). 1720-50. *515*
Connecticut (Norwich). Social Change. Women. 1750-1800. *174*
Connecticut (Norwich, Hartford, Fairfield). Family (political domination). Office-holding patterns. 1700-60. *69*
Connecticut (Windsor). Community structure. Geographic mobility. 17c. *374*
Conservatism. Social Change. 1960-79. *26*
Conte, Stephen G. (account). Genealogy. Italy (Andretta). Travel. 1971. *867*
Converts. Christians. Intermarriage. Jews. 1971. *183*
Cookery. Men. Sex roles. Stereotypes. 20c. *580*
Cooperative households. Cities. Family life. 1850-1976. *158*
Copper, Fannie Adams. Homesteading and Homesteaders. Memoirs. Oregon. 1889-99. *1146*
Copperheads. Civil War. Delaware (Newark). Vallandigham family. 1861-69. *1010*
Corbit, William (family). Delaware (Odessa). Economic Conditions. Indiana (Richmond). Wilson, David (family). 1768-1925. *848*
Corporation, family. Jews. Lilienthal family pact. New York. 1814-1904. *1117*
Cost of Living. Day Nurseries. Employment. Government. 1970's. *354*
Cotton. Child Labor. Occupational segregation. Sex. Textile industry. 1910. *489*
Cotton industry. Quebec. Women. 1910-50. *382*
Country life. Agricultural Production. Alberta. Capital. 20c. *457*
—. Brookwood Farm. Children. Delaware. Douglas, Elinor Thompson (account). Thompson, Mary Wilson. Travel. 1900's-20's. *78*
—. Buell, John L. (family register). Diaries. New York (Morristown). 1844-88. *985*
—. Civil War. Mississippi (Pontotoc County). Smith, Andrew Jackson (account). 1864-69. *155*
—. Diaries. Farmers. Gillespie, Emily Hawley. Iowa. Women. 1858-88. *1006*
—. Drawing. Lyndes, Stanley Horace. Teaching. Vermont. 1918-75. *9*
—. Economic Conditions. Mexican Americans. Occupations. Social Organization. Washington (Yakima Valley). 1971. *433*
—. Ethnicity. Immigrants. Marriage. Minnesota (Kandiyoki County). Swedish Americans. 1870-1905. *729*
—. Farms. German Americans. Illinois. Irish Americans. Land transfers. 1975-78. *539*
—. Farms. Illinois (southern). Lentz, Lula Gillespie (reminiscences). 1883-1929. *996*
—. Frost, Margaret Fullerton. Oklahoma. Personal Narratives. 1901-07. *913*
—. Hecker, Friedrich Karl. Illinois (St. Clair County). Köhler, Carl. Letters. 1851. *1129*
—. Kansas (Decatur County). Webb, Bernice Larson (reminiscences). 1930's. *319*
—. Land transfers. Minnesota, east-central. Swedish Americans. 1885-1915. *224*
—. Social Customs. Women. 18c-1976. *643*
Courts. *Blair* v. *Blair* (Virginia, 1773). Jefferson, Thomas. Virginia (Williamsburg). 1771-73. *415*
—. Massachusetts (Salem). Sex roles. Women. 1636-83. *458*
Courtship. Diaries. Indiana. Mennonites. Sprunger, David. 1893-95. *1111*

—. Howells, William Dean. Mead, Elinor Gertrude. 1860-62. *1019*
—. Logan, Ernest. Logan, Lizzie Walker. Wyoming (Cheyenne). 1871-1910. *1091*
Courtship narratives. Folklore. 1974-76. *793*
Covenant theology. Bulkeley, Peter. Massachusetts (Concord). Puritans. 1635-1731. *1060*
Coverlets. Brenneman family. Genealogy. Mennonites. Pennsylvania. 1631-1971. *948*
Cowley, Josephine Hutmacher. Cowley, Malcolm. Personal narratives. ca 1890-1940. *870*
Cowley, Malcolm. Cowley, Josephine Hutmacher. Personal narratives. ca 1890-1940. *870*
Creativity. Food Industry. Jews. Knishes. Social Customs. 1980. *652*
Cree Indians. Chippewa Indians. Indians. Rego, Mary. Women. 20c. *828*
Creek Indian War (1813-14). Alabama. Indian-White Relations. Lott, Arthur. Louisiana. Meredith, Thomas. Murders. 1812-14. *1156*
Creoles. Blacks. Louisiana. 1970's. *704*
—. Louisiana (Cane River, Natchitoches). Race relations. Social status. 1767-20c. *1022*
Crisp, Minnie A. (reminiscences). Homesteading and Homesteaders. New Mexico (Union County). 1910-33. *992*
Crop yields. Apple industry. Genealogy. Nova Scotia. Prescott, Charles Ramage. 1772-1970's. *944*
Crothers, Rachel. Boothe, Clare. Drama. Hellman, Lillian. Women. 1920-69. *30*
Cuba. Hawthorne, Sophia Peabody. Letters. 1833-35. *815*
Cuban Americans. Employment. Sex roles. Women. 1960's-70's. *426*
—. Marriage. 1957-74. *581*
Culture. Bransten, Florine Haas. Business. California (San Francisco). Jews. Lilienthal, Alice Haas. ca 1900-81. *880*
Culture, youth-oriented. Aged. Mass media. Stereotypes. 1960's-70's. *665*
Cunningham, Jane Elizabeth. California. Steamboat. Terschuren, Gerhard Frederick. 1860-1947. *1094*
Curricula. Domesticity. Home economics. Progressivism. Sex roles. 1900-20. *673*
Custis, Martha Dandridge. Virginia. Washington, George. Weddings. 1759. *1040*
Customs and behavior. Marriage. New England. 1632-1783. *687*
Czech Americans. Agriculture. Colorado. Migration, Internal. Mines. Slovak Americans. 1860-1920. *161*
—. Family life. Iowa (Pocahontas). Johnson, Anna Dockal (memoir). 1900-20. *674*

D

Daedalus(periodical). Biology. Feminism. Lasch, Christopher. Social change. 1975-77. *44*
Daily Life. Alger, Hugh Wesley. Farms. Pennsylvania (Bradford County). Personal Narratives. 1890-99. *5*
—. Autobiography. Civil War. Genealogy. Martin, Frances Martha Atkinson. Social organization. Texas. 1857-75. 1979. *200*
—. Battle, Lucy Martin. Battle, William Horn. North Carolina. Plantations. 1805-74. *918*
—. Bavaria. Hartlieb, Louise Marie Katherina Boehner. Immigration. New York (Buffalo). Reminiscences. 1825-1918. *1114*
—. Bradford, Phoebe George (diary). Delaware. 1832-33. *1150*
—. British Columbia (Victoria). Point Ellice House. 1861-89. 1968-80. *2*
—. California. Civil War. Gold Rushes. Letters. Pennsylvania. Shuler family. 1849-64. *1051*

—. California (Los Angeles). Mott, Thomas. Sepúlveda y Ávila, María Ascensión. 1844-61. *1151*

—. California (Martinez). Letters. Muir, John. 1890-1914. *1089*

—. Chandler, Cornelia C. Cherokee Indians. North Carolina. Personal narratives. Removals. 1867-1918. *231*

—. Cherokee Indians. Indians. Tennessee. Wolf, Lucyann Davis (family). 1900-35. *1108*

—. Cheyenne Indians. Comenha (woman). Indians. Women. 1860-1900. *832*

—. Colorado. Smith, John Guy. 1878-1937. *1106*

—. Diaries. Drinker, Elizabeth Sandwith. Pennsylvania (Philadelphia). Women. 1758-1807. *872*

—. Eichholtz, Leonard (family). Pennsylvania (Lancaster). 1750-1817. *1079*

—. Fort Washakie. Indians. Letters. Winne, Caroline. Wives. Wyoming. 1879-80. *845*

—. Great Britain. Household goods. Massachusetts. Social Change. 1650-1775. *743*

—. Howells, William Dean. Ohio (Hamilton). 1841-50. *946*

—. Humphrys, James (and family). Saskatchewan (Cannington Manor). 1880's-1908. *965*

—. Indians. Personal Narratives. Sioux Indians. Swan, Lucy. Women. 1900-71. *1059*

—. Letters. Maryland (Baltimore). Preston, Madge. Preston, William P. 1855-67. *827*

—. Waugh, Jesse (reminiscence). West Virginia. 1830-1900. *993*

Daily Life (conference). Diaries. Great Britain (London). Sanderson, Mr. USSR. 1937. *875*

Daily Life (photo-essay). Coal Mines and Mining. Kentucky (Harlan County). Poor. Sergent family. 1946. *994*

Daley, Richard (and family). Democratic Party. Illinois. Ireland (County Cork; Old Parish, Ring). Irish Americans. State Politics. 19c-1976. *1061*

D'Antonio, William V. (autobiography). Assimilation. Connecticut. Ethnicity. Italian Americans. ca 1926-73. *70*

Darley family (papers). Colorado, University of (Western Historical Collections). 1875-1970. *808*

Dating. Blacks. Mexican Americans. Race Relations. Whites. 1978-79. *691*

Daughters. Bibliographies. Literature. Mothers. Women. 1800-1979. *680*

Davis, James Dick. Genealogy. Harbormaster. History (societies). Old Folks of Shelby County. Tennessee (Memphis). 1810-80. *822*

Davis, Rebecca Harding. Fiction. Industrial Revolution. Realism. Social Organization. Women. Working Class. 1861. *234*

Davis, Richard Harding. Reporters and Reporting. War correspondents. ca 1890-1916. *933*

Day care *See also* Child care.

—. Children. Employment. Women. 1890-1977. *500*

Day care centers. Children. Social reform. Women's liberation movement. 1854-1973. *533*

Day care movement. Child Welfare. Fiscal Policy. Research. 1960's-70's. *385*

Day care system. Children. Race Relations. 1967-73. *572*

Day nurseries. Children. Florida (Jacksonville). Georgia (Swainsboro). North Carolina (Durham). 1960-80. *490*

—. Cost of Living. Employment. Government. 1970's. *354*

—. Federal policy. Politics. 1960-77. *575*

Day Nurseries (effect). Employment. Wages. Women. 1971-72. *336*

Death and Dying. Birth. Marriage. Rites and Ceremonies. Social Customs. Tennessee, eastern. 20c. *693*

—. Chesapeake Bay area. Kinship. Parents. Virginia (Middlesex County). 1650-1710. *735*

—. Chesapeake Bay area. Marriage. Maryland. 1630-1720. *777*

—. Childbirth. Diaries. Diseases. Massachusetts (Westborough). Parkman, Ebenezer. Social Organization. 1724-82. *702*

—. Infants. New England. Parents. Theology. 1620-1720. *277*

Decisionmaking. Budgets. Pennsylvania (Philadelphia). 1870-80. *437*

Degler, Carl N. Berkin, Carol R. Dublin, Thomas. Kennedy, Susan. Lovett, Clara M. Women (review article). 1770's-1980. *243*

—. DuBois, Ellen Carol. Suffrage. Women's Liberation Movement (review article). 19c-20c. 1980. *403*

Degler, Carl N. (review article). Women. ca 1750-1980. *41*

Delaware. Aid to Families with Dependent Children. Attitudes. Poor. Public Welfare. 1949-75. *373*

—. Bradford, Phoebe George (diary). Daily life. 1832-33. *1150*

—. Brookwood Farm. Children. Country Life. Douglas, Elinor Thompson (account). Thompson, Mary Wilson. Travel. 1900's-20's. *78*

—. DuPont family. Reading. Social Customs. Women. 1810-35. *957*

—. Higgins, Anthony (reminiscences). Memoirs. Thompson, Mary Wilson. 1770-1947. *953*

—. Memoirs. Thompson, Mary Wilson. 1870-1918. *954*

Delaware (Brandywine Valley). Bauduy, Victorine Du Pont. Business. Domesticity. DuPont, Sophie. Eleutherian Mills. Women. 1803-52. *975*

—. DuPont de Nemours, Pierre Samuel. DuPont, Victorine. Education. 1800-17. *974*

Delaware (Lewes). Assimilation. Genealogy. Jews. Nunez family. 18c. *241*

Delaware (New Castle County). Canby, Edmund (diary). Friends, Society of. Milling. 1822-35. *959*

Delaware (Newark). Civil War. Copperheads. Vallandigham family. 1861-69. *1010*

Delaware (Odessa). Corbit, William (family). Economic Conditions. Indiana (Richmond). Wilson, David (family). 1768-1925. *848*

Delaware (Wilmington). Ward, Christopher L. (autobiography, family). 1850-1900. *1071*

Delicatessens. Bakeries. Broder family. Cadish family. California (Los Angeles). Jews. Settlement. 1922-70. *1162*

Democracy. Camping. New England. 1978. *395*

Democratic Party. Daley, Richard (and family). Illinois. Ireland (County Cork; Old Parish, Ring). Irish Americans. State Politics. 19c-1976. *1061*

Demographic transition. Family history. 1600-1800. *321*

Demography. Birth Rate (decline). Canada. 1961-71. *725*

—. Blacks. Family structure. Fertility trends. 1880-1940. *637*

—. British West Indies. Family structure. Slavery. South. 19c. *98*

—. California (Los Angeles). Economic Conditions. Family (structure). Methodology. Social change. 1850-75. *181*

—. California (Los Angeles). Economic Conditions. Marxism. Social change. 1850-70. *182*

—. Canada. Family size ideals. Social Surveys (methodology). 1945-74. *601*

—. Divorce. 1967-79. *796*

—. Employment. 1968-79. *455*

—. Federal Policy. Liberalism. Sex. 1940-80. *393*

Demos, John. Boocock, Sarane Spence. Hareven, Tamara K. Life course (concept). Methodology. 1800-1980. *318*

Denlinger family. Genealogy. Mennonites. Pennsylvania. Switzerland. 1594-1803. *886*

Depressions. Berkeley Guidance Study. California. Employment. Women. 1930-70. *367*

—. Biography. Family history. Interviews. Louisiana State University. Students. Works Progress Administration. 1930's. 1978. *66*

—. Labor. Middle Classes. Values. Women. 1930's. *377*

Derrico family. Assimilation. Italian Americans. 1904-1970's. *853*

Desertion. Jews. Social Problems. 1900-26. *100*

DeWitt, Zachariah Price (family). Kentucky. Migration. New Jersey. New Netherland. Ohio. 1650-1820's. *981*

Diaries. Arkansas. Frontier and Pioneer Life. Simms, Mary Ann Owen. 1855-61. *1147*

—. Bean, Warren G. Farmers. Pennsylvania (Skippack Township). 1899. *1032*

—. Belknap, Kitturah Penton. Family life. Frontier and Pioneer Life. Iowa. 1839-48. *1075*

—. Bruce, Mazie. Maryland (Cumberland). McKaig, Mrs. William W. Upper Classes. Women. 1857-89. *821*

—. Buell, John L. (family register). Country Life. New York (Morristown). 1844-48. *985*

—. Byrd, William, II. Social Organization. Virginia. 1700-20. *1161*

—. Childbirth. Death and Dying. Diseases. Massachusetts (Westborough). Parkman, Ebenezer. Social Organization. 1724-82. *702*

—. Country Life. Farmers. Gillespie, Emily Hawley. Iowa. Women. 1858-88. *1006*

—. Courtship. Indiana. Mennonites. Sprunger, David. 1893-95. *1111*

—. Daily Life. Drinker, Elizabeth Sandwith. Pennsylvania (Philadelphia). Women. 1758-1807. *872*

—. Daily Life (conference). Great Britain (London). Sanderson, Mr. USSR. 1937. *875*

—. Frontier and Pioneer Life. Missions and Missionaries. Oregon (Forest Grove). Tshimakain Indian Mission. Walker, Mary Richardson. Washington. 1833-97. *962*

Dickinson, Emily. Dickinson, Lavinia Norcross. Dickinson, Susan Gilbert. ca 1850-86. *1029*

Dickinson, Lavinia Norcross. Dickinson, Emily. Dickinson, Susan Gilbert. ca 1850-86. *1029*

Dickinson, Susan Gilbert. Dickinson, Emily. Dickinson, Lavinia Norcross. ca 1850-86. *1029*

Didion, Joan. Cheever, John. Fiction. Irving, John. Isolation. Stegner, Wallace. 1970's. *651*

Direct mail. Birth control information. Information diffusion. 1972. *723*

Directory of Worship. Presbyterian Church. Worship. 1788-1979. *550*

Discipline. Factories. Massachusetts (Webster). Rhode Island (Slatersville). 1790-1840. *562*

Discrimination. Florida (Miami area). Mulattos. Pioneers. Wagner, William (family). 1850-1901. *802*

—. Mexican Americans. Political familialism. Sex roles. 1970-75. *17*

Diseases. Biography. Edel, Leon (interview). James, Henry (1811-82; and family). Literature. Psychology. 1811-1916. 1979. *806*

—. Childbirth. Death and Dying. Diaries. Massachusetts (Westborough). Parkman, Ebenezer. Social Organization. 1724-82. *702*

—. James, Alice. James, William. Letters. 1886. *1157*

Divorce. Aged. Marriage. Middle Age. 1970's. *593*

—. Agricultural Labor. Blacks. Men. Moynihan, Daniel P. ("The Negro Family"). 1965-78. *536*

—. Blacks. Marriage. 1970. *763*

—. Blair, James. Documents. Jefferson, Thomas. Legislation. Virginia. 1770-73. *416*

—. California. Family Law Act (1970). Law. ca 1970-80. *578*

—. California. Women. 1850-90. *122*

—. Child care. Economic problems. Family, single-parent. Women. 1970's. *383*

—. Child custody. Law. Mental health. Social workers. 1970's. *463*

—. Children. Separation. 1973. *606*

—. Cities. Marriage. Mortality. Rural Settlements. Tennessee. 1970. *326*

—. Connecticut. 1757-97. *617*

—. Demography. 1967-79. *796*

—. Economic Conditions. Higher education. Identity. Occupations. Social Status. Women. 1971-77. *461*

—. Economic Conditions. Women. 1970-81. *571*

—. Feminism. Marriage. Reform. Stanton, Elizabeth Cady. 1840-90. *120*

—. Labor. Wives. 1960's-70's. *443*

—. Louisiana. Mahon, Samuel S. Speeches and Addresses. State Legislatures. 1806. *419*

—. Mormons. Personal narratives. Raynes, Marybeth. ca 1975-80. *524*

—. Motherhood. Race. 1968-72. *716*

—. Religion. Western States. 1972-76. *590*

—. Social organization. South. Supreme courts, state. Women. 1800-60. *394*

Divorce (grounds). Law. Massachusetts. Women, status of. 1692-1786. *622*

Divorce rates. Canada. Law and Society. Legal access. 1867-1973. *519*

Divorce records. Family life. Massachusetts. 18c. *623*

Documents. Baptisms. Birth. Blacks. Virginia (Mannikintown). Vital Statistics. 1721. *292*

—. Blacks. Genealogy, black. Public Records. Research. 19c-20c. *229*

—. Blacks. Mortality. Pennsylvania (Chambersburg). Sellers Funeral Home. 1866-1933. *254*

—. Blacks. Mortality. Pennsylvania (Franklin County; Chambersburg). Sellers Funeral Home. 1866-1933. *253*

—. Blair, James. Divorce. Jefferson, Thomas. Legislation. Virginia. 1770-73. *416*

—. Historiography. Lincoln, Abraham. Lincoln, Mary Todd. Marriage. 1842-65. 1885. 1947-82. *916*

Domestic education. Industrialization. Protestantism. Womanhood, sentimental. 1830-70. *389*

Domestic roles. Massachusetts (Salem). Social Change. Women. 1660-1770. *753*

Domesticity. Adams, Louisa Catherine. Middle Classes. 1797-1812. *868*

—. Attitudes. Lincoln, Mary Todd. Stanton, Elizabeth Cady. Stowe, Harriet Beecher. 1830-80. *1104*

—. Bauduy, Victorine Du Pont. Business. Delaware (Brandywine Valley). DuPont, Sophie. Eleutherian Mills. Women. 1803-52. *975*

—. Curricula. Home economics. Progressivism. Sex roles. 1900-20. *673*

—. Feminism. Howe, Julia Ward. Motherhood. Reform. 1844-85. *656*

—. Iowa. Photographs. Women. ca 1890-1910. *592*

—. Pennsylvania (Philadelphia). Suburbs. Women. 19c. *208*

Dominican Americans. Immigration. 1962-76. *108*

Dominis, John Owen (and ancestors). Hawaii. Liliuokalani. 1437-1891. *988*

English Canadians. Alberta. Homesteading and
Homesteaders. Personal Narratives. Rowell,
Gladys M. Stephenson family. 1904-06. *1084*
—. Canada. Woman suffrage. 1877-1918. *18*
—. French Canadians. Ontario (Alfred, Caledonia).
Stereotypes. 1800-81. *105*
Enlightenment. Civic culture. Mothers, Republican.
Political theory. 18c. *679*
Entrepreneurs. Arizona. Jews. Zeckendorf, Aaron.
Zeckendorf, Louis. Zeckendorf, William.
1853-1906. *906*
—. Jews. 1750-1949. *261*
Environment. Children. Medical care. 1970's. *527*
Epidemics. Exogamy. Marriage. Quebec. 1700-60.
705
Episcopal Church, Protestant. Christian Biography.
Huntington, Frederick. New York. 1869-1904.
1039
Epitaphs. Allen Family. Burial plots. Vermont.
1770-1834. *857*
Equality. Blacks. Marriage. Sex roles. Whites. 1976.
362
Erickson sisters. Homesteading and Homesteaders.
Letters. North Dakota (Hettinger County).
1910-11. *831*
Erikson, Erik. Childhood (review article).
Historiography. Hunt, David. Psychology.
1960-71. *166*
Errington family. Genealogy. Great Britain
(Northumberland; Denton). Massachusetts
(Cambridge). 16c-17c. *824*
Essex Institute. Massachusetts (Forge Village).
Prescott, Olive Adams. Social history. Weaving.
1780-1860. *900*
Ethnic Groups. Aged. 1970's. *790*
—. Assimilation. Greek Americans. Moskos,
Charles C., Jr. (reminiscences). 1898-1976. *1031*
—. Capitalism. Social organization. 1970's. *513*
—. Employment. Family roles. Rhode Island.
Women's attitudes. 1968-69. *631*
—. Family land. Farmers. Illinois. Land Tenure.
1975-77. *540*
—. Fertility. Marriage. Pennsylvania (Philadelphia).
1850-80. *659*
—. Fur Trade. Marriage. Mountain men. Rocky
Mountains. Settlement. 19c. *297*
—. Government. Morality. Religious institutions.
1960's-70's. *504*
—. Massachusetts (Holyoke). 1880. *717*
—. Pennsylvania (Philadelphia). Women. Working
Class. 1910-30. *476*
Ethnic studies. Genealogy. Schools. 1979. *118*
Ethnicity. 1970's. *141*
—. Age. Education. New York City. Puerto
Ricans. 1958-79. *248*
—. Assimilation. Connecticut. D'Antonio, William
V. (autobiography). Italian Americans. ca
1926-73. *70*
—. Birth Rate. Marriage. Massachusetts (Boston;
South, South End). Occupations. 1880. *131*
—. Canada. Jews. Schools. Youth groups. 20c. *294*
—. Country Life. Immigrants. Marriage. Minnesota
(Kandiyoki County). Swedish Americans.
1870-1905. *729*
—. Dutch Americans. Roosevelt, Franklin D.
Roosevelt, Theodore. 19c-20c. *910*
—. Economics. Immigration. Italians. Quebec
(Montreal). Social Conditions. 1900-30. *239*
—. Education. Employment. Mexican Americans.
Women. 1970's. *577*
—. Irish Americans. Marriage. Migration. South
Carolina. 1970-80. *662*
—. Jews. 20c. *84*
Ethnocentrism. Industrial Relations. Modernization.
New Hampshire (Manchester). 1912-22. *452*
Ethnography. Indians. Navajo Indians. Tradition.
Women. 1850-1980. *101*

Europe. Birth Control. Elites. Fertility.
Pennsylvania (Philadelphia). ca 1750-1869. *677*
—. Education. Letters. Yale University (Beinecke
Library). Youth. 1779-84. 1970's. *1009*
—. Income. Occupations. Women. 1968-75. *522*
—. Poor. Public housing. 1949-73. *104*
Europe, Western. Budgets. Income. Life cycles.
1889-90. *448*
Evangelicalism. New York (Utica). Revivals.
Women. 1800-40. *258*
Exogamy. Anglicization. French Canadians.
Language. 1971. *54*
—. Epidemics. Marriage. Quebec. 1700-60. *705*

F

Factories. Discipline. Massachusetts (Webster).
Rhode Island (Slatersville). 1790-1840. *562*
Fairweather, David (and descendants). Nova Scotia
(Pictou County). 19c-20c. *935*
Familism, rural. Far West. Regionalism. Southeast.
1940's. *664*
Family. Blacks. Employment. Women workers.
1969-75. *508*
Family background. Occupational aspirations.
Roles. Women. 1973. *685*
Family cycle. Household structure. Massachusetts
(Worcester). Social Change. Urbanization.
1860-80. *59*
Family, death of the. Women. 1973. *39*
Family dynasties. Business. Capital. Elites. Law.
Texas (Galveston). ca 1890-1980. *488*
—. Elites. Meritocrats. Social Classes. 1960's-70's.
147
Family heads. Labor force. Women. 1960-75. *492*
Family heads (female). Blacks. Cities. Women. 19c.
647
Family history. 1970-80. *309*
—. Archives. Genealogical Society of Utah.
Mormons. 1500-1900. *328*
—. Archives, National. Census Bureau. Libraries,
local. Research. 1960's-70's. *242*
—. Artifacts. History Teaching. Massachusetts. Old
Sturbridge Village. 1790-1840. 1980. *22*
—. Biography. Depressions. Interviews. Louisiana
State University. Students. Works Progress
Administration. 1930's. 1978. *66*
—. Buschow family. City directories. Local
History. Ohio (Cleveland). 1883-1900. 1979.
316
—. Community history. Nevins, Allan. Oral
history. 1940's-70's. *268*
—. Demographic transition. 1600-1800. *321*
—. Genealogy. National Characteristics. 18c-20c.
301
—. Haley, Alex (interview). History teaching.
Instructor(periodical). 1976. *338*
—. History teaching. Methodology. 1977. *230*
—. History Teaching. Painting. Photographs.
Teaching Aids and Devices. 1980. *185*
—. History Teaching. Questionnaires. Teaching
Aids and Devices. 1970's. *40*
—. Illinois (Chicago). Local History. Newberry
Library. 1972-77. *51*
—. Information Storage and Retrieval Systems.
Mormons (Genealogical Department). 1979. *276*
—. Lasch, Christopher (review article).
Modernization theory. Women. ca 1400-1976.
136
—. Louisville, University of. Oral history. Perry,
Barbara. 1977. *259*
—. Methodology. 1750-1979. *281*
—. Slavery. South. 1790-1872. *1093*
—. Women's history. 1960-80. *74*
Family interaction processes. Achievement
syndrome. Secondary Education. Social Status.
1962-73. *703*

—. Congregationalism. Connecticut. Ohio. Western Reserve. Wright, Elizur (and family). Yale University. 1762-1870. *911*

—. Conine family. Letters. North Central States. 1852-63. *819*

—. Diaries. Missions and Missionaries. Oregon (Forest Grove). Tshimakain Indian Mission. Walker, Mary Richardson. Washington. 1833-97. *962*

—. Felton, Jacob. Indiana. Ohio. Personal narratives. Settlement. 1820-40. *904*

—. French Americans. Merchants. Military officers. North America. Picoté de Belestre family. 1659-1820. *861*

—. Great Plains. Sod houses. Women. 1855-1910. *587*

—. Letters. Nebraska, southeastern. Sim, Francis (family). 1856-59. *1099*

—. Men. Overland Journeys to the Pacific. Wagon trains. Women. 1840's-50's. *639*

—. Mormons. Polygamy. Richards, Franklin D. (family). Utah. Women. 1852-90. *646*

—. Thorington, J. Monroe (family history). 1758-1887. *1126*

Frost, J. William (review article). Family life. Friends, Society of. 17c-18c. 1973-75. *774*

Frost, Margaret Fullerton. Country life. Oklahoma. Personal Narratives. 1901-07. *913*

Fuller, Henry Blake (pseud., Harry S. Free). *Chicago Tribune*. Letters. Marriage. 1875. *740*

Fultz County Restoration Society. Fultz, Johann Andreas (family). Houses. Museums. Nova Scotia (Halifax, Sackville, Windsor Junction). 1751-1801. *942*

Fultz, Johann Andreas (family). Fultz County Restoration Society. Houses. Museums. Nova Scotia (Halifax, Sackville, Windsor Junction). 1751-1801. *942*

—. Genealogy. Nova Scotia (Halifax County; Sackville). 1751-1881. *983*

Funeral homes. Florida. Genealogy. 1981. *164*

—. Florida. Genealogy. Methodology. ca 1880-1982. *165*

Fur trade. Drouet de Richerville family. Great Lakes. Indiana. 1720's-1841. *860*

—. Ethnic Groups. Marriage. Mountain men. Rocky Mountains. Settlement. 19c. *297*

G

Galbraith, John Kenneth. Capitalism. Housework. Oakley, Ann. Sex roles. Women. 1950-70's. *436*

Gallaway, Lowell. Great Britain. Immigrants. Ireland. Settlement. Vedder, Richard. 1897-98. *80*

Gambling. Legalization. Social problems. 1975. *417*

Games. Children. Folk Songs. Kentucky, eastern. 20c. *325*

—. Children. Plantations. Slaves. Socialization. South. 1820-60. *786*

—. Hispanic Americans. Indians. Southwest. Toys. 16c-20c. *762*

Gay family. Borden family. Connecticut. Massachusetts. 1635-91. *807*

Gay, Sydney Howard. Abolition movement. Values. 1830's-40's. *926*

Genealogical Society of Utah. Archives. Family history. Mormons. 1500-1900. *328*

Genealogies. Bond, John (descendants). Massachusetts. 17c-19c. *1086*

—. Immigration. McKay, John. McLennan, Roderick. Nova Scotia. Scottish Canadians. 1805-1927. *923*

Genealogists. Historians. Research. 1975. *175*

Genealogy. 1975-81. *10*

—. American Revolution. St. Clair, Arthur (and family). 1762-1818. *876*

—. Apple industry. Crop yields. Nova Scotia. Prescott, Charles Ramage. 1772-1970's. *944*

—. Archival Catalogs and Inventories. Baptismal certificates. Birth certificates. Pennsylvania Folklife Society (archives). 19c. *103*

—. Archival Catalogs and Inventories. Long Island Historical Society. New York City. 17c-20c. *270*

—. Archives. Mormons. Utah. 17c-20c. *267*

—. Archives, National. Cherokee Indians. Indians. North Carolina (western). 1906-10. *332*

—. Armies. Civil War. Ladd, Nathaniel Eustis. 1861-65. *917*

—. Assimilation. Delaware (Lewes). Jews. Nunez family. 18c. *241*

—. Autobiography. Civil War. Daily life. Martin, Frances Martha Atkinson. Social organization. Texas. 1857-75. 1979. *200*

—. Banks, Joshua. Banks, Moses. Nova Scotia (Granville). 1739-1843. *1014*

—. Bibliographies. Blacks. Research. 1977. *160*

—. Bibliographies. Massachusetts. Research. 17c-20c. *129*

—. Bibliographies. Methodology. 1977. *121*

—. Blacks. Howard University (Moorland-Spingarn Research Center). 1867-1981. *67*

—. Blacks. Methodology. 1981. *312*

—. Brenneman family. Coverlets. Mennonites. Pennsylvania. 1631-1971. *948*

—. Brigham Young University Library. Immigration studies. Mormons. Utah (Provo). 1830-1978. *215*

—. Bristol Public Library. Georgia. History. Information file. Tennessee. Virginia. 1970's. *20*

—. Brunk family. Immigrants. Mennonites. 1750-1850. *843*

—. Canada. Ireland (Waterford). Prime Minister. Thompson, John S. D. 1796-1903. *1013*

—. Cemeteries. 1978. *293*

—. Census. Cities. Local history. Methodology. 1980. *266*

—. Computers. 20c. *289*

—. Conte, Stephen G. (account). Italy (Andretta). Travel. 1971. *867*

—. Davis, James Dick. Harbormaster. History (societies). Old Folks of Shelby County. Tennessee (Memphis). 1810-80. *822*

—. Denlinger family. Mennonites. Pennsylvania. Switzerland. 1594-1803. *886*

—. Errington family. Great Britain (Northumberland; Denton). Massachusetts (Cambridge). 16c-17c. *824*

—. Ethnic studies. Schools. 1979. *118*

—. Family history. National Characteristics. 18c-20c. *301*

—. Fellows family. Massachusetts. Nova Scotia (Granville). 1635-1977. *869*

—. Florida. Funeral homes. 1981. *164*

—. Florida. Funeral homes. Methodology. ca 1880-1982. *165*

—. Florida Society for Genealogical Research, Inc. 1972-79. *169*

—. Fox Indians. Indians. North Central States. Potawatomi Indians. Sauk Indians. Thorpe, Jim. 1786-1868. *1127*

—. Fultz, Johann Andreas (family). Nova Scotia (Halifax County; Sackville). 1751-1881. *983*

—. Germany. Methodology. 1600's-1978. *315*

—. Gibson family. Pennsylvania (Muncy, Nisbet). 1802-1946. *1131*

—. Gloor family. Iowa (Tell City). Ohio (Cincinnati). Swiss Colonization Society. 1850's-1970's. *925*

—. Goranson, Greta K. (personal account). Immigration. Sweden. 1832-1973. *929*

—. Great Britain. Massachusetts. Morris family. Nova Scotia. 18c-19c. *874*

—. Guam. Letters. Souder, Paul. 1710-1958. *1109*
—. Harvie, John (and family). Nova Scotia. 1730-1945. *941*
—. Hawthorne, Nathaniel. Manning, Nicholas (and family). 1680-1841. *898*
—. Hershey family. Land Tenure. Pennsylvania (Lancaster County). 1730's-1870's. *973*
—. History Teaching. 1977. *327*
—. History teaching. 1978. *154*
—. History Teaching. Methodology. Research. 1976. *151*
—. Hoar family. New England. 18c-19c. *958*
—. Howe, John (and family). Nova Scotia (Halifax). 18c-19c. *1065*
—. Howells family. Wales (Hay). 18c-19c. *899*
—. Hurd family. Massachusetts (Boston). 17c-19c. *940*
—. Indians. Massasoit. Plymouth Plantation. Wampanoag Indians. 1620-1931. *1041*
—. Iowa. Mennonites. Settlement. 1839-1974. *114*
—. Land records, federal. Research. 19c-20c. *176*
—. LaVache family. Nova Scotia (Cape Breton; Arichat). 1774-20c. *1145*
—. Ledgers. Rhode Island (Glocester). Shippee, Welcome Allen. 1834-70. 1970's. *1090*
—. Levy, Asher. New Amsterdam. New Jersey. 1630-1785. *1115*
—. Lewis, Waitsill (family). Methodology. Nova Scotia (Yarmouth). 1976. *16*
—. Libraries. Massachusetts, western. Research. 1978. *64*
—. Maine. Research. 17c-19c. *102*
—. Migration, Internal. Research. 1725-1850. *36*
—. Migration, Internal. Vermont. 1760-1979. *130*
—. Mississippi Gulf Coast. 18-19c. *997*
—. New England. Shaw family. 17c-19c. *1144*
—. New Hampshire. Research. 20c. *73*
—. North Central States. Northeastern or North Atlantic States. Seymour family. 1760's-1860's. *1096*
—. Nova Scotia (Cornwallis). Walton, Jacob (identity). ca 1811-1914. *897*
—. Nova Scotia (Hants County). Weatherhead family. ca 1820-1946. *930*
—. Research. Social history. Statistics. 19c-1980. *299*
—. Social history. Social surveys. 1850-1980. *71*
Genealogy, black. Blacks. Documents. Public Records. Research. 19c-20c. *229*
Generation conflict, basis. Identity. Quebec (Quebec City). Social integration. 1968. *75*
Generations. Adams family. Attitudes. Communications Behavior. 1764-1919. *1036*
—. Assimilation, patterns of. Attitudes. Jewish families. 1925-75. *532*
—. Canada. Family unit. Immigrants. Italians. 20c. *330*
—. Communications Behavior. James, William (d. 1832; and family). Values. 1811-1910. *903*
—. Education. Fertility. Mexican Americans. Women. 1976. *23*
Genetics. Kentucky. Morgan, Thomas Hunt (and family). 1866-1945. *1069*
—. New York. Noyes, John Humphrey. Oneida Community. Stirpicultural experiment. 1848-86. *791*
Genovese, Eugene D. Family (review article). Gutman, Herbert G. Slavery. 17c-20c. *167*
Geographic mobility. Assimilation. Immigrants. Mexican Americans. Social status. 1890-1977. *303*
—. B'nai B'rith. Jews. Occupations. Oregon (Portland). Social status. 1910-30. *305*
—. Community structure. Connecticut (Windsor). 17c. *374*
—. Economic development. Family structure. Quebec (Laterrière). 1851-1935. *37*

—. Housing. Public policy. Research. 1920's-82. *251*
—. Ontario (Toronto Gore). Population. 1820-90. *203*
Geographic space. Cities. Federal Policy. Households. Labor. Women. 1977-80. *198*
Georgia. Appalachia. Cherokee Indians. Indian-White Relations. Oklahoma. Ridge family. 1785-1907. *901*
—. Black-white differentials. Family size preferences. Florida. Youth. 1969. *123*
—. Bristol Public Library. Genealogy. History. Information file. Tennessee. Virginia. 1970's. *20*
—. Catholic Church. O'Connor, Flannery (ancestry). ca 1733-1949. *908*
—. Indexes. Milledgeville *Southern Recorder*. Newspapers. 1820-1981. *15*
—. Land grants. Women. 1755-75. *556*
—. New Hampshire. Wadleigh, Joseph (and descendants). 1711-1920. *915*
—. Piedmont Plateau. Pottery. 19c-1970's. *847*
Georgia (Atlanta). Blacks. Social Mobility. 1870-80. *454*
—. Haas (family). Immigration. Jews. 1845-65. *1082*
Georgia (Dougherty County). Freedmen. Land. 1870-1900. *79*
Georgia (Savannah). American Revolution. Jews. Sheftall (family). 1730-1800. *1028*
Georgia (Swainsboro). Children. Day nurseries. Florida (Jacksonville). North Carolina (Durham). 1960-80. *490*
German Americans. Aged. Farmers. Illinois. Land tenure. 1976-77. *738*
—. Assimilation. Goettsch family. Higher education. Immigration. Iowa (Davenport). 20c. *927*
—. Atzeroth, Joseph (family). Florida (Terra Ceia Island). Homesteading and Homesteaders. Immigrants. 1840's-1910. *1105*
—. Blacks. Indiana (Vanderburgh County; Evansville). 1880. *29*
—. Country Life. Farms. Illinois. Irish Americans. Land transfers. 1975-78. *539*
German Russians. Colorado (South Platte Valley). Farmers. Frontier and Pioneer Life. Immigration. 1890-ca 1907. *88*
—. Farms. Hildebrand, Bernhard (and family). Manitoba (Rosenthal). Mennonites. 1795-1915. *1042*
Germany. Farmers. Minnesota. Standke family. 1873-1978. *1027*
—. Genealogy. Methodology. 1600's-1978. *315*
Germany, East. Birth rate. Child care. Education. Employment. Women. 1970's. *85*
Geronimo (wives). Fort Marion. 1885-1918. *1167*
Gibson family. Genealogy. Pennsylvania (Muncy, Nisbet). 1802-1946. *1131*
Gibson family records. Births. Marriage. South Carolina. 1750-1800. *1132*
Gifford, William (and descendants). Massachusetts (Dartmouth area). New York. 18c-19c. *881*
—. New England. 1640's-1840. *882*
—. New England. 18c-19c. *883*
—. New England. 18c-19c. *884*
—. New England. 18c-19c. *885*
Gillespie, Emily Hawley. Country Life. Diaries. Farmers. Iowa. Women. 1858-88. *1006*
Gloor family. Genealogy. Iowa (Tell City). Ohio (Cincinnati). Swiss Colonization Society. 1850's-1970's. *925*
Godchaux family. California (San Francisco). French language. Music. Teachers. 1880's-1920's. *811*
Goettsch family. Assimilation. German Americans. Higher education. Immigration. Iowa (Davenport). 20c. *927*

H

—. Dominis, John Owen (and ancestors). Liliuokalani. 1437-1891. *988*

Hawaii (Niihau). British Columbia. New Zealand. Sinclair, Eliza. 1840-1980. *1018*

Hawthorne, Elizabeth. Hawthorne, Nathaniel *(Scarlet Letter)*. 1800-50. *825*

Hawthorne, Nathaniel. Genealogy. Manning, Nicholas (and family). 1680-1841. *898*

Hawthorne, Nathaniel *(Scarlet Letter)*. Hawthorne, Elizabeth. 1800-50. *825*

Hawthorne, Sophia Peabody. Cuba. Letters. 1833-35. *815*

Hayden, Dolores. Family (review article). Feminism. Housing. 19c-20c. *115*

Hayes, Rutherford B. Social Conditions. 19c-20c. *920*

Health. Birth rate. Minorities. Social Conditions. 1867-1935. *404*

—. Children. Women. Working hours. 1972. *541*

Health professionals. Appalachia. Social integration. 1950-77. *484*

Hecker, Friedrich Karl. Country Life. Illinois (St. Clair County). Köhler, Carl. Letters. 1851. *1129*

Hellman, Lillian. Boothe, Clare. Crothers, Rachel. Drama. Women. 1920-69. *30*

Hemings family. Jefferson, Thomas. Monticello. Virginia. 1730's-1830's. *826*

Hemings, Sally. Jefferson, Thomas (and descendants). Miscegenation. Virginia. ca 1780-1976. *839*

Hemingway, Ernest. Faulkner, William. Middle Classes. World views. 1900-50. *1083*

Henderson, Lucy Ann. Oregon Trail (Applegate Cutoff). Overland Journeys to the Pacific. 1846. *1122*

Heron family. Hill family. Ontario. Theater. Touring companies. 1840-60. *1100*

Hershberg, Theodore. City Life (review article). Pennsylvania (Philadelphia). 19c. *62*

Hershey family. Genealogy. Land Tenure. Pennsylvania (Lancaster County). 1730's-1870's. *973*

Heterogeneity. Intermarriage. Metropolitan areas. Social Organization. 1970. *598*

Higgins, Anthony (reminiscences). Delaware. Memoirs. Thompson, Mary Wilson. 1770-1947. *953*

High Schools. Attitudes. Blacks. Social Organization. Students. Tennessee (Rutherford County). 1970. *586*

—. Indiana (Muncie). Lynd, Helen Merrell. Lynd, Robert S. Students. 1924-77. *589*

Higher education. Assimilation. German Americans. Goettsch family. Immigration. Iowa (Davenport). 20c. *927*

—. Divorce. Economic Conditions. Identity. Occupations. Social Status. Women. 1971-77. *461*

—. Socialization. Youth. 18c. *565*

Hildebrand, Bernhard (and family). Farms. German Russians. Manitoba (Rosenthal). Mennonites. 1795-1915. *1042*

Hill family. Heron family. Ontario. Theater. Touring companies. 1840-60. *1100*

Hispanic Americans. Blacks. Households. Income. Social Organization. Whites. 1976. *11*

—. Games. Indians. Southwest. Toys. 16c-20c. *762*

Historians. Genealogists. Research. 1975. *175*

Historical Sites and Parks. Indiana. Wolcott, Anson (family; home). 1628-1975. *907*

Historical sources. Blacks. Family records. New England. 1973. *235*

Historiography. 1620-1800. *279*

—. Adams, Brooks. Adams, Henry. Adams, John Quincy. 1767-1848. 1880-1920. *1030*

—. Americas (North and South). Blacks. Slavery. ca 1550-1850. *256*

—. Bailyn, Bernard (review article). Education. 1915-74. *65*

—. Blacks. Census. City Life. Indiana (Vanderburgh County; Evansville). 1865-80. *27*

—. Childhood (review article). Erikson, Erik. Hunt, David. Psychology. 1960-71. *166*

—. Documents. Lincoln, Abraham. Lincoln, Mary Todd. Marriage. 1842-65. 1885. 1947-82. *916*

—. Family structure. Massachusetts (Boston). 19c. *132*

—. Fertility. Marriage. Methodology. Occupations. Pennsylvania. 1850-80. *125*

—. Lasch, Christopher. Middle Classes. Stone, Lawrence. 1500-1980. *304*

—. Leftism. *Radical History Review* (periodical). Slavery. 17c-20c. 1970's. *106*

—. Modernization. Social change. ca 19c-20c. *134*

—. Oral history. 1980. *274*

—. Slavery. 18c-20c. *344*

History. Bristol Public Library. Genealogy. Georgia. Information file. Tennessee. Virginia. 1970's. *20*

—. Households. Kinship. Methodology. 1970's. *210*

—. Life cycles. Methodology. Research. Sociology. 1950's-70's. *34*

—. Research. Social Sciences. 20c. *340*

History (societies). Davis, James Dick. Genealogy. Harbormaster. Old Folks of Shelby County. Tennessee (Memphis). 1810-80. *822*

History Teaching. Adelphi University. Social History. 1976. *97*

—. Artifacts. Family history. Massachusetts. Old Sturbridge Village. 1790-1840. 1980. *22*

—. Family history. Haley, Alex (interview). *Instructor*(periodical). 1976. *338*

—. Family history. Methodology. 1977. *230*

—. Family history. Painting. Photographs. Teaching Aids and Devices. 1980. *185*

—. Family history. Questionnaires. Teaching Aids and Devices. 1970's. *40*

—. Genealogy. 1977. *327*

—. Genealogy. 1978. *154*

—. Genealogy. Methodology. Research. 1976. *151*

—. Methodology. Oral history. 1977. *204*

—. New Mexico State University. Oral history. Women. 1976. *152*

Hoar family. Genealogy. New England. 18c-19c. *958*

Hoblit family. Illinois (Logan County). Lincoln, Abraham. ca 1840-66. *1043*

Hodgdon, Elizabeth. Hodgdon, Sarah. Labor. Letters. Massachusetts (Lowell). New Hampshire (Rochester). Textile Industry. 1830-40. *889*

Hodgdon, Sarah. Hodgdon, Elizabeth. Labor. Letters. Massachusetts (Lowell). New Hampshire (Rochester). Textile Industry. 1830-40. *889*

Hoff, John George (and sons). Clockmaking. Pennsylvania (Lancaster County). 1769-1822. *1153*

Holsman, Virginia (reminiscences). Child-rearing. Children. Oregon (Hillsboro). Recreation. 19c-1920's. *961*

Home (concept). Metaphor. Popular Culture. Women. 1980. *711*

Home Economics. Child-rearing. Colorado. Frontier and Pioneer Life. Oral history. Women. 1895-1920. *585*

—. Curricula. Domesticity. Progressivism. Sex roles. 1900-20. *673*

Home Missionary Society. Children's Aid Society. Foster care. Pennsylvania (Philadelphia). 1880-1905. *398*

Home ownership. 1750-1850. *390*

I

Illinois (Polo). Letters. Thomas, Lewis (family). 1878-79. *863*
Illinois (St. Clair County). Country Life. Hecker, Friedrich Karl. Köhler, Carl. Letters. 1851. *1129*
Illinois (southern). Country Life. Farms. Lentz, Lula Gillespie (reminiscences). 1883-1929. *996*
Illinois (Springfield). Dresser, Nathan (family). Dresser, Rebecca. 1800-1982. *950*
Immaculate Conception Primary School. Educational attainment. Lithuanian Americans. Missouri (St. Louis). Occupations. 1948-68. *109*
Immigrants. Assimilation. Geographic mobility. Mexican Americans. Social status. 1890-1977. *303*
—. Assimilation. Jews. Literature. ca 1900-20. *792*
—. Atzeroth, Joseph (family). Florida (Terra Ceia Island). German Americans. Homesteading and Homesteaders. 1840's-1910. *1105*
—. Brunk family. Genealogy. Mennonites. 1750-1850. *843*
—. Canada. Family unit. Generations. Italians. 20c. *330*
—. Country Life. Ethnicity. Marriage. Minnesota (Kandiyoki County). Swedish Americans. 1870-1905. *729*
—. Family structure. Polish Americans. Social control. Values. 20c. *724*
—. Gallaway, Lowell. Great Britain. Ireland. Settlement. Vedder, Richard. 1897-98. *80*
—. Irish Americans. Pennsylvania (Scranton). Social mobility. Welsh Americans. 1880-90. *376*
—. Japanese Americans. Marriage. Picture brides. Women. 1900-24. *467*
—. Labor. Stereotypes. Women (review article). 1850-1950. *307*
—. Maryland. Plantations. Social Conditions. Women. 1632-1700. *611*
Immigration. Alberta (Calgary). Jews. USSR. 1974. *998*
—. Aquino, Salvatore A. (reminiscences). City Life. Italian Americans. New York City. 1914. *13*
—. Assimilation. German Americans. Goettsch family. Higher education. Iowa (Davenport). 20c. *927*
—. Bavaria. Daily Life. Hartlieb, Louise Marie Katherina Boehner. New York (Buffalo). Reminiscences. 1825-1918. *1114*
—. British Columbia (Oliver, Osoyoos). Portuguese Canadians. 1952-78. *216*
—. Burns family. Ireland. Nova Scotia (Annapolis County; Wilmot Township). 1764-20c. *1012*
—. Canada. Chinese Canadians. Federal Policy. Legislation. 1885-1971. *187*
—. Canada. Chinese Canadians. Social change. 1850's-1970's. *153*
—. Carnevale, Achille. Italian Americans. 1884-1978. *1026*
—. Cities. Italian Americans. Jews. Rhode Island. 1880-1940. *548*
—. Colorado (Denver). Jews. Shwayder family. 1865-1916. *833*
—. Colorado (South Platte Valley). Farmers. Frontier and Pioneer Life. German Russians. 1890-ca 1907. *88*
—. Dominican Americans. 1962-76. *108*
—. Economics. Ethnicity. Italians. Quebec (Montreal). Social Conditions. 1900-30. *239*
—. Genealogies. McKay, John. McLennan, Roderick. Nova Scotia. Scottish Canadians. 1805-1927. *923*
—. Genealogy. Goranson, Greta K. (personal account). Sweden. 1832-1973. *929*
—. Georgia (Atlanta). Haas (family). Jews. 1845-65. *1082*
—. Great Britain (Hertfordshire). New England. 1630-40. *1140*

—. Irish Canadians. Ontario (Upper Canada). Settlement. 1825. *50*
—. Mennonites. North America. Surnames. Swiss Brethren. 1680-1880. *263*
—. Minnesota. Persson, Johan. Settlement. Sweden. 1874-75. *976*
—. New Netherland. 1630-64. *244*
—. Poland. 1945-74. *213*
—. Working class. 1890-1940. *375*
Immigration studies. Brigham Young University Library. Genealogy. Mormons. Utah (Provo). 1830-1978. *215*
Income. 1951-76. *357*
—. Amish. Fertility. Indiana. Women. 20c. *197*
—. Blacks. Hispanic Americans. Households. Social Organization. Whites. 1976. *11*
—. Blacks. Moynihan, Daniel P. ("The Negro Family"). Whites. Women. 1965-77. *380*
—. Budgets. Europe, Western. Life cycles. 1889-90. *448*
—. Canada. Fertility. Labor. 1951-76. *246*
—. Children. Cities. Pennsylvania (Philadelphia). 1880. *438*
—. Children. Employment. Literacy. Men. Wives. 1901. *428*
—. Europe. Occupations. Women. 1968-75. *522*
—. Family size, expected. Mexican Americans. -1973. *359*
—. Family (two-earner). Housing. Labor. Land use. Suburbs. Women. 1976. *487*
—. Family (two-earner). Housing. Prices. Women. 1970's. *529*
—. Industrial structure. Metropolitan areas. 1969. *408*
—. Inflation. Social classes. 1971-75. *345*
—. Methodology. Poverty line. 1860-1909. *422*
—. Nurses and Nursing. Women. 1953-70. *602*
Income, family. Ozark Mountains. Social status orientation. Youth. 1962-73. *514*
Income inequality. Educational opportunity. Jencks, Christopher. Minorities. -1973. *579*
—. Labor Unions and Organizations. Race Relations. 1947-74. *360*
Indentured servants. Pennsylvania. Religion. Women. 18c. *171*
Indexes. Georgia. Milledgeville *Southern Recorder.* Newspapers. 1820-1981. *15*
India. International Trade. Lee family. Maryland. Russell family. Scotland. 1707-1857. *1063*
Indian culture (hostility to). McBeth, Sue L. Missions and Missionaries. Nez Percé Indians. Presbyterian Church. 1873-93. *61*
Indian Territory. Beams family. Freedmen (status). Law. 1823-58. *1008*
Indiana. Amish. Fertility. Income. Women. 20c. *197*
—. Conine family (letters). Pioneers. 1849-51. *817*
—. Conine family (letters). Pioneers. 1852-63. *818*
—. Courtship. Diaries. Mennonites. Sprunger, David. 1893-95. *1111*
—. Drouet de Richerville family. Fur trade. Great Lakes. 1720's-1841. *860*
—. Felton, Jacob. Frontier and Pioneer Life. Ohio. Personal narratives. Settlement. 1820-40. *904*
—. Great Britain. Ireland. Surnames. 18c-1981. *245*
—. Historical Sites and Parks. Wolcott, Anson (family; home). 1628-1975. *907*
—. Marriage, interfaith. 1962-67. *714*
Indiana (Indianapolis). Poverty, types of. Residence, spatial distribution of. 1959-73. *388*
Indiana (Jasper). Durlauf, Michael (and family). Tombstones. 1858-1962. *840*
Indiana (Muncie). High Schools. Lynd, Helen Merrell. Lynd, Robert S. Students. 1924-77. *589*

—. Inequality. Lifestyles. Lynd, Helen Merrell. Lynd, Robert S. Occupations. Social Classes. 1920-78. *392*

—. Small business. 1865-1980. *919*

Indiana (Richmond). Corbit, William (family). Delaware (Odessa). Economic Conditions. Wilson, David (family). 1768-1925. *848*

Indiana (Vanderburgh County; Evansville). Blacks. Census. City Life. Historiography. 1865-80. *27*

—. Blacks. Census. Migration, Internal. 1880-1900. *28*

—. Blacks. German Americans. 1880. *29*

Indians. Acculturation. Bureau of Indian Affairs. California (San Francisco Bay area). Navajo Indians. Relocation. Women. 1950-80. *207*

—. Acculturation. Canada. Sex roles. Wisconsin. Women. 1901-70. *168*

—. Archives, National. Cherokee Indians. Genealogy. North Carolina (western). 1906-10. *332*

—. Arizona. Assimilation. Education. Industrial Arts Education. Phoenix Indian School. 1890-1901. *561*

—. Blacks. Child-rearing. Mexican-Americans. Values. 1979. *573*

—. British Columbia. Households. Industrialization. Kinship. 1971. *715*

—. California. Chumash Indians. Marriage. Mission Santa Barbara. Social Organization. Yanunali, Pedro. 1787-1806. *1141*

—. Cherokee Indians. Daily Life. Tennessee. Wolf, Lucyann Davis (family). 1900-35. *1108*

—. Cherokee Indians. Leadership. McIntosh family. 1765-1897. *850*

—. Cheyenne Indians. Comenha (woman). Daily Life. Women. 1860-1900. *832*

—. Childhood. Folklore. Oral tradition. Prehistory-1970's. *595*

—. Child-rearing. Minipoka (concept). Social status. 19c-1979. *727*

—. Chippewa Indians. Cree Indians. Rego, Mary. Women. 20c. *828*

—. Clans. Sioux Indians. Social Organization. Villages. 19c-20c. *145*

—. Daily life. Fort Washakie. Letters. Winne, Caroline. Wives. Wyoming. 1879-80. *845*

—. Daily Life. Personal Narratives. Sioux Indians. Swan, Lucy. Women. 1900-71. *1059*

—. Ethnography. Navajo Indians. Tradition. Women. 1850-1980. *101*

—. Fox Indians. Genealogy. North Central States. Potawatomi Indians. Sauk Indians. Thorpe, Jim. 1786-1868. *1127*

—. Games. Hispanic Americans. Southwest. Toys. 16c-20c. *762*

—. Genealogy. Massasoit. Plymouth Plantation. Wampanoag Indians. 1620-1931. *1041*

—. Indian-White Relations. Social Change. 1937-78. *712*

—. Lévi-Strauss, Claude. Social Customs. 17c-19c. *184*

Indians (captivities). Arizona, southwestern. Oatman, Roys (and family). Westward Movement. Yavapai Indians. 1851-1903. *630*

Indian-White Relations. Alabama. Creek Indian War (1813-14). Lott, Arthur. Louisiana. Meredith, Thomas. Murders. 1812-14. *1156*

—. Appalachia. Cherokee Indians. Georgia. Oklahoma. Ridge family. 1785-1907. *901*

—. Cherokee Indians. Christianity. Missions and Missionaries. Property. Social Change. Women. 19c. *329*

—. Indians. Social Change. 1937-78. *712*

Individualism. Autobiography. Emerson, Ralph Waldo. Franklin, Benjamin. Interpersonal Relations. Malcolm X. 18c-1980. *669*

—. Collectivism. Family (review article). Zimmerman, Carle C. 1945-70's. *324*

—. Government. Lasch, Christopher. Narcissism. 1889-1979. *273*

Industrial Arts Education. Arizona. Assimilation. Education. Indians. Phoenix Indian School. 1890-1901. *561*

Industrial Relations. Ethnocentrism. Modernization. New Hampshire (Manchester). 1912-22. *452*

Industrial Revolution. Davis, Rebecca Harding. Fiction. Realism. Social Organization. Women. Working Class. 1861. *234*

Industrial structure. Income. Metropolitan areas. 1969. *408*

Industrialization. British Columbia. Households. Indians. Kinship. 1971. *715*

—. Domestic education. Protestantism. Womanhood, sentimental. 1830-70. *389*

—. Economic Conditions. Research. Social History. 1950's-70's. *475*

—. Education. Social change. 1920's-70's. *278*

—. Labor, unskilled. Quebec (Montreal). 1860-99. *381*

—. New York (Oneida County). Ryan, Mary P. (review article). Urbanization. 1790-1865. *518*

—. Periodicals. Urbanization. 1741-1865. *178*

—. Urbanization. 1800-1977. *661*

Industrialization (impact). Railroad expansion. Women, role of. 1890's. *608*

Industry. Business. Women. 19c. *567*

Inequality. Indiana (Muncie). Lifestyles. Lynd, Helen Merrell. Lynd, Robert S. Occupations. Social Classes. 1920-78. *392*

Infants. Canada. Childbirth. MacMurchy, Helen. Mortality. Whitton, Charlotte. 1919-39. *386*

—. Death and Dying. New England. Parents. Theology. 1620-1720. *277*

—. Mortality. Slaves. 1850-60. *676*

Inflation. Income. Social classes. 1971-75. *345*

—. Social Surveys. 1976. *391*

Information diffusion. Birth control information. Direct mail. 1972. *723*

Information file. Bristol Public Library. Genealogy. Georgia. History. Tennessee. Virginia. 1970's. *20*

Information Storage and Retrieval Systems. Family history. Mormons (Genealogical Department). 1979. *276*

Inglis, Charles. Apple industry. Calkin(s) family. Halliburton, Robert Grant. Nova Scotia. Starr family. 19c. *943*

Inheritance. 1964-65. *560*

—. Children. Connecticut. Probate. Wealth. 1930-46. *494*

—. Connecticut (Guilford). Migration. 1650-1775. *779*

—. Connecticut (Hartford County). Massachusetts (Essex County). Property rights. Widows. 1638-81. *732*

—. Farms. Illinois. Iowa. 1870-1950. *431*

—. Patriarchy. Plantations. South Carolina (Charleston). 1800-60. *675*

Institutionalization. Handicapped children. 1900. *430*

Institutions. Public Welfare. Social Organization. Western Nations. 1c BC-19c. *477*

Instructor(periodical). Family history. Haley, Alex (interview). History teaching. 1976. *338*

Insurance. Architecture. California (Los Angeles). Marks, David X. Marks, Joshua H. Philanthropy. 1902-77. *1163*

Intellectuals. Jews. Youth. 1940-78. *744*

Interest groups. Education. Parents. Political Participation. 1977-81. *410*

Intermarriage *See also* Marriage, interfaith; Marriage, interreligious; Miscegnation.

—. Christians. Converts. Jews. 1971. *183*

—. Great Britain. 1960-70. *262*
—. Heterogeneity. Metropolitan areas. Social Organization. 1970. *598*
—. Language. Quebec (Montreal). 1971. *56*
International Company of Mexico. Bernstein, Max. California. Gold Rushes. Jews. Mexico (Baja California). 1854-1971. *1116*
International Trade. India. Lee family. Maryland. Russell family. Scotland. 1707-1857. *1063*
Interpersonal contact. Race Relations. Students. Taiwan. 1933-73. *188*
Interpersonal Relations. Autobiography. Emerson, Ralph Waldo. Franklin, Benjamin. Individualism. Malcolm X. 18c-1980. *669*
—. Behavior. James, Mary. James, William. ca 1842-1914. *805*
—. Canada. Kinship. Marriage. Suicide. 1951-71. *625*
—. Jews. Marriage. 1975-78. *708*
—. Location. 20c. *641*
Interstate commerce. Children. Franklin & Armfield (firm). Manifests. Slave Trade. Virginia (Alexandria). 1828-36. *557*
Interviews. Biography. Depressions. Family history. Louisiana State University. Students. Works Progress Administration. 1930's. 1978. *66*
—. Slavery. South. Works Progress Administration. 1850's-60's. 1930's. *179*
Invalidism. James, Henry (1811-82; and family). Neurasthenia. New England. Social Conditions. 1811-1916. *902*
Investment. Wages. Women. 1967. *339*
Iowa. Belknap, Kitturah Penton. Diaries. Family life. Frontier and Pioneer Life. 1839-48. *1075*
—. Country Life. Diaries. Farmers. Gillespie, Emily Hawley. Women. 1858-88. *1006*
—. Domesticity. Photographs. Women. ca 1890-1910. *592*
—. Farms. Illinois. Inheritance. 1870-1950. *431*
—. Genealogy. Mennonites. Settlement. 1839-1974. *114*
—. Irish family. State Historical Society of Iowa, Irish-Preston Papers. 1832-1972. *922*
—. Minnesota. VanDuzee family (papers). Westward Movement. Wyoming, University of. 1808-1932. *877*
Iowa (Davenport). Assimilation. German Americans. Goettsch family. Higher education. Immigration. 20c. *927*
Iowa (Marshall County). Blacks. Warren, Edward (family). 1864-91. *972*
Iowa (Pocahontas). Czech Americans. Family life. Johnson, Anna Dockal (memoir). 1900-20. *674*
Iowa (Tell City). Genealogy. Gloor family. Ohio (Cincinnati). Swiss Colonization Society. 1850's-1970's. *925*
IQ. Academic achievement. Fathers. Linkage hypothesis. Occupations. Personality. Sons. 1964. *485*
Ireland. Burns family. Immigration. Nova Scotia (Annapolis County; Wilmot Township). 1764-20c. *1012*
—. Gallaway, Lowell. Great Britain. Immigrants. Settlement. Vedder, Richard. 1897-98. *80*
—. Great Britain. Indiana. Surnames. 18c-1981. *245*
Ireland (County Cork; Old Parish, Ring). Daley, Richard (and family). Democratic Party. Illinois. Irish Americans. State Politics. 19c-1976. *1061*
Ireland (Waterford). Canada. Genealogy. Prime Minister. Thompson, John S. D. 1796-1903. *1013*
Irish Americans. Architects. Kansas. Martin, Joseph. 19c. *1015*
—. Country Life. Farms. German Americans. Illinois. Land transfers. 1975-78. *539*

—. Daley, Richard (and family). Democratic Party. Illinois. Ireland (County Cork; Old Parish, Ring). State Politics. 19c-1976. *1061*
—. Ethnicity. Marriage. Migration. South Carolina. 1970-80. *662*
—. Family life. Massachusetts (Holyoke). Tenement housing. 1860-1910. *423*
—. Farmers. Illinois (Finnegan area). Kinship. 1860's-1980. *739*
—. Immigrants. Pennsylvania (Scranton). Social mobility. Welsh Americans. 1880-90. *376*
Irish Canadians. Burns, Francis (and family). Farms. Nova Scotia (Wilmot Township). 18c. *1011*
—. Immigration. Ontario (Upper Canada). Settlement. 1825. *50*
—. Nova Scotia (Halifax). Tobin, Thomas (and descendants). ca 1759-1936. *1066*
Irish family. Iowa. State Historical Society of Iowa, Irish-Preston Papers. 1832-1972. *922*
Ironmonger, Elizabeth Hogg (reminiscences). Kitchens. Virginia (York County). 1890's. *672*
Ironworks. Chesapeake Bay area. Slavery. 1730's-1862. *481*
Irving, John. Cheever, John. Didion, Joan. Fiction. Isolation. Stegner, Wallace. 1970's. *651*
Isolation. Cheever, John. Didion, Joan. Fiction. Irving, John. Stegner, Wallace. 1970's. *651*
Israel. Agricultural Technology and Research. Fiji. Japan. Social Change. 1689-1975. *618*
Italian Americans. Aquino, Salvatore A. (reminiscences). City Life. Immigration. New York City. 1914. *13*
—. Assimilation. Connecticut. D'Antonio, William V. (autobiography). Ethnicity. ca 1926-73. *70*
—. Assimilation. Derrico family. 1904-1970's. *853*
—. Carnevale, Achille. Immigration. 1884-1978. *1026*
—. Cigar industry. Florida (Tampa). Women. 1890-1930. *212*
—. Cities. Immigration. Jews. Rhode Island. 1880-1940. *548*
Italian Americans (review article). Acculturation. Social Organization. 20c. *227*
Italian Canadians. Ontario (Toronto). Social Mobility. 1935-60. *295*
Italians. Canada. Family unit. Generations. Immigrants. 20c. *330*
—. Economics. Ethnicity. Immigration. Quebec (Montreal). Social Conditions. 1900-30. *239*
Italy (Andretta). Conte, Stephen G. (account). Genealogy. Travel. 1971. *867*

J

Jackson, John Jay, Jr. (and family). Law. Political Leadership. West Virginia (Parkersburg). 1715-1847. *814*
Jackson, Millie. Blacks. Husband sharing. Music, soul. Women. 1973-80. *756*
Jacobs, Mark Israel (and family). Arizona. Business. California, southern. Jews. 1851-94. *928*
James, Alice. Diseases. James, William. Letters. 1886. *1157*
James, Henry (1811-82; and family). Biography. Diseases. Edel, Leon (interview). Literature. Psychology. 1811-1916. 1979. *806*
—. Invalidism. Neurasthenia. New England. Social Conditions. 1811-1916. *902*
James, Mary. Behavior. Interpersonal Relations. James, William. ca 1842-1914. *805*
James, William. Behavior. Interpersonal Relations. James, Mary. ca 1842-1914. *805*
—. Diseases. James, Alice. Letters. 1886. *1157*

James, William (d. 1832; and family). Communications Behavior. Generations. Values. 1811-1910. *903*
Japan. Agricultural Technology and Research. Fiji. Israel. Social Change. 1689-1975. *618*
Japanese Americans. Acculturation. California (San Francisco Bay area). 1905-76. *1124*
—. Immigrants. Marriage. Picture brides. Women. 1900-24. *467*
—. Marriage, interracial. 1960-73. *683*
Japanese Americans (Issei). Economic Conditions. 1924-79. *574*
Japanese Americans (Issei, Sansei). Assimilation. Social Mobility. ca 1900-. *186*
Javits, Jacob. Javits, Marian. Marriage. Personal narratives. Politics. 1947-80. *469*
Javits, Marian. Javits, Jacob. Marriage. Personal narratives. Politics. 1947-80. *469*
Jefferson, Thomas. Blair, James. Divorce. Documents. Legislation. Virginia. 1770-73. *416*
—. *Blair* v. *Blair* (Virginia, 1773). Courts. Virginia (Williamsburg). 1771-73. *415*
—. Farms. Great Britain. 1776-1808. *12*
—. Hemings family. Monticello. Virginia. 1730's-1830's. *826*
Jefferson, Thomas (and descendants). Hemings, Sally. Miscegenation. Virginia. ca 1780-1976. *839*
Jencks, Christopher. Educational opportunity. Income inequality. Minorities. -1973. *579*
Jenkins, Thomas (family). Economic growth. Illinois (Jackson County; Grand Tower). Merchants. 1818-90's. *1005*
Jewish families. Assimilation, patterns of. Attitudes. Generations. 1925-75. *532*
Jewish Family and Children's Service. Americanization. Community organization. Education. Michigan (Detroit). 1876-1976. *479*
Jews. Alberta (Calgary). Immigration. USSR. 1974. *998*
—. American Revolution. Georgia (Savannah). Sheftall (family). 1730-1800. *1028*
—. Arizona. Business. California, southern. Jacobs, Mark Israel (and family). 1851-94. *928*
—. Arizona. Entrepreneurs. Zeckendorf, Aaron. Zeckendorf, Louis. Zeckendorf, William. 1853-1906. *906*
—. Assimilation. California (Los Angeles). Sichel, Carolyn Meyberg (reminiscence). 1902-31. *1102*
—. Assimilation. Delaware (Lewes). Genealogy. Nunez family. 18c. *241*
—. Assimilation. Immigrants. Literature. ca 1900-20. *792*
—. Assimilation. Mental Illness. Novels. Race. Singer, Israel Joshua *(Family Carnovsky)*. 1943. *113*
—. Bakeries. Broder family. Cadish family. California (Los Angeles). Delicatessens. Settlement. 1922-70. *1162*
—. Bernstein, Max. California. Gold Rushes. International Company of Mexico. Mexico (Baja California). 1854-1971. *1116*
—. B'nai B'rith. Geographic Mobility. Occupations. Oregon (Portland). Social status. 1910-30. *305*
—. Bransten, Florine Haas. Business. California (San Francisco). Culture. Lilienthal, Alice Haas. ca 1900-81. *880*
—. Buildings (iron front). California (San Luis Obispo). Sinsheimer, Aaron Zachary (2d family). 1878-1956. *1118*
—. Business. California (Fort Bragg). Russia. Shafsky family. 1889-1976. *1166*
—. California. Census. Fertility. 1970. *568*
—. California (Santa Ana). Nasatir, Morris (family). Retail Trade. 1888-1915. *1038*
—. Canada. Ethnicity. Schools. Youth groups. 20c. *294*

—. Christians. Converts. Intermarriage. 1971. *183*
—. Christians. Marriage. 1962-79. *746*
—. Cities. Immigration. Italian Americans. Rhode Island. 1880-1940. *548*
—. Colman, Blanche. Colman, Nathan. Frontier and Pioneer Life. South Dakota (Deadwood). 1877-1977. *799*
—. Colorado (Denver). Immigration. Shwayder family. 1865-1916. *833*
—. Corporation, family. Lilienthal family pact. New York. 1814-1904. *1117*
—. Creativity. Food Industry. Knishes. Social Customs. 1980. *652*
—. Desertion. Social Problems. 1900-26. *100*
—. Durkheimer family. Olympia beer. Oregon. Retail Trade. 1862-1978. *924*
—. Entrepreneurs. 1750-1949. *261*
—. Ethnicity. 20c. *84*
—. Georgia (Atlanta). Haas (family). Immigration. 1845-65. *1082*
—. Intellectuals. Youth. 1940-78. *744*
—. Interpersonal relations. Marriage. 1975-78. *708*
—. Lipsitz family. Michigan (Detroit). 1868-1982. *1120*
—. Maryland (Baltimore). 1770-1810. *249*
—. Socialization. 1970's. *781*
Jews, Sephardic. American Revolution. Massachusetts (Leicester). Rhode Island (Newport). 1777-83. *1142*
Johnson, Anna Dockal (memoir). Czech Americans. Family life. Iowa (Pocahontas). 1900-20. *674*
Johnston, John D. Lincoln, Abraham. 1819-59. *801*
Journalism. Alabama. Hall family. 1908-79. *960*
Juvenile Delinquency. Mormons. Utah (Salt Lake City). 1850-81. *31*
—. Youth. 19c-1974. *112*

K

Kansas. Architects. Irish Americans. Martin, Joseph. 19c. *1015*
Kansas (Decatur County). Country Life. Webb, Bernice Larson (reminiscences). 1930's. *319*
Katz, Michael. Boarders. Households. New Brunswick (Moncton). Ontario (Hamilton). 1851-61. 1975. *493*
Katz, Michael B. (review article). Ontario (Hamilton). Social Classes. 1850-80. *7*
Kealey, James (and family). Folklore. Oral history. Quebec (Hull). 1974-75. *77*
Kennedy family. Behavior. Fantasy. Risk-taking. Violence. ca 1940-79. *1152*
—. Canada. 18c-1973. *1098*
Kennedy, Susan. Berkin, Carol R. Degler, Carl N. Dublin, Thomas. Lovett, Clara M. Women (review article). 1770's-1980. *243*
Kent, Duke of (Edward). Armies. Great Britain. Lyons, Charles (family). Nova Scotia (Halifax). 1812-63. *938*
Kentucky. Attitudes. Blacks. Breckenridge family. Elites. Race. 1760-1935. *987*
—. DeWitt, Zachariah Price (family). Migration. New Jersey. New Netherland. Ohio. 1650-1820's. *981*
—. Feuds. Law. Violence. West Virginia. 1820-1903. *170*
—. Genetics. Morgan, Thomas Hunt (and family). 1866-1945. *1069*
Kentucky (Butler, Warren Counties). Farms. Folklore. Language. Stewart family. Toponymy. 1850-1978. *1037*
Kentucky, eastern. Children. Folk Songs. Games. 20c. *325*
Kentucky (Gallatin County). Blacks. Public Records. 1866-1913. *33*

—. Historiography. Middle Classes. Stone, Lawrence. 1500-1980. *304*

—. Sexuality. 1982. *591*

Lasch, Christopher (review article). Capitalism. Women. 1900-75. *642*

—. Family history. Modernization theory. Women. ca 1400-1976. *136*

Latin America. Blacks. 16c-1976. *257*

Latta, Eli Chambers (and family). Letters. 1855-72. *1081*

LaVache family. Genealogy. Nova Scotia (Cape Breton; Arichat). 1774-20c. *1145*

Law. Beams family. Freedmen (status). Indian Territory. 1823-58. *1008*

—. Birth control. Medicine and State. Public Policy. 19c. *453*

—. Business. Capital. Elites. Family dynasties. Texas (Galveston). ca 1890-1980. *488*

—. California. Divorce. Family Law Act (1970). ca 1970-80. *578*

—. Child abuse. 1970's. *660*

—. Child custody. Divorce. Mental health. Social workers. 1970's. *463*

—. Divorce (grounds). Massachusetts. Women, status of. 1692-1786. *622*

—. Feuds. Kentucky. Violence. West Virginia. 1820-1903. *170*

—. Jackson, John Jay, Jr. (and family). Political Leadership. West Virginia (Parkersburg). 1715-1847. *814*

—. Liberty. North Carolina. Whites. Women. 1700-76. *780*

Law and Society. Canada. Divorce rates. Legal access. 1867-1973. *519*

Law reform. Battered women's shelter movement. Organizations. Wife beating. 1850-1981. *472*

Lawsuits. Fraud. Land (claims). Local Government. Nurnberger, Frederick (and family). 1854-1923. *1062*

Leadership. Cherokee Indians. Indians. McIntosh family. 1765-1897. *850*

Learning disabilities. Bureaucracy. Children. Mental Illness. 1975. *370*

Ledgers. Genealogy. Rhode Island (Glocester). Shippee, Welcome Allen. 1834-70. 1970's. *1090*

Lee family. India. International Trade. Maryland. Russell family. Scotland. 1707-1857. *1063*

Lee, Mary Edmunds Tabor. Louisiana (Shiloh). 1840's-1926. *1004*

Leftism. Historiography. *Radical History Review*(periodical). Slavery. 17c-20c. 1970's. *106*

Legal access. Canada. Divorce rates. Law and Society. 1867-1973. *519*

Legal devices. Adoption. Massachusetts. 1650-1850's. *368*

Legal status. New York. Virginia. Women. 18c. *446*

Legalization. Gambling. Social problems. 1975. *417*

Legislation. Blair, James. Divorce. Documents. Jefferson, Thomas. Virginia. 1770-73. *416*

—. Canada. Child welfare. Mothers' allowances. 1916-70's. *554*

—. Canada. Chinese Canadians. Federal Policy. Immigration. 1885-1971. *187*

—. Canada. Mothers. Public Welfare. ca 1900-39. *555*

Lehman, Hans (and family). Clergy. Mennonites. Pennsylvania (Lancaster County; Rapho Township). Swiss Americans. ca 1727-1909. *995*

Leisure. Farmers. Labor. Sex roles. 1920-55. *773*

—. New York (Corning). Social History. Upper Classes. ca 1880-1913. *1107*

Lentz, Lula Gillespie (reminiscences). Country Life. Farms. Illinois (southern). 1883-1929. *996*

Leonard, Nathaniel (descendants). Cattle Raising. Houses. Missouri (Cooper County). Ravenswood (residence). 1825-1980. *1139*

Leshe, Mary Jane Conly (biography). Louisiana (Bienville Parish). 1849-1932. *1017*

Letters. Advice. Great Britain (London). Nova Scotia (Halifax). Uniacke, Norman Fitzgerald. Uniacke, Richard John. 1798. *627*

—. Arkansas. Lockridge family. Morris, Joseph. Pioneers. 1856-68. *1125*

—. Barry, John Waller. US Military Academy. 1826-30. *866*

—. Bleser, Carol. Hammond family (review article). Social change. South Carolina. 19c-1950's. *1155*

—. Brown family. Frontier and Pioneer Life. New England. 1792-1852. *934*

—. Byrd, William, I. Byrd, William, II. Byrd, William, III. Tinling, Marion (review article). Virginia. 1684-1776. *887*

—. California. Civil War. Daily life. Gold Rushes. Pennsylvania. Shuler family. 1849-64. *1051*

—. California. Ehrman, Theresa. France (Paris). Music. Stein, Gertrude. 1901-67. *1121*

—. California (Martinez). Daily Life. Muir, John. 1890-1914. *1089*

—. Cannon, Martha Hughes. Great Britain. Mormons. Polygamy. Utah (Salt Lake City). Women. 1885-96. *1000*

—. *Chicago Tribune*. Fuller, Henry Blake (pseud., Harry S. Free). Marriage. 1875. *740*

—. Civil War. Lewis, Charlotte. Lewis, Enoch. Pennsylvania (Altoona). 1863. *650*

—. Conine family. Frontier and Pioneer Life. North Central States. 1852-63. *819*

—. Country Life. Hecker, Friedrich Karl. Illinois (St. Clair County). Köhler, Carl. 1851. *1129*

—. Cuba. Hawthorne, Sophia Peabody. 1833-35. *815*

—. Daily life. Fort Washakie. Indians. Winne, Caroline. Wives. Wyoming. 1879-80. *845*

—. Daily Life. Maryland (Baltimore). Preston, Madge. Preston, William P. 1855-67. *827*

—. Diseases. James, Alice. James, William. 1886. *1157*

—. Education. Europe. Yale University (Beinecke Library). Youth. 1779-84. 1970's. *1009*

—. Erickson sisters. Homesteading and Homesteaders. North Dakota (Hettinger County). 1910-11. *831*

—. France. Louisiana. Ruelle, François (1821-77). Ruelle, François (1790-1855). 1818-56. *873*

—. Frontier and Pioneer Life. Nebraska, southeastern. Sim, Francis (family). 1856-59. *1099*

—. Genealogy. Guam. Souder, Paul. 1710-1958. *1109*

—. Hodgdon, Elizabeth. Hodgdon, Sarah. Labor. Massachusetts (Lowell). New Hampshire (Rochester). Textile Industry. 1830-40. *889*

—. Illinois (Polo). Thomas, Lewis (family). 1878-79. *863*

—. Latta, Eli Chambers (and family). 1855-72. *1081*

—. Lincoln, Abraham. Lincoln, Robert T. 1865-1980. *952*

—. Mormons. Smith, Joseph. Smith, Lucy Mack. 1829. *971*

Letters, family. Brigham (family). Massachusetts (Marlborough). Migrants. Vermont (Bakersfield). 1800-26. *194*

Lévi-Strauss, Claude. Indians. Social Customs. 17c-19c. *184*

Levy, Asher. Genealogy. New Amsterdam. New Jersey. 1630-1785. *1115*

Lewis and Clark expedition. Charbonneau family. Western States. 1759-1866. *804*

Lewis, Charlotte. Civil War. Letters. Lewis, Enoch. Pennsylvania (Altoona). 1863. *650*

Lewis, Enoch. Civil War. Letters. Lewis, Charlotte. Pennsylvania (Altoona). 1863. *650*

Lewis, Waitsill (family). Genealogy. Methodology. Nova Scotia (Yarmouth). 1976. *16*

Liberalism. Demography. Federal Policy. Sex. 1940-80. *393*

Liberty. Government. Political socialization. 1980. *495*

—. Law. North Carolina. Whites. Women. 1700-76. *780*

Libraries. Genealogy. Massachusetts, western. Research. 1978. *64*

Libraries (holdings). Colorado, University of (Western Historical Collections). Patterson, Thomas M. (family). 1850-1925. *809*

Libraries, local. Archives, National. Census Bureau. Family history. Research. 1960's-70's. *242*

Life course (concept). Boocock, Sarane Spence. Demos, John. Hareven, Tamara K. Methodology. 1800-1980. *318*

—. Fertility. 1930-70. *636*

Life cycles. Budgets. Europe, Western. Income. 1889-90. *448*

—. History. Methodology. Research. Sociology. 1950's-70's. *34*

—. Women. 1900-70. *285*

Life histories. Assimilation. Colorado (Denver). Greek Americans. 20c. *1052*

Life insurance. Children. Social Classes. 1875-1980. *576*

Life patterns. Marital timing. Women, white. 1925-76. *635*

Lifestyles. Fertility. Social Change. 1970-79. *684*

—. Indiana (Muncie). Inequality. Lynd, Helen Merrell. Lynd, Robert S. Occupations. Social Classes. 1920-78. *392*

Lilienthal, Alice Haas. Bransten, Florine Haas. Business. California (San Francisco). Culture. Jews. ca 1900-81. *880*

Lilienthal family pact. Corporation, family. Jews. New York. 1814-1904. *1117*

Liliuokalani. Dominis, John Owen (and ancestors). Hawaii. 1437-1891. *988*

Lincoln, Abraham. Documents. Historiography. Lincoln, Mary Todd. Marriage. 1842-65. 1885. 1947-82. *916*

—. Elites. Myths and Symbols. 1770's-1860's. *1067*

—. Hoblit family. Illinois (Logan County). ca 1840-66. *1043*

—. Johnston, John D. 1819-59. *801*

—. Letters. Lincoln, Robert T. 1865-1980. *952*

Lincoln, Mary Todd. Attitudes. Domesticity. Stanton, Elizabeth Cady. Stowe, Harriet Beecher. 1830-80. *1104*

—. Documents. Historiography. Lincoln, Abraham. Marriage. 1842-65. 1885. 1947-82. *916*

Lincoln, Robert T. Letters. Lincoln, Abraham. 1865-1980. *952*

Lindbergh, Charles A., Sr. (early career). Minnesota (Little Falls). 1884-1906. *991*

Linkage hypothesis. Academic achievement. Fathers. IQ. Occupations. Personality. Sons. 1964. *485*

Lipsitz family. Jews. Michigan (Detroit). 1868-1982. *1120*

Literacy. Children. Employment. Income. Men. Wives. 1901. *428*

Literature. Assimilation. Immigrants. Jews. ca 1900-20. *792*

—. Bibliographies. Daughters. Mothers. Women. 1800-1979. *680*

—. Biography. Diseases. Edel, Leon (interview). James, Henry (1811-82; and family). Psychology. 1811-1916. 1979. *806*

—. Canada. History (image). 1950-80. *645*

—. Farms. Sex roles. Social Status. South. Women. 1800-60. *605*

Lithuanian Americans. Educational attainment. Immaculate Conception Primary School. Missouri (St. Louis). Occupations. 1948-68. *109*

Litoff, Judy Barrett. Bogdan, Janet. Childbirth (review article). Donegan, Jane. Scholten, Catherine. Wertz, Dorothy C. Wertz, Richard W. 17c-1980. *633*

Local Government. Fraud. Land (claims). Lawsuits. Nurnberger, Frederick (and family). 1854-1923. *1062*

Local History. Buschow family. City directories. Family history. Ohio (Cleveland). 1883-1900. 1979. *316*

—. Census. Cities. Genealogy. Methodology. 1980. *266*

—. Family history. Illinois (Chicago). Newberry Library. 1972-77. *51*

—. Family (review article). Massachusetts (Salem). Witchcraft. 18c. *111*

Local politics. Congregationalism. Connecticut (Canterbury). Great Awakening. Schisms. 1742-50. *470*

Location. Interpersonal Relations. 20c. *641*

Lockridge family. Arkansas. Letters. Morris, Joseph. Pioneers. 1856-68. *1125*

Logan, Ernest. Courtship. Logan, Lizzie Walker. Wyoming (Cheyenne). 1871-1910. *1091*

Logan, Lizzie Walker. Courtship. Logan, Ernest. Wyoming (Cheyenne). 1871-1910. *1091*

Long Island Historical Society. Archival Catalogs and Inventories. Genealogy. New York City. 17c-20c. *270*

Lott, Arthur. Alabama. Creek Indian War (1813-14). Indian-White Relations. Louisiana. Meredith, Thomas. Murders. 1812-14. *1156*

Louisiana. Alabama. Creek Indian War (1813-14). Indian-White Relations. Lott, Arthur. Meredith, Thomas. Murders. 1812-14. *1156*

—. Blacks. Creoles. 1970's. *704*

—. Divorce. Mahon, Samuel S. Speeches and Addresses. State Legislatures. 1806. *419*

—. Dubuclet, Antoine. Reconstruction. Treasurers. 1868-78. *1138*

—. France. Letters. Ruelle, François (1821-77). Ruelle, François (1790-1855). 1818-56. *873*

—. St. Denis, Louis Antoine Juchereau de. St. Denis, Louise Marguerite Juchereau de. ca 1712-60. *1023*

Louisiana (Bernice). Elam, Margaret Fuller. 1874-1975. *1003*

—. Mabry, Catherine Cook. Women. 1885-1913. *1002*

Louisiana (Bienville Parish). Leshe, Mary Jane Conly (biography). 1849-1932. *1017*

Louisiana (Cane River, Natchitoches). Creoles. Race relations. Social status. 1767-20c. *1022*

Louisiana (Claiborne Parish, Murrell settlement). Miller, Frederick (descendants). 1820-20c. *859*

Louisiana (Shiloh). Baptists. Burns, Bertha Porter. Burns, Marion Van. Clergy. Teachers. 1884-1975. *1001*

—. Lee, Mary Edmunds Tabor. 1840's-1926. *1004*

Louisiana State University. Biography. Depressions. Family history. Interviews. Students. Works Progress Administration. 1930's. 1978. *66*

Louisville, University of. Family history. Oral history. Perry, Barbara. 1977. *259*

Lovett, Clara M. Berkin, Carol R. Degler, Carl N. Dublin, Thomas. Kennedy, Susan. Women (review article). 1770's-1980. *243*

Loyalists. American Revolution. Massachusetts. Oliver family. Political Leadership. 1632-1860. *856*

—. Michigan (Mackinac, Straits of). Migration, Internal. Mitchell, David. Mitchell, Elizabeth. 1780-1832. *810*

Lumber trade. Barton, Stephen, Jr. North Carolina (Hertford County, Bartonsville). Rural Settlements. 1856-65. *1049*

Lutheran Church (lifestyles). Parsonage. 1974. *600*

Lynd, Helen Merrell. High Schools. Indiana (Muncie). Lynd, Robert S. Students. 1924-77. *589*

—. Indiana (Muncie). Inequality. Lifestyles. Lynd, Robert S. Occupations. Social Classes. 1920-78. *392*

Lynd, Robert S. High Schools. Indiana (Muncie). Lynd, Helen Merrell. Students. 1924-77. *589*

—. Indiana (Muncie). Inequality. Lifestyles. Lynd, Helen Merrell. Occupations. Social Classes. 1920-78. *392*

Lyndes, Stanley Horace. Country Life. Drawing. Teaching. Vermont. 1918-75. *9*

Lyons, Charles (family). Armies. Great Britain. Kent, Duke of (Edward). Nova Scotia (Halifax). 1812-63. *938*

M

Mabry, Catherine Cook. Louisiana (Bernice). Women. 1885-1913. *1002*

MacArthur family. Military. Wisconsin (Milwaukee). 1849-1951. *803*

MacMurchy, Helen. Canada. Childbirth. Infants. Mortality. Whitton, Charlotte. 1919-39. *386*

Mahon, Samuel S. Divorce. Louisiana. Speeches and Addresses. State Legislatures. 1806. *419*

Mahurin, Hugh (family). Massachusetts (Taunton, Bridgewater). New Jersey (Morris County). 17c-20c. *966*

Maine. Africans. Paris, Pedro Tovookan (biography). Parris family. 1845-60. *1050*

—. Durrell, Philip (and descendants). 18c-19c. *892*

—. Genealogy. Research. 17c-19c. *102*

Maine (Mount Desert). Migration, Internal. Pioneers. Richardson, James. 1761-89. *937*

Maine (Portland). Cemetery records. Eastern Cemetery. ca 1717-1900. *977*

Malcolm X. Autobiography. Emerson, Ralph Waldo. Franklin, Benjamin. Individualism. Interpersonal Relations. 18c-1783. *669*

Manifests. Children. Franklin & Armfield (firm). Interstate commerce. Slave Trade. Virginia (Alexandria). 1828-36. *557*

Manitoba (Red River). Anglican Communion. Missionary wives. Missions and Missionaries. Women. 1820-37. *765*

Manitoba (Rosenthal). Farms. German Russians. Hildebrand, Bernhard (and family). Mennonites. 1795-1915. *1042*

Manitoba (Winnipeg area). Personal Narratives. Poets. Woodcock, George (ancestors). 1780-1981. *1154*

Manning, Nicholas (and family). Genealogy. Hawthorne, Nathaniel. 1680-1841. *898*

Manuscripts. New England. Pierce, John. Social history. 1800-50. *206*

Marital status. Fertility. Migration, Internal. 1967. *731*

Marital timing. Life patterns. Women, white. 1925-76. *635*

Markley family. Cemeteries. Pennsylvania (Skippack area). Restorations. 1738. 1926. *905*

Marks, David X. Architecture. California (Los Angeles). Insurance. Marks, Joshua H. Philanthropy. 1902-77. *1163*

Marks, Joshua H. Architecture. California (Los Angeles). Insurance. Marks, David X. Philanthropy. 1902-77. *1163*

Marriage. 1959-73. *342*

—. Adams, Henry Brooks. Adams, Marian Hooper. Monuments. Saint-Gaudens, Augustus. Suicide. 1872-85. *912*

—. Adolescence. Purity. Sexual reform. Social organization. 1830's-40's. *549*

—. Age. Fertility. Massachusetts (Sturbridge). 1730-1850. *225*

—. Age. North Carolina (Perquimans County). 1661-1775. *649*

—. Aged. Divorce. Middle Age. 1970's. *593*

—. Aged. Employment. 1900. *283*

—. Birth. Death and Dying. Rites and Ceremonies. Social Customs. Tennessee, eastern. 20c. *693*

—. Birth control. Blacks. Fertility. 1880-1980. *710*

—. Birth Rate. Ethnicity. Massachusetts (Boston; South, South End). Occupations. 1880. *131*

—. Births. Gibson family records. South Carolina. 1750-1800. *1132*

—. Blacks. Divorce. 1970. *763*

—. Blacks. Equality. Sex roles. Whites. 1976. *362*

—. Blacks. Family life. Pennsylvania. 18c. *603*

—. Blacks. Kentucky (Todd County). 1866-72. *25*

—. Blacks. Kentucky (Todd County). 1866-84. *24*

—. Blacks. Youth. 1960's. *87*

—. California. Chumash Indians. Indians. Mission Santa Barbara. Social Organization. Yanunali, Pedro. 1787-1806. *1141*

—. California (Los Angeles). Catholic Church. Mission Santa Barbara. Social Customs. 1786-1848. *209*

—. Canada. 1851-91. *110*

—. Canada. Interpersonal Relations. Kinship. Suicide. 1951-71. *625*

—. Census. New York. 1845-75. *310*

—. Chesapeake Bay area. Death and Dying. Maryland. 1630-1720. *777*

—. *Chicago Tribune.* Fuller, Henry Blake (pseud., Harry S. Free). Letters. 1875. *740*

—. Childlessness. Women. 1960-77. *412*

—. Christians. Jews. 1962-79. *746*

—. Cities. Divorce. Mortality. Rural Settlements. Tennessee. 1970. *326*

—. Country Life. Ethnicity. Immigrants. Minnesota (Kandiyoki County). Swedish Americans. 1870-1905. *729*

—. Cuban Americans. 1957-74. *581*

—. Customs and behavior. New England. 1632-1783. *687*

—. Divorce. Feminism. Reform. Stanton, Elizabeth Cady. 1840-90. *120*

—. Documents. Historiography. Lincoln, Abraham. Lincoln, Mary Todd. 1842-65. 1885. 1947-82. *916*

—. Education. Employment. Fertility. Poor. 1910-70. *202*

—. Education. Social Organizations. Women. 1960-67. *333*

—. Employment. Sex roles. Women. 1890-1978. *460*

—. Employment, part-time. Women. 1940-70. *482*

—. Epidemics. Exogamy. Quebec. 1700-60. *705*

—. Ethnic groups. Fertility. Pennsylvania (Philadelphia). 1850-80. *659*

—. Ethnic Groups. Fur Trade. Mountain men. Rocky Mountains. Settlement. 19c. *297*

—. Ethnicity. Irish Americans. Migration. South Carolina. 1970-80. *662*

—. Family life. Slavery. 1800-60. *173*

—. Fertility. Historiography. Methodology. Occupations. Pennsylvania. 1850-80. *125*

—. Freedmen. Kentucky (Owensboro). 1866. *334*

—. Freedmen. Kentucky (Paducah). 1865-66. *343*

—. Friends, Society of. Nova Scotia (Dartmouth). 1786-89. *681*

—. Immigrants. Japanese Americans. Picture brides. Women. 1900-24. *467*

—. Interpersonal relations. Jews. 1975-78. *708*

—. Javits, Jacob. Javits, Marian. Personal narratives. Politics. 1947-80. *469*

—. Labor. 1980-81. *456*

Massachusetts (Lynn). Methodology. Poverty.
Working Class (family history). 1915-40. *879*
Massachusetts (Marlborough). Brigham (family).
Letters, family. Migrants. Vermont
(Bakersfield). 1800-26. *194*
Massachusetts (Marlborough, Sudbury). Bruce,
Thomas (family). 17c-19c. *1054*
Massachusetts (Newburyport). Age. Men.
Remarriage. Women. ca 1800-30. *657*
Massachusetts (Oak Knoll). Whittier, John
Greenleaf (family). Woodman, Phebe.
1876-1929. *1160*
Massachusetts (Quincy). Adams family. 1775-1927.
846
Massachusetts (Salem). Courts. Sex roles. Women.
1636-83. *458*
—. Domestic roles. Social Change. Women.
1660-1770. *753*
—. Family (review article). Local history.
Witchcraft. 18c. *111*
—. Population. Towne, William (family).
1630-1700. *1143*
—. Verin, Philip (sons). 1635-90. *1128*
Massachusetts (Sandwich). Migration, Internal.
Settlement. Vital Statistics. 1650-1805. *60*
Massachusetts (Southwick). Connecticut
(Colebrook). New York (Liberty). Russell,
Stephen (and descendants). 1749-1820. *1087*
Massachusetts (Sturbridge). Age. Fertility.
Marriage. 1730-1850. *225*
Massachusetts (Talbot County). Architecture. Land.
Sherwood Manor. Tilghman, Lloyd. 1718-1823.
1048
Massachusetts (Taunton, Bridgewater). Mahurin,
Hugh (family). New Jersey (Morris County).
17c-20c. *966*
Massachusetts (Webster). Discipline. Factories.
Rhode Island (Slatersville). 1790-1840. *562*
Massachusetts (Westborough). Childbirth. Death
and Dying. Diaries. Diseases. Parkman,
Ebenezer. Social Organization. 1724-82. *702*
Massachusetts, western. Genealogy. Libraries.
Research. 1978. *64*
Massachusetts (Weymouth). Ford, Andrew
(descendants). 17c-20c. *896*
Massachusetts (Woburn). Social History.
Widowhood. Women. 1701-10. *682*
Massachusetts (Worcester). Family cycle.
Household structure. Social Change.
Urbanization. 1860-80. *59*
Massasoit. Genealogy. Indians. Plymouth
Plantation. Wampanoag Indians. 1620-1931.
1041
Material culture. Child-rearing. Family structure.
Painting. Portraits. 1730-1860. *47*
Material relationships. Social Classes. 1970's. *240*
Materialism. Parental control. Values. 1965-75. *784*
Maternal deprivation. Children. Upper Classes.
1950-74. *758*
Maternity. Mortality, Maternal. New York City.
Obstetrics. Physicians (accountability). 1915-40.
584
Matteson, Joel. Doolittle, Clara Matteson
(reminiscences). Douglas, Stephen A. (statue).
Governor's mansion. Illinois. Sculpture.
1850's-65. *951*
Maxner family. Nova Scotia. 1730-1978. *890*
May, Elaine Tyler (review article). Marriage.
1880-1920. *741*
Mayer, Francis Blackwell (family). Maryland
(Annapolis). Painting. Preservation. 1876-98.
1047
McBeth, Sue L. Indian culture (hostility to).
Missions and Missionaries. Nez Percé Indians.
Presbyterian Church. 1873-93. *61*
McIntosh family. Cherokee Indians. Indians.
Leadership. 1765-1897. *850*

McKaig, Mrs. William W. Bruce, Mazie. Diaries.
Maryland (Cumberland). Upper Classes.
Women. 1857-89. *821*
McKay, John. Genealogies. Immigration.
McLennan, Roderick. Nova Scotia. Scottish
Canadians. 1805-1927. *923*
McLennan, Roderick. Genealogies. Immigration.
McKay, John. Nova Scotia. Scottish Canadians.
1805-1927. *923*
Mead, Elinor Gertrude. Courtship. Howells,
William Dean. 1860-62. *1019*
Medical care. Children. Environment. 1970's. *527*
Medical Care (costs). Children. 1969. *478*
Medicine and State. Birth control. Law. Public
Policy. 19c. *453*
Mellon family. Bibliographies. Pennsylvania.
1885-1978. *1034*
Memoirs. Copper, Fannie Adams. Homesteading
and Homesteaders. Oregon. 1889-99. *1146*
—. Delaware. Higgins, Anthony (reminiscences).
Thompson, Mary Wilson. 1770-1947. *953*
—. Delaware. Thompson, Mary Wilson. 1870-1918.
954
—. Gold Rushes. Oregon. Pioneers. Postal Service.
Shively, John M. 1843-51. *1007*
Men. Age. Massachusetts (Newburyport).
Remarriage. Women. ca 1800-30. *657*
—. Agricultural Labor. Blacks. Divorce. Moynihan,
Daniel P. ("The Negro Family"). 1965-78. *536*
—. Blacks. Feminism, black. Sexism. Social
Problems. 1970's. *754*
—. Children. Employment. Income. Literacy.
Wives. 1901. *428*
—. Cookery. Sex roles. Stereotypes. 20c. *580*
—. Employment. Women. 1970-82. *466*
—. Frontier and Pioneer Life. Overland Journeys
to the Pacific. Wagon trains. Women.
1840's-50's. *639*
Mennonites. Brenneman family. Coverlets.
Genealogy. Pennsylvania. 1631-1971. *948*
—. Brunk family. Genealogy. Immigrants.
1750-1850. *843*
—. Cemeteries. Pennsylvania (Dauphin County;
Lower Swatara Township). Shope Mennonite
Cemetery. 18c-1981. *1159*
—. Clergy. Lehman, Hans (and family).
Pennsylvania (Lancaster County; Rapho
Township). Swiss Americans. ca 1727-1909. *995*
—. Courtship. Diaries. Indiana. Sprunger, David.
1893-95. *1111*
—. Denlinger family. Genealogy. Pennsylvania.
Switzerland. 1594-1803. *886*
—. Farms. German Russians. Hildebrand,
Bernhard (and family). Manitoba (Rosenthal).
1795-1915. *1042*
—. Genealogy. Iowa. Settlement. 1839-1974. *114*
—. Immigration. North America. Surnames. Swiss
Brethren. 1680-1880. *263*
—. Rhodes families. Virginia. 1770's-1900. *1101*
Mental health. Child custody. Divorce. Law. Social
workers. 1970's. *463*
—. Mothers. Nuclear accidents. Pennsylvania.
Three Mile Island power plant. 1979. *384*
Mental Illness. Assimilation. Jews. Novels. Race.
Singer, Israel Joshua *(Family Carnovsky)*. 1943.
113
—. Blacks. Mothers. 1977. *626*
—. Bureaucracy. Children. Learning disabilities.
1975. *370*
Mentally Handicapped. Children. Fogarty, John E.
Parents Council for Retarded Children. Rhode
Island. Social change. Trudeau, Arthur.
1951-70. *350*
Merchants. Economic growth. Illinois (Jackson
County; Grand Tower). Jenkins, Thomas
(family). 1818-90's. *1005*

N

Nurnberger, Frederick (and family). Fraud. Land (claims). Lawsuits. Local Government. 1854-1923. *1062*
Nurses and Nursing. Income. Women. 1953-70. *602*

O

Oakley, Ann. Capitalism. Galbraith, John Kenneth. Housework. Sex roles. Women. 1950-70's. *436*
Oatman, Roys (and family). Arizona, southwestern. Indians (captivities). Westward Movement. Yavapai Indians. 1851-1903. *630*
Oberholtzer family. Farms. Pennsylvania (Terre Hill). Switzerland. 1720's-1850's. *1045*
Obstetrics. Maternity. Mortality, Maternal. New York City. Physicians (accountability). 1915-40. *584*
Occupational aspirations. Family background. Roles. Women. 1973. *685*
Occupational mobility. State Department (Foreign Service). Wives. 1974. *351*
Occupational movements, intergenerational. College students, male. -1974. *718*
Occupational segregation. Child Labor. Cotton. Sex. Textile industry. 1910. *489*
Occupational systems. Social Organization. 1970's. *538*
Occupations. Academic achievement. Children. Mothers. North Central States. Occupations. 1977. *352*
—. Academic achievement. Children. Mothers. North Central States. Occupations. 1977. *352*
—. Academic achievement. Fathers. IQ. Linkage hypothesis. Personality. Sons. 1964. *485*
—. Attitudes. Behavior. Education. Social Classes. 1972-80. *411*
—. Birth Rate. Ethnicity. Marriage. Massachusetts (Boston; South, South End). 1880. *131*
—. Blacks. Women. 1964-75. *346*
—. B'nai B'rith. Geographic Mobility. Jews. Oregon (Portland). Social status. 1910-30. *305*
—. Country Life. Economic Conditions. Mexican Americans. Social Organization. Washington (Yakima Valley). 1971. *433*
—. Divorce. Economic Conditions. Higher education. Identity. Social Status. Women. 1971-77. *461*
—. Educational attainment. Immaculate Conception Primary School. Lithuanian Americans. Missouri (St. Louis). 1948-68. *109*
—. Europe. Income. Women. 1968-75. *522*
—. Fertility. Historiography. Marriage. Methodology. Pennsylvania. 1850-80. *125*
—. Indiana (Muncie). Inequality. Lifestyles. Lynd, Helen Merrell. Lynd, Robert S. Social Classes. 1920-78. *392*
O'Connor, Flannery (ancestry). Catholic Church. Georgia. ca 1733-1949. *908*
Office-holding patterns. Connecticut (Norwich, Hartford, Fairfield). Family (political domination). 1700-60. *69*
Ogburn, William F. Affectional function hypothesis. Sociology. 1920's-81. *233*
Ohio. Congregationalism. Connecticut. Frontier and Pioneer Life. Western Reserve. Wright Elizur (and family). Yale University. 1762-1870. *911*
—. DeWitt, Zachariah Price (family). Kentucky. Migration. New Jersey. New Netherland. 1650-1820's. *981*
—. Felton, Jacob. Frontier and Pioneer Life. Indiana. Personal narratives. Settlement. 1820-40. *904*
Ohio (Cincinnati). Adams, John Quincy (family). Catholics. 1843-1930. *1148*
—. Genealogy. Gloor family. Iowa (Tell City). Swiss Colonization Society. 1850's-1970's. *925*

Ohio (Cleveland). Buschow family. City directories. Family history. Local History. 1883-1900. 1979. *316*
Ohio (Hamilton). Daily Life. Howells, William Dean. 1841-50. *946*
Ohio (Kirtland). Mormons. Women. 1831-38. *509*
Ohio (Maumee City). Wolcott, James (and family). 1630-1873. *1133*
Oklahoma. Appalachia. Cherokee Indians. Georgia. Indian-White Relations. Ridge family. 1785-1907. *901*
—. Country life. Frost, Margaret Fullerton. Personal Narratives. 1901-07. *913*
Old Folks of Shelby County. Davis, James Dick. Genealogy. Harbormaster. History (societies). Tennessee (Memphis). 1810-80. *822*
Old Sturbridge Village. Artifacts. Family history. History Teaching. Massachusetts. 1790-1840. 1980. *22*
Oliver family. American Revolution. Loyalists. Massachusetts. Political Leadership. 1632-1860. *856*
Olympia beer. Durkheimer family. Jews. Oregon. Retail Trade. 1862-1978. *924*
Onderdonk family. Painting. Texas. ca 1879-1964. *1164*
Oneida Community. Foster, Lawrence. Kern, Louis J. Mormons. Sex (review article). Shakers. 19c. 1981. *707*
—. Genetics. New York. Noyes, John Humphrey. Stirpicultural experiment. 1848-86. *791*
—. New York. Noyes, John Humphrey. Religion. Sex. 1848-80. *302*
Ontario. Archives of Ontario. Bibliographies. Women. 18c. *190*
—. Brink, Nicholas (family). 1797-1857. *838*
—. Feminism. Social reform. 1875-1900. *503*
—. Heron family. Hill family. Theater. Touring companies. 1840-60. *1100*
Ontario (Alfred, Caledonia). English Canadians. French Canadians. Stereotypes. 1800-81. *105*
Ontario (Hamilton). Boarders. Households. Katz, Michael. New Brunswick (Moncton). 1851-61. 1975. *493*
—. Katz, Michael B. (review article). Social Classes. 1850-80. *7*
Ontario (Toronto). Italian Canadians. Social Mobility. 1935-60. *295*
Ontario (Toronto Gore). Geographic Mobility. Population. 1820-90. *203*
Ontario (Upper Canada). Elites. Government. 1788-1841. *14*
—. Immigration. Irish Canadians. Settlement. 1825. *50*
Oral History. Alabama (Yell County). Methodology. Slavery. 1852-60. *226*
—. Child-rearing. Colorado. Frontier and Pioneer Life. Home Economics. Women. 1895-1920. *585*
—. Community history. Family history. Nevins, Allan. 1940's-70's. *268*
—. Family history. Louisville, University of. Perry, Barbara. 1977. *259*
—. Folklore. Kealey, James (and family). Quebec (Hull). 1974-75. *77*
—. Historiography. 1980. *274*
—. History Teaching. Methodology. 1977. *204*
—. History Teaching. New Mexico State University. Women. 1976. *152*
Oral tradition. Childhood. Folklore. Indians. Prehistory-1970's. *595*
Oregon. Boswell, Ben D. Boswell, Emma. Boswell Springs (resort). Civil War. Military. Spas. 1860-1908. *1033*
—. Copper, Fannie Adams. Homesteading and Homesteaders. Memoirs. 1889-99. *1146*

—. Durkheimer family. Jews. Olympia beer. Retail Trade. 1862-1978. *924*
—. Gold Rushes. Memoirs. Pioneers. Postal Service. Shively, John M. 1843-51. *1007*
Oregon (Forest Grove). Diaries. Frontier and Pioneer Life. Missions and Missionaries. Tshimakai Indian Mission. Walker, Mary Richardson. Washington. 1833-97. *962*
Oregon (Hillsboro). Child-rearing. Children. Holsman, Virginia (reminiscences). Recreation. 19c-1920's. *961*
Oregon (Portland). B'nai B'rith. Geographic Mobility. Jews. Occupations. Social status. 1910-30. *305*
Oregon Trail (Applegate Cutoff). Henderson, Lucy Ann. Overland Journeys to the Pacific. 1846. *1122*
Organizations. Battered women's shelter movement. Law reform. Wife beating. 1850-1981. *472*
Overland Journeys to the Pacific. California. Frontier and Pioneer Life. Missouri. Morris, Sally Dodge. Nebraska. Personal narratives. 1821-77. *932*
—. Frontier and Pioneer Life. Men. Wagon trains. Women. 1840's-50's. *639*
—. Henderson, Lucy Ann. Oregon Trail (Applegate Cutoff). 1846. *1122*
Overland Trail. Westward Movement. Women. Work roles. 1842-67. *93*
Owen, Robert (family). Point of Honor (home). Virginia (Lynchburg). 1830-1978. *1097*
Ownership. Education. Farms. Social origins. Wisconsin. 1970-79. *692*
Ozark Mountains. Income, family. Social status orientation. Youth. 1962-73. *514*

P

Paine, Thomas. American Revolution. Authority (symbols of). 1776. *157*
Painting. Audubon, John James. Audubon, John Woodhouse. Audubon, Victor Gifford. Wildlife. 1785-1862. *1074*
—. Child-rearing. Family structure. Material culture. Portraits. 1730-1860. *47*
—. Family history. History Teaching. Photographs. Teaching Aids and Devices. 1980. *185*
—. Maryland (Annapolis). Mayer, Francis Blackwell (family). Preservation. 1876-98. *1047*
—. Onderdonk family. Texas. ca 1879-1964. *1164*
Palmer, Alice Freeman. Bryn Mawr College. Feminism. Sex roles, traditional. Thomas, Carey. Wellesley College. 1875-1918. *569*
Parental control. Materialism. Values. 1965-75. *784*
Parent-child relations. Family structure. Middle Classes. Social change. Women, role of. 1970's. *594*
Parents. Academic achievement. Blacks. Children. Human Relations. Teachers. 1970's. *612*
—. Adolescence. Attitudes. 1975-76. *709*
—. Adolescence. Attitudes. Education. ca 1954-74. *347*
—. Aged. Children. 1970's. *770*
—. Attitudes. Children. 18c. *778*
—. California (Alum Rock). Education. Public Schools. Vouchers. 1960's-70's. *401*
—. Chesapeake Bay area. Children. Maryland. Values. Virginia. 18c. *749*
—. Chesapeake Bay area. Death and Dying. Kinship. Virginia (Middlesex County). 1650-1710. *735*
—. Childhood, fear of. Elementary Education. Teachers. 19c. *427*
—. Children. Educational Policy. Poor. 1960-78. *543*
—. Death and Dying. Infants. New England. Theology. 1620-1720. *277*

—. Education. Interest groups. Political Participation. 1977-81. *410*
—. Marriage partners, selection. Virginia. 17c-18c. *745*
Parents Council for Retarded Children. Children. Fogarty, John E. Mentally Handicapped. Rhode Island. Social change. Trudeau, Arthur. 1951-70. *350*
Parents, single. Housing. Massachusetts. 1970's. *570*
Parent-youth conflict. Catholic Church. Educational system. French Canadians. Quebec. Social change. 1960-70. *473*
Paris, Pedro Tovookan (biography). Africans. Maine. Parris family. 1845-60. *1050*
Parish registers. Catholic Church. Government. Quebec. 1539-1973. *379*
—. Catholic Church. Population. Quebec. 1616-1700. *252*
Parkman, Ebenezer. Childbirth. Death and Dying. Diaries. Diseases. Massachusetts (Westborough). Social Organization. 1724-82. *702*
Parris family. Africans. Maine. Paris, Pedro Tovookan (biography). 1845-60. *1050*
Parsonage. Lutheran Church (lifestyles). 1974. *600*
Patriarchy. Inheritance. Plantations. South Carolina (Charleston). 1800-60. *675*
—. New England. 1619-1776. *644*
Patterson, Thomas M. (family). Colorado, University of (Western Historical Collections). Libraries (holdings). 1850-1925. *809*
Paul, Thomas (and family). Blacks. Church, black (first). Clergy. Massachusetts (Boston). 1773-1973. *1024*
Peale family. Art. Science. 1770-1823. *1020*
Peasants. Land. Massachusetts (Barnstable County). Values. 1620's-1720's. *317*
Pennsylvania. Bibliographies. Mellon family. 1885-1978. *1034*
—. Blacks. Family life. Marriage. 18c. *603*
—. Brenneman family. Coverlets. Genealogy. Mennonites. 1631-1971. *948*
—. California. Civil War. Daily life. Gold Rushes. Letters. Shuler family. 1849-64. *1051*
—. Denlinger family. Genealogy. Mennonites. Switzerland. 1594-1803. *886*
—. Fertility. Historiography. Marriage. Methodology. Occupations. 1850-80. *125*
—. Fisher, William Logan (memoir). 1781-1862. *1134*
—. Friends, Society of. Schools. Social Customs. ca 1740-76. *196*
—. Indentured servants. Religion. Women. 18c. *171*
—. Klein, Randolph Shipley (review article). Methodology. Shippen family. Social sciences. 1668-1776. 1975. *1053*
—. Mental health. Mothers. Nuclear accidents. Three Mile Island power plant. 1979. *384*
—. Rural-Urban Studies. Social Classes. Wives. 1947-71. *449*
Pennsylvania (Altoona). Civil War. Letters. Lewis, Charlotte. Lewis, Enoch. 1863. *650*
Pennsylvania (Bradford County). Alger, Hugh Wesley. Daily Life. Farms. Personal Narratives. 1890-99. *5*
Pennsylvania (Chambersburg). Blacks. Documents. Mortality. Sellers Funeral Home. 1866-1933. *254*
Pennsylvania (Christiana). Broomell family. Business community. Christiana Machine Company. Social status. 1880-1900. *1025*
Pennsylvania (Dauphin County; Lower Swatara Township). Cemeteries. Mennonites. Shope Mennonite Cemetery. 18c-1981. *1159*
Pennsylvania (Delaware Valley). Children. Friends, Society of. Theology. 1681-1735. *698*

Quebec (Quebec City). Generation conflict, basis. Identity. Social integration. 1968. *75*
Questionnaires. Family history. History Teaching. Teaching Aids and Devices. 1970's. *40*
Quitrents. Land Tenure. Money. Tobacco. Virginia (Isle of Wight County). 1704-14. *220*

R

Race. Assimilation. Jews. Mental Illness. Novels. Singer, Israel Joshua *(Family Carnovsky)*. 1943. *113*
—. Attitudes. Blacks. Breckenridge family. Elites. Kentucky. 1760-1935. *987*
—. Divorce. Motherhood. 1968-72. *716*
Race Relations. Blacks. Dating. Mexican Americans. Whites. 1978-79. *691*
—. Children. Day care system. 1967-73. *572*
—. Creoles. Louisiana (Cane River, Natchitoches). Social status. 1767-20c. *1022*
—. Income inequality. Labor Unions and Organizations. 1947-74. *360*
—. Interpersonal contact. Students. Taiwan. 1933-73. *188*
Radical History Review (periodical). Historiography. Leftism. Slavery. 17c-20c. 1970's. *106*
Railroad expansion. Industrialization (impact). Women, role of. 1890's. *608*
Ranches. Business. Cattle Raising. Montana. Sheep raising. Sieben, Henry. 1864-1937. *1046*
Ranching. Beckton, Ernest. Beckton, William. Saskatchewan (Cannington Manor). Upper Classes. 1888-97. *964*
Ravenswood (residence). Cattle Raising. Houses. Leonard, Nathaniel (descendants). Missouri (Cooper County). 1825-1980. *1139*
Raynes, Marybeth. Divorce. Mormons. Personal narratives. ca 1975-80. *524*
Reading. Delaware. DuPont family. Social Customs. Women. 1810-35. *957*
Realism. Davis, Rebecca Harding. Fiction. Industrial Revolution. Social Organization. Women. Working Class. 1861. *234*
Reconstruction. Blacks. Texas. 1865-70. *748*
—. Dubuclet, Antoine. Louisiana. Treasurers. 1868-78. *1138*
Reconstruction (economic, cultural forces). Blacks. Family life (perpetuation). Slavery (review article). 1850's-1970's. *323*
Recreation. British Columbia (Victoria). 1880-1914. *57*
—. Child-rearing. Children. Holsman, Virginia (reminiscences). Oregon (Hillsboro). 19c-1920's. *961*
—. Cities. Social Change. Working conditions. 1830-90. *520*
Reform. Divorce. Feminism. Marriage. Stanton, Elizabeth Cady. 1840-90. *120*
—. Domesticity. Feminism. Howe, Julia Ward. Motherhood. 1844-85. *656*
—. Marriage. Taxation. Women. 1969-81. *424*
Reform (antebellum). 1820-70. *313*
Reform school, girls'. Adolescence. Family, make-believe. 1973. *52*
Refugees. Vietnamese Americans. Virginia, northern. 1975-80. *658*
Regionalism. Birth Control. Childlessness. 1900. *306*
—. Familism, rural. Far West. Southeast. 1940's. *664*
Regions. Fertility. Slaves. 1820-60. *755*
Rego, Mary. Chippewa Indians. Cree Indians. Indians. Women. 20c. *828*
Religion. Abortion. Attitudes. Family size preferences. 1972. *525*

—. Attitudes. Child-rearing. Education. Family (review article). Sex. 18c. *228*
—. Attitudes. Cohabitation. Youth. 1974-80. *358*
—. Cheney Family Singers. Vermont. 1839-91. *955*
—. Child-rearing. Church attendance. Women. 1972-80. *414*
—. Divorce. Western States. 1972-76. *590*
—. Indentured servants. Pennsylvania. Women. 18c. *171*
—. Marriage, interfaith. 1973-75. *583*
—. New York. Noyes, John Humphrey. Oneida Community. Sex. 1848-80. *302*
—. Puritans. 1620-1800. *501*
—. Social control. 1982. *406*
Religiosity. California (Los Angeles). Catholic Church. Fertility. Mexican Americans. Women. 1973. *737*
Religious differences. Catholics. Family size preferences. Teenagers. 1971-74. *42*
Religious institutions. Ethnic groups. Government. Morality. 1960's-70's. *504*
Relocation. Acculturation. Bureau of Indian Affairs. California (San Francisco Bay area). Indians. Navajo Indians. Women. 1950-80. *207*
Remarriage. Age. Massachusetts (Newburyport). Men. Women. ca 1800-30. *657*
Reminiscences. Bavaria. Daily Life. Hartlieb, Louise Marie Katherina Boehner. Immigration. New York (Buffalo). 1825-1918. *1114*
Removals. Chandler, Cornelia C. Cherokee Indians. Daily Life. North Carolina. Personal narratives. 1867-1918. *231*
Reporters and Reporting. Davis, Richard Harding. War correspondents. ca 1890-1916. *933*
Republicanism. Books. Child-rearing. Education. Pennsylvania (Philadelphia). Protestantism. 1780-1835. *728*
Research. Archives, National. Census Bureau. Family history. Libraries, local. 1960's-70's. *242*
—. Bibliographies. Blacks. Genealogy. 1977. *160*
—. Bibliographies. Genealogy. Massachusetts. 17c-20c. *129*
—. Blacks. Documents. Genealogy, black. Public Records. 19c-20c. *229*
—. Blacks. Social Organization. 17c-1979. *138*
—. Child Welfare. Day care movement. Fiscal Policy. 1960's-70's. *385*
—. Children. 1960-79. *396*
—. Economic Conditions. Industrialization. Social History. 1950's-70's. *475*
—. Educators. Social Policy. 1960's-79. *94*
—. Genealogists. Historians. 1975. *175*
—. Genealogy. History Teaching. Methodology. 1976. *151*
—. Genealogy. Land records, federal. 19c-20c. *176*
—. Genealogy. Libraries. Massachusetts, western. 1978. *64*
—. Genealogy. Maine. 17c-19c. *102*
—. Genealogy. Migration, Internal. 1725-1850. *36*
—. Genealogy. New Hampshire. 20c. *73*
—. Genealogy. Social history. Statistics. 19c-1980. *299*
—. Geographic Mobility. Housing. Public policy. 1920's-82. *251*
—. History. Life cycles. Methodology. Sociology. 1950's-70's. *34*
—. History. Social Sciences. 20c. *340*
—. Marriage, interracial. 1940's-75. *582*
—. Mexican Americans. ca 1970-75. *713*
—. Photographs. 1978. *142*
—. Photography. Postcards. 19c-20c. *286*
—. Rhode Island. 17c-20c. *96*
—. Slavery. South. 1750-1925. *53*
—. Social change. 1960's-70's. *89*
—. *Social Indicators, 1976* (report). Statistics. 1973-76. *320*

S

Sexism. Blacks. Feminism, black. Men. Social Problems. 1970's. *754*
Sexual reform. Adolescence. Marriage. Purity. Social organization. 1830's-40's. *549*
Sexual relationships. Family patterns. Marriage (motivations). Power patterns. Romantic love. 1825-50. *177*
Sexuality. Lasch, Christopher. 1982. *591*
—. Slavery. Values. 1800-60. *604*
—. Social Theory. Sumner, William Graham. 1870's-1910. *68*
Seymour family. Genealogy. North Central States. Northeastern or North Atlantic States. 1760's-1860's. *1096*
Shafsky family. Business. California (Fort Bragg). Jews. Russia. 1889-1976. *1166*
Shakers. Foster, Lawrence. Kern, Louis J. Mormons. Oneida Community. Sex (review article). 19c. 1981. *707*
Sharples (family). Alberta, southern. Homesteading and Homesteaders. 1870's-1902. *820*
Shaw family. Genealogy. New England. 17c-19c. *1144*
Sheep raising. Business. Cattle Raising. Montana. Ranches. Sieben, Henry. 1864-1937. *1046*
Sheftall (family). American Revolution. Georgia (Savannah). Jews. 1730-1800. *1028*
Shepherd's Tent (church). Congregationalism. Connecticut (New London). Great Awakening. New Lights. Separatism. 1720-50. *515*
Sherwood Manor. Architecture. Land. Massachusetts (Talbot County). Tilghman, Lloyd. 1718-1823. *1048*
Shippee, Welcome Allen. Genealogy. Ledgers. Rhode Island (Glocester). 1834-70. 1970's. *1090*
Shippen family. Klein, Randolph Shipley (review article). Methodology. Pennsylvania. Social sciences. 1668-1776. 1975. *1053*
Shively, John M. Gold Rushes. Memoirs. Oregon. Pioneers. Postal Service. 1843-51. *1007*
Shope Mennonite Cemetery. Cemeteries. Mennonites. Pennsylvania (Dauphin County; Lower Swatara Township). 18c-1981. *1159*
Shuler family. California. Civil War. Daily life. Gold Rushes. Letters. Pennsylvania. 1849-64. *1051*
Shwayder family. Colorado (Denver). Immigration. Jews. 1865-1916. *833*
Sichel, Carolyn Meyberg (reminiscence). Assimilation. California (Los Angeles). Jews. 1902-31. *1102*
Sieben, Henry. Business. Cattle Raising. Montana. Ranches. Sheep raising. 1864-1937. *1046*
Sikhs. Acculturation. British Columbia (Vancouver). 1904-72. *613*
Sim, Francis (family). Frontier and Pioneer Life. Letters. Nebraska, southeastern. 1856-59. *1099*
Simms, Mary Ann Owen. Arkansas. Diaries. Frontier and Pioneer Life. 1855-61. *1147*
Sinclair, Eliza. British Columbia. Hawaii (Niihau). New Zealand. 1840-1980. *1018*
Singer, Israel Joshua *(Family Carnovsky).* Assimilation. Jews. Mental Illness. Novels. Race. 1943. *113*
Sinsheimer, Aaron Zachary (2d family). Buildings (iron front). California (San Luis Obispo). Jews. 1878-1956. *1118*
Sioux Indians. Clans. Indians. Social Organization. Villages. 19c-20c. *145*
—. Daily Life. Indians. Personal Narratives. Swan, Lucy. Women. 1900-71. *1059*
Skinner, John Stuart. *American Farmer* (newspaper). Physical Education and Training. Women. 1825-30. *372*
Slave Trade. Children. Franklin & Armfield (firm). Interstate commerce. Manifests. Virginia (Alexandria). 1828-36. *557*

Slavery. Alabama. Civil War. Social Change. Whites. 1850-70. *21*
—. Alabama (Yell County). Methodology. Oral History. 1852-60. *226*
—. Americas (North and South). Blacks. Historiography. ca 1550-1850. *256*
—. Bancroft, Frederic. Missouri (Boone County). Stampp, Kenneth. 1820-65. *205*
—. Birth Rate. Engerman, Stanley L. Fogel, Robert William. Methodology. 19c. *771*
—. Birth Rate. Plantations. South Carolina. ca 1721-1803. *701*
—. British West Indies. Demography. Family structure. South. 19c. *98*
—. Chesapeake Bay area. Ironworks. 1730's-1862. *481*
—. Clarke, Lewis G. (family history). 1833-82. *1136*
—. Family history. South. 1790-1872. *1093*
—. Family life. Marriage. 1800-60. *173*
—. Family (review article). Genovese, Eugene D. Gutman, Herbert G. 17c-20c. *167*
—. Fannie (slave). Norfleet (slave). Texas. 1862. *852*
—. Historiography. 18c-20c. *344*
—. Historiography. Leftism. *Radical History Review*(periodical). 17c-20c. 1970's. *106*
—. Interviews. South. Works Progress Administration. 1850's-60's. 1930's. *179*
—. Maryland. Social Organization. Virginia. 1650-1790. *172*
—. Research. South. 1750-1925. *53*
—. Rocks (plantation). South Carolina. 1786-1833. *616*
—. Sexuality. Values. 1800-60. *604*
—. Women. 1619-1800. *619*
—. Women. 17c-1865. *607*
Slavery (review article). Blacks. Family life (perpetuation). Reconstruction (economic, cultural forces). 1850's-1970's. *323*
Slaves. Children. Games. Plantations. Socialization. South. 1820-60. *786*
—. Fertility. Regions. 1820-60. *755*
—. Good Hope Plantation. South Carolina. 1835-56. *785*
—. Infants. Mortality. 1850-60. *676*
Slovak Americans. Agriculture. Colorado. Czech Americans. Migration, Internal. Mines. 1860-1920. *161*
—. British Americans. Rudinsky, Mary Louise (family). 16c-20c. *1085*
Small business. Indiana (Muncie). 1865-1980. *919*
Smith, Andrew Jackson (account). Civil War. Country Life. Mississippi (Pontotoc County). 1864-69. *155*
Smith, Jedediah Strong. Bacon, Julian Smith. California. Smith, Peter (family). 19c-20c. *1130*
Smith, John Guy. Colorado. Daily Life. 1878-1937. *1106*
Smith, Joseph. Letters. Mormons. Smith, Lucy Mack. 1829. *971*
Smith, Lucy Mack. Letters. Mormons. Smith, Joseph. 1829. *971*
Smith, Peter (family). Bacon, Julian Smith. California. Smith, Jedediah Strong. 19c-20c. *1130*
Snobbery. Elites. New England. ca 1605-20c. *126*
Social Change. 17c-20c. *76*
—. Agricultural Technology and Research. Fiji. Israel. Japan. 1689-1975. *618*
—. Alabama. Civil War. Slavery. Whites. 1850-70. *21*
—. Alcott, Bronson. Child-rearing practices. Transcendentalism. 1830-60. *794*
—. Armies. Family (structure). Women. 1950's-70's. *545*
—. Attitudes. 1970's. *180*

—. Biology. *Daedalus* (periodical). Feminism. Lasch, Christopher. 1975-77. *44*
—. Blacks. Christianity. Values. War. 1960's-70's. *191*
—. Blacks. Family life. 1974. *290*
—. Bleser, Carol. Hammond family (review article). Letters. South Carolina. 19c-1950's. *1155*
—. Busing. Child care centers. 1975. *402*
—. California (Los Angeles). Demography. Economic Conditions. Family (structure). Methodology. 1850-75. *181*
—. California (Los Angeles). Demography. Economic Conditions. Marxism. 1850-70. *182*
—. California (Los Angeles). Mexican Americans. Modernization. 1850-80. *413*
—. Canada. Chinese Canadians. Immigration. 1850's-1970's. *153*
—. Catholic Church. Educational system. French Canadians. Parent-youth conflict. Quebec. 1960-70. *473*
—. Cemeteries, rural. Tombstones. 1830's-40's. *288*
—. Cherokee Indians. Christianity. Indian-White Relations. Missions and Missionaries. Property. Women. 19c. *329*
—. Children. Education. 1946-76. *3*
—. Children. Fogarty, John E. Mentally Handicapped. Parents Council for Retarded Children. Rhode Island. Trudeau, Arthur. 1951-70. *350*
—. Cities. Recreation. Working conditions. 1830-90. *520*
—. Connecticut (Norwich). Women. 1750-1800. *174*
—. Conservatism. 1960-79. *26*
—. Daily Life. Great Britain. Household goods. Massachusetts. 1650-1775. *743*
—. Domestic roles. Massachusetts (Salem). Women. 1660-1770. *753*
—. Education. Industrialization. 1920's-70's. *278*
—. Egalitarianism. Women. 1960's-70's. *787*
—. Family cycle. Household structure. Massachusetts (Worcester). Urbanization. 1860-80. *59*
—. Family structure. Middle Classes. Parent-child relations. Women, role of. 1970's. *594*
—. Family studies. Ideology. Sex roles. 1945-79. *298*
—. Fertility. Lifestyles. 1970-79. *684*
—. Historiography. Modernization. ca 19c-20c. *134*
—. Indians. Indian-White Relations. 1937-78. *712*
—. Labor. Marriage. 20c. *720*
—. Labor. Social work. Wives. 1950's-80. *468*
—. Research. 1960's-70's. *89*
—. Suburbanization. 1890-1950. *499*
Social Classes. Abortion. Ideology. 1970's. *506*
—. Abortion. Values. 1973-78. *747*
—. Attitudes. Behavior. Education. Occupations. 1972-80. *411*
—. Blacks. Fathers. Socialization. 1960's-70's. *668*
—. Children. Life insurance. 1875-1980. *576*
—. Elites. Family dynasties. Meritocrats. 1960's-70's. *147*
—. Fertility. 1855-1915. *159*
—. Fertility. Protestant Churches. Theology. Whites. 1965. *195*
—. Happiness. Television. 1978-80. *559*
—. Income. Inflation. 1971-75. *345*
—. Indiana (Muncie). Inequality. Lifestyles. Lynd, Helen Merrell. Lynd, Robert S. Occupations. 1920-78. *392*
—. Katz, Michael B. (review article). Ontario (Hamilton). 1850-80. *7*
—. Material relationships. 1970's. *240*
—. Pennsylvania. Rural-Urban Studies. Wives. 1947-71. *449*
Social Conditions. Birth rate. Health. Minorities. 1867-1935. *404*

—. Economic Conditions. Emigration. Great Britain (Wiltshire). 1630-60. *260*
—. Economics. Ethnicity. Immigration. Italians. Quebec (Montreal). 1900-30. *239*
—. Employment. Mothers. 1970-80. *445*
—. Hayes, Rutherford B. 19c-20c. *920*
—. Immigrants. Maryland. Plantations. Women. 1632-1700. *611*
—. Invalidism. James, Henry (1811-82; and family). Neurasthenia. New England. 1811-1916. *902*
Social control. Appalachia. Kindergarten. 1970's. *378*
—. Behavior. Pregnancy. Sex, premarital. 1640-1971. *797*
—. Family structure. Immigrants. Polish Americans. Values. 20c. *724*
—. Religion. 1982. *406*
Social customs. Adams, Thomas Boylston. Codman family. Massachusetts (Lincoln). Personal Narratives. Upper Classes. 1890-1920. *798*
—. Amish. Weddings. 20c. *654*
—. Birth. Death and Dying. Marriage. Rites and Ceremonies. Tennessee, eastern. 20c. *693*
—. Blacks. Folklore. Mississippi (Homochitto River Valley). 1973. *8*
—. California (Los Angeles). Catholic Church. Marriage. Mission Santa Barbara. 1786-1848. *209*
—. Country Life. Women. 18c-1976. *643*
—. Creativity. Food Industry. Jews. Knishes. 1980. *652*
—. Delaware. DuPont family. Reading. Women. 1810-35. *957*
—. Friends, Society of. Pennsylvania. Schools. ca 1740-76. *196*
—. Indians. Lévi-Strauss, Claude. 17c-19c. *184*
—. New York (Utica). Polish Americans. Weddings. 1900-40's. *629*
Social History. Adelphi University. History Teaching. 1976. *97*
—. Burrough, James. Burwell, Lewis (letter). Virginia. 1734. *844*
—. Cities. Population change. 1750-1975. *133*
—. Economic Conditions. Industrialization. Research. 1950's-70's. *475*
—. Essex Institute. Massachusetts (Forge Village). Prescott, Olive Adams. Weaving. 1780-1860. *900*
—. Genealogy. Research. Statistics. 19c-1980. *299*
—. Genealogy. Social surveys. 1850-1980. *71*
—. Leisure. New York (Corning). Upper Classes. ca 1880-1913. *1107*
—. Manuscripts. New England. Pierce, John. 1800-50. *206*
—. Massachusetts (Woburn). Widowhood. Women. 1701-10. *682*
Social History (review article). Colonial experience. New England. 17c-18c. *119*
Social Indicators, 1976 (report). Research. Statistics. 1973-76. *320*
Social integration. Appalachia. Health professionals. 1950-77. *484*
—. Generation conflict, basis. Identity. Quebec (Quebec City). 1968. *75*
Social Mobility. Assimilation. Japanese Americans (Issei, Sansei). ca 1900-. *186*
—. Blacks. Georgia (Atlanta). 1870-80. *454*
—. College graduates. Women. 1961-68. *353*
—. Immigrants. Irish Americans. Pennsylvania (Scranton). Welsh Americans. 1880-90. *376*
—. Italian Canadians. Ontario (Toronto). 1935-60. *295*
—. Musical comedy. Sex roles. 20c. *49*
Social Organization. Acculturation. Italian Americans (review article). 20c. *227*

—. Adolescence. Marriage. Purity. Sexual reform. 1830's-40's. *549*
—. Amish, Old Order. Pennsylvania (Lancaster County). Sex roles. Women. 1981. *91*
—. Appalachia. 1880's-90's. *90*
—. Attitudes. Blacks. High Schools. Students. Tennessee (Rutherford County). 1970. *586*
—. Attitudes. Fisk, Elizabeth (family). Frontier and Pioneer Life. Montana (Helena). Women. 1867-1902. *1056*
—. Autobiography. Civil War. Daily life. Genealogy. Martin, Frances Martha Atkinson. Texas. 1857-75. 1979. *200*
—. Blacks. Hispanic Americans. Households. Income. Whites. 1976. *11*
—. Blacks. Research. 17c-1979. *138*
—. Byrd, William, II. Diaries. Virginia. 1700-20. *1161*
—. California. Chumash Indians. Indians. Marriage. Mission Santa Barbara. Yanunali, Pedro. 1787-1806. *1141*
—. Capitalism. Ethnic groups. 1970's. *513*
—. Childbirth. Death and Dying. Diaries. Diseases. Massachusetts (Westborough). Parkman, Ebenezer. 1724-82. *702*
—. Childlessness. Norms. 1960's-70's. *730*
—. Cities (decline). 1700-1977. *349*
—. Clans. Indians. Sioux Indians. Villages. 19c-20c. *145*
—. Country Life. Economic Conditions. Mexican Americans. Occupations. Washington (Yakima Valley). 1971. *433*
—. Davis, Rebecca Harding. Fiction. Industrial Revolution. Realism. Women. Working Class. 1861. *234*
—. Divorce. South. Supreme courts, state. Women. 1800-60. *394*
—. Family policy. Welfare state. 1960's-70's. *502*
—. Federal Policy. 1970's. *523*
—. Heterogeneity. Intermarriage. Metropolitan areas. 1970. *598*
—. Institutions. Public Welfare. Western Nations. 1c BC-19c. *477*
—. Maryland. Slavery. Virginia. 1650-1790. *172*
—. Occupational systems. 1970's. *538*
Social Organizations. "All in the Family" (program). Television. 1970's. *314*
—. Education. Marriage. Women. 1960-67. *333*
Social origins. Adolescence. Attitudes (formation). Fertility aspirations. Women. 1977. *621*
—. Education. Farms. Ownership. Wisconsin. 1970-79. *692*
Social pathologies. Motherhood, early. Role transition. 1970's. *588*
Social Policy. Blacks. Women. 1970-74. *149*
—. Educators. Research. 1960's-79. *94*
Social Problems. Blacks. Children, treatment of. Illinois. Moynihan Report (1965). 1965-74. *369*
—. Blacks. Feminism, black. Men. Sexism. 1970's. *754*
—. Blacks. Motherhood. 1977. *223*
—. Desertion. Jews. 1900-26. *100*
—. Gambling. Legalization. 1975. *417*
—. Wife beating. 1970's. *767*
Social Psychology. Attitudes. Sex roles (influences). Students. 1969. *640*
Social reform. Academic achievement. Teachers. Wellesley College. Women. 1880-1920. *721*
—. Blacks. Massachusetts (Boston). ca 1800-60. *144*
—. Children. Day care centers. Women's liberation movement. 1854-1973. *533*
—. Cities. Illinois (Chicago). Playgrounds. Progressivism. 1894-1917. *491*
—. Feminism. 1960-80. *450*
—. Feminism. Ontario. 1875-1900. *503*
Social Sciences. History. Research. 20c. *340*

—. Klein, Randolph Shipley (review article). Methodology. Pennsylvania. Shippen family. 1668-1776. 1975. *1053*
—. Methodology. Mexican Americans. 1970's. *331*
Social Security. Federal Policy. Taxation. 1934-79. *366*
Social services. Child abuse. 1921-80. *507*
Social status. Achievement. Ascription. 1970's. *511*
—. Achievement syndrome. Family interaction processes. Secondary Education. 1962-73. *703*
—. Assimilation. Fertility. Puerto Ricans. 1969-77. *620*
—. Assimilation. Geographic mobility. Immigrants. Mexican Americans. 1890-1977. *303*
—. Birth Control. Feminism, domestic. ca 1870's-1900. *750*
—. B'nai B'rith. Geographic Mobility. Jews. Occupations. Oregon (Portland). 1910-30. *305*
—. Broomell family. Business community. Christiana Machine Company. Pennsylvania (Christiana). 1880-1900. *1025*
—. Canada. French Canadians. Success, chances for. 1965-66. *117*
—. Census. Economic Conditions. Households, heads of. Texas, east. 1850-60. *192*
—. Child-rearing. Indians. Minipoka (concept). 19c-1979. *727*
—. Creoles. Louisiana (Cane River, Natchitoches). Race relations. 1767-20c. *1022*
—. Divorce. Economic Conditions. Higher education. Identity. Occupations. Women. 1971-77. *461*
—. Employment. Women. 1960-70. *528*
—. Farms. Literature. Sex roles. South. Women. 1800-60. *605*
—. New Jersey. Provincial Government. 1703-76. *237*
—. Poverty. 1960's-70's. *517*
Social status orientation. Income, family. Ozark Mountains. Youth. 1962-73. *514*
Social surveys. Genealogy. Social history. 1850-1980. *71*
—. Inflation. 1976. *391*
Social Surveys (methodology). Canada. Demography. Family size ideals. 1945-74. *601*
Social Theory. Poster, Mark (review article). Psychology. Sex roles. 1930's-60's. *250*
—. Sexuality. Sumner, William Graham. 1870's-1910. *68*
Social work. Labor. Social change. Wives. 1950's-80. *468*
Social workers. Child custody. Divorce. Law. Mental health. 1970's. *463*
Socialization. 1965. *628*
—. Blacks. Fathers. Social Classes. 1960's-70's. *668*
—. Blacks. Sex roles. 1975. *699*
—. Children. Games. Plantations. Slaves. South. 1820-60. *786*
—. Children. Massachusetts. Sewall, Samuel (family). 1670-1720. *1113*
—. Children. Sex roles. Technology. Toys. 1920-40. *726*
—. Higher education. Youth. 18c. *565*
—. Jews. 1970's. *781*
Socialization, political. Blacks. Children. Cities. Family structure. 1973. *397*
Society, alternative. Communes (review article). 1960's-70's. *219*
Society for the Preservation of New England Antiquities (Codman Family Manuscripts Collection). Archives. Codman Family. Massachusetts. 1715-1979. *963*
Society for the Prevention of Cruelty to Children. Child abuse. New York City. 1820's-80's. *552*
Sociology. Affectional function hypothesis. Ogburn, William F. 1920's-81. *233*

—. History. Life cycles. Methodology. Research. 1950's-70's. *34*

—. Marriage, second. North America. Women, single. 1974. *742*

Sod houses. Frontier and Pioneer Life. Great Plains. Women. 1855-1910. *587*

Somerville, Nellie Nugent. Federal government. Howorth, Lucy Somerville. Mississippi. New Deal. State Legislatures. 1923-57. *947*

Sons. Academic achievement. Fathers. IQ. Linkage hypothesis. Occupations. Personality. 1964. *485*

Sons, preadolescent. Rural families. School achievement. Values. 1974. *214*

Souder, Paul. Genealogy. Guam. Letters. 1710-1958. *1109*

South. Academies. Education. Planter class. Women. 1800-40. *400*

—. Aged. Blacks. Economic Structure. Whites. 1880-1900. *751*

—. British West Indies. Demography. Family structure. Slavery. 19c. *98*

—. Children. Games. Plantations. Slaves. Socialization. 1820-60. *786*

—. Divorce. Social organization. Supreme courts, state. Women. 1800-60. *394*

—. Family history. Slavery. 1790-1872. *1093*

—. Farms. Literature. Sex roles. Social Status. Women. 1800-60. *605*

—. Interviews. Slavery. Works Progress Administration. 1850's-60's. 1930's. *179*

—. Research. Slavery. 1750-1925. *53*

South Carolina. American Revolution (personal narratives). Pinckney, Eliza Lucas (letters). 1768-82. *1057*

—. Birth Rate. Plantations. Slavery. ca 1721-1803. *701*

—. Births. Gibson family records. Marriage. 1750-1800. *1132*

—. Bleser, Carol. Hammond family (review article). Letters. Social change. 19c-1950's. *1155*

—. Ethnicity. Irish Americans. Marriage. Migration. 1970-80. *662*

—. Good Hope Plantation. Slaves. 1835-56. *785*

—. Governors. Morton (Mourton), Joseph (parentage). 17c. *1137*

—. Rocks (plantation). Slavery. 1786-1833. *616*

—. Wigg family. 1705-1860. *999*

South Carolina (Charleston). Blacks, free. Women. 1850-60. *596*

—. Inheritance. Patriarchy. Plantations. 1800-60. *675*

South Dakota (Deadwood). Colman, Blanche. Colman, Nathan. Frontier and Pioneer Life. Jews. 1877-1977. *799*

Southeast. Familism, rural. Far West. Regionalism. 1940's. *664*

Southwest. Armies. Military Camps and Forts. 19c. *148*

—. Education. Pioneers. 19c. *512*

—. Fertility. Mexican Americans. 1970. *696*

—. Games. Hispanic Americans. Indians. Toys. 16c-20c. *762*

Spas. Boswell, Ben D. Boswell, Emma. Boswell Springs (resort). Civil War. Military. Oregon. 1860-1908. *1033*

Speeches and Addresses. Divorce. Louisiana. Mahon, Samuel S. State Legislatures. 1806. *419*

Sperry-Steele, Fannie. Montana (Lincoln). Rodeos. 1887-1965. *1119*

Spinsterhood. Massachusetts. Sedgwick, Catharine Maria. Women. 1811-54. *678*

Spock, Benjamin (*Baby and Child Care*). Behavior. Child-rearing. Labor Department (Children's Bureau). Mothers. West, Mary Mills (*Infant Care*). 1914-76. *782*

Sprague, Edward (and family). Great Britain (Dorset). Massachusetts (Charlestown). Settlement. 16c-17c. *888*

Sprague family. Great Britain (Dorchester; Fordington St. George, Puddletown). Massachusetts (Charlestown). 1565-1692. 1923. 1978. *982*

Sprunger, David. Courtship. Diaries. Indiana. Mennonites. 1893-95. *1111*

Stampp, Kenneth. Bancroft, Frederic. Missouri (Boone County). Slavery. 1820-65. *205*

Standard of living. Child labor. French Canadians. Massachusetts (Lowell). Migration. 1870's. *82*

—. Employment. Women. 1950-73. *564*

—. Pennsylvania (Philadelphia). Working class. 1750-1800. *547*

Standke family. Farmers. Germany. Minnesota. 1873-1978. *1027*

Stanton, Elizabeth Cady. Attitudes. Domesticity. Lincoln, Mary Todd. Stowe, Harriet Beecher. 1830-80. *1104*

—. Divorce. Feminism. Marriage. Reform. 1840-90. *120*

Starkey, J. B., Sr. (family). Agriculture. Florida (Pasco, Pinellas counties). Personal narratives. Umberton Ranch. 1980. *1165*

Starr family. Apple industry. Calkin(s) family. Halliburton, Robert Grant. Inglis, Charles. Nova Scotia. 19c. *943*

State Department (Foreign Service). Occupational mobility. Wives. 1974. *351*

State Government. Aid to Families with Dependent Children. Public Welfare. 1973. *432*

State Historical Society of Iowa, Irish-Preston Papers. Iowa. Irish family. 1832-1972. *922*

State Legislatures. Divorce. Louisiana. Mahon, Samuel S. Speeches and Addresses. 1806. *419*

—. Federal government. Howorth, Lucy Somerville. Mississippi. New Deal. Somerville, Nellie Nugent. 1923-57. *947*

State Politics. Daley, Richard (and family). Democratic Party. Illinois. Ireland (County Cork; Old Parish, Ring). Irish Americans. 19c-1976. *1061*

Statism. ca 1945-72. *255*

Statistics. Genealogy. Research. Social history. 19c-1980. *299*

—. Research. *Social Indicators, 1976* (report). 1973-76. *320*

Steamboat. California. Cunningham, Jane Elizabeth. Terschuren, Gerhard Frederick. 1860-1947. *1094*

Steevens family. Bradford, William (descendants). Connecticut (Killingworth). 1752-1800. *823*

Stegner, Wallace. Cheever, John. Didion, Joan. Fiction. Irving, John. Isolation. 1970's. *651*

Stein, Gertrude. California. Ehrman, Theresa. France (Paris). Letters. Music. 1901-67. *1121*

Stephenson family. Alberta. English Canadians. Homesteading and Homesteaders. Personal Narratives. Rowell, Gladys M. 1904-06. *1084*

Stereotypes. Aged. Culture, youth-oriented. Mass media. 1960's-70's. *665*

—. Attitudes. Children. Welfare, recipients of. 1970's. *486*

—. Cookery. Men. Sex roles. 20c. *580*

—. English Canadians. French Canadians. Ontario (Alfred, Caledonia). 1800-81. *105*

—. Family models. Mexican Americans. 1968-74. *300*

—. Immigrants. Labor. Women (review article). 1850-1950. *307*

Sterilization. Family planning services. Poor. 1970's. *534*

Stevens family. Architecture. Landscaping. New Jersey (Hoboken). 1820-60. *909*

Stewart family. Farms. Folklore. Kentucky (Butler, Warren Counties). Language. Toponymy. 1850-1978. *1037*

Stirpicultural experiment. Genetics. New York. Noyes, John Humphrey. Oneida Community. 1848-86. *791*

Stockbridge, John (and descendants). Massachusetts. New Hampshire. 17c-18c. *978*
—. New England. 17c-18c. *980*
—. New England. 18c. *979*

Stone, Lawrence. Donzelot, Jacques. Family (review article). France. Great Britain. Lasch, Christopher. ca 1500-1970. *269*
—. Historiography. Lasch, Christopher. Middle Classes. 1500-1980. *304*

Stowe, Harriet Beecher. Attitudes. Domesticity. Lincoln, Mary Todd. Stanton, Elizabeth Cady. 1830-80. *1104*

Students. Attitudes. Blacks. High Schools. Social Organization. Tennessee (Rutherford County). 1970. *586*
—. Attitudes. Family organization. Pennsylvania (Philadelphia). 1970's. *648*
—. Attitudes. Sex roles (influences). Social Psychology. 1969. *640*
—. Biography. Depressions. Family history. Interviews. Louisiana State University. Works Progress Administration. 1930's. 1978. *66*
—. High Schools. Indiana (Muncie). Lynd, Helen Merrell. Lynd, Robert S. 1924-77. *589*
—. Interpersonal contact. Race Relations. Taiwan. 1933-73. *188*

Suburbanization. Fertility. Pennsylvania (Philadelphia). Public schools. 1880-1920. *498*
—. Social Change. 1890-1950. *499*

Suburbs. Domesticity. Pennsylvania (Philadelphia). Women. 19c. *208*
—. Family (two-earner). Housing. Income. Labor. Land use. Women. 1976. *487*

Success, chances for. Canada. French Canadians. Social Status. 1965-66. *117*

Suffrage. Degler, Carl N. DuBois, Ellen Carol. Women's Liberation Movement (review article). 19c-20c. 1980. *403*

Suicide. Adams, Henry Brooks. Adams, Marian Hooper. Marriage. Monuments. Saint-Gaudens, Augustus. 1872-85. *912*
—. Canada. Interpersonal Relations. Kinship. Marriage. 1951-71. *625*

Sumner, William Graham. Sexuality. Social Theory. 1870's-1910. *68*

Superstitions. Childbirth. Folklore. Pregnancy. Tennessee (Chester County). 18c-1974. *666*

Supreme courts, state. Divorce. Social organization. South. Women. 1800-60. *394*

Surette family. Nova Scotia. 18c-1979. *835*

Surnames. Great Britain. Indiana. Ireland. 18c-1981. *245*
—. Immigration. Mennonites. North America. Swiss Brethren. 1680-1880. *263*

Swan, Lucy. Daily Life. Indians. Personal Narratives. Sioux Indians. Women. 1900-71. *1059*

Sweden. American Revolution. Congress. Hanson, George A. Hanson, John. Maryland. 18c. 1876. *855*
—. Genealogy. Goranson, Greta K. (personal account). Immigration. 1832-1973. *929*
—. Immigration. Minnesota. Persson, Johan. Settlement. 1874-75. *976*

Swedish Americans. Country Life. Ethnicity. Immigrants. Marriage. Minnesota (Kandiyohi County). 1870-1905. *729*
—. Country Life. Land transfers. Minnesota, east-central. 1885-1915. *20*
—. Emigration. Finnish Americans. North America. 1865-95. *4*

Swiss Americans. Clergy. Lehman, Hans (and family). Mennonites. Pennsylvania (Lancaster County; Rapho Township). ca 1727-1909. *995*

Swiss Brethren. Immigration. Mennonites. North America. Surnames. 1680-1880. *263*

Swiss Colonization Society. Genealogy. Gloor family. Iowa (Tell City). Ohio (Cincinnati). 1850's-1970's. *925*

Switzerland. Denlinger family. Genealogy. Mennonites. Pennsylvania. 1594-1803. *886*
—. Farms. Oberholtzer family. Pennsylvania (Terre Hill). 1720's-1850's. *1045*

T

Taiwan. Interpersonal contact. Race Relations. Students. 1933-73. *188*

Tattrie, George (family). Nova Scotia. 1785-1977. *936*

Taxation. Federal Policy. Social Security. 1934-79. *366*
—. Marriage. Reform. Women. 1969-81. *424*

Teachers. Academic achievement. Blacks. Children. Human Relations. Parents. 1970's. *612*
—. Academic achievement. Social reform. Wellesley College. Women. 1880-1920. *721*
—. Baptists. Burns, Bertha Porter. Burns, Marion Van. Clergy. Louisiana (Shiloh). 1884-1975. *1001*
—. California (San Francisco). French language. Godchaux family. Music. 1880's-1920's. *811*
—. Childhood, fear of. Elementary Education. Parents. 19c. *427*

Teaching. Country Life. Drawing. Lyndes, Stanley Horace. Vermont. 1918-75. *9*

Teaching Aids and Devices. Family history. History Teaching. Painting. Photographs. 1980. *185*
—. Family history. History Teaching. Questionnaires. 1970's. *40*

Technology. Children. Sex roles. Socialization. Toys. 1920-40. *726*
—. Economic Conditions. 20c. *275*

Teenagers. Catholics. Family size preferences. Religious differences. 1971-74. *42*

Television. "All in the Family" (program). Social Organizations. 1970's. *314*
—. Children. 1982. *387*
—. Happiness. Social Classes. 1978-80. *559*

Tenement housing. Family life. Irish Americans. Massachusetts (Holyoke). 1860-1910. *423*

Tennessee. Bristol Public Library. Genealogy. Georgia. History. Information file. Virginia. 1970's. *20*
—. Cherokee Indians. Daily Life. Indians. Wolf, Lucyann Davis (family). 1900-35. *1108*
—. Cities. Divorce. Marriage. Mortality. Rural Settlements. 1970. *326*

Tennessee (Chester County). Childbirth. Folklore. Pregnancy. Superstitions. 18c-1974. *666*

Tennessee, eastern. Birth. Death and Dying. Marriage. Rites and Ceremonies. Social Customs. 20c. *693*

Tennessee (Grand Junction). Ames, Hobart C. Ames Plantation. Moorman, Micajah Clark. Plantations. Tennessee, University of, College of Agriculture. 1820-1979. *409*

Tennessee (Memphis). Black Capitalism. Church, Robert Reed, Sr. Wealth. Wills. 1912. *1021*
—. Davis, James Dick. Genealogy. Harbormaster. History (societies). Old Folks of Shelby County. 1810-80. *822*

Tennessee (Rutherford County). Attitudes. Blacks. High Schools. Social Organization. Students. 1970. *586*

US Military Academy. Barry, John Waller. Letters. 1826-30. *866*
USSR. Alberta (Calgary). Immigration. Jews. 1974. *998*
—. Daily Life (conference). Diaries. Great Britain (London). Sanderson, Mr. 1937. *875*
—. Sex. Women. 1930's-70's. *143*
Utah. Antipolygamy campaign. Mormons. Woodruff, Wilford (letter). 1885. *663*
—. Archives. Genealogy. Mormons. 17c-20c. *267*
—. Attitudes. Catholic Church. Mormons. Protestant Churches. 1974. *19*
—. Frontier and Pioneer Life. Mormons. Polygamy. Richards, Franklin D. (family). Women. 1852-90. *646*
—. Mormons. Polygamy. 19c. *688*
Utah (Kanab). Mormons. 1874-80. *706*
Utah (Provo). Brigham Young University Library. Genealogy. Immigration studies. Mormons. 1830-1978. *215*
Utah (Salt Lake City). Cannon, Martha Hughes. Great Britain. Letters. Mormons. Polygamy. Women. 1885-96. *1000*
—. Illinois (Nauvoo). Migration, Internal. Mormons. Young, Brigham (and family). 1841-48. *970*
—. Juvenile Delinquency. Mormons. 1850-81. *31*

V

Vallandigham family. Civil War. Copperheads. Delaware (Newark). 1861-69. *1010*
Values. Abolition movement. Gay, Sydney Howard. 1830's-40's. *926*
—. Abortion. Social Classes. 1973-78. *747*
—. Age. Youth. 1970's. *271*
—. Agriculture. Capital. Commerce. Frontier and Pioneer Life. 1607-1758. *337*
—. Agriculture. Capital. Frontier and Pioneer Life. 1607-1830. *139*
—. Baptists. 17c-1970's. *768*
—. Blacks. Child-rearing. Indians. Mexican-Americans. 1979. *573*
—. Blacks. Christianity. Social change. War. 1960's-70's. *191*
—. Blacks. Fertility. 1880-1910. *694*
—. Chesapeake Bay area. Children. Maryland. Parents. Virginia. 18c. *749*
—. Communications Behavior. Generations. James, William (d. 1832; and family). 1811-1910. *903*
—. Depressions. Labor. Middle Classes. Women. 1930's. *377*
—. Economic Conditions. Population. 1920's-50's. *58*
—. Family structure. Immigrants. Polish Americans. Social control. 20c. *724*
—. Land. Massachusetts (Barnstable County). Peasants. 1620's-1720's. *317*
—. Materialism. Parental control. 1965-75. *784*
—. Rural families. School achievement. Sons, preadolescent. 1974. *214*
—. Sexuality. Slavery. 1800-60. *604*
VanDuzee family (papers). Iowa. Minnesota. Westward Movement. Wyoming, University of. 1808-1932. *877*
VanRensselaer family. Dutch Americans. English Americans. Land. New York (Albany, Beverwyck). Rural-Urban Studies. 1620-1750. *496*
Vedder, Richard. Gallaway, Lowell. Great Britain. Immigrants. Ireland. Settlement. 1897-98. *80*
Verin, Philip (sons). Massachusetts (Salem). 1635-90. *1128*
Vermont. Allen Family. Burial plots. Epitaphs. 1770-1834. *857*
—. Cheney Family. Singers. Religion. 1839-91. *955*

—. Country Life. Drawing. Lyndes, Stanley Horace. Teaching. 1918-75. *9*
—. Genealogy. Migration, Internal. 1760-1979. *130*
Vermont (Bakersfield). Brigham (family). Letters, family. Massachusetts (Marlborough). Migrants. 1800-26. *194*
Vermont (Burlington). Fletcher, Thaddeus. Philanthropy. 1871-85. *854*
Vietnam War. Behavior. Missing in action. Prisoners of war. 1965-80. *670*
Vietnamese Americans. Refugees. Virginia, northern. 1975-80. *658*
Villages. Clans. Indians. Sioux Indians. Social Organization. 19c-20c. *145*
Violence. 1967-82. *193*
—. 1973. *291*
—. Behavior. Fantasy. Kennedy family. Risk-taking. ca 1940-79. *1152*
—. Feuds. Kentucky. Law. West Virginia. 1820-1903. *170*
—. Marriage. 1960-80. *759*
—. Women. 1966-80. *614*
Violence, political. Fertility. France. Great Britain. Population. 1700-1900. *201*
Virgin Islands (St. John). Blacks. Women. 1717-1975. *221*
Virginia. Argall, Samuel (ancestors). 1560-1620. *800*
—. Blair, James. Divorce. Documents. Jefferson, Thomas. Legislation. 1770-73. *416*
—. Bristol Public Library. Genealogy. Georgia. History. Information file. Tennessee. 1970's. *20*
—. Burrough, James. Burwell, Lewis (letter). Social History. 1734. *844*
—. Byrd, William, I. Byrd, William, II. Byrd, William, III. Letters. Tinling, Marion (review article). 1684-1776. *887*
—. Byrd, William, II. Diaries. Social Organization. 1700-20. *1161*
—. Chesapeake Bay area. Children. Maryland. Parents. Values. 18c. *749*
—. Custis, Martha Dandridge. Washington, George. Weddings. 1759. *1040*
—. Elites. Emotion. 1690-1775. *700*
—. Hemings family. Jefferson, Thomas. Monticello. 1730's-1830's. *826*
—. Hemings, Sally. Jefferson, Thomas (and descendants). Miscegenation. ca 1780-1976. *839*
—. Legal status. New York. Women. 18c. *446*
—. Marriage partners, selection. Parents. 17c-18c. *745*
—. Maryland. Slavery. Social Organization. 1650-1790. *172*
—. Mennonites. Rhodes families. 1770's-1900. *1101*
—. Townley (family). Warner (family). ca 1500-1900. *1016*
Virginia (Alexandria). Children. Franklin & Armfield (firm). Interstate commerce. Manifests. Slave Trade. 1828-36. *557*
Virginia (Charles Parish). Chesapeake Bay area. Mortality. 17c-18c. *280*
Virginia (Isle of Wight County). Land Tenure. Money. Quitrents. Tobacco. 1704-14. *220*
Virginia (Louisa County). Blacks. Household composition. Rural Settlements. 1880. *272*
Virginia (Lynchburg). Owen, Robert (family). Point of Honor (home). 1830-1978. *1097*
Virginia (Mannikintown). Baptisms. Birth. Blacks. Documents. Vital Statistics. 1721. *292*
Virginia (Middlesex County). Chesapeake Bay area. Death and Dying. Kinship. Parents. 1650-1710. *735*
Virginia, northern. Refugees. Vietnamese Americans. 1975-80. *658*
Virginia (Richmond). Artists (miniaturists). Peticolas family. Portraits. 1800-50. *1103*
Virginia (Spotsylvania County). Alrich family. Civil War. 1830-1979. *989*

Virginia (Williamsburg). *Blair* v. *Blair* (Virginia, 1773). Courts. Jefferson, Thomas. 1771-73. *415*
Virginia (York County). Ironmonger, Elizabeth Hogg (reminiscences). Kitchens. 1890's. *672*
Vital Statistics. Baptisms. Birth. Blacks. Documents. Virginia (Mannikintown). 1721. *292*
—. Births. Blacks. Connecticut (Bridgeport). 1855-85. *45*
—. Massachusetts (Sandwich). Migration, Internal. Settlement. 1650-1805. *60*
Vocational guidance. Education. National Institute of Education. Poor. Western States. 1970's. *546*
Vouchers. California (Alum Rock). Education. Parents. Public Schools. 1960's-70's. *401*

W

Wadleigh, Joseph (and descendants). Georgia. New Hampshire. 1711-1920. *915*
Wages. Day Nurseries (effect). Employment. Women. 1971-72. *336*
—. Investment. Women. 1967. *339*
Wagner, William (family). Discrimination. Florida (Miami area). Mulattos. Pioneers. 1850-1901. *802*
Wagon trains. Frontier and Pioneer Life. Men. Overland Journeys to the Pacific. Women. 1840's-50's. *639*
Wales (Hay). Genealogy. Howells family. 18c-19c. *899*
Walker, Mary Richardson. Diaries. Frontier and Pioneer Life. Missions and Missionaries. Oregon (Forest Grove). Tshimakain Indian Mission. Washington. 1833-97. *962*
Walton, Jacob (identity). Genealogy. Nova Scotia (Cornwallis). ca 1811-1914. *897*
Wampanoag Indians. Genealogy. Indians. Massasoit. Plymouth Plantation. 1620-1931. *1041*
War. Blacks. Christianity. Social change. Values. 1960's-70's. *191*
War correspondents. Davis, Richard Harding. Reporters and Reporting. ca 1890-1916. *933*
War of 1812. American Revolution. Brennan (and similar surnames). Military Service. 1775-83. 1812-14. *836*
Ward, Christopher L. (autobiography, family). Delaware (Wilmington). 1850-1900. *1071*
Warner (family). Townley (family). Virginia. ca 1500-1900. *1016*
Warren, Edward (family). Blacks. Iowa (Marshall County). 1864-91. *972*
Washington. Diaries. Frontier and Pioneer Life. Missions and Missionaries. Oregon (Forest Grove). Tshimakain Indian Mission. Walker, Mary Richardson. 1833-97. *962*
Washington, George. Custis, Martha Dandridge. Virginia. Weddings. 1759. *1040*
Washington (Yakima Valley). Country Life. Economic Conditions. Mexican Americans. Occupations. Social Organization. 1971. *433*
Waugh, Jesse (reminiscence). Daily Life. West Virginia. 1830-1900. *993*
Wealth. Black Capitalism. Church, Robert Reed, Sr. Tennessee (Memphis). Wills. 1912. *1021*
—. Children. Connecticut. Inheritance. Probate. 1930-46. *494*
Weatherhead family. Genealogy. Nova Scotia (Hants County). ca 1820-1946. *930*
Weaving. Essex Institute. Massachusetts (Forge Village). Prescott, Olive Adams. Social history. 1780-1860. *900*
Webb, Bernice Larson (reminiscences). Country Life. Kansas (Decatur County). 1930's. *319*
Weddings. Amish. Social Customs. 20c. *654*
—. Custis, Martha Dandridge. Virginia. Washington, George. 1759. *1040*

—. New York (Utica). Polish Americans. Social Customs. 1900-40's. *629*
Welfare, recipients of. Attitudes. Children. Stereotypes. 1970's. *486*
Welfare state. Family policy. Social organization. 1960's-70's. *502*
Wellesley College. Academic achievement. Social reform. Teachers. Women. 1880-1920. *721*
—. Bryn Mawr College. Feminism. Palmer, Alice Freeman. Sex roles, traditional. Thomas, Carey. 1875-1918. *569*
—. College graduates. Human Relations. Women. 1880-1910. *348*
Welsh Americans. Immigrants. Irish Americans. Pennsylvania (Scranton). Social mobility. 1880-90. *376*
Wertz, Dorothy C. Bogdan, Janet. Childbirth (review article). Donegan, Jane. Litoff, Judy Barrett. Scholten, Catherine. Wertz, Richard W. 17c-1980. *633*
Wertz, Richard W. Bogdan, Janet. Childbirth (review article). Donegan, Jane. Litoff, Judy Barrett. Scholten, Catherine. Wertz, Dorothy C. 17c-1980. *633*
West, Mary Mills *(Infant Care)*. Behavior. Child-rearing. Labor Department (Children's Bureau). Mothers. Spock, Benjamin *(Baby and Child Care)*. 1914-76. *782*
West Virginia. Daily Life. Waugh, Jesse (reminiscence). 1830-1900. *993*
—. Feuds. Kentucky. Law. Violence. 1820-1903. *170*
West Virginia (Parkersburg). Jackson, John Jay, Jr. (and family). Law. Political Leadership. 1715-1847. *814*
Western Nations. Institutions. Public Welfare. Social Organization. 1c BC-19c. *477*
Western Reserve. Congregationalism. Connecticut. Frontier and Pioneer Life. Ohio. Wright Elizur (and family). Yale University. 1762-1870. *911*
Western states. Armies. Frontier and Pioneer Life. Wives. 19c. *217*
—. Charbonneau family. Lewis and Clark expedition. 1759-1866. *804*
—. Divorce. Religion. 1972-76. *590*
—. Education. National Institute of Education. Poor. Vocational guidance. 1970's. *546*
Westward Movement. Arizona, southwestern. Indians (captivities). Oatman, Roys (and family). Yavapai Indians. 1851-1903. *630*
—. Iowa. Minnesota. VanDuzee family (papers). Wyoming, University of. 1808-1932. *877*
—. Myres, Sandra L. Trans-Mississippi West. Women (review article). 1800-1915. *150*
—. Overland Trail. Women. Work roles. 1842-67. *93*
White House Conference on Families. Fleming, Patsy. 1960's-80. *6*
Whites. Aged. Blacks. Economic Structure. South. 1880-1900. *751*
—. Alabama. Civil War. Slavery. Social Change. 1850-70. *21*
—. Blacks. Dating. Mexican Americans. Race Relations. 1978-79. *691*
—. Blacks. Employment. Family (one-parent). Women. 1970's. *471*
—. Blacks. Equality. Marriage. Sex roles. 1976. *362*
—. Blacks. Hispanic Americans. Households. Income. Social Organization. 1976. *11*
—. Blacks. Income. Moynihan, Daniel P. ("The Negro Family"). Women. 1965-77. *380*
—. Fertility. 1886-99. *769*
—. Fertility. Protestant Churches. Social Classes. Theology. 1965. *195*
—. Law. Liberty. North Carolina. Women. 1700-76. *780*

—. Cannon, Martha Hughes. Great Britain. Letters. Mormons. Polygamy. Utah (Salt Lake City). 1885-96. *1000*

—. Capitalism. Galbraith, John Kenneth. Housework. Oakley, Ann. Sex roles. 1950-70's. *436*

—. Capitalism. Lasch, Christopher (review article). 1900-75. *642*

—. Carter, Jimmy (administration). Cities. Federal Policy. 1977-80. *429*

—. Cherokee Indians. Christianity. Indian-White Relations. Missions and Missionaries. Property. Social Change. 19c. *329*

—. Cheyenne Indians. Comenha (woman). Daily Life. Indians. 1860-1900. *832*

—. Child care. Divorce. Economic problems. Family, single-parent. 1970's. *383*

—. Child care. Employment. 1977. *521*

—. Childlessness. Marriage. 1960-77. *412*

—. Childlessness (voluntary). 1973. *775*

—. Child-rearing. Church attendance. Religion. 1972-80. *414*

—. Child-rearing. Colorado. Frontier and Pioneer Life. Home Economics. Oral history. 1895-1920. *585*

—. Child-rearing. Handbooks. Sex roles. 1913-76. *783*

—. Children. Day care. Employment. 1890-1977. *500*

—. Children. Health. Working hours. 1972. *541*

—. Chippewa Indians. Cree Indians. Indians. Rego, Mary. 20c. *828*

—. Cigar industry. Florida (Tampa). Italian Americans. 1890-1930. *212*

—. Cities. Federal Policy. Geographic space. Households. Labor. 1977-80. *198*

—. College graduates. Human Relations. Wellesley College. 1880-1910. *348*

—. College graduates. Social mobility. 1961-68. *353*

—. Colorado, northeastern. Frontier and Pioneer Life. Methodist Episcopal Church (North, South). Propst, Missouri Powell. 1874-91. *1064*

—. Connecticut (Norwich). Social Change. 1750-1800. *174*

—. Cotton industry. Quebec. 1910-50. *382*

—. Country Life. Diaries. Farmers. Gillespie, Emily Hawley. Iowa. 1858-88. *1006*

—. Country Life. Social Customs. 18c-1976. *643*

—. Courts. Massachusetts (Salem). Sex roles. 1636-83. *458*

—. Cuban Americans. Employment. Sex roles. 1960's-70's. *426*

—. Daily Life. Diaries. Drinker, Elizabeth Sandwith. Pennsylvania (Philadelphia). 1758-1807. *872*

—. Daily Life. Indians. Personal Narratives. Sioux Indians. Swan, Lucy. 1900-71. *1059*

—. Davis, Rebecca Harding. Fiction. Industrial Revolution. Realism. Social Organization. Working Class. 1861. *234*

—. Day Nurseries (effect). Employment. Wages. 1971-72. *336*

—. Degler, Carl N. (review article). ca 1750-1980. *41*

—. Delaware. DuPont family. Reading. Social Customs. 1810-35. *957*

—. Depressions. Labor. Middle Classes. Values. 1930's. *377*

—. Divorce. Economic Conditions. 1970-81. *571*

—. Divorce. Economic Conditions. Higher education. Identity. Occupations. Social Status. 1971-77. *461*

—. Divorce. Social organization. South. Supreme courts, state. 1800-60. *394*

—. Domestic roles. Massachusetts (Salem). Social Change. 1660-1770. *753*

—. Domesticity. Iowa. Photographs. ca 1890-1910. *592*

—. Domesticity. Pennsylvania (Philadelphia). Suburbs. 19c. *208*

—. Education. Employment. Ethnicity. Mexican Americans. 1970's. *577*

—. Education. Fertility. Generations. Mexican Americans. 1976. *23*

—. Education. Larson, Agnes. Larson, Henrietta. Larson, Nora. Minnesota. 1883-1972. *968*

—. Education. Marriage. Social Organizations. 1960-67. *333*

—. Egalitarianism. Social Change. 1960's-70's. *787*

—. Employment. Fertility. 1970-75. *474*

—. Employment. Marriage. Sex roles. 1890-1978. *460*

—. Employment. Men. 1970-82. *466*

—. Employment. Social Status. 1960-70. *528*

—. Employment. Standard of living. 1950-73. *564*

—. Employment, part-time. Marriage. 1940-70. *482*

—. Ethnic Groups. Pennsylvania (Philadelphia). Working Class. 1910-30. *476*

—. Ethnography. Indians. Navajo Indians. Tradition. 1850-1980. *101*

—. Europe. Income. Occupations. 1968-75. *522*

—. Evangelicalism. New York (Utica). Revivals. 1800-40. *258*

—. Family background. Occupational aspirations. Roles. 1973. *685*

—. Family, death of the. 1973. *39*

—. Family heads. Labor force. 1960-75. *492*

—. Family history. Lasch, Christopher (review article). Modernization theory. ca 1400-1976. *136*

—. Family (two-earner). Housing. Income. Labor. Land use. Suburbs. 1976. *487*

—. Family (two-earner). Housing. Income. Prices. 1970's. *529*

—. Farms. Literature. Sex roles. Social Status. South. 1800-60. *605*

—. Fertility. 1930's-70's. *610*

—. France (Roubaix). New Hampshire (Manchester). ca 1900. *135*

—. Frontier and Pioneer Life. Great Plains. Sod houses. 1855-1910. *587*

—. Frontier and Pioneer Life. Men. Overland Journeys to the Pacific. Wagon trains. 1840's-50's. *639*

—. Frontier and Pioneer Life. Mormons. Polygamy. Richards, Franklin D. (family). Utah. 1852-90. *646*

—. Georgia. Land grants. 1755-75. *556*

—. History Teaching. New Mexico State University. Oral history. 1976. *777*

—. Home (concept). Metaphor. Popular Culture. 1980. *711*

—. Immigrants. Japanese Americans. Marriage. Picture brides. 1900-24. *467*

—. Immigrants. Maryland. Plantations. Social Conditions. 1632-1700. *611*

—. Income. Nurses and Nursing. 1953-70. *602*

—. Indentured servants. Pennsylvania. Religion. 18c. *171*

—. Investment. Wages. 1967. *339*

—. Labor force participation. Residential mobility. 1970's. *483*

—. Labor market. Poverty. Sex discrimination. ca 1950-70's. *542*

—. Labor Unions and Organizations. Massachusetts (Lowell). Textile Industry. 1830-60. *420*

—. Law. Liberty. North Carolina. Whites. 1700-76. *780*

—. Legal status. New York. Virginia. 18c. *446*

—. Life cycles. 1900-70. *285*

—. Louisiana (Bernice). Mabry, Catherine Cook. 1885-1913. *1002*

—. Marriage. Reform. Taxation. 1969-81. *424*

Y

Z

Zeckendorf, William. Arizona. Entrepreneurs. Jews. Zeckendorf, Aaron. Zeckendorf, Louis. 1853-1906. *906*

Zimmerman, Carle C. Collectivism. Family (review article). Individualism. 1945-70's. *324*

Author Index

A

Abbott, Walter F. 345
Abu-Laban, Sharon McIrvin 1
Adams, John 2
Adams, Thomas Boylston 798
Adamski, Władysław 3
Adler, Thomas A. 580
Aguirre, B. E. 581
Akerman, Sune 4
Albin, Mel 903 1036
Aldridge, Delores P. 582
Alexander, Thomas G. 688
Alger, Hugh Wesley 5
Allen, Walter R. 346
Alschuler, Al 799
Alsop, James D. 800
Alston, Jon P. 583
Alter, Jonathan 6
Ames, Marilyn G. 801
Ammerman, David L. 735 777
Ammidown, Margot 802
Anderson, Harry H. 803
Anderson, Irving W. 804
Anderson, James William 805 806
Anderson, Kristine L. 347
Anderson, Michael 7
Anderson, Robert C. 807
Anderson, Solena 8
Andrews, Dale K. 9
Andrews, Peter 10
Angel, Ronald 11
Antler, Joyce 348 584
Appleby, Joyce O. 12
Aquino, Salvatore A. 13
Arguimbau, Ellen 808 809
Ariés, Philippe 349
Armitage, Susan 585
Armour, David A. 810
Armstrong, Frederick H. 14
Armstrong, Thomas F. 15
Arnstein, Flora J. 811
Aseltine, Gwendolyn Pamenter 586
Ashkenazy, Elinor 812
Ashkenazy, Irvin 812
Atkin, Charles K. 387
Auman, Dorothy Cole 813
Austin, Ellen 587
Austin, John D. 1096
Auwarter, Ruth 16
Avery, Valeen Tippetts 509

B

Baas, Jacob C., Jr. 814
Baca, Beverly 152
Baca Zinn, Maxine 17
Bacchi, Carol 18
Bacon, Lloyd 588
Badaracco. Claire M. 815
Bahr, Howard M. 19 589 590
Bair, Barbara 350
Baird, Anne Foster 816
Baker, Donald E. 817 818 819
Baker, Katharine Gratwick 351
Baker, Mary Holland 352
Baker, Therese L. 353
Baldwin, Alice Sharples 820
Baldwin, Hélène L. 821
Baldwin, Wendy 521
Ballard, Elsie Miner 822
Bane, Mary Jo 354 355
Banks, Ben Wayne 1044
Barclay, Richard L. 20

Barlow, Claude W. 823
Barney, William L. 21
Barrett, Carol J. 356
Barrett, Michèle 591
Bartlett, Robin L. 357
Bate, Kerry William 824
Bayer, Alan E. 358
Baym, Nina 825
Beall, Pamela 22
Bean, Frank D. 23 359
Bean, Lee L. 276
Bear, James A., Jr. 826
Beauchamp, Virginia Walcott 827
Beck, E. M. 360
Becker, Gary S. 361
Beckett, Joyce O. 362
Bedford, Denton R. 828
Bell, Carolyn Shaw 363 364
Bellard, Lewis 24 25
Belous, Richard S. 480
Belzile, Bertrand 365
Benham, Lee 333
Bennett, Carol T. F. 366
Bennett, Mary 592
Bennett, Mildred 829
Bennett, Sheila Kishler 367
Ben-Or, Joseph 368
Benton, Robert M. 830
Berardo, Donna Hodgkins 593
Berger, Alan S. 369
Berger, Brigitte 370
Berkin, Carol Ruth 322 453
Bern, Enid 831
Bernard, Jessie 26
Bernstein, Blanche 371
Berry, Carolyn 832
Berry, Hannah Shwayder 833
Berryman, Jack W. 372
Bertolino-Green, Dianne 535
Bettelheim, Bruno 594
Bieker, Richard F. 373
Bierhorst, John 595
Bigham, Darrel E. 27 28 29
Billman, Carol 30
Bingham, Afred M. 834
Bissell, Linda Auwers 374
Bitton, Davis 31
Blackburn, George 596
Blake, Judith 597
Blake, Tona 1119
Blau, Peter M. 598
Block, James E. 599
Blum, Terry C. 598
Blumin, Stuart M. 32
Bobbitt, Randy 164 165
Bodnar, John 375 376
Bogardus, Carl R., Sr. 33
Bolin, Barbara 152
Bolin, Winifred D. Wandersee 377
Bomberger, Herbert L. 600
Boocock, Sarane Spence 34 89 99 278 475 549
Borman, Kathryn M. 378
Bosher, J. F. 35
Bosworth, Timothy W. 36
Bouchard, Gérard 37 379
Boucher, Neil 835
Bould, Sally 380
Boyd, Monica 601
Boyer, Dorothy M. 169
Boyers, Robert 38 39
Boylan, Anne M. 40 41
Bracher, M. D. 725
Brackbill, Yvonne 42
Bradbury, Bettina 381

Braito, Rita 602
Brandes, Stanley H. 43
Brandt, Gail Cuthbert 382
Brandwein, Ruth A. 383
Breines, Wini 44
Brennan, John A. 808 809
Brennan, Thomas A., Jr. 836 837
Brewster-Walker, Sandi J. 45 46
Brink, Andrew 838
Brislin, Joann 372
Brobeck, Stephen 47
Brodie, Fawn M. 839
Brody, Elaine M. 48
Bromet, Evelyn 384
Bronner, Simon J. 840
Brophy, Frank Cullen 841
Brouwer, Merle G. 603
Brown, Janet 49
Brown, Steven E. 604
Brubaker, Landis H. 842
Bruce-Briggs, B. 385
Brunger, Alan G. 50
Brunk, Ivan W. 843
Bryant, Keith L., Jr. 605
Bryson, William Hamilton 844
Buckley, Suzann 386
Bueckner, Thomas R. 845
Buerkel-Rothfuss, Nancy L. 387
Bullamore, Henry W. 388
Bumpass, Larry L. 606 763
Bunkle, Phillida 389
Burleigh, Anne Husted 846
Burnham, Dorothy 607
Burrison, John A. 847
Burstyn, Joan N. 608
Bushman, Claudia 848
Bushman, Richard L. 390
Bycel, Benjamin 578

C

Callahan, Brian P. 559
Calvert, Karin 609
Camden, Thomas E. 849
Campbell, Arthur A. 610
Campbell, D'Ann 51
Campbell, David G. 850
Campbell, Janet 850
Campbell, Joan Bourque 851
Campbell, Randolph B. 192 852
Caplovitz, David 391
Caplow, Theodore 392
Capozzola, Barbara 853
Carlisle, Lilian Baker 854
Carlson, Allan C. 393
Carlson, Elwood 796
Carlsson, Sten 855
Carr, Lois G. 611
Carson, Christopher Seberian 856
Carter, Barbara L. 52
Carter, Donald E. 612
Carter, Joseph C. 857
Casper, Trudie 858
Cassity, Michael J. 53
Castonguay, Charles 54 55 56
Cauthers, Janet 57
Cawthon, John Ardis 859
Censer, Jane Turner 394
Cerullo, Margaret 44 395
Chadney, James G. 613
Chadwick, Bruce A. 392
Champoux, Edouard 75
Chaput, Donald 860 861
Charbonneau, Hubert 252
Chegwidden, Paula 614

277

REFERENCE

FOR

USE IN LIBRARY ONLY

Randall Library – UNCW
HQ535 .A587 1984   NXWR
American family history : a historical bibliograph

304900290447%